dog ~~toe~~trot

Harris County
Historical
Society

Houston
Historical
Harris C.

May 9

Dove - 1901
McComb
Spindletop
Beaumont
David

PLEASANT BEND

Pilgrim Rest Church 1865

1860's
Rich planters
came w 200-300
slaves.

Wm. Betk

Antioch 1866
Baptist

Houston came out

St Peter's church
on
Longpoint

250,000 slaves in
Texas 1865

1940's Houston
4 L -
lot of Italian

Windemere subdivision

Freedman Town.

Pilgrim's Rest → Jeramillo

1830 San Felipe Trail to Harrisburg / Houston

Cotton was thing til spindletop.
Houston

South of 4 L-prairie

Blacksmith
teamster

1831
Joel + Eliz Wheaton
Inn

1830-35 1st settlers down San Felipe

$3 - food -
1 yoke
of oxen -

Canfield
Piney Pt. Farm 1830

1848 - German -
north of Buffalo Bayou

PLEASANT BEND

Upper Buffalo Bayou *and the* San Felipe Trail *in the* Nineteenth Century

Dan M. Worrall

Concertina Press

Fulshear, Texas

Pleasant Bend: Upper Buffalo Bayou and the San Felipe Trail in the Nineteenth Century
by Dan M. Worrall

First Edition
Published in 2016 by Concertina Press,
Fulshear, Texas USA

ISBN: 978-0-9825996-2-4
LCCN: 2016914197

Cover:
An Ox Wagon on the Texas Frontier,
Linoeum cut by Barbara Mathews Whitehead,

Map:
Stephen F. Austin's Connected Map of 1837,
courtesy of the General Land Office, Austin

Book and cover design by
Barbara Mathews Whitehead

For Fiona, Danny, Elizabeth *and* Teddy

CONTENTS

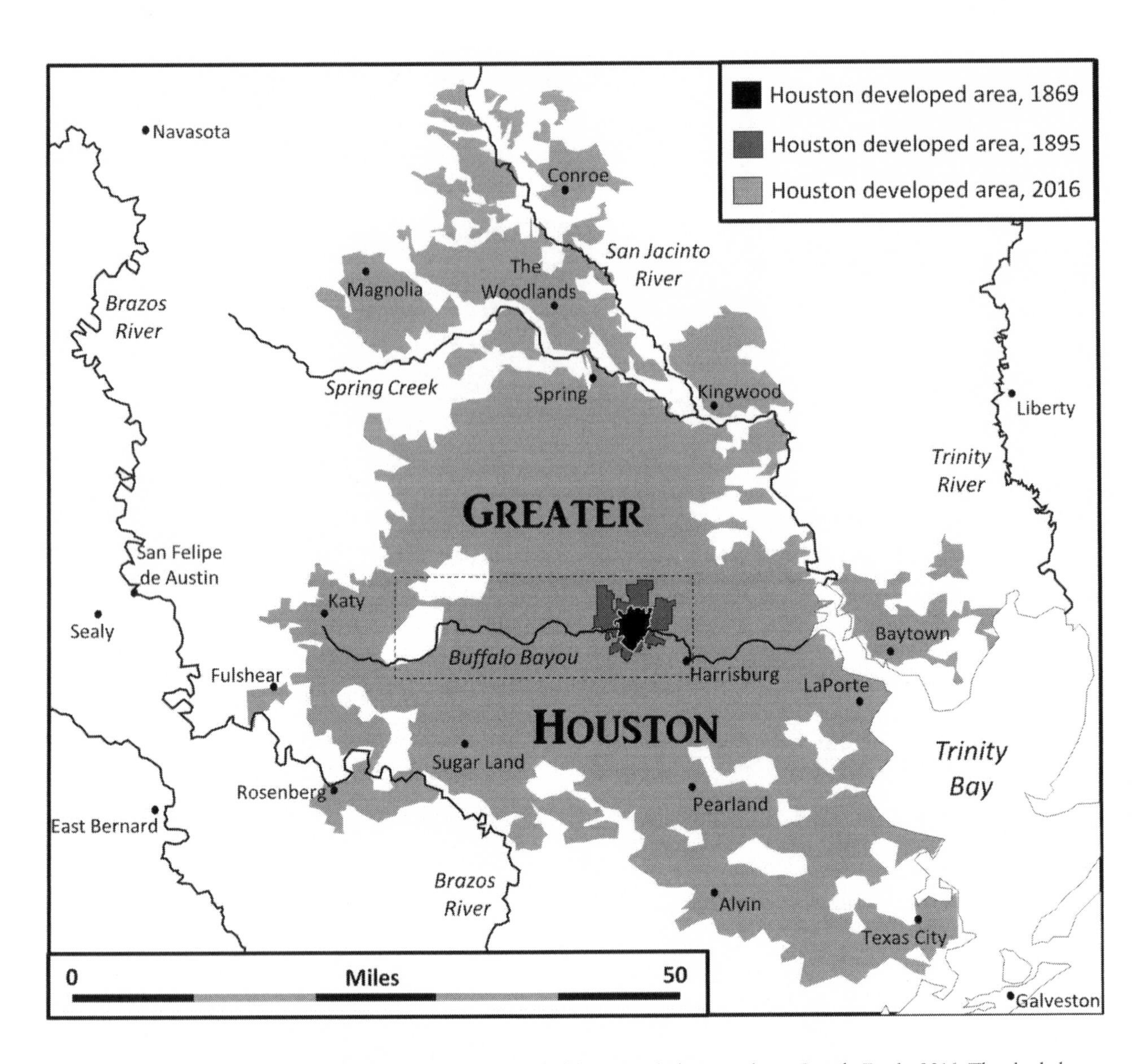

Figure 1. The extent of modern day Greater Houston, compiled from aerial photographs in Google Earth, 2016. The shaded area depicts the urban areas and industrial zones of the City of Houston and its more or less contiguous suburban developments. Insets show the approximate developed area of Houston in 1869 and 1895. A dashed rectangle shows the focus area of this book *(see next figure)*.

INTRODUCTION

TODAY'S Houston is a vast urban place, stretching some eighty miles from its northernmost suburbs in the Conroe area to Texas City in the south, and some fifty miles from the western limits of Katy on its west to Baytown on its east. In the nineteenth century, however, Houston was a relatively small place, and its modern footprint would seem unimaginably large to area pioneers. They lived in an era when a trip by ox wagon from what is now downtown Houston to Katy, then a rural settlement called Cane Island, would take three days.

Open a book about the history of the city of Houston, and you will read about those who lived within and built that great metropolis, and how the city grew from a collection of log cabins to the nation's fourth largest city. You can read of the Allen Brothers selling town tracts on the south bank of Buffalo Bayou, within months of the battle of San Jacinto; of John Harris and the eclipse of Harrisburg by Houston; of the growth of the Ship Channel and the city's exports of cotton, rice and petroleum; of the skyscrapers, of William Marsh Rice, T. W. House, Roy Cullen and Jesse Jones, and of course of Judge Hofheinz and the famed Astrodome. However, you will find little about the surrounding rural land that was consumed by the city's vast twentieth-century expansion, or of the everyday people who had lived there. Perhaps like many other Houstonians, I've always blithely assumed that as the city of Houston has sprawled ever westward toward Katy and the Brazos River, it did so at the expense of mere cow pasture, and I never much considered that such cow pasture had history of its own. Yet part of this rural area was settled for over a decade before Houston itself was founded, and the area contained a number of completely separate settlements during the nineteenth century.

The objective of this book is to examine the largely forgotten history of the early settlers of the rural land over which urban Houston has expanded in a westward direction. It focuses on a strip of land about twenty miles long and ten miles wide that surrounds Buffalo Bayou in its upper reaches, above the core of the original city. It is what some term a "microhistory," concerned with recording the lives of pioneer Anglo-American and immigrant German farmers and ranchers; of African American slaves, sharecroppers, and freemen; of sawmill workers, inn keepers, cow herders and soldiers; and of an oft-forgotten pioneer trail that witnessed many events of early Texas history. Not for us the larger-than-life stories of Sam Houston, the Allen brothers, or even a William Marsh Rice; they were part of the city that ultimately overran the now forgotten rural world of our story.

Whereas lower Buffalo Bayou, extending eastward from Allen's Landing along the Ship Channel, arguably contains Houston's commercial heart, upper Buffalo Bayou west of Allen's Landing contains its residential soul. Here are the stately homes of River Oaks and Tanglewood, the forested villages of Piney Point and Hunter's Creek, and the suburban streets of Memorial, Spring Branch, West Memorial, Briar Meadow and Briar Forest. It is also the city's demographic heart, with the city's highest population density, a fact underscored by the elegant high rises and townhomes of the Uptown Houston district and the humbler apartment dwellings stretching along Interstate 10, Highway 59, and Long Point.[1]

All of these residential developments, as well as the extensive commercial shopping districts that accompany them, are products of the twentieth century. Within living memory, formerly rural areas have become in turn exurban, suburban, and then densely urban, at each stage losing physical evidence of their history. With older pioneer farming families long since displaced by development, and with the arrival of floods of new residents from all over the globe building a new metropolis, it is no surprise that the past has been somewhat difficult to remember. For many, there is a feeling of rootlessness that is an unfortunate side-effect of our city's rapid expansion. History can provide a connection to the deep roots that lie beneath us, beneath the concrete and glass.

Pioneer beginnings

At one time this land was an endless tallgrass prairie, broken only by the riparian forest that hugged the banks of Buffalo Bayou. In a time more ancient than that of our first European settlers, there were Native Americans living here, and bison, wolves, cougars, deer, turkey and prairie chickens. Early Anglo settlers and enslaved African Americans enlarged a wilderness track south of the bayou into a frontier wagon road, the San Felipe Trail. These settlers set up farms, ranches and sawmills on the southern edge of upper Buffalo Bayou in the early nineteenth century. The San Felipe Trail was Harris County's first commercial road, and it served a vital role in colonial times, providing an export route for cotton raised on newly established Brazos River plantations to seaborne craft on Buffalo Bayou – the raison d'être for the locations of both Harrisburg and its successor, Houston.

The area south of Buffalo Bayou along the San Felipe Trail was first settled by Anglo farmers. The earliest to arrive were John and Maria Taylor, who built a cabin at Piney Point in 1824. Joel and Elizabeth Wheaton as well as Buckman and Harriet Canfield established farms and travelers' inns along the San Felipe Trail in 1831 and 1838, respectively. During the Texas Revolution of 1836, this trail played a part in the great Runaway Scrape, when settlers fled east toward safety at Harrisburg, Lynchburg and ultimately the Sabine River.

Although most of the plantations of Austin's early colony lay in the rich bottomlands of the Brazos and Colorado river valleys, a large antebellum cotton and timber plantation briefly flourished on land that later contained all of the modern-day Tanglewood and Post Oak/Galleria area as well as most of the River Oaks and West University Place neighborhoods. The story of the rise of the Agur T. Morse family's Pleasant Bend plantation—of his forward-thinking experiments with cotton production on the bald Houston prairie outside the classic setting of the fertile Brazos River bottomlands, and of the abrupt crash of his plantation after the Civil War—is virtually unknown to Houstonians today.

In the years immediately following Texas statehood in 1845, a wave of German immigrants arrived on ships at Galveston, traveled by steamboat to the small town of Houston, and then took the San Felipe Trail toward settlements in Cat Spring, Industry and New Ulm. Some of these immigrants stayed behind to establish three early German settlements along on the north side of upper Buffalo Bayou, at Bear Creek, Spring Branch, and White Oak.

The Civil War years were especially tough on all the settlers of this area, and most of its young men served for the duration of the war either as eager enlistees or as reluctant conscripts. Many did not return. After the war, large numbers of African Americans, freed from their bondage on Brazos and Colorado River plantations, trekked eastward along the San Felipe Trail, many staying in the rural upper Buffalo Bayou area to become sharecroppers and farmers. A few of them, along with their former Anglo masters, took thousands of longhorn cattle up the famed Chisholm Trail from cattle gathering pens built along the San Felipe Trail, near modern-day Shepherd Drive. The prairie that extended for many miles west of early small-town Houston was an unfenced open range until nearly the end of the nineteenth century, and cattle ranching has deep roots here. With the arrival of a narrow-gauge railroad in 1875 along what is now busy Westheimer Road, Houston expanded westward to Shepherd Drive, although the rest of upper Buffalo Bayou remained an area of small farms until well into the early twentieth century.

Our narrative begins with the founding of

Stephen F. Austin's colony in the early 1820s and ends with the Galveston storm of 1900. That storm did a fair amount of damage to rural parts of the county, but its main impact was in boosting the economic ascendancy of Houston over Galveston as the main port of Texas, which—along with the discovery of oil at Spindletop in 1901—caused the small town of Houston to grow by leaps and bounds, changing forever the idyllic rural neighborhood to its immediate west. The end of the nineteenth century is thus a perfect stopping point.

Reconstructing the past

Giving voice to the early settlers of this area is not an easy task. The lifespans of these area pioneers occurred five to eight generations prior to Houstonians of today, which is out of living memory of even the oldest among us. Moreover, the subjects of our story were not the relatively well-recorded movers and shakers of Houston, but the ordinary (and often extraordinary) folk who settled a raw frontier to its west. To find records of them and their world, one must head to the archives of the General Land Office in Austin to look at early Texas land grants, or to various Harris County archives to research property deeds and tax records. Federal census records and genealogical databases of various sorts help flesh out the vital statistics: where and when these pioneers were born and died, and who the members of their families were. In some cases, those simple facts are all the information that exists. In other cases, however, there is much more: an old diary, a family member's autobiography, a newspaper story, an old tintype. What follows is an attempt to bring forward the stories of as many of these pioneer settlers of the area that is now west Houston as is possible, given the constraints of the known and available record.

This work grew out of an effort to save a long-forgotten mid-nineteenth-century graveyard of the pioneer Morse family that was under threat of imminent development. The Morse-Bragg Cemetery on South Wynden Drive in the Post Oak/Galleria area is a tiny remnant of the aforementioned Agur Morse plantation. It was used by the Morse family and their neighbors from the early 1850s to the 1890s, but by 2010 it had been lost to living memory of all but one or two descendants. In the effort to defend it from development by contacting descendants of those buried there—it has now been designated a Harris County pocket park—we descendants had much to learn about our family histories. In my

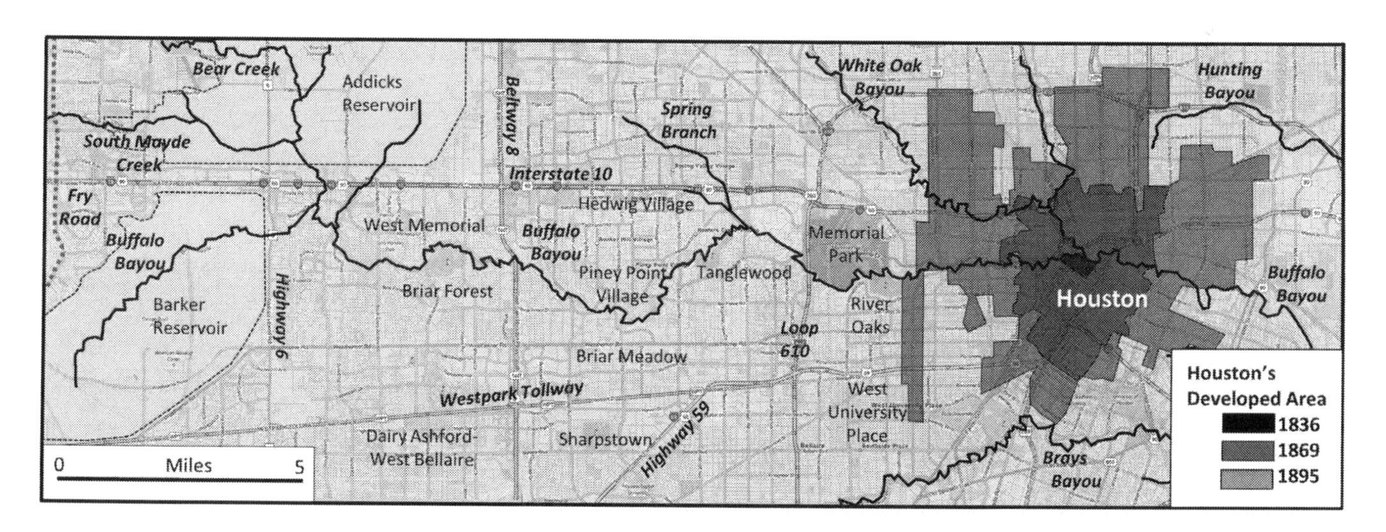

Figure 2. A part of western Harris County and the upper reaches of Buffalo Bayou. Gray shaded areas show the approximate developed area of Houston in 1869, taken from a map of that year by C. E. Wood, and in 1895, taken from a map by Whitty and Stott; both maps are at the Houston Metropolitan Research Center, Houston Public Library. Modern street map base is courtesy of OpenStreetMap.

own case, I knew that my great-great-grandfather, Rev. John Kell Morse, was a frontier Methodist preacher but not that he lived on the edge of a brother's large plantation. Neither did I know that his son, orphaned in boyhood, was adopted by German immigrants living in the neighborhood, and that this son later married into another area pioneer family, the Silliman-Thorntons, who had operated a frontier inn and tavern on the San Felipe Trail.

As we connected with formerly unknown distant relatives as well as descendants of other families buried in the cemetery, in our effort to save the old burial ground, we learned of the pioneer Buckman Canfield family of old Piney Point, of the Old Three Hundred settler Thaddeus Bell, and of the African American family of Jordan and Rachel Banks. We followed other threads that took us to the pioneer Habermachers from Alsace and to the early German settlers of Bear Creek, Spring Branch and White Oak. The lives and stories of these pioneer families, who lived in a sparsely populated rural area, were thoroughly interconnected, and surprising relationships are everywhere.

Our focus is a twenty-mile-long strip of Harris County stretching from Fry Road in the west, just west of Barker Reservoir, to the western edge of early Houston town at its various stages of growth (Figure 2, the map of which extends a short distance east of Houston). Upper Buffalo Bayou is at its center. There are frequent diversions in our story that will take us as far east as Houston and Harrisburg, and as far west as Cane Island (modern Katy) and San Felipe, as required by the events of the day. To separate this rural zone from Houston, however, is not to say that it was of no consequence to the city's development—far from it. The commerce of Houston town in its earliest decades—the access to goods to be shipped in and out of the new inland port—depended on the San Felipe Trail, the slender pathway cut through the endless prairie to the west, until the first railroads arrived in the area. But this rural focus area was culturally and physically distinct from Houston, with a fascinating story of its own.

A word on style, detail and content

This book is a lingering amble through forgotten local history. There are no famous leaders to analyze and few big ideas to discuss or heroic deeds to recount. Instead, the focus is on people's everyday lives.

I confess a tendency toward long quotes from first-hand sources. Rather than repackaging the content of documents uncovered from the period, I prefer to treat those documents as the voices of people from the past, and to listen to them at some length. Imagine an unexpected time travel where we encounter a mid-nineteenth-century Texan strolling along a country lane. Our natural tendency would be to stop, lean on a fence post, and listen for as long as the stroller wanted to talk. Old family diaries, hand-me-down stories, and yellowed newspaper clippings are here treated in the same way: quoted at length where I was fortunate enough to find them.

There are a large number of 'before-and-after' maps included here. A sense of place is always useful when sorting out the past, and the maps are designed to help present-day residents find historically interesting places in the urban areas where they live.

Besides serving an admitted curiosity, this work aims to record what happened during the nineteenth century along upper Buffalo Bayou. As mentioned, my research began by finding and contacting descendants of the area pioneers buried in a forgotten cemetery. With the generous help of these descendants and other sources, many diaries, photographs, and family letters came out of musty attics. Some of those items are unlikely ever to see the light of day in public again and could be lost forever; if the treatment of everyday people seems at times unduly detailed, that is why.

A further aim is to help modern Houstonians with roots in the area to connect with ancestors who may have lived in upper Buffalo Bayou. For persons discussed in the narrative I include birth and death years and usually list the names of their children.

While this risks a tinge of "Joshua begat Jacob," it stops short of full genealogical treatment—there are too many families involved for that. But I hope it provides leads for those interested in linking their family trees to the story. Finally, for those who know they have family links to this area but do not find their forebears mentioned, I'm sure I missed many more interesting people than I found. I apologize in advance for errors of omission–as well as errors of other kinds.

Figure 1.1. Tallgrass prairie at the Attwater Prairie Chicken National Wildlife Refuge near Eagle Lake, Colorado County, 2014.

ONE

The Grand Prairie

We [crossed] the grand prairie—this prairie abounds with deer and Mustangs or wild horses. It is beautiful to behold their lofty gambols and wild maneuvers unconstrained and unshackled by the thraldom of Man . . . .
[The prairie] is all clothed with grass from one to two feet in height. The eye in its wanderings is lost for a resting place and returns to the mind nought but the resemblance of a boundless ocean—its billows, the pliant bendings of successive swards before the unbroken blasts—its canopy the same cloudless azure of the skies or dark pavilion of the threatening storm.

—Joseph C. Clopper (1802–1861),
on traveling through western Harris County in 1828[1].

TO IMAGINE THE BEGINNINGS of the settlement of western Harris County, one must first visualize this place back before the arrival of the city of Houston—a tall order, given the thoroughness of its urban transformation today. The task is best done by finding a place high up with a view—perhaps a high rise office or residential tower, or a public building with a third- or fourth-floor view. Once there, look around. You are surrounded by a lush green vista of trees, with here and there a high rise office or residential building. The trees grow in the yards of ubiquitous suburban homes, and a panoramic, bird's eye view of miles and miles of such development reveals an urban forest. Imagine that same ground with no trees and houses, no high rise buildings, no roads, and no fences. Here once was only an endless coastal prairie, with its tall grasses waving in the breeze as far as the eye could see. This prairie, which extended from the coastal marshes of Galveston Bay westward to the Post Oak Belt, was known to the early settlers only as "the prairie," but in later years has been variously and locally called the Fayette prairie, the Houston prairie, and the Katy prairie. Until the 1850s large herds of bison periodically visited that prairie, along with herds of wild mustangs and longhorn cattle.

That view of seemingly endless prairie was broken only by the bank-hugging riparian forest along Buffalo Bayou, the slow-moving stream that transects the area in an east-west direction. Locally, to the north of the bayou, are the southernmost stands of pine of the great southern upland pine forest that

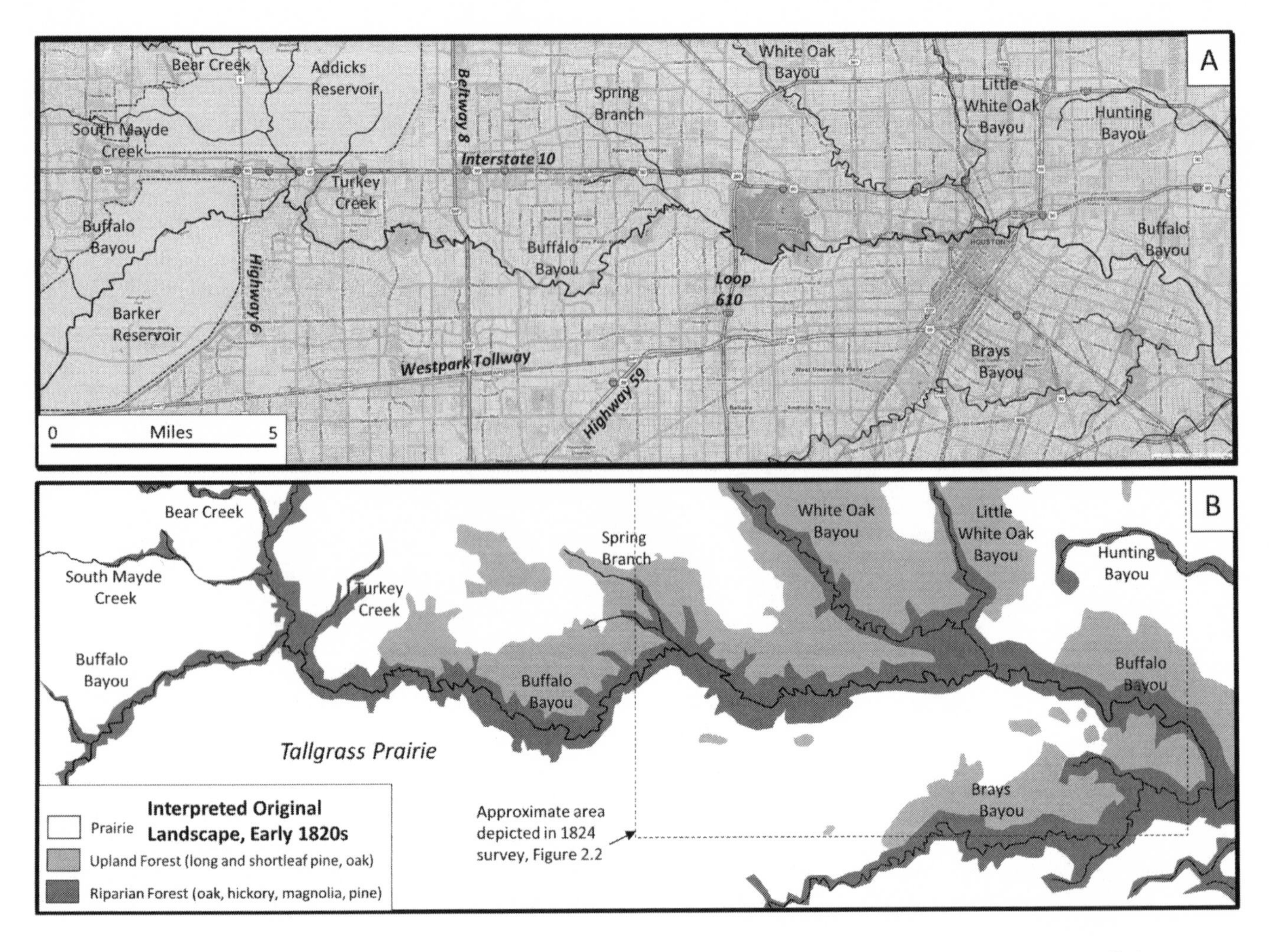

Figure 1.2. (Adjacent page) **A:** Modern road map of the upper Buffalo Bayou study area, courtesy of OpenStreetMap. **B:** Interpreted areas of original forest cover, 1820s. The edge of the trees and the distinction between riparian and upland forests were reconstructed using U.S. Geological Survey topographic maps made in 1915, when most of this area was still rural, as well as a survey made by John Cooke in 1824 (next figure).

stretches from the Carolinas to East Texas. The local name for this great forest in East Texas is the piney woods, and it was noted in pioneer days for its dense stands of tall, straight longleaf, shortleaf and loblolly pines as well as its oaks, sweetgums, and fragrant magnolias. In the early nineteenth century, before railroad transport arrived, only those parts of the forest that lay close to water transport were accessible for harvesting, hence the importance of Buffalo Bayou to early lumberjacks.

These three ecosystems—the prairie, the riparian forest, and the upland pine forest—constituted the whole of western Harris County in the era before Anglo, African American, and German settlement. Their former extent has been reconstructed (Figure 1.2) 1915 U.S. Geologic Survey topographic map, made when most of this area was still rural, and a survey map made in 1824 of the area around what would become central Houston and Harrisburg (Figure 1.3). The various land grants mentioned on the latter map are discussed in Chapter 2.

The best way to understand the primeval appearance and beauty of this area is through the written first-hand accounts of the early travelers and settlers of the 1820s and 1830s, and such is the purpose of this chapter. These early visitors described a Garden of Eden of lush vegetation and plentiful and varied wildlife—albeit with too many mosquitoes. It is a landscape that has today all but vanished—not only in urban Houston but throughout rural areas of

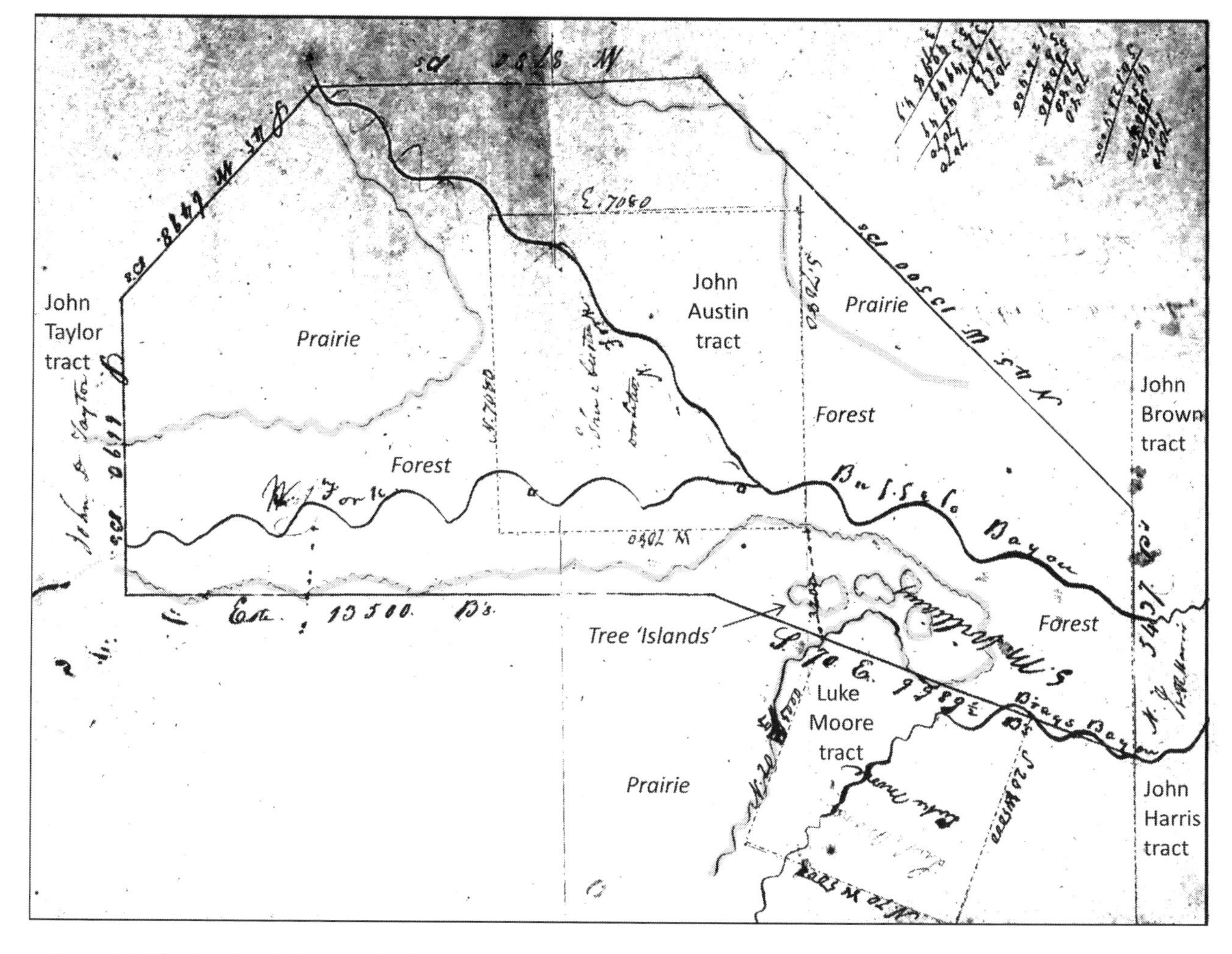

Figure 1.3. The first detailed map of the future area of Houston, before it existed. The survey was made by surveyor John Cooke in 1824. The boundaries of land grants of 1824 are highlighted with dashed lines. The map outline of the forest edge (highlighted with broad gray shading) shows the extent of wooded areas before settlement and urbanization. Courtesy of the General Land Office, Austin; English Field Notes volume 2, p. 224a.

coastal Texas—although it strongly shaped human activities along upper Buffalo Bayou throughout the nineteenth century. Also vanished today are nearly all traces of the Native Americans who once lived in the area surrounding the bayou; a brief accounting of their former presence is also included here.

The Spanish, the first Europeans to come into Texas, had numerous exploratory expeditions that traveled through areas surrounding Buffalo Bayou during the sixteenth through early eighteenth centuries, but no permanent settlements were made there. They established a number of missions along the San Antonio River to the west and southwest, and a mission east of the Trinity River to the northeast, all founded in the eighteenth century, but none in Harris County.[2] Excepting a well-known Native American presence, that county and its upper Buffalo Bayou area remained a wilderness until Anglo settlers arrived in the early nineteenth century.

The great coastal prairie

One of the earliest of Texas travelogues was that of an unknown visitor who came to Texas in 1831 to check up on a troubled real estate purchase from the Galveston Bay and Texas Land Company; he had been swindled. His name is unknown, and over the years his book of 1834, entitled *A Visit to Texas in 1831: Being the Journal of a Traveller through Those Parts Most Interesting to American Settlers*, has been variously attributed to M. Fiske, Colonel Morris, and Asahel Langworthy.[3] For the purposes of this history, we shall call the author Fiske. He left a riveting account of his travels, including detailed descriptions and images of the great coastal prairie and its wildlife, as he journeyed through the area between Brazoria, San Felipe, and Galveston Bay:

> *I was very much struck with the uniformity of the surface in the Prairie; which I had often heard of so particularly, but never observed before. I had now run a mile or more over it, without meeting a single irregularity or obstacle, a stone, a pebble, or even a shrub. Scarcely a blade of grass seemed to rise above the ordinary height, which, as I have before remarked, was about six inches. And thus this extensive plain, neglected by man, and tended only by the hand of nature, presented a surface as level as the most carefully rolled garden walk, and was covered with a coat of green as uniform as a smooth shaven lawn, or a vast sheet of velvet. And this scene was not confined to a small vale or meadow, or bounded by a range of neighboring hills: but stretched off to a vast distance on almost every side . . . . There was nothing elevated, or rough, or wild, to contrast with the flat surface of green; and after a few moments spent in contemplating the plain, finding it varied only by the distant groves which were seen towards the north, the mind feels a kind of surprise at finding, that the senses are almost useless where there is so little to give them exercise. Such were some of my feelings at the first sight of a Prairie.*[4]

Some weeks later, he expounded again on the utter vastness of it, romantically comparing it to the vastness of an ocean:

> *We proceeded somewhat carelessly over the verdant and boundless lawn that spread before us, in some places apparently to the horizon. What acres, what miles, what leagues square of the most fertile land were now in sight without a human inhabitant! And how easy would it be for a stranger to become bewildered in travelling over them! There was not a road to be traced, not even the slightest appearance of a path, or of a single footstep. . . . An unbroken surface of grass, intermingled here and there with beautiful flowers, extended on every side of us a great distance: in some places bounded by a distant grove or range of trees, and in others stretched far between points and islands of woodland, till lost in the thickness of air . . . there was nothing to vary the scene, more than is found in the midst of the ocean.*[5]

Fiske mentioned being overwhelmed with the beauty of the Texas coastal prairie in the spring and early summer:

> *I had never been at all prepared for the indescribable beauty of a Texas Prairie at this season of the year, which I now could not avoid admiring, even under such unpleasant circumstances. The wild flowers had greatly multiplied, so that they were often spread around us in the utmost profusion, and in wonderful variety. Some of those which are most cultivated in our northern gardens were here in full bloom and perfection, intermingled with many which I had never before seen, of different forms and colors. I should despair of giving my reader any adequate idea of the scenes which were thus so richly adorned, and through which we often passed for acres in extent, breaking for ourselves the only path perceptible on the whole Prairie. Among the flowers were the largest and most delicate I had ever seen, with others the most gaudy.*[6]

Although there is no purely native prairie left in the upper Buffalo Bayou portion of Harris County today, the same feeling of awe can be experienced each spring, albeit in somewhat smaller patches of earth, in preserves of the Katy Prairie Conservancy of Austin and Harris counties to the north (Figure 1.4) and in the virgin prairie of the Attwater Prairie Chicken Reserve in nearby Colorado County.

Another very early Anglo visitor to the area was Joseph C. Clopper (1802–1861), one of several sons of Nicholas Clopper (1766–1841). Nicholas Clopper came to Texas in 1821 to start a family enterprise,

Figure 1.4. Williams Prairie, a part of the Katy Prairie ecosystem, northwest of Houston. Photograph by Michael Morton, courtesy of the Katy Prairie Conservancy and Wikimedia Commons.

part of which involved operating merchandise stores in the frontier towns of San Felipe and Harrisburg in the late 1820s. In 1828 his son Joseph traveled the then roadless and unpopulated prairie between the two settlements on an ox wagon, a fifty-mile journey that took him directly through what was to become metropolitan Houston and its western suburbs, including Piney Point:

> *We passed over very little land of productive fertility, most of the country being prairie. We crossed the grand prairie—this prairie abounds with deer and Mustangs or wild horses. It is beautiful to behold their lofty gambols and wild maneuvers unconstrained and unshackled by the thraldom of Man. The grand prairie is here about 20 miles across. Its length is said to be about 80 to 100 miles without a tree and scarce a shrub to obstruct the view. It is all clothed with grass from one to two feet in height. The eye in its wanderings is lost for a resting place and returns to the mind nought but the resemblance of a boundless ocean—its billows, the pliant bendings of successive swards before the unbroken blasts—its canopy the same cloudless azure of the skies or dark pavilion of the threatening storm.*
>
> *After passing through pine island [modern day Pattison near Buffalo Bayou], a small cluster of that species of timber, we reach for a distance of 15 miles and the only watering place for the same distance. We journey three miles before entering the Brazos bottom . . . . San Felipe is situated on the west bank on a high rolling prairie that here runs into the [Brazos] river. It is composed of about 20 houses principally of hewn logs. Col. Austin's is quite a commodious and respectable dwelling.*[7]

Joseph Clopper described the Brazos bottomlands as "choice" lands for sugar and cotton, although subject to flooding–in contrast to the prairies of modern Houston and Katy, which he called land of little "productive fertility." This sort of judgment against prairie farming had a negative impact on early settlement along western Buffalo Bayou, until Agur Morse proved otherwise on his Pleasant Bend Plantation in the 1850s (Chapter 7).

Also observing the prairies west of Houston in frontier times was Moravian-born Carl Anton Postl (1793–1864), writing under the pseudonym Charles Sealsfield. Postl spent some years in the United States in the 1820s and early 1830s, and some scholars think he spent time in Texas and the Southwest, although that is uncertain. His German language novel of 1841, *Das Kajütenbuch (The Cabin Book)*, has descriptions of frontier coastal Texas with details that have the ring of truth to them but that could have been influenced by Fiske's 1831 travelogue.[8] Here Postl's narrator tells of his stay at a cattle plantation that year in what would have been the Katy/Houston prairie:

> *We were at one of these plantations; it lay a few miles off the trail which leads from Harrisburg to San Felippe de Austin, and belonged to Mr. Neal [who] devoted himself exclusively to cattle breeding . . .. His herds consisted of about seven or eight hundred head of cattle, and from fifty to sixty horses, all mustangs. The plantation, like most of those we had seen, was as yet little improved; the log house was built in that style which is so common in our south-western states, was spacious and comfortable. It was standing at the skirt of an island [motte], on clumps, between two sycamores, which sheltered it from the sun and wind. Before it, the endless prairie, with its waving grass and flowers, extended to an immeasurable distance; in the background rose a Texian primitive forest in its glorious majesty, overgrown with grape vines, climbing a hundred feet or more, along the trees, and spreading their shoots all over the island.*

"Mr. Neal" may have been the real-life William Neal, whose abode was in the large "neighborhood" of ranches near Stafford's Point (modern Stafford) by early 1834.[9] Invited by Neal to venture out onto the unfenced open prairie to help round up some longhorn cattle for sending to New Orleans, the narrator became separated from his companions and found himself alone on the vastness of the Katy/Fayette prairie:

> *I stopped, listened—a profound silence all around —the very birds in the islands were silent. . . . As far as the eye could reach, one waving, undulating sea of grass, here and there with a cluster of trees, but not a trace of the existence of man. . . .*
>
> *I had ridden on in this way for several hours, stopping, listening, if nothing could be heard—no shout, no cry. But something struck my sight; a discovery which was nothing less than delightful to me. For in the direction in which we had proceeded in the morning, the grass had been more abundant; flowers were rare; whilst the prairies through which I now was riding resembled more a flower garden—a flower garden in which scarcely any grass was to be seen. There was the most brilliant carpet of red, yellow, violet and blue flowers I had ever seen; millions of the most splendid prairie roses, sunflowers, dahlias, and asters, such as are to be found in no botanical garden in the world. My mustang was scarcely able to get through this profusion of flowers.*[10]

Prairie fires. The prairies had been kept open of brush and trees for time immemorial by means of periodic brush fires, some set by lightning, others by Native Americans who saw the value in keeping the land open for bison, horses and cattle (Figure 1.5). Ferdinand Roemer, an early German visitor of 1846, described one such prairie fire near present day Waco:

> *We were entertained before going to sleep by the beautiful spectacle of a prairie fire. Like a sparkling diamond necklace, the strip of flame a mile long*

Figure 1.5. The earliest known image of western Harris County depicts a prairie fire in 1835, west of what would become the town of Houston. From A. A. Parker, *A Trip to the West and Texas, Comprising a Journey of Eight Thousand Miles* (Concord, N.H.: William White, 1836).

raced along over hill and dale, now moving slowly, now faster, now flickering brightly, now growing dim. We could the more enjoy this spectacle undisturbed, since the direction of the wind kept it from approaching us. My companion was of the opinion that the Indians had without doubt started the fire, since they do this often to drive the game in a certain direction, and also to expedite the growth of the grass by burning off the dry grass.[11]

Fiske, too, was fascinated by uncontrollable fires in the limitless coastal prairie:

Everywhere in the Prairie were to be seen traces of the fire by which it had been overrun and devastated only a few weeks before. The young grass had begun to spring, but it was not yet high enough entirely to conceal the blackened surface and thin layers of ashes which contributed to its luxuriance. In one place however we came to a considerable tract of ground where the fire had not been, as it was overgrown with a thick cane brake about five feet high. So far apparently from all habitations, and in the midst of a region which had been but lately swept by the flames, we never thought that any evil could arise from a little amusement of the kind; and feeling curious to see the burning of a Prairie, we determined to set a small portion of it on fire. Dismounting therefore, by snapping our guns we soon obtained a flame, which we touched to a few of the tall canes, at this season as dry as fishpoles, and were surprised at the rapidity with which it spread. It rose fast in the air to their tops, communicating with others around, and soon began to roar and extend with greater and greater rapidity. . . .

As we stood gazing at the effects of our sport, the conflagration fast retired from us, levelling a broad track before us, where nothing was to be seen but a smooth, blackened and smoking surface, between two walls of standing canes. We now for the

Figure 1.6. Cowboys branding cattle on the open prairie, Texas, from a sketch by James E. Taylor, in *Frank Leslie's Illustrated Newspaper*, June 25, 1867. Courtesy of the Library of Congress.

> *first time began to ask, whether there might not be some habitation in its path, or at least some person or domestic animal, exposed to be surrounded and burnt to death in an instant; but as it was evidently out of our power to do anything to stop the devastation which we had commenced, we remounted and pursued our way. We often turned back to see the progress of the fire, which at length was to be traced only by a distant column of smoke rising from the vast level around us; and we could but flatter ourselves that no serious consequences would result from it.*[12]

Wild cattle, horses and bison. Longhorn cattle and Spanish mustangs abounded over the grand prairie. Some of the first cattle in Texas were brought in by the Spanish in 1690 as they established the Mission San Francisco de los Tejas. The seed stock for the mission included two hundred head of cattle from south of the Rio Grande.[13] Escaped and abandoned mission cattle propagated rapidly. By 1715 a pair of Spaniards traveling in the bottomlands of the Trinity River reported seeing "wild cattle left by the Spaniards on their first expedition into Texas. They killed a fat cow and some turkeys."[14] In 1778 a Frenchman in the service of the Spanish named Athanase de Mézières was traveling between San Antonio ("Bejar") and a new settlement called Nuestra Señora del Pilar de Bucareli on the Trinity River, a route that took him just north of this area. He noted:

> *After leaving the Guadalupe River I crossed the Colorado and Brasos, where there are great quantities of all kinds of fish and birds, valuable timber and quarries, an incredible number of Castilian cattle, and herds of mustangs that never leave the banks of these streams. The region, from one river*

to another, is no less bountifully supplied with buffalo, bear, deer, antelopes, wild boars, hares, partridges, and turkeys, which live in luxuriant and spacious plains, that are endowed with a healthful climate . . . with richest pastures, various medicinal herbs, and permanent arroyos, along the banks of which are paths shaded by lofty trees.[15]

A visitor to Brazoria in 1831 described some of these abundant wild Spanish cattle, which by that time had been branded by an early settler named Westall and were kept on the open range:

The cattle, scattered over the spacious plain before us, were feeding, or lying down or straying about as they pleased. . . . It would be difficult to imagine a landscape more expressive of tranquility and repose. The most distant cattle were apparently reduced to so small a size, that one could not have distinguished them from much smaller animals had they been alone. Now it was easy to realize that the numerous spots on the Prairie, one two and three miles distant, were large, sleek and vigorous cattle like those near us, and belonged to the same great herd to which that vast pasture ground was appropriated.[16]

In 1837, the numerous wild cattle in the near vicinity of brand-new Houston town were variously estimated at 500 to 4,000 head; "but included no dairy animals; butter was seventy-five cents a pound. The one cheap food was beef, which was good and plentiful at two to four cents per pound."[17]

As Carl Anton Postl (Sealsfield) noted, the periodic collection and branding of wild cattle by ranchers was already well underway by the late 1820s and early 1830s. The Katy/Houston prairie was kept as open, unfenced range until the 1870s and even later

Figure 1.7. "Lazooing a Horse on the Prairie," somewhere between Brazoria and San Felipe, 1831. From Anonymous, *A Visit to Texas* (New York: Goodrich and Wiley, 1834).

Figure 1.8. Bison on a ranch near Chappell Hill, Texas. The Lyda Hill Texas Collection in Carol Highsmith's America Project, Library of Congress

in western areas, and ranchers, who were not necessarily land owners, kept track of their stock by branding new calves every year in community roundups. W. C. Moore described this process from his Houston boyhood in the 1860s:

> *There were hundreds of unbranded cattle and calves all over South Texas, and no one was permitted to brand any of these cattle, unless they had cattle on the range. I have heard my father laugh and comment upon an emigrant that reached this territory in the fall, soon after the civil war in a covered wagon drawn by a yoke of oxen. He turned his oxen loose on the range and next spring, branded twenty-eight calves.*[18]

Wild mustangs abounded on the prairie and had only to be lassoed, branded and tamed by the settler, as Fiske observed (Figure 1.7):

> *We saw several small droves of wild mustangs as we travelled on, which betrayed greater interest or curiosity towards us. They would start off at their slow gallop, with their long [manes] and tails flying, while their thick fetlocks and foretops gave them a wild, untutored aspect; and sweeping off in a semicircle to the right or left, scour over half a mile or a mile of the Prairie, and then stop to survey us until we again approached them. After repeating this manoeuvre several times, they generally changed their course and disappeared. . . .*[19]
>
> *The small horses of the country, called mustangs, introduced by the Spaniards, and now numerous in the more northern prairies, run wild in droves over these parts of Texas, and are easily taken and rendered serviceable by the inhabitants. . . . These horses are very useful in the country, and may perhaps become at some future time a valuable article of export, as they are innumerable, and cost only the trouble of catching. This is done with a strong noosed cord, made of twisted strips of raw hide, and called [a] lazo [lasso], which is the Spanish word for a band or bond. . . . A man on horseback, with a rope of this kind coiled in his left hand, and one end of it fastened to the horse, whirls the noosed end in the air over his head as he approaches the animal he intends to seize: and, on finding an opportunity, throws it over its head or horns, and checks his horse. The noose is instantly drawn tight, and the poor creature is thrown violently down, without the power of moving.*[20]

Buffalo in large traveling herds were also plentiful on the coastal prairie in those early days but were only periodically seen (Figure 1.8).. Mrs. Dilue Rose Harris (1825 –1914) arrived in Harrisburg, Texas, with her family in 1835, having moved from St. Louis; they were to settle at Stafford's Point in what is now nearby Fort Bend County. She described one large herd of bison that they saw on the great coastal prairie in 1836, during the Texas Revolution. The herd crossed the Brazos near present day Richmond, which at that time was known as Fort Bend:

> *Just as the people began to quiet down and go to work, a large herd of buffaloes came by. There were three or four thousand of them. They crossed the Brazos River above Fort Bend, and came out of the bottom at Stafford's Point, making their first appearance before day. They passed in sight of our house, but we could see only a dark cloud of dust, which looked like a sand storm. Father tried to get a shot at one, but his horse was so fractious that it*

Figure 1.9. Hunting deer on the Texas coastal prairie, somewhere between Brazoria and San Felipe, 1831. From Anonymous, *A Visit to Texas.*

was impossible. As the night was very dark we could not tell when the last buffalo passed. We were terribly frightened, for it was supposed that the Indians were following the herd. The buffaloes passed and went on to the coast, and the prairie looked afterwards as if it had been plowed.[21]

Buffalo Bayou

Buffalo Bayou cuts east-west across the prairie, and its steep banks and tributaries supported a hardwood riparian forest (Figure 1.10).. In frontier times the bayou was spring-fed, with water that was clear enough to see the bayou's bottom. One of the earliest written descriptions of Buffalo Bayou was by Joseph C. Clopper, who in 1828 wrote of sailing ten miles up the San Jacinto River,

where we enter the mouth of Buffalo bayou—this is the most remarkable stream I have ever seen. At its junction with the San Jacinto it is about 150 yards in breadth having about three fathoms of water with little variation in depth as high up as Harrisburg—20 miles—the ebbing and flowing of the tide is observable about 12 miles higher, the water being of navigable depth close up to each bank giving to this most enchanting little stream the appearance of an artificial canal in the design and course of which Nature has lent her masterly hand; for its meanderings and beautiful curvatures seem to have been directed by a taste too exquisite for human attainment—most of its course is bound in by timber and flowering shrubbery which overhang its grassy banks and dip and reflect their variegated hues in its unruffled waters. These impending shrubs are in places overtopped by the evergreen magnolia rising in the grandeur of its excellence to the reach of deserved pre-eminence where it unfolds

Figure 1.10. A scene along Buffalo Bayou near Houston, around 1904. *From Artwork of Houston, Texas,* MSS 114-0852, courtesy of the Metropolitan Research Center, Houston Public Library.

its far-scented magnificence; softening to the eye of admiration the dazzling lustre of its expansive bloom by agreeable blendings with the deep sea-green of its umbrageous foliage.

The banks of this stream are secured from the lavings of the water by what are here termed "cypress knees"—these are apparently exuberences of cypress roots and shoot up along the margin of the waters to the height of three and four feet and from 3 to 10 inches in diameter without leaf or branch; and so closely and regularly are they often found standing in lines as to resemble piles driven in pur-

posely as security against the innovation of the tides. Often along these shady banks have I rowed my little skiff and wondered if ever some Bard had consecrated its border shades by a correspondent flow of song—if some native Ossian had ever breathed forth in his artless strains the dictates of an inspired Muse. I thought of other streams immortalized, and thought that this might by its enchanting beauty give immortality to some future Bard—for it cannot forever be "by fame neglected and unknown to song" and "creep inglorious like a vulgar stream."[22]

Clopper was writing to his family in Ohio. He, his brothers and father hoped to eventually coax the women of the family down to Texas, once the Cloppers' commercial dreams were realized (*see Chapter 2*), which may account for the promotional tone of his note. George Bonnell described the bayou in 1840, when it was already the site of the growing small town of Houston:

Buffalo Bayou enters the San Jacinto bay, near the [San Jacinto] battleground. It is about fifty-five miles in length, and navigable at all seasons of the year for steamboats drawing six feet of water, to Houston, about thirty-five miles from its junction with the San Jacinto [River]. It rises from Austin County, and runs in nearly an eastern direction . . . . From the mouth of the bayou to Houston, the country is about equally divided between prairie and timber. The land is very low, and in the winter extremely muddy; in other respects the land is of a very good quality. The timber is pine, oak, ash, magnolia, hickory, mulberry, cypress, etc. Several steam mills have been located upon this stream, which furnish large quantities of lumber. Four miles above Houston the bayou extends into the extensive prairies and has only a narrow fringe of timber upon the margin of the stream, and the bayou in the summer season becomes almost dry.[23]

Fiske described the vegetation in Buffalo Bayou:

The growth was large, and consisted principally of pine and cypress, with some cedar, ash, peccan, oak, and walnut and a little locust. Red grapes and introduced china trees . . . live oak, red oak, wild peach, holly, cottonwood, peccan.

Wild game was plentiful and an important part of the diet of early settlers. Walter C. Moore (1857–1943) grew up in Harrisburg and Houston and recalled that a great variety of wild game was still to be had even in settled areas into the early 1860s. He also remembered why the bayou was named "Buffalo." It was not for the bison:

When I was born in Harris County, Houston was young, and the country was wild. My father lived on the east bank of Buffalo Bayou, about four hundred yards south of the elevator, where I was born.

There were many wild cattle and horses roaming the ranges, and bear, wild cats, catamounts [mountain lions] and wild hogs. All wild hogs, when they are cornered, will fight, and the boars are especially very vicious. As soon as they hear the bark of dogs on their trail, they bunch up and the boar or boars stand guard, and woe to the dog whose temerity brings him near the boar, as happened to one of our dogs that was hauled home on the wagon with several of the hogs that had been killed. Many a wild turkey was brought home before breakfast as his gobble could be heard from our home. My father killed three black bear around his field fence. . . . We boys killed a large catamount in Magnolia Park [east of Houston]. My two brothers, and a little negro boy and myself, none of us over 11 years old, about half a mile south of my father's farm, jumped a bear and the dogs brought it to [bay] in a big briar thicket. About that time, four small boys were back-tracking at a rapid rate.

Buffalo Bayou was full of fish, consisting primarily of catfish, buffalo [fish], several varieties of perch, some trout, and occasionally an alligator would come along. My father would bait a place and catch so many buffalo until he boiled them in an iron kettle and fed them to his hogs. I cannot say authoritatively but I have understood that the name "Buffalo" prefixed by bayou resulted from so many buffalo fish in the bayou.[24]

Figure 1.11. The Ivory-Billed Woodpecker, drawn in 1837 by John J. Audubon from specimens collected along Buffalo Bayou. Courtesy of the Library of Congress.

John J. Audubon famously visited the brand-new town of Houston in 1837, when it was little more than a collection of log cabins connected by muddy paths. He spent a month there, working on drawings for his Birds of North America, during which time he was able to explore the bayou thoroughly. Among the birds he captured along Buffalo Bayou were four specimens of the now extinct Ivory-Billed Woodpecker, which were the basis for his painting of that bird (Figure 1.11).

In addition to the continuous strip of riparian forest that followed Buffalo Bayou, there were also mottes of trees sparsely placed in the prairie. Some of the larger of these are marked on the south side of the bayou on the maps in Figure 1.3. These mottes were universally called "islands" by the early settlers and visitors. Fiske described them:

> *The only interruption [to the open Prairie] is caused by clusters of trees of different forms and sizes, scattered at distant intervals here and there. These clumps and groves, apparently possessing all the neatness and beauty which could have been given them if planted by the hand of man, and tended by his greatest care, added the charm of variety to the eye, while they promised thick and convenient shelter from sun and storm to man or beast. Without such variety and such a refuge, the aspect of the Prairie, with all its verdure, would have been monotonous to the sight, and disheartening to the traveller. It would be almost impossible for a person who has never seen them, to imagine the appearances of these groves. Although they are wholly the work of nature, they often present all the beauty of art: for the trees are of nearly equal size, and grow near together, without underwood, and present outlines perfectly well defined, and often surprisingly regular. Some appear to form exact circles or ovals, while others are nearly square or oblong. . . . These groves are called islands, from the striking resemblance they present to small tracts of land surrounded by water. Nothing can be more natural, than the comparison. The Prairie assumes the uniform appearance of a lake, both in surface and color; and in the remoter parts the hue melts into that of distant water; and it requires no very great effort of the imagination.*[25]

Another type of "island" was made of canes, forming a "cane brake" (Figure1.12):

> *They are tracts of land low and often marshy, overgrown with the long reeds which we know in the Northern States as fishing rods. They are sometimes found as underbrush in woods and forests, and sometimes are not intermingled with trees, but form one thick growth, impenetrable when the cane is dry*

Figure 1.12. Traveling through a cane brake in the Texas coastal prairie, 1831.
From Anonymous, *A Visit to Texas*.

and hard. Our way led us the next day through one of the latter description; and such a sight I never before witnessed. The frequent passage of men and horses keeps open a narrow path, not wide enough for two mustangs to pass with convenience. The reeds grow to the height of about twenty feet, and are so slender, that having no support directly over the path, they droop a little inward, and so meet and intermingle their tops, forming a complete covering overhead. We rode thus about a quarter of a mile, along a singular avenue, arched overhead, and with the view of the sky shut out. The sight of a large tract, covered with so rank a growth of an annual plant, which rises to such a height, decays and is renewed every twelvemonth, affords a striking impression of the fertility of the soil. Cane brakes often occur of great extent. Those of a league, indeed of several leagues, are not uncommon. . . . The reeds are eaten by cattle and horses in the winter, and afford a valuable and inexhaustible resource of food in that season when the Prairies yield little or none. At that time they are young and tender. When dry they are generally burnt, to clear the ground.[26]

One such island of cane was formed along an upper tributary of Buffalo Bayou, in present day Katy, which before the coming of the Missouri, Kansas and Texas Railroad in 1895 was a rural area known as Cane Island. According to Carol Adams of the Katy Heritage Society, "What . . . early visitors [found] was a small area in the middle of a large prairie with a cane-filled creek. An 'island' of cane was surrounded by an ocean of tall grass, thus the area became known as Cane Island."[27] By 1880 that cane brake had disappeared.[28] Today the name Cane Island is being revived for use in a large housing development there.

Native Americans in the Buffalo Bayou area

Early Spanish explorers described sizeable populations of Native Americans all along the Gulf Coast. There are no remnant, intact populations of Native Americans in western Harris County today, and their previous presence is known mainly

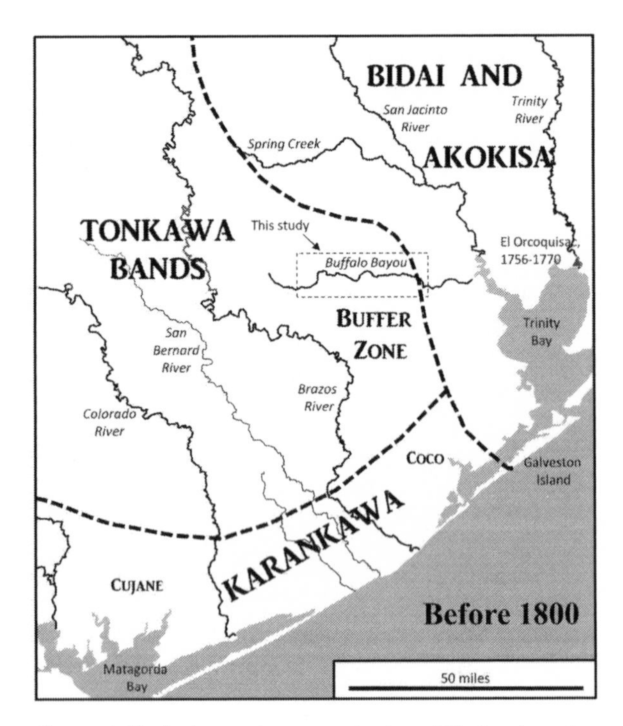

Figure 1.13 A. Approximate territories of Native American groups of Southeast Texas in the early eighteenth century, prior to Anglo settlement. Boundaries are as shown in Lawrence Aten's *Indians of the Upper Texas Coast* (New York: Academic Press, 1983). Also shown is the location of El Orcoquisac, the Spanish fort and mission to the Akokisa and Bidai.

through the diaries of these Spanish explorers and missionaries as well as those of early Anglo settlers, along with results of archeological excavations at numerous sites. Using such information, anthropologist Lawrence Aten reconstructed the eighteenth-century locations of Native American groups along the Texas coast (Figure 1.13 A). He reasons that Buffalo Bayou and the future western Harris County were a "buffer zone" in the eighteenth century between the Akokisa, Karankawa, and Tonkawa tribes—subject to seasonal visits—and were not part of any tribe's core area.[29] The Tonkawa were nomadic Indians of the central Texas plains; they hunted buffalo and deer, which provided the bulk of their food.[30] The Karankawa linguistic group, consisting of the Cocos (Capoques), Cujane (Copanes) and Guapite subgroups, were coastal nomadic hunter-gatherers who, according to Spanish observers, also raised dogs for food.[31] The Akokisa were a western branch of the Atakapa linguistic group, an indigenous people of the southeastern woodlands surrounding the Gulf of Mexico.[32] Their core area was on the lower Trinity River, and they were closely related to the small Bidai group with whom they seem to have merged by the time of Anglo colonization.[33]

Archeologist Robert Ricklis described the coastal groups:

> *When European explorers and colonists first arrived in the region, beginning in the 1500s, the indigenous coastal peoples (Karankawa, Akokisa and other tribal groups) practiced a mix of subsistence economies: intensive fishing in the shoreline bays and lagoons, hunting of deer, antelope, and bison that foraged and grazed on the prairies and woodlands of stream floodplains, and gathering of a wide range of aquatic and terrestrial plant foods. . . . At the time of initial contact with Europeans, the coastal tribes must have placed great value on the abundant opportunities that existed within their homelands, and they maintained clear territorial boundaries between their lands and those of Native peoples living in the interior. Such was the richness of their environment that coastal population density was relatively high, and people spent much of the annual cycle living in large shoreline fishing camps that housed several hundred people during peak fishing seasons.*[34]

By the middle of the nineteenth century most of these native groups had either disappeared or were in small remnant populations, hence their scarcity in many of the travelogues written by Anglo and German visitors. This disappearance was partly the result of the introduction of disease by Spanish explorers and more prominently to the dense colonization of coastal Texas by early Anglo settlement.

Spanish and French contacts with Native American groups

Álvar Núñez Cabeza de Vaca was famously shipwrecked on Galveston Island in 1528. He and his men brought a stomach disease which infected the natives, who were probably members of the Karakawa group. According to Cabeza de Vaca,

> *Within a very short time only fifteen of the eighty men . . . who had reached the island were left alive; and after the death of these men, a stomach ailment afflicted the Indians of the land from which half died. . . . They believed that it was we who were killing them, and they were wholly convinced of this, they agreed among themselves to kill those who were left.*[35]

De Vaca and his men became medicine men, attempting to heal sick natives, and this proved their salvation.

Cabeza de Vaca also wrote about encountering the Han and Coaque (Coke, Akokisa) tribes in 1528. French traders from New Orleans and from Nacogdoches encountered Akokisa (Orcoquisa) and Bidai tribes from the 1720s, and the French built a short-lived trading post in 1754 on the bank of the Trinity River, a few miles up from Trinity Bay. The Spanish soon put an end to that, arriving later that year with a small military force aided by Akokisa and Bidai Indians who were promised part of the spoils.[36] The Spanish then founded a mission on that site in 1756, to protect their boundary with Louisiana. The Mission of Nuestra Señora de la Luz (also called El Orcoquisac) had an accompanying military garrison, Presidio San Agustín de Ahumada. Located near modern day Anahuac, thirty miles east of downtown Houston, it was an unhappy place, marred by frequent flooding, bouts of dysentery from unsuitable drinking water, and hordes of mosquitoes. It was abandoned in 1770.

A French explorer, Louis LeClerc Milfort, encountered a European living among the Akokisa in 1781. This European, of whom little but his name (Joseph) is known, related:

> *We are in the habit of dividing ourselves into two or three groups in order to follow the buffalo, which in the spring go back into the west, and in autumn come down into these parts; there are herds of these buffalo, which go sometimes as far as the Missouri; we kill them with arrows; our young hunters are very skillful at this hunting. You understand, moreover, that these animals are in very great numbers, and as tame as if they were raised on a farm; consequently, we are very careful never to frighten them. When they stay on a prairie or in a forest, we camp near them in order to accustom them to seeing us, and we follow all their wanderings so that they cannot get away from us. We use their meat for food and their skins for clothing.*[37]

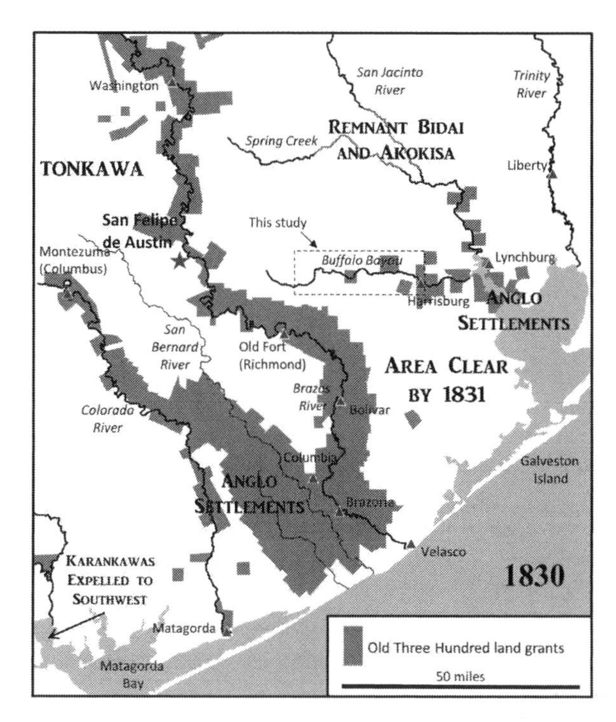

Figure 1.13 B. Same area as the previous figure, showing the distribution of Native American groups by 1830. Locations of early nineteenth-century Native American groups are as shown in Aten's Indians of the Upper Texas Coast. Also shown are the locations of the earliest land grants of the Old 300 settlers, compiled from General Land Office data by Wolfram Von-Maszewski, *Austin's Old Three Hundred: The First Anglo Colony in Texas* (Waco: Eakin Press, 2011).

The Spanish attempted to subdue the coastal Karakawas, who lived farther down the coast from the Akokisa, beginning with a garrison and mission at La Bahia on the Guadalupe River in 1722, near a destroyed earlier fort founded in 1685 by the French explorer Robert Cavelier, Sieur de La Salle. La Bahia was moved to a site on the San Antonio River by José de Escandón in 1745; this site is located at modern day Goliad, in South Texas.[38] The mission was never successful in converting significant numbers of Karankawas, but the military purpose of the garrison allowed the site to thrive. Other Spanish efforts to colonize the Karankawa were at Mission Nuestra Señora de Rosario, located a short distance west of modern Goliad and abandoned in 1781, and another at Nuestra Señora del Refugio (modern Refugio), founded in 1793. These latter missions were to have little success with the Karankawas, who saw the Spanish as useful for protection from marauding Lipan Apaches but for little else.[39]

Disappearance of Native American groups with Anglo colonization

With Mexican independence from Spain in 1821 and the coming of large numbers of Anglo settlers in the 1820s, Native Americans were soon to nearly disappear from the area. The primary reason that Anglo settlers came to Austin's colony, then a part of Mexico, was to grow cotton along the rich bottomlands of eastern Texas; they brought thousands of enslaved African Americans with them.[40] The Anglos settled primarily along the Brazos, Colorado and San Bernard rivers, with a few others settling along the San Jacinto River River (Figure 1.13 B). Their slaves cleared woodlands in the river bottoms and planted cotton in vast plantations. By 1833, Texas produced 900,000 pounds of cotton,[41] and by 1835, production grew to 3,000,000 pounds;[42] there were fortunes to be made. A scene from a Colorado River plantation in Texas, painted in about 1860, shows the critical ingredients of early Texas cotton culture (Figure 1.14). A group of enslaved African American women cultivates cotton that is growing in river bottom soil, working under the menacing stare of an overseer who carries a whip. In the background are dead trees, likely girdled in the effort to clear the river bottom land for planting.

This rapidly growing cotton economy wiped out vast amounts of prime bottomland habitat for the wild game that had sustained Native Americans, leaving many of them with nowhere else to go in coastal Texas. Clashes between Anglo settlers and the Karankawa and Akokisa were frequent during the early years of Stephen F. Austin's colony, and the settlers favored severe retribution. In 1823 at San Felipe, Austin appointed early settler Josiah Bell as a lieutenant in the colony's militia, granting him authority to act independently in case of Indian attack on Brazos settlements: "Bell will adopt all necessary measures to protect the said settlements from the attacks of the Karankawas, Cokes [Akokisa], or any other Indians, and to chastise them for any depredations they may commit within said limits without waiting for orders from his Superior officer."[43] By 1840, as a result of pressures due to Anglo settlement along the Brazos and Colorado rivers, as well as on Galveston Bay, the western Harris County area was largely empty of these three groups (Figure 1.13B).

Karankawa. The Karankawa, and in particular the Cocos subgroup that inhabited coastal Harris and Galveston counties (Figure 1.15) had a particularly difficult relationship with Stephen F. Austin's early colonists. Proud and warlike, they were known by settlers to practice cannibalism. A first-hand account of an early interaction between settlers and the Karankawa was written by Richard Hancock Hunter (1813–1902), who came to settle in Texas in 1822 with his father, Johnson Calhoun Hunter (1787–1855). They first landed in San Jacinto Bay, and after a rough time of it made their way to Galveston and then to what was later called variously New Washington, Clopper's Point, and (today) Morgan's Point in San Jacinto Bay, near the mouth of Buffalo Bayou. At this time there were a number of emigrants landing in the area, and encounters with Indians began:

> *The Tankaway Indians [Tonkawas], & Cronks [Karankawas], ware hostile & troubled the whites. Tha lernt how to give a signal, by putting up a white flag. There was two fameleys come up from Galveston in two small boats. The Cronks put a white flag on the beach at little seder Bayou & the boats went a shore. The Cronks run on them & kild them, 3 men 2 wimmen & 4 or 5 children. One man got a way, by jumping out in to the bay swim-*

Figure 1.14. Watercolor, Cotton Plantation near Columbus Texas, c. 1860, artist unknown. Enslaved African American women on a Colorado River plantation are cultivating cotton under the gaze of an overseer. Courtesy of the Museum of Fine Arts, Houston.

Figure 1.15. Cocos Indians of the Karankawa linguistic group, from Jean-Louis Berlandier's *The Indians of Texas in 1830*, courtesy of the Smithsonian Institution Library, Washington.

Figure 1.16. "Indians of several Nations bound for New Orleans, 1735," by Alexandre de Batz. The group includes various members of the Illinois tribes of the Mississippi Valley, a Fox woman who was a captive slave *(seated)*, a negro boy, and an Atakapan male *(right)*. The Atakapan people lived in southern Louisiana and southeastern Texas, where their westernmost bands were the Akokisa and Bidai. Courtesy of the Peabody Museum, Harvard.

> *ing & wading a bout 4 or 5 miles a cross to the point, & came a round to Pas. Pa & a man by the name of Fowler, got in thare boats & collected some 10 or 15 men, & went down to little seder Bayou that night, & found the Indians, a kooking the peoples hands & feet & eating & dancing. The whites lay close in the grass by them untill day light, & fiard in to them, & kild 15 or 20 of them, & the balance left. Tha never bothered us any more.*[44]

Stephen F. Austin led a raid in 1824 that drove the Karankawas to seek sanctuary in La Bahía Mission (modern day Goliad), but that outcome was not a permanent solution from the Texian perspective, and there were many more clashes with the tribe, each successive one thinning the native group's population. By the time of Texas Independence in 1836 the Indians were greatly diminished in numbers, and by 1840 there were only scattered remnants along the coast. A final clash in 1858 near Rio Grande City apparently finished off the last remaining band of the tribe.[45]

Akokisa and Bidai. Encounters with such early European travelers, missionaries and traders seem to have caused the demise of the Akokisa and Bidai, two groups who lived between the Brazos and Trinity rivers. Both were considered subgroups of the Atakapa, a Southeastern Woodland people of coastal southeastern Texas and southwestern Louisiana. Infectious diseases decimated the Atakapa before the Anglo settlement of Texas in the early nineteenth century, and most of the few survivors then joined Caddo and other surrounding tribes (Figure 1.16).[46] Accounts of sightings of Akokisa and Bidai after the Texas Revolution are rare. Surprisingly, one small group of Bidai existed in northern Harris County into the early 1920s. They lived along Cypress Creek on land homesteaded by Matthew Burnett in 1836. Burnett's daughter, Rebecca Burnett Lee, wrote about these people, and their chief, Francisco. The Burnett land was eventually purchased by German immigrants named Telge in the 1850s. Chester Telge, born on that property in 1918, recalled that the Bidai were still there in his youth. In an interview with archeologists Roger A. Moore and Madeleine Donachie, Telge described how they lived in hide tents on pimple mounds, and said:

> *His father and grandfather gave the Indians beef and hides periodically, and [he] went on to describe a charming incident of reciprocity. On baking day, his grandmother would wrap up a large loaf of bread and leave it on the back porch. By sundown, the Indians would have exchanged it for a large catfish. . . . The end of the Bidai's occupation was marked by the day in the early 1920s when the loaf of bread remained on the porch past sundown. Chester's grandmother brought the bread back into the house, and announced in German that "the Indians are no more."*[47]

Tonkawa. The Tonkawa, a group of Plains Indians, were only periodic visitors to the Houston and the Brazos River areas; their core area was farther west and southwest, between the Colorado and San Antonio rivers, so they were less impacted by the cotton plantations. They were allies of the Anglo settlers in battles with the Comanches, after Stephen F. Austin entered into a treaty with them in 1824. Tonkawans fought with the Texas Rangers against Comanches at the Battle of Plum Creek in 1840 and were granted a reservation on the Brazos River, near present day Graham, Texas, in 1854. At the Battle of Little Robe Creek in 1858, in Oklahoma, a large number of Tonkawans again assisted the Texas Rangers against the Comanche. They assisted the 4th U.S. Army in anti-Comanche campaigns of the 1870s. Nonetheless, Anglo settlers pressed for their removal, and they were forcibly relocated to Indian Territory (Oklahoma) in 1885, where members of that tribe still reside today.[48]

The Alabama-Coushatta. While the Karankawas and Akokisa were being displaced and decimated by Anglo settlement, a new group of Native Americans moved into Texas, forced westward from their homes in Alabama and Mississippi, pushed from there by yet earlier Anglo settlement. They began crossing the Sabine River into Spanish Texas by the 1780s. A small group of Alabama-Coushatta traded with settlers in early Houston and settled briefly on the north bank of Buffalo Bayou.

Robert Hunter wrote of peaceful relationships with this group in the 1820s:

> *Pa ust to traid up the San Jancinto river with the Coshatta Indians, would buy deer skins bare skins coon skins & all kinde & bares oil. I all ways went with him. We went in a boat. The old chief Francisco treated us fine. When we would leave them, Francisco would give us as much bare meat as we wanted to take home with us. He would say to pa, for you scaw & poppass [for your squaw and papoose]. Pa would take his bare deer skins & oil to Attakapas [Louisiana] & sell them for sugar, molases, rum, red flannel broad cloth, for the indians. Pa don write smart traiding with the indians.*[49]

Relationships between Anglo settlers and this tribe were generally peaceful, but there were occasional flare-ups. General Sam Houston wrote to them in October 1838:

> *There is much talk of war. It is useless. There is no sense in it. I know that my brothers, the Alabamos and Coosatties, will not deceive me. A few bad men may have gone from amongst you and been killed with the enemy. This shall not destroy your band. Remember the words which I have spoken to you.*

The little chiefs of the Texas nation shall not hurt you. My words have been spoken and the winds shall not scatter them. Remember me and be happy with your women and children. Winter is coming and cold weather and you may be unhappy unless with your women and children. Stay with them until the spring comes and you shall receive a talk from the chief of this nation. You must not take up the tomahawk. Nor will I allow other men to raise it against you.[50]

The Alabama-Coushatta periodically visited German settlers in the Bear Creek community, north of Addicks, in the period 1847–1875. Early settler Dorothea Hillendahl Groschke, who moved to the Bear Creek area in about 1850, recalled how "Indians" bartered with her and others there, trading wild game for food.[51] A grandson of Wilhelm and Christiana Rummel, a pair of German immigrants who had moved to frontier Spring Branch in 1848 and opened a trading post there, wrote of this remembered incident, in the late 1840s:

It was . . . at this time that they had the scare of their lives. Indians, fifteen of them, coming right up to them in the trail that led to their place. Grandpa came running, telling Grandma "Run for your life, the Indians are coming," but Grandma was thinking something entirely different. She told him to set the table, put the dried beef on the table, all the sweet potatoes and a water bucket full of milk on the table, and she would do the rest. She couldn't even speak English but she went out to meet the chief and she held up her hands, palms turning outward, indicating that they wanted to be friends, then pointed to the house and they all followed her. She pointed to the food on the table and the milk they could drink. The Indian chief was so pleased that she fed them when they were tired from their long hike. They stayed two days and the chief showed my father's oldest brother how to make buckskin clothes, and then Grandma gave them some steel sewing needles. Those were the little Polk County Indians, the Alabama Coushattas, and were peaceable. They had no intention of fighting anyone.[52]

These Alabama-Coushatta had migrated from the southeastern United States to Polk County in the East Texas piney woods, where they received a reservation in 1853. An Addicks area resident remembered how "the Indians came in large numbers and camped near Buffalo Bayou near the Habermacher Crossing [Wheaton's Ford, now at Highway 6]. In 1875, they suffered from a severe winter and many died. This was the last time that a large tribe ever came."[53]

Legacy

The natural world that was so glowingly described by early Texas visitors is all but gone in Harris County today. Only a few small remnants of "grand prairie" native habitat remain, chiefly at the Attwater Prairie Chicken National Wildlife Refuge in Eagle Lake, Colorado County, and on Katy Prairie Conservancy land in Harris and Waller counties. Nonetheless, the open range of the grand prairie existed in western Harris County throughout the nineteenth century and was to shape the lives of area pioneers for several generations, as we shall see in following chapters.

There are few traces left of early Native Americans in the upper Buffalo Bayou area, save a few artifacts on display at scattered local historical sites and museums. Archeological evidence of Native American groups' residence in western Harris County is strong but is little known outside the ranks of academic archeologists and professional historians. The Smithsonian Institution conducted an archeological survey in 1943 of nine midden sites along Buffalo Bayou and its tributaries as part of an effort to study them before completion of the Addicks and Barker Dams.[54] An archeological excavation of 1953 on the north bank of Buffalo Bayou just west of Voss Road yielded large amounts of flint and chert arrowheads, spear points and hand tools, possibly related to use of the site by Indians from the interior.[55] Well-studied excavations of burial sites on Mitchell Ridge in Galveston, undertaken in the early 1990s, show a range of dates from around 50 BC to the historic period, for a people who may well have been the Akokisa.[56]

Figure 2.1. An early dog trot cabin, coastal Texas, 1920s.
Photograph by J. M. Heiser, Jr, MSS 246-283,
courtesy of the Houston Metropolitan Research Center, Houston Public Library.

TWO

Dreams of a Commercial Empire

We are doing well as it respects worldly things and much pleased with the country,
and although some of the Indian tribes are troublesome yet, they will soon
be brought to peaceable terms and the country will settle. . . .
The situation is handsome & the land around [is] rich. . . .
there are not many large plantations yet open,
but those who are industrious are well paid for their labour.
Corn & Cotton grow remarkably large, & the increase of cattle & stock of every kind surpass
any thing I ever witnessed in any country. The first settlers here as in all new Countries
are a Class of people who do not Labour, but soon make way
and are succeeded by those of a more industrious description.

—Nicholas Clopper, San Felipe, Texas, July 26, 1826[1]

THE DESCRIPTIONS by early Texas travelers of an untrammeled, empty prairie, home to abundant wild game and few Indians, are often a bit promotional in tone, but nonetheless capture the awe of early visitors gazing upon an unfenced wilderness. Except for a few small settlements surrounding earlier Spanish missions and the town of San Antonio, Texas was a nearly unpopulated frontier. In 1809 the Spanish governor of Texas, Manuel de Salcedo, counted only 352 soldiers and 3,122 mostly impoverished citizens of European origin in the unimaginably vast province of Texas. By the time the new country of Mexico had won its independence in 1821, it is estimated that the population of Texas was even smaller.[2]

As Anglo settlers began to pour into Texas in the early 1820s, an unheralded stream called Buffalo Bayou assumed strategic importance for the early Texian colony. This chapter examines some of the upper bayou's early settlers and then explores the beginnings of an early colonial transport route from the bayou to the capital of Austin's colony at San Felipe de Austin. That route developed along a wilderness track that followed the course of the upper bayou; it later became known as the San Felipe Trail. The development of the early trade route was enabled by the foundation of Harrisburg by John Harris in 1826, and by the efforts of Nicholas Clopper and his family to establish a Texas mercantile empire utilizing that trail.

Stephen F. Austin's Colony

Land-hungry American would-be settlers had been anticipating the opening of Texas to settlement for decades. A number of unsuccessful military filibustering expeditions had been undertaken to seize the province from a weak Spanish administration, among them the Gutiérrez-Magee "Republican Army of the North" of 1812, the Mina-Perry expedition of 1817, and the Long expedition of 1819.[3] Meanwhile, Connecticut-born Moses Austin (1761–1821), a formerly wealthy owner of lead mines in Virginia and Missouri who had lost his fortune in unsuccessful ownership of a bank in St. Louis, tried a more peaceful approach than the filibusterers, appealing directly to the Spanish government in San Antonio to establish an American colony in Texas. Moses Austin's efforts to gain a Texas land grant from the Spanish government of Mexico were rewarded by that government in 1820.[4]

Moses Austin, however, died on returning to his home in Missouri in June 1821. His son Stephen F. Austin sought to reauthorize the grant in his name, brought a few settlers with him into Texas, and then traveled to New Orleans to recruit more. Complications arose when Mexico became independent of Spain in 1821, potentially threatening the future of the venture, so Austin went to Mexico City in early 1822 to petition for reauthorization from the new Mexican authorities. The State of Coahuila y Tejas received the authority to administer public lands in 1824, and 272 titles were granted in Austin's colony by the end of 1824, with a few more granted in 1827 and 1828. These early settlers have later been called the "Old 300."[5] Stephen F. Austin founded his colony's capital at San Felipe de Austin on the west bank of the Brazos River in 1824.

As mentioned earlier, the vast majority of the Austin Colony's Old 300 land grants were located along fertile bottomlands of the Brazos, Colorado, and San Bernard river valleys (Figure 2.2). Most of the Old 300 were planters from the southern United States, and they came with their African American slaves to set up cotton plantations on the rich soil of those bottomlands. Their migration from other earlier plantations in the South happened because intensive cultivation of cotton, in an age before widespread use of industrial fertilizer, was damaging to the soil. Austin's new colony had plenty of fertile land for these migrating Southern planters. The grants were for a labor of 177 acres for farmers, and a sitio (league) of 4,428 acres for stock raisers, with the possibility of a labor and a sitio for those wishing to do both. Yet more land could be granted to those bringing multiple families, establishing new industries, or somehow being useful in other ways.[6]

Early settlers on Buffalo Bayou

By 1822 a number of settlers had entered Galveston Bay and the mouths of the San Jacinto River and Buffalo Bayou. Some, perhaps most, were attracted by Austin's promotional activities. Among these early settlers was Nathaniel Lynch, who settled near the mouth of Buffalo Bayou on the San Jacinto River and began a ferry operation there. John D. Taylor settled on the north side of that river, at a place later called Midway.[7]

Also among the 1822 settlers were the Mason and Phelps families from Florence, Alabama. An elderly Robert Mason led the party from Florence, but he and his wife soon died. His daughter, a widow named Jane Mason Wilkins (1787-ca. 1848), ascended Buffalo Bayou to the prairie in a place later called Frostown (or Frost Town), east of today's downtown Houston, where she settled temporarily with her two daughters. Jane Wilkins did not obtain a land grant at this site, and she later moved to San Felipe. Dr. James Phelps, a physician recruited by Stephen F. Austin, started a farm at this site with Stephen Holston. Phelps also moved on and later was granted a sitio and two labors of land in Brazoria County.[8]

By 1824 there were a few more undocumented settlers living on lower Buffalo Bayou, including the Vince brothers, Ezekiel Thomas, and Moses A. Callahan.[9] That same year the Mexican government allowed Stephen F. Austin to issue titles to settlers in areas outside the boundaries of his original colony, including in particular the areas along the

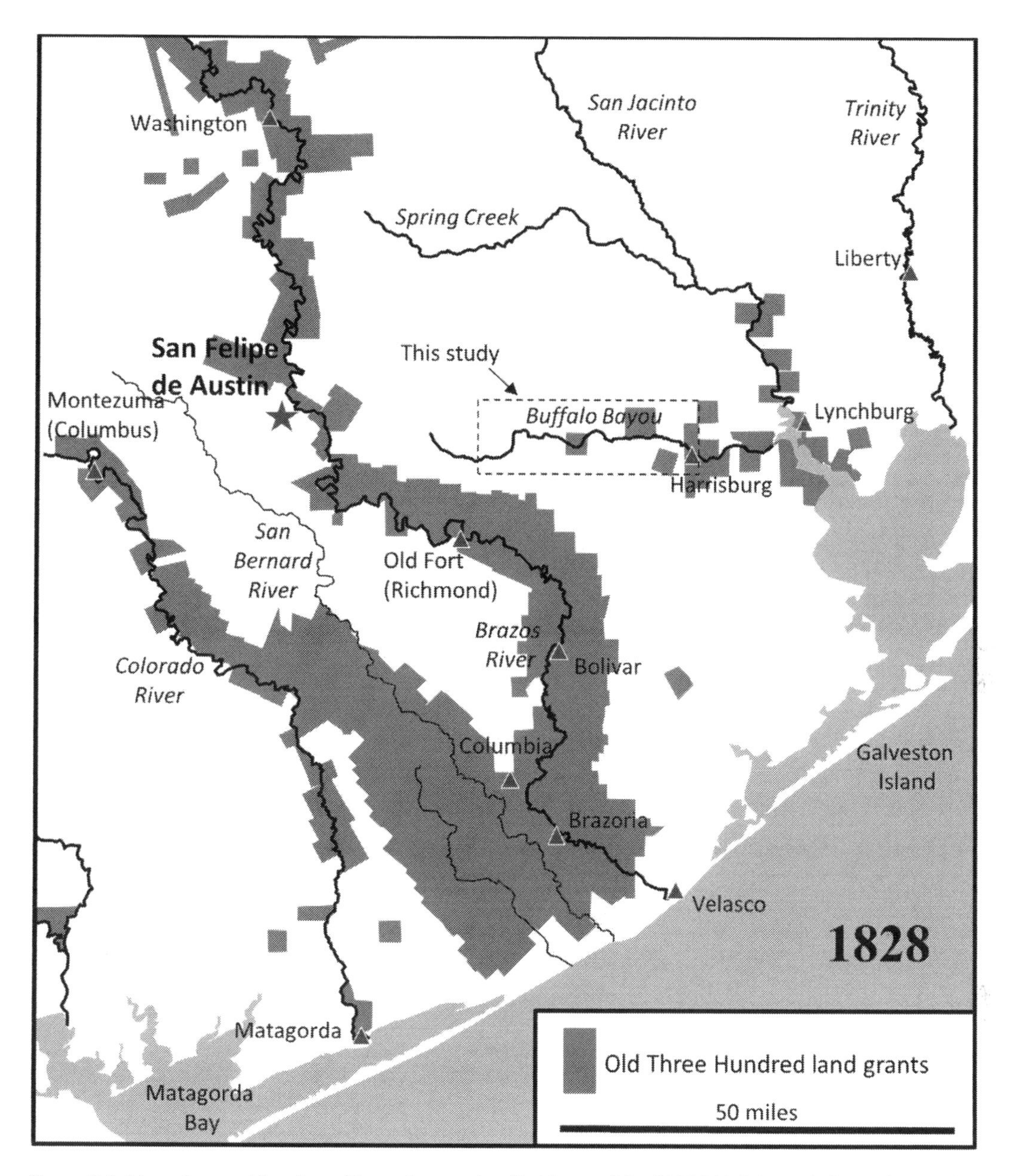

Figure 2.2. Map of part of Southeast Texas showing landholdings of the "Old 300," Austin's first colonists, by 1828. Compiled from General Land Office data by Wolfram Von-Maszewski, *Austin's Old Three Hundred* (Waco: Eakin Press, 2011).

southern San Jacinto River, Buffalo Bayou, and Cedar Bayou. In July–August 1824 Stephen F. Austin, along with his secretary, Samuel May Williams, and his land commissioner, Felipe Enrique Neri, the self-styled "Baron de Bastrop," visited the area to award the first set of these grants. The appointments were made in John D. Taylor's former home at Midway Point, which had by that time been sold to William Scott; Taylor had his eye on a plot along upper Buffalo Bayou.[10]

Buffalo Bayou, being a much smaller waterway than the Brazos or Colorado, did not have the wide fertile bottomlands of the larger Texas rivers and thus did not receive a large number of these colonists of 1824. A few settled on the lower bayou, close to the navigation possibilities of Trinity Bay. Robert and Allen Vince, Ezekiel Thomas, Thomas Earle, Moses Callahan and a few others received grants on the heavily timbered lower bayou. David Carpenter and William Harris received a grant at the mouth of the river, at its confluence with the San Jacinto River, and just upstream of Trinity Bay. Of more interest to this narrative, however, are a few settlers and land speculators who settled still farther up that bayou, into areas that later became parts of Houston.

John Austin's leagues of 1824

Yet farther upstream was the two-league tract granted in 1824 to John Austin, part of which would much later, in 1836, become the core of the town of Houston (Figure 2.3). John Punderson Austin (1801–1833) came from New Haven, Connecticut. An adventurer in spirit, he went to sea as a sailor in his teenage years and eventually found his way to New Orleans, where he signed on to the Long expedition of 1819. This was one of the "filibustering" expeditions undertaken by Anglo-Americans—some jointly with Mexican rebels, some not—that attempted to take Texas from a weak Spanish colonial government. This expedition's organizer, James Long, promised a league of land in Texas to each soldier, which perhaps was the draw for young John Austin. After a series of mishaps for the group, its last remnants were captured by Spanish troops at La Bahía (Goliad) in October 1821. Long was taken to Mexico City, where he eventually was executed.[11]

John Austin and some of the others were released, and while in Mexico City in 1821 he contacted Stephen F. Austin, who was there to receive his land grant for his new colony; they became friends. After a brief return to the United States in 1822, John Austin traveled to San Felipe and joined Stephen F. Austin's colony, making a bond as constable of the district of San Felipe de Austin on January 26, 1824.[12] On his way to San Felipe in 1822, John Austin may have made his way up Buffalo Bayou. At any rate, in 1824 he selected a site located four miles upstream of Harrisburg, at the farthest inland point at which there were any tidal effects in the bayou.

John Austin and John D. Taylor, who settled yet farther west along the bayou (discussed later) requested a surveyor to be sent, and District Surveyor John Cooke arrived in winter 1824, at which time he surveyed several properties along the bayou (Figure 1.3). The first was Taylor's Pine Point league, located at the site later to become Piney Point Village. Second was John Austin's two-league tract, located at the confluence of White Oak and Buffalo bayous. That tract, with its three streams, was almost entirely timbered, suggesting that Austin had timbering in mind when he chose it.

John Austin received title to this league on July 5, 1824, when he met with Stephen Austin, Austin's secretary Sam Williams, and Commissioner Baron de Bastrop, in the home at Point Pleasant that Taylor had just sold to Scott.[13] At the same meeting several other early settlers obtained land near future Harrisburg: John Harris, John D. Taylor, Nicholas Clopper, John Brown, and Luke Moore.

By 1825 John Austin had purchased a cotton gin (probably financed by Stephen F. Austin) and appears to have constructed a mill near the site of present day Allen's Landing. But he quickly lost interest in his land on the bayou. Perhaps John Austin saw poor initial results with cotton cultivation in the gumbo soil around his new cotton gin and became discouraged. By late 1825 he entered a partnership with J.E.B. Austin, Stephen F. Austin's younger brother, and both partners moved to the new town of Brazoria that they founded on the lower Brazos River; they opened a mercantile store there.[14] With this move, John Austin left the Buffalo Bayou area, although he continued to own the property.

At his new home in Brazoria, John Austin operated a cattle ranch and shipping business, becoming a port officer in 1831 and the *alcalde* of Brazoria in 1832. He later became involved in an early attempt at insurrection against Mexican authorities when he led Texian troops against the fort at nearby Velasco (modern day Surfside Beach, near Freeport). Mexican customs agents and the military authorities in

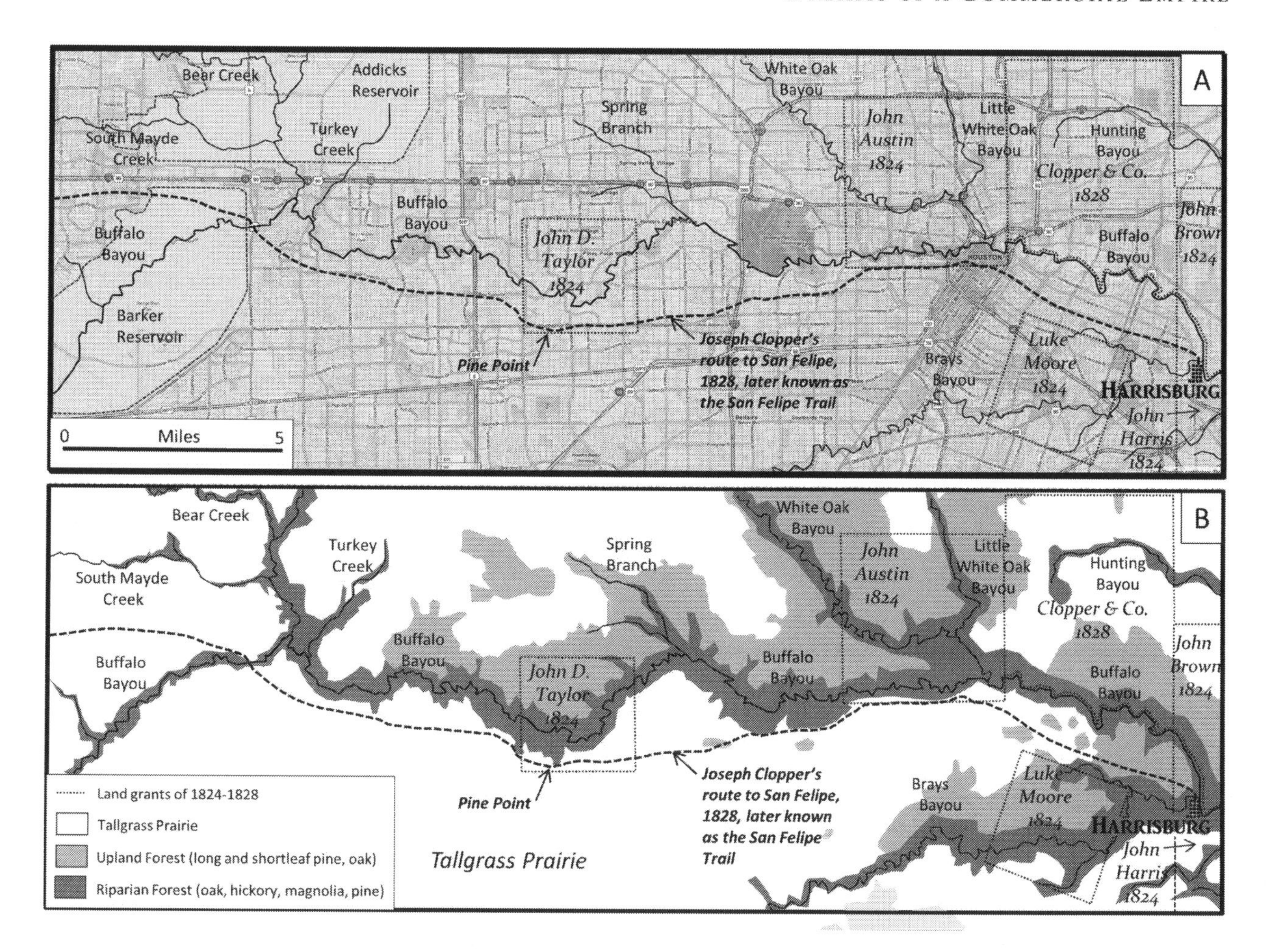

Figure 2.3. Land grants (dashed lines) along upper Buffalo Bayou in the 1820s.
A: Modern base map courtesy of OpenStreetMap.
B: Locations of forest and prairie (as in Figure 1.2), along with the approximate trade route of the Cloppers in 1828.

the garrison there had objected to movement of a cannon from Brazoria. The Texians intended to take the cannon to Anahuac, where an insurrection and siege were taking place. John Austin led the Texians in the battle of Velasco, on June 25–26, 1832, and the Mexican garrison was forced to surrender in the first military engagement of what would later become the Texas War of Independence.[15]

In August 1833 John Austin and two of his children died of cholera at Gulf Prairie. His wife Elizabeth survived and inherited his real estate interests, including his tract on Buffalo Bayou, and she married Thomas Parrott in 1834. Austin's father, named John Punderson Austin (1774–1834), traveled to Texas from his home in New Haven, Connecticut, to settle his son's estate, and Elizabeth turned over the upper part of her late husband's two-league tract to him. He too contracted cholera and died in Texas in 1834; he was buried in New Haven. In 1836 Elizabeth, by now remarried to Thomas F.L. Parrott, sold the southern part of the tract to the Augustus C. and John K. Allen, and that part of the tract shortly became the site of the new town of Houston.[16]

John Taylor and the Pine Point league of 1824

The earliest settler along upper Buffalo Bayou was John D. Taylor (d. 1829). Nearly nothing is known of him prior to his arrival in Texas by 1822, but by early 1824 he was living on the east side of the San Jacinto River near modern Baytown, where he built a log home overlooking the river. That year Taylor sold this home to William Scott, a newly arriving settler who named the home Point Pleasant. For reasons unknown, Taylor turned his attention to western Buffalo Bayou, away from any existing claims, in a frontier area far from any roads and considerably upstream of the part of the bayou that was accessible by steamboat traffic. By any estimate, it was in the middle of the frontier, and far from the nascent plantations of the Brazos and other rivers. With the help of surveyor John Cooke in 1824, Taylor laid out a league of 4,428 acres at Pine Point (Figure 2.3; also see Figure 1.3).

Taylor received title to this league on the same day as did John Austin, on July 5, 1824, at the meeting already mentioned with Stephen F. Austin, Samuel May Williams and Baron de Bastrop, in the home at Point Pleasant that Taylor had just sold to Scott.[17] Stephen F. Austin signed a statement indicating that Taylor was qualified to be "admitted as resident of this new Colony on account of his good qualities and circumstances and notorious application to agriculture and reading of cattle and industries, in consideration of which one league of land can be granted to him."[18]

At the location of Taylor's grant, there is a bend in the course of Buffalo Bayou, along which the bayou projected southward out into the prairie. A steep gully, named Piney Point Gully, fed into the bayou from the south, and it was surrounded by the southern tip of the forest. At or near that place was the stand of very tall pine trees that formed a beacon to travelers crossing the featureless prairie, leading to the name Pine (or Piney) Point (Figure 2.4). Pine Point was mentioned by name in the 1824 survey notes for Taylor's property and was already at that time becoming a landmark and a noted stopping point for travelers along the east-west path that would soon become the San Felipe Trail. A nearby spring became an important campground for travelers on the trail. The trail swerved south at Pine Point to miss the steep banks of Piney Point Gully.

John Taylor had a wife, Maria, as well as a daughter and two servants.[19] Upon arriving at their new land at Pine Point in 1824 they began the required cultivation to prove up the grant, and built a house. John and Maria Taylor had owned their one-league tract for a little over a year when Taylor sold the land for $1,095 in October 1825 to Charles S. Hudson, another member of the Old 300. Hudson soon died, and his note to Taylor was in default, so Taylor bought the land back at public auction for $173, in 1828. Taylor immediately resold the property to Stephen F. Austin, except for the southwestern part of the league where his house was situated, which became known as "Taylor's Reserve." Taylor and his wife moved to Harrisburg, where they both died of fever in 1829.[20]

The exact site of their house at Pine Point is not precisely known. When the Taylor property was transferred by title bond to John R. Harris in 1829, the deed mentioned an "old improvement near pine point spring" on the property east of Piney Point Gully; this improvement was most likely the Taylor house. Some 300 acres of the former Taylor land was sold to Buckman Canfield in 1838 (discussed later), including the "old improvement," and it is thought that Canfield may have used the earlier Taylor house, perhaps improving it or even rebuilding it. Other parts of the Taylor land were sold to Stephen F. Austin, and following Austin's death in 1836 that land went into litigation among Austin's heirs. At the time of the litigation's settlement in 1846 the land was divided into lots, and a map of those lots was made in 1854, filed with Harris County land records. That map indicates the approximate location of the Canfield home, south of the bayou and east of Pine Point Gully (Figure 2.4), within what is today the Windermere subdivision.

The Canfields' log house was described by a German visitor, Karl von Sommer, in 1846 when he stayed at the residence, then in the possession of

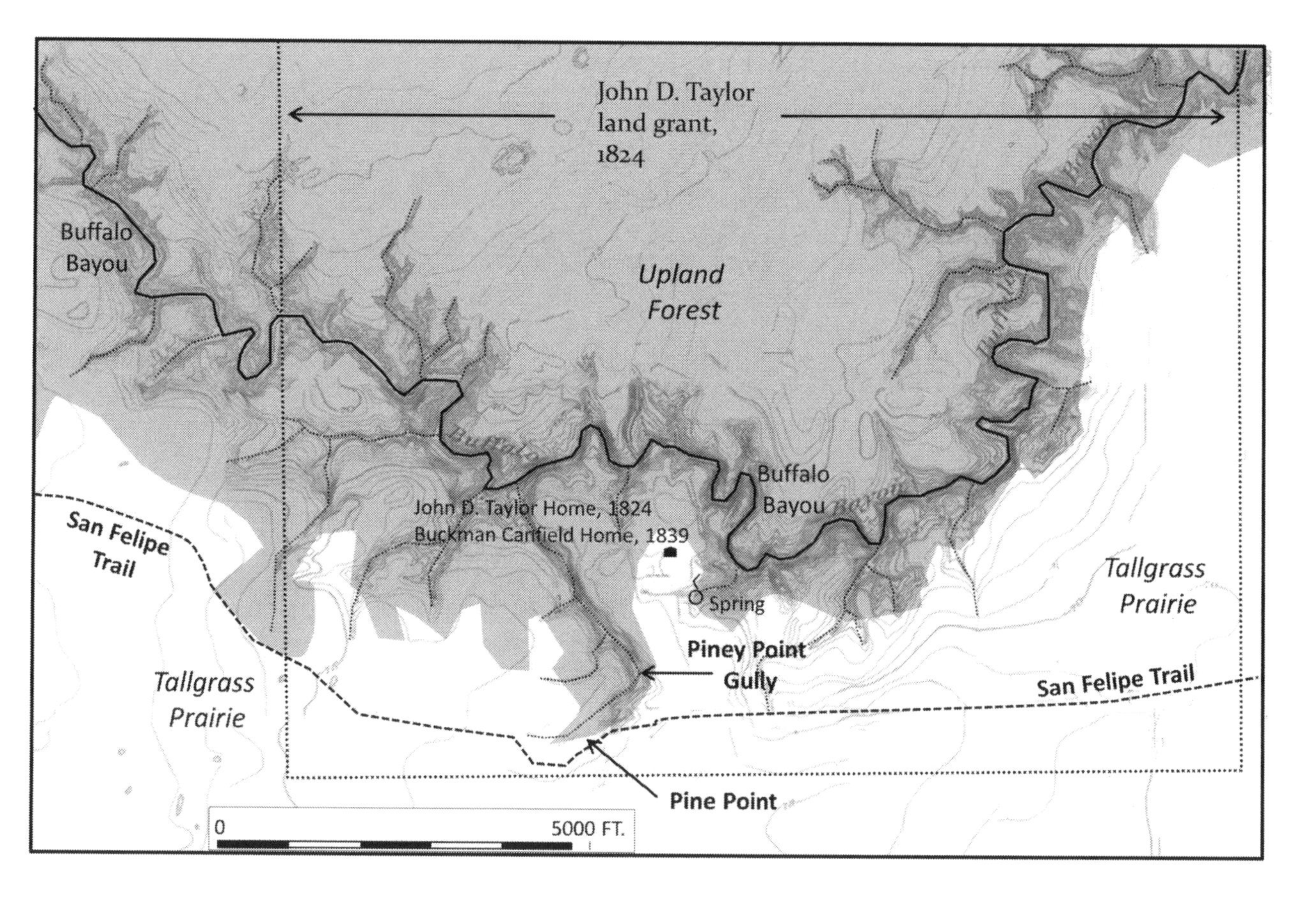

Figure 2.4. Cultural features of the Piney Point area in the 1830s, plotted on a 1915 U.S. Geological Survey topographic map. The estimated extent of original forest cover is shaded in gray.

Buckman's widow Harriet and her new husband, Benjamin George: "I searched for a path and was soon at the Pine Point Farm of a farmer named Mr. George, where we were given lodging. The farm house contains two rooms in which beds are available, and a kitchen, and also has, like almost all farm houses, a porch."[21] This is a description of the classic dog-trot house famously used throughout colonial Texas, where two log pens are constructed with an intervening open porch, the whole construction covered by one roof (examples are shown in Figures 2.1 and 2.5).

Buckman Canfield's widow replaced their early log home with a new frame house in the 1850s, and this home burned down in 1912 (Chapter 5). Large-scale sand removal operations that occurred in the 1950s prior to the construction of homes in the Windermere subdivision have obliterated all potential traces of the Canfield (and possible Taylor) home site.

John D. Taylor's stay in the area had been very brief, and there is little to indicate that he had done much to improve the property in his year of residency other than by building his home. It would appear that his intention, like that of many other early land speculators, was simply to prove up the purchase and sell it at a profit. Because his tenure at the property was so short it is not altogether clear whether he built a sawmill here, although the tract was heavily timbered. At the time of its purchase, Taylor's league was far from both San Felipe and the Brazos, and for that matter from any other settlement or any other land grant. Taylor may well have seen its potential utility both as a timber property and also as a waystation—with water and a prominent landmark—for travelers along the San Felipe

Figure 2.5. Dog-trot cabin at the Mc-Neal Plantation near Brazoria Texas, 1834. From Anonymous, *A Visit to Texas* (New York: Goodrich and Wiley, 1834).

Trail, which was then in all likelihood only a wilderness path from Harrisburg to San Felipe. The strategic importance of that path to Austin's colony was soon noted by others.

A problem, with a Buffalo Bayou solution

While Stephen F. Austin's new frontier colony was taking shape, it soon became apparent that planters had problems in getting their cotton to market. Because Texas had no cotton mills or textile industry, their produce needed to find its way to a saltwater port for export to New Orleans and beyond. Neither of the two main rivers in the colony—the Colorado or the Brazos—was easily or reliably navigable from the sea to its upstream plantations, nor to the colonial capital of San Felipe de Austin.

The Colorado River had an immense driftwood "raft" (logjam) that filled its channel in the coastal counties that it traversed, leaving it impassable for twenty miles. This massive logjam had existed for centuries, and was first noted by Spanish explorer Alonso de Leon in 1690. Following his visit, a cartographer, Manuel Joseph de Cardenas, attempted to ascend the Colorado from its mouth, but was stopped by the logjam, about ten to fifteen miles upriver. That raft was still there a century and a half later. The Texas congress enacted a law incorporating the Colorado Navigation Company in 1837, but the company failed to sell enough stock to act on removing the jam.[22] Colorado River farmers were reduced to unloading their export produce at the head of the jam, near modern day Bay City, and moving the freight by ox wagon to a small port at Matagorda.[23]

The Brazos River, which serviced the colony's capital at San Felipe as well as the plantations along its trace stretching from Brazoria to Washington counties, had a shallow, shifting sand bar at its mouth that rendered it generally impassable to saltwater vessels. Water depth at the bar was perhaps two or three feet at best. Only small sailing craft and keelboats were able to squeeze past the bar and navigate the river. As J. C. Clopper observed in 1828, "Vessels do not yet approach nearer than within 60 miles of Sanfelipe."[24] This meant that shipping goods to the colony's capital necessitated an overland segment of at least that length. An ox-drawn wagon could travel perhaps 12 to 15 miles per day on a good road, so reducing the overland transport distance by even a few miles could save days of travel and expense.

A first attempt at bringing a steamboat up the

Brazos was made in 1830, when Henry Austin, a cousin of Stephen F. Austin, brought the Ariel to test the feasibility of steamboat trade on that river. He decided that he could not make such a business profitable, and when attempting to return the boat to New Orleans, he nearly wrecked it while attempting to cross the shallow sand bar at the mouth of the Brazos.[25] When the steamboat *Cayuga* was brought to the Brazos by planters in 1834, it was the only steamboat operating in Texas and ascended as far as Washington—after waiting for three rises in river level while going upstream and enduring another three in returning downriver.[26] The Brazos was clearly not made for river trade, but the simple necessity of exporting cotton spurred on efforts at it. The *Yellow Stone* was brought to the Brazos in 1835 and was famously commandeered for moving Texian soldiers by Sam Houston at Groce's Landing in 1836 before disappearing somewhere on the Brazos in 1837.[27] As noted by Texas steamboat historian Leonard Kubiak,

> *Although the Brazos River carried a tremendous volume of water at times, the flow of the river was so uncertain and erratic that navigation on a regular basis proved to be impossible. Parts of the river were dredged and snags removed, but seasonal rises silted in manmade channels and left behind new snags to catch the unwary navigator. Elaborate plans were initiated to "improve" the river for navigation, but most were never begun.*[28]

What was needed was a protected port with sufficient draft, close to the plantations of the Brazos River bottom. A letter of 1824 from a J. Child to Stephen F. Austin suggested that goods could perhaps be moved up one of the streams entering Trinity Bay and then across the prairie to San Felipe.[29] Attention was focused on Buffalo Bayou, and the reason is clear from an inspection of the map in Figure 2.2. The major rivers of coastal Southeast Texas all flow from a north-northwesterly direction except for Buffalo Bayou, which flows from west to east (as does the smaller Spring Creek), providing a potential water highway far into the interior, allowing imported goods to be landed closer to San Felipe than by other routes. Early wagon roads of Austin's colony converged at San Felipe, which was situated more or less in a central position within the colony. John McFarland operated a ferry at San Felipe by 1822, even before the town was laid out, so crossing the Brazos River at that point—to service farmers living farther west—was possible.[30]

Getting oceangoing vessels to Buffalo Bayou did not present a particular problem. At Bolivar Pass, the water depth across the sand bar was ten to twelve feet, more than sufficient for saltwater vessels of the day to enter protected Galveston Bay. The rear side of Galveston Island made an attractive potential port, but before Texas Independence in 1836, it was too remote for much use. Its growth came later.[31]

Early settler and businessman Joseph C. Clopper (1802–1861) observed in 1828 that the bayou had "about three fathoms water with little variation in depth as high up as Harrisburg—20 miles—[and] the ebbing and flowing of the tide is observable about 12 miles higher[,] the water being of navigable depth close up to each bank, giving to this most enchanting little stream the appearance of an artificial canal."[32] The observation that the bayou was deep and looked like a canal was significant in an era when the Erie Canal was an important water highway in the northern United States. Along with the bayou's placid, canal-like appearance, it had fewer shifting sand bars, less log debris, and less seasonal flooding than did the Brazos and Colorado rivers. In a 1943 retrospective analysis, historian Andrew Forest Muir summed up the bayou's strategic importance to early Texas:

> *Buffalo Bayou, it would seem, was the means by which salt water navigation might safely penetrate the interior, free from the persistent danger of inundation. . . . In addition to its canal-like appearance, Buffalo Bayou had another peculiar advantage in respect to the trade of the Brazos River area. Unlike most significant Texas streams, it flows almost due east and west. With the Brazos extending in a general northerly direction, this meant that the head of navigation on the Bayou was but twenty miles or*

Figure 2.6. A scene along Buffalo Bayou, Houston, 1873. From Edward King, *The Great South: A Record of Journeys* (Hartford, Conn.: American Publishing Company, 1875).

so from the heart of the fertile agricultural region of the Brazos.[33]

Such transport seems to have been the general rationale for several land grants of 1824 and 1828 in interior parts of Buffalo Bayou. As mentioned earlier, Buffalo Bayou had no great swath of fertile bottomland soil along its course and was thus seemingly of little use to planters for cotton cultivation. Therefore the few land grants made along it in early times would likely have been requested either for the bayou's strategic use as a transport medium or for transporting timber to be harvested along its banks.

John Harris and Harrisburg

John Richardson Harris (1790–1829) was to sense the importance of the bayou waterway. Born in New York State, he was a veteran of the War of 1812. By 1819 he and his wife, Jane Birdsall Harris, were living in St. Genevieve, Missouri, where they met Moses Austin and decided to throw in with the Texas colony. By 1822 or 1823 Harris was in Texas, where he applied for and received a land grant in 1824 on Buffalo Bayou at its confluence with Brays Bayou (Figure 2.3). The spot was strategic, as it lay about twenty-five miles inland from the edge of Trinity Bay (ten miles upstream from the mouth of the San Jacinto River in Trinity Bay, and another fifteen miles up Buffalo Bayou). The bayou at Harris's site was deep enough to allow steamboat traffic to pass easily, and Harris considered that spot to be the head of practical navigation on the bayou. Having an inland position, the site was relatively protected from Gulf storms—certainly a better location in this regard than Velasco or Matagorda. The spot was also thickly timbered. Harris laid out the town of Harrisburg there in 1826, and built a trading post and a sawmill.

The town was laid out in 1826. John Harris and his brother David, by 1828 joined by their brothers William and Samuel, also operated a trading post at Bell's Landing on the lower Brazos, and they owned sloops that plied the Gulf between those locations and New Orleans.[34] Joseph Clopper wrote an early description of Harrisburg in 1828:

Harrisburg is laid out on the west side of this bayou [Buffalo Bayou] just below its junction with Bray's Bayou—it is yet in the woods consisting of 6 or 8 houses scatteringly situated—the timber consisting primarily of tall pine and oaks so excludes the prairie breezes as to render the Summer's heat almost intolerable, but this can be the case but for a short time—being situated at the head of navigation without any local cause for unhealthiness and surrounded by a vast quantity of timber which in this country must prove immensely valuable[;] there is only wanted a population a little more dense and a few capitalists of enterprise and energy to render it one of the most important towns in the colony.35

Soon the town had a blacksmith shop, a carpenter's shop, and a fine mercantile.[36] By 1829 Harris was building a steam sawmill/gristmill, but he contracted yellow fever and died while on a trip to New

Orleans for supplies for the mill. His operations then went to his brothers David, Samuel and William. This milling operation was the beginning of the industrial use of shipping along Buffalo Bayou. The mill thrived, as is clear from the descriptions of its operation by Fiske, who visited in 1831:

> *At this place was the only steam saw mill at that time in the country. The engine works also a flour mill, where one fifth is taken for a toll. It was found very profitable, although not worked with proper attention to economy, as the lumber is admitted into all the Mexican ports without duty, while from the United States it was almost excluded. They did not heat the boilers until after breakfast, and emptied them daily at sunset. The price of boards was forty dollars a thousand. The mill is on Buffalo Bayou, about thirty miles from the Brazos River, and is accessible to vessels drawing five or six feet of water. The timber, yellow pine and oak, is floated to the mills. Three vessels were there on the 1st of April, waiting for loads of lumber for Tampico and Matamoros. Mr. Harris told me that he had orders for more than he could supply. They might saw from three to five thousand a day with proper industry.*
>
> *The town had its name from Mr. Harris, the owner of the mill. It contained only about twenty houses, built almost entirely of logs, with only two or three frame dwellings, and being laid out without much regard to regularity.*[37]

After the death of John Harris in 1829, the property went to his brothers, his wife, and other heirs amid litigation. It was still in litigation when the town was burned down by Santa Anna's army in 1836, during the Texas Revolution. It was a place of great strategic potential in a day of water travel. When two real estate promoters from New York, John Kirby Allen and Augustus Chapman Allen, came up Buffalo Bayou soon after the Battle of San Jacinto, looking for a site for a new commercial center, they offered to buy the Harrisburg site, then in ashes. However, when it became clear that the title was not clear, they moved six miles upstream and purchased a southern part of the John Austin leagues from his widow, Elizabeth Parrott (discussed later); that became the founding site of Houston and the new seat of government for the new Texas Republic.[38] Harrisburg had been bypassed.

An adjacent league of land granted to Luke Moore, also in 1824, was located on a heavily forested part of Brays Bayou and appears from both its position and orientation to have been selected for its timber (Figure 2.3). Moore, of whom little is known, was later a soldier in the Texas Revolution, and appears to have died shortly after the war, in 1837.[39] Also in 1824 a tract just to the north of Harris's grant went to John Brown (b. ca. 1789, d. probably 1836), a Kentuckian who appears to have had only a speculative interest in the property, as he soon sold it to Nicholas Clopper (see next section). By 1830 Brown was apparently living in San Antonio.[40]

Dreams of empire: Nicholas Clopper and his family

The first person both to understand the commercial potential of the bayou for moving goods to and from the Austin Colony and to act upon this realization was Nicholas Clopper (1766–1841; Figure 2.7). He was born in New Jersey in the decade before the American Revolution.[41] His great-great-grandfather Cornelius Clopper (1630–1686) had emigrated from the Netherlands to New Amsterdam (the future New York City) in 1653, and the family had lived on the eastern seaboard ever since. Nicholas married Rebecca Chambers (1767–1814) in Pennsylvania in 1790, and the couple had eleven children between 1791 and 1809. There were seven boys, of whom four reached adulthood (Andrew May, 1791–1853; Nicholas Jr., 1794–1822; Joseph, 1802–1861; and Edward Nicholas, 1803–1828), and four daughters, none of whom ever married (Rebecca C., 1792–1845; Caroline C., 1800–1875; Mary Ann Catherine, 1807–1875; and Rachel Ruhamah, 1809–1845).[42] Nicholas Sr.'s wife Rebecca died in 1814, leaving him to manage the upbringing of the family on his own. By 1820 he was living in Cincinnati, Ohio.

When Nicholas Clopper heard Stephen F. Austin's call for colonists, he planned to establish a new home in Texas for his family. Nicholas and three of his sons—Andrew, Nicholas Jr., and Joseph—resolved to open a mercantile in the new colony, testing Texas to see if it might make an appropriate new home for his close-knit family. By May 1822 Nicholas and Andrew were in Texas, leaving Joseph, for the time being, in Cincinnati. Nicholas Jr. arrived in October 1822, with a flatboat loaded with merchandise intended for sale in the Clopper mercantile, and was killed by Karankawa Indians, probably at the mouth of the Colorado River. The details were never clear to family members, who long held out hope that he might have been captured. His Aunt Ann wrote to his sister Rebecca Clopper, living in Ohio, on July 5, 1823:

> *Poor Nicholas, I cannot bear to think of his fate but I will not think he is lost to you entirely, if it had been their intention to kill they would have done it at once . . . and while there is life there is hope and you may still see your dear brother. . . . Poor Peter [a companion who accompanied Nicholas Jr. on the flatboat] how different a fate from what he looked forward to. . . . I expect they found him too high spirited to submit was the reason they murdered him. Your father must have hopes or he would not stay in that hateful place.*[43]

Figure 2.7. Nicholas Clopper (1766–1841), from Edward Nicholas Clopper, *An American Family* (Cincinnati: Standard Print and Publishing Company, 1950).

Nicholas Sr. and Andrew returned to the United States at the end of 1823. But the attractions of Texas had taken effect on Nicholas Sr., and by 1826 he left for Texas a second time, along with the Ludlow brothers, relatives of his wife. They arrived on March 26 at the mouth of the Brazos on the schooner The Rights of Man and unloaded the merchandise that they had brought. After journeying to San Felipe, intent upon starting a mercantile store there, he wrote to his children on July 26, 1826:

> *We are doing well as it respects worldly things and much pleased with the country, and although some of the Indian tribes are troublesome yet, they will soon be brought to peaceable terms and the country will settle. I have purchased a Lott in this place [San Felipe] & Building a store house & dwelling, and have a farm near Town on which there is a natural vineyard, the grapes are large & fine & am making Wine and Vinegar very good. . . . This Town is but in a state of infancy, only about 9 familys & 10 or 12 Log houses. The situation is handsome & the land around [is] rich . . . there are not many large plantations yet open, but those who are industrious are well paid for their labour. Corn & Cotton grow remarkably large, & the increase of cattle & stock of every kind surpass any thing I ever witnessed in any country. The first settlers here as in all new Countries are a Class of people who do not Labour, but soon make way and are succeeded by those of a more industrious description. We are now ready to receive and encourage a goodly number of the latter kind, this [is] one of our principal wants at present.*[44]

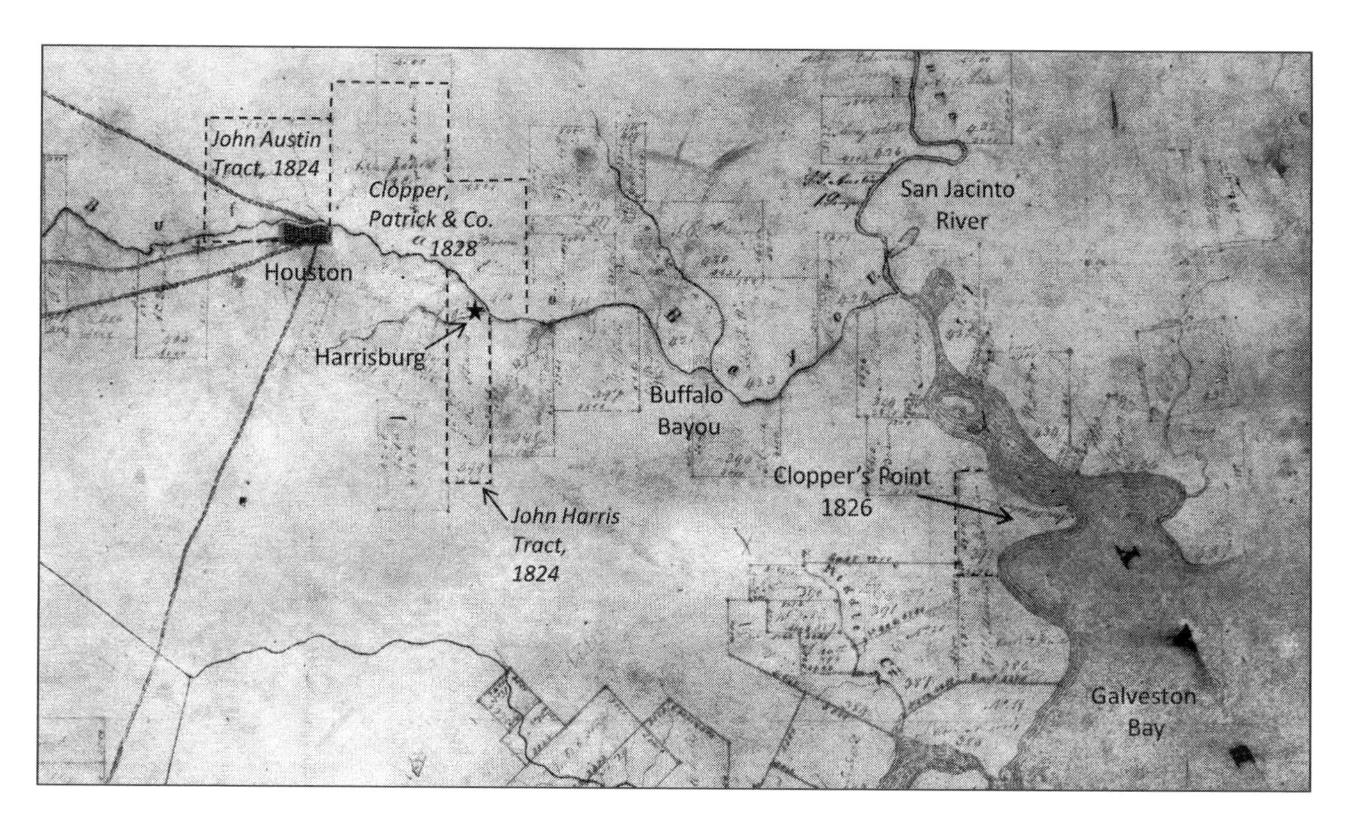

Figure 2.8. A portion of the Connected Map of Austin's Colony by Stephen F. Austin and J. F. Perry, 1837, showing lower Buffalo Bayou. Tracts discussed in the text are highlighted with dashed lines.
Courtesy of the General Land Office, Austin.

Clopper's tract in San Felipe was Lot 17, adjacent to Commerce Square, and his mercantile building was an 18-foot by 18-foot- square hewn log cabin with plank floors and a front porch.[45]

Nicholas was intent upon creating and securing the colony's trade route to the coast from San Felipe, and he quickly turned to the second leg of his scheme. Also in 1826, he purchased a peninsula of land that divided Galveston Bay from the estuary of the San Jacinto River, from Johnson Calhoun Hunter (1787–1855) for $1,450. Hunter had lived there for four years with his family and had made a living ferrying emigrants from Galveston to the mainland, farming, and trading supplies with the Coushatta Indians.[46] The peninsula, newly named Clopper's Point (and today, Morgan's Point; Figure 2.8), projected farther eastward into a submerged sand bar that was a menace to trade on Buffalo Bayou. The tiny settlement there—primarily Hunter's trading post—was called New Washington. Later that year Nicholas Clopper also bought John Brown's tract opposite and to the north of John Harris's new town of Harrisburg, with an intent to establish a mercantile emporium there. Clopper was thinking large.

After a visit to Cincinnati in early 1827 to purchase merchandise and supplies, Nicholas Clopper returned in November with his son Andrew and, for the first time, his sons Joseph Clopper (Figure 2.9) and Edward Clopper. Young Joseph, like others in his family, was a learned man, having studied the classics and law. The four Cloppers plus Captain James Lindsay, Dr. George Patrick, and surveyor Darius Gregg, all headed to Texas on the same boat from Cincinnati, and formed the Texas Trading Association (TTA), of which Nicholas Clopper was named president. On board the vessel were 10,300 pounds of materials for their planned mercantile establishments in both San Felipe and Harrisburg, the endpoints for their planned land route from middle Buffalo Bayou to the Brazos River plantations. These items included "whisky, wine, tobacco, powder, hardware, tinware, glassware, nails, beans, flour, mackerel, soap, and candles." A shipment intended for their store at Harrisburg included "dry goods, clothing, shoes, table utensils, lamps, hardware, tools, tomahawks, powder, and books." Another shipment, bound for their emporium in San Felipe, held "blankets, stockings, gloves, reticules, buckles, spectacles, brushes, combs, mirrors, scales, tumblers, snuffboxes, spices, writing paper, and medicine."[47]

In New Orleans they purchased a schooner named Little Zoe, and they arrived in Texas with their merchandise in January 1828. The party ascended Buffalo Bayou to Harrisburg, where they were to establish their next mercantile operation. Joseph Clopper's enthusiastic description of Buffalo Bayou, related esarlier, dates from this time.

Figure 2.9. Joseph C. Clopper (1802–1861), painted by Richard Verbryck, Cincinnati, 1827. From Clopper, *An American Family.*

At Harrisburg, on January 5, 1828, Edward Clopper wrote in his diary:

> *Were busy this day discharging the cargo of the schooner at the Landing at Harrisburgh where we rented a ware house @ 6$ p mo to put our goods in. During the ensuing week we went into the woods and commenced clearing a spot of ground whereon to build a store house &c. It is a privilege granted by the Proprietors of this burgh, that every settler who wishes to build in the town is entitled to a lot, we selected one of the best, on the bank of the river, at the junction of Braes and Buffalo Bayou, the river opposite our lot is about one hundred yards wide and 12 to 15 feet deep, and well stored with various kinds of fishes, turtle, crabs &c not excepting the vile and hideous aligators.*
>
> *Commenced gardening on the twelfth of this month—planted some beans, onions, potatoes, & transplanted some corn which I found growing about the old houses, had a great deal of rain during this month, some heavy thunder and sharp lightning. In consequence of the almost continual rains, we were very much retarded with our building. We however being strong handed, went to work with willing minds and a determined spirit, and soon got our lot cleared off, our logs cut and hewn, shingles made, and the house erected, and moved into it in about one month after our first landing in this Burgh, bravo.*
>
> *Find plenty of game of almost every kind in this country, very frequently see from forty to fifty or an hundred deer in a herd. Wild cattle, horses, and hogs are also numerous, one of our Hunters killed a wild turkey that weighed twenty pound . . . caught a turtle (loggerhead) that weighed eighty-five pounds, the head after being severed from the body weighed 10 3/4 lbs.*[48]

At Harrisburg the TTA purchased the Clopper's Point and John Brown tracts from Nicholas, and at this time Darius Gregg withdrew from the company.

Andrew assumed control of the store at Harrisburg. Shipments between the two TTA stores (at Harrisburg and San Felipe) commenced, and a raft of supplies was sent downriver to open a third store at the tiny settlement of New Washington, on Clopper's Point.[49] After nearly losing the raft, the association members assembled at the point, and according to Joseph's diary, built a small cabin and a warehouse, and planted a garden. With that work in hand, they returned to Harrisburg.

In April 1828 Nicholas Sr. and Edward headed to San Felipe with a wagon of supplies for the store there, followed by Joseph, Captain Lindsay, and Dr. Patrick. Joseph's joyful description of the great prairie that they encountered on this trip, and the distinctive tall pine trees at Pine Point along that trail, were included in the previous chapter. The route they took to San Felipe was the unimproved path–later known as the San Felipe Trail–that followed the southern edge of the riparian forest along Buffalo Bayou from Harrisburg to San Felipe (Figure 2.3). It is likely that Stephen F. Austin, Sam Williams, and Baron de Bastrop all used this same trail in 1824 on their way from San Felipe to Point Pleasant to sign the aforementioned land grants.

The Cloppers' transit of this trail probably marked the beginning of commercial overland trade between the new port on Buffalo Bayou at Harrisburg and inland regions of Texas. The route had the advantage of being out in the open prairie for fast travel but close to the trees for shade, protection, and water when needed. The south side of the bayou did not have nearly as many tributaries coming into the bayou as on the north side (e.g., White Oak Bayou, Spring Branch, Bear Creek and South Mayde Creek), obviating the necessity of crossing a lot of steep water-filled gullies on the way west (Figure 2.3).

At San Felipe, Joseph described the small town and its setting before turning to the agricultural potential of the region:

> *[They] will turn out more than 100 bales of cotton, & sugar cane proportionally—it is thought there will be a sufficiency of sugar made this year to supply both colonies—Austin's & De Witt's—tho' in the former alone the census of last Spring makes a total of 3,000 souls. There are several planters already engaged in erecting sugar mills & they have resolved to dispose of it at 10 cts, this is cheaper than it can be sold at here by purchasers & shippers from N. Orleans—Many have their cotton gins in operation & the establishment of a cotton factory is already agitated. Here also is raised some of the fattest & most delicious beef & bacon in the world at no expense nor trouble, the grass of the prairies & mast of the bottoms makes it all—salt is made abundantly & sold remarkably low & the waters abound with the finest fish, oysters, crabs, turtles &c—the forests with Buffalo, deer, bear et cetera.*[50]

As if the TTA hadn't enough to do, they purchased about thirty longhorn cattle with the intent to drive them to San Antonio to market them. While rounding them up in early July—no small feat in the unfenced Brazos River bottom—Edward fell ill and died. Shortly thereafter, while in mourning, Nicholas Sr. also fell ill, telling Joseph, "I fear we have been here too long." As his father was recovering, Joseph returned to the task of taking the cattle to San Antonio, catching up with Lindsay and Patrick in Gonzales, where the latter two were also very ill. After a pause there to recover, the group began again for San Antonio, with a still very sick Patrick in the wagon. Darius Gregg, with the group herding the cattle, was likewise ill, but Joseph by this time seems to have been healthy and "already acclimated tho' not yet wedded to Texas." Joseph remained in San Antonio for some months, nursing the invalided association members.[51]

By November they were off for Brazoria and the coast to meet more expected shipments. On January 8, 1829, Joseph left for Cincinnati to rejoin his fiancée, Mary Este, never to return to Texas. Edward's death in Texas, following the earlier death of Nicholas Jr., was a hard blow to the spirits of this close-knit family. In Ohio, Nicholas's daughter Rebecca reflected on the death of her second brother in far off Texas:

My heart is sad, my harp unstrung,
Upon the willow branch 'tis hung—
The silver chord has lost its pow'r
To cheat the mind in sorrow's hour . . .
A brother far from me doth lie
In unknown land, 'neath the southern sky;
Then keep my harp upon the tree—
Its cheerful notes are lost on me.[52]

Andrew remained in Texas, where he was rejoined by his father Nicholas after a brief trip to Ohio. Nicholas's intention all along had been to build up a trading empire in Texas, centered along Buffalo Bayou, but things were beginning to unravel. Certainly Rebecca and her sisters were not keen on leaving a comfortable life in Ohio for the frontier in Texas, and by this time Joseph and Mary were in this camp as well. Their pastor, Rev. Joshua Wilson, penned some verses that found their way into Rebecca's album:

They sail to Brazos' rolling flood,
To Texas wilds they go,
Where men and beasts, athirst for blood,
No ties of friendship know.
Where Liberty, more dear than life,
Sheds no enliv'ning ray.
Where demon plots and savage strife
Becloud meridian day.[53]

Back in Texas, trade was not as brisk as hoped. Little by little the company gave up its empire, first the shop at San Felipe, then the one at Harrisburg, leaving only the New Washington store at Clopper's Point. On June 8, 1929, a departing Darius Gregg's shares were repurchased by the remaining members, Nicholas, Patrick, and Andrew, and then the company quietly folded. Andrew commented in a letter of 1830 that immigration had been stopped by the Mexican government, surely a bad sign for any international trading operation.

Nicholas Clopper, sixty-four years old when his company dissolved, spent the rest of his years traveling between his home just west of Clopper's Point, which he called Highland Cottage, and his family's homes in Ohio; the family's move to Texas never occurred.[54] He grew oranges and lemons at Highland Cottage and lived the quiet life. Ever dreaming of a trading empire, he obtained a grant on the Colorado River above the town of Matagorda in 1830, thinking of establishing a "City of Portland" there, but those dreams were never acted upon during his lifetime.[55] When the tide of revolution came in 1835 he traveled to Cincinnati, where he rallied support for the Texas cause among the citizens of that city, who purchased and sent to Texas the famed Twin Sisters cannons, which were put to good use at the Battle of San Jacinto the following year.[56] In 1836 Clopper sold Clopper's Point to pioneer Texas merchant James Morgan (1787–1866), who laid out the town of New Washington on that peninsula. That land has been called Morgan's Point ever since, and is today the site of the massive Barbours Cut container terminal of the Port of Houston. Nicholas Clopper died in Ohio in 1841.

Andrew Clopper stayed on in Texas, living as a bachelor at Highland Cottage, which was a part of the Clopper's Point land not sold to Morgan. He fought in the Texian Army during the Texas Revolution and died in Houston in 1853. He is buried at the Founders' Memorial Cemetery in Houston, on West Dallas Street, where his tombstone is the only remaining physical reminder of the family's dream of a Texas empire along Buffalo Bayou (Figure 2.10).

Legacy

The early commercial foundation of the city of Houston that was to come was in many ways built upon the vision and efforts of John Harris and Nicholas Clopper. Both men recognized the strategic location of Buffalo Bayou for Austin's young colony. Harris's port and lumber operation at Harrisburg, where timber was cut and lumber shipped to Mexico, proved the viability of international shipping from an interior port on Buffalo Bayou. That port

Figure 2.10. Headstone of Andrew M. Clopper (1791–1853) at Founders Memorial Park cemetery, West Dallas Street, Houston.

has grown to become the Port of Houston on the Houston Ship Channel, one of the world's busiest ports. Nicholas Clopper, often overlooked today, established a company that built three early mercantile stores, at Morgan's Point, Harrisburg and San Felipe. Those commercial establishments utilized a combined water and land route to open up Austin's colony to a more efficient export route for its produce. Clopper's easternmost trading place is now the location of the Port of Houston's Barbour's Cut cargo container shipping center at Morgan's Point—evidence of the farsightedness of the Cloppers' vision of empire along the bayou. The overland shipping route that the Cloppers spearheaded in 1828 from the new port at Harrisburg to San Felipe was soon to be converted to a wagon road by the government of Austin's Colony, the first of a number of commercial wagon routes—and later railroad and highway routes—that were to radiate outward from the Greater Houston area, bringing the fruits of oceangoing commerce to inland locations across Texas and the nation.

Figure 3.1. Man with ox wagon, sketched by Texas German frontier artist Friedrich Richard Petri (1824-1857). Friedrich Richard Petri collection, Image di10673, Dolph Briscoe Center for American History, the University of Texas at Austin.

THREE

The San Felipe Trail in Colonial Times

The oxen were hitched—four yoke to each wagon—and urged on by encouraging shouts, the horned beasts of burden were on their way. All commerce is carried on in this manner in Texas. Many farmers occupy themselves with hauling goods during the winter months, when work in the field does not require their presence at home. . . .
The use of oxen is a decided advantage, as they subsist almost entirely upon the grass found on the prairies. Their broad hoofs also do not sink into the mud as easily as do those of a horse or mule. . . . Of course, the slow pace with which they travel is a decided disadvantage. A heavily laden wagon of three thousand pounds, drawn by four yoke of oxen, can travel on the average only ten to fifteen miles daily.

—Ferdinand Roemer,
traveling on the San Felipe Trail in 1846[1]

Nicholas Clopper's Texas Trading Association failed, but its bold experiment resonated in Austin's capital of San Felipe. Stephen F. Austin and others realized that a real road connecting San Felipe to the growing port of Harrisburg—not just a trail through the wilderness—would shorten the route of the Colony's exported cotton produce to a port that was in a relatively protected inland setting.

The Ayuntamiento builds a new road along Buffalo Bayou

After an initial four-year period when Stephen F. Austin had broad powers over nearly all aspects of his colony's government, an ayuntamiento (council) was formed in 1828 to regulate local affairs of the colony permanently, including establishment and maintenance of roads among other items like crime, taxation, public welfare, etc.[2] Its members were elected from the various parts of the colony. One might think of such an august body meeting in palatial surroundings, but this was frontier San Felipe, which consisted of a ramshackle collection of log buildings. Noah Smithwick (1808–1899), an early

San Felipe resident, described the meeting place as follows:

> *The alcalde's office was in a large double log house standing back some distance from the main thoroughfare almost immediately in the rear of the Whiteside Hotel, which building it much resembled. By whom it was built, or for what purpose, I do not now remember, but my impression is that it was designed for a hotel. The walls of hewn logs were roofed in and abandoned at that stage. It was here the ayuntamiento held its sittings, and this windowless, floorless pen, through the unchinked cracks of which the wild winds wandered and whistled at will, was presumably the Faneuil Hall of Texas.*[3]

The issue of the San Felipe to Harrisburg road was taken up first on August 4, 1830:

> *The Report of the Road Commissioners Saml. C. Hirams, Martin Allen and Randal Johns [Jones] authorizing them to lay out a road from San Felipe to Harrisburg was taken up, and deferred to the next meeting of the Ayunto.*

They approved the construction of the road on September 13, 1830:

> *The several Reports of the commissioners Saml C. Hirams[,] Martin Allen, John Jones[,] Randall Jones[,] and William Pettus to view out a road from the town of [San Felipe de] Austin to John Jones on the San Jacinto by way of Harrisburg were read, discussed, and adopted with the amendments thereon. Martin Allen, William Andrews and Thos. Davis were appointed superintendents of Said road, and it was ordered that the President acquaint them with their appointment and give them their necessary instructions as decreed on that subject this day, by ordinance No. 5.*[4]

The construction of a road in those days does not imply a provision of a hard surface, as it would today. Ferdinand Roemer, who visited Texas in the mid-1840s, observed that "up to this time, road building was confined chiefly to indicating the directions between important points; to fell trees along the river banks where necessary; to lower the inclines at the fords; and to install ferries at the larger

Figure 3.2. A modern reconstruction of Stephen F. Austin's residence and office, at the San Felipe de Austin Historical Site, San Felipe, Texas.

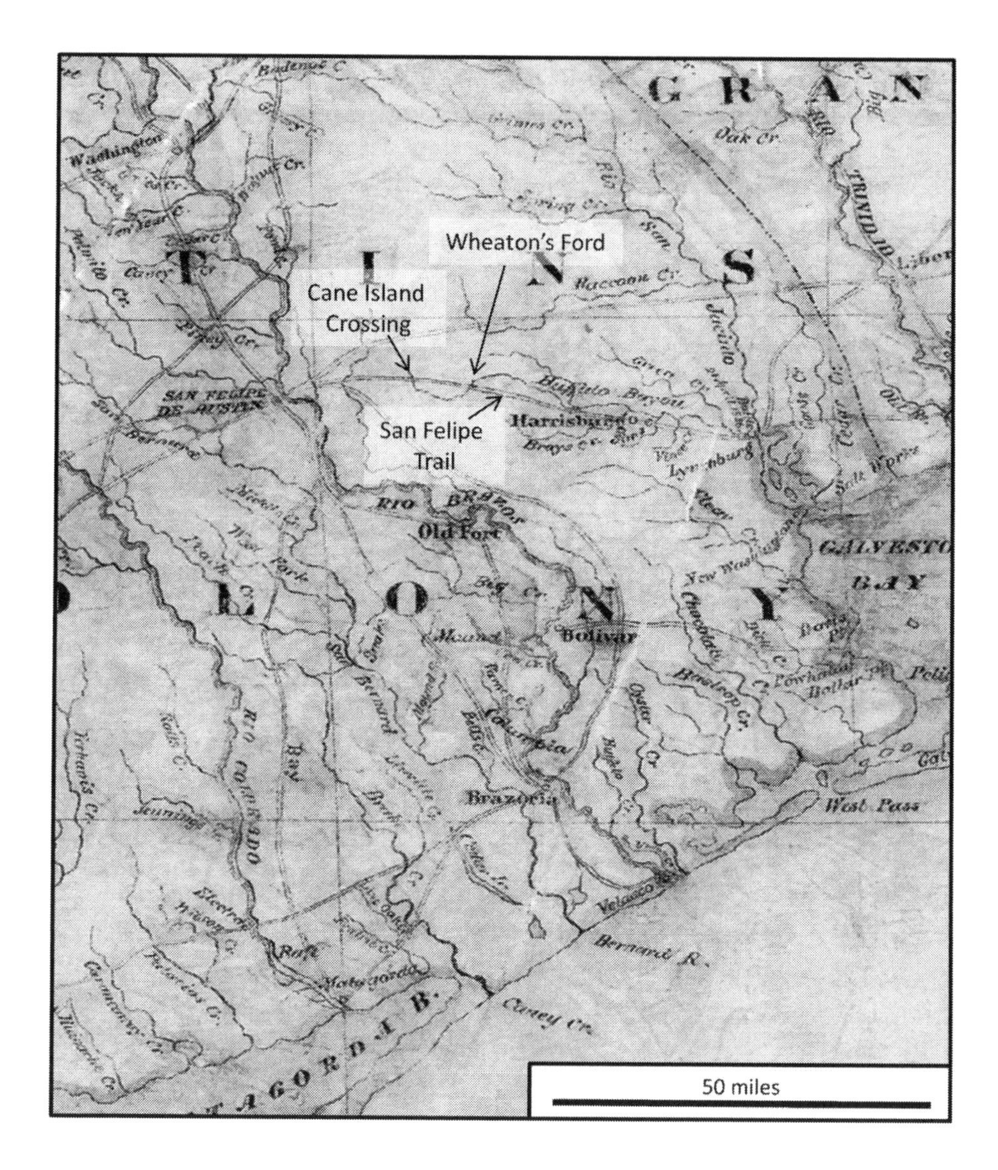

Figure 3.3 A portion of *Map of Texas with parts of the Adjoining States* by Stephen F. Austin, published by H. S. Tanner, 1837. The first version of this map came out in 1830, and the roads and towns shown are those existing at that time (note that the town of Houston is not yet present). The location of the new San Felipe to Harrisburg wagon road, cleared in 1830, is shown, along with the crossings at Cane Island (modern Katy) and at Wheaton's Ford. Location and scale are approximately the same as in Figure 2.2. Courtesy of the General Land Office, Austin.

rivers."[5] Nonetheless, it was an enormous improvement over a wilderness trail.

The general route is known from several early large-scale maps of Texas. Stephen F. Austin compiled a map of Texas published by H. S. Tanner in 1830 that showed the new San Felipe Road (Figure 3.3).[6] In general, the route followed the southern edge of the riparian forest of Buffalo Bayou, at a sufficient distance to avoid its various meanders (Figure 3.4). The road made two crossings of Buffalo Bayou and its tributaries, neither large enough to warrant a ferry. The first was a ford approximately halfway between San Felipe and Harrisburg, at the farm of Joel and Elizabeth Wheaton, and the second, farther west, was at the cane brake at Cane Island Branch of Buffalo Bayou (just north of what would later be Katy, Texas).

The precise original route of the wagon road has been poorly remembered, because its western meandering portions in Harris County do not follow

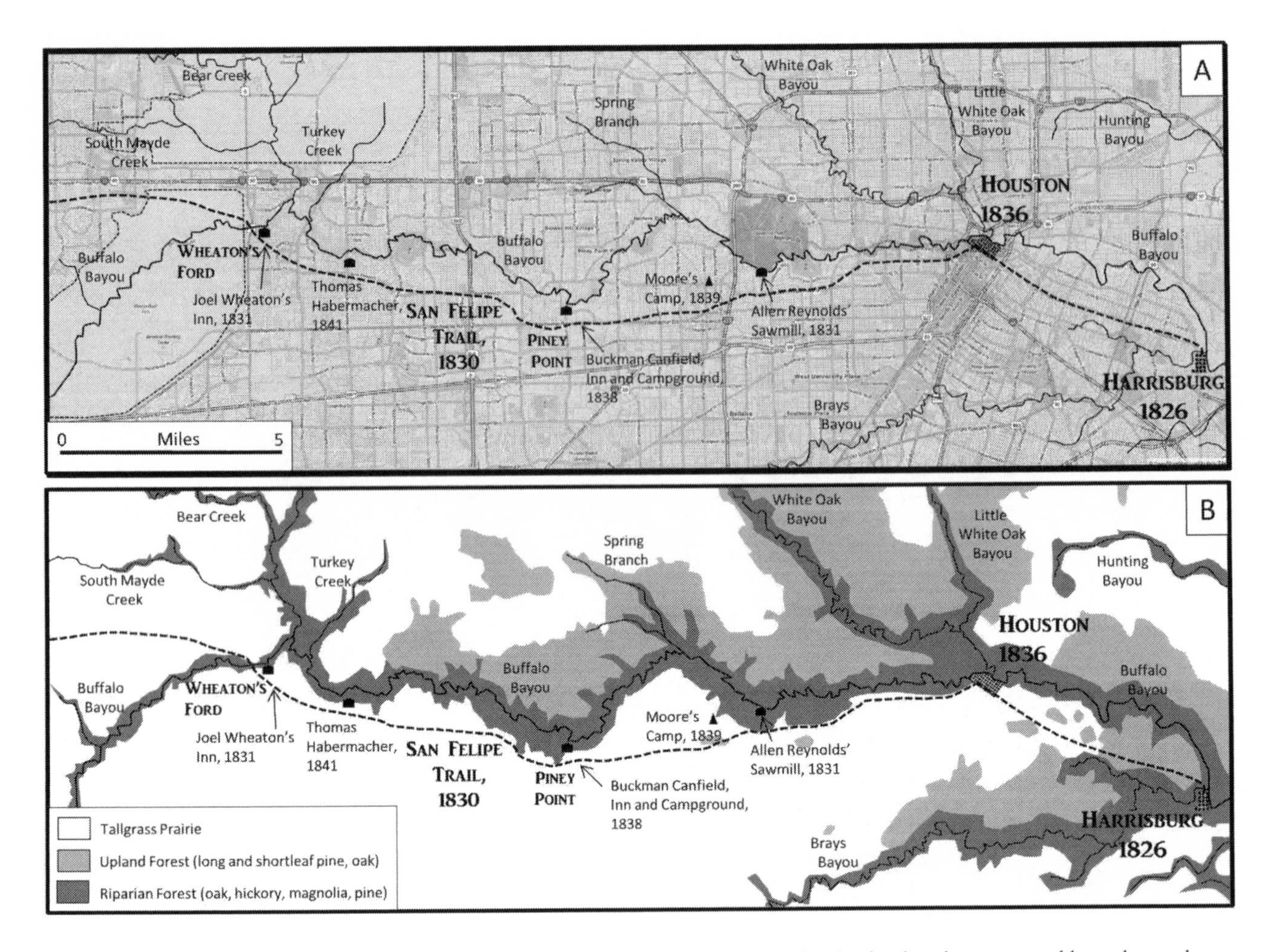

Fig. 3.4. The San Felipe Trail (wagon road) of 1830 in western Harris County, with a few landmarks mentioned by early travelers. A: Modern road map courtesy of OpenStreetMap. B: Interpreted areas of original forest cover, as in Figure 1.2.

modern roads, which tend to be rectilinear. Other than a mention on a tablet at Founder's Memorial Cemetery on San Felipe Road near downtown Houston, and another along River Oaks Boulevard, it is not memorialized by historical markers.[7] Its former route from Cane Island to Harrisburg was reconstructed from a variety of archival sources (Figure 3.5). In the east, an 1869 map of the City of Houston by W. E. Wood shows "San Felipe Road" running west from the city; later maps depict that road as West Dallas Street, by which name it is known today. Farther west, a 1915 U.S. Geological Survey topographic map of the Houston Heights Quadrangle shows "San Felipe Road" extending west from Shepherd Drive to about the present location of Loop 610—still known as San Felipe Road (Figure 3.5). It is likely that, as is the case for West Dallas Street, this segment of modern San Felipe Road was close to the original wagon road, as both locations stay just south of the original riparian forest (Figure 3.4)—although it is clear that both West Dallas and this part of San Felipe were straightened during their construction as urban streets. Parts of modern San Felipe Road extending farther west from Loop 610 are younger, however (dating from the 1920s), and clearly do not follow the early trail.

The route of this early wagon road in the western part of Harris County was noted on the detailed

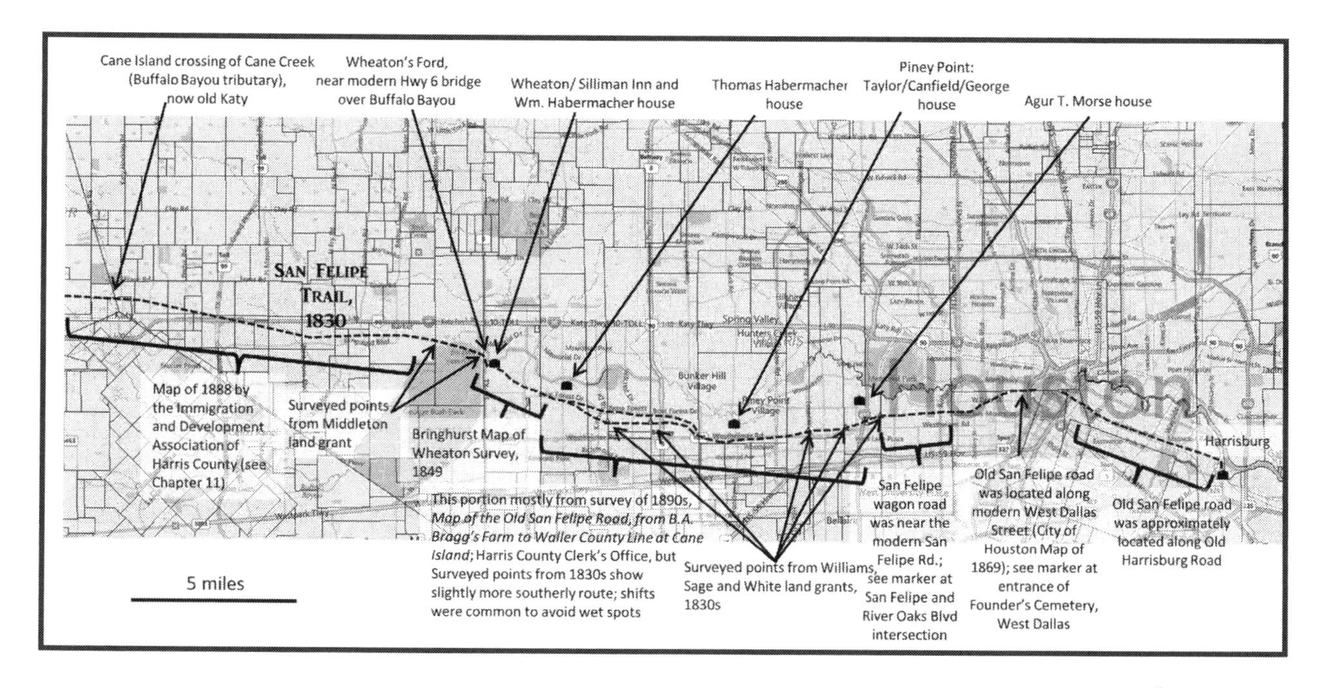

Figure 3.5. Reconstructed location of the San Felipe Trail, Cane Island (Katy) to Harrisburg, compiled from various indicated sources. Modern base map, courtesy of the General Land Office, Austin, shows outlines of original Texas land grant boundaries.

survey field notes of several early land grants, notably those of Middleton, Williams, Sage and White (Figure 3.5). A map of the by then "old" San Felipe road was surveyed by Harris County in 1890, when new railroads and other roads were rapidly replacing parts of it; portions of that map are shown in Chapter 11.[8] The road was also shown on a map for new immigrants in 1888, by the Immigration and Development Association of Harris County, as part of a "Home-Seekers' Journal" that displayed both the new railroad lines and the older wagon routes (see Chapter 11).

The construction of the San Felipe to Harrisburg wagon road in 1829–1830 began to change trade routes in the colony almost immediately, as it became apparent that the overland route for freight to Harrisburg was an efficient alternative to taking cotton partly overland and partly by river to the Brazos River port at Matagorda. On the new route, cotton was shipped overland on the San Felipe road to Harrisburg by ox cart, for trans-shipment by steamboat down Buffalo Bayou either to the port at Galveston or directly to New Orleans. Wagon trains of cotton-laden ox wagons were a common sight on the road after harvest (Figure 3.6). Oxen had the advantage of being available (one had only to capture and train wild cattle), strong, and with large hooves that helped them keep negotiate the often muddy trail.

In historical documents, this road is variously called "San Felipe Road" and "San Felipe Trail." Because this early road can be confused with the modern road of that name, which only partly overlies it, the usage "San Felipe Trail" is preferred in this book.

The new San Felipe Trail began to attract a few pioneer residents to the area of upper Buffalo Bayou, including Joel and Elizabeth Wheaton as well as Allen and Harriet Reynolds. Both families arrived in the early 1830s.

Joel and Elizabeth Wheaton and the Inn at Wheaton's Ford

Joel Wheaton and his wife Elizabeth Hawkins Wheaton were to operate an inn and traveler's waystation at a critical crossing of Buffalo Bayou along the new wagon road. Joel Wheaton (1788–

Figure 3.6. An ox-drawn cart. Drawing by James W. Champney, from Edward King, *The Great South: A Record of Journeys* (Hartford, Conn.: American Publishing Company, 1875).

1838) was born in New York State and joined the New York State Militia during the War of 1812, with the rank of private. He married Tennessee-born Elizabeth Hawkins (b. ca. 1805) in Jefferson, Mississippi, in 1826, and they had three daughters while living there: Argive H. M. Wheaton (1825–1903), Amanda Wheaton (1828–1854; she later married Lawrence Habermacher), and Sara Martha Jane Wheaton (1829–1866). The family traveled to Texas in 1830, arriving in December that year. A son, James Perry Wheaton (ca. 1830–after 1880), was probably born as they arrived in Texas. An entry in Stephen F. Austin's Register of Families, written when Joel Wheaton applied at San Felipe for his land grant, lists Joel as a blacksmith with a wife, four children, and one other dependent: John T. Vince.[9]

On December 24, 1831, Joel Wheaton received a grant for a league and a labor of land (4,605 acres) along Buffalo Bayou (Figure 3.7) and established his home on the south side of the bayou at the ford for the new San Felipe to Harrisburg wagon road (Figure 3.4). He had arrived in Texas the year that the San Felipe ayuntamiento ordered the construction of the road, and it seems possible that Stephen F. Austin may have guided Wheaton's choice of land grants, figuring that the major ford on Buffalo Bayou on the colony's new road would need someone to assist travelers, both with an inn and the services of a blacksmith. At times of high water, wagon teamsters would wait for days or even weeks at this crossing for the water to recede. A detailed survey showing the route of this road across the Wheaton tract was made by surveyor George Bringhurst in 1849 (Figure 3.8) when that property was being subdivided by the family following Joel's death.[10] The Wheaton home and inn was on the south side of the ford, as indicated the accounts of early travelers, notably Karl von Sommer in 1846.

The earliest account of Joel Wheaton at this ford underscores his generosity and helpfulness. In 1834 the Robert Kleberg family, emigrating from Germany, were shipwrecked on a then wild Galveston Island. They had intended to settle at Friedrich Ernst's settlement at Cat Spring. Kleberg's account of their desperate struggles that winter is included in Chapter 6; suffice it to note here that they survived the winter after making their way to Harrisburg and set out for Cat Spring in the fall of 1835, following the San Felipe–Harrisburg road. Kleberg's wife, Rosa von Roeder Kleberg (1813–1907), recalled their encounter with Joel Wheaton on that trip:

> *In the fall my husband, who had been in Cat Spring, came to Harrisburg with a team of oxen to take us with him. The roads in the Brazos bottom being impassable on account of the mud, we*

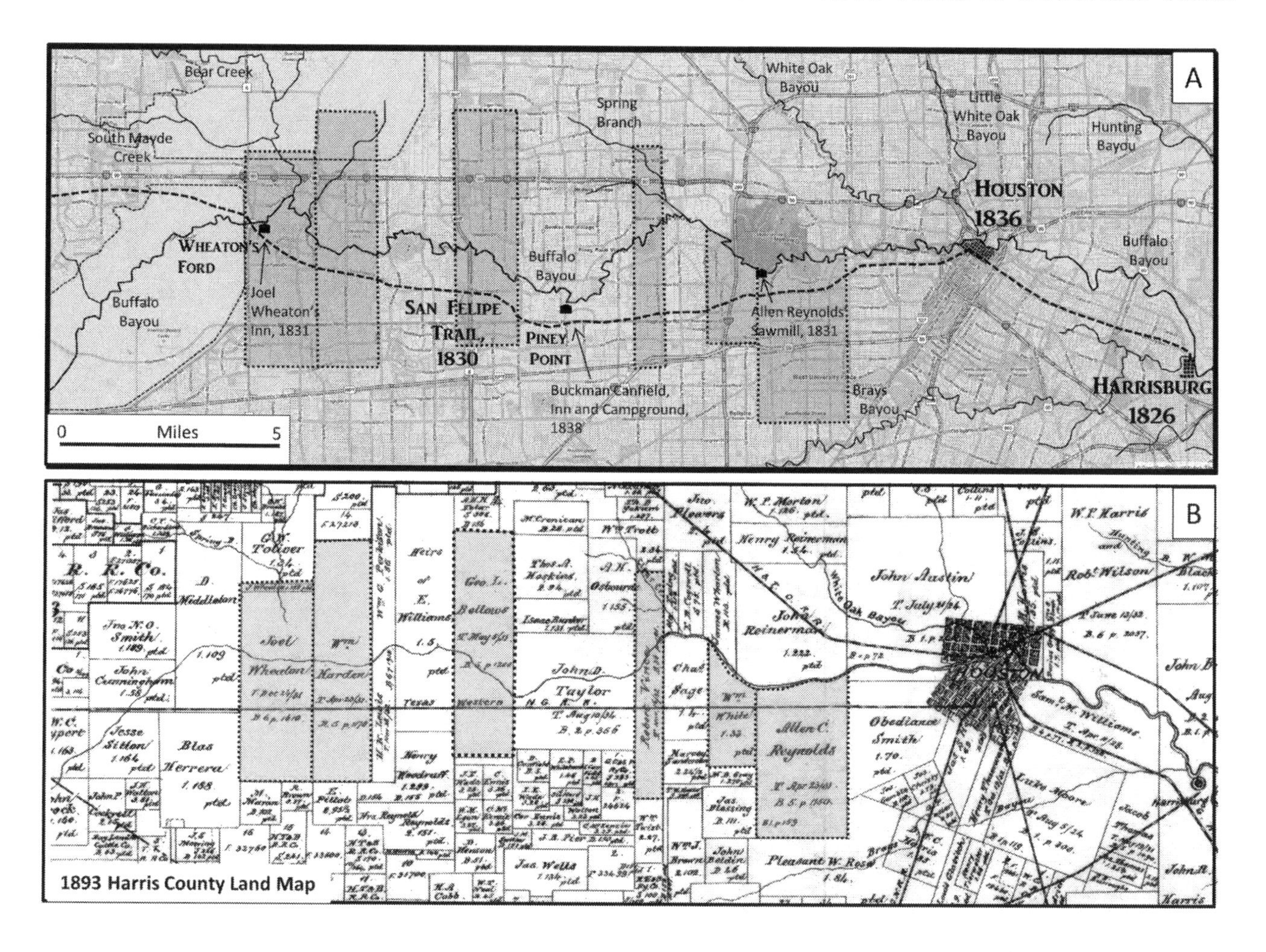

Figure 3.7. Post Old-300, pre-Independence land grants, upper Buffalo Bayou (dashed outlines). A: Superimposed on a modern base map, courtesy of OpenStreetMap. B: Superimposed on a Harris County land grant map of 1893, showing grantees' names, courtesy of the General Land Office, Austin.

camped at Weeton's [Wheaton's]. This was the first house on the road from Harrisburg to Cat Spring, and was a good day's journey from the former place. Weeton was backwoods American, and carried on the trade of a "teamster." He was the very personification of whole-souled generosity and hospitality. We also stopped at Hoff's [Hoffman's]. Hoff was a Pennsylvania Dutchman.[11]

Joel Wheaton died on October 6, 1838, possibly of yellow fever. By that time he had seven children, all but one of them minors. On his deathbed, he asked a friend, John Perry, to look out after his estate, because he was unable to write a will.[12] His widow Elizabeth would continue to live on the property, operating the farm, the inn, and raising a large family as a single woman in the frontier.

Joel Wheaton's estate was inventoried in March, 1839 by neighbors Buckman Canfield of Piney Point and John Woodruff, who lived in what is now the Fourth Ward; both were among the few who lived along the San Felipe Trail at that time. The inventory provides a good description of what it took to live in what was then a frontier outpost. Wheaton was a slave-owner, with two enslaved African Americans listed as possessions in the inventory, as was the practice of the time. The slaves' combined assessed value, at $1,200, shows their great importance to the farm and inn; without their work the Wheatons could not easily succeed. Wheaton's

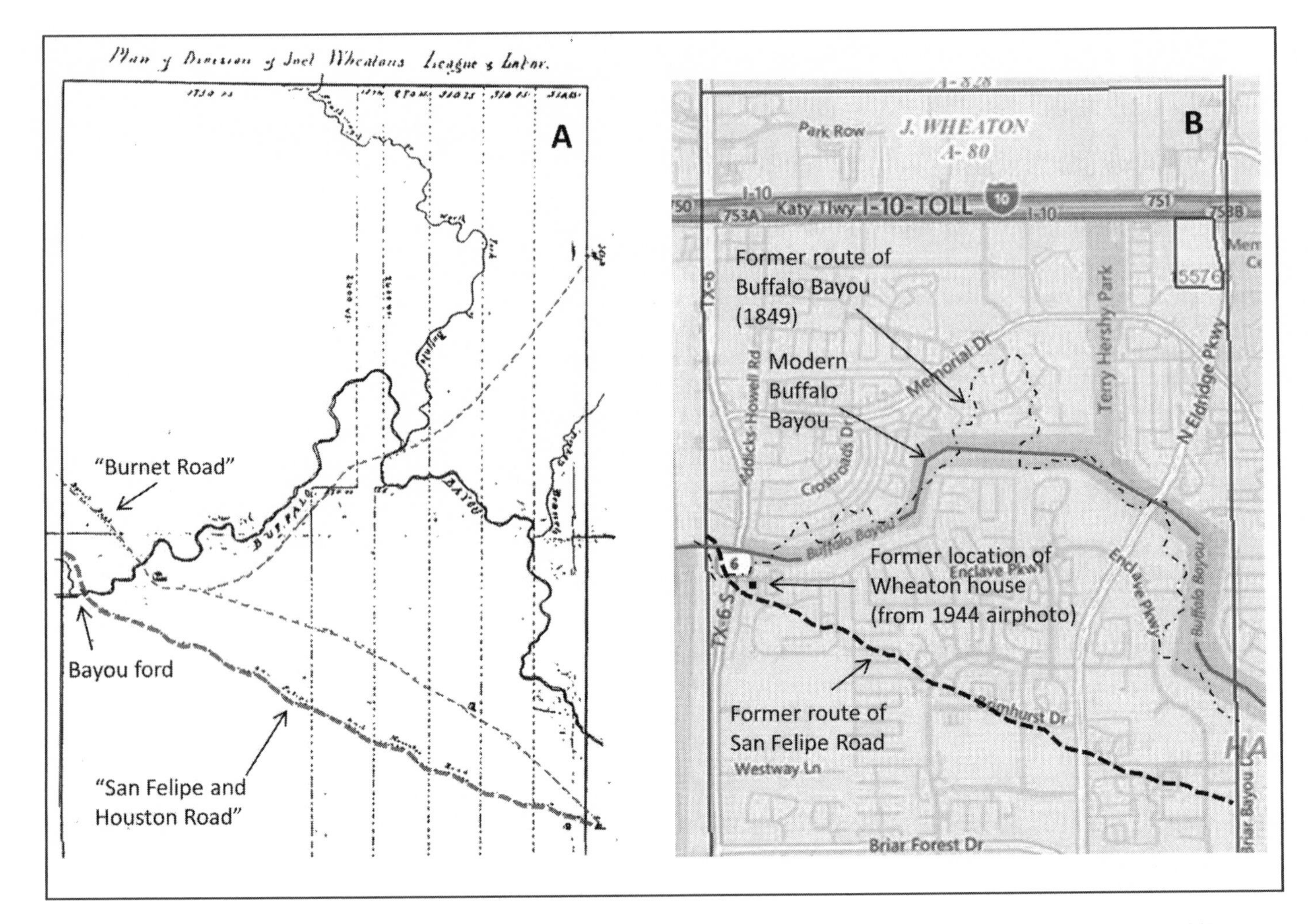

Figure 3.8. A: Northern portion of a survey of the Joel Wheaton league, made by surveyor George Bringhurst on February 9, 1849 for the subdivision of Joel Wheaton's land for Wheaton's heirs, showing the location of the San Felipe wagon road. B: Same area today. Note the significant straightening of the bayou, done as part of 1940s flood control efforts; its former course is shown in a dashed line. Bringhurst map courtesy of Harris County Clerk's Office; modern base map, with outlines of original land grants, courtesy of the General Land Office, Austin.

4,605 acres of land was valued at a little over $1.24 per acre, which included their inn and other improvements. His numbers of cattle, horses and hogs were average for small farmers of his time, and his farm equipment and household items were minimal. It was a frugal life in a lonely outpost.[13]

At the time of Joel Wheaton's probate hearing in 1841, Elizabeth listed five children: Elizabeth Amanda (1828–1854), Sarah Martha Jane (1829–1866), John (1831–1853), James P. (1834–after 1880), and Travis (b. ca. 1837). She also listed one married daughter, Argive, who had married Young Settoon (or Settune) in 1840.[14] Elizabeth received the western half of the land, and the rest was divided among the children, including Argive; this property division was the reason for the Bringhurst survey of 1849 (Figure 3.8). Travis is not mentioned in the division and had likely died by that time.

Elizabeth Wheaton continued to manage the farm and stagecoach inn, and it figures in the accounts of several early travelers. On December 12, 1838, soon after her husband's death, she was visited by the quartermaster of the 1st Regiment of Texas Cavalry, who was headed for Indian territory. That quartermatser, Major Valentine Bennet, had been severely wounded in the Texian's clash with Mexican troops at Velasco in 1832 and was appointed quartermaster during the Siege of Bexar in 1835. In late 1838 he and his son, Miles S. Bennet, were with two cavalry companies headed west, and Bennet Sr. purchased food for the troops from Elizabeth Wheaton, including one shoat and 60 pounds of salt beef at 12½ cents per pound, for a total of $17.25, "For the 1st Regt. Cavalry commanded by S. Wells."[15] Of that period, Bennet's son Miles wrote: "Dec. 1838. During this month we furnished transportation, beef and corn to two companies of troops ordered to the Western frontier, they were commanded by Captains Jordan and Howard. On the route I drew all the drafts on the dept. for the supplies."

Two months later, in February 1839, Miles Bennet was back. He was heading west from Houston during a wet winter in 1839:

> *On February again left Houston, with three ox wagons loaded with military stores. . . . The weather was very inclement, an unusual storm of sleet delayed us. Buffalo Bayou at Mrs. Wheaton's crossing was swollen out of its banks, making necessary for us to change our route, and the van became so heavy that we had to unload our wagons and place the stores in a house.*[16]

His personal diary read:

> *Sat Feb 2. I started from Hd. Qrs. With a Lieut. Some soldiers and wagons with supplies for the post at San Antonio, wintry weather, delayed at Mrs. Wheaton's at the crossing of Buffalo Bayou first by high water, then by a heavy sleet which broke a great deal of timber. The bayou and prairie were flooded, I had some adventures killing wild game and exploring for a practicable route. Was constrained to diverge from our road and cross the Brazos at Richmond. Teams much fatigued. Worked on toward Columbus, in crossing Feb 26th the Colorado, the ferryboat sank with one of our largest wagons, delaying us in recovering it and its contents several days, the weather being very inclement.*[17]

Inventory of the Estate of Joel Wheaton

Appraised by John Woodruff and Buckman Canfield, March 26, 1839
Harris County Probate Record, vol. H, p. 236

1 League and Labor of Land	$5,715
Two Negroes	$1,200
Seven head of horses	$210
One pair of work steers	$150
57 to 75 head of cattle, $6 per head	
Twenty head of hogs	$100
One waggon	$65
1 clock	$30
Small library	$20
Two beds and furniture	$50
One table, one desk and medium chest	$12
One rifle gun and two brace of pistols	$30
Crockery ware & kitchen furniture	$30
Water barrels and two trunks	$8
Two saddles	$14
Two ploughs	$12
One set of plough gear & ox chains	$10
One broad axe and one narrow axe	$7
Two spades and two hoes	$4
One small ring and staple	$2

A roving Republic of Texas tax collector, Henry Walton Raglin, passed through on July 24, 1841, when he paid three dollars for dinner and lodgings for himself and his mule; the receipt has survived (Figure 3.9), along with Elizabeth's signature. The previous night, Raglin had stayed with Buckman Canfield at Piney Point (Chapter 4). The bill of fare was pricier at the Canfield home, at four dollars and fifty cents.

Dr. Ferdinand Roemer, a geologist sent in 1845 by Prince Carl of Solms-Braunfels to scope out Texas as a home for German immigrants, provides a brief mention of a stop at Wheaton's. Like Bennet, he was traveling in midwinter and met bad travel conditions. On his second day out from Houston:

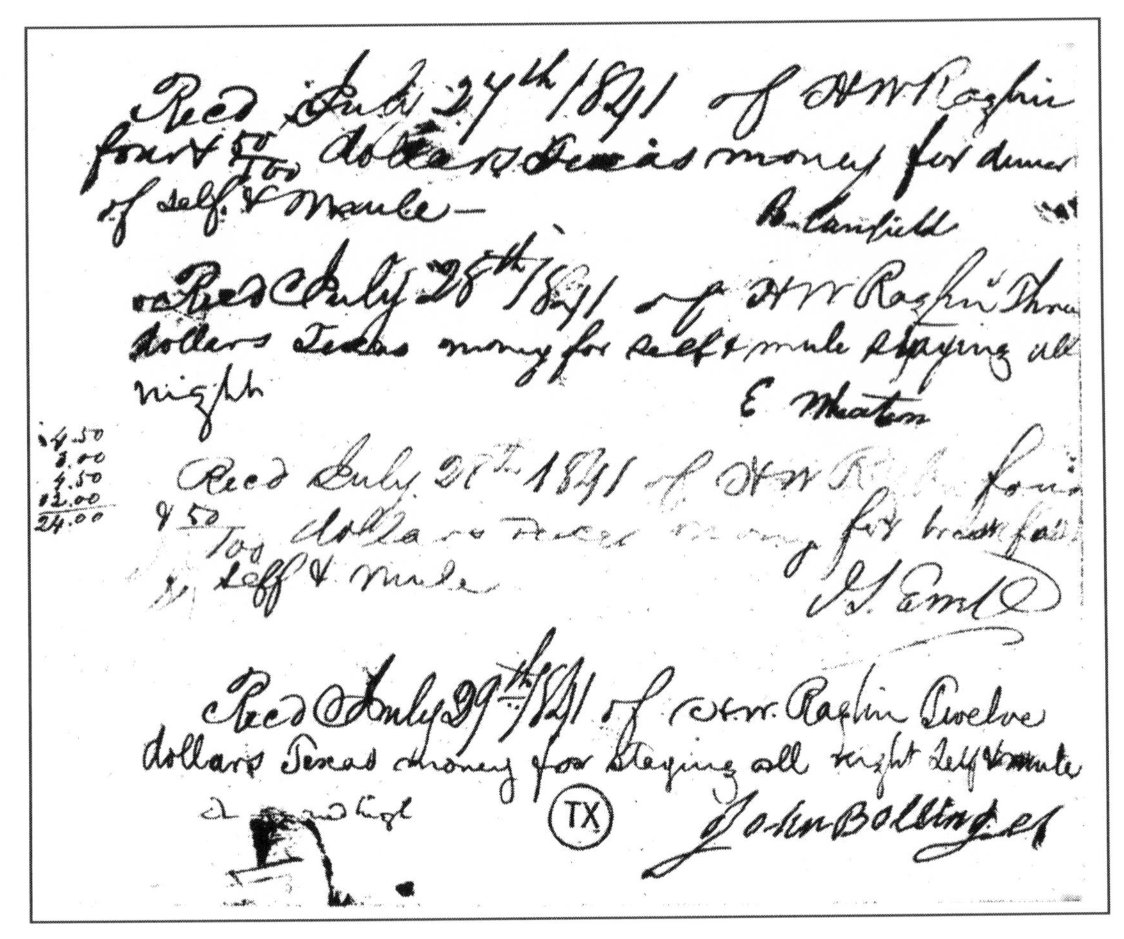

Rec'd July 27th 1841 of H W Raglin four & 50/100 dollars Texas money for dinner of self & mule — B. Canfield

Rec'd July 28th 1841 of H W Raglin Three dollars Texas money for self & mule staying all night E. Wheaton

Rec'd July 28th 1841 of H W R[illegible] four & 50/100 dollars Texas money for breakfast [illegible] self & mule [illegible]

Rec'd July 29th 1841 of H. W. Raglin Twelve dollars Texas money for staying all night self & mule John Bollinger

4.50
3.00
4.50
12.00
24.00

TX

Figure 3.9. A claim for several nights' lodging for a Republic of Texas tax collector, Henry Walton Raglin, in July 1841. The first claim is with Buckman Canfield of Piney Point, who charged $4.50 for lodging and dinner for the man and his mule. The second stay was at Elizabeth Wheaton's inn and farm. She charged Raglin three dollars. Courtesy of Republic Claims, Texas State Library and Archives Commission, claim # 6365.

NOTICE.

ON the evening of the 19th of June, A. D. 1848, the subscriber has lost, between Houston and Mrs. Wheaton, a leathern pocket book, containing a bill of sale for a horse and an honorable discharge from Col. J. Hays for services rendered in the United States Army in Mexico. If said certificate is not recovered or heard from within sixty days from date, the subscriber will apply for a dupiicate. JOHN STORK,

9 tf53* At Francis Dungen's, Market Square, Houston.

Figure 3.10. A notice from the *Houston Democratic Telegraph and Texas Register* of August 10, 1848.

We were confronted with the same obstacles met with on the previous day. An extensive, level prairie, now and then broken by a sparse grove of oaks, partially covered with water, lay before us. We moved very slowly, occasionally passing isolated and rather miserable-looking farms. In the afternoon, we arrived at a larger and more pretentious looking farm, belonging to a Mrs. Wheaton, where the road to San Felipe led us over Buffalo Bayou. The latter, a shallow stream in the dry season, was swollen to such an extent that we were unable to ford it.[18]

Fuller accounts of Roemer's trip and that of another German, Karl von Sommer, who traveled the San Felipe road in 1846 and also met the problem of high water at the ford, are in Chapter 4. With the help of Elizabeth's sons, von Sommer was able to cross.

Wheaton's inn at the ford was a well-known landmark along the road between Houston and San Felipe, as a newspaper "lost and found" advertisement of 1848 demonstrates (Figure 3.10). Life at such a frontier spot must have been difficult for this family, with disease a constant threat—especially mosquito-borne malaria and yellow fever, as well as cholera from tainted bayou water and the open wells of that period. Elizabeth's son John married Mary Jane Echols in 1844, but she was dead by the 1850 census.[19] Argive's husband, Young Settoon, died before 1845.[20] Argive married Archilaus (Archie) Kirkland Brookshire (1823–1885) in 1848, after a short time living on her inheritance acreage on the Wheaton survey. They moved to nearby Austin County and raised six children in a healthier environment on the prairie, away from Buffalo Bayou.

Sarah (Martha Jane) also married a Brookshire, James Seborn Brookshire (1824–1880), in 1846. James was a brother of Archilaus, and their father Nathan Brookshire (1786–1853) owned land west of the Wheaton property and south of the bayou. Nathan, a veteran of the Creek Indian Wars of 1813 and the Battle of New Orleans in 1814, came to Texas in 1835 and obtained a large colonial land grant in southeastern Waller County. He joined the Texian Army in 1836, and after the war was a noted Indian fighter with the Texas Rangers. After Indian threats were locally diminished, he tried cattle ranching but reportedly grew bored with it. He sold most of that land to his children; modern Brookshire, Texas rests on some of it. He and his wife opened a shop in Richmond, Texas, in 1841, and sometime before 1850—probably before James's marriage to Sarah Wheaton in 1846—they moved to western Harris County in the vicinity of the Wheatons, where they were enumerated by the census taker. It was at that time that the two Wheaton daughters, Argive and Sarah, married two of his sons.[21] Sarah and James Brookshire were living in Harris County in 1850, probably on part of the above-mentioned Nathan Brookshire family land. They had five children between 1846 and 1858, but must have divorced, because James married again (to Henrietta Streppe, a German immigrant) in 1859; Sarah died in 1866.[22]

Elizabeth's other daughter Amanda had married Lawrence Habermacher (b. 1822) in 1846, and thus had also left home, but had not left the area. Lawrence was the son of early settler and Alsatian immigrant Thomas Habermacher, who lived near the bayou to the east on the Hardin tract (see Chapter 6). Amanda died in 1854.[23]

Meanwhile, Elizabeth continued to operate the inn and farm. By the 1850 census her sons John and James both still lived at home; John was listed as a farmer and James as a carpenter. The agricultural portion of that census shows that Elizabeth Wheaton cultivated 20 acres out of 820 acres reportedly owned at that time. She owned a horse but no oxen and had 70 beef cattle running in the surrounding open range. There were 12 swine, and the family harvested 200 bushels of corn (about 4–5 acres' worth). Her land and improvements were valued at $1,500—a high amount, probably reflecting the value of the inn. Her livestock was valued at $550 and her farm equipment at $75. The agricultural produce was low for someone with that amount of land, but then much of her income would have come from her inn.

Elizabeth Wheaton died in November 1851, and her son John died in 1853; this was clearly not a healthy place to live. By 1855 only James P. Wheaton remained on the original Wheaton property, on his small inherited portion of it. Elizabeth's larger, 2,303-acre tract, to the west, which included the inn at the ford, was sold in 1854. It passed briefly through the hands of David Cole, and then Whitacker Baines, neither of whom seemed to have lived on the property, before it was sold to Mary Frisby Silliman in 1855.[24]

Mary Frisby Silliman at Wheaton's Ford

Mary Frisby Silliman (1808-1864) bought the land on January 9, 1855, as trustee for the benefit of her children, and operated the crossing and its inn for the next nine years.[25] Mary Silliman's late husband was Abram Benson Silliman (1802-1842), who was born in Fairfield, Connecticut, but moved to Jefferson County, Mississippi, where the couple were married in 1825. Abram and his brother William S. Silliman (1806-ca. 1838) visited Texas in 1830, and William stayed, eventually obtaining a headright grant in Matagorda County. Abram returned to Mississippi, where his wife had remained. After the War of Independence, Abram returned to settle in Texas with his wife Mary. Notes by Abram Benson Silliman's granddaughter, Florence Genevera Thornton (1864-1950), tell the family's story:

> *My grandfather Abram Benson and grandmother Mary Frisby [born in Mississippi], his wife, came to Texas for my grandfather's health. . . . Grandfather died at Cane Island [in 1842]. Grandmother [Mary Frisby] Silliman returned to Mississippi [with her new baby, Isaac Benson Silliman (1842–1863)]. Did not live in Mississippi long. [She] returned to Texas and settled on the Bayou in the Habermacher neighborhood. It was when she lived on the Bayou that my grandmother . . . had a large farm on the Brazos.*

The "Habermacher neighborhood" was named for German immigrant farmer Thomas Habermacher, who settled along the bayou a mile or so east of Wheaton's Ford in 1841 (Figure 3.4 and Chapter 6). The precise location of Mary Silliman's home at that time is not known. Mary Frisby Silliman would have lived there from the 1840s to the early 1850s before resettling at the Wheaton farm. While living at the former place, her daughter, Mary Jarvis Silliman (ca. 1833-ca. 1868) was married to John Wesley Thornton (1832-1918). As the wedded couple's daughter Florence Genevera Thornton told it:

> *My father, John Wesley Thornton, who had known my mother, Mary Jarvis Silliman [daughter of Mary Frisby Silliman] back in Mississippi where they both lived . . . came to Texas and married at the old Silliman home in Old Beeler neighborhood, married March 17, 1853, taking her back to Mississippi as a bride in 1853, but a few years later they moved back to Texas.*[26]

The "Old Beeler neighborhood" was another name for the Habermacher neighborhood; the Beelers lived in the same vicinity, along the bayou near where the Beeler Cemetery is today in the Energy Corridor (see Chapter 9). By the time they moved back to Texas, Mary Frisby Silliman (the widowed mother) had purchased the old Wheaton place, in 1855, and relocated there.[27]

Mary Frisby Silliman and her husband Abram had five children between 1825 and 1842: Abram Frisby Silliman (1825-1891), Mary Jarvis Silliman (1834-1871), Harris Warson Silliman (1836-1862), James Monroe Silliman (b. 1840), and Isaac Benson Silliman (1842-1863). All but Isaac were born in Mississippi, prior to moving to Texas. The eldest child, Abram Frisby Silliman, reached adulthood in Mississippi and married Sarah Talbot Hall there in 1847; she died in 1855, and he married Jane Ann Louisa Pratt in 1856, in Fort Bend County. The second child, Mary Jarvis Silliman, as noted, also married in Mississippi, in 1853. She and her new husband John Wesley Thornton briefly moved into

Figure 3.11 The William Habermacher home, ca. 1885, was formerly Joel and Elizabeth Wheaton's home and inn of 1831, and after 1855, Mary Frisbee Silliman's inn and tavern. The house was destroyed by fire in 1956.
Courtesy of Marie Neuman Gray.

the old Wheaton farm and inn with the widow Mary Frisby Silliman when they returned to Texas, helping to run that property and a farm along the Brazos that the Sillimans also owned. The Thorntons stayed in the area but purchased land and lived in now vanished Pittsville, Texas—once located between Brookshire and Fulshear—and later lived near Sealy, Texas.[28] Mary Frisby Silliman's youngest three sons, Harris, James and Isaac, lived at Wheaton's Ford with their mother; all were teenagers when the property was purchased in 1855.

By the time Mary Frisby Silliman bought the old Wheaton place, there was a bridge under construction at the old ford. The 1855 Baines-to-Silliman deed record states that the property included "the bridge under construction on San Felipe Road to Houston. Habermacher to have free use of bridge as long as bridge timbers last." From this we may infer that Elizabeth Wheaton charged a toll for use of the bridge, and that the heirs of immigrant Thomas Habermacher (1777–ca. 1848), who continued to live in the area, may have played some part in its construction. There was no bridge present during the visits of Miles Bennet in 1839, Dr. Roemer in 1845, or von Sommer in 1846, but their experiences of being denied passage because of high water there certainly underscored the need for one.

The widow Silliman was to have a rough time during the Civil War, losing her sons Harris and Isaac, both of whom died in the Vicksburg campaign (see Chapter 8). She died in 1864, no doubt heartbroken, and her heirs, including sons Abram and James and the Thorntons, sold the old place. Ownership of the western half of the Wheaton survey and the old Wheaton home and inn passed in 1869 to August Marks, and in 1871 to William J. "Billy"

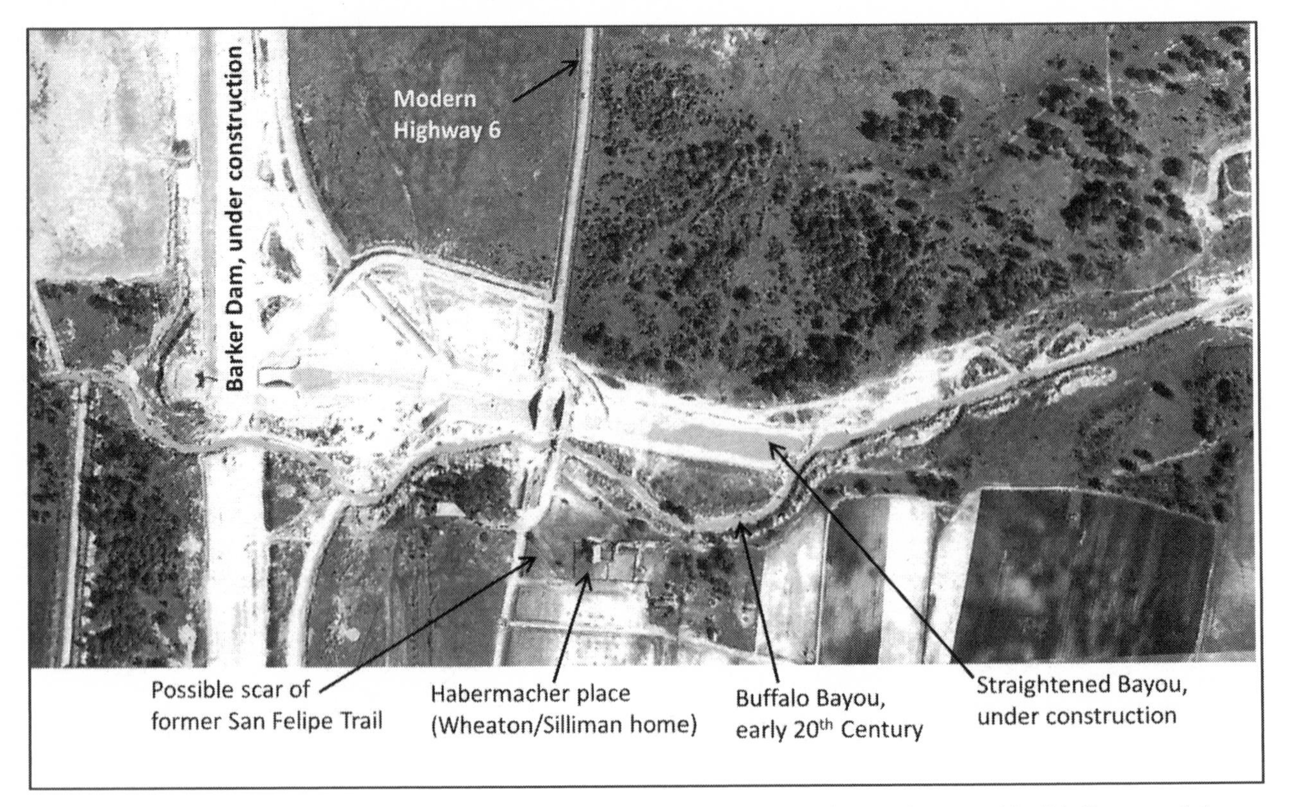

Figure 3.12. Aerial photograph of 1944 showing the construction of Barker Dam, the straightening of Buffalo Bayou, and the construction of a modern bridge along Addicks Road (now Highway 6). Visible are the Wheaton/Silliman/Habermacher house (once the inn and tavern at the crossing) and remnant portions of early 20th century Buffalo Bayou adjacent to the newly straightened bayou. The area is now heavily developed. Photo courtesy of the Texas Natural Resources Information System, Austin.

Habermacher.[29] Habermacher used the old home and inn only as a home, and within a few years closed the ford, by then used only sporadically as a crossing.

The house and inn

Remarkably, the old Wheaton home survived intact until 1956, when it burned to the ground. A story about the home appeared in the Houston Chronicle in 1949, when William Habermacher's daughter Kate Habermacher still lived in the home.[30] A photograph of the home dating from the late nineteenth century, when the Habermachers owned it, has survived (Figure 3.11).[31] The house had two front entrances, one for the owners and a second for travelers who stayed at the inn. According to the newspaper story, the house had four rooms and a detached kitchen in the rear; placing the kitchens in a separate building was common practice and a precaution against fire. There were two fireplaces, one on either end of the building; Wheaton's slaves had fired the bricks using clay that outcropped nearby in the bank of Buffalo Bayou. The sills were hewn oak and the walls hand-sawn pine. A Habermacher relative noted that most of the house was put together with wooden pegs, and that "I have been in the attic and tried nailing into the old rafters, but they are just too hard."[32] Kate Habermacher reportedly delighted in telling visitors, "Ours was the only house with glass windowpanes."[33]

The house can be seen on a 1944 aerial photograph (Figure 3.12), at a time when Kate Habermacher was living there. The Barker dam was under construction at the time. The course of Buffalo Bayou was being significantly straightened and relocated to streamline its flow, and a bridge was built over the original crossing, for State Highway 6. That bridge is still there today. During construction, workmen found traces of the old San Felipe Trail. They "came upon the bayou's crossing site. Buried beneath several layers of topsoil they found the ruts where the heavy wheels of the stage coaches had cut deep into the damp soil. The ruts were still intact. Time had changed them into petrified mud."[34] The entire area around the house and bayou was developed in the late twentieth century, including the site of the former inn. A further description of the house and a photograph of Habermacher's daughter Kate taken in these later years is included in Chapter 11.

Joel Wheaton Road, perhaps one mile south-southeast of the old ford in the modern West Oaks subdivision, commemorates the Wheatons and the ford where they built their inn. Silliman Street in Sealy was named for Mary Frisby Silliman's son Abram, who died in nearby San Felipe in 1891 and is buried in San Felipe cemetery.

Allen C. Reynolds and his sawmill

Figure 3.13. Allen C. Reynolds (1786-1837), early settler along Buffalo Bayou. Courtesy of La Quencis Gibbs Scott.

Another early resident along the new San Felipe to Harrisburg road was Allen C. Reynolds (1786–1837), who established one of the earliest sawmills on Buffalo Bayou, years in advance of the founding of the town of Houston (Figure 3.13). According to a brief biography by Reynolds's descendant La Quencis Gibbs Scott, Reynolds was born in Connecticut in 1786 and lived in New York in his teenage years, with his parents.[35] He married Harriet A. Baisley (1789–1843) in 1810, and by 1819 they had five children.[36] A lawyer by profession, he enlisted as a second lieutenant, Third New York Volunteers, during the War of 1812 and was later a captain of the United States Twenty-seventh Infantry.

A well-to-do gentleman looking to expand his fortune, he emigrated to Texas and travelled to San Felipe with his wife Harriet and one daughter. He registered his family there in February 1830.[37] The couple may have temporarily left their other children behind in New York with relatives, or in Harrisburg during their trip to San Felipe. On March 15, 1831, having searched for and selected an appropriate piece of vacant land, Reynolds petitioned Austin for a league of land "situated on the creek called Buffalo Bayou, between the tracts granted to John Austin and John D. Taylor, for which reason I apply to you so that you may be pleased to admit me and put me in possession of said tract, with the understanding that I offer to settle and cultivate it in accordance with the provisions of the law and to comply with the other obligations of the same." His application for a league of 4,428 acres was approved on April 23, 1831; its location is shown in Figure 3.7, to the southwest of the John Austin tract where the town of Houston was later founded.[38] Reynolds's grant encompassed most of the modern River Oaks and West University neighborhoods.

Reynolds moved into a wilderness along the bayou. John Taylor and John Austin had both left the bayou in 1825, and except for Joel Wheaton, six miles to the west of Reynolds, there were no other known upper Buffalo Bayou residents in 1831 (and of course the city of Houston was not yet in existence). Reynolds arrived with a number of slaves and built a sawmill and a gristmill on the south side of the bayou.[39] The mill was probably located a short distance to the east of the present day Union Pacific Railroad bridge over the bayou. An inactive mill was noted at that site in 1848 by surveyor George H. Bringhurst, who surveyed that part of the bayou.[40] It is possible that Reynolds tried this spot first for his sawmill and then abandoned it in favor of a site farther east along the bayou on his tract, which was more than a decade later utilized for a flour mill by Charles Shearn (Shearn's mill, discussed in Chapter 8, was also noted in Bringhurst's 1848 survey). There is apparently no documentary evidence linking Reynolds' mill to Shearn's mill site, however.

It has been suggested that Reynolds used the bayou to ship his timber products to Harrisburg.[41] The bayou has never been considered particularly navigable above Allen's Landing in modern Houston; if he shipped lumber by bayou, it would have been placed on a small flat-bottomed barge, and taken downstream to Harrisburg for trans-shipment elsewhere. An alternate route would be to take it by ox wagon to Harrisburg utilizing the new San Felipe Trail that had just been built across his land, a short distance from the mill. Either way, he was a long way away from potential markets.

The location of the Reynolds house is not known. It would seem likely that it, like many later such farmhouses, would rest in the shade of the trees along the south side of the bayou's riparian forest, near the San Felipe Trail. Water was a necessity, and proximity to the bayou would have been important until a well could be dug by hand.[42] Reynolds probably tried his hand at raising crops on the prairie, almost certainly including cotton, as well as corn to feed his gristmill.

Despite his location on the frontier, Allen Reynolds lived the life of a wealthy planter, like many of the well-to-do planters of the "old 300" who had preceded him to Texas. He arrived at his new home on Buffalo Bayou with a fully equipped household. His probate inventory listed household goods that included a bureau, three beds, bedding and bedsteads, brass andirons and shovel tongs, a hearth brush, two inkstands, a card table, a large looking glass, four oil paintings, fourteen yards of carpeting, a kitchen table, nine chairs, four brass candlesticks, one lot of queensware (glazed earthenware, one lot of china, glasses, one set of britannia ware (lathe-spun pewter), forty-four dinner plates, three large dinner dishes, two glass decanters, one lot of tinware, one lot of candle molds, and several books.[43] Such luxury was a far cry from the humble inventory of James Wheaton to his west, who died in 1839. These goods would have shipped from his former home in New York, and the forty-four dinner plates attested to a man and his wife who had big plans for prospering and for socializing in a new land.

An invoice for a shipment of luxury foodstuffs from the South Street seaport in New York City in 1832, while Reynolds was living on his tract on the bayou, underscores his relative prosperity (Figure 3.14). Groceries that we might consider normal today were true luxuries at this time on the frontier and had to be shipped from New York to Harrisburg, and then by wagon to his home. This included items like spices, horseradish, flour, pepper, raisins, coffee, pickled oysters, and soap, but also five gallons each of brandy, gin, Irish whiskey and peach brandy—and four hundred Havana cigars. Presumably these items took the frontier edge off the local fare of wild game, beef, pork and cornbread. The purchase amount for these comestibles, $156.96, is equivalent to about $3,600 in modern currency, and apparently did not include shipping.[44] Given that there were no grocery stores within a day's ride on horseback, the purchases were perhaps not too extravagant from the perspective of a prosperous settler.

Such comforts could not hide the fact that the environment and setting was harsh. Shipping his mill's produce was expensive and time-consuming, and it may well be that Reynolds was disappointed with the limited opportunity to transport timber goods by water at this upstream location on Buffalo Bayou. Water depth at his site was at most a few feet, and the channel immediately downstream was narrow in many places. More importantly, he and his family members seem to have contracted malaria at the site, because orders for large quantities of qui-

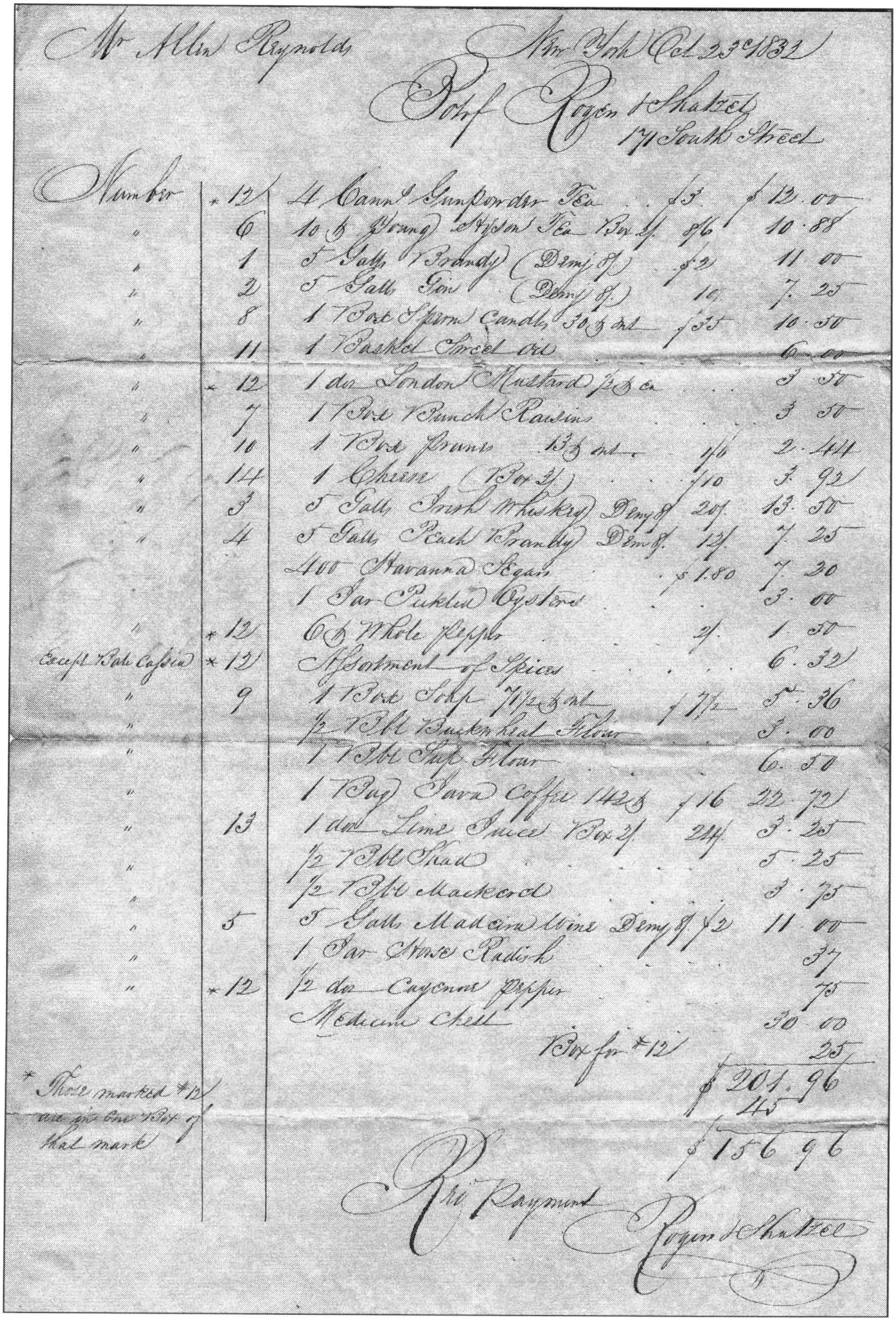

Mr Allen Reynolds — New York Oct 23d 1832

Bot of Rogen & Shatzel
171 South Street

Number		Article	Price	Amount
Number	*12	4 Canns Gunpowder Tea	$3	$12.00
"	6	10 lb Young Hyson Tea Box 2/	8/6	10.88
"	1	5 Galls Brandy (Demij 8/)	$2	11.00
"	2	5 Galls Gin (Demij 8/)	10/	7.25
"	8	1 Box Sperm Candles 30 lb nt	$.35	10.50
"	11	1 Basket Sweet oil		6.00
"	*12	1 doz London Mustard ½ lb ea		3.50
"	7	1 Box Bunch Raisins		3.50
"	10	1 Box Prunes 13 lb nt	1/6	2.44
"	14	1 Cheese (Box 2/)	$.10	3.92
"	3	5 Galls Irish Whiskey Demij 8/	20/	13.50
"	4	5 Galls Peach Brandy Demij 8/	12/	7.25
		400 Havanna Segars	$1.80	7.20
		1 Jar Pickled Oysters		3.00
"	*12	6 lb Whole Pepper	2/	1.50
Except Box Cassia	*12	Assortment of Spices		6.32
"	9	1 Box Soap 71½ lb nt	$7½	5.36
"		½ Bbl Buckwheat Flour		3.00
"		1 Bbl Sup Flour		6.50
"		1 Bag Java Coffee 142 lb	$.16	22.72
"	13	1 doz Lime Juice Box 2/	24/	3.25
"		½ Bbl Shad		5.25
"		½ Bbl Mackerel		3.75
"	5	5 Galls Madeira Wine Demij 8/	$2	11.00
"		1 Jar Horse Radish		37
"	*12	½ doz Cayenne Pepper		75
		Medicine Chest		30.00
		Box for *12		25
				$201.96
				45
				$156.96

* Those marked *12 are in one Box of that mark

Recd Payment
Rogen & Shatzel

Figure 3.14. An invoice of 1832 for a shipment of luxury foodstuffs to Allen Chapman Reynolds from a vendor in New York City. Courtesy of La Quencis Gibbs Scott.

nine water are among his papers from this time period.[45] He sold his Buffalo Bayou tract in 1835 to James Spillman, and moved to Washington County, selecting a site on the Brazos River located between Independence and Washington-on-the-Brazos. Here Reynolds built a new home on Hidalgo Bluff overlooking the Brazos River, and became a founder of the town of Washington-on-the-Brazos. At the first election of officers for that town, in July 1835, he was elected *síndico procurador* (town attorney), and he also helped Stephen F. Austin with legal matters related to immigration.[46]

He did not last long at this new site, however. He died suddenly at Washington-on-the-Brazos in 1837 at the relatively young age of 51, perhaps due to the yellow fever epidemic that ravaged Houston and other coastal settlements that year. As he lay dying, he dictated a last will and testament to his physician, and its unusual status caused a probate that took many years to settle, but which left us with his detailed inventory, discussed earlier. Wealthy to the last, he left an estate valued at about $100,000, a princely sum in early Texas.[47] He and his wife are buried in the Reynolds cemetery on Hidalgo Bluff, now on private property.

Post-Old 300
Land grants on the bayou, before Independence

Wheaton and Reynolds appear to have been the only permanent settlers along the western bayou in the years leading up to the Texas Revolution. However, there were several land speculators, who signed up for Mexican land grants that they seem to have intended only as investments. They are listed below, from west to east (see Figure 3.7).

William B. Hardin (1801–1839) was born in Franklin County, Georgia, and raised in Tennessee. In 1825 he became angry about an affair between his brother's wife and another man, Isaac Porter. Hardin shot and killed both Porter and a man who accompanied Porter and was indicted for the murder, along with his brothers. He escaped to Texas and was arrested for extradition twice but escaped both times. With his experience in law and order, he was elected commissary of police in Anahuac and secretary of the board for the town of Liberty, in 1831, at which time he was a leader of the Anahuac Disturbances, resulting in his election as alcalde of Anahuac in 1832 and 1835; he also became that municipality's first judge. A practicing lawyer, he was a member of the Galveston Bay Land Company and was a noted land speculator. After the Battle of San Jacinto, he and his wife, Sarah Looney, cared for many Mexican officers at their Liberty plantation. When Hardin died in Galveston in 1839, of yellow fever, he was one of the republic's wealthiest landowners, with an estate that included 114,222 acres plus a number of city lots in Galveston.[48]

One of Hardin's many speculative acquisitions was a league of land granted in Austin's colony on April 23, 1831, next to Joel Wheaton's league (Figure 3.7). There is no evidence that he lived on the land any longer than the bare minimum time required to prove it up. By 1841 Alsatian immigrant Thomas Habermacher had purchased some of this land and had built a farm on it.

Henry K. Lewis was an early grantee of whom very little is known. On November 28, 1832, he was granted 885 acres next to and east of William Hardin, south of Buffalo Bayou (Figure 3.7). This occurred just days after he had obtained a grant for an entire 246-acre island in San Jacinto Bay.[49] He appears to have vanished without much of a trace.

George L. Bellows (1798–1831) was born in Walpole, Cheshire, New Hampshire, and married Charlotte Louisa Stoddard in 1829 in New London, Connecticut. They lived briefly in Ogdensburgh, New York, before George traveled to Texas to seek his fortune. He received a league of land in Austin's colony on May 5, 1831. However, by August 27 of that year he died.[50] His grant was immediately to the west of John D. Taylor's league at Pine Point (Figure 3.7).

Robert Vince (ca. 1793–ca. 1837) was born in Tatnall County, Georgia, and migrated to Texas in 1822 along with three brothers, Allen, William and Richard, and a sister, Susan. They lived along what came to be known as Vince's Bayou, and they together received a sitio there from Austin's colony in 1824; that land straddled Vince's Bayou. They built a bridge across the bayou near their dwelling. The census of 1826 placed Robert at that dwelling place on Vince's Bayou.

In 1830 Robert Vince applied for his own land from the colony and was subsequently granted half a league, in 1832. The location of that half league is shown in Figure 3.7, just east of the John Taylor League. In 1833, however, he was still living on Vince's Bayou with his family, so it is questionable how much he had done to perfect his grant over what was minimally required. By 1836 or 1837 Robert died, and the land went to his heirs; his brother Richard was named administrator of his estate in February 1837. Vince's bridge became famous during the Battle of San Jacinto in 1836. Both armies crossed that bridge en route to the battle, and Texian general Sam Houston ordered Deaf Smith to burn it. Mexican general Santa Anna fled the battlefield on Allen Vince's horse but could not cross the rain-swollen bayou without the bridge.[51]

Charles Sage is little known, save that he appeared in San Felipe in February 1836 to apply for a land grant. The register states that he was from New York[52]. The grant was finally patented on March 18, 1845. His application was noted as follows:

> *Charles Sage personally appears claiming one league and labor, has taken the oath prescribed by law. Witnesses Christopher Williams and Jesse Benton being duly sworn deposeth and says that they knew the said C[harles] Sage previous to the declaration of independence and that he did not leave the Country to avoid participating in the wars of the Country. He is at present a citizen. Issued for one third.*[53]

Although he applied for a league and a labor, his received grant of one third of a league reflected his status as a single man residing in Texas before the declaration of independence. The grant was along the bayou, adjacent to that of William White (Figure 3.7). Sage may have been a businessman, as he is shown in multiple passenger lists for the schooner Kosciusko, traveling between Galveston and New Orleans, in 1837 and 1838.[54]

The Texas Revolution and its Runaway Scrape

The tumultuous events of the Texas Revolution of 1835–1836 were to profoundly affect the residents of the frontier region of upper Buffalo Bayou.

Anglo settlers, who by 1834 vastly outnumbered native Mexicans in the Mexican state of Coahuila y Texas, chafed under the Mexican government's abolition of slavery in 1829.[55] They objected to a bill calling for the cessation of new immigration from the United States, passed by President Bustamente in 1830.[56] In this political climate, it is not surprising that such entrepreneurs as the Cloppers were disheartened; their dream of a vibrant trade route along the San Felipe to Harrisburg road depended upon an influx of new settlers, and the worsening political climate no doubt contributed to their decision to fold their venture. When Antonio López de Santa Anna ousted Bustamente in a revolt in 1832, Texian settlers responded by expelling Mexican troops from eastern Texas and held conventions to see what could be done to weaken or abolish the 1830 laws.[57] In 1835 Santa Anna overturned the Mexican constitution of 1824, which led to widespread unrest throughout Mexico, not least in Coahuila y Texas. Texians began to mobilize as militias, and a skirmish at Gonzales led to a siege at Bexar, in which the Mexican garrison surrendered in December 1835.

With Texas in open revolt, General Santa Anna and more than six thousand Mexican soldiers began to march northward that same month.[58] A Declaration of Texas Independence was passed by Texian delegates at a political convention in Washington-on-the-Brazos on March 2, 1836, but that declaration was soon followed by news of the disastrous Texian defeat at the Alamo on March 6 and the massacre of captive Texian soldiers at Goliad on March 27.

These events, proceeding in rapid-fire order in early 1836, took the war out of south central Texas and thrust it eastward. Sam Houston, selected as commander in chief of Texian forces at the same

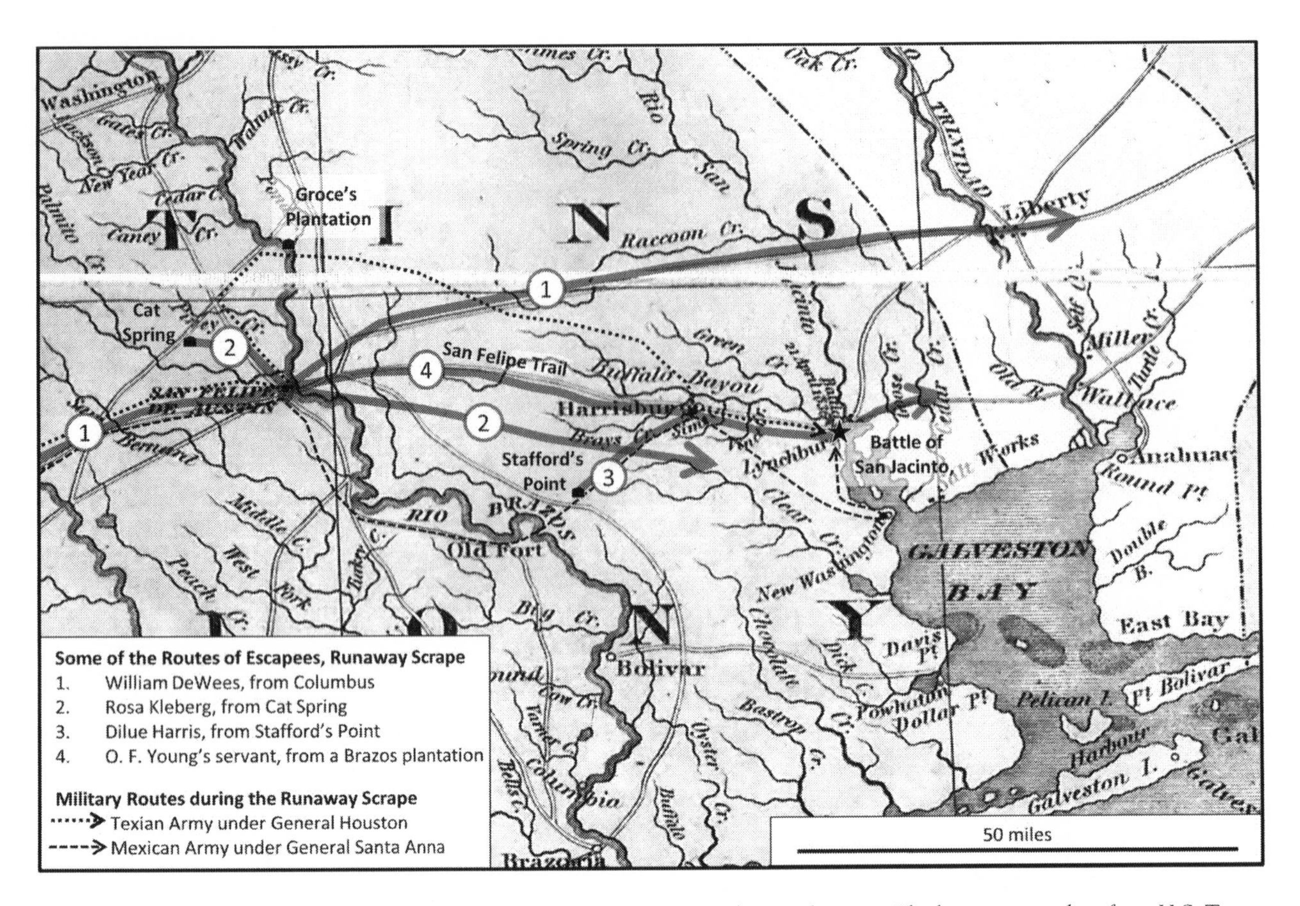

Figure 3.15. Some of the exit routes taken during the Runaway Scrape, as discussed in text. The base map is taken from H.S. Tanner's "Map of Texas with Parts of the Adjoining States, Compiled by Stephen F. Austin, 1837," courtesy of the Library of Congress, Geography and Map Division. Routes of the armies of Generals Houston and Santa Anna are taken from "Military Map of Texas and Coahuila, 1835-1836," by Andrew Jackson Houston, 1938.

convention that declared independence, was in Gonzales on March 13 when news of the fall of the Alamo reached the town. With Santa Anna's army moving eastward, Houston and his ill-equipped army began an eastward retreat, which in turn caused the mass evacuation of civilians who lay in the path of these two armies. Thus began the infamous Runaway Scrape, much of which happened in the countryside on either side of Buffalo Bayou (Figure 3.15).

Houston and the Texian army moved east to La Grange, then Columbus, then San Felipe, before heading north to Groce's Bernardo Plantation on the Brazos River, where they arrived on March 29. Here they stayed for two weeks, training the hundreds of new recruits who had left their families to defend their new republic. Meanwhile, roads and ferries were choked with thousands of women, children, old men, and African American slaves who fled in front of Santa Anna's advance. The dangers were real; Santa Anna's army had divided into five columns that were ransacking and burning any and all farms that they encountered as they moved across the prairie. Their intention was to start a panic, and they were successful.[59]

Several accounts describe the chaos and tragedy of those days for the women, children, and slaves who were left behind to fleeis when their husbands and sons joined up with General Houston. William DeWees (1799–1878) had been in Texas since 1822 and lived with his family in Columbus. When the Texian army began to retreat across the Brazos, he left the army to protect his feeling family and others, apparently with Sam Houston's concurrence. They crossed the Brazos at San Felipe and camped on the

Figure 3.16. Rosa Kleberg, from John Henry Brown, *Indian Wars and Pioneers of Texas* (Austin: L. E. Daniell, 1896).

Figure 3.17. Dilue Rose Harris. Courtesy of Nesbitt Memorial Archive Library, Columbus, Texas.

prairie, but when the Mexican army crossed the Brazos eight miles below San Felipe, the remaining Texians (under the leadership of Moseley Baker) burned the town, and the DeWees party headed east across the prairie, eventually camping at Spring Creek while they tried to figure out the movements of the two armies. This campsite was likely along the San Felipe to Liberty Road along modern day Cypress Creek, which was named Raccoon Creek on the Tanner map of 1830 (Figure 3.3); it seems to have been regarded as a branch of Spring Creek, which is arguably the case on modern maps as well.

> *It seemed as though the whole country was panic struck . . . the roads were literally crowded with wagons, men, women and children, hurrying with the greatest speed to a place of safety. On they went, one after another, through woods and through prairies, seeming to have nothing in view but to go eastward. . . . Here might be seen delicate ladies wading through mud and dirt, striving to hasten their footsteps and free themselves from the marshes; but at every step they would bog in deeper and deeper. . . . Loaded wagons rolled on one after another in the greatest haste, till they came to a stream, then each would strive to be first and foremost, in order that they might be soonest across the stream; now you might behold children falling from the wagons which still kept on, leaving them behind, till another wagon came along and picked them up. Mothers have in this manner been separated from their children for days, and some for weeks, as the wagons often take a different course.*[60]

They eventually crossed the Trinity River and camped, awaiting their next step. There were about 150 to 200 families there.[61]

Rosa Kleberg (1813–1907; Figure 3.16) was living at Cat Spring, not far from Groce's plantation, and fled along a similar route. She and her family had arrived only a year earlier, after a long and arduous trip from Germany (see Chapter 6), and lived in a log cabin in an area settled by other German immigrants. When the news came of the fall of the

Alamo, the family discussed what to do. Typical of what happened in many families, her husband and brothers left to join Houston's army, while her aged father stayed behind to help with the escape:

> *As the men left their families began to move, intending to cross the Sabine River; and we set out like the rest. . . . Having only one big ox-wagon, and being compelled to take in it four families and their baggage, we were compelled to leave behind much that was valuable. My father and I drove our cattle and packed horses; and I carried my daughter Clara, who was then a child of only a few months, upon the saddle in front of me. Most of the families travelled separately until they reached the Brazos, where all were compelled to come to a halt. It was necessary to drive the cattle across before people could pass over, and this was attended with a good deal of difficulty. In this way there were collected from forty to fifty families who were trying to cross with their cattle, and the noise and confusion were terrible. There was only one small ferryboat, which carried a wagon and a few passengers. Many of the people were on foot.*[62]

The Klebergs proceeded across the prairie to camp at Clear Creek along the modern Harris County–Brazoria County boundary, and then headed yet farther east. It would appear that they were avoiding the main east-west San Felipe to Harrisburg road (San Felipe Trail); they may have assumed that the Mexican army would take that road in their pursuit of President Burnet and the members of the Texian government, who were by then in Harrisburg. Other families, especially those living south of Buffalo Bayou, did use the San Felipe to Harrisburg road and/or its extension that leading farther east to the Lynchburg ferry across the San Jacinto River, whence they could continue to Liberty and the Sabine River. Dilue Rose Harris (1825–1914; Figure 3.17) came to Texas in 1833 with her parents, Dr. Pleasant W. Harris and Margaret Wells Rose, settling at Stafford Point (modern Stafford, southwest of Houston and northeast of Richmond). In her old age she wrote perhaps the most detailed account of the Runaway Scrape, which includes a description of African American slaves fleeing along with their white owners:

> *By the 20th of February the people of San Patricio and other western settlements were fleeing for their lives. . . . On the 12th of March came the news of the fall of the Alamo. A courier brought a dispatch from General Houston for the people to leave. Colonel Travis and the men under his command had been slaughtered, the Texas army was retreating, and President Burnet's cabinet had gone to Harrisburg. . . .*
>
> *We left home at sunset, hauling clothes, bedding, and provisions on the sleigh with one yoke of oxen. Mother and I were walking, she with an infant in her arms. Brother drove the oxen, and my two little sisters rode in the sleigh. . . . We camped the first night near Harrisburg, about where the railroad depot now stands. Next day we crossed Vince's Bridge and arrived at the San Jacinto in the night. There were fully five thousand people at the ferry. The planters from Brazoria and Columbia with their slaves were crossing. We waited three days before we crossed. Our party consisted of five white families: father's, Mr. Dyer's, Mr. Bell's, Mr. Neal's, and Mr. Bundick's. Father and Mr. Bundick were the only white men in the party, the others being in the army. There were twenty or thirty negroes from Stafford's plantation. They had a large wagon with five yoke of oxen, and horses and mules, and they were in charge of an old negro man called Uncle Ned. Altogether, black and white, there were about fifty of us. Everyone was trying to cross first, and it was almost a riot. We got over the third day, and after travelling a few miles came to a big prairie. It was about twelve miles further to the next timber and water, and some of our party wanted to camp; but others said that the Trinity river was rising, and if we delayed we might not get across. So we hurried on.*
>
> *When we got about half across the prairie Uncle Ned's wagon bogged. The negro men driving*

the carts tried to go around the big wagon one at a time until the four carts were fast in the mud. . . . The negro men put all the oxen to the wagon, but could not move it; so they had to stay there until morning without wood or water. Mother gathered the white children in our cart. They behaved very well and went to sleep, except one little boy, Eli Dyer, who kicked and cried for Uncle Ned and Aunt Dilue till Uncle Ned came and carried him to the wagon. He slept that night in Uncle Ned's arms . . . .

Our hardships began at the Trinity. The river was rising and there was a struggle to see who should cross, first. Measles, sore eyes, whooping cough, and every other disease that man, woman or child is heir to broke out among us. . . . The horrors of crossing the Trinity are beyond my power to describe. One of my little sisters was very sick, and the ferryman said that those families that had sick children should cross first. When our party got to the boat the water broke over the banks above where we were and ran around us. We were several hours surrounded by water. Our family was the last to get to the boat. We left more than five hundred people on the west bank. . . . The sick child was in convulsions. It required eight men to manage the boat. When we landed the lowlands were under water, and everybody was rushing for the prairie. . . . All we carried with us was what clothes we were wearing at the time. The night was very dark. We crossed a bridge that was under water. As soon as we crossed, a man with a cart and oxen drove on the bridge, and it broke down, drowning the oxen. . . . Father and mother hurried on, and we got to the prairie and found a great many families camped there.[64]

It was an event never to be forgotten by participants. Unfortunately, most did not record their memoires in writing, and the memories were lost. Dr. Orceneth Fisher Allen (1851–1947) wrote a history of his birthplace, the city of Houston—a city founded after the Texas Revolution was concluded—and mentioned the role of San Felipe wagon road during the Runaway Scrape as part of an epilogue of regrets about what had been left out of his opus; he hoped others would somehow formally remember the road in the future. That never happened, but he did write down some of his own family memories from the difficult flight that occurred along the San Felipe Trail:

> *In closing my book may I speak of two matters that I think have been neglected, both of which I hope Houston's patriotic and business organizations will look to. . . . First, the restoration of San Felipe [street] from Dallas avenue east of the old Cemetery Park, and continue same [to the west] as far as the city may build. Thence on as the old trail over which those pioneer men, women and children fled before Santa Anna toward Harrisburg and other points of safety beyond. A story related to me in my boyhood by my old black mammy slave, told what she endured as a barefoot fifteen year old girl as her white folks fled from San Felipe. She trod the old trail with blistered feet. Her white folks would hide in the brush and rest, and had no food but roasted grains of corn for three days. By all means these pioneer sufferers should be remembered with markers on this trail, and its name remembered.*[65]

While the women and children, the elderly and the slaves were fleeing eastward along various routes across the coastal prairie, two major armies were in the same general vicinity, jockeying for position for an expected confrontation. General Houston and the Texian army had been camped across the Brazos River from Groce's plantation, on the west side of the river near an oxbow lake (Figure 3.15), where Houston had been training the soldiers and gathering supplies and more recruits. While there, the Texian army received the Twin Sisters cannons, a gift of the people of Cincinnati. Nicholas Clopper, whose Texas Trading Association had by now crumbled, had been in that Ohio city in 1835 rallying support and funds for the revolution from its citizens, who purchased the cannon (Chapter 2). Houston and his Texian troops stayed at their camp on the Brazos

River from the end of March until April 12 and 13, when they departed across the river using the steamboat Yellow Stone, which had been loading cotton at Groce's when Houston arrived. They then moved southeastward.[66]

Santa Anna left Bexar on March 29, joining General Ramírez y Sesma as he headed eastward. When Houston had earlier left for Groce's Landing, he had left behind a small force under Captain Mosely Baker (1802–1848) to protect the crossing at San Felipe, and Baker burned the town on March 30 to keep it from falling into Santa Anna's hands.[67] Santa Anna's army marched into San Felipe on April 7 and learned from a Texian captive that Houston's army planned to retreat further if the Mexican forces crossed the Brazos.[68] Prevented from crossing there by fire from Baker's force across the river to the east, Santa Anna left with 700 men on April 14, crossing the Brazos at Fort Bend (Old Fort, Figure 3.15; modern Richmond), intending to capture Burnet and the government at Harrisburg. The Mexicans arrived in Harrisburg on April 15, but Burnet and the others had left. Santa Anna's troops sent a column under Juan Almonte to New Washington, Nicholas Clopper's home, to intercept them. Almonte nearly captured them, arriving as the Texians fled by boat to Galveston. Almonte burned New Washington and then rejoined Santa Anna, who burned Harrisburg and headed to Lynchburg, where they expected to find the main Texian force.[69]

By April 16 Houston's army had reached a crossing of the Atascosita Road that headed to Liberty and Nacogdoches (Figure 3.15). Many of his restive troops had families who were fleeing in the Runaway Scrape. Not wishing to retreat further, they marched toward Harrisburg. They arrived at the smoldering ashes of Harrisburg on April 18.[70] Both forces arrived at Lynch's Ferry on April 20, the Texians making camp near Buffalo Bayou and Santa Anna near the San Jacinto.

On the morning of April 21 Mexican General Cos arrived with 540 more troops, bringing Santa Anna's army to 1200 men. Santa Anna allowed the tired troops to rest and reportedly himself took a nap. At 4:30 p.m. the Texians crept up and surprised the Mexicans, who within eighteen minutes abandoned the field with Texians in pursuit; a bloodbath awaited the Mexicans as they fled into the marshes.[71] Santa Anna was captured the following day and, on May 14, signed the Treaties of Velasco, wherein Texas was declared an independent state, and Mexican troops were ordered to retreat south of the Rio Grande. The war was over, at least for the time being. The Mexican government never recognized the treaties because they were signed while Santa Anna was held prisoner, and the issue was finally resolved during the Mexican-American war the following decade.[72]

The fleeing Texian families, many camped out around the San Jacinto and Trinity rivers, received the good news by horseback. Dilue Rose Harris reported:

> *We heard someone calling [from] the direction of Liberty. We could see a man on horseback waving his hat; and, as we knew there was no one left at Liberty, we thought the Mexican army had crossed the Trinity. The young men came with their guns, and when the rider got near enough for us to understand what he said, it was "Turn back! The Texans have whipped the Mexican army and the Mexicans are prisoners. No danger! No danger! Turn back. When he got to the camp he could scarcely speak he was so excited and out of breath. When the young men began to understand the glorious news they wanted to fire a salute, but father made them stop. He told them to save their ammunition, for they might need it. Father asked the man for an explanation, and he showed a despatch from General Houston giving an account of the battle and saying it would be safe for the people to return to their homes.*[73]

Their time of despair and deprivation was not over, as most returned to find their farms ravaged and destroyed. In Dilue Harris's account:

Early the next morning we were on the move. . . . We could hear nothing but sad news. San Felipe had been burned, and dear old Harrisburg was in ashes. There was nothing left of the Stafford plantation but a crib with a thousand bushels of corn. . . . The burning of the saw mill at Harrisburg and the buildings on Stafford's plantation was a calamity that greatly affected the people. On the plantation there were a sugar-mill, cotton-gin, blacksmith-shop, grist-mill, a dwelling-house, negro houses, and a stock of farming implements. The Mexicans saved the corn for bread, and it was a great help to the people of the neighborhood.[74]

Rosa Kleburg had a somewhat similar tale:

It was our intention to return home, but we heard that the Indians were in the country, and so we . . . went to Galveston Island. . . . We received some supplies from the people of the United States, but we nevertheless here passed through some of our hardest experiences. Many of us were sick. . . . My sister-in-law Ottilie v. Roeder died here and we buried her under the Three Lone Trees. . . . When we came home [to Cat Spring] we found everything we had left was gone. We had buried our books, but the place had been found and they were torn to pieces. We had to begin anew, and with less than we had we started.[75]

Figure 4.1. A cotton wagon train. From Edward King, 1875, *The Great South: A Record of Journeys* (Hartford, Conn.: American Publishing Company, 1875).

FOUR

The Town of Houston and the San Felipe Trail After Independence

For the last three or four weeks all our streets in the business part of the city
have been so blocked up with wagons and teams
that it is almost impossible to pass between them,
even on foot, in any direction.

—The *Houston Weekly Telegraph*, May 7, 1856.

Some days, as many as eight hundred bales of cotton have been brought into town upon waggons,
for sale and shipment. Our merchants are "up and at it," early and late;
everyone appears busy, hopeful, happy....Boats are constantly arriving and departing,
travellers coming and going, steam engines snorting, everybody working, politicians scheming,
the Germans smoking, and the Irish joking, the ox-drivers cursing, the churches praying,
debtors paying, and finally the clouds are raining, while some sidewalks
and most of the street crossings are perfectly too bad.

—The *Houston Weekly Telegraph*, May 14, 1856.

THE EVENTS of March and April 1836, profoundly affected the frontier settlements along Buffalo Bayou. Both endpoints of the San Felipe Trail were burned to the ground, never to regain their past political or commercial prominence. Indeed, the three lynchpins of what had been the Clopper's dreamed-of Texas trading empire were all destroyed (the third was New Washington). The political capital of Stephen F. Austin's colony was gone, but in its place a new capital of the independent Republic of Texas arose almost overnight, along the same wagon road. This chapter explores the early years of Houston; the earliest suburbanization of its west side, largely along the San Felipe Trail, as the town began to grow; and the peak years for trade and travel along that road, in the Republic and early statehood era.

The founding of Houston

Two New York land speculators, Augustus C. Allen and his brother John K. Allen, had arrived in

Texas in 1832 and settled in Nacogdoches. They seem to have spent their time during the war for Texas independence as supply agents. Following the Texian victory at San Jacinto they moved quickly to capitalize on an unparalleled opportunity. Realizing the commercial importance of the site at Harrisburg, with its accessibility by sea and proximity to the cotton fields of the Brazos–via the San Felipe Trail–they soon traveled to what remained of the town of Harrisburg and attempted to purchase it. However, its patriarch, John Richardson Harris, had recently died, and his estate was in litigation, so a sale was not immediately possible. The brothers then continued up Buffalo Bayou, where on August 26, 1836, they purchased the south half of the John Austin tract from Elizabeth E. Parrott, the remarried widow of John Austin. In a canny move, they named the town after their friend and hero of the moment, Sam Houston. Houston was elected president of the Republic of Texas and inaugurated on October 22, 1836, for a two-year term, and the new town was declared the new country's capital.[1]

Houston very soon replaced Harrisburg in its role as the western terminus of waterborne shipping along Buffalo Bayou and the point of embarkation on land-based routes to the interior on the San Felipe, Washington, Fort Bend (Richmond) and Brazoria wagon roads (Figure 4.2). When a young Francis R. Lubbock arrived about January 1, 1837, however, all he found were survey stakes, a few tents (one of them a saloon), and a few houses under construction. When Sam Houston arrived on April 26, he noted that there were "upwards of 100 houses finished, and going up rapidly (some of them fine frame buildings) and 1500 people, all actively engaged in their respective pursuits."[2] Those pursuits included land speculation that accompanied the awarding of land bounties that had been promised to soldiers during the war.

By all accounts, it was a frontier town with rough edges, including muddy streets, unfinished cabins, an element of uncouth and sometimes violent citizenry, a dank and humid climate, and dangerous diseases. Gustav Dresel (1818–1848), a businessman from Germany who visited frontier Texas in 1837–1840, left one of the most vivid pen portraits of early Houston life from his visit of 1838:

> *There was lively and varied activity going on in Houston at that time. Steamboats from Galveston tied up daily. The owners of land certificates, who had selected the finest free land, and tradesmen of all sorts arrived on horseback from the interior of the county, among them many a Mexican smuggler. They brought news from the frontier, pointed out the beauty of newly discovered regions, and described their adventures with the Indians and wild beasts.*
>
> *As may easily be imagined, the social conditions in Texas were still very unsettled in that period. The Revolution was hardly over, and the number of those who had participated in it and were unemployed were very great. A chummy companionship among those who had shared suffering and joy for so long was unavoidable. All of them lived and dwelled indiscriminately. When fall came with its northers and there were only three stoves in the whole of Houston, we used to light fires in front of the saloon in the evening, stand around them and enjoy—not excepting the President—hot drinks with merry speeches.*
>
> *The City Hotel was then the chief gathering place. In that spacious wooden shack we were often 100 and 150 at the table. All the nations were represented. One could hear the most interesting careers. There were frequent brawls, pistols were drawn, bowie knives flashed, and as everyone walked about well armed, these incidents looked rather dangerous. I twice witnessed scenes where first in the barroom and afterwards in the street, men were wounded in this manner. . . . Games of hazard were forbidden, but nevertheless the green tables were occupied by the gamblers for whole nights. What is more, these blacklegs even formed a regular guild, against which any opposition was a risky matter. The resident citizens, however, who were intent on the peace and good reputation of their new dwelling place, checked with all their might the nuisance that had gained ground.*[3]

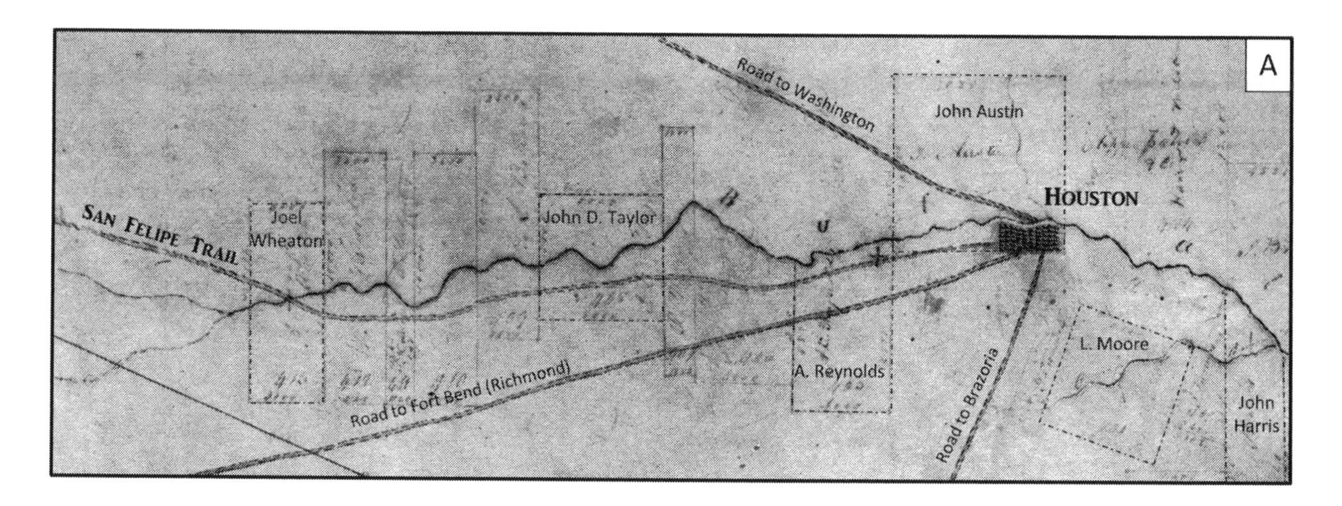

Figure 4.2. **A:** A portion of Stephen F. Austin's *Connected Map of Texas,* 1837, courtesy of the General Land Office, Austin. It shows tracts that were granted before the Texas Revolution as well as several roads leading to the new town of Houston, founded in 1836. The street grid of Houston is not to scale and not oriented properly. A few of the tracts are highlighted for clarity. **B:** Same area, with a modern road map as base, highlighting some significant settlements of the republic era. Roads in the early town of Houston (downtown) are highlighted and shown to proper scale. Base map courtesy of OpenStreetMap. **C:** Same area, showing the natural environment that existed at the time (as in Figure 2.1).

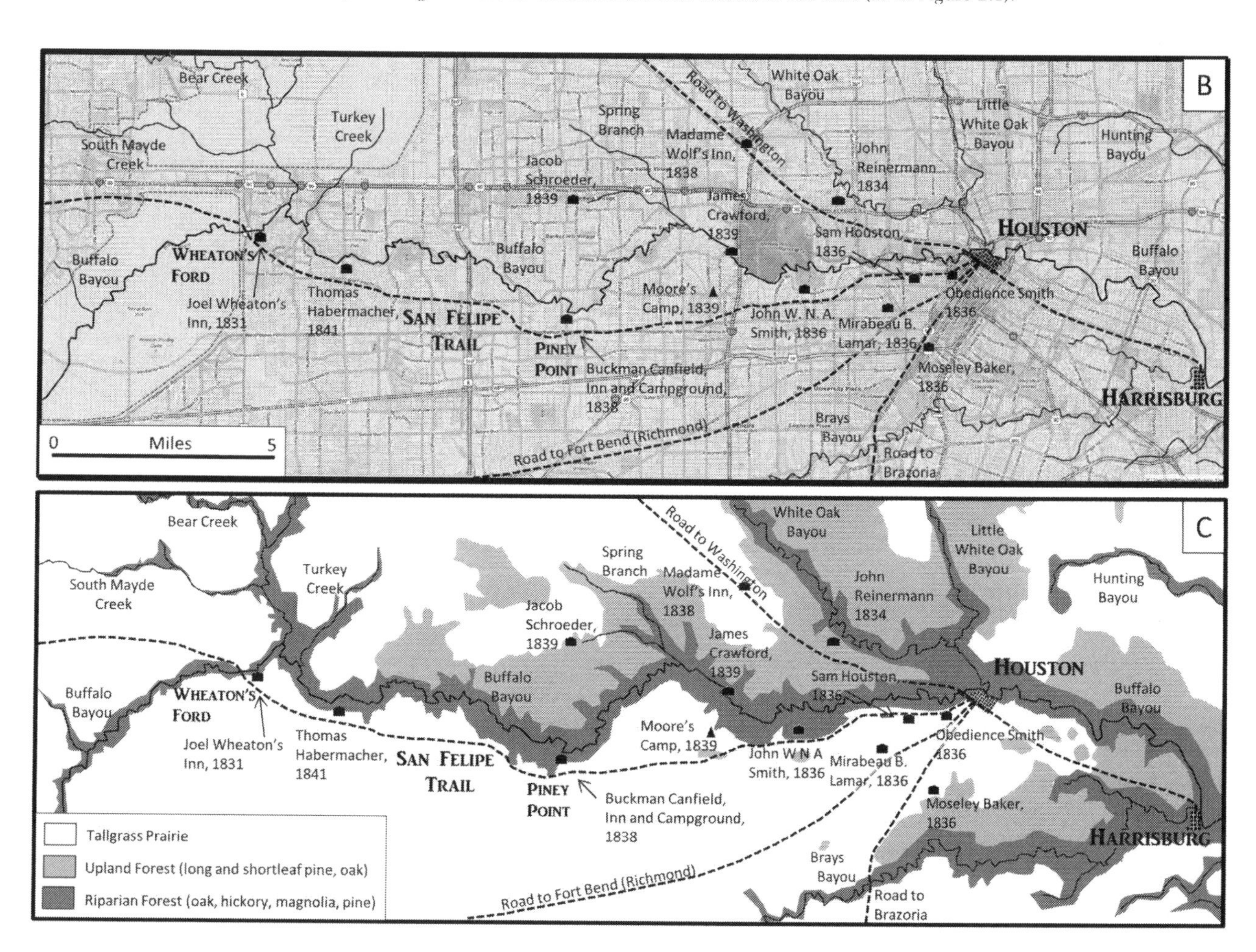

The following year, 1839, a yellow fever epidemic struck the new city and brought home to all the dangers of living in the swampy area. Dresel described it in stark terms. He was visiting at "Madame (Teresa) Wolf's" inn on the Washington Road (located in Figure 4.2 B and C) when he heard about the epidemic from his innkeeper, a recent German immigrant:

> *Her description of the state of sickness in the capital was horrifying. I was anxious to find out the truth about all the rumors. It was a gloomy Sunday afternoon, which further intensified the sad impression made anyway by an epidemic-stricken city. I had my first view of Houston from the bluff on Buffalo Bayou opposite the city. Everything was dead. The formerly so animated streets were deserted by people; all the shops were closed. The water of the bayou looked so lazy and dark-green, and the air was so oppressively sultry and ghastly.*
>
> *In the City Hotel was the same amazement—followed by an enumeration of all the acquaintances who had already died, and of others who had saved themselves by escaping into the country. . . . I was quickly reminded of the epidemic, for the whole house was animated in such a manner as to rob the most fearless of their sleep. The rooms consisted of mere compartments that, being open above, had the whole extent of the roof in common as their ceiling. What therefore, was discussed in one chamber was heard in all the others. My neighbor groaned, vomited, and wailed frightfully; his "O Lord's" vividly recalled the Methodist meetings; he died the next day. A few rooms away there was a party of Texian army officers who played at cards, drinking grog and punch. They paid no heed to their sick neighbors and expressed their opinion one time after another that, if they really were to die, they wanted at least to have some jolly hours before they died. They became silent only before daybreak. The coughing, vomiting, and groaning continued throughout the night . . . but the worst was still to come: when I got up from my couch in the morning, I perceived traces of blood and suppuration on it. I as much as flew away from it. It was clear that a sick person or even a dead man had occupied it before me! . . . The attendant, who was not very well himself, had neglected to change the used linen and had taken me to the wrong compartment.*[4]

During the yellow fever epidemic of 1839, some 240 persons—reportedly 12 percent of the town's population—were buried between May and November at what was then the City Cemetery (now called Founders Memorial Park, discussed later in this chapter).[5]

The suburbs begin

In such an unhealthy town environment—unhealthy not just because of disease but also because of the constant mud and the often unsavory characters—it is not surprising that many citizens found a way to leave town for much of the year and occupy a second country residence. That situation was what led to the establishment of Houston's first suburbs, as townspeople spread in the same western direction that they continue to do today, some 180 years later. Many of those first suburbs lay along the San Felipe Trail.

Obedience Smith. One of the first to dwell in the near-west area of Houston spurned a town home completely. She was a hardy pioneer woman named Obedience Smith (1771–1847; Figure 4.3 A), who built a log cabin half a mile southwest of town in 1836, near where modern Clay and West Dallas streets intersect (Figures 4.2 C and 4.4). Her fascinating life has been recently documented in a biography by Audrey Barrett Cook.[6] Smith was a native of North Carolina, and her husband David Smith had been a soldier in the Revolutionary War, the War of 1812, and the Creek War of 1813–1814. The couple were pioneer residents of both Kentucky and Mississippi. When David Smith died in 1835, Obedience left to join her son Benjamin Fort Smith (1796–1841) in Texas, where he had been since 1833. He had a Brazos River plantation in Brazoria County, not far from where Dilue Rose Harris lived. Obedience arrived in February 1836, just in time for the Runaway Scrape, when she, her daughter Sarah

Figure 4.3. Houston's first suburbanites, these neighbors escaped the squalor of early city life by living all or part of the time on the new town's western fringe in 1837. **A**: Obedience Smith, ca. 1841, with grandsons A. J. and C. L. Terry, courtesy of Audrey Barrett Cook. **B:** Sam Houston, as he appeared in 1850, courtesy of the Sam Houston Memorial Museum.. **C:** Mirabeau B. Lamar, from Lucien Lamar Knight, Reminiscences of Famous Georgians (Atlanta: Franklin-Turner Company, 1907). **D:** Mary Smith Jones, former wife of John Woodruff (later wife of Anson Jones), from Adele Looscan, "The Women of Pioneer Days," in Dudley G. Wooten, ed., *A Comprehensive History of Texas, 1685 to 1897* (Dallas: William G. Scarff, 1898).

Smith Terry, and a number of African American slaves fled for the Sabine River.[7] Her son Benjamin Fort Smith served in the Texian army at Gonzales and at the siege of Bexar and was in Mirabeau B. Lamar's cavalry (serving under Henry Karnes) at the battle of San Jacinto. Politically astute, he was quick to move his family to Houston after the war and used proceeds from the sale of his Brazos plantation to build the first substantial building in the new city, which he originally named "Major Ben Fort Smith's Tavern House" but which soon became known as the City Hotel, already described in Dresel's account. It was located at present day 915 Franklin, at Travis.[8]

How much of the Smiths' Brazos plantation survived the war is not known, but Obedience's daughter Sarah died in August 1836, and it was at this time that Obedience moved to join her son in Houston. The log cabin her son built for her was near the San Felipe Trail just a half mile from town. As a widow arriving before the Declaration of Texas Independence was signed, she pursued a claim to a league and labor of land.[9] She placed her cabin on the league that she wanted, which was located immediately south of John Austin's grant (Figure 4.4). The Texas Land Office was closed during and just after the revolution, from 1836 to 1838, and so Smith had to wait. When the Republic of Texas Land Office opened in February 1838, Mrs. Smith was granted a tract of 3,368 acres—somewhat less than the 4,605 acres of a league and labor that she was theoretically due, but by then her preferred tract was landlocked. She received the headright on February 5, 1838, having already lived on it for nearly two years; the grant was patented in 1845.[10]

In 1837 Mrs. Smith moved yet farther out, to a spot near present day 2616 Louisiana at Dennis, over a mile from frontier Houston town. That was close enough for a pioneer woman! Here she built a more substantial home, elevated above the ground and made from lumber that was cut, pre-numbered, and shipped from Mobile, Alabama.[11]

By the time Obedience Smith was awarded her tract in 1838, it already had several prominent persons living on it, due no doubt to the long period of time it was without clear ownership (1836–1838). Captain Moseley Baker was one such interloper, and moreover, he reportedly sold a 150-acre tract on what became Mrs. Smith's tract to Mirabeau B. Lamar. Sam Houston had a "Rancho" of 50 acres, as did John Woodruff.[12] There was also a City Cemetery on the land that was active as early as 1836 (now Founders Memorial Park). Following are brief profiles of these other owners and entities.

Moseley Baker. Captain Moseley Baker, a prominent veteran of the Texian war, kept a country cabin on Smith's tract as an adjunct to his home in town, which was on Main Street not far from the City Hotel. The town house was a small clapboard home in which the first anniversary ball celebrating the Battle of San Jacinto was held on April 21, 1837, attended by President Houston (just back from recuperating in New Orleans from the wound he received in the battle) and by nearly every dignitary in town. President Houston and Mrs. Baker led the first dance, and at midnight the dancers repaired to the City Hotel for supper.[13] Baker's country place was about two miles southwest of Houston (Figure 4.4), not far from the modern intersection of San Jacinto Street and U.S. Highway 59. When Obedience Smith won her land, she effectively pushed him off her tract just to the east, onto land owned by James Holman.[14]

Sam Houston's Farm. Sam Houston's country property faced the San Felipe Trail, and its odd nonrectilinear layout probably reflected the crooked nature of the frontier road when he obtained the land (Figure 4.4). The road was later squared up to its current east-west location at the south edge of John Austin's tract, between 1837 and 1847 (now West Dallas Street); that new alignment of the road is noticeable on an 1890 map (Figure 4.5). Mrs. Smith apparently quit-claimed this land to the president after she acquired the property.[15] At the time, Sam Houston had a small, badly built home in town—probably at the corner of Main and Preston, built in early 1838.[16] He had a cabin on his small ranch, built in 1836 during his first term as president (1836–1838). Houstonians were to remember that place for over a century, as it remained largely undeveloped acreage well into the early twentieth century. In an article in

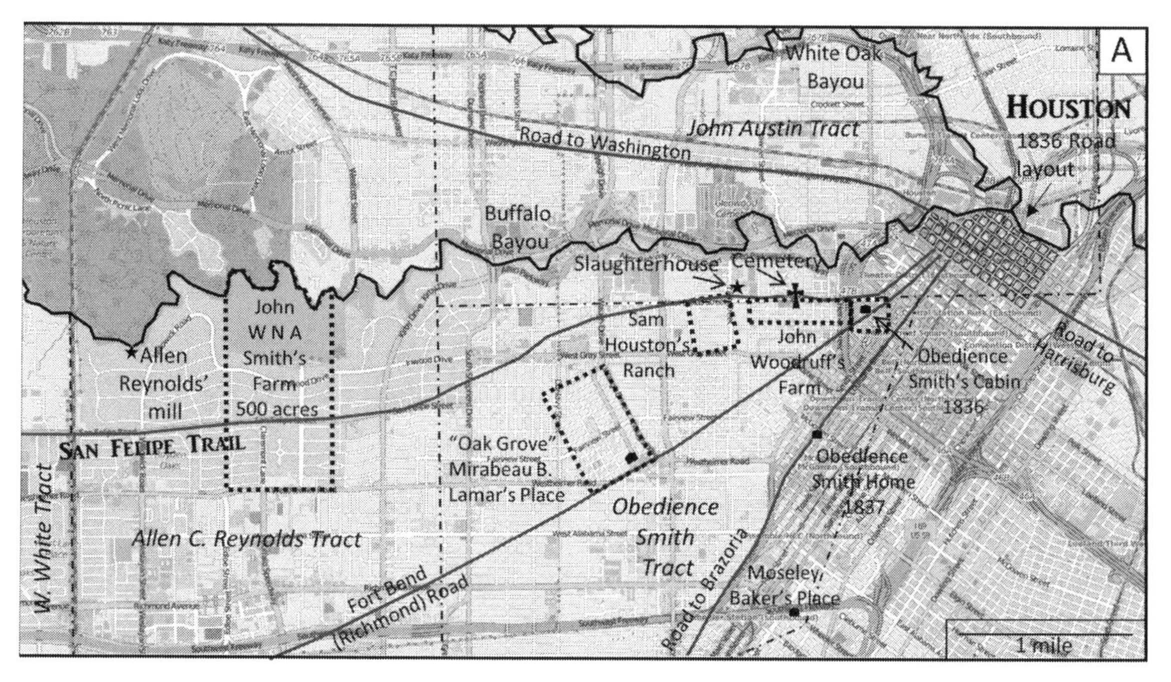

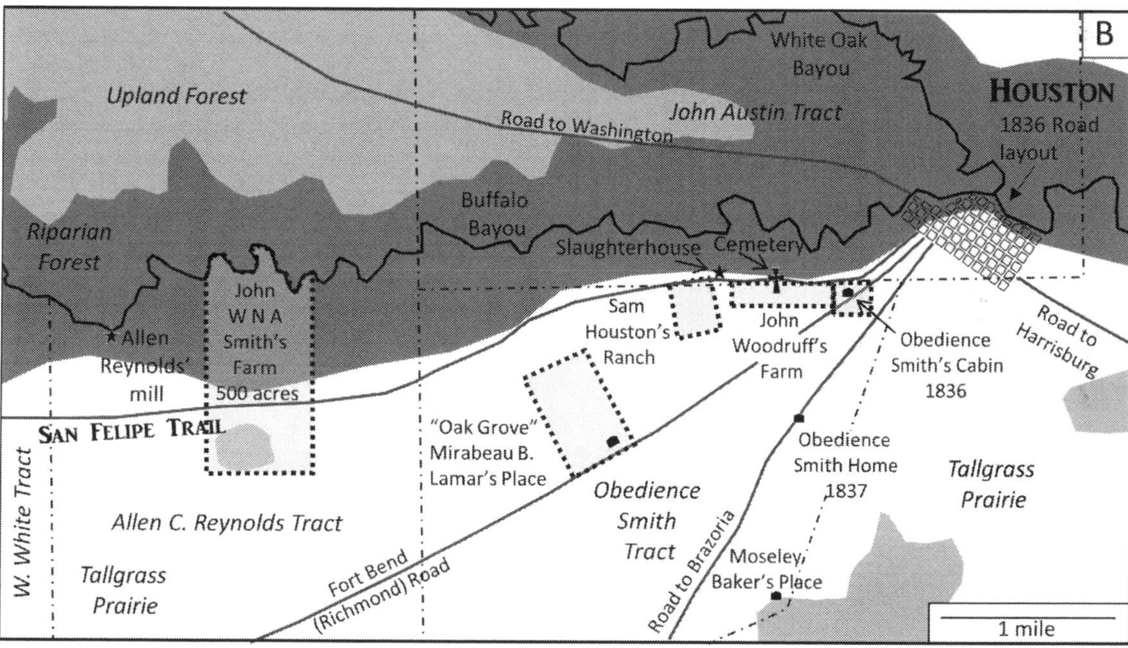

Figure 4.4. **A:** The area immediately west of the town of Houston in 1837, highlighting homes of various early settlers. The locations of the San Felipe, Brazoria and Fort Bend roads are reconstructed from various documents and should be considered approximate. Bayou locations shown are modified slightly from the U.S. Geological Survey topographic map of 1915, which was made before straightening and channelization of the bayous. Houston town road layout is from a *Plan of the City of Houston*, 1836. **B:** Natural features of the period. Forest outlines are as in Figure 1.2.

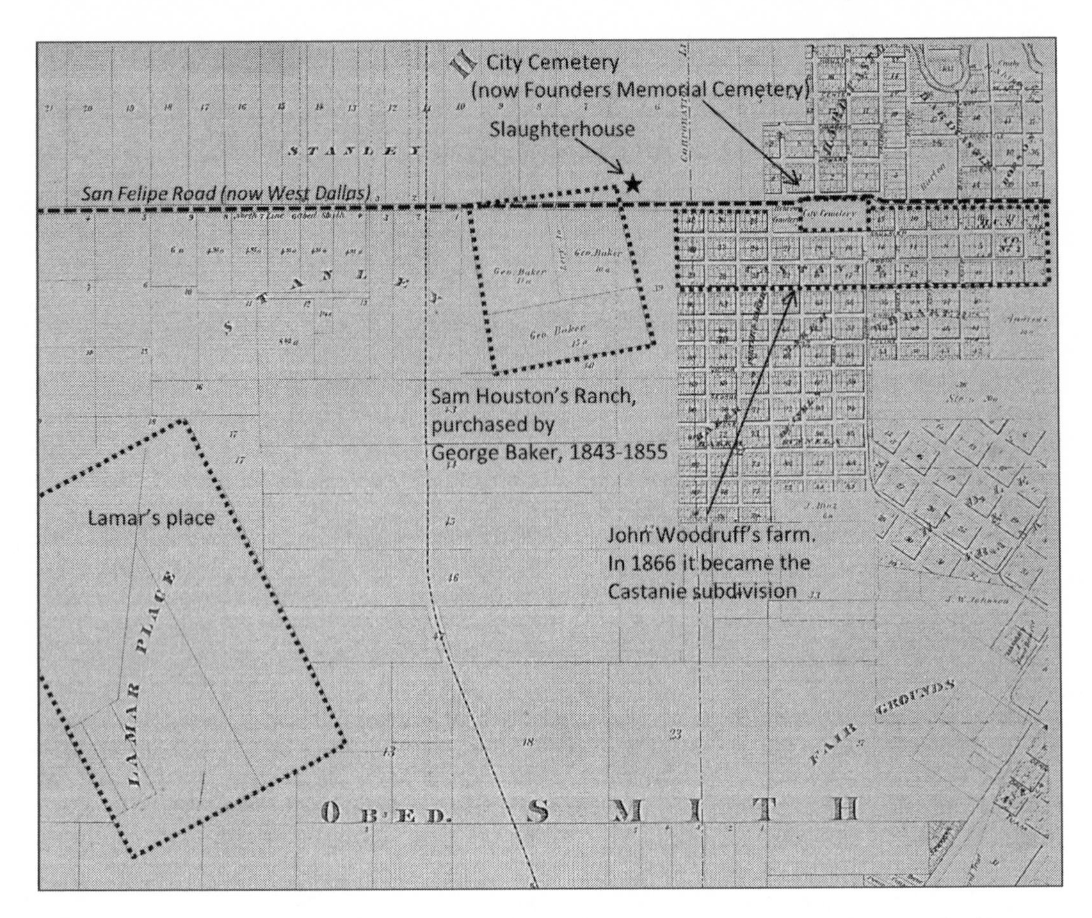

Figure 4.5. A portion of a *Map of the City of Houston, 1890*, by Porter, Pollard and Ruby, courtesy of Harris County Archives. The map focuses on the area around eastern San Felipe Road. The boundaries of the former Sam Houston ranch and Mirabeau B. Lamar's place (highlighted) are oriented differently than those of properties developed later. The railroad located near the center of the map became Montrose Boulevard in the early twentieth century.

the *Houston Chronicle* on July 27, 1930, the vacant plot on San Felipe Road was noted as Houston's farm:

> *Houston had a farm here. . . . it was of good size and it was situated along what is now West Dallas Street, which was then the famous San Felipe Trail or San Felipe Road, as it was variously called, and which led to San Felipe, the capital of Austin's colony. . . . In the course of time, Houston was president for another term [1841–1844]. . . . General Sam Houston then became United States Senator, and later governor. But by then the capital had been moved to Austin and Houston, the political center, was on the road to becoming the great commercial center that it is today. But there is to be recalled one more scene in this drama as it was played. Came the war between the states, and Sam Houston, a Union man, was in the governor's chair in Austin. He would not consent to secession, and so he was deposed. . . . His son, however, grown to manhood, went along with the Confederacy. He enlisted in the 2d Texas regiment, and was sent to Camp Lubbock here at Houston to train. The campsite was right next to his old farm on the San Felipe Road. Later the camp was the site of the old J. W. Baker [home; actually George W. Baker's home].*
>
> *Sam Houston came out of retirement to visit his son at Camp Lubbock. People would not go along with him on his views of secession, but they loved him still, and respected him. He reviewed the troops of the Second Texas, his son among them, although he had sacrificed his political career in his futile attempt to keep them from going to war.*[17]

George W. Baker (1812–1890), a German immigrant, purchased the land in 1843 (Figure 4.5), along with some adjoining pieces His house was across San Felipe Road to the north, where he had purchased 13 acres from Lewis A. Levi in 1846.[18] The property was used for gathering and selling longhorn cattle after the Civil War (see Chapter 10).

The Lamar Place. Mirabeau B. Lamar (1798–1859; Figures 4.4 and 4.5) came to Texas in 1835 and joined Houston's army while it was in training at Groce's Landing. Distinguishing himself at San Jacinto, he briefly became secretary of war and then was elected vice president in 1836. A rival of Sam Houston, he was elected president in 1838 after Houston's term expired. The Lamar place was called "Oak Grove" and had two homes on it, facing the southeastern edge of the property.[19] That southeastern edge was along the Hodges Bend (Fort Bend) Road that led to what is now Richmond. Its siting along that road accounts for the northwestern orientation of the property lines. That odd orientation is preserved to this day in the streets and property boundaries of the Hyde Park subdivision (Figure 4.4 A). The southeastern boundary accounts for the bend in Westheimer Road; that piece seems to be the only locally preserved part of the frontier road to Fort Bend, the rest having been developed in the twentieth century into north-south and east-west home sites. Modern Waugh Drive marks the eastern side of Lamar's place; the 150-acre tract was partly subdivided as the Cherryhurst subdivision in 1908 and then later became known as part of Hyde Park.

As mentioned, Lamar was sold the vacant tract by Moseley Baker in 1836, even though Baker had no title to it. Mrs. Smith confronted Lamar about her ownership of the property, pointing out his lack of title, and he reportedly shrugged his shoulders and walked away.[20] She later sold the place to B. F. Tankersly in January 1846, disregarding any claim Lamar may have had.[21] But by 1839 Lamar moved the capital to Austin, so the issue was moot. While living at his home "Oak Grove" on the "Lamar Place," Lamar forcibly removed all Cherokee Indians from Texas and established a school system funded by public lands.[22]

John Woodruff. Baptist preacher John Woodruff (1790–1847) had a home to the east of Sam Houston's ranch. Born in Kentucky, Woodruff married Mary Anderson (1805–1826) in Ohio in 1823. She died in 1826, and he married Dorothy "Rhoady" Smith (b. 1810), also in Ohio, in 1829. In 1831 they moved to Brazoria County, Texas, where they had a plantation between the Brazos River and Oyster Creek. Dorothy seems to have passed away after the birth of a son, John J. Woodruff (b. 1831). John then married a widow, Sarah "Sallie" Pevehouse Smith (1800–1845), in 1835 in Brazoria. She was a Tennessee native who had earlier been married to John McCutcheon Smith, in 1819 in Arkansas.

John Woodruff was an early ranching partner to Ben Fort Smith. In February 1834 he and Smith were involved in cattle purchases at the Rose plantation at Stafford Point, which was described earlier in an account by Dilue Rose Harris.[23]

John and his family were caught up in the Runaway Scrape with others of their area, like those of the nearby Ben Fort Smith family. They fled to the timbers of Clear Creek, and after the Battle of San Jacinto they returned to a home that had been destroyed by the Mexican army.[24] The family then moved to Houston. The location of their town home, if indeed they ever had one, is not known, but they settled a 50-acre place on the San Felipe Road, east of the Sam Houston ranch and bounded mostly by the San Felipe Trail (now West Dallas) in the north and what is now Andrews Street in the south. That property included what is now Founders Memorial Park cemetery (Figures 4.4, 4.5; already a burial ground when the Woodruffs lived there) and would later include modern day Beth Israel Cemetery. Woodruff was a close associate of Ben Fort Smith, and it may be that Woodruff never owned the land where he resided, but lived there by an agreement with the Smith family. In any event, that land was sold in 1842 by Obedience Smith to Robert C. Campbell (b. 1811),[25] and still later it became the Castanie subdivision of 1866.

One of John and Sarah Woodruff's several children was Mary Smith (1819–1907; Figure 4.3 D), who lived in the Woodruff country home with her mother and stepfather John Woodruff. Mary married Texian soldier Hugh McCrory in 1837, in the city of Houston's first recorded marriage ceremony.[26] He died six weeks later, probably in the yellow fever epidemic of that year. While Mary was living at the Woodruff home on San Felipe she met Anson Jones, who boarded with the Woodruff family. Jones had been President Houston's secretary of state. Mary Smith and Anson Jones were married in Austin in 1840, and Jones became the last president of the Republic of Texas in 1845. In 1891 Mary Smith Jones became the first president of the Daughters of the Republic of Texas.[27]

John W.N.A. Smith. John William Nicholas Arthur Smith (1797–1843) was the second child of Obedience Smith. He served in the Creek Indian Campaign of 1813–1814 alongside his father, David Smith, and brother, Benjamin Fort Smith. He married his maternal first cousin, Mary Fort, in 1817, and lived on his father's mill property in Kentucky. Both John and Mary were born in Tennessee. John and Mary Smith arrived in Texas in February 1836 at more or less the same time as Obedience, and all moved to Benjamin's plantation in Brazoria County. He obtained a headright grant in Harris County in 1838, but for some reason it was never patented.[28]

In 1838, however, he purchased 500 acres of the Allen C. Reynolds tract that lay along the San Felipe Trail and was adjacent to Buffalo Bayou (Figure 4.4). Smith purchased it from James Spillman, who had purchased the entire Reynolds tract from Allen C. Reynolds in 1835 and subsequently split it up for resale.[29] John had lived and worked at the mill owned by his father back in Tennessee, and it is possible that he built a mill on Buffalo Bayou. His brother Ben bought the tract from him in 1840, after which John and Mary left for Brazoria County. John had had money trouble, and when he died in Brazoria County in 1843, his probate listed only a few cows, a yoke of oxen, and a mule.[30] By 1848 Charles Shearn (1794–1877) owned this property, where he operated a grist mill and supplied flour to his partner, early Houston grocer T. W. House (Chapter 7). The property is now the site of the River Oaks Country Club and its golf course.

A visitor ambles through the rural neighborhood. In 1838 a young businessman visited Houston, and his diary gives us an interesting look not only at early Houston but at the aforementioned people with country properties along the San Felipe Trail, just to the west of the new town. John Hunter Herndon (1813–1878) left his home in Kentucky, new law degree in hand, and arrived in Galveston in January 1838. He became a law clerk for the House of Representatives of the Republic of Texas that year, while living in Houston.[31] Herndon kept studying law while in Houston and lived in town. Often restless, he would take long ambles through the areas surrounding Houston in order to observe nature, socialize with prosperous people in the area, and meet their marriageable daughters. Favorite places of his for visiting included the Obedience Smith, John Woodruff, John W.N.A. Smith, and Moseley Baker homes. The following snippets give a glimpse of life in the rural neighborhood at the time:

Sunday, March 18, 1838: Rode out to Mr. Woodruff's and got a drink of his well water.

Monday, March 26: Supped at John Woodruff's where I had Milk, Corn bread and butter.

Tuesday, March 27: Morning cloudy and warm. Went out to Woodruff's for breakfast. Took a wash in well water. Counted nineteen young cows in the pen. Returned by the slaughterhouse where I saw upwards of two hundred beeve's heads, a little further and I saw a pretty girl—how great the contrast? Dined at Woodruff's. Saw Judge Smith [John W.N.A. Smith] who invited me out to see him. Went to the ball at 9 O'clock and returned at 4, forty gentlemen and as many ladies in attendance.

Saturday, March 31: Lovely weather. . . . In the afternoon Dr. Price and self took a ride in the country. Went to Holland's [Andrew G. Holland, d. 1840] where we spent an hour with Misses Holland and Bond. Thence to Judge Smith's where we had the pleasure of seeing Miss Smith, an interesting young lady. Thence over the prairie beautifully clad with the grass and wildflowers by M [Moseley] Baker's to Mrs. [Obedience] Smith's where we had an excellent supper and fine society. Invited to board. Miss Smith [a daughter of Obedience] walked me out into the garden to behold the beautiful results of her industry. Returned to town at 8 O'clock.

Thursday, April 5. Foggy and windy. . . . Rode out to Mrs. Smith's from there to Judge Smith's where I was entertained an hour or two by [daughter] Miss Margaret. Returned by way of Holland's. Got some spring water and saw some ladies. Went to Woodruff's for supper. Had buttermilk and fresh butter. Became acquainted with Dr. [Anson] Jones, a member of Congress. Came by the Capital where there was preaching.[32]

All the places that he visited are within the area of the map shown in Figure 4.4 and were well within a morning's horseback ride. Herndon never mentions visiting either Sam Houston or Mirabeau Lamar; as he was a young law clerk, perhaps they were a bit above his pay grade. Herndon carefully mentions his encounters with fresh well water and spring water on his jaunts. At that time, roughly a year and a half into Houston's existence, many Houstonians were bathing in and drinking from Buffalo Bayou, which initially had run clear. Cholera and dysentery were inevitable results at a time when no one yet understood how these deadly diseases were spread. Finally, Herndon lovingly mentions having milk, buttermilk and butter on his country visits. Most landholding townspeople in Houston typically still lived on country lots, and many kept milk cows, but he was a bachelor boarding at Floyd's Hotel, and no doubt his diet was suffering for lack of fresh dairy products.

Herndon moved in 1839 to Richmond, Texas, became involved in a sugar plantation, and by the start of the Civil War was reportedly the richest man in the state. A Confederate patriot, he was financially ruined by the war and eventually moved to Hempstead.[33]

City Cemetery (now Founders Memorial Park). There was a graveyard in the tract where John Woodruff had his farm (Figure 4.4). Known burials date from at least 1837, and some 850 burials are estimated to exist at the site.[34] The cemetery is located at 1217 West Dallas at Valentine Street.

Of note to this narrative, John Woodruff and his wife Sarah Pevehouse Smith Woodruff are buried there, as are Sarah's son William Smith (d. 1837) and daughters Sarah Ann Smith (d. 1845), Rachel Francis Smith Bollinger (1827–1856), and Mary Smith Jones McCrory. Mary is buried next to her husband Hugh McCrory (d. 1837). All are listed on a memorial stone in the cemetery. Other burials include Robert C. Campbell, who bought the Woodruff place. Mirabeau B. Lamar's mother Rebecca Lamar Lamar is also buried there (she and her husband were first cousins); she died in July 1839 while they were still living at Oak Grove. John N.O. Smith is buried there; he died in 1851. There are many other notables, not least of whom are John Kirby Allen (1810–1838), co-founder of the city of Houston, and Andrew Clopper.[35]

The San Felipe Trail after independence

One might have expected that the important town of Harrisburg, port to the burgeoning trade from the Brazos River via the road, would soon have been rebuilt. But by founding the city of Houston upstream of Harrisburg, and shrewdly arranging for it to become the capital of the new republic, the Allen brothers stole a march on the destroyed town of Harrisburg, which could never recover. They and others could see that Houston lay essentially on the already existing San Felipe wagon road, and thus cut a day's ox cart ride off the freight journey from the Brazos to a port. The effect was almost immediate. As Andrew Muir pointed out in his 1943 treatise on Buffalo Bayou,

Houston quickly and deftly undermined the position of importance on Buffalo Bayou that Harrisburg had maintained. More significantly, it immediately began to drain the business of the Brazos valley; this, above all else, was the motive of the Allens in

Figure 4.6. An ox wagon laden with cotton bales being driven to market by an African American teamster, while other slaves pick cotton. From W. O. Blake, *The History of Slavery and the Slave Trade, Ancient and Modern* (Columbus, Ohio: J and H. Miller, 1857).

locating on Buffalo Bayou. The two steamers, Laura and Yellowstone, deserted the Brazos and began plying the Bayou. Despite the wet prairies extending between the Brazos and Houston [along the San Felipe Trail], a large traffic moved between the two places. In April, 1840, twenty-three freight wagons from the upper Brazos arrived in Houston in one day. . . . In March, 1838, four steamships made weekly runs on the Bayou, and others ran occasionally.

Long wagon trains loaded with cotton and sugar wended their way across the prairies to Houston, and steamboats churned up and down the Bayou carrying staples to Galveston or New Orleans for reshipment to the North and to England, and returning with processed goods to be loaded into wagons and distributed along the Brazos River. In 1856, Houston handled over its wharves 45,557 bales of cotton.[36]

Once Houston was founded, the San Felipe Trail was extended into Houston; this was not much of a stretch, because the new town lay only slightly north of the old road. A map of Texas published by Jacob de Cordova in 1849 shows how the war and resulting independence was to affect both Houston and the region (Figure 4.7). A wealth of early wagon roads that once radiated outward from San Felipe (Figure 3.3) now radiated outward from Houston, which captured the trade of Brazos cotton in all western and southern directions. Harrisburg appears on that map as if it were an afterthought, with no new roads heading toward it. The San Felipe wagon road was still the main western artery, but by 1837 shared the trade with roads to Washington, Richmond, and Brazoria (Figure 4.2). The coming of the railroads in the next decade further accentuated this radial dominance of Houston town.

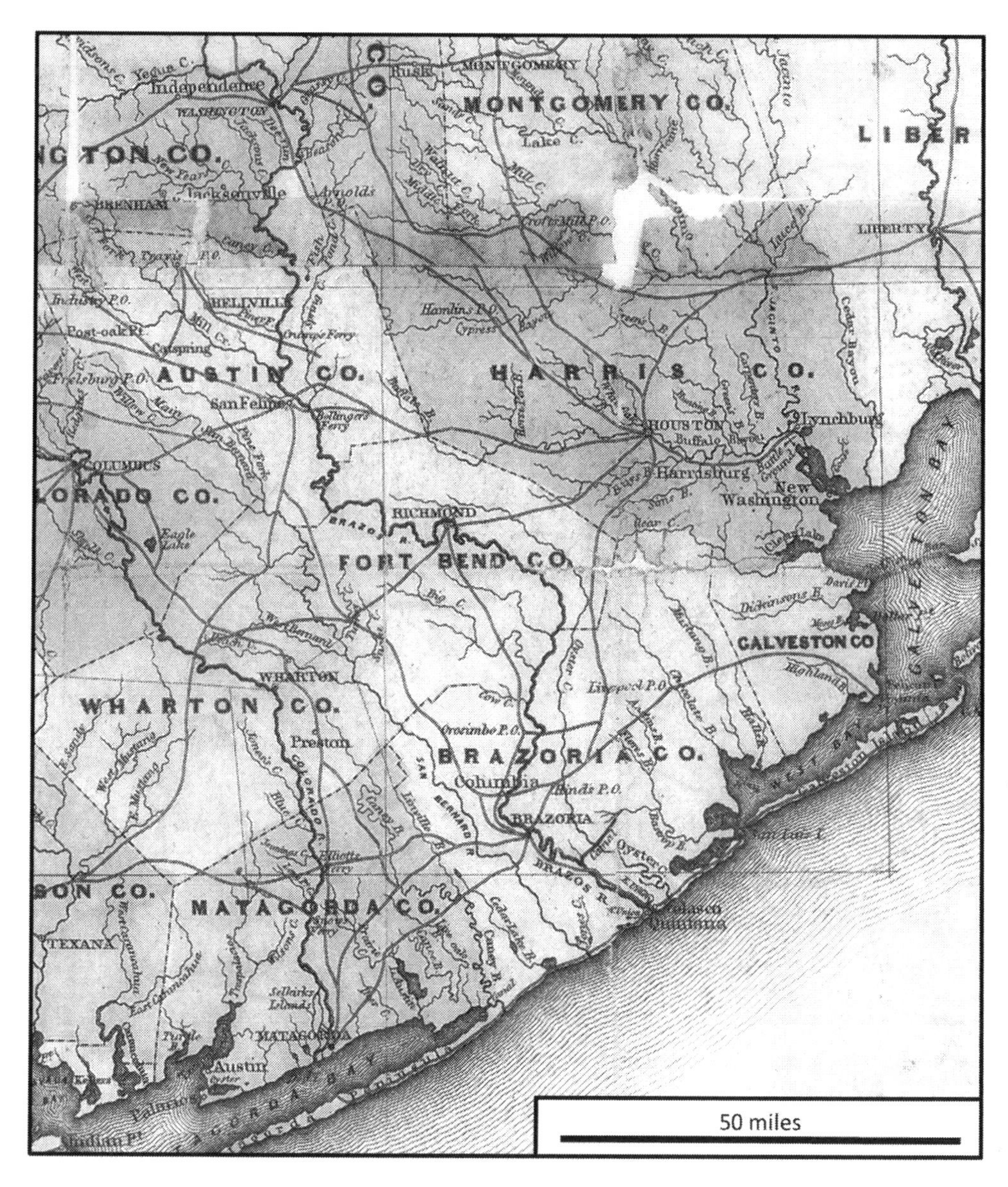

Figure 4.7. A portion of a map of Texas by Jacob de Cordova, 1849. The area and scale are the same as for Figures 2.2 and 3.3. Note the growth in wagon roads radiating outward from Houston, which by the 1840s had captured the trade of Brazos cotton in all western and southern directions.
Map courtesy of the General Land Office, Austin.

Early travelers on the San Felipe Trail

A number of early travelers to Texas have left fascinating accounts of their journeys into the interior of Texas along this frontier wagon road. Except for J. C. Clopper's account of 1828 (which predated the formal construction of the road), all these postdate independence and the foundation of the town of Houston. Friedrich Wilhelm von Wrede traveled from San Felipe to Houston in October 1836 and noted that in "the forty-six miles to that place [the new Houston town site], I had to go over a twenty-two mile-long, practically waterless prairie before and after which there were only a few farms."[37] In the summer the San Felipe road lacked water west of Houston, except at Wheaton's Ford, Pine Point (now called Piney Point)—where the trail came close to the Bayou—and at a spring two or three miles east of Pine Point.

In 1839 Tennessean Clinton Harrison Moore

traveled through much of Austin's colony, with a brother, sister, brother-in-law and uncle, and left an evocative portrait of the wilderness surrounding the early settlements, including a visit to that spring (Figure 4.2). Here is an excerpt, picking up his travelogue at Washington on the Brazos, as he headed to San Felipe, then Houston and Galveston:

> *On the 30th we made an early start and in a short time we struck those beautiful prairies that lie between the Brazos and the Colorado. Here is doubtless the most beautiful country in the world. Here all animated nature seems to flourish in perpetual youth. The wild horse rest in luxury uncontrolled. Here you see thousands of [wild] cattle feeding at large where the green prairies are snugly bound by the blue vault of Heaven. . . .*
>
> *May 1st 1839 I awoke early in the morning and heard rain falling heavily upon our tent, but it soon stopped. We drove on till 12:00 and stopped in the edge of a prairie to let our horses graze. While we were here the lightning began to play in the north and all at once the clouds shifted from the north to the south and the wind blew with great violence. The tall grass of the prairie waved like a wheat field in June. My horse became frightened, threw his head, struck back his ears and ceased to graze. At length the rain stopped and the balance of the evening was fine. We traveled 18 miles this day and encamped on a large creek that runs into the Colorado.*

Moore spent a few weeks in Bastrop and in Austin before eventually coming to San Felipe:

> *Next morning we . . . came to San Phillipe De Austin, situated on the west side of the Brazos River. This place was settled by Austin and his company of 90 men. . . . In this Colony the first settlement was made by Anglo-Saxon race and formed a nucleus for other settlements which finally led to the Independence of Texas. . . . We crossed the river at St. Phillipe [San Felipe, Texas, which by the time of Moore's visit had been burned to the ground]. Here we saw signs of the Revolution, an engagement took place here between the Texans and Mexicans. The former being on the east and the latter being on the west side of the river. The tops of the cottonwood trees that skirted the banks had been shot off by cannon balls.*
>
> *The Brazos bottom here is very fertile. The land is of a dark red color. The principal timber is ash, elm, some black walnut, some red oak, wild cherry, with scattering cane. In this bottom we crossed a small creek. The water looked so clear and beautiful that I concluded that I would have a good drink, but found that it was so full of copper as that I only took one swallow and it operated on me like salt.*
>
> *We soon found ourselves in an open prairie about 25 miles wide. We had become very thirsty. About a quarter of a mile to the right a small grove pointed us to a puddle of water. By knocking off a thick green skum we got enough to quench our thirst, but none for our team, we again set out and a little while after night reached a skirt of timber on the head of Buffalo Bayou. Here we found a small seeping spring where we got water. This day's travel was through a low white prairie.*
>
> *Next morning we made an early start and traveled about 25 miles. The country was the same as the day before excepting we were generally in sight of timber and the country was lower. In the evening we came in sight of pine timber. The tops of evergreen as they stood elevated above the other timbers presents a sight of admiration and wonder to an individual who had resided in the western part of Texas.*

Moore is referring to Pine Point, the southernmost part of the riparian forest and its local pine fringe; that point was near the modern intersection of Westheimer Road and Fondren Road (Figure 4.2 C). Modern day Piney Point Village is named after this point, but this actual "Pine Point" of frontier days is some distance south of the modern village.

> *At night we struck camp about 3 miles from Houston. . . . We found a spring near our encampment of the best water I had found in western Texas. We*

stayed at this camp 2 or 3 days and then moved into the edge of the city.

This was almost certainly the former spring on a short tributary of Buffalo Bayou, which was located near San Felipe Street a block west of that street's intersection with North Post Oak Road (Figure 4.2 C). That creek and its spring have been buried and covered by tall buildings in modern Houston. Moore continues:

> *[Houston] has been settled for about 4 years and was the seat of the government for the Republic. It was the most flourishing place in Texas. . . . Houston is situated on the head of Buffalo Bayou, about 60 miles from Galveston. At this time there was one boat that ran from Houston to Galveston.*
>
> *After staying at Houston about a week we got ready, got on the boat and started for Galveston. We left about dusk, the Bayou at Houston has a very narrow channel. The boat was obliged to run slowly for many miles. The boatman frequently stood in the fore end of the boat and with long poles kept it from running against the bluff. Night with its dark curtains soon closed around us and hid the landscape from view. But by day break we got to the mouth of the Bayou. Here it was more than a mile wide and toward the south the gulf spread out into the sea. The adjoining country was not much higher than the sea. Some scattering trees were to be seen.*[38]

Dr. Ferdinand Roemer, a geologist sent in 1845 by Prince Carl of Soms-Braunfels to scope out Texas as a home for German immigrants, provides another early travelogue of travel along this road, from a German perspective. Roemer traveled by boat up Buffalo Bayou to the small town of Houston and set off on the San Felipe Trail west to San Felipe town. In wet mid-January the wagon road was a sea of mud that did not escape his ascerbic attention. His first day's segment began from Houston's early town center south of Allen's Landing and ran to the modern southern tip of Piney Point, in the trees near Buffalo Bayou:

> *We started our journey in the afternoon of January 15. The train consisted of two loaded wagons, one drawn by four, the other by two, horses. . . . We had advance notice that the road to the Brazos was bad, owing to continuous rains. This information was correct. Hardly had we left the city when the flat Houston prairie loomed up as an endless swamp. Large puddles of water followed one another and at several places a large section of land was under water. The long, yellow dry grass and barren trees added to the drab appearance of the landscape. All of the low coastal region presents a similar picture during this time of the yea. . . .*
>
> *The wagons sank deeply into the mud, compelling the horses to pull them slowly, step by step. Often the wagons became so mired that it required the help of members of our company to push them out of a bog. We moved forward in this manner. Darkness fell and still we had not reached the end of the prairie, nor did we find a dry place to lie down. Impatient over the delay, I rode ahead for about an hour on the dim trail now barely discernible due to the darkness. Just as I was about to give up hope of finding a better camping place, I saw a fire in the distance and this revived my hopes of finding a camp, and also human beings. Soon I heard the tinkling bells of grazing oxen and upon riding up a small incline, I found a group of men camping under the trees near a big fire. Several prairie schooners, shaped like boats, were nearby. The men were American farmers from the Colorado [River], who were bringing corn to Houston. . . . They informed me that this was Piney Point, only nine miles distant from Houston, which was often used as the first stopping place by wagons travelling between Houston and San Felipe on the Brazos.*
>
> *On the following morning . . . [their] oxen were hitched—and urged on by encouraging shouts, the horned beasts of burden were on their way. All commerce is carried on this way in Texas. . . . Usually oxen are used, but horses and mules are also employed.*[39]

After their night at Piney Point, Roemer and his party continued west, coming to the ford across the bayou at Wheaton's farm, as described previously.

A trip to Katy and back, in 1846

An extensive travel guide for German immigrants in Texas was prepared by Karl von Sommer in 1846 and published in Bremen, Germany, under the title Bericht über meine Reise nach Texas im Jahre 1846 (The story of my trip to Texas in 1846). He published a table of distances for German immigrants traveling between Houston and the German colony at New Braunfels (Figure 4.8) that includes Pine Point, "Mrs. Weathen am Buffalo" (Elizabeth Wheaton's farm at the ford across Buffalo Bayou), and "Caney Island" (modern Katy). In one segment of his travelogue, von Sommer and his son described a trip along the San Felipe road from Houston to Cane Island, where they were stopped by a swollen Cane River—a tributary of Buffalo Bayou—and were forced to return. Their writing constitutes the most complete and detailed account of travel on the old wagon road that now exists.

Die directe Reiseroute von Houston nach Neu-Braunfels ist folgende:

Von Houston	
nach Pine-Point	9 engl. M.
" Mr. Hoffmanns Farm	6 "
" Mrs. Weathen am Buffalo	3 "
" Caney-Island	12 "
" Pine-Island	10 "
" Judge-Wahr	3 "
" San Felipe de Austin am Brazos	7 "
" Mr. Amsler am Wild-oat-Spring	15 "
" Industry (Mr. Ernst) am Mill-Creek	16 "
" Mr. Stevens Farm	15 "
" Ruthelrsville	4 "
" Lagrange	6 "
" Black-jack-Spring	12 "
" Mr. Brockhaus am Peach-Creek	28 "
" Gonzales	10 "
" Kiny	9 "
" Seguin	26 "
" Neu-Braunfels	14 "

Figure 4.8. "The direct trip-route from Houston to New Braunfels," a table from Karl von Sommer, *Bericht über meine Reise nach Texas im Jahre 1846* (Bremen, Germany: Johann Georg Hesse, 1847). Distances from Houston to various places are given in miles. The first part of the route, from Houston to San Felipe, occurred on the San Felipe Trail. "Mrs. Weathen am Buffalo" is a misspelling of Mrs. Wheaton on Buffalo Bayou (at Wheaton's Ford). Caney Island refers to Cane Island, now Katy, Texas.

A modern round trip from downtown Houston to Katy and back again, along Interstate Highway 10, takes a little over thirty to forty minutes each way if traffic is light, with a round trip distance of 58 miles. In 1846 the San Felipe wagon road was the interstate highway of its day, and the round trip took six toilsome and dangerous days by ox wagon and horse. Although the von Sommers were traveling in the dry season of July, they were beset by a tropical storm, and the ensuing flooding was similar to that earlier experienced by Roemer and by Bennet:

On 14 July, a preacher of the Methodists sect was travelling together with his wife and two children to his new station at Santer Hill, in the country beyond the Brazos River; he came from St. Louis, Missouri. Getting acquainted with this learned and helpful man prompted me to plan to visit the western area with him; I took my son with me. Not until noon were the ox-cart and the family ready to go. The preacher, like me, was on horseback. After heading two to three English miles in a westerly direction, we had passed through the small prairies and woodlands with which Houston is surrounded, and we now entered the great prairie.

In the distance to the right was the wooded horizon of Buffalo [Bayou], and on the left the unlimited horizon; ahead were some groves of trees ("islands"). There were many visible pathways from which one had to choose the main path. It is easy to lose the main path picking shortcuts, and then there is a danger of getting lost. Only after a long, dry spell is defining the path somewhat easier.

So it was with me. I was alone riding ahead of the group, because the ox-wagon could only move very slowly, and after a few miles I came into very marshy terrain. Wagon tracks were only visible now and then, and people were riding back and forth to find them; it was difficult to follow them with the eyes through the hardy prairie grasses because the prairie was half submerged under water.[40]

Von Sommer's experience with the difficulty of following the trail was similar to that of other travelers of his day. On the open prairie there were many boggy patches, and the wagon road had to move around those impediments in wet weather, which led to many competing tracks at a time when there were no real trail markers. The sharply defined trace of the road on the map of Figure 4.2 was clearly not nearly that sharp and straight on the ground, where it was perhaps more like the trace of a meandering river.

I rode on keeping well to the west, and I could not see the way back because the objects located behind me were no longer clearly visible, because of their great distance. The clouds drew together and a very violent storm broke almost on top of me. I held my umbrella all the way to southwest and turned as much as possible in the saddle, but I was soaked and the whirlwind threatened to knock me off my horse. Then the darkness broke and I considered that I might have to descend and spend the night standing in the water, but I rode further through the over-flowing Prairie, step by step, and luckily discovered to my right an intersection of enclosure fences, built for buffalo exclusion.

I searched for a path and was soon at the Pine Point Farm of a farmer named Mr. George, where we were given lodging. The farm house contains two rooms in which beds are available, and a kitchen, and also has, like almost all farm houses, a porch. I immediately set out a light, so that the wagon would have a sign in the gloomy night, which was very useful. Two hours later, I arrived at the wagon, where my son was. We had both been very worried about the separation that had taken place. Also, the wagon had to overcome very huge trouble.

The night and the following day it rained almost incessantly, the bayous overflowed and the prairie was more than partly under water; we could therefore not leave. On the second day, even though it was not raining, it was not possible to get through the mud with the wagon. My son obtained a horse, and after I had put on my pistols, he and I rode on together [without the others in the wagon]. I had paid Mr. George two and one half dollars for the lodging.

The woman of the house had married her second husband. The first husband was shot to death by his own Negro [slave] while they were fishing. After they found out that the Negro had shot and robbed the man, they hanged him. In accordance with local customary legal practice, twelve resident farmers got together and delivered the sentence. The execution was carried out when the lawbreaker was placed on a cart under a tree, tied to an overhanging tree branch, and the cart was removed.

The farmer whom von Sommer met at Pine Point was Benjamin George, who had married his wife Harriet Putnam only the preceding April. Harriet's previous husband, the man who had been murdered, was Buckman Canfield, who had purchased part of John Taylor's League at Piney Point in 1838. The Canfields form the main subject of the following chapter.

After we travelled six English miles we came to the farm of a German (Hoffman), which lay in the wet prairie. Three English miles farther, we came to the farm of the widow Weathon [Wheaton] on Buffalo [Bayou]. The river was transformed by the rain fallen in a raging current, so we could not swim the horses while riding them; they were therefore driven unloaded across the water. A kind of bridge was made across the river, in which two large trees on opposing banks were toppled together. Clambering over this, we brought our things over piecemeal.

By the time of von Sommer's trip Joel Wheaton had died, and Elizabeth Wheaton ran the inn at what became known as Wheaton's Ford, located where modern Highway 6 crosses the bayou. Helping travelers in distress at that crossing earned the daily bread for her and her sons.

> *Then we rode twelve English miles further, all alone in the great prairie, the horses sometimes in water partly above the knees, and at other times the water reached their bellies. We arrived at the farm of Mr. Scott, Cane Island.*

Here von Sommer describes the beginnings of a settlement at Cane Island (modern Katy) in 1846. Like Elizabeth Wheaton, Scott was running an inn at a troublesome ford on the wagon road.

Before the farm, two Bavarian emigrant families were camped on the Prairie who had intended to settle beyond the Brazos to the little fertile area of Santer Hill; they had come on the same ships with us from Europe and had been left at this spot by a corrupt Negro. They understood not a word of English, therefore could not inquire their location, and then beheld their fraud. They now believed their destiny was not in Texas and were on their way back to Houston, thence to travel to the northern United States.

> *Their wagon was not far from here, beyond the Caney river, and the wagon could not be brought across the river because the current was so high and rising. A few days ago, they said, they could still swim across, but now this would not be possible, and the horses would be swept away by the current. Mr. Scott said that because of all the rain it could take eight days before the river would lower again, so I decided that my son and I would return the following day back to Houston. We paid him $3 [for lodging].*
>
> *The return trip was even worse than the way had been previously. More rain had fallen during the night which raised the water everywhere, and the sun's heat was very oppressive. The horses were covered with horse flies and were bleeding everywhere from the bites of these insects. We tried to give them some rest, but the horses were very restless and we were glad to be back out again and in motion. . . .*
>
> *Apart from a few flocks of pelicans, prairie chickens, prairie turtles and crabs, we saw swimming tarantulas and a few tracks of prairie wolves, but not a single person. When we returned to Buffalo [Bayou], the river was flooded a half a mile wide, and only the tops of the bushes were out of the water. We approached the shore sensing danger, because the horses were too tired from the arduous journey to Caney Island. Finally we got to the farm belonging to the widow Wheaton, and we made ourselves known by waving and calling.*
>
> *We had to drive the horses through the river. We then dismounted, where we got into the water up to our waists, took down the luggage and carried it up to the place where the tree bridge was. The two downed trees where we had previously crossed were now partly under water. Mrs. Wheaton's son came over and helped us bring across the luggage; then we crossed ourselves. We still knew the location of the submerged, back and forth-swaying tree trunks from the previous day.*
>
> *We had had a sample of the danger of traveling into the interior, and it has happened more than once, that travelers—even apart from attacks by the Indians—disappear without a trace by becoming lost or by drowning. In the storerooms of Mr. Grübler in Houston there are trunks and boxes that were deposited a prior year and a day there, and up to now are still not claimed by their owners. The luggage spoils in the humid locale, but Mr. Grübler chooses not to open the trunks.*
>
> *We used the afternoon to dry our stuff on tree branches. The river [Bayou] is rich with alligators and water snakes. The latter, especially the kind that is called the Chicken Snake, comes at night into chicken coops—and also probably into the rooms of houses when they are not driven out by the farm dogs. They don't bother people, and we were therefore able to safely bathe and swim in Buffalo [Bayou]. We stayed the night at the farm of those worthy people [the Wheatons] and rode back the next day, July 18 to the farm of Mr. George, near Houston.*

Here von Sommer's travelogue ends; he probably returned to Houston the following day, for a total round trip of sixty miles traveled in six days.

The Mr. Scott who ran the inn at the Cane Island crossing was succeeded by 1864 by a John White, who ran a two-story stagecoach inn at that location. Early Katy residents recalled that White and his wife were robbing some of the wayfarers who stayed at the inn and even killed one. As the story goes, the early residents rose up and lynched White and his wife, and then burned all of the buildings. Early Katy resident Water Rosenbush found the charred remains of the inn and its cistern in 1888, when he was a boy, "along Cane Island Creek just back of the present residence of Charlie Peck."[41]

Peak use of the San Felipe Trail and its ultimate replacement by railroads

The San Felipe wagon road was a frontier solution to transportation and was responsible in a significant way—along with Buffalo Bayou—for the success of modern Houston and Harris County. Capturing the all-important Brazos freight trade for the port of Harrisburg, and later Houston, ensured the latter town's early commercial success. By the late 1830s, wagon traffic to the town of Houston was already heavy. The Telegraph and Texas Register of May 5, 1838, reported: "Hundreds of baggage wagons have been constantly arriving from the upper country, and return loaded with merchandise." Houston quickly became the trading center for an inland area that reached as far as Navasota to the northwest and Bastrop to the west.

In the early years the San Felipe Trail was little more than a widened pioneer path through the prairie, and with heavy use in wet weather, it became impassable. The inevitable shortcuts taken by travelers in the open prairie around mud wallows and swampy places made the trail ever wider, to the point that—as we have seen—it was difficult to follow. Because of this road's importance, as well as that of other such early wagon roads, to Houston's commercial health, it is no surprise that Harris County formed a Board of Roads and Revenue early on to deal with issues of transportation. They met in January 1844, with the following proclamation:

> *Whereas, the bad state of roads through this country tend greatly to . . . prevent commercial transactions and render [it] almost impossible for the inhabitants . . . to procure the supplies necessary to the comfort of a civilized life; and whereas the City of Houston is particularly interested in the good state of the roads leading to the city, without which there is a danger of said City losing its trade altogether by obliging the inhabitants of the Brazos and other points of the county to look for other channels of exportation and other markets, all of which is greatly detrimental . . . to the City and county.*[42]

The proclamation went on to form a committee for road improvements, approve a road tax, and plan some new roads to the Brazos to replace the old wagon roads. At that time there were four or five main roads plus the Lynchburg ferry to be tended, and three of them involved transportation to the all-important Brazos River. These three were the San Felipe road, the Washington road—which started on modern day Washington Avenue and headed northwest across Cypress Creek, ultimately ending at Washington-on-the-Brazos in Washington County—and the Richmond road, which headed from Houston more or less directly to that town. In later decades, each of these three wagon roads was to be replaced by a railroad, but until that time they were vital commercial highways.

The county officials divided the main roads of the county into precincts and recommended persons to be appointed overseers of each road. There were two overseers chosen for the San Felipe road in that session. Buckman Canfield lived at Pine Point and was chosen to oversee the segment from Houston to Piney Point. Stephen Habermacher, son of early settler Thomas Habermacher, who lived along the western segment of the road (Figure 4.2), was chosen to oversee the portion from Pine Point to the county line (west of Wheaton's Ford). Presumably "overseeing" meant keeping the road passable and limiting the numbers of shortcuts around wet spots in the now surveyed road. It may have included oversight of the aforementioned bridge that was under construction at Wheaton's Ford in 1855, when Mary Silliman bought the inn.

Beyond the important issue of road maintenance, the transportation of heavy goods by ox wagon was labor intensive, slow, unpredictable, and expensive—and the amount of trade carried by ox wagons was exploding. The amount of cotton coming into Houston along the three main western roads grew to 47,008 bales in 1856, and the ox traffic was crowding the streets, as noted in this 1866 history of the city:

> *From 1854 to 1855, ox wagons were used exclusively. Imagine if you can the number of horned animals required to transport to the city in one year 47,008 bales of cotton, and an idea may be formed of the immense crowds of wagons and teams which blocked up the business thoroughfares of the city. In 1857 and 1858 a great deal of produce was yet conveyed by this means although railroads began to exhibit their utility.*[43]

Jesse Ziegler, a Galvestonian who first visited Houston in 1872, described this period in Houston's history, including the campgrounds for wagon drivers and warehouses for the materials shipped to Houston:

> *Houston derived her first impetus and growth toward her present metropolitan status from the patronage of immense wagon-trains from outlying counties and the interior of the state. The motive power employed was either long yokes of oxen or four- to eight-mule teams. The wagons were loaded top-high with baled cotton, hides and wool, bacon, lard, hogsheads of molasses, barrels of sugar, grain, butter, cheese and eggs.*
>
> *The merchants and brokers of early Houston had to provide suitable facilities for sheltering these incoming wagon-trains and storage for their cargoes. Hence originated the old camping grounds and warehouses of pioneer Houston. The first cotton warehouse and camping-ground of which we appear to have record was the large two-story warehouse of Tom Whitmarsh, erected about 1850. . . . It was so erected that long wooden chutes were used to slide the cotton and the other baled and bagged commodities from the great sliding doors of the first stories down to the waiting steamboats and barges on the bayou. From there, the cargo was freighted to Galveston and other nearby ports for either consumption or transshipment. . . . Later came the renowned Macatee warehouse, built in 1858 . . . it received the greatest portion of trade coming in from the Brazos and Colorado section on Washington and San Felipe roads, and being just across from [the old camping ground at] "Vinegar Hill," where the Southern Pacific depot now stands, was one of the most popular stopping points in the county. . . .*
>
> *I have seen as many as two hundred wagons unload at the Macatee place in a single day. The charge for storage, sampling, and weighing cotton was fifty cents per bale—in addition the farmers had the privilege of camping for the remainder of their stay. . . . Their stay usually depended upon the weather and conditions of the roads. . . . Somewhat later, Henke and Pillot erected a warehouse and free camping ground . . . taking in nearly two blocks. Where the Martha Hermann Square now lies was an entire block fenced in for a wagon yard to take care of a portion of the business coming in from the Brazos on the San Felipe Road.*
>
> *These wagon trips usually required about three weeks to come and go and complete their transactions. . . . I have seen as many as three hundred wagons arrive in the course of a morning. As late as 1877–78, one could see ox-wagons lying all day in front of the Barnes House (where the Rice Hotel now stands) waiting for orders from their owners, who had stopped at the Barnes House. A similar scene was at the corner of Main and Franklin, where the First National Bank now stands. Closely adjacent was the T. W. House plantation commissary and wholesale grocery; and here the ox-wagons remained half a day waiting on a load of bacon, flour, beans, bagging, ties, and other staple commodities for the interior farms.*[44]

Figure 4.9. Transporting cotton by ox wagon. A postcard from the author's collection.

The city of Houston's wide streets of today were not planned with automobiles, buses and trains in mind but for the needs of these hordes of ox wagons bearing bales of cotton. Streets needed to be wide to accommodate this traffic as well as to give the teams room to turn, as Ziegler pointed out: "Oxen, once they started the turn, held an utter disregard for anything in their way. Many times the light posts or carts were caught in the turn and demolished."[45]

The Houston newspapers of the ox wagon days kept a careful eye on this traffic, as it portended the health of the town's all-important trading. That traffic was heavily dependent upon weather, as muddy roads could all but shut down business in the town:

> *Owing to the heavy rains that have fallen recently, the small streams in the interior have swollen to an unusual height, and a cessation, to a limited degree, in wagon arrivals and in business generally has been the result. The roads are now in a very bad condition.*
>
> —Weekly Telegraph, *February 6, 1856*

> *There has been little or no animation in any department of trade during the past week. Owing to the heavy rains and bad roads, we have to note a considerable falling off in the wagon arrivals and receipts of cotton at this point. The weather has materially moderated, however, and we have no doubt that Spring has already set in. Our merchants are receiving heavy supplies of Spring Goods, counting upon a brisk trade the coming season.*
>
> —Weekly Telegraph, *March 26, 1856*

> *Since our last report, business has assumed a decided and permanent activity in every department. Wagon arrivals are becoming very numerous, and our streets are crowded with merchants, and planters from the country, who seem to be taking advantage of the fine condition of the roads to secure their supplies.*
>
> —Weekly Telegraph, *April 9, 1856*

> *For the last three or four weeks all our streets in the business part of the city have been so blocked up with wagons and teams that it is almost impos-*

sible to pass between them, even on foot, in any direction.

—Weekly Telegraph, *May 7, 1856*

Again we have to congratulate our friends upon the increased and daily increasing business. Some days, as many as eight hundred bales of cotton have been brought into town upon waggons, for sale and shipment. Our merchants are "up and at it," early and late; everyone appears busy, hopeful, happy. . . . Boats are constantly arriving and departing, travellers coming and going, steam engines snorting, everybody working, politicians scheming, the Germans smoking, and the Irish joking, the ox-drivers cursing, the churches praying, debtors paying, and finally the clouds are raining, while some sidewalks and most of the street crossings are perfectly too bad. By the way, these crossings should be mended; somebody ought "to take heed to their ways."

—Weekly Telegraph, *May 14, 1856*

With the condition of the roads always at risk due to inclement weather, and with the city's business so dependent upon them, it is not surprising that Houstonians and residents of Harris County turned their attention to railroads. The first three railroads constructed in the state were aimed squarely at providing an alternative way to market for Brazos Valley freight. Construction was begun on the Buffalo Bayou, Brazos and Colorado Railroad in 1850, and it reached from Harrisburg to the lower Brazos River in 1856. Threatened by the potential reemergence of the old competitor Harrisburg, City of Houston backers constructed a "Tap Road" to connect Houston with the BBB&C railroad in 1856, thereby protecting city interests as an international shipping port. A second line, the Houston and Texas Central, headed northwest, reaching Hempstead in 1856, and within four years it had reached the upper Brazos.[46] By 1857 these railroads began to take commerce away from the San Felipe, Washington, and Richmond wagon roads, because railroad freight rates were approximately half of those charged by teamsters.[47]

Soldiers and land speculators along upper Buffalo Bayou in the Republic period

Beginning in Republic of Texas days, increasingly numbers of Texans settled along the San Felipe Trail and along adjacent Buffalo Bayou. Some of them were soldiers who claimed land bounties along the bayou for their service. Legislation granting those bounties had been passed during the revolution, when the need for soldiers was intense:

Ordinance Granting Bounties of Land to Volunteers

Whereas many individuals, from the United States and elsewhere, have left their homes of peace and comfort, to volunteer to the service of this country, and endured the hardships and peril of war in its struggle against Mexican tyranny; and thereby their generous patriotism and gallant conduct in the field earned our warmest gratitude:

Therefore resolved, That bounties of land be granted and are hereby granted to said volunteers, as follows, viz:

To all who are now in service, and shall continue in service faithfully during the war, twelve hundred and eighty acres.

To all who have served faithfully, or who shall have served faithfully, for a period not less than six months, six hundred and forty acres.

To all who have served faithfully for a period not less than three months, three hundred and twenty acres.

To all who shall enter the service previous to the first day of next July, and shall continue in service faithfully during the war, provided the war shall continue for a period of six months, nine hundred and sixty acres. . . .

Passed in Convention, March 16, 1836
Richard Ellis, President of the Convention[48]

From 1825, when frontiersmen John Taylor and John Austin had abandoned the Buffalo Bayou area and left, until 1829–1830, when the San Felipe wagon road was cleared to Harrisburg, western Harris County south of Buffalo Bayou had not seen much settlement, and the area was still essentially a wilderness. The new wagon road, however, provided east-west access to both Harrisburg and San Felipe, and as we have seen, Joel Wheaton and Allen Reynolds had both taken advantage of the new road by 1831 and had settled. They were apparently the only settlers in the area before the end of the War of Independence.

After San Jacinto, there was renewed interest in Texas lands along Buffalo Bayou, if not settlement. Soldiers traveled to Houston, the new capital of Texas, to collect upon their government's promises, as did new immigrants, attracted by the government's promises of free land. The scene was ripe for speculators, who preyed upon the indigent soldiers. The next tier of lands to be sold along upper Buffalo Bayou fell to this process. An anonymous observer from Ohio paints a vivid picture of the shenanigans going on in frontier Houston town in 1837:

> *While speaking of the different ways in which the people of Houston were employed, I ought not to omit to mention the modus operandi of the speculator, who finds a fine field here for the exercise of his shrewdness and energies. Some were engaged in purchasing the discharges of the soldiers, each of whom is entitled, beyond his pay of eight dollars a month in government paper, to six hundred and fifty acres of land for each six months service, and in proportion for a less period. For this he gets a certificate from the government.*
>
> *The discharged soldier comes to Houston, hungry, and next to naked, with nothing but his claims upon the government; which his situation compels him to sell. If he gets ten per cent for his money scrip, and fifty dollars for a six month's discharge, he receives quite as much as these claims were selling for during the summer.*
>
> *When the storm-beaten soldier thus sees the reward of all his sufferings reduced to a few dollars, he has too much reason to lament over the time which he has worse than thrown away; and often in despair gives himself up to total abandonment. Upon this subject I might say much; but as Texas may have need for more soldiers, it is well that I should be silent.*
>
> *Another class of citizens were busy in buying what in the language of the country are called head rights. In order that the reader may understand what these are, I will add that the constitution of Texas provides that all white males of a specified age, who were in the country on the second of March, 1836, the date of the declaration of independence, provided such persons are married, shall be entitled to a league and labor of land [4,605 acres]; and if single to one third of a league [1,476 acres]. As the land office has been closed since the commencement of the revolution, these rights are nothing more than claims upon the government, but are more valuable than soldiers' discharges, or government land scrip, as the constitution provides further, that all such rights have a priority of location, for six months, when the office is opened. Such rights have been known to sell for twenty-five cents an acre, and in some instances for much more. Those however, who contracted to take such claims through all the legal steps necessary to procure a title from the government when the land office is opened, for the one half, and pay all attendant expenses, made the safest and most profitable speculation.*[49]

Besides the military grants and the "first class" headrights to single men and to families who had lived in Texas before independence, as just described, smaller second, third and fourth class headrights of 640 or 320 acres were available for persons arriving from 1836 to 1842, meant to encourage settlement of the frontier. Even after statehood, from 1845 to 1854 "pre-emption" grants of 320 acres were available for those homesteading vacant land. In addition, military grants of varying amounts were available for who had served in the Texian Army during the war.[50]

After independence was won, applications were made for these military and headright grants. One seeking a headright would find a desirable vacant

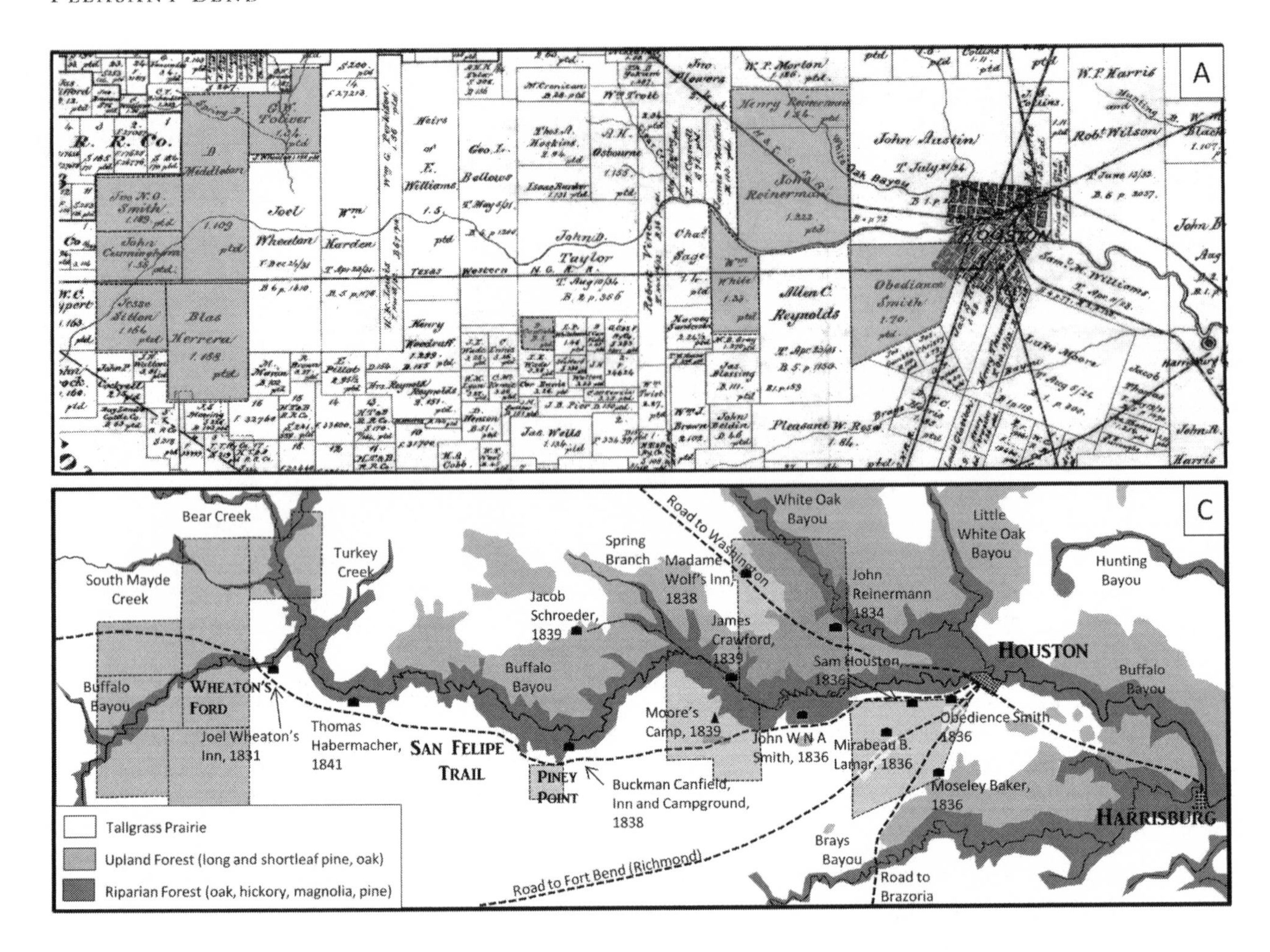

Figure 4.10. **A:** A portion of a land grant map of Harris County, 1893, highlighting those grants made in upper Buffalo Bayou during the republic period (1836–1845) that are discussed in Chapter 4. Map courtesy of the General Land Office, Austin. **B:** Same highlighted grants, superimposed on a map of the natural environment (as explained in Figure 1.2), with selected cultural features of the republic era. The street grid of the town of Houston in 1836 is shown to scale.

plot, have it surveyed, and apply. Most of the grants discussed later were applied for in 1837 and 1838 and officially patented in 1844–1845. Many early residents already had a homestead elsewhere, and would apply for a headright grant and then sell their rights to that headright to a land speculator, shortly after their application was made. In such cases there was no intention of occupying the property, nor was such a requirement. Of the several Republic of Texas era land grants discussed in the rest of this section, each located directly on either Buffalo Bayou or the San Felipe Trail or both, only one was settled by its original grantee (that of German immigrant John Reinermann).

Thus most of the land along Buffalo Bayou continued to be a vacant wilderness for the time being; large-scale settlement west of Houston generally waited until after Texas joined the United States in 1845—an event assuring many that an investment in Texas land would be safe. Nonetheless, by the end of the republic period of 1836–1845, all the land directly along the bayou and the San Felipe wagon road was claimed; any vacant land lay only farther to the north and south in the open prairie. Following are descriptions of some of these republic era grants (Figure 4.10), from east to west, not including that of Obedience Smith, already discussed.

Johann Gerhard (John) Reinermann (1775–ca. 1836) arrived in Texas from Oldenburg, Germany in December 1835 with his wife, Anna Adelheld Strodtmann, and two grown but unmarried sons, John Jr. and Henry, aged 24 and 27. John Sr. was 60 years of age. He selected a tract to the west of John Austin's two leagues, north of Buffalo Bayou in an application for a grant made on March 20, 1835.[51] They settled there, in the general area of modern Memorial Park, where John died, probably in 1836 but certainly before 1838. After independence his heirs were awarded a first class family headright of one league and a labor. The league of 4,428 acres was granted in 1838, and an additional labor of 177 acres was granted in 1847 (Figure 4.10).[52] His son, Henry Reinermann, received a one-third league headright immediately to the north of John Reinerman's tract. John Reinermann was among the first of a wave of German immigrants to western Harris County, and he is discussed in more detail in Chapter 6.

Figure 4.11. William White (1815–1880), soldier in the Texas War of Independence. Courtesy of Sharon Felfe Howell.

William White (1815–1880) was born in St. Martin Parish, Louisiana. After his father, also William White (1766-1821) died, William Jr. came with his mother Amy Comstock White (1775-1853) and several siblings to Texas (Figure 4.11). They settled on The San Jacinto River at Highlands, in eastern Harris County. William White was a soldier in the War of Independence and fought at the battle of San Jacinto; his rifle and powder horn are on display at the San Jacinto Museum. White applied for a first class headright grant on February 3, 1838, following the War of Independence.

The William White tract lies between the John Taylor and John Austin tracts (Figure 4.10 A). White never intended to live on the tract, but sold it immediately to N. Dobie, who in turn sold it to George M. Patrick, all in March 1838. On his bill of sale, White writes that he is a resident of "Harrisburg" County, leaving little doubt that he is the William White from Highlands. The deed was patented by the State on October 28, 1844, at which time the grant went back to White, for reasons unknown. The following June 4, 1845, White sold the lower half of his grant to Darius Gregg (1804–1870).[53] Gregg, who immigrated to Texas in 1827, later became a surveyor in Houston in the 1850s–1860s, and surveyed for the Buffalo Bayou, Brazos and Colorado Railroad in 1862–1863.[54] Another part of White's tract was sold back to George Patrick, on the same day. From 1849 to 1852 Darius Gregg sold his holdings to several other early landholders along the bayou: George Foos, Neil Robison, Alex McGowen, and Agur T. Morse. The latter two became long-term residents.

A farmer, William White married Martha Margaret Ryan (1818-1857) in 1838, and the couple had eight children between 1842 and 1857. He and many family members are buried in the Sterling White chapel and cemetery in Highlands, in eastern Harris County. His land grant today comprises the bulk of the Uptown Houston district of the city of Houston.[55]

Buckman Canfield (1800–1844) received a grant south of John Taylor's league at Piney Point and lived on his property. His story is told in the next chapter.

George Washington Toliver (b. ca. 1813) came

from Mississippi and arrived in Texas in 1836. He applied for a first class headright in 1838, due north of the Wheaton survey. He sold his rights to the land that same year, 1838, to former soldier and Harris County surveyor George M. Patrick, who in turn sold it to surveyor Darius Gregg.[56] Gregg then sold it in pieces to a number of Bear Creek German immigrants in the 1840s and 1850s. Toliver never lived on the land and may never even have seen it. He was working as a "laborer" in Harris County in 1850, according to the federal census of that year.

David Middleton (ca. 1810–1840) was born in Quebec, Canada, in about 1810 and married Mary Armstrong there in 1833. He came to Texas in November 1834 and was a soldier in the Texas War of Independence, afterwards living in Liberty County, Texas, where he died in 1840. He applied for a headright grant in February 1838, which was located immediately to the west of the Wheaton tract (Figure 4.10 A). It was patented on May 20, 1857, but only after litigation between James Morgan, to whom Middleton had signed his rights prior to his death, and Middleton's heirs. Each claimed rights to the by then dormant land. His wife, Mary Middleton, attempted in 1855 to have the tract located elsewhere, saying that it was "located on the head of Buffalo Bayou in Harris County on land wholly worthless . . . being mostly wet boggy prairie [and] that the same was located there without the procurement or knowledge to the wishes of affiant [herself] and her said children." Morgan proclaimed a few months later that the land was "precisely where he [Middleton] wanted it, that is, the nearest point to Houston where vacant land could be found."[57] From these arguments we can deduce that the land was still vacant as late as 1855. That "wet boggy prairie" land is still mostly vacant today, most of it lying within the Barker Reservoir in west Houston.

Blas María Herrera (1802–1878) was a Hispanic Texian soldier who claimed land after the War of Independence as a headright. He was born in San Antonio and grew up in a home on the Military Plaza there. Herrera served under Juan Seguín during the siege of Bexar in 1835, and in early 1836 earned the nickname "Paul Revere of Texas" when he warned the city of the advance of Mexican General Santa Anna's troops. A scout and courier as well, he escorted José Navarro and José Ruiz to Washington-on-the-Brazos, where they signed the Texas Declaration of Independence on March 2, 1836. He also is reported to have served as scout for General Sam Houston at the battle of San Jacinto.[58] For his military service Herrera was granted a league and a labor of land, which he received in two pieces, both patented in 1845. The first, 1,535 acres, lay along Simms Bayou southeast of Houston, and a second of 3,070 acres lay west of Joel Wheaton's tract, along modern Westpark Drive, west of Highway 6 (Figure 4.10 A).[59] Herrera did not live on either tract, however; he sold them both to E. A. Rhodes and returned to Bexar County, where he was a successful rancher and farmer.

John N. O. Smith (1815–1851), born in Massachusetts, was a soldier in the war, participating in the Battle of San Jacinto as a sergeant major. He applied for a headright grant in 1838 for a 1,476-acre tract to the west of David Middleton's tract (Figure 4.10 A), then lost his certificate, had it replaced, and sold it in 1845, when it was finally patented. A citizen of Houston, he published the Houstonian in 1841 and published several other short-lived newspapers there in 1843–1844. He served as a representative for Harris County in the first Texas Legislature in 1846 and is buried at Founders Memorial Park in Houston.[60]

John Cunningham (b. 1800) arrived from Ohio with his wife Susan and three children in 1831. He served in the Texian army, enrolling in 1836. A farmer, he applied for and received a headright grant of 1,476 acres in 1838, west of David Middleton's grant.[61] Little is known of the precise identity of Cunningham beyond those facts. He may be the John R. Cunningham who was captured by Mexican General Adrian Woll in San Antonio in 1842, where the raiding Mexican forces imprisoned an entire courtroom that was in session, including Cunningham, then marched them to prison in Mexico City.

That John Cunningham died of malaria on the Leona River, en route to Mexico.[62] Alternatively, he might be the John C. Cunningham who was a friend of Moses Austin and Stephen F. Austin, prior to moving to Texas.[63] The grant was patented in 1845.

Jesse Sitton came from Missouri and was in Milam's Colony with his wife by 1832. He served in the war and afterwards was granted a one-third league (1,476-acre) tract due west of Herrera's tract (Figure 4.10 A), patented in 1847.[64] Most of this tract lies within George Bush Park within Barker Reservoir.

Legacy

The siting of the city of Houston along Buffalo Bayou was to be the dominant factor in the development of the upper Buffalo Bayou area to its west throughout the rest of the nineteenth century, even though the city itself did not extend west of Shepherd Drive (well inside modern Loop 610) until the twentieth century. The trade for all of the rural settlements that were to come in the upper Buffalo Bayou area—Piney Point, Pleasant Bend, the Habermacher Settlement, Spring Branch, Bear Creek, and White Oak—involved marketing their produce in Houston, typically in the market stalls on Market Square, or in the cattle pens that lined the San Felipe Trail on the town's western perimeter. Nonetheless, these rural settlements were independent entities, each with a fascinating history different from that of Houston. The story of the earliest of them, Piney Point, is discussed in the next chapter.

Figure 5.1. A stand of virgin East Texas pine, ca. 1910. Courtesy of the Texas A&M University Forest Service

FIVE

The Canfield-George Family of Piney Point

We purchased horses the day after our arrival in town [Houston].
We loaded them with our meager possessions, camping gear and provisions and
departed toward evening, hoping to reach Piney Point, a distance of nine miles. . . .
We began to worry when the sun went down, it rained hard and the horses got stuck.
With words of encouragement we drove them out of the swamp. We reached the woods
where the trees' low branches pummeled our bodies in the worst manner.
Staying close together, our sighs and—pardon me—our profanity kept us in touch.
Suddenly a light became visible in the distance, like a friendly star. We followed it to a
farm house where its owner extended his hospitality, much to our delight.

—Traveler Alvin Sorgel, at the Piney Point home
of Benjamin and Harriet Canfield George, 1846[1]

ANOTHER RECIPIENT of a Republic of Texas land grant, Buckman Canfield, together with his wife, Harriet Putnam Canfield (later Harriet George), built a lasting legacy at Piney Point, by then already a landmark on the San Felipe Trail. Upon Stephen F. Austin's death in December 1836, the former John D. Taylor league of land, excepting Taylor's Reserve, was broken up into lots and sold (see Figure 2.3 and Chapter 2). Taylor's Reserve itself had apparently been promised to John R. Harris, and after John Harris's death, his heir William Harris sold 300 acres of the reserve to Buckman Canfield.[2]

Buckman Canfield (1800–1844) was born in New York State, the son of Thomas Canfield and his wife Martha Underwood.[3] Harriet Putnam (1809–1892; Figure 5.2) was born in Stonington, Connecticut, the daughter of Jedediah Putnam and Lois Chesebrough.[4] They married in New York State on January 13, 1829, and settled in Volney, Oswego, New York. A first son, William Byron Canfield (1832–1862) was born in New York. In 1833 they traveled to New Orleans and then to Texas, where they arrived on February 6; their daughter Hannah Canfield (1835–1894) was born there.[5] There is a record of Buckman Canfield traveling from Brazoria, Texas, to New Orleans in June 1833 on the schooner Helen Mar, perhaps to pick up supplies or tend to other business.[6] Buckman Canfield was a soldier in the Texas War of Independence, serving in Captain Martin's Company.[7]

Figure 5.2. Harriet Putnam (1809–1892), wife of Buckman Canfield and later Benjamin George. Photograph from Kathy Monaghan Phillips, from the Canfield/Putnam family Bible.

Buckman and his wife Harriet became the first long-term residents of Piney Point. Buckman Canfield purchased 300 acres of the Taylor League, including "an old improvement near pine point spring"—undoubtedly the John Taylor home—in 1838. After he and Harriet took residence, a seemingly well-to-do Canfield then expanded his land holdings. Also in 1838, Canfield purchased another part of the Taylor league called Lot 1, just to the east of their existing property, from heirs of Stephen F. Austin. In 1841 Canfield received a patent to a military claim of 320 acres for his service in the War of Independence as well as a headright grant to a labor of 177 acres. Both tracts were immediately to the south of their homestead and outside the John Taylor League. He received his main headright of land, one league, in Montgomery County, but did not reside there. He then purchased the rest of the Taylor Reserve, 548 acres, in 1842 from John Harris's heirs, and purchased another 360 acres to the south in 1844 from Edward Whitehead, in between his headright and military claim parcels. By his death, he had a sizeable holding of 1,893 acres at Piney Point (Figure 5.3 outlines the entire parcel), along with a 2,583-acre tract on the Brazos River, 18 acres near Houston, and 4,428 acres on Mill Creek in Montgomery County.[8]

The Canfields had two more sons while living at Piney Point, Milam Canfield (1839–1843), who died as a child, and John Dewitt Canfield (1842–1863).[9] In addition to growing corn and other produce, Buckman Canfield kept cattle on the adjacent open range. In 1840, when John W. Pitkin of Houston outfitted a mounted company of infantry to fight Comanche Indians in central Texas, his first lieutenant and quartermaster, Ebenezer B. Nichols, purchased beef from Canfield for the company's provisions:[10]

Camp Pitkin, near Houston
March 16th & 18th 1840

Received of Buckman Canfield five hundred and twenty five pounds of fresh Beef at 25 cts per pound it being for the use of the mounted company of Infantry raised by order of the War Department of the 18th Feby 1840
To the Hon. Wm. G. Cooke, Qr. M. General
E.B. Nichols 1st Lt. Mounted Infantry, Acting Assistant Quarter Master
Approved C. Peirce Capt. By order of Brig. Genl Morebank [11]

Many travelers heading west from Houston on the San Felipe wagon road were barely able to make Piney Point before nightfall; there they found a welcoming campground, inn, and watering place at the Canfield farm at Piney Point. The Canfields most likely lived in the log cabin built by John Taylor a decade earlier (see Chapter 2) or perhaps built themselves a newer version of it. A description of their two-room dogtrot home was provided by German visitor Karl von Sommer in 1846. By that time Buck-

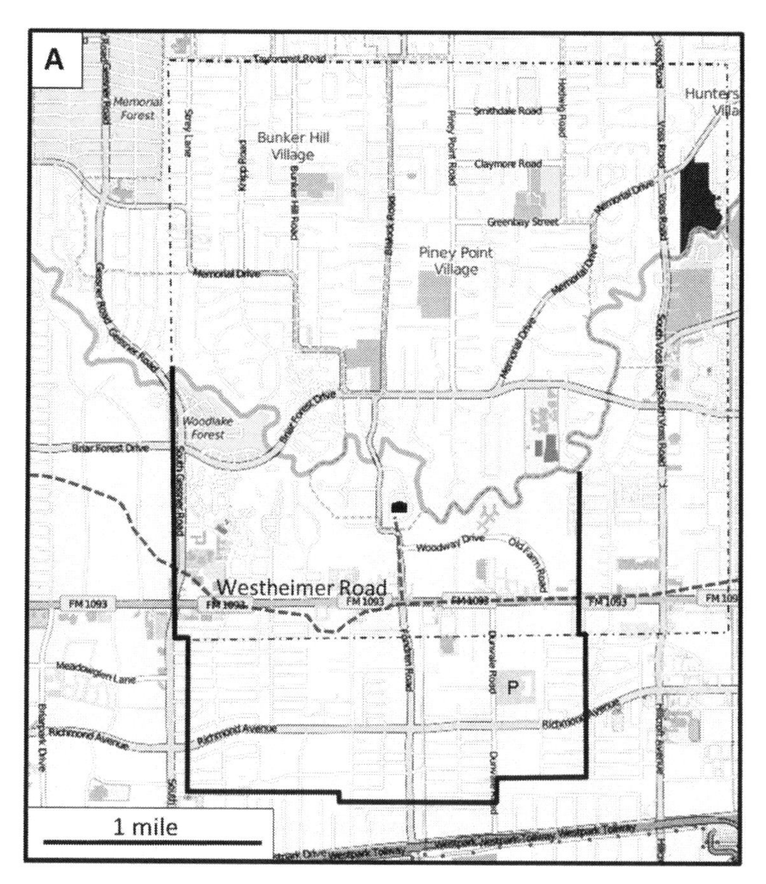

Figure 5.3. Map showing mid-nineteenth-century features of the Piney Point area. **A:** Features superimposed on a modern road map, courtesy of OpenStreetMap. **B:** Natural setting, as described in Figure 1.2. The outline of Buffalo Bayou is taken from a 1915 topographic map by the U.S. Geological Survey and differs slightly from its position today.

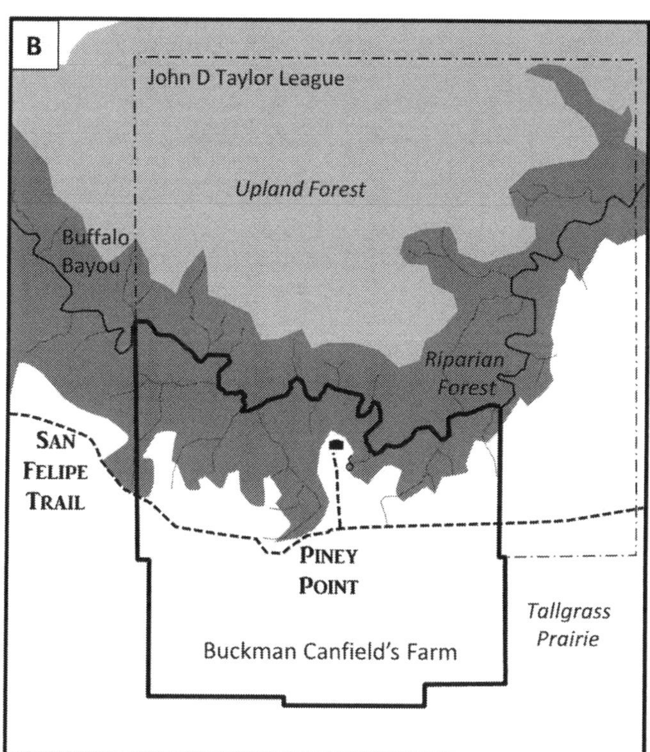

man Canfield had died, and Harriet had married Benjamin George, (of whom later): "I searched for a path and was soon at the Pine Point Farm of a farmer named Mr. George, where we were given lodging. The farm house contains two rooms in which beds are available, and a kitchen, and also has, like almost all farm houses, a porch."[12]

Here is another such account of an early traveler, from 1846, when German immigrant Alvin Sorgel stopped there on the way to New Braunfels:

> *We purchased horses the day after our arrival in town [Houston]. We loaded them with our meager possessions, camping gear and provisions and departed toward evening, hoping to reach Piney Point, a distance of nine miles. The town's young people laughed at our boldness on account of our inferior Mexican horses, the bad road ahead and our departure into the prairie late in the day. We began to worry when the sun went down, it rained hard and the horses got stuck. With words of encouragement we drove them out of the swamp. We reached the woods where the trees' low branches pummeled our bodies in the worst manner. Staying close together, our sighs and—pardon me—our profanity kept us in touch. Suddenly a light became visible in the distance, like a friendly star. We followed it to a farm house where its owner extended his hospitality, much to our delight.*[13]

A traveling tax agent for the Republic of Texas, Henry Walton Raglin (1817–1882) stayed overnight at Buckman Canfield's farm, and a signed receipt has survived (Figure 3.9): "Recd July 27th 1841 of H W Raglin four & 50/100 dollars Texas money for dinner [and lodging] of self & mule–B. Canfield."[14] Visitors from the San Felipe Trail brought extra income to the Canfields, and it is no surprise that Buckman Canfield was assigned early in 1844 as the county-appointed overseer for the part of the San Felipe Trail that extended from Houston to his farm.[15]

Death of Buckman Canfield

Carving a farm out of a wilderness of forest and prairie was a large and labor-intensive undertaking. It was certainly a wilderness at the beginning; the Canfields' nearest neighbors were the Joel Wheaton family, some three miles to the west, and the John Reinermann family, across the bayou and about five miles to the east. Like many relatively prosperous Anglo farmers in the days of the Texas Republic, Canfield made use of slave labor to build and maintain his farm, and he purchased two slaves from Houston slave trader Samuel Smith in 1837.[16]

Life at Piney Point must have been unimaginably hard for those slaves. The Canfields had moved to a wilderness forest. Fields and gardens needed to be cleared, planted and hoed. The old Taylor home, assuming it still existed, would need extensive renovation by its new owners, or a new one would need to be built. Slave quarters would have to be built, in addition to barns and other outbuildings, plus fences to keep grazing animals out of the gardens. For those enslaved, this was an enormous amount of work with little or no reward, and the remote location of the farm meant that opportunities for socializing with other African Americans would be scarce. With a generous master, life might be bearable, but with a harsh one, there was always the chance for escape to Mexico, where slavery was illegal. *The Telegraph and Texas Register* of January 20, 1838 (Figure 5.4) carried an advertisement from Buckman Canfield, who sought the return of a runaway "mulatto boy, named Shelby (familiarly styled) Doctor." He was described as twenty years in age "with a long scar on the right eye slanting down toward the nose." Canfield promised one hundred dollars for his return, a sizeable reward but small compared to the purchase price of a mature, prime enslaved field hand, which could reach a thousand dollars or more.[17]

There is no record that that slave was ever found, but by 1844 Shelby was not on the scene when Buckman Canfield was murdered by another slave. *The Houston Telegraph and Texas Register* recorded the crime in its edition of June 12, 1844:

> *Assassination. The body of Mr. B. Canfield, whose residence is about 9 miles from Houston, at Piny Point, was found in Buffalo Bayou a short distance below his dwelling, on the 6th inst. He went out to catch some fish the day before, and not returning,*

a search was instituted. The body was found by three gentlemen who went from Houston for that purpose. Upon examination, it was discovered that he had been shot in the face and neck with fourteen buck shot by some person unknown, and the Jury returned a verdict accordingly. Appearances show that he was shot in a sitting posture near the edge of the water on a steep bank. The foot steps as well as the range of the ball holes, prove that the assassin discharged the fatal shot from an eminence on the opposite bank, 40 feet higher than his victim was sitting.[18]

The indicted murderer was a slave named Castro, belonging to an attorney named Campbell, who lived near Richmond. Castro may have been hired out to Canfield. Robbery appears to have been the motive, as $582 in cash was found on the slave when he was captured. Also indicted were two other slaves: Hester, a female slave belonging to the Canfields, who had three children, and John, a slave belonging to a J. Benton Johnson. These two were dropped from the case, as they were found to be accessories to murder before the fact. Castro was convicted on November 9, 1844, and sentenced to be hanged. *The Telegraph and Texas Register* of November 27 announced the execution:

On Friday next will take place the execution of the negro Castro, belonging to Judge Campbell. This negro has been convicted, during the present term of the Court, of the murder of Mr. Canfield last summer.[19]

As noted in the preceding chapter, his execution was described by von Sommer.[20] Hester, found to be an accomplice, was treated harshly. Harriet Canfield, Buckman's widow, petitioned the court as part of probate to sell Hester and her newborn infant child, for "it is not only unpleasant but unnatural for her to keep said negro."[21] She sold Hester and the infant for $415 in June 1845 but kept Hester's two children, Ellen and Judah. Separation of families was one of the cruelest practices of slavery times.

Harriet was named administratrix of Buckman

STOLEN NEGROES FOUND.

NOTICE is hereby given to the owner of two Negroes named **Joe** and **Henry,** who were stolen from Louisiana in July last, that they have been captured at Columbus, Colorado county, Texas, and are now in charge ot the undersigned. These Negroes say they belong to a Mr. Burr, who resides about sixty miles above New Orleans. STEPHEN TOWNSHEND, Sheriff of Colorado co.

Columbus, Jan. 13, 1838. '10-3t

$100 REWARD.

THE above reward will be given by the undersigned to any one who will restore to him a mulatto boy, named Shelby (familiarly styled) Doctor. Said boy is about twenty years old, five feet eight inches high, stout built, has a long scar on the right eye slanting down towards the nose; he escaped on the night of 14th inst.

B. CANFIELD,

Piney Point, Jan. 9, 1838. '10-4t

Figure 5.4. Two notices for runaway slaves in the *Houston Telegraph* and *Texas Register* of January 20, 1838. The second reports a runaway slave from the farm of Buckman Canfield in Piney Point.

Canfield's estate. An inventory of the estate, undertaken by neighbors Stephen and Casper Habermacher and C. W. Buckley, provides a thorough and detailed look at the belongings of a prosperous farmer of frontier Texas (see box). By far his largest investment was in land, worth $10,182. His residential acreage at Piney Point was valued at only $1.00 per acre, whereas fertile bottomland on the Brazos at 16 Mile Point was valued much higher, at $2.32 per acre. This valuation took into account the low regard with which prairie land such as that at Piney Point was held for growing cotton and corn. Timber land on Mill Creek in Montgomery County, which constituted his headright league, brought only $0.50 per acre, half that of his Piney Point land. In an age when transport costs on muddy roads were a major factor, timber lands on Buffalo Bayou or on any navigable stream would be valued much higher than those farther away. The inventory also mentioned a relatively unvalued claim on an unspecified piece of land, and that claim was later patented as one third of a league of land in Milam County, on Grimes

Creek.[22] Canfield's four slaves were valued at $1,000, but these were women and children, typically valued at far less than mature male slaves.

The value of Canfield livestock holdings was rather modest. Not included is the value of cash crops like cotton and corn, which would have been sold before the inventory was taken. Significantly absent is any mention of a sawmill, on a property that today has a remnant millpond. Buckman Canfield's widow Harriet and her new husband, Benjamin George, got that industry going at Piney Point after Buckman Canfield's death.

Harriet Putnam Canfield soon remarried, first to James Todd (d. 1846) on January 22, 1845. One daughter was born to that couple, Mary (b. 1845). Todd died by early 1846, and Harriet then rather quickly married Benjamin George, on April 5, 1846. Benjamin was the "Farmer George" noted earlier, in von Sommer's account of travel in July 1846. This last marriage resulted in one son, Edward W. George (b. ca. 1848).[24]

The early timber business along Buffalo Bayou

One may well wonder what would attract people like the Canfield family to live along a remote backwater like the Buffalo Bayou area at this frontier time—especially its upstream, non-navigable sections. The proximity to the San Felipe Trail was useful, of course, but not a reason in and of itself. The largest draw to the bayou for many was its virgin stands of timber, needed not only for the building of growing towns like Harrisburg and later Houston but for export to markets along the Gulf Coast. The future Houston Heights, Memorial Park, and Memorial Villages areas offered large virgin stands of pine, the southern tip of the massive upland pine forest that stretched northward to the future Houston Intercontinental Airport, thence to Lufkin and Tyler—and from there eastward, across the southern United States, all the way to the Atlantic Ocean. For the most part this pine forest to the north of Houston was inaccessible to economic development in the era before railroads. For this reason, the exploitation of most of the East Texas pine forest did not gain major investment until the 1880s, after the end of Reconstruction.

However, there was a huge and—because of the new San Felipe wagon road—fairly accessible forest resource along Buffalo Bayou, consisting largely of oak, hickory, gum, and most important, pine. The northern edge of this riparian forest merged into the southernmost part of the upland pine forest of the East Texas pineywoods. The shading of forest cover shown in Figure 5.3 shows an approximation of the original extent of the wilderness forest near the Canfield's property. Buffalo Bayou also provided water power for sawmills and local transport for felled logs. Upstream of Houston, the San Felipe Trail provided a way for finished sawn products to find a market.

In order to exploit this resource, Benjamin George built an unusual, ox-powered sawmill by October 1848, as first mentioned in an article in the *Democratic Telegraph and Texas Register*, which described it as "simply the old inclined wheel, without cogs." The writer recommended that Gail Borden, the Houston printer, visit the saw:

> *We advised him to visit "George's" and examine his inclined wheel. He did so, and wrote as follows:*
>
> *"Dear General,*
>
> *I went out last evening to see George's mill power. I agree with you in every respect as to the superiority of this mode of producing power for ordinary mill work. I shall look no further for plans or modes: George's power and Pages [patented circular] saw mill will answer my purpose."*
> *From what we have witnessed, we have no doubt that George's wheel, worked by 8 oxen, will give all the power that will be required.*[25]

The George sawmill was described a year later in more detail in the *Democratic Telegraph and Texas Register* of July 12, 1849:

Probate Inventory,
Buckman Canfield Estate
December 30, 1844

Farm implements, tools and livery

1 crosscut saw	$4.00
1 ox yoke	$3.00
1 crowbar	$2.00
1 adz	$1.00
3 chairs	$3.00
1 ox cart	$25.00
1 lot ploughs	$10.00
1 tro (froe?)	$0.75
1 stone hammer	$0.75
1 weeding hoe	$0.25
2 axes	$3.00
1 broad axe	$2.00
1 ditto	$5.00
1 spade	$1.25
1 scaith for scythe	$0.50
1 bench screws	$0.50
1 pitch fork	$0.25
1 box sundry screws etc.	$2.00
1 pr. steelyards	$1.50
1 lot carpenters tools	$25.00
Saddles etc.	$8.00
1 grind stone	$2.00

Livestock

1 bay horse	$60.00
1 mare and colt	$60.00
1 yoke oxen	$30.00
21 head cattle	$63.00
40 head stock hogs	$30.00

Furniture and household goods

1 lot bedding and bedsteads	$104.00
1 marble top bureau	$35.00
1 card table	$15.00
1 dressing table	$20.00
1 bureau	$12.00
1 clock	$5.00
1 rocking chair	$5.00
10 chairs	$2.50
1 pine table	$1.00
1 leather trunk	$ 2.00
1 valice (valise)	$.050
1 hair trunk	$1.00
1 leather trunk	$5.00
Cooking utensils	$10.00

Silver goods

1 castor (silver)	$20.00
1 fruit basket	$20.00
4 large silver candlesticks	$25.00
2 large cut glass decanters with stands	$8.00
1 small decanter	$1.00
1 pr. snuffers (silver) and tray	$4.00
1 silver soup ladle	$7.50
9 table spoons	$22.50
14 tea spoons	$10.50
1 fish knife	$5.00
1 butter knife	$1.00
12 ivory handle knives with silver forks	$30.00
2 German silver butter knives	$0.50
1 pr. sugar tongs	$0.25

Personal possessions

1 rifle and shot bag`	$10.00
2 large pistols	$12.00
1 double barrel shotgun	$15.00
1 lot game bags & contents	$0.50
2 gold watches & 1 gold chain	$150.00
1 looking glass	$0.50
1 lot miscellaneous books	$8.00

Land

1893 acres land (including residence etc.)	$1893.00
18 acres below Houston	$50.00
2583 acres on Brazos at 16 mile point	$6000.00
4428 acres on Mill Creek in Montgomery County	$2214.00
1 milocated (?) claim for 1/3 league land	$25.00

Slaves

1 negro woman named Hester (at present charged with murder of intestate)	$500.00
Hester's two children	$200.00
1 negro girl Maria	$300.00

Grand Total **$12,100.00**

DOMESTIC SAWMILL. We visited the saw mill of Mr. George, at Piney Point, a few days since, and were agreeably surprised to notice the remarkable ingenuity and mechanical skill, evinced in its construction. Mr. George has completed nearly every part of the mill himself and with materials chiefly obtained on his own land. The saw and a few ropes and bands of cloth are almost the only materials that were procured abroad. The main wheel is about forty feet in diameter and turns another large wheel by the friction of its surface upon a small wooden drum. The driving wheel propels the machinery which works the saw with a band of cotton cloth, and a band of ropes moves the log carriage. The main wheel is so admirably constructed that a small dog could propel it readily. It is usually turned by four oxen walking upon its inclined surface. Mr. George has displayed a remarkable degree of mechanical knowledge, in adapting cheap materials to answer the purpose of expensive bands, cog wheels and rack work, in making the machinery.

The cost of running this mill is but one dollar and a half a day, and he saws about twenty four hundred feet of lumber daily. A mill of this description could be erected in any of the pine forests in the interior, by a carpenter and a blacksmith, and at a comparatively trifling expense. A grist mill is attached to this saw mill capable of supplying the whole neighborhood, including Houston, with meal. With the addition of Pages patent circular saws, this mill might probably be made more profitable than any mill in the country propelled by steam or water power. The materials of which it is constructed are cheap and durable, and the oxen that propel it feed upon the prairie grass so that the expense of working it is limited almost entirely to the wages of the man that tends it.[26]

Animals and people have powered mills for centuries, but not so much in Texas, where water power was abundant, and where, after 1829, steam power was introduced at the Harris sawmill at Harrisburg. However, Piney Point was a frontier setting, and Benjamin George was evidently inspired by the power of readily available oxen. The rig described has no known parallels locally. The challenge of using animal power is capturing energy from the feet of beasts and turning it into a reciprocating saw motion. Horse-powered treadmills (not unlike the modern exercise treadmill) became commercially available in the 1880s.[27] But the description of the George sawmill is of a large, homemade, inclined wheel, 40 feet in diameter, "turned by four oxen walking upon its inclined surface." This is reminiscent of European people-powered grain mills that used inclined wheels (Figure 5.5).

However eloquently the newspaper reporter waxed on the huge machine's inspired design, there appear to have been problems. The same issue of the newspaper that carried the detailed story of the George sawmill also carried an advertisement from George of a young slave woman for sale (Figure 5.6), suggesting that there may have been some financial difficulty at the farm. George may also have faced some stiff competition. Just below his advertisement is one from a man named D. Russell of Houston, seeking return of a runaway slave from a steam sawmill owned by William Purvis.[28] That was not the only steam sawmill around; William Ahrenbeck was building one in Spring Branch at this same time.[29]

For whatever reason, Benjamin George's marriage with Harriet was on the rocks, and by the federal census of 1850, just a year following the newspaper article, Benjamin George was no longer living at Piney Point with his wife, child, and stepchildren. The census states that Harriet's son, William Canfield, age eighteen, was the family sawyer. According to family history, Benjamin George deserted Harriet.[30] Perhaps he was weary of the life of isolation on the bayou, although his fifteen minutes of fame as an acclaimed local inventor had just begun. Perhaps more likely is that his machine was a failure and he (or she) had difficulty dealing with that. There are no known records of similar machines in Texas inspired by his invention, which suggests that it was less successful than the newspaper reporter predicted.

Benjamin George, though gone from Piney Point, remained in the region. In the 1860s Cecelia Morse—wife of a Confederate soldier from nearby

FOR SALE.

A VERY likely Negro woman, twenty-four years old, good house servant or field hand, cheap for cash, apply to

B. M. GEORGE, Piney Point, Harris County.

3t704

Runaway or Stolen,

FROM the Steam Mill of William Purvis, about the 8th inst., a Negro man named Jim, about 5 feet, 9 or 10 inches high, very black complexion; speaks slow, is about 30 years of age, formerly the property of John W. Cloud. I am apprehensive he has been persuaded away by some white person. He has a wife at Mr. Smith's, near Seguine, and his old master, I understand, lives near San Felippe. I will give $25 reward for the apprehension and delivery of said Negro in any jail in the State, or if stolen, I will give $100 for the conviction of the thief.

The Austin Democrat and Western Texian will please advertise 4 weeks and send their bills to

D. RUSSELL.

Houston, June 20th, 1849. w4t 706

Above: Figure 5.6. An advertisement by Benjamin George, Piney Point, for the sale of a slave woman. *Democratic Telegraph and Texas Registry*, July 12, 1849.

Left: Figure 5.5. An early human-powered inclined wheel treadmill operating a grain mill. Wikipedia.

Pleasant Bend Plantation (see Chapter 7)—mentions him as a courier for Morse family news to and from her husband and her brother-in-law, who served in the Army of Northern Virginia during the Civil War. George died sometime before 1880.

Harriet builds a new sawmill

Benjamin George's desertion no doubt caused Harriet George to take stock of her situation. She was a single mother, thrice married, living on an isolated frontier farm along Buffalo Bayou. She was not without resources, however. Certainly she had her land, although most of the Canfield land outside Piney Point had gone to her children at the time of Buckman Canfield's probate. A federal agricultural census of 1850 showed that she had 50 improved acres on her farm, the rest being unimproved prairie pasture and timber land. To work the farm, she had 6 horses and 4 oxen. Other livestock included 25 milk cows and 150 head of beeves, 50 sheep, and 80 hogs, for a total livestock value of $1,100. She was growing corn and had harvested 500 bushels (probably about 10 acres); cotton was not mentioned. Her farm's cash value was placed at $1,100. It was a reasonably prosperous but hardly wealthy farm. She needed to maintain a steady income for her children, and this need must have weighed heavily on her mind.

At some time after Benjamin George left, Harriet obtained some new machinery for a different sawmill, "machinery she had hauled by ox team from Alabama."[31] Why Alabama? Gideon Hotchkiss (1797–1860) was a civil engineer and inventor living in the small town of Windsor in New York State, with patents in the 1830s for a threshing machine, a grist mill, and a "reacting water wheel" for sawmills. These were enclosed small vertical wheels, hung on a horizontal shaft, which turned under the force of injected water, something like a modern turbine (Figure 5.7). The advantage of this system over the age-old large overshot or undershot water wheels typically seen in old prints was a faster sawing motion for less water used. As a testimonial, an 1846 advertising broadside included this statement from Alabama governor Ben Fitzpatrick:

> *The . . . Hotchkiss Water Wheels have recently been applied to my Saw Mill, and I state with pleasure, that with one-fifth less water, my Mill now cuts double the quantity of lumber than she ever did while using the common flutter wheel. When properly applied, I regard the Vertical water wheel as vastly superior to any that I have seen used at Saw Mills.*[32]

In short, the Hotchkiss wheel required less water to make more lumber, with a device that was still of a size that could readily be transported. Hotchkiss licensed the sale of his device in several locations, the closest to Texas being the firm of House and Lundy in the small town of Wetumpka, Alabama. A broadside advertising this system in 1846 in Montgomery, Alabama, has survived (Figures 5.8, 5.9). All that needed hauling to Texas was a pair of the cast-iron turbine-like wheels, which at the sizes commonly used of 28 inches to 40 inches in diameter were of reasonable size for an ox cart to carry; the rest of the rig could be fabricated locally.

It is known that Jacob Croft was building Hotchkiss-style mills for timber companies in the Buffalo Bayou and Spring Creek areas from as early as 1838, so it is possible that Harriet and her son went to him for help in assembly.[33] Ironically, the same article in the *Democratic Telegraph and Texas Register* on October 12, 1848, in which Gail Borden praised Benjamin George's ox-powered sawmill also devoted upwards of two full columns to describing and promoting the Hotchkiss Vertical Water Wheel, then being sold by Conklin and Lillie in Houston, for use in sawmills, so Harriet George would likely have been aware of it. She hired a German builder named Wilhelm Betke to construct the wooden housing for the mill (more on him later).

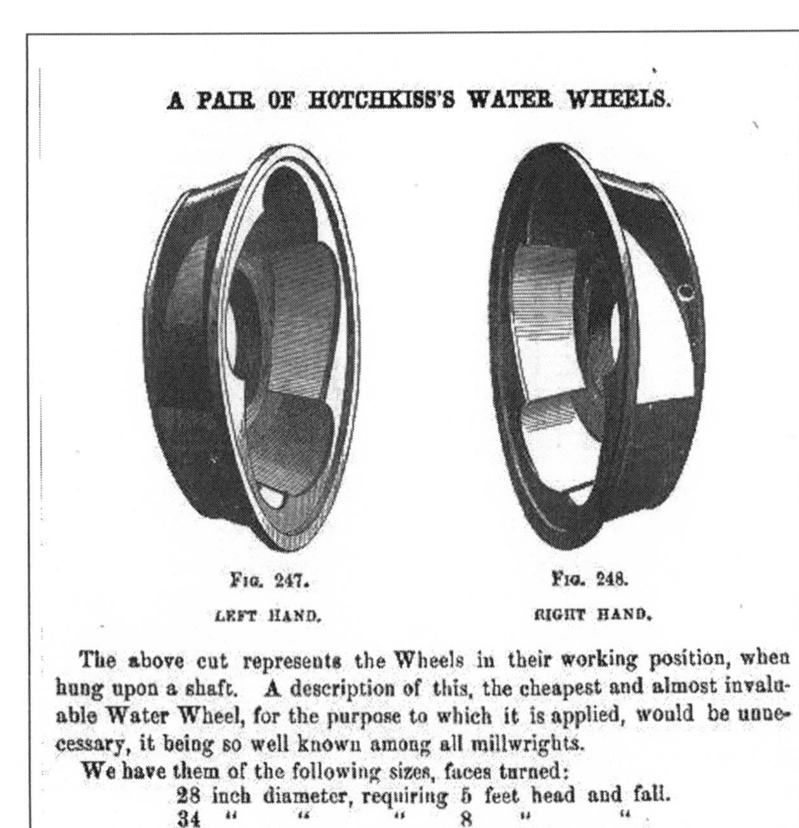

A PAIR OF HOTCHKISS'S WATER WHEELS.

FIG. 247. LEFT HAND.

FIG. 248. RIGHT HAND.

The above cut represents the Wheels in their working position, when hung upon a shaft. A description of this, the cheapest and almost invaluable Water Wheel, for the purpose to which it is applied, would be unnecessary, it being so well known among all millwrights.

We have them of the following sizes, faces turned:

28 inch diameter, requiring 5 feet head and fall.
34 " " " 8 " "
40 " " " 12 " "

Left: Figure 5.7. Hotchkiss's water wheel. From Tredwell and Jones Illustrated Catalogue of Agricultural Implements and Machinery (New York, 1859).

Opposite top: Figure 5.8. Broadside for a "Premium Vertical Waterwheel," published by Gideon Hotchkiss in Alabama, 1846. MSS.3731, courtesy of University Libraries Division of Special Collections, University of Alabama.

Opposite below: Figure 5.9. Hotchkiss water wheels mounted on a sawmill. Enlargement from Figure 6.10.

HOTCHKISS'

PREMIUM VERTICAL WATERWHEEL

AND APPENDAGES.

From the constant operation of nearly four thousand of these **WHEELS** and **APPENDAGES**, in different sections of the Country, and the very high popularity which they have attained with all that have had an opportunity of witnessing their extraordinary power, the subscriber feels justified in giving publicity to the following statement.

The use of these wheels, when properly introduced, nearly doubles the value of the mills, and enables them to do a business which far exceeds the most sanguine expectation of their owners. For this invention, (Hotchkiss' Water Wheel,) the managers of the Seventeenth Annual Fair of the American Institute awarded a Silver Medal, in October, 1844.

GIDEON HOTCHKISS, *Patentee.*

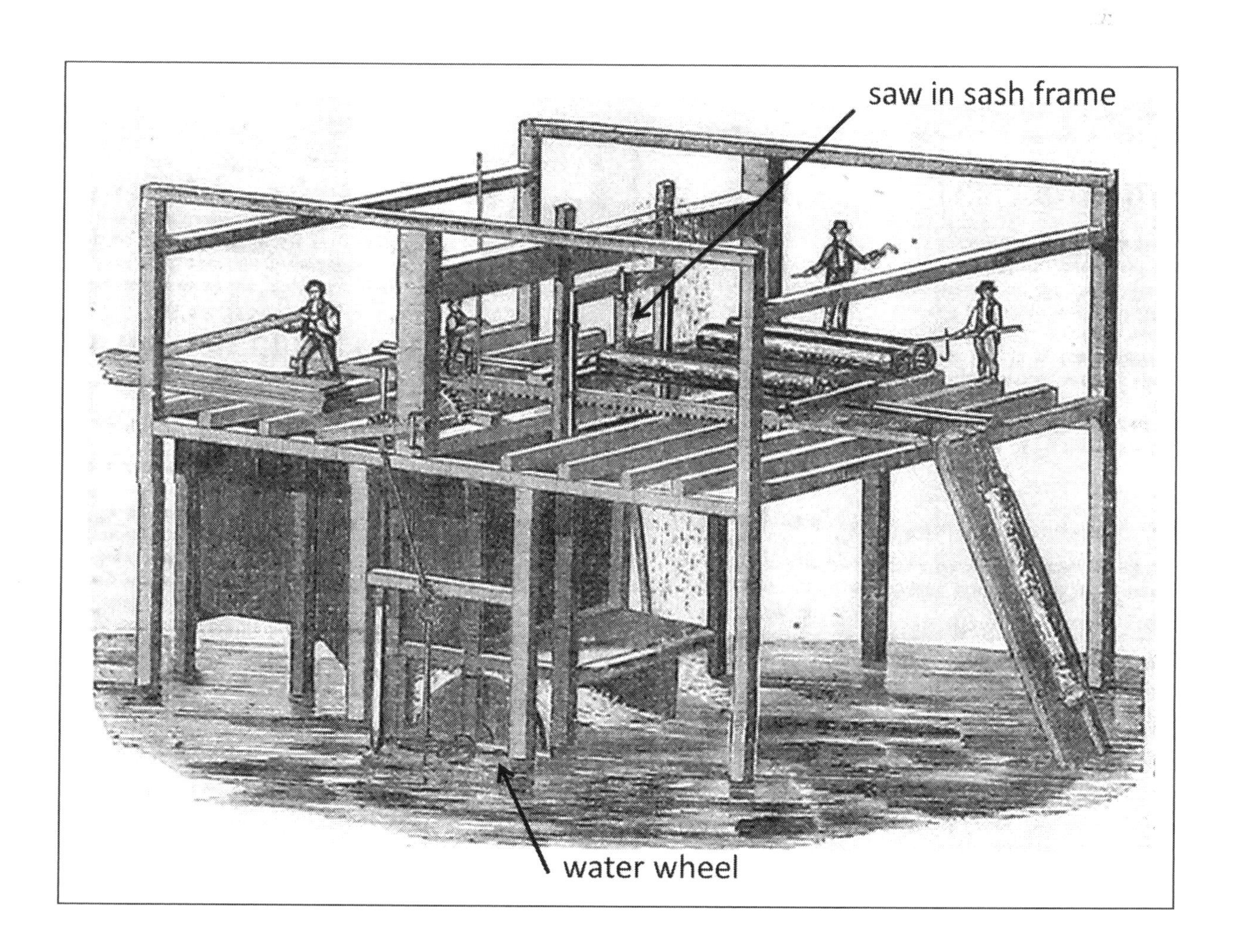

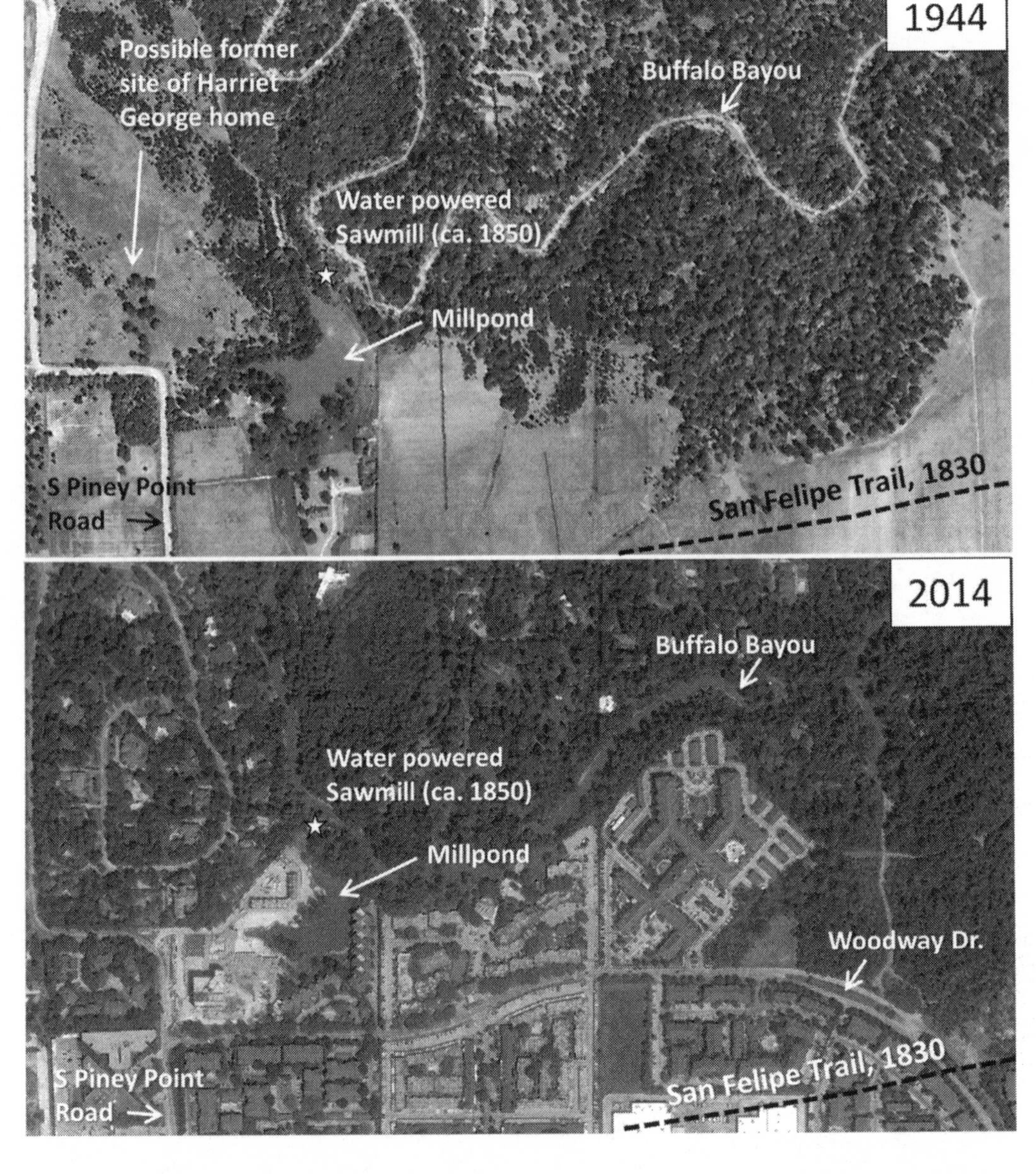

Figure 5.10. The Harriet George sawmill site at Piney Point. Upper figure, an aerial photo of December 1944, when the area was still rural and the (approximate) original prairie-woodland boundaries can still be seen. Lower figure, 2014. Photos courtesy of the Texas Natural Resources Information System, Austin.

The sawmill required the construction of a millpond (Figure 5.10). A gully draining into Buffalo Bayou was fed by a spring, which had been the source of water for the homestead since the time of John Taylor. They dammed the gully just short of its drop into Buffalo Bayou. In normal water conditions, the water level in the bayou is about 20 to 30 feet lower than that of the millpond, yielding a great deal of potential energy for a water wheel. The millpond also kept the logs moist while they waited to be cut, which helped prevent them from cracking and checking, and kept them within easy reach of the chain hoist that carried them to the mill floor. Harriet's millpond has survived until today relatively intact. Until recently it formed a verdant backdrop to the once popular Vargo's restaurant, and it is now surrounded by the high rise condominiums of "Vargo's on the Lake."

As earlier noted, Harriet George's eldest son William Canfield became the sawyer of the mill by 1850, according to the federal census of that year. In the slave schedule that accompanied the 1860 federal census, William is credited with owning one unnamed male slave and Harriet with two unnamed female slaves; the male slave probably worked in the sawmill. When landscaping operations at Vargo's restaurant site—which included the pond area that was the scenic backdrop for the venue—were underway in the late 1960s, it is said that a groundskeeper and an owner discovered several graves, one of which was marked simply as the grave of "Noah Cambeaux, New Iberia Parish, La., 1861."[34] It would seem reasonable to conclude that Noah Cambeaux was a millworker, buried near the mill site. It seems likely that he was an African American slave, perhaps from Louisiana.

A house for freedom

With the sawmill complete, Harriet George turned her attention to the house; she and her family were probably still living in the dog-trot home visited by von Sommer in 1846, and she needed more room. In particular, her sawyer son William would need a home for his future family. At the time of the 1850 census, German cabinetmaker "Wm. Bathke" (Wilhelm Betke, b. ca. 1824, Germany) was living with the Canfield family. He arrived in Galveston on the ship Neptune in late December 1846, and appears to have been hired by Harriet George to help construct the new sawmill.[35] According to family history, he built a substantial new home for Harriet and her family, sometime before 1854. There is a family story on how that house came to be built, recounted in the 1920s by Nancy Thornton Eatwell (whose grandmother Mary Silliman operated the inn and farm at nearby Wheaton's Ford in the late 1850s):

> *[The] William Canfield home [was] built at Piney Point by a German builder and contractor (Betke) who fell in love with one of Canfield's negro slave women. He was so enamored or in love with this woman that he agreed to build this Canfield residence, taking for his pay this negro woman, which he did. A son, Leander Betke, lives at Hempstead.*[36]

Eatwell's story is supported by the sale of "a negro woman Maria belonging to the estate of said Canfield about twenty years of age & of a light complexion" to "William Batka" for $705 in 1854, as reported in Harris County probate records.[37] Maria was mentioned as a young girl in Buckman Canfield's probate inventory of 1844, and as a seventeen-year-old female slave living in the Harriet George household, nameless but "quite white, " in the slave schedule of the U.S. Census of 1850.[38] The $705 price quoted for her in 1854 apparently reflects the cash value of the barter: a big house built for Maria's freedom. German immigrants had few of the race prejudices of Anglo-Texans, and very few had slaves; the implied marriage of William Batke and Maria fits with those general facts.

Mixed-race marriages were outlawed in the Republic of Texas in 1837, so there was probably not a formal marriage.[39] Nancy Thornton Eatwell's account shows that the romance was well known to the extended Canfield, George, Morse and Thornton families in the area, who seem to have chosen to remain silent in regard to the authorities. William and Maria left the area, no doubt to get a new start, and were living together as man and wife in the now defunct town of Pittsville, Fort Bend County, Texas, in 1860, under the (badly misspelled) name "Buthie," according to the 1860 federal census. They were working for a wealthy farmer named John Patterson. William (age 34) of Lippe-Detmold, Germany, and "Morcoh" (age 28) of Louisiana, had two daughters: Louisa (30, and Emily (1). Maria (Morcoh) was clearly "passing" as white, under the radar. By the time of the 1870 Federal census, Maria Batka (age 34), "white," is keeping house in Fort Bend County with seven children: Louisa, Emma, Leander, Theodore, Rena, Florence, and Mina. William is not listed, and may have passed away by then.

Most telling is the 1932 death certificate of Louise E. (Batke) Carter, Maria's eldest daughter.

Louise (Louisa) was born on July 27, 1857, to "Batke" (father) and "M. Canfield" (mother). Maria, like most Texas slaves in the 1850s, had no recognized, legal last name. Like many slaves, she had taken the last name of her former slave master, Buckman Canfield.[40] The death certificates of Emma (1859–1938) and Leander (1861–1926) both list "William Batke born in Germany" as father, but "unknown" as the name of the mother, perhaps intending to keep the family secret hidden in a repressive age of Jim Crow.[41]

Maria's eldest son, Leander Betka (1861–1926), mentioned in Nancy Thornton Eatwell's account as living in Hempstead, Texas, was buried in Hempstead Cemetery in Waller County in 1926.[42] He has living descendants in Texas and California.

Jeannette Morse Hollady, a Morse cousin of Hannah Canfield's husband William Morse, described the old house that Bethke built to win his lover's freedom:

> *Grandma George's land [Grandma George being her name for Harriet] . . . had a large white colonial house on it built from lumber and heavy timbers that had been milled on the place with machinery she had hauled by ox team from Alabama. Later, this home was inherited by Charlie Morse, whose wife was Joy and they had a daughter named Hattie. . . . Charlie Morse sold Grandma George's home to Sam Bongio, an Italian immigrant.*[43]

"Joy" was Abby Ivie Beeler (1861–1896); she and her husband Charles Morse are discussed in Chapter 11. Harriet lived in that house until her death in 1892. Harriet's grandson Charles Canfield Morse (1855–1905), the son of Hannah Canfield and William Morse, inherited the house after Harriet's death. Jeannette was a niece of Nancy Thornton Eatwell; she continues:

> *In the meantime [early in the twentieth century], Sam Bongio had sold the Grandma George estate to Colonel A. B. Nibbs, who ostentatiously lived the old-type Southern aristocratic life with his son, Alan B. Nibbs. Young Mrs. Nibbs and daughter, Mollie lived there. Col. Nibbs had built a fairly large one-room school house on the corner of the land on Westheimer Road, adjoining our land, and Mollie and I, being of the same age, became good friends. . . .*
>
> *As Mollie's and my friendship grew, I had the rare privilege of spending many hours in Grandma George's magnificent home, now Col. Nibbs'. Both of Mollie's aunts furnished a grand library with a wealth of the finest literature. . . .*
>
> *Col. Nibbs died and the Grandma George place was then sold to young Tom C. Dunn, Jr. He took his bride there, furnished it extravagantly, so we were told, as I never was there after the Col. Nibbs family left. But young Mr. Dunn and his wife didn't like the country. The house and all contents burned to the ground to the consternation and regret of all around. The colored help said there was plenty of time and they could have saved much if not all of the furnishings, but Tom Dunn Jr. wouldn't permit anyone to even try. The home and the furnishings were insured.*[44]

According to Albert C. Timme (1906–2001), a neighbor who watched the fire as a small boy in January 1912, the pipes had frozen, and the hired help were using lighted hay to try to defrost them when the old home caught fire. Timme was born in the nearby George Edward Morse family home, where Jeannette Morse Hollady was born, which Timme's parents had purchased from Jeannette's father George Edward Morse (1853–1901), of whom more in Chapter 11. There were close familial bonds between Grandma (Harriet) George and the Morse family throughout the late nineteenth century.

Timme remembered that the house was square in shape, with two stories and a "widow's walk" on the roof (a small high deck with porch railings), typical of Greek Revival southern homes of the mid-nineteenth century.[45] The *Houston Daily Post*, writing about the fire, described the house as a "two-story, twelve-room structure . . . built on the Southern colonial style, and [it] was one of the historical landmarks of Harris County." The house and its contents were valued at $25,000, according to the *Post*.[46] Using a CPI-based currency calculator, that amount would be worth around $600,000 today, although a house of that history and size in the Piney Point area today would likely be worth several times that amount.

By the end of the 1850s Harriet had a large farm with a water-powered sawmill, two sons and an unknown number of slaves living on the estate to help work it, and a daughter and son-in-law living nearby. With the events of the Civil War, this situation was to change drastically. She was to lose both sons to the war, and lose her son-in-law within months after the end of the conflict (Chapter 8).

Figure 6.1. Two German settlers on horseback, sketched by Texas German frontier artist Friedrich Richard Petri (1824-1857). Friedrich Richard Petri collection, Image di03143, Dolph Briscoe Center for American History, the University of Texas at Austin.

SIX

German Immigration to Upper Buffalo Bayou

They came from a very cold country . . . and when they arrived at Spring Branch it was so warm and the sun was shining brightly and even some flowers were still blooming in the early part of December. What a wonderful country they said, it isn't even necessary to build a house; we will live under the trees. But they didn't know that in Texas the weather may change overnight or sometimes in a few hours. So two weeks later one of those cold ice northers came and two of the children almost froze to death. . . . But the good neighbors were right there to help them and they gave them shelter until they had their log cabin finished.

—A grandson of pioneer settler Wilhelm Rummel[1]

GERMAN COLONIZATION in Texas began with Friedrich Ernst (1796–1848). Fleeing a charge of embezzlement in his native Oldenburg, Germany, Ernst brought his family to Texas in 1831, settling on Mill Creek in Austin's colony, in what eventually became Industry, Texas. Glowing written reports about Texas that Ernst sent back to Germany encouraged many others to emigrate.[2] They emigrated for a variety of reasons related to economic, social, and military conditions in their homeland. Although many if not most of these immigrants headed inland for Ernst's Industry, or to later settlements in New Braunfels and Fredericksburg, a large number stayed in the coastal zone, especially in northern and northwestern Harris County. This included several early German immigrants who settled on or close to the banks of upper Buffalo Bayou, at what would become rural communities at Spring Branch, Bear Creek, White Oak, and Habermacher (Figure 6.2). Others settled along Cypress Creek in northwestern Harris County, in what is now Spring-Cypress. Some of the settlers of these communities were sawyers, but most were farmers. They raised corn, vegetables and other crops along with cattle, hogs and chickens for markets in Houston, and often planted small fields of cotton as a cash crop. Bringing with them from Germany the practice of intensive agriculture on family-run farms, German farmers tended to settle on relatively small plots of land, typically less than 200 acres, rather than on the leagues of land occupied by earlier Anglo settlers. By and large they were not slave owners, and the contrast between the appearance of their farms and those of Anglo farmers, especially those who depended upon forced slave labor, was noticeable to Frederick Law Olmstead, who described these German farms in the New Braunfels area in 1857. He noted that small amounts of market cotton were grown along with food crops:

> *They lived in little log cabins, and had enclosures of ten acres of land about them. . . . The greater variety of crops which had been grown on their allotments, and the more clean and complete tillage they had received, contrasted favorabl[y] with the patches of corn-stubble, overgrown with crab-grass, which are usually the only gardens to be seen adjoining the cabins of the poor whites and slaves. The people themselves were also to be seen, women and children, busy at some work. . . . It caused us a sensation to see a number of parallelograms [plots] of "Cotton—Free Labor Cotton." These were not often of more than an acre in extent. Most of them looked as if they had been judiciously cultivated, and had wielded a fine crop, differing, however, from that we had noticed on the plantations the day before, in this circumstance—the picking had been entirely completed, and that with care and exactness, so that none of the cotton . . . had been left to waste.*[3]

Only one German family, that of Johann Gerhard (John) Reinermann (1775–ca. 1836), was to come to the upper Buffalo Bayou area early enough to apply for a colonial era land grant, before the revolution. For this reason, by the time most Germans arrived in the mid-to-late 1840s the south bank land along the San Felipe Trail—which tended to be better drained—was already mostly taken by Anglo settlers and land speculators. Consequently the German pioneers purchased small tracts of land to the north of Buffalo Bayou, and in northwestern Harris County as well. The land north of Buffalo Bayou was distinctly different from that of the south bank. Several tributaries spilled into the bayou from the north, among them Bear Creek, Spring Branch, and White Oak Bayou (Figure 6.2). When heavy rains came, these tributaries backed up and tended to flood. That flooding produced swampy land with pockets of water after rains—perfect breeding grounds for disease. Yellow fever and malaria were frequent visitors. In addition, there were large stands of upland pine forest on the north side of Buffalo bayou that had to be cleared for farming. Several of the German immigrants operated sawmills.

The three German settlements that grew up in the land north of Buffalo Bayou in the 1840s and 1850s were each named for a tributary of the bayou: Bear Creek, Spring Branch, and White Oak. We begin the story, however, with the settler and his family who came to rural Harris County at the end of colonial days: John Reinermann, whose league of land is outlined on Figure 6.2.

The John Reinermann League

Johann Gerhard (John) Reinermann (1775–ca. 1836), sailed from Oldenburg, Germany, in 1834 with his wife, Anna Adelheld Strodtmann, and two sons, John Jr. (1808–1835) and Henry (b. 1808), bound for New Orleans.[4] The Reinermanns settled on land that encompassed all of present day Memorial Park and most of the modern Timbergrove subdivision.

The Reinermanns were with a party of emigrants led by Robert Kleberg, who later founded Cat Spring, Texas, and by Kleberg's father-in-law, Lieutenant Ludwig von Roeder. These men and others in the party had read the letters of recent Texas immigrant Friedrich Ernst, praising life in Texas, and they sought freedom from military despotism in Prussia at the time. An advance party of five emigrants was sent ahead to select a place to live. When the rest (including Reinermann and his family and about twenty others) received word that the earlier party had successfully landed, they sailed from Oldenburg in September 1834.[5] The story of this party's arduous trip to Texas, recounted years later by Robert Kleberg, is worth including here as a testimony to the hardships endured by many early Texas immigrants. They landed in New Orleans in November 1834:

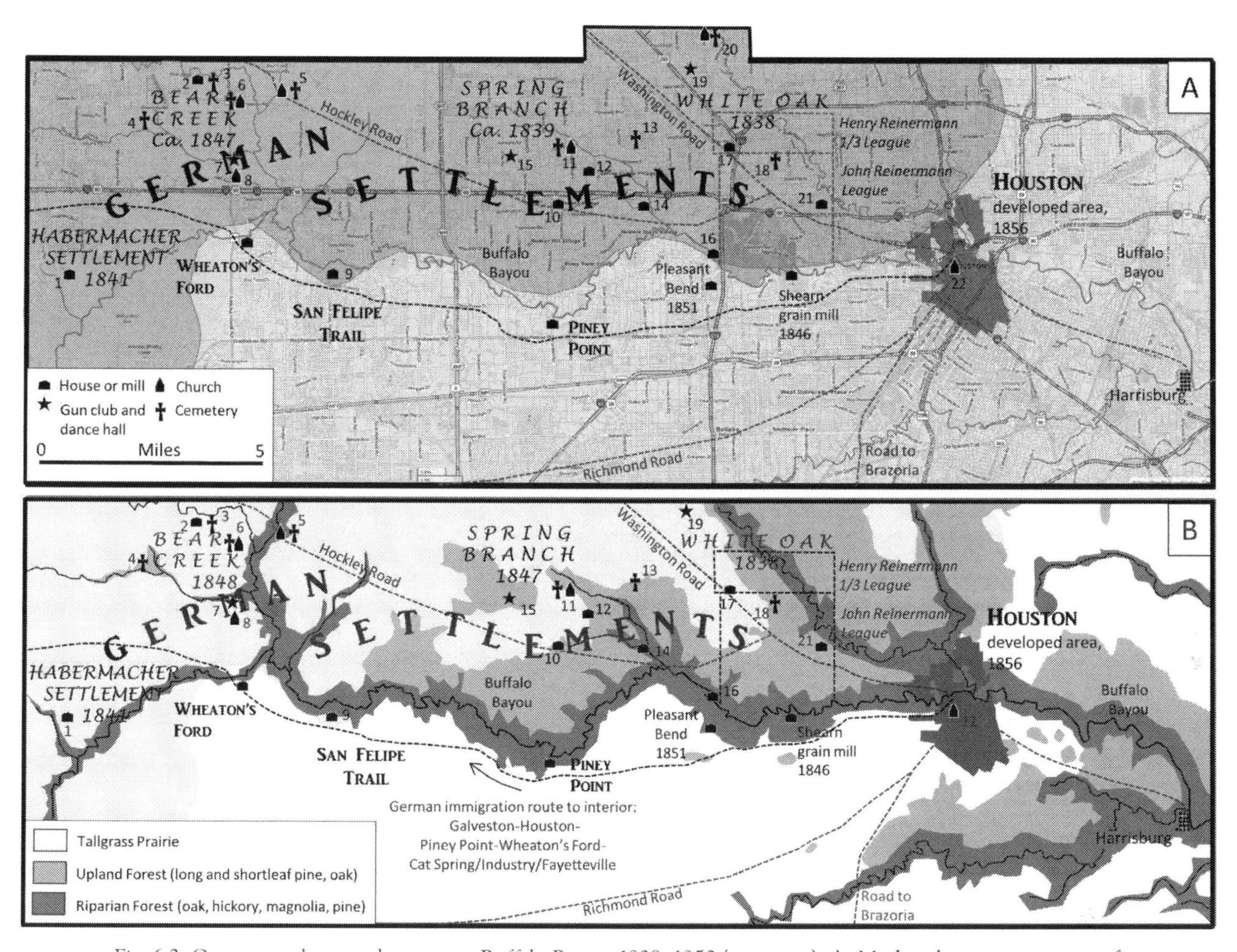

Fig. 6.2. German settlement along upper Buffalo Bayou, 1838–1850 (next page). **A:** Modern base map courtesy of OpenStreetMap. **B:** Original forest cover, as in Figure 1.2.

1. Joseph Habermacher, 1851
2. Marks, Groschke farms ca. 1847
3. Groschke family cemetery
4. Koch-Schmidt cemetery, Cullen Park
5. Location of Bear Creek Methodist Church in 1890 and the Hillendahl-Eggling cemetery
6. Location of Bear Creek Methodist Church in 1903 and the Addicks Bear Creek Methodist Cemetery today, Highway 6 at Patterson Road
7. Bear Creek Schuetzen Verein (Gun Club), 1900 location
8. Addicks United Methodist Church, location since 1940s
9. Thomas Habermacher, 1841
10. Jacob Schroeder, 1839
11. St. Peter United Church of Christ (formerly Evangelical Lutheran) and cemetery, and Bauer families, 1847–1848
12. Karl Kolbe, 1852
13. Hillendahl family cemetery, 1854, Long Point at Pech Road
14. Ahrenbeck sawmill, 1851
15. Spring Branch Schuetzen Verein (Gun Club), before 1876
16. James Crawford farm, 1839; Karl Kolbe farm, 1846
17. Madam Wolf's inn and farm, 1838
18. Vollmer cemetery, 1848, Timbergrove Manor subdivision
19. White Oak Schuetzen Verein (Gun Club), 1873
20. St. John Evangelical Lutheran Church and cemetery, 1860
21. Farm of John Reinermann heirs, 1838
22. Bering Memorial Methodist Church, 1857, Milam at McK-inney

Figure 6.3. German immigrants in a wagon near Brenham, Texas, 1874. Drawing by J. Wells Champney, from Edward King, *The Great South: A Record of Journeys* (Hartford, Conn.: American Publishing Company, 1875).

Here we heard very bad accounts about Texas, and were advised not to go there, as it was said that Texas was infested with robbers, murderers, and ferocious Indians. But we were determined to risk it, and could not afford to disappoint our friends who had preceded us. As soon, therefore as we succeeded in chartering the schooner Sabine, about two weeks after we had landed in New Orleans, we sailed for Brazoria, Texas. After a voyage of eight days, we were wrecked off Galveston Island, on December 22, 1834 . . . it was about 10 miles from the present site of the city of Galveston.

The island was a perfect wilderness inhabited only by deer, wolves and rattlesnakes. All the passengers were safely brought to shore and were provided with provisions, partly from those on board ship and partly but the game on the island.

Two or three days after our vessel was beached, the steamer Ocean hoved in sight, and observing our distress signal, anchored opposite our camp and sent a boat ashore with an officer to find out the situation. The captain agreed to take two of us to Brazoria. . . . I, with . . . Roeder, took passage on it as an agent of the remaining passengers to charter a boat, to take them and their belongings to the main land.

Finding no boat at either Brazoria or Bell's Landing, the only Texas ports at that time, I proceeded on foot to San Felipe, where I was told I would find a small steamer. . . . I found the steamer, but . . . the price of $1000 asked for [was] too high. In San Felipe I heard for the first time of the whereabouts of my relatives who had preceded us. Here I also made the acquaintance of Colonel Johnson and Captain Moseley Baker, under whose command I afterward fought at the battle of San Jacinto. These gentlemen informed me that my two friends, Louis and Albert von Roeder, had located about 14 miles from San Felipe on a league of land, the present Cat Spring, but that [two others] had died. I found Louis and Albert in a miserable hut and in a pitiful condition. They were emaciated by disease and want of proper treatment and nourishment. Tears of joy streamed from their eyes when they beheld me and my companion.

After a few days of rest I continued my search for a boat. . . . Fortunately, I succeeded in chartering a small vessel from Mr. Scott . . . for three trips *to Galveston, for $100, and immediately returned to Galveston, landing on the bay side, opposite the camp of the stranded passengers, just four weeks after I had left it. I found all the passengers in good health and spirits. They had spent most of their time hunting and fishing. Those who could not shoot were employed to drive the deer to the hunters. There were deer by the thousands.*

The next day I left with the first cargo of passengers . . . after a stormy trip we arrived in the evening of the same day at Mr. Scott's place, where we were hospitably treated. I was fortunate to find quite a comfortable house in Harrisburg, which I rented, as we intended to remain there until all passengers had arrived from the island. The last passengers did not come until the fall of 1835, although I had hired another small sloop from Captain Smith in Velasco, that also made three trips. The winter of 1836 was unusually severe.[6]

John Reinermann was likely with the first group to be picked up by Kleberg and Scott, because he showed up in San Felipe on March 20, 1835, with his wife, stating in an application for land that he "wants to live about 11 miles below Wheatons on Buffalo Bayou near John Austin's two leagues on N. side of bayou."[7] The Reinermann headright of a league of land (4,338 acres) was not officially granted until February 20, 1838, following the hiatus from late 1835 to 1838 in the process of making land grants, a result of the tumultuous Texas War of Independence.[8] An additional labor of land (177 acres) was issued in June 1847; it was not adjacent to the league and was later sold.[9] Both league and labor were patented in March 1847, with an accompanying survey of the league by surveyor George Bringhurst.[10]

While the Reinermanns awaited the certificate for their land, their son John Jr. died in Harrisburg, in August 1835.[11] A few months later the Texas War of Independence began. The siege of Bexar started in December 1835, the Alamo fell in March 1836, and Harrisburg was burned to the ground on April 16. Where the newly arrived Reinermanns were during this time is unclear, although the approval of their land application in 1838 attests to the fact that they remained in Texas. It would seem likely that in the months preceding the onset of the siege of Bexar, John Reinermann and his family were beginning to clear and plant their land as they waited for their grant application to be approved. The men of the Kleberg family in Cat Springs, the former shipmates of the Reinermanns, joined with the Texian army at the siege of Bexar, but there is no record of John Reinermann having joined. At age sixty in early 1836, he was likely considered exempt.

After the battle of the Alamo in March 1836 the Texian women, children, old men and slaves took part in the frantic exodus of the Runaway Scrape of March–April 1836. It would seem very likely that the Reinermanns were part of that flight. Rosa Kleberg wrote that members of several families were with them as they fled from Cat Spring, but she did not name these families (Chapter 3). It was a difficult time, and many participants died from exposure. One thing only is certain: by the time the Reinermann headright grant was approved in 1838, John Reinermann was dead. He may have been buried at a family cemetery on their farm.[12] The aforementioned land grants were made to his widow and heirs.

The Reinermann league included the land where Memorial Park now lies, plus a considerable amount more to the north and east (Figure 6.2). John Reinermann's son Henry, single when he entered Texas with his parents in 1835, received one third of a league at the same time, immediately north of the John Reinermann tract; this was a standard headright grant for single men living in Texas before the Texas Revolution.[13] He was living on the Reinermann estate with his mother, Anna, in 1840.[14] Two years earlier, on March 17, 1838, they sold the southern half of the John Reinermann tract to McHenry Winburn, and its boundary was certified in a lawsuit between Winburn and the Reinermann family in 1849.[15]

The story of the Reinermann heirs is intricate. Anna Reinermann appears to have passed away by the early 1840s. In December 1840 John Reinermann's German-born son Henry Reinermann (1808–1844)—apparently his only heir—married

Figure 6.4. Preliminary sketch for "The pioneer cowpen," by Texas German frontier artist Friedrich Richard Petri (1824–1857). Friedrich Richard Petri collection, Image di04969, Dolph Briscoe Center for American History, the University of Texas at Austin

Louisa Margarette Agnes Schiermann (1813–1867), of Hanover, Germany. Louisa had been married twice previously and was a mother of two children, named Anna Maria Louisa Gerding (1836–1916) and Frederick Hobein (ca. 1838–1862). It is not apparent from the German historical record that these were recognized marriages.[16] She arrived in Houston with her children in 1839. Henry legally adopted the two children in 1841 and changed their surname to Reinermann, in order to enable them to inherit his property. Henry died in 1844, and Louisa married Joseph Sandman in 1845. In April 1846, they had twins, Joseph Jr. (1846–1867) and Josephine (1846–1848). Louisa's husband Joseph Sr. died that same year of 1846, and Louisa then married Christian Lodovic Bethje (1822–1876) in 1847. Finally, Louisa had found a (fifth) husband with whom she would grow old; she and Christian were married until her death in 1867. The Bethjes had four daughters, two of whom, Bertha (b. 1850) and Eliza, married and had children.[17]

By 1850, in the survey of agriculture in the 1850 U.S. Census, Christian and Louisa Bethje's farm had 20 improved and 2,194 unimproved acres, for a total land value of $2,250. They had 3 horses and 4 working oxen, with other livestock including 60 milk cows, 140 beeves, and 60 hogs, valued in total at $120. They raised corn, as nearly everyone did, and harvested 400 bushels of it from about 8 cultivated acres. It was a reasonably prosperous farm. In addition, Christian Bethje built a sawmill along White Oak Bayou.

In 1849 Louisa, now the legal guardian of the two minor Reinermann heirs (her children), petitioned the District Court to replace the old John Reinermann log home and pay for it from the heirs' trust.[18] The newer home was probably built near the old one, and the family was living in the new home by the time of the Civil War. On August 23, 1865, some errant Union soldiers of the First Texas Cavalry attempted to rob the family, and one was killed in an ensuing gunfight (the story is told in Chapter 8).

A 1915 *Houston Chronicle* story featured the old house, including its scars resulting from the 1865

Figure 6.5. Louisa Bethje's house of ca. 1849 in Cottage Grove, Houston, at about 5302 Darling Street, as it looked in 1915, before it fell to urbanization in the 1920s. Houston Chronicle, August 4, 1915.

gunfight (Figure 6.5). The house was at 5306 Darling Street in the twentieth-century Cottage Grove subdivision.[19] The Reinermann house, by 1905 sold and abandoned by the family, was left stranded when the Cottage Grove subdivision was carved out of surrounding farmland, and the house was slated for demolition until a man named John L. Bryant, recognizing its age, purchased it to restore and live in it:

> *"Born in Houston, I wanted to save this relic of the past. I bought it. It cost me about $80. I have patched it up in spots. I had to preserve it. But mostly I have left it just as it was. . . .*
>
> *"This house will be here when houses that ain't built yet are gone . . . look at those joints. She's pinned all through—built like a ship. That weatherboard was ripped out by hand. The only nails used were old cut-iron nails. You don't see 'em any more. Look at those rafter poles. You could search Texas today and you couldn't find 'em like that. They're hard as flint. You can't drive a nail in 'em. And the sills are one piece, 40 and 50 feet long. See, they're hand-hewed. You don't get 'em like that these days. . . ."*
>
> *Mr. Bryant then led the way to an old well. It is maybe four feet across. Its stagnant, dark water looks fifty feet down. Probably no water has been drawn from it in years. "Mrs. Brunner fell down this well when she was a baby," he explained. "But they fished her out. Her name was Bertha Bethje [daughter of Louisa Schiermann Reinermann Sandman Bethje]. When she grew up she married Antoine Brunner . . . Mr. and Mrs. Brunner are living still. . . .*
>
> *"Here is my abstract of title to the place. It shows that on June 18, 1847, E. Simmler, Justice of the Peace, united in marriage Christian Lodovic Bethje and Louisa Sandman.*
>
> *"Do you know, this place was way out in the country for a long time. It used to be hunting ground in my memory. And in the days it was a farm, heaps of fine watermelons were raised out here. . . . Then one day they platted the place off in*

village lots. . . . Since then 1000 people have drifted in to make their homes. Odd are the ways of the world."[20]

In spite of John Bryant's efforts to maintain the home, the house was destroyed in the 1920s. The story of the house's identity is given credence by the reference to Bertha Bethje, who was still alive at the time the newspaper article was written, and by the number of bullet holes in the home that were pointed out by Bryant at the time of his interview; they evidenced the robbery attempt and gunfight of 1865.

A family cemetery, on Inker Street adjacent to the Houston and Texas Central Railroad tracks, was left out of the Cottage Grove development but was finally sold in 1910, with a proviso that the bodies be reinterred elsewhere.[21] Louisa Bethje, who died in 1867, and her son with Joseph Sandman, Joseph Jr. (1846–1867), are both buried in Glenwood Cemetery, along with Louisa's last husband Christian Bethje, who died in 1876.[22] Because the burials of Louisa and Joseph Jr. predate the formation of Glenwood Cemetery in 1867, it is likely that they were reinterred from the family burial plot in Cottage Grove. Moreover, their deaths in 1867 coincide with a severe yellow fever epidemic that left 492 dead in nearby Houston, a quarantine imposed, and a shortage of coffins.[23]

Thomas Habermacher and the Habermacher settlement

In the autumn of 1844 Price Carl of Solms, a German nobleman touring frontier Texas, was heading eastward and paid a visit:

Saturday, October 5th. Left 5 minutes to five. On to Old Habermacher, an Alsatian, his wife was born in Turin. A pleasant area, flat prairie aspect. 28 miles. Rested until 1:30. Then another 16 miles to Houston. The pony became lame, no willpower.[24]

"Old" Habermacher, indeed. Thomas Habermacher (1777–ca. 1848) was about sixty-seven years old when that visit took place, quite an advanced age even in a city of the era but especially so in frontier Texas. Ethnically German, he was born in Alsace, a German-speaking province of France that has been sometimes French and sometimes German. He married his wife Mary Ann (ca. 1782–after 1850) sometime before 1814; she was from Sardinia. While in Alsace the couple had six children: Stephen (1814–after 1880), Joseph (ca. 1817–1882), Casper (1820–1883), Lawrence (1822–1895), John (1825–ca. 1853), and Catherine (1827–1900). They emigrated from Alsace to Pennsylvania in about 1827, where two more sons were born: Thomas (1828–after 1910) and Peter (1831–after 1884). The 1830 census shows them living in Cambria County, Pennsylvania, east of Pittsburgh.[25] By June 1834 the Thomas Habermacher family had moved to Fort Bend County. At this time he was working at William Stafford's cotton gin on Oyster Creek in Brazoria County. Mrs. Dilue Rose Harris, who grew up in frontier Harrisburg and in Stafford's Point on Oyster Creek in Brazoria County, recalled meeting two of the Habermachers at the Rose home on Oyster Creek in May 1834. At that time, there had been reports of a runaway slave in the neighborhood. Young Dilue's father and brother were away in Harrisburg, and she and the rest of her family were kept up during the night by the barking of dogs, as the desperate slave raided their chicken coop. When her mother finally got to sleep, near dawn, there was another interruption:

She had slept only a few minutes when there was another commotion among the dogs. It was daylight. We could see between an opening between the logs two men with a cart and oxen, and mother opened the door. The travelers were Germans, Mr. Habermacher and son, Stephen, from Harrisburg, going to Mr. Stafford's to work on the cotton gin [at Stafford's Point, on the Brazos River, where several cotton planters had settled]. It was a great relief to see them. They had met father, and he said he would be home the next day. The old gentleman [Thomas Habermacher] could not speak English, but the son could. They had camped near our house and had heard the dogs and thought they were after game. They said the [runaway] negro must have heard them, as they were singing. The Germans stayed with us till Uncle James came home. They expected to have gotten to our house by eight o'-clock, but could not see the house.[26]

Those were hardscrabble years for the Habermachers, according to a biography of Peter L. Habermacher, son of Thomas Habermacher's son Casper. The then young Casper and the rest of the Habermacher family in those years

were in very straightened circumstances, and the family labored at anything they could find to do, such as picking cotton, corn, etc. Frequently Casper would labor at cotton picking, obtain a little corn in this way and carry it on his back ten miles to the mill to have it ground into meal. Thus the family existed for some time, but through their energy and perserverance, better times soon came to them and they began farming on their own account.

The family were in the "run away" from the Mexicans in 1834 [should be 1836]. Mr. Habermacher harnessed a yoke of oxen to a slide on which he placed their beds and the bedding and such of the children that could not walk, and the remainder of the family made their way on foot to a place of safety.[27]

By 1841 Thomas Habermacher shows up on the Harris County tax rolls, living just off the San Felipe wagon road on 107 acres of the southern William Hardin League (Figure 6.2).[28] His house would have been somewhere in the vicinity of the intersection of modern Briar Forest and Dairy Ashford streets in west Houston. Several travelers on the San Felipe trail in the mid-1840s mention stopping at his farm.

His adult sons began to acquire property in the area, establishing their own farms. Thomas Habermacher died in about 1848, and by 1850 the U.S. Census shows five Habermacher households in the area, including that of his widow, Mary Ann. These farms extended from the Thomas Habermacher farm in the northeast to Joseph Habermacher's place in what is now Barker Reservoir. The vicinity became known as the Habermacher Settlement.[29] The early Habermacher Settlement residents were as follows:

Stephen Habermacher married Anne Sophia Coates (b. 1828) in 1846, and was living in 1850 with his brother Peter Habermacher. He was listed as a farmer and by this time worked 12 out of a total 150 acres owned at the settlement. As listed in the 1850 federal census of agriculture, he had about 3 or 4 acres in corn, yielding 150 bushels a year, a horse, 9 milk cows, 15 beeves and 17 hogs. His farm was worth $200, plus $75 in farm equipment and $175 in livestock. He was a Harris County overseer of a portion of the San Felipe wagon road in 1844. Eventually he sold this farm, and resettled in Fort Bend County.[30]

Lawrence Habermacher married Amanda Jane Wheaton (1825–before 1854), the daughter of Elizabeth and Joel Wheaton, their nearest neighbors at Wheaton's Ford to the south (Figure 6.2). In 1850 they were just starting their farm, and had 5 improved acres out of 369 owned. They had one horse, 5 milk cows, fourteen beeves, and 25 hogs. Their corn crop made 120 bushels from about 2 to 3 acres under cultivation. The value of their farm was reported at $500, plus $125 in equipment and $140 in livestock. The Habermacher couple had two children: Amanda (b. 1851), and George (b. 1854). In 1854, following the death of Amanda Jane, Lawrence married a second time, to Jane Hall, and this couple had two children: Sarah (b. 1856), and Frank (b. 1860). By 1899 a widowed Jane Habermacher lived on 11 acres of the old Wheaton survey and received a Confederate soldier's pension.[31]

Casper Habermacher, also a farmer in 1850, married Eliza Jane Coates (b. 1825) in 1844 and by 1850 had two children, Mary Ann (b. ca. 1846) and Susan (b. ca. 1848). Mary Ann became good friends with Mary Jarvis Silliman in the late 1860s, and Silliman saved her portrait (Figure 6.6). In 1850 Casper Habermacher had about 8 acres in corn yielding 400 bushels a year, 3 horses, 2 oxen, 30 milk cows, 70 beeves and 20 hogs. He farmed 33 improved acres out of 100 owned. His farm was worth $1,000–the higher amount than that of Stephen's farm probably reflects the greater number of improved acres–plus

$100 in equipment and $675 in livestock. Casper eventually moved to Austin County, where he was a prosperous rancher.

John Habermacher (1825–ca. 1853) and Arthemise McFarland married in 1849; her family had a neighboring farm in 1850. They had no children in 1850, and there is no record of their property, so it is likely that John was working the farm of a brother (probably that of Casper, who had a much larger improved acreage than the others). The same could be said for the youngest brother, Thomas Jr. (1828–after 1910), who was living in 1850 with his mother, Mary Habermacher, then 68 years old.

Catherine Habermacher (1827–1900), a daughter of Thomas and Mary, married William Henry Baker, a member of a local family. They were not in the Habermacher Settlement but lived along Buffalo Bayou a mile or so southeast of Thomas Habermacher's original house.[32]

Joseph Habermacher (ca. 1817–1882), Thomas's son, initially stayed behind in Pennsylvania when his parents moved to Texas in 1841. Joseph married a Pennsylvania woman named Petronilla Rutler (1813–1861) and had started a family. But he, his wife and four Pennsylvania-born children moved to Texas in 1846, and their last child was born there in 1847.[33] Joseph claimed 160 acres of vacant land on the western rim of what is now Barker Reservoir in 1851, on a small brook then called Waterhole Gully (later named Mason Creek), and after three years residing on this land and cultivating it, he had it surveyed in 1854 for a State of Texas homestead "donation" grant. His application was certified in July 1858 by Harris County Chief Justice (and local flour miller) Charles Shearn. The land was granted officially on September 15, 1860, by local rancher and then Harris County Chief Justice J. S. Stafford (item 1, Figure 6.2).[34] Joseph was probably the first resident on the bald prairie land that was to become Barker Reservoir. By 1880 he was the postmaster at Habermacher Settlement.[35] By that time, in addition to the post office and dwellings, the Habermacher Settlement had a church, a school, and a train depot (Habermacher Station on the old Texas Western narrow gauge railway; see Chapter 11). The post office was discontinued in 1881, as the town declined.[36]

Figure 6.6. Mary Ann Habermacher (b. 1846) as a young woman (the back of the photo reads "Mae Habermacher"). She was a daughter of Casper Habermacher, and a friend of Mary Jarvis Silliman, who saved the portrait. Courtesy of the late Mrs. Arch B. Marshall.

The early sojourn in Pennsylvania, before the Thomas Habermachers came to Texas, tugged mightily at the heartstrings of the extended family, especially when the Civil War came. As just noted, Joseph had not come to Texas immediately when the rest of the Thomas Habermacher family left Pennsylvania in 1834, but had stayed behind and married Petronilla Ellen Rotter Rutler (1813–1861), who was born in England. Their four children born in Pennsylvania were Thomas M. (1836–1864), Mary Ellen (1838–1914), Susanna (1838–1926), and Theresa (1844–1881). In about 1846 the Joseph Habermacher family left Pennsylvania to follow Joseph's parents to Texas, where Joseph's last child, John Charles (1847–1923) was born on Buffalo Bayou in Harris County, probably at the Thomas Habermacher home. Both of Joseph's sons, Thomas M. and John Charles Habermacher, returned to Pennsylvania with their mother at about the time that the war started, for schooling. Petronilla died there in 1861. Young Thomas became a Union soldier during the war and died in battle (Chapter 8). John Charles returned to Texas from Pennsylvania after the Civil War and became postmaster of Quinan, Fort Bend County, before owning the Shiner Gazette newspaper in Lavaca County.[37]

The nursery of James Crawford and Karl Kolbe

Just west of present day Interstate 610 on the north side of Buffalo Bayou, in a small and little-visited part of Memorial Park, an early settler from Tennessee named James Crawford started Houston's first plant nursery, which was later purchased by early German immigrant Karl Kolbe and his wife. The farm was on the north bank of Buffalo Bayou, sandwiched between John Reinermann's League on the east and the German settlement of Spring Branch to the west (Figure 6.2).

James Johnson Crawford (1811–1844) had traveled to Texas his birthplace in Williamson County, Tennessee, arriving in newly founded Houston around 1837. At some time between 1839 and 1843 he entered into a contract for a sale agreement with Isaac Brashear, for 100 acres in the Wharton survey that Brashear had bought in 1837.[38] Crawford's aim was to found a nursery for the new town of Houston, importing plant stock from his home in central Tennessee. From 1839 to 1843 Crawford made several plant collecting and purchasing trips back to Tennessee, and while there in 1841 he married Elizabeth T. Hogan, in Davidson County.[39] He then brought Elizabeth and his widowed and remarried mother, Elizabeth Crenshaw (1787–1854), to frontier Texas. They settled in at their new farm and, with the help of four slaves, built several cabins, cleared some of the land, and planted their nursery stock. This was likely the first plant nursery in Houston.[40]

Houston was beset with an epidemic during a very wet August 1844. A fever "similar to yellow fever" had caused a number of deaths, among them James Crawford, who died on August 22, and his wife Elizabeth, who may have died slightly earlier.[41] One of their slaves appears to have died at the same time. James's half-brother, Charles D. Crenshaw, administered the estate, preparing the inventory and readying the property for sale. Besides the 100 acres, the couple had left behind several cabins and "considerable" fencing, farm animals, farm equipment, household items, some Windsor chairs, and a library of five books. When listed for sale in the Houston Telegraph and Texas Register in November 1844, the farm was described as a lot of 100 acres,

> *on which is a small farm of about ten acres, enclosed and in cultivation, with a variety of fruit trees: 10 kinds of peaches, 3 plumbs, 2 cherrys, 3 apples, 3 raspberrys, strawberrys, figs, oranges, pomegranates, shaddocks [a type of grapefruit], quineys, lemons, almonds, 11 kinds of rose, 6 flower shrubs, pinks, herbs, sage, rhue, thime, horse radish, worm wood, balm teney, hops &c &c. This tract of land is about six miles above the city of Houston, on the North bank of Buffalo bayou–is heavily timbered–has 2 fine springs, well calculated for a spring house.*[42]

James Crawford had indeed been busy during his five-year ownership of the property. The property was purchased by William Lyons in December 1844, and he sold it on to Karl Kolbe only eighteen months later.[43]

Karl Julius Kolbe (1819–1894) was born in Gotha, Theuringen, Germany. In December 1845, in Antwerp Belgium, he purchased 160 acres of Texas land near Fredericksburg and signed an immigration contract with the Society for the Protection of German Immigrants to Texas.[44] He and his brother Bernhard Kolbe left from Antwerp on the Hamilton that same month, arriving in Galveston in early 1846.[45] His brother Bernhard died, and Kolbe thought the better of moving to central Texas; he sold the Fredericksburg land.[46] As noted earlier, on July 3, 1846, Karl Kolbe bought the former Crawford property for $125 from William Lyons, who as noted had owned it only briefly, with a promise from Lyon to remove persons "presently living and renting" there. In January 1850 Kolbe married Dorothea

Figure 6.7. Karl and Dorothea Kolbe. Photographs courtesy of Nelda Blackshere Reynolds.

Durkop (1826–1885), another recent German immigrant (Figure 6.7), and the couple were counted in the 1850 federal census. In that year's agricultural census, their farm was evaluated as follows: five acres cultivated out of a total landholding of 25 acres; one horse, two oxen, 9 milk cows, 15 beeves and 10 hogs. They had raised 100 bushels of corn. Their land was valued at $100, plus $40 in equipment and $200 in livestock. It was a start.

In 1852 the Kolbes left the old Crawford farm and moved upstream to an 84-acre plot on the A. M. Osbourne survey (Figures 6.2 and 4.10) purchased from George Bringhurst. That property lay between Spring Branch Creek to the north and Briar Creek to the south. Karl later purchased an additional 75 acres on the Osbourne Survey from George Schmidt as well as 250 acres of the adjacent Taylor League, from William A. Morse.[47] The Osborne and the northern Taylor tracts lay within what later became known as the community of Spring Branch. It has been widely and erroneously reported that Karl Kolbe "arrived in Spring Branch in 1830" and that he thus founded the German community of Spring Branch,[48] but as mentioned earlier he only came to Texas in 1846, and by the time he took up residence in the Osborne survey in 1852 there were a number of other pioneer German families in the area (see below).

Karl and Dorothea Kolbe had four sons and three daughters between 1850 and 1865: Frank Charles Kolbe (1850-1922), Mary Kolbe Peters (1852-1932), Elizabeth Kolbe Fries (1854-1927), Annie Kolbe Minster (1856-1931), Louis L. Kolbe (1859-1930), Charles Kolbe (1860-1934), and Henry August Kolbe (1865-1938).[49]

In 1852, Kolbe sold 75 acres of the old Crawford farm to Henry Vollmer, a German immigrant who settled in the White Oak area (more on that settlement below).[50] Kolbe retained the 25 acres with the cabins, nursery and gardens, however, and rented the place out to persons who maintained the nursery plants. By the federal census of 1870 it was being rented by Martha Rodgers, a widow from Alabama, with her three children; her husband, Col. William P. Rodgers, had died a hero's death at the Civil War Battle of Corinth (Chapter 8). Karl Kolbe held that property until 1888, when he sold it to Frederick Minster (d. 1908), a gardener who became manager of the Fred and Fritz Weber Grocery and Dry Goods Store on Washington Avenue, where farm produce was marketed.[51] Fred was the husband of Karl Kolbe's daughter Annie. The Minster's produce was also marketed in the market stalls at Market Square (the old City Hall Square) in downtown Houston (Figure 6.8). The Minsters sold their nursery to A. C. Tenzler in 1894.[52]

Spring Branch Community

Before discussing the history of the pioneer German community of Spring Branch, which developed to the west of the early Reinermann and Kolbe properties, it is perhaps useful to define the boundaries of the place. Spring Branch today is considered a "district" of greater Houston, an area that is bounded on its south by Interstate 10, to the east by Loop 610 and Hempstead Highway, to the west by Addicks Reservoir, and to the north by Tanner Road. In frontier times the area of Spring Branch more closely resembled that of the modern Spring Branch School District, which includes the land just described but also extends south to the northern bank of Buffalo Bayou. In the 1950s an effort was made to join this large area into a formally incorporated government entity as a defense against incorporation into the growing city of Houston, but that effort failed, resulting in a number of small villages being formed. These modern "Memorial villages," each of which was part of the greater Spring Branch area of pioneer days, include Bunker Hill Village, Hedwig Village, Hilshire Village, Spring Valley Village, and the majority parts of Hunters Creek Village and the City of Piney Point Village that lie north of Buffalo Bayou. Spring Branch also includes portions of what is now the City of Houston. An approximate outline of what is here described as pioneer Spring Branch is shown encircled by a heavy gray line in the map of Figure 6.9 A.

Starting in the Republic of Texas era, a few hardy German pioneers entered the area, and that migration became a flood as Europe tilted toward war in the late 1840s. Most arriving Germans who stayed in Harris County settled in the northwestern part of the county, along Spring and Cypress creeks, but a significant number were to settle on the northern bank of Buffalo Bayou in three distinct rural German settlements: from west to east, they were Bear Creek, Spring Branch, and White Oak. The land in the Spring Branch area was somewhat less flood prone than in either Bear Creek or White Oak. Only one stream of any size transected the Spring Branch area, a tributary of Buffalo Bayou. A

Figure 6.8. Houston's market house, 1874. Drawing by J. Wells Champney, from King, *The Great South*.

story is told that a surveyor asked Karl Kolbe the name of the stream, and he replied, "Spring Branch," because the tributary was fed by a spring.[53] That name began to be applied to the surrounding area. There were large riparian forests along the gullies and low cliffs that surrounded both Buffalo Bayou and Spring Branch and dense stands of pine in a large expanse of upland forest north of the bayou (Figure 6.9 B). Settlers immediately took advantage of the forest, operating a number of early sawmills and then establishing farms on cleared forest land. Farther north was tallgrass prairie with abundant grass for livestock; several pioneer settlers soon established dairy farms. The area was reasonably close to Washington Road, the preferred route to Houston for selling produce and mill products.

Following John Reinermann's lead in settling the area just east of Spring Branch in 1834, four families settled in Spring Branch by 1848: Schroeder (1839), Ahrenbeck and Bauer (1847), and Rummel (1848), with the Kolbes living nearby by 1846. By the time of the 1850 federal census, there were thirteen German households in the area, with 37 adults and 26 children. Nearly all were farmers on small holdings, with the exception of two teachers (even in this sparsely settled pioneer area), two blacksmiths and

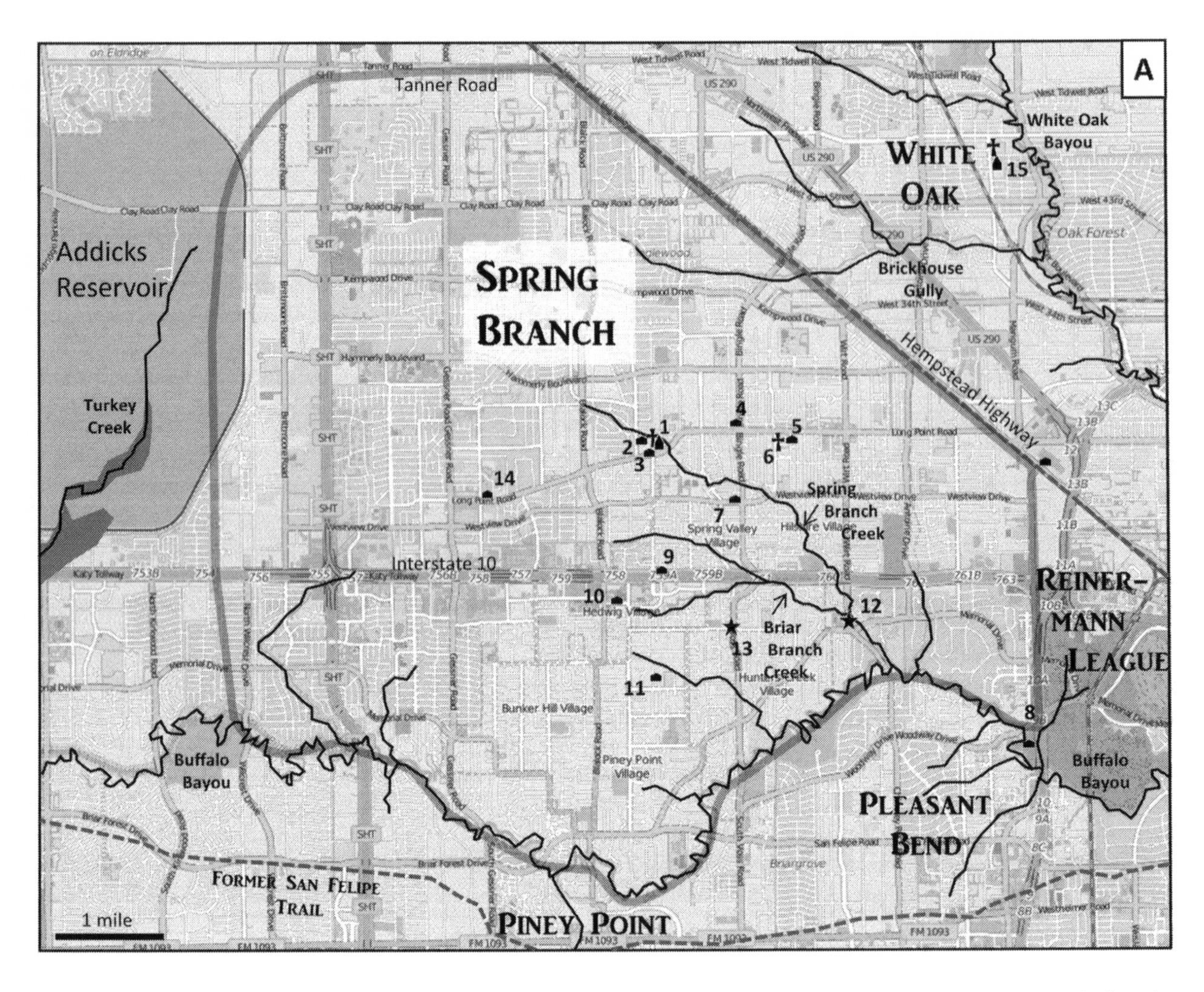

Figure 6.9. Maps of the pioneer Spring Branch community. **A:** Modern base map with locations of former home sites of selected early settlers as well as the St. Peter Church. The thick gray line shows the approximate areal extent of the nineteenth century Spring Branch community, which is grossly equivalent in area to that of the modern Spring Branch School District. **B:** Same area, showing an interpretation of natural features and roads as they existed in the nineteenth century. Locations of forested areas as well as wagon tracks are modified slightly from the U. S. Geological Survey topographic map of 1915.

one baker. The pioneer families of this time, listed on the 1850 census, included Ahrenbeck, App, Bleke, Diederick, Pifer, Hillendahl, Kreuse, Luedge, Look, Bauer, Proetzle, Rummel, and Schroeder. The Kolbes moved into Spring Branch proper in 1852 from their nursery farm at the old Crawford place. By 1856 the graveyard of St. Peter Church—the central pioneer cultural organization in Spring Branch, of which more later—contained burials from families named Bauer, Beinhorn, Beutel, Deumeland, Eichler, Feuerschuetz, Hillendahl, Holm, Koehn, Neuen, Oberpriller, Ojeman, Proetzel, Reichardt, Rummel, Sauer, Schaper, Schroeder, Schultz, Spanuth, Struebing, Tappenbeck, Throing, and Williamsen.[54]

Most of the earliest homes were built near either the Spring Branch or Briar Branch tributaries of Buffalo Bayou, for access to water. Later farmsteads were placed farther from water and used hand-dug wells. Unlike the Anglo and African American communities south of Buffalo Bayou, residents of which visited Houston by traveling the San Felipe Trail, Spring Branch residents used Washington Road (now Hempstead Highway) to market their farm produce in Houston. A system of wagon tracks con-

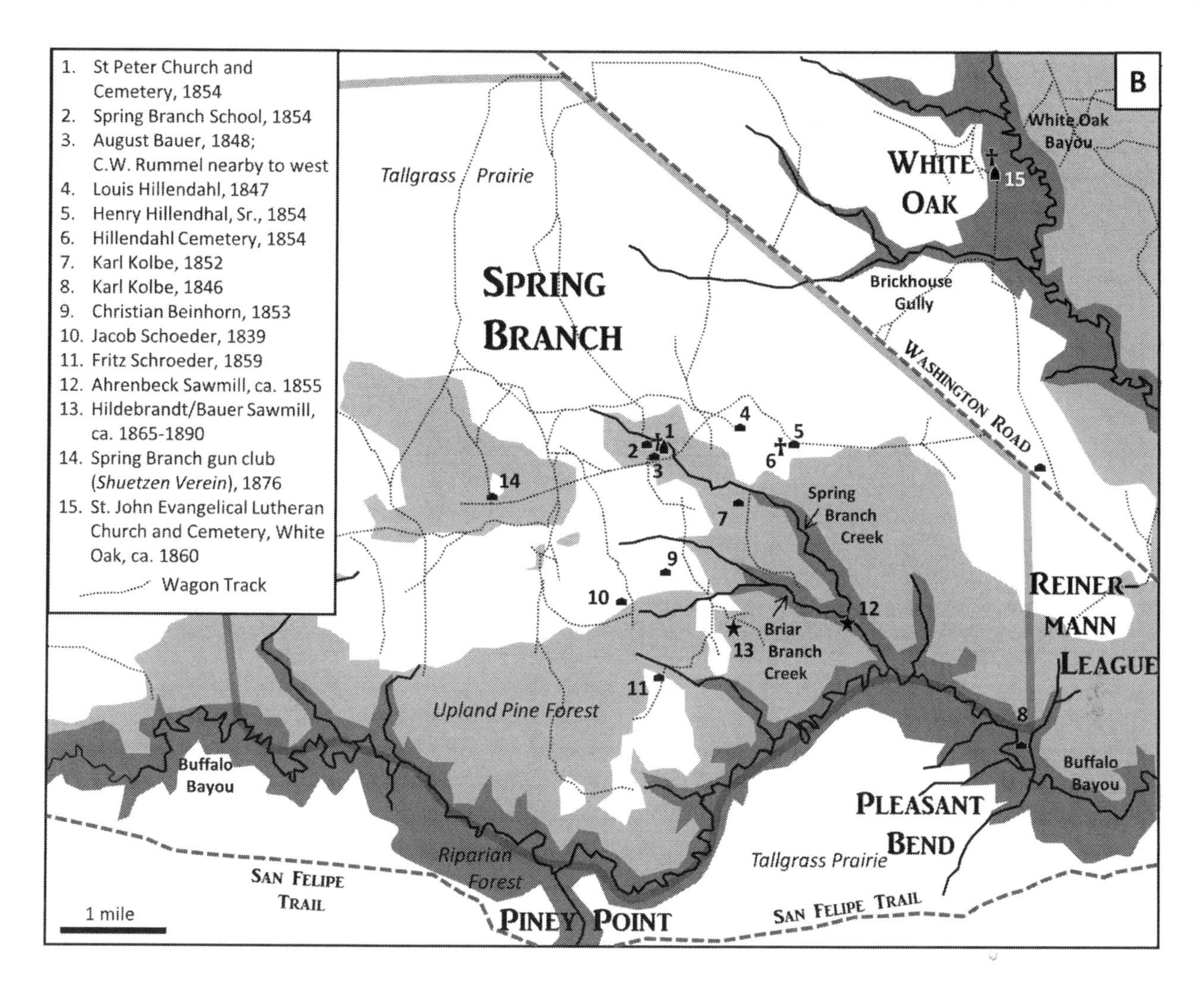

nected that road, the early settlers' homes, and St. Peter Church; those tracks are shown in Figure 6.9 B. The locations of the tracks were taken from a U.S. Geological Survey topographical map of 1915, which was surveyed when the area was still rural. The web-like appearance of this system of tracks is starkly different from the rectilinear grid of roads in use today (compare Figures 6.9 A and B). Before the advent of barbed wire fencing in the late nineteenth century, property boundaries were usually unfenced, and uncultivated areas were part of the open range, so wagon tracks were haphazard in plan and tended to follow natural terrain features. After about 1890, modern and largely straight east-west and north-south roads were built that followed equally rectilinear property boundaries.

The Jacob Schroeder family, 1839. The earliest known European inhabitants of Spring Branch were Jacob and Dorothea Schroeder. Jacob Schroeder (ca. 1804–1888; Figure 6.10) was born in Braunschweig, Lower Saxony, Germany, according to the 1870 federal census. On February 19, 1839, he arrived in the three-year-old frontier town of Houston to apply for a third class Republic of Texas land grant for 640 acres; this land was officially granted to him by the Bureau of Land Commissioners for Harris County in 1842, although he had probably been living on it since the date of his application.[55] Third class Republic of Texas land grants were issued for persons arriving in Texas between October 1, 1837, and January 1, 1840. Heads of families were eligible for 640 acres and single men were eligible for 320 acres.[56] Schroeder may have been in Texas as early as 1838, when a Jacob Schroeder, perhaps the same person, took a trip from Galveston to New Orleans on the sailing ship *Cuba*.[57]

Figure 6.10. Some Spring Branch pioneers. Top Row, left to right: Jacob Schroeder and Carl Wilhelm Rummel. Bottom row: Carl Siegismund Bauer and Christiane Caroline Bauer. Images courtesy of Evelyn Schroeder Kingsbury, the Round Top Area Historical Society, Inc., and Melanie Parkett.

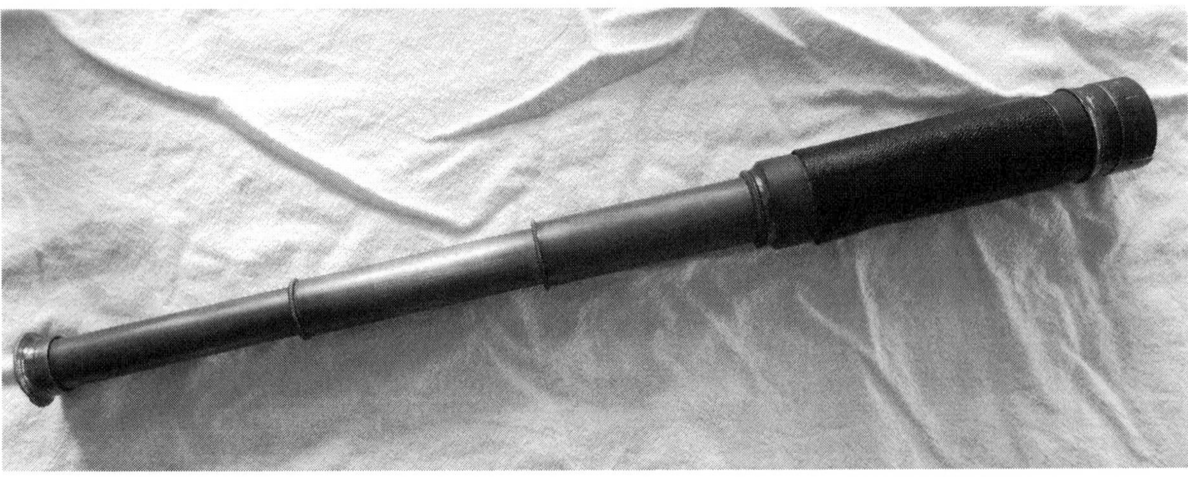

Figure 6.11. A frontier emergency warning system: Jacob Schroeder's small telescope, approximately 16 inches in length. Courtesy of Evelyn Schroeder Kingsbury.

Jacob Schroeder was in Houston again in 1840, when he was one of 53 Harris County German inhabitants to form the German Society of Texas, the first such German heritage organization in the state. Joining with him was a William Schroeder, of whom nothing else is known.[58]

His wife Dorothea Schroeder (b. ca. 1798) was also from Germany, according to the 1850 federal census, which lists two sons born in Germany, Frederick in 1833 and Heinrich, born ca. 1837. From this we can conclude that the family arrived in Texas no earlier than 1837, and certainly no later than 1839. Jacob's wife was listed as "Katrina" by the census taker, but she was called Dorothea in family records and in legal documents of 1858 that she signed, discussed later.

Family lore has it that Jacob initially built a log cabin. According to descendant Ida Schroeder Warwick, that home was located on the Isaac Bunker survey, on a small farm lane near where modern Blalock Street intersects Interstate 10 (Figure 6.9). According to his great-granddaughter, Jacob lived at that site into his old age; his grandson Henry Hillendahl (1864–1940) often brought him food there from Fritz Schroeder's home nearby, of which more later.[59] In December 1848 the newly immigrated families of Carl Bauer and Carl Rummel arrived in Spring Branch by ox cart from Galveston—where they had just arrived by ship from Germany—and stayed in the Schroeder home. They had stopped first at a temporary dwelling built by Carl Bauer's son, August Bauer, the previous year. August had arrived earlier to prepare the way but fell ill from malaria. August's small dwelling was located to the southwest of where St. Peter United Church of Christ is today, on modern Long Point Drive. According to Carl Rummel's descendant Lena Rummel,

> *[The families'] first disappointment was that there was no house for them, except an old weather-beaten shack, too small for both families. The roof leaked and when an icy cold, wet norther blew up, they found it disagreeable and cold. But after the third day, they found better quarters in the home of Mr. Jacob Schroeder.*[60]

Schroeder's home was their only nearby alternative; the area was a wilderness. In 1850, the Federal census taker estimated the value of the Schroeder family's total holdings as $100; it was a tenuous start. Ten years later, when Jacob Schroeder's holdings were examined as part of the Agricultural Schedule of the 1860 census, he owned farmland worth $100, farm equipment worth $50, and livestock worth $350, so things were slowly improving. Those livestock included three horses, ten milk cows, four working oxen, thirty-six sheep, and ten swine. He raised 80 bushels of corn that year. Jacob, like nearly all German immigrants, did not own slaves.

An artifact has survived from that era (Figure 6.11). Jacob Schroeder's small telescope was used as part of a frontier emergency warning system. At that time there was a clear line of site between Schroeders' place, the Rummel and Bauer homes, and St. Peter Church on Spring Branch Creek, because the intervening one to two miles consisted entirely of open prairie. The neighbors had an agreement to place a white flag on a pole and attach it to a fence if they needed help for any reason. Once or twice a day, Jacob would scan the horizon with this small telescope, checking up on his neighbors.[61]

In 1858 a significant and unpleasant event took place. In a legal transaction dated April 9, 1858, Jacob separated himself from his wife and two sons, Friederich (later "Fritz") and Heinrich.[62] To each son he deeded 100 acres plus $50 and a horse. To his wife he gave 100 head of cattle, one wagon, four yoke of oxen, and half of his stock of horses. The sons agreed henceforth to support their mother and not to make any further claims on their father or ask for any support from him. His wife Dorothea, for her part, agreed to make no further claims on Jacob's property and renounced any right to community property. It was a separation, in an age when divorce was not in the cards. One can wonder what caused

Figure 6.12. Dorothea and Jacob Schroeder, ca. 1865.
Courtesy of Evelyn Schroeder Kingsbury.

this—there is no further source of information than this agreement—but a clear potential factor was the stress caused by the poverty, disease and deprivation inherent in living with few resources on the edge of a wilderness. The Bauer and Rummel families wrote extensively on their own travails in the early years, which are discussed in the next section.

Almost immediately after this agreement was reached, Jacob began to sell land and buy more. Between 1858 and 1882 he sold about 29 small tracts of 11 to 75 acres to German immigrants, nearly all in the Isaac Bunker and Thomas Hoskins surveys in central Spring Branch (for reference, Figure 4.10 A shows the locations of early land grants).[63] Because Jacob's home is also reported to have been located on the Bunker tract, it seems safe to assume that Jacob's initial land was located in those two tracts and that he was selling parcels from it.

Whatever caused the separation of Jacob from his family, it seems eventually to have been mended. A surviving photograph shows the couple in their old age (Figure 6.12). Sometimes, things just work out.

On March 29, 1859, Jacob's son Fritz purchased 150 acres of the northern part of the John D. Taylor league for $200 from William Canfield (Buckman Canfield's son). That land was bounded by what later became Piney Point Road, Beinhorn Road, Smithdale Road, and (approximately) Hunters Park Lane. He later purchased another 100 acres to the south of this tract, from Canfield heirs.[64] Fritz Schroeder (1833–ca. 1903), Jacob and Dorothea's older son, was born in Germany, and married Dorathe Bleker (1842–1919), another German immigrant, in about 1860.[65] He soon built a frame house on that property, which against all odds has survived to the present day. That house was originally located on Fritz's property purchased in 1859, a few hundred feet north of Smithdale Road, near the cul de sac of modern Wexford Court (item 11, Figure 6.9). The single-story six room clapboard house contained cypress logs in its ceiling and was likely constructed with sawn timber from the nearby Rummel-Hildebrandt-Bauer sawmill. It was slated for demolition by developers in the early 1990s but was donated to the Memorial Villages Water Authority, and was moved a few blocks to their property at 435 Piney Point, where it rests today (see Chapter 12).[66] It is today almost certainly the oldest remaining home in Houston that is west of Shepherd Drive.

Fritz and Dorathe Schroeder had five children while living at that house, including Henry Schroeder, Fritz Schroeder Jr., Louis Schroeder, Elizabeth Schroeder Golbow, and Dora Schroeder Knigge. Henry (1864–1940) inherited the land and married Hedwig Jankowski (1887–1983). It was divided into five-acre lots and sold during the Depression. After Henry's death Hedwig donated land for what was named Hedwig Road in her honor, and modern Hedwig Village also bears her name.[67]

Dorothea Schroeder seems to have died at some time before 1870. She is missing in the census of that year, and sixty-six-year old Jacob was living only with a small boy named Joseph Bower (probably Bauer), whom Jacob was step-parenting.

Carl Bauer and William Rummel families, 1847 and 1848. Carl Siegismund Bauer (1792–1873) was born in Annaberg, Saxony, and married his wife Christiana Malzer (1791–1849) in 1813. The story of their wedding was perhaps not unusual for the time:

In 1813, much of Germany was involved with the Napoleonic wars in Europe. Carl was twenty-one years old at the time and his mother was worried that her only child would have to go to war. His mother thought that if Carl Siegismund were married, he would not have to go fight in the war. She invited a special girl over to the house, fixed a big meal and introduced Christiana Malzer to her son with hopes that he would propose to her. As time went on, Carl's mother saw that he was not proposing so she did it for him. She explained to Christiana that she could not bear to see her son go to war and if he were married he might not have to go. Christiana felt sorry for the mother and she accepted. Christiana and Carl were married three weeks later. They had eight children between the years 1813 and 1830, Charlotte, Carolina, Karl, Augustin, Christliebe, Wilhelmine, Carl Ergott, and Carl Traugott.[68]

By the 1840s Germany was at war again, this time with the revolutions of 1847–1849. Carl Bauer, perhaps influenced by letters from Karl Kolbe, sent his son Augustin (August) Bauer (1820-1854) to Texas so that he might avoid that war. August Bauer (1820–1854) and his wife Emilie Ficke (1818–1859) traveled to Texas in 1847 on the ship Franziska, landing at Galveston. August moved to the Spring Branch area near Kolbe, joining Daniel Ahrenbeck and Jacob Schroeder, two other new arrivals. August wrote favorable reviews of Texas in his letters to his parents in Germany. Carl Bauer at that time was operating an oil mill in Germany with his partner, Carl Wilhelm Rummel (1812–1867; Figure 6.10). Based on August's letters from Texas, the two partners sold their mill and decided to move there.[69] Carl Wilhelm Rummel had married Christiane Caroline Bauer (1816–1899), Carl Bauer's daughter, in 1836 (Figure 6.10).

On December 15, 1848, the sailing ship Neptune arrived in Galveston from Bremen, Germany, carrying a number of German immigrants, among them Carl Bauer, Christiana and their youngest three children, and Carl Wilhelm Rummel, Christiana, and two children, Emma and Carl William (variously called "William," "C. W.," or "Junior"). The trip had been an arduous one, as the ship had been blown off course by a hurricane and then becalmed for days. A number of passengers and crew perished of a scurvy-like disease.[70] The Bauers and Rummels immediately took a steamer for Houston, where they met Karl Kolbe, Daniel Ahrenbeck and Jacob Schroeder, who took them to August's land on Spring Branch Creek, north of Buffalo Bayou. Wilhelm Rummel's grandson relates the tale:

Somehow they got to Houston and there they found an old Jewish merchant who lived across the street from the market place. . . . The old merchant took them to [some] Spring Branch farmers who had sold their produce [Kolbe, Ahrenbeck, and Schroeder], and they offered to haul all their big oak chests and whatever they had to Spring Branch. All those who were able to walk would follow that ox wagon while the tired ones would ride awhile. When they arrived in Spring Branch, where St. Peter's Evangelical Lutheran Church now stands, my Grandfather and his brother-in-law asked them to stop their oxen and they told them to unload their belongings right there. They admired the beautiful oak trees, and a little further over were thirteen beautiful pine trees, and there they decided to live.[71]

They were at August's new farm, as Carl Bauer's grandson, Louis C. Rummel, related,

where they were cordially welcomed by . . . August Bauer, who had written so enthusiastically about Texas. The family hardly recognized their kinsman. He was pale and emaciated. That fever which so many of the early comers to Texas had contracted [malaria] had him in its grip for several months. August's little hut was entirely too small to harbor all the newly arrived kin. A man by the name of Schroeder offered to take care of them temporarily.[72]

Another grandson related again the story of the cold weather:

They came from a very cold country . . . and when they arrived at Spring Branch it was so warm and the sun was shining brightly and even some flowers were still blooming in the early part of December. What a wonderful country they said, it isn't even necessary to build a house; we will live under the trees. But they didn't know that in Texas the weather may change overnight or sometimes in a few hours. So two weeks later one of those cold ice northers came and two of the children almost froze to death and had to be washed with snowy sleet to bring them back to life. But the good neighbors were right there to help them and they gave them shelter until they had their log cabin finished.[73]

When they arrived, it is said that August Bauer, who had been appointed religious leader of the group, held a thanksgiving service. August and his wife Emilia Ficker Bauer purchased 110 acres, 10 in timber and 100 in prairie, on the south bank of Spring Branch in 1851 from George Bringhurst, a surveyor, for $153.75; this was the land he had been living on since his arrival in 1847. The Bauers later donated a small part of this land to St. Peter Church, which still rests there today (Figure 6.9).[74] Carl Wilhelm Rummel bought 45 acres of prairie and 10 acres of wooded land, which was adjacent to and west of the Bauer land and also on the south bank of Spring Branch Creek; here Carl Wilhelm built his log cabin.

These families had been in their new Spring Branch homes only a matter of months in 1849 when both families were struck down by malaria. Carl Wilhelm Rummel's son William later wrote:

1849 was an unusually wet year. It rained so much that it brought on a very unhealthful condition. The mosquitoes came in such droves that at night we could sleep only by keeping cover over us even during the hot summer time. One after another we were down with malaria, spending more time in bed than working. My father had a siege of eighteen months; we others from four to six months.

William Rummel's mother, Carolina Bauer Rummel, and wife of Carl Wilhelm Rummel, later wrote that:

All my family were down with malaria; I was the only one able to wait on them. I was so busy attending to them day and night, I had no time for the family washing. When they finally recovered, I took my soiled clothing of many weeks out to wash; and was heartsick to discover that all the clothes on the bottom of the heap had rotted from the damp. The rabbits had done much harm to the garden; but even more havoc had been wreaked by roving cattle and hogs, which broke down the fences and ate our beans and potatoes.[75]

Carl Siegismund Bauer's wife Christiana – Carolina's mother – was not to survive that epidemic of 1849, as her grandson, William Rummel, Jr. wrote:

The wife of Carl Siegismund Bauer, my dear grandmother, was sick of malaria for months. She was just able to walk when one of those cold northers blew up—she took a severe cold and took to her bed again, and never recovered; soon to be followed by our sweet little sister, Minna. The cooler weather eventually helped the other ailing ones and one by one they left their beds.[76]

Such were the travails of many early area pioneers. After the death of his wife, Carl Siegismund Bauer and two of his sons left Spring Branch in 1851 and moved to Round Top, where there was a larger German settlement. Carl was a stonemason, and helped build many of the limestone buildings in Round Top, where he died in 1873.[77] His son August Bauer remained in Spring Branch, along with the Carl Wilhelm Rummel family.

Soon after the Christmas season of 1849, the pioneer Spring Branch families cut logs for a church. The logs were somehow stolen (railroad tie-cutting crews for the nearby Houston and Texas Central Railroad, being built along Washington Road, were suspected), but new logs were cut and stored at Wil-

Figure 6.13. A gathering of the congregation in front of St. Peter Church, March 29, 1907. Courtesy of Nelda Blackshere Reynolds.

helm Rummel's place, and by 1854 a log cabin church named for St. Peter was completed, on a quarter-acre plot donated by Carl Wilhelm Rummel and his wife. An additional four acres were donated by August Bauer and his wife. When the log church was damaged by fire in 1864, it was replaced with a frame church using sawn lumber from a sawmill that had been built by a man named McGuffey, where Carl Wilhelm Rummel and his son worked.[78] That church, still standing, is the St. Peter United Church of Christ (formerly St. Peter Evangelical Lutheran Church), near the intersection of Campbell and Long Point (Figure 6.13). It became the centerpiece for the frontier community. A school was started at the church as early as 1854, to be replaced only in 1889 by the community's first public school.[79]

August Bauer died of yellow fever in 1854, during an epidemic that wiped out thirty-six members of the St. Peter Church's congregation, all of whom were buried in the church's cemetery. August Bauer's wife Emilie remarried, her new husband a man named Kurtz who was deeply in debt. Emilie had a hard life; she died in 1859.[80]

Most of the German families who settled Spring Branch were subsistence farmers, and Carl Wilhelm and Christiana Rummel were no exception. By the agricultural census of 1850, they had 2 improved acres out of a total of 50 that they owned. They had one horse and two oxen, 3 milk cows, 15 beeves and ten hogs. They raised 50 bushels of corn. Their farm was worth $62 in land, $40 for equipment, and $110 in livestock. It was a tenuous but hopeful start. Such a frontier life, living off farm produce with few other fallback options and an ever-present threat of disease, is today difficult for most of us to imagine. William Rummel described their farming activities and mishaps in the early years:

Grandfather [Bauer] and my father [Carl Wilhelm] bought a pair of half-tame oxen, for which

Figure 6.14. Preliminary sketch for "Going Visiting," by Texas pioneer artist Friederich Richard Petri (1824-1857). Friedrich Richard Petri collection, Image di10669, Dolph Briscoe Center for American History, the University of Texas at Austin.

they paid $28.00, and a very light wagon for $21.00. When spring came, we were busy preparing ground for a garden and putting fences around it, but these were not strong enough. There were many rabbits, and they ate all our beans and sweet potato vines, and what was left of the corn and potatoes the hogs and cattle destroyed, while all of us were ill [in the 1849 epidemic]. Inexperienced as we were, most of our work was in vain.

During this time [while they were ill] we lost all our cows and oxen. . . . Also we were without money. After I was able to be up, I went to look for the animals. After eleven days on horseback trying to round them up, I found only one ox. The cows we never saw again.

One night [on the search] my horse went through water up to his knees and swam several creeks. Night came on and the horse could not be made to go any farther. There was nothing else to do but to spend the night in the open prairie between Cedar Island and Lang's Bayou. A cold norther blew up and the horse and I were chilled to the bone. . . .

The cattle had to be replaced. For the second time, we bought cows and oxen, the latter because my brother, Louis, and I could haul and sell the several hundred logs split during the winter.

Carl Wilhelm Rummel started a trading post on their land, and worked at other tasks as well. Their grandson told of these years:

A few years later Grandpa made his first ox cart and Grandma was making tarcheon lace, and sold it in Houston and walked all the way. They lived twelve miles from the courthouse. After she had sold enough lace to buy a pair of oxen and he had completed his cart and everything was paid for, then they celebrated for a few hours by all getting in the cart and taking a ride to try it out. Grandpa did quite a bit of hauling with it and a year later he bought another yoke of oxen and a large wagon, and he hauled furniture and all sorts of merchandise from Houston to Brenham and cotton from Brenham to Houston. He finally had two big cotton wagons. . . . Grandpa made good with his teams and Grandma with her trading post; every time she had saved some money she would invest it in real estate.[81]

Carl Wilhelm Rummel's daughter, Lena M. Rummel (1854–1928) was born in Spring Branch and married Heinrich August Sauer in 1876 at St. Peter Church.[82] Their son, Conrad Louis Sauer (1892–1965), left these notes about his grandmother Carolina (Bauer) Rummel, Carl Wilhelm's wife, who was faced with another epidemic—again yellow fever—in 1867:

Yellow fever struck the Houston area anew in 1867, again wiping out entire families. When the epidemic reached the city, many terrified people fled to the country. Some got as far as Grandmother's house in Spring Branch before succumbing. Grandmother was now faced with the supreme test of her faith. Should she barricade her family against the stricken refugees, or play the good Samaritan? She chose the latter course, and opened her house and her porch to the sick. Those were terrible days, and neighbors were hard to find to help with the nursing; even harder, to find men to bury the dead. Granma's youngest daughter was called to help inter the corpses because there were not enough people to draw the cross-pieces to let the coffins down into the graves.[83]

Sawmills. The Rummel and Bauer clans were involved in the lumber business throughout the late nineteenth century, utilizing the abundant pine that grew in the extensive upland pine forest nearby. As mentioned, a man by the name of McGuffey built a sawmill in Spring Branch in the early 1860s. Possibly it was the William McGuffey who was living as a single man in a Houston boarding house, employed as a carpenter, in the 1860 census. Once McGuffey's sawmill was up and running, he hired both Carl Wilhelm Rummel and Carl's son William Rummel to work there. The Rummels hand-picked the twelve-inch timbers used in construction of the new St. Peter Church, built in 1864 after fire damaged the original log church.[84]

William Rummel (1837–1915) survived a stint in the Confederate army during this time (see Chapter 9), and his father died in 1867. In January 1868 William Rummel married German immigrant Clara Hildebrandt (1814–1918) in Round Top, where some of his Bauer kinfolk now lived, and the couple returned to Spring Branch, where their son William Rummel (1869–1899) was born in 1869. According to the 1870 federal census, William owned a sawmill there by 1870, probably by purchasing it from McGuffey. The census lists William Rummel, at age thirty-three, as the owner of the sawmill, with Herman Hildebrandt (b. ca. 1837)—probably Clara's brother—employed as a sawyer, and Henry Fech, age forty-three, as a sawmill laborer. Both Hildebrandt and Fech were German immigrants.

The manufacturing schedule of the 1870 census gives some detail about the mill's operation and production. The six men who ran the mill (three are not listed in the population census) operated it only three months of the year, most likely in the dry months when it was easiest for ox teams to pull the logs to the mill; during the rest of the year, farming activities took top priority for the self-sufficient German farmers who worked there. The mill itself, worth $2,000, had an eighteen-horsepower Shearn steam engine with a Phoenix circular saw. They cut 1,000 pine logs a year and turned them into 100,000 board feet of lumber destined for the building trade. The mill returned $1,600 per year in revenue, of which $500 was paid as wages to the six employees. A similar steam sawmill owned by Henry and George Morse, also visited by the tax man that year (see Chapter 8) returned about four times the product and revenue, but with ten employees who ran the mill six months per year.

The pull of Round Top was strong on Clara, and Carl Wilhelm Rummel purchased about 160 acres of land there in three tracts in 1871. For the land he

Figure 6.15. The Herman Bauer sawmill, ca. 1885, formerly located near the intersection of modern Voss and Beinhorn roads. **A:** Exterior, showing a group of families with an empty mule-drawn wagon, and an ox-drawn wagon carrying logs.

paid $2,500 in gold and a promissory note for 9,000 feet of first class pine lumber from his sawmill in Spring Branch. Carl Wilhelm and Clara then moved to Round Top, leaving the sawmill with her brother Herman Hildebrandt. A house that they lived in and may have built still stands on Mill Street in Round Top, where he lived until his death in 1915, and Clara lived until 1918.[85] They raised five children there.

Back in Spring Branch, Herman Hildebrandt continued to operate the sawmill, located near the intersection of modern Voss and Bienhorn (item 13, Figure 6.9). August Bauer's son, Herman August Bauer (1852–1932) began to work there. After his father's death of yellow fever in 1854, when Herman was two years of age, Herman had been raised by an aunt in Round Top, but he returned to Spring Branch in the 1870s to work at the mill. Herman eventually bought the mill from Hildebrandt, beginning a three-generation period of Bauer sawmill operation in the area.[86]

Two photos of the Herman Bauer sawmill at this time have survived (Figure 6.15). The second of the two photos was labeled "Voss + Beinhorn, Bauer Sawmill" on the back, leaving little doubt as to its provenance (neither road existed at the time the photographs were made). The first photo shows a gathering of sawmill families in front of the mill building. At the left, men are standing on stacks of drying lumber behind a wagon pulled by mules. At the right, well behind a group of women and children, is a wagon laden with pine logs, pulled by two

B: Interior, showing the circular saw, driven by overhead belts and pulleys. The steam engine is not shown.
Photos courtesy of Nelda Blackshere Reynolds.

oxen. The second picture shows the interior of the mill. Pulleys and belts overhead deliver steam power to the circular saw, left; a cradle on iron tracks at the right pulled the logs past the saw.

John Bauer (1861–1950) was a grandson of Carl Siegismund Bauer and was raised in Round Top. Orphaned, he moved to Spring Branch to work in his cousin Herman's sawmill. John took over the operation of the mill from Herman in the 1890s. He moved it to near what is now the intersection of modern Rosslyn Road at 34th Street. It was moved to Karen, Texas, in 1904, then to Humble in 1908 as a response to the oil boom. A new generation, Jerry and Albert Bauer, took over the mill in 1914 and moved it to Rummel Creek, near the present site of Rummel Creek School. John Edwin Bauer took over Albert's interest in 1918 and moved it to where Memorial City shopping mall is today. In 1936 John bought out Jerry Bauer and moved the mill to its final home, north of Old Katy Road at Gessner, where an Exxon station is today. It was closed in 1955, after having provided building materials for Houston's expansion for many decades.[87]

Bernard, Daniel and William Ahrenbeck. Another immigrant family was engaged in the sawmill business in Spring Branch, although for a much shorter duration of time. Bernard Ahrenbeck (1795–bef 1860) was born in 1795 in Prussia and married Wilhelmina Martens (1798–1859) in Germany in 1820. Between 1820 and 1836 the couple had eight children, Minna (1820–1911), Daniel (1822–1907), Johannes Christian (1824–1867), Loise Wilhelmine

(1826–1827), William (1828–1886), Carl Friedrich (1832–?), John Bernhard (1833–1905) and Heinrich Ludewig (1836–1837). The family sailed from Bremen, Germany, to Galveston on board the barque Franziska, arriving in November 1847.[88] August Bauer and his wife Emilie were on the same voyage.

The family, along with August and Emilie Bauer, made their way to Spring Branch area, where they settled near where the Kolbes and Hillendahls would later live. By 1850 Bernhard and Wilhelmina were living with three children: William, Daniel, and Bernard. Bernard senior was a farmer, and his son William was listed as a blacksmith. In the agricultural census of 1850, Bernard Ahrenbeck was reported as owning a farm of 35 acres, of which only four were improved by cultivation. He had one horse, a pair of oxen, nine milk cows, 12 beeves, and 14 hogs, and the family raised 45 bushels of corn. His farm was valued at $150, his equipment at $50, and his livestock at $200. In the 1850s, on land belonging to Bernard that was outside but adjacent to the Vince tract, the Ahrenbecks operated a steam sawmill (item 12, Figure 6.9). Daniel and William Ahrenbeck sold that land in 1857 to S. D. Hewes, with the mill, along with another 200 acres in the northeastern Vince tract.[89]

After selling that land in 1857, most of the family seems to have moved to Hempstead in Austin County (part of Waller County in 1873), where William became alderman and later postmaster. Daniel was living there by 1860 and became mayor in 1867. Daniel's future son-in-law wrote of their activities in Hempstead, where William returned to his trade as a blacksmith:

> *They were building a cotton seed oil mill, then the first one in the state. Will Ahrenbeck, a brother, before the war had large blacksmith shop and wagon shop in town. During the war the Confederacy leased the plant and made wagons for the army. At the end of the war the Confederate states owed him a lot of money in promises to pay signed by General Mc Gruder. All was lost when the south lost and the Ahrenbeck brothers had to start from the beginning. D. Ahrenbeck had a corn mill and a small flour mill and cotton gin in connection. W. Ahrenbeck had been in the mercantile business but had lost out. He had a little left so he got Daniel to go in with him again and decided to go in the plow and wagon business again. While they were putting up the building a salesman happened in; and when he saw a large pile of cotton seed in the yard going to waste, he told them they made oil out of that in New Orleans. He knew a Mr. Callahan of Dayton Ohio who was making machinery for oil mills. He gave them the address. They wrote to him and later got acquainted with him. He was a jolly Irishman. They told him of the financial conditions after the war. He was liberal and sold them the machinery mostly on credit. I was anxious to see the oil going so I made myself useful wherever I could and was only anxious to please, especially Daniel and his daughter Minnie. I could not keep her out of my mind.*
>
> *When the first oil was made, W. Ahrenbeck was running the press. Later we had seven, in fact 14, according to the capacity of the first. As we put in double mats, making two cakes instead of one. The arrangement for pumping the oil in large tanks was not finished, so I was employed for that day to dip the oil out of a small tank into a barrel with a dipper. When the barrel was full, I was told by W. Ahrenbeck to go tell John Tuffy, old citizen of Hempstead, to come and bring his spoon, that the barrel of oil was ready for him. He had promised to eat all the oil they could get out of seed. He came but no spoon. One half of Hempstead came to see the show. This was 1870.*[90]

Both William and his wife Justine Auguste Froelich (1835–1908), and Daniel and his wife Maria Bartman (1827–1885) are buried in the Hempstead cemetery. Their father Bernhard died around 1860, probably in Hempstead.

Louis and Henry Hillendahl. Franz Ludwig "Louis" Hillendahl (1812–1874) was a bootmaker from Hanover, Niedersachsen, Germany. He married his wife, Sophie Dorothea Schulz (1811–1881), from Weyhausen, Saxony, in 1835 in Fallersleben, Saxony. They arrived in Galveston in 1847, bringing four surviving children who had been born between 1837 and 1847: Dorothea "Doris" Hillendahl (1838–1915), Ludwig "Louis" Hillendahl (1840–1921), Theodore W. Hillendahl (1844–1931), and George Christian Hillendahl (1847–1915).[91] On September 1, 1848, Louis Hillendahl paid surveyor George Bringhurst ten dollars for ten acres of land in the Osborne survey. The agricultural census of 1850 reported that Louis and his wife had ten acres, of which five were cultivated. They owned three horses, eight milk cows, 16 beeves, and 18 hogs and raised 40 bushels of corn. One may well wonder how all those animals plus the corn crop and their home could fit on only ten acres. All these frontier settlers in early Harris County made good use of the surrounding open range, where their branded stock could roam free. In westernmost Harris County, that open range lasted until the 1880s, although in areas farther east in the county, heavier settlement made an end to the practice a decade or so earlier. The Hillendahls' small property was valued at a generous $250, with equipment valued at $20 and livestock $250.

It may have been a rough frontier, but the Hillendahls looked to better things for their children. Living with the Hillendahls at the time of the 1850 federal census was a German schoolteacher, Otto Behne, who educated the children of the area in the 1850s.

That ten-acre piece of land was enough to get a foothold but insufficient to raise his family. In 1856 Louis purchased 150 acres in the Trott survey and built his permanent home and farm there.[92] That home was not far from the modern intersection of Bingle Road and Long Point. They were connected by a wagon track to St. Peter Church (Figure 6.9 B).

When grown, their children George and Dorothea moved to Bear Creek, where Louis had purchased a 480-acre tract in 1860. His son Theodore, after a stint in the Confederate army, moved to White Oak (discussed later). Louis Jr. stayed with the family farm in Spring Branch. Both Louis Sr. and his wife Dorothea are buried at St. Peter Church cemetery on Long Point Drive.

Wilhelm Heinrich ("Henry") Hillendahl (1814–1870) was Louis's younger brother. He came to Spring Branch in 1851 with his wife Elizabeth Heine (1810–1854) and three daughters, Auguste Johanne Hillendahl Tappenbeck (1842–1927), Johannne Dorothea (1845–1851), and Friederike Wilhelmine Elise Johann Hillendahl (1850–1867). They moved to the Spring Branch area, probably to be near his brother Louis. After Dorothea died in 1854, Henry married Maria Schmidt (1828–1907), and the couple had at least five children, including Arnold Hillendahl, Sr. (1855–1939) and Henry Hillendahl, Jr. (1857–1948); three of their children died young.

In 1854 Henry Hillendahl Sr. bought 80 acres located at the intersection of modern Long Point and Pech Road, where he farmed and was also self-employed as a shoemaker and cordwainer. Arnold Sr. grew up on that farm in the late 1850s and early 1860s and in his later years longed for the free life of a young ox cart driver; ox carts were the main method of ferrying anything during his youth. The San Felipe Trail was still in frequent use at the time of the Civil War, although it faded in importance once the Texas Western Narrow Gauge Railroad was built in 1875 and Westheimer Road developed as a dirt track on its north side (see Chapter 10). Arnold, at age seventy-one in 1927, was the subject of a story in the *Houston Chronicle:*

> *They sometimes went as far as Pittsville—30 miles—to haul cotton to Taylor's wagon yard for $2.50 a bale. Nine or ten bales to the load—that made $25. Yes sir, there was good money in "ox whip," as they called it. It only took about a week to cover the 30 miles, you see, with five yoke of oxen making 10 miles a day and resting every fifth day. Soon, the boy was driving with the rest, in regular hauling caravans. Sometimes 30 huge-wheeled, ungainly wagons, pulled by 300 oxen.*
>
> *The roads? Oh, it was a path, and when heavy hauling made it rutty you just pulled off to one side. Everyone did that at the worst spot of all, "Dead*

Figure 6.16. Hillendahl brothers and cousins, ca. 1900. Back row, left to right: Brothers Theodore W. Hillendahl, George Hillendahl, and Ludwig "Louis" Hillendahl Jr., all of whom were sons of Ludwig "Louis" Hillendahl and his wife Dorothea Schulz. Front row, left to right: Henry Hillendahl, Jr. and Arnold Hillendahl, both of whom were sons of Wilhelm Heinrich (Henry) Hillendahl, Sr., who was Ludwig Sr.'s younger brother. Courtesy of Walker Richard Gray Jr. and David Hornburg.

Man's Island," on the Westheimer road just this side of Piney Point. They kept doing it until the road was a mile wide! . . . There was no bridge across Buffalo Bayou . . . you forded what you could, and went roundabout mostly.

Pittsville, now vanished, lay about three miles north of modern Fulshear. That distance from Spring Branch to old Pittsville can be traversed today in a little less than an hour, if the traffic is light.

Henry Hillendahl's farm was passed down to his son Arnold, Sr. and then to his grandson Arnold Louis Hillendahl, who continued to farm it until 1962, when city taxes made its continuation untenable and it was sold. The farm was paved over for a giant Kmart parking lot, except for the family cemetery, which was kept intact at the corner of Long Point and Pech Road, where it rather oddly sits on the edge of a parking lot for an auto service shop (see Chapter 13).[93]

An old photograph taken in about 1910 of the five sons of pioneers Louis Hillendahl Sr. and Henry Hillendahl Sr. has survived (Figure 6.16). Beards were clearly a "thing" for the early Hillendahls.

Beinhorn. After the first hardy pioneers of 1846–1848 had put Spring Branch on the map and began writing to their relatives back in Germany, a flood of new families came in the 1850s. One of these families was that of Johann Heinrich Dietrich Beinhorn (1798–1866) and his wife Anna Marie Dorothea Lehn. Dietrich, from Fallersleben, Germany, married Anna Marie in 1824. They had five children in Germany: Heinrich Dietrich (b. 1825), Johann Heinrich Jacob (1827–1869), Marie Dorothea (b. 1829), Johann Heinrich Christian (1833–1905), Dorothea Sophia Henriette, Elizabeth, and Johann Heinrich (1847–1866). All but son Heinrich Dietrich and daughter Marie Dorothea appear to have sailed on the Suwa from Bremerhaven to Galveston in 1853 and made their way to Spring Branch.[94]

Their daughter Dorothea Sophia Henriette seems to have crossed to Texas first and married J. H. Tendler in June 1853. She may have coaxed the rest of the Beinhorn family to Texas. Her brother Johann Heinrich Jacob also married a Tendler, Wilhelmine Tentler, in 1856 in Spring Branch, so there was a close connection between the two families. They had four daughters before his death, after which she married William Beutel. Those families are interred at St. Peter Church cemetery.

After serving in the Confederate Army (Chapter 8), their son Johann Heinrich Christian ("Christian") married Marie Mueller in 1866. They lived at a home near modern day Old Katy Road at Campbell (Figure 6.9), and modern Beinhorn Road honors their memory. It is not known where the elder Beinhorns are buried, and it is thought that they may have perished in one of the early yellow fever epidemics and thus may be buried in an unmarked mass grave at St. Peter Church.[95]

Matzke and Weimann families. Many arriving families in Spring Branch have, for one reason or another, left few descendants in the area, and the Matzke and Weiman families provide examples. Christian Matzke Sr. (1799–1886) and his wife Johanna Dorothea Pipjahle (1802–1875) left Klein Lahse, Silesia, Poland, with their eight children as part of the Adelsverein (German Emigration Company). Before the family sailed from Bremen on August 1, 1846, their contract was modified, probably due to arriving news that the Adelsverein main settlement at New Braunfels was faring very poorly (see discussion later in this chapter of the Bering family's arrival). Their ship, the Mathilde, arrived in Galveston on October 3, 1846. Family lore holds that the family settled in Washington County but could not make a living farming the sandy soil. They left after harvest, around 1850, for the German settlement at Spring Branch. The Matzkes traveled in a wagon train, and had to leave a sick son, Carl Matzke, behind with a family. A runner found them around Chappell Hill to tell them the boy had died.

The family settled east of Spring Branch Creek in the area of present day Woodlawn Cemetery. Christian Matzke Sr. became a trustee of St. Peter Evangelical Lutheran Church. Three of his remaining children died young and are buried in unmarked graves in St. Peter Church's cemetery: Gottfried, who died unmarried in 1856, Gottlieb, who died in 1865 shortly after returning from service in the Confederacy, and Rosina, who died as a newlywed with her husband, Joachim Wiglow, in the 1867 yellow fever epidemic. Christian Matzke Jr., also a Confederate soldier (Chapter 8), married Dorothea Hoffmeister of Spring Branch and then moved to the Cypress area. Wilhelm Matzke married Elisabeth "Bertha" Weimann of Spring Branch and moved to Horsepen Bayou south of Houston. Susanna Matzke first married Joseph Koch of Bear Creek in 1851 (see Bear Creek community account, following). After their divorce in 1879, she married Frederick August Schmidt in 1882. Dorothea married the Lutheran minister in Bear Creek, Christian David Ankele, in 1854, and they left Texas to minister in the Midwest. The patriarch Christian Sr. moved to Houston after his wife Johanna Dorothea died in 1875, married the widow Fredericka Mohre Ellenberger in 1884, and died in 1886 from malaria.

Samuel Weimann (1809–1867) was born in Munich but worked as a mason Braetz, Poland. He married Louise Johanna Paelchen (1815–1873) in 1837, and the couple had seven children (all but one were daughters) before leaving for North America in 1855. By 1858 Samuel Weimann was listed on the tax rolls in Harris County. In 1865 he was elected secretary of St. Peter Evangelical Lutheran Church in Spring Branch. An eighth child, Lydia Rosalia, was born in 1861 in Spring Branch.

Over the years, most of the Weiman children moved away from Spring Branch. Lydia married Henry Hillendahl, Jr. in 1880, and the family moved

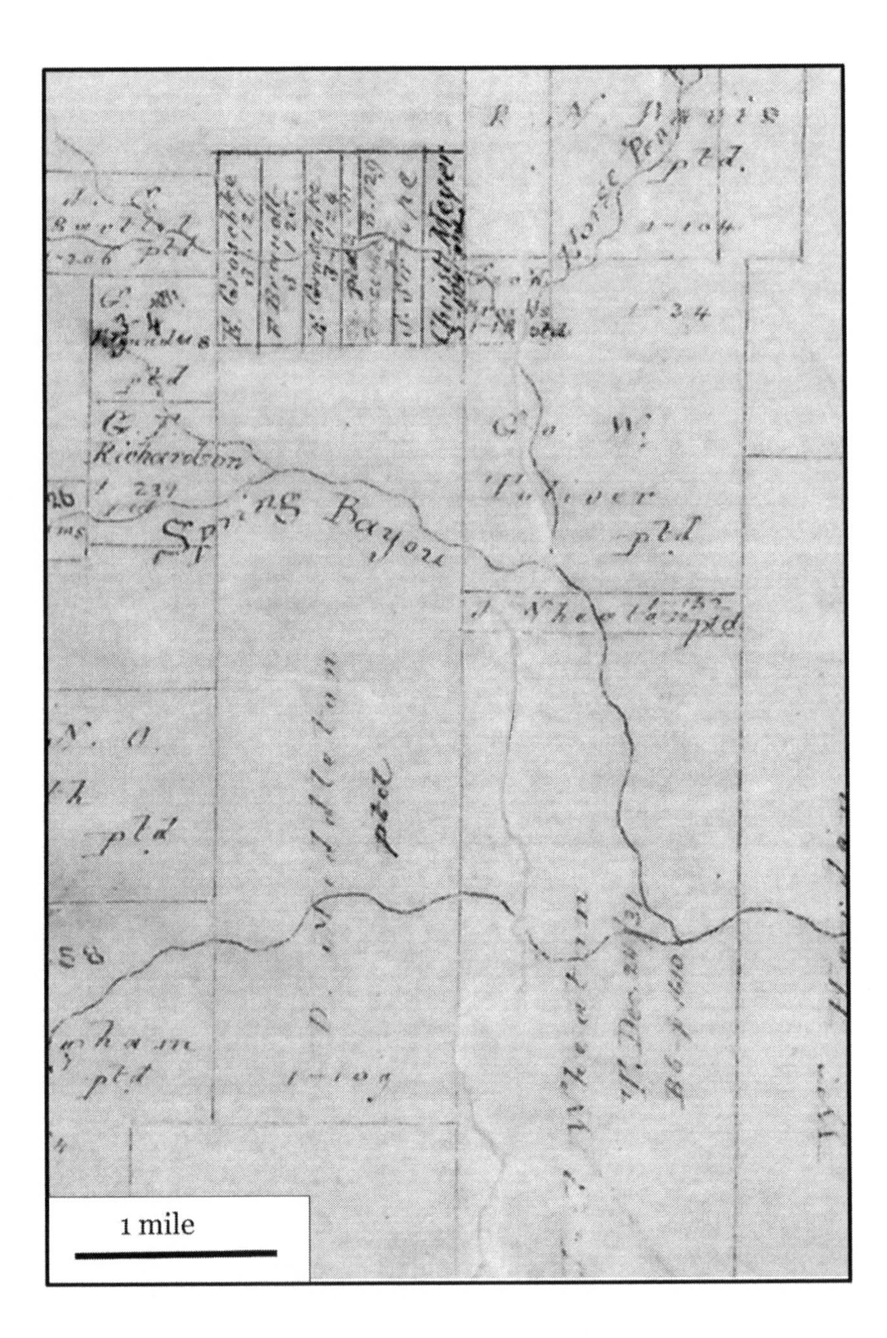

Figure 6.17. A portion of an 1847 Harris County land map. The small strips of land of the Groschke, Brandt, Striepe and Meyer families straddle Bear Creek, a tributary of Buffalo Bayou, at the northern part of the image. The annotations of these German purchases appear to have been added to the map at some time in the 1850s. Courtesy of the General Land Office, Austin.

to California. Another daughter, Louise Bertha (1842–1911) married the Lutheran minister John Frederick Flath, who served at St. Peter Evangelical Lutheran Church until his transfer to Indianola. Family lore states that the Flath family left on a Union gunboat for New York during the Civil War and lived at New Lots Township in Kings County, New York. Another daughter, Elisabeth "Bertha" (1853–1941), married Wilhelm Matzke of Spring Branch and moved to Horsepen Bayou in southeastern Harris County. The Weimanns had one son, Albert Carl (1855–1943), who married Mary Molly Prunier, and they also moved to Horsepen Bayou. Some of the grown children of Bertha Matzke and Albert Carl Weimann later lived in the Bear Creek settlement.

Samuel Weimann died on August 31, 1867, in Harrisburg from yellow fever. Since his daughter Augusta (b. 1845), had recently lost her husband, Dr. John Butscher, in June 1867 to yellow fever, it is possible that Samuel had gone to Harrisburg to assist her. Samuel's wife Louise Johanna Paelchen died in Spring Branch in 1873.[96]

There are many, many more names of German settlers who came to Spring Branch in the pioneer era of 1847 to about 1861–too many to detail. Besides those already discussed, they include the families named Beutel, Bingle, Clay, Emnora, Fredrich, Hedwig, Hufmeister, Koehn, Kuhlman, Mueller, Neuen, Oberpriller,Ojeman, Reichart, Pech,Reidel, Sauer, Tappenback, Telchow, Tendler, and Witte, many of whom have roads named for them and their early farms.

The Bear Creek Community

Most of the early pioneer sites in Houston have long since been covered with urban buildings, roads, and parking lots. Not so those of the old Bear Creek Community (Figure 6.2), a German settlement that dates back to the late 1840s, and where viable German vegetable, beef and dairy farms existed until the mid-1940s. A disastrous 1935 flood in central Houston resulted in the authorization of construction of both the Barker and Addicks reservoirs in 1938 for flood control along Buffalo Bayou, and almost all of Bear Creek lay within the Addicks Reservoir. Purchase of most of the farms in the community followed this authorization, some if not most by eminent domain, and all the buildings were leveled by the Army Corps of Engineers after 1946. Bear Creek residents were dispersed from farms that had been owned and worked by their families for nearly a century, and the pioneer community ceased to exist. The Addicks dam and reservoir were completed in 1948.[97] Most of the historic sites there have reverted to a near wilderness setting.[98] The story of the Bear Creek pioneers is little known today, although a subject of a well-researched MA thesis by area descendant Andrea Stahman Burden in 2004.[99]

Like Spring Branch to the east, the Bear Creek community was first settled in the 1840s by recent immigrants from Germany, including the Marks, Koch, Striepe, Meier, Brandt and Groschke families (Figures 6.17, 6.18). They settled on lands that had been earlier granted to Anglo land owners; there had been little or no Anglo settlement in the immediate area. The one-third league of land on which the earliest-arriving families settled was granted in 1838 as a first class headright to Flournoy Hunt, who was a citizen of Texas before March 2, 1836. Hunt died in 1842; the land became vacant and the title voided. The arriving settlers heard of the vacant land, which was later open to claims under the Texas Homestead Act of 1854. Under its terms, one could claim a 160-acre homestead on vacant land if one could show proof of having lived there for three years or more. These German immigrants took advantage of the act, claiming 160-acre grants in the Hunt tract on which they had been residing as early as 1847. In 1855 these families all applied for "pre-emption" grants (right to purchase) for 160-acre homesteads on the same day: Christian Meier, Sophia Striepe, Frederick Brandt, a widow named Charlotte Groschke, and her sons Carl Ernst Groschke and Friedrich Emil Groschke.

Like their Spring Branch neighbors, these German immigrants settled on relatively small plots of land, favoring intensive agriculture techniques on farms worked by the families; in general this area was slave-free. The main Bear Creek landholders centered their landholdings on Bear Creek for its water and timber and farmed the adjacent upland prairie. Corn was the crop of choice, with some cotton added as a cash crop. They raised cattle, hogs and chickens. Their nearest neighbors to the south were Elizabeth Wheaton and her two sons, who operated the inn at Wheaton's Ford on the San Felipe Trail. The nearby Hockley wagon road took them into Houston for trading their produce (Figure 6.18); they traveled on it to Market Square. Houston was a long, seventeen-mile trip by ox wagon or on foot, and they would camp overnight there, sleeping either on the ground or in the wagons, and would return the following day with supplies purchased there.[100]

The Marks-Striepe family. One of the earliest Bear Creek area German families to arrive in Texas was that of Gotthilf Marks (1800–1850) of Sachsen-Anhalt and his wife Sophia (1824–1882) of Prussia. They arrived in Galveston in August 1845, along

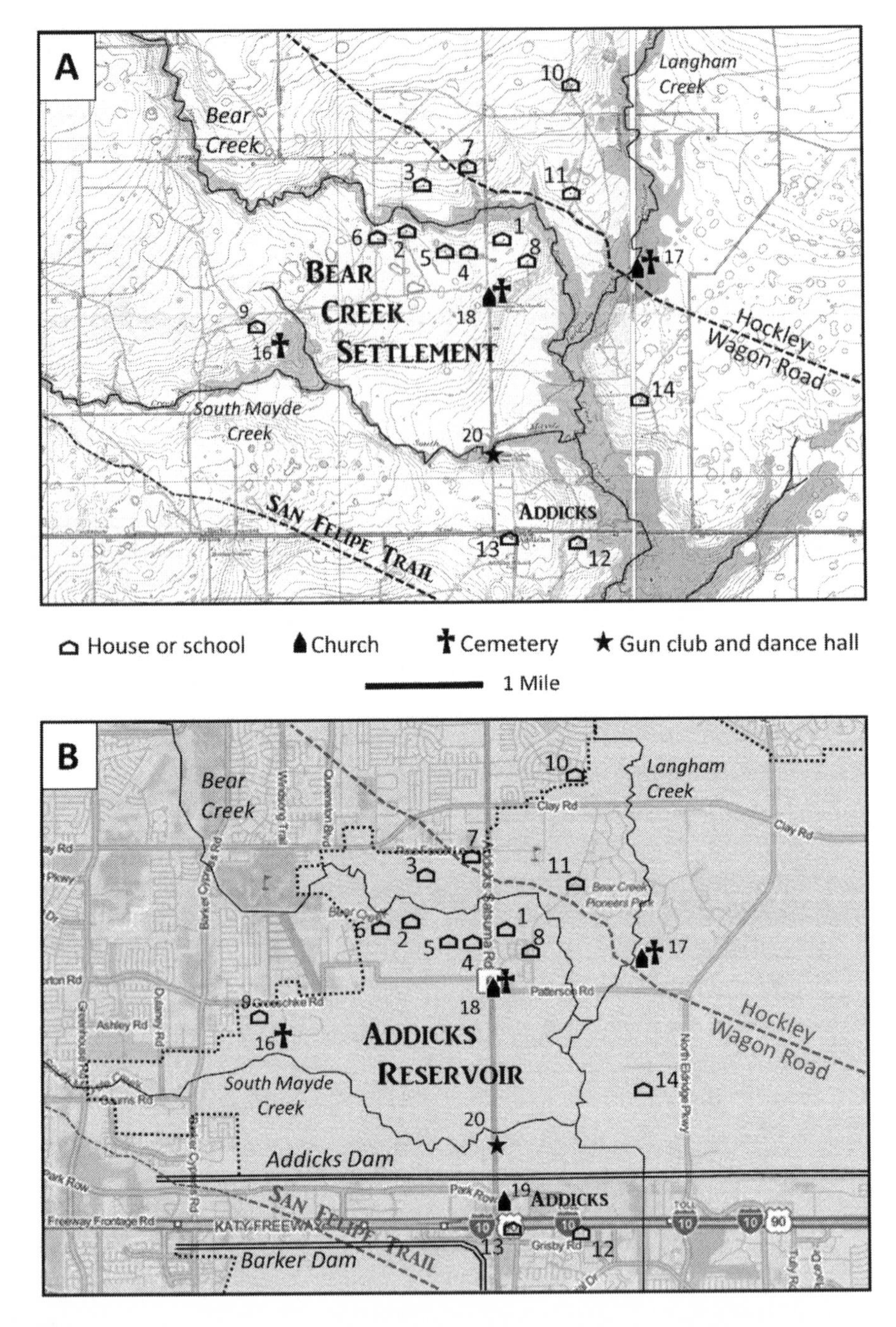

Figure 6.18. Locations of the farmhouses of selected pioneer families and other cultural features of the Bear Creek area.
A: On a topographic base map made by the U.S. Geological Survey in 1915, when the farms were still intact.
B: Same area today; former farm locations and other features are shown on a modern road map.
Base map courtesy of OpenStreetMap.

Locations of features:

1. Sophie Marks (later Sophie Striepe), later owned by her sons Adolph and Hilf Marks
2. Frederick Brandt and his wife Katherine Meier Brandt
3. Emil Fritz Brandt (Fred Brandt's son) and his wife Hulda Kobs
4. Ludwig Friedrich Carl Groschke and his wife Charlotte Henrietta Groschke; later sold to their daughter Albertine Marianne Groschke and her husband Frederick "Fritz" Hoffman
5. Carl Ernst Groschke (son of Ludwig and Charlotte Groschke) and his wife Dorothea Hillendahl

with two sons Albert (1842–1910) and Hilf (ca. 1843–1863). A third son August Texas Marks (1845–1891), was born onboard their ship on August 15, 1845, as the ship lay off Galveston harbor—hence his name. Their ship had earlier attempted to land in Indianola but had been waved off due to an epidemic of yellow fever and smallpox there. Galveston was also infested with yellow fever, so the family placed their belongings on a two-wheeled cart and walked to Houston. Two Gotthilf's brothers never made it out of Galveston, where they were killed by thieves. Another brother drowned in Cypress Creek. According to family history, Gotthilf, Sophia and their three sons arrived with their cart at an already partly settled German settlement at Bear Creek; they settled near South Mayde Creek.[101]

Gotthilf soon registered the family's "Wet Hat" brand in Houston.[102] That brand gave the Marks family the right to brand wild cattle on the adjacent open range, and Gotthilf seems to have had plans to supply beef in nearby Houston town. He left the family and traveled to Galveston, in order to work at the du Pont gunpowder factory there, and was never seen again—a not uncommon fate on a dangerous frontier. When Gotthilf did not return, Sophia married Christian Striepe in 1850 in what may have been a marriage of convenience, in order to obtain land.[103]

Christian Striepe (1806–1870) was born in Hanover, Germany, and arrived in Texas in 1848.[104] The record is unclear, but he apparently arrived in Texas already married (his wife's name is unknown) and with at least three children, all daughters, who were born in Germany between 1832 and 1836 and are listed in the 1850 federal census: Dorothea, Christian, and Henrietta. The federal census of agriculture for 1850 reported that Christian Striepe had cultivated 12 of a total of 100 acres reported. He had four horses, two pairs of oxen, four milk cows, six beeves, and twelve hogs, and harvested 50 bushels of corn (about one acre). His farm land was valued at $150, equipment at $35, and livestock at $180.

We do not know what happened to Christian's first wife, but either she died or they were divorced, as he married the widow Sophia Marks in 1850. Sophia brought to this marriage her three sons, August, Albert and Hilfe, and Christian brought his three daughters by his earlier marriage; all six children are listed in the 1850 census. The couple had one more child, Mary Striepe, born in 1852.

Then Christian "disappeared" by 1853; he moved to Austin County, near Industry, by 1860 and married Sophia Willhams in 1859. The later record on Christian is uncertain. He married Mrs. Wilhelmine Brine (possibly Brune) in 1866, in Austin County.[105] But he appeared on the 1870 census at Pittsville with a wife named Mary (possibly Mary Backner); the site of Pittsville is today between Brookshire and Fulshear (present day Waller County). He died later that same year.

His second wife Sophia resumed using her Marks name and was approved for a State of Texas

Continued fron opposite page:

6. Friedrich Emil Groshke and his wife Catharine Koch
7. Henry Moers and his wife Katie Hoffman Moers
8. Christian and Dorothea Meyer (Meier); later Heinrich Addicks and Charles Kunze
9. Johann Koch and his wife Anna Elisabetha Koch; later Susanna Matzke family
10. Ludwig Koch and his wife Sophia Addicks Koch
11. Joseph Koch, and later Susannah Koch Golbow and her husband Henry Golbow
12. Carl Golbow (originally spelled Goldbaum) and his wife Dorothea Shulz; approximate location
13. Johann Joachim Friedrich Schulz and his wife (and first cousin) Sophie Schulz
14. Carl Frederick Wilhelm (Fritz) Kobs and his wife Dorothea Louise Meier Kobs
15. Ludwig Louis Hillendahl and his wife Dorothea; house built by his son George Hillendahl
16. Koch-Schmidt Cemetery (1854)
17. Bear Creek Methodist Church, from 1890 to 1903, and Hillendahl-Eggling Cemetery (1875)
18. Bear Creek Methodist Church, from 1903 to 1948, and Cemetery
19. Bear Creek (now United) Methodist Church, from 1948 to present
20. Bear Creek Gun Club, second location, from 1900

Figure 6.19. Albert Marks and his wife, Mina Walter, in front of Sophie Marks's former home. Photo courtesy of Doris Cook and Marie Neuman Gray.

pre-emption grant of 160 acres on Bear Creek in 1854 (Figure 6.18, site number 1), and the property was surveyed in 1855.[106] An 1847 land map of Harris County (Figure 6.17) lists her landholding under the name S. Striepe; it is likely that this marking and others were additions to the initial map. She may have needed a marriage of convenience to Christian Striepe to be able to get the homestead grant. At any rate, Sophia married again, to John Rinkel.[107] On her gravestone, she is remembered as Sophia Marks.

By the time of the 1870 federal census, Sophia was the head of her own household with two surviving sons (August and Albert; Hilf was to die in the Civil War; see Chapter 8) and a daughter, Mary (b. 1852). Albert Louis Marks (1842–1910) bought his mother's land in 1874 for $350 and an annual delivery of twenty-five bushels of corn. Albert married Mina S. Walter (1858–1910), and they had seven children (Figure 6.19). On their deaths, the property passed to their sons, Gotthilf and Adolph.[108]

Sophia's son August Texas Marks (1845–1891) and her grandson Emil Henry Marks (1881–1969) would become famed local ranchers in the Barker-Clodine area. August owned about 1,600 acres and participated in many of the storied early Texas cattle drives to Kansas. He married Elizabeth Schulz in 1870; she was the daughter of John and Sophie Schulz (profiled later in this section). Elizabeth died during the birth of her sixth child, in 1887. August died in the 1891 smallpox epidemic. Her parents and later her brother, William "Uncle Billy" Schulz, cared for the orphans. Emil became one of the founders of the Houston Livestock Show and Rodeo.[109]

The Brandt family. Frederick Brandt (1829–1923) was a woodcarver who emigrated from Oldenburg, German, reportedly to avoid military service (Figure 6.18, site number 2; Figure 6.20). He sailed from Bremen on the same ship as the Groschke family, the Solon; in 1850–1851 he lived with them as a bachelor. He applied for a 160-acre land grant at the same time as the Groschkes, in 1855; it was patented in 1861. He married a widow, Catherine Meier Suhr (b. 1831), in 1854. According to Andrea Burden's interview of a descendant, Catherine "was told by some young men who came to her door that her hus-

Figure 6.20. Fred Brandt and Catherine Meier Suhr Brandt with their children, ca. 1878. Back row: Emil Fritz, Henrietta Suhr, Adolph, and Catherina. Front row: Bettje, Catherine Brandt, Fred Brandt, and Carolina. Courtesy of Marie Neuman Gray.

Figure 6.21. The abandoned home of Frederick Brandt and Catherine Meier Suhr Brandt, built ca. 1854, as photographed by the U.S. Army Corps of Engineers in 1944, prior to its demolition. Courtesy of Martha Doty Freeman and USACE.

Figure 6.22. Emil Fritz Brandt and Hulda Kobs Brandt home, ca. 1884, on the north side of the Brandt survey, as it appeared in 1944. Courtesy of Martha Doty Freeman and USACE.

Figure 6.23. Photographs of the barns and outbuildings of the Brandt-Pasche farmstead. **A:** Feed shed and barn enclosure. **B:** Implement shed. **C:** Barn with loft. Photographed by the U. S. Army Corps of Engineers in 1946, prior to their demolition. Courtesy of Martha Doty Freeman and USACE.

band had been killed by mistake [hung as a horse thief] and was dead. Fred felt sorry for her and her little girl so he married Catherine."[110] They had five children between 1856 and 1870: Adolph, Catherina, Emil Fritz, Carolina and Bettje. Catherine already had a daughter, Henrietta Suhr (1853–1942) by her previous marriage.

Reluctant to join the Confederacy when war broke out, Frederick (by now, Fred) was drafted but was allowed to work as a wagon maker and repairer for the Texas State Troops; he stayed in Texas and survived the war. Catherine died sometime after 1880, and he remained on the land until he died of pneumonia in 1923 after a tree fell on him, breaking his pelvis.[111] He is buried at the Addicks Bear Creek Methodist cemetery.

Fred Brandt's farm was described in the 1850 federal census of agriculture, when he was a single man, prior to his marriage with Catherine. He was reported as having two cultivated acres out of a total of 22 acres (his full homestead claim of 160 acres was made in 1855, after his marriage). He had a horse, six milk cows, three hogs and a pair of oxen, but no beeves, and he harvested 40 bushels (about an acre) of corn. His farm was valued at just $32, his equipment at $35, and his livestock at $120. These are low figures, but at this time he was living with (and helping) Louis Groschke, according to the 1850 federal census.

Brandt's step-daughter Yetta (Henrietta) continued to live on the farm and in the family home until her death in 1942, after which time the old house and farm buildings became derelict (Figure 6.21). Typical of early German dwellings in coastal Texas, the pier and beam frame house lacked indoor plumbing or electricity. It was razed by the Army Corps of Engineers in 1947–1948.

Frederick's son, Emil Fritz Brandt (1861–1901), settled on the north half of his father's 160-acre tract in 1884 (Figure 6.18, site number 3; Figure 6.22) and bought it in 1898. He, his wife Hulda Kobs (1863–1916), and six children raised hogs, chicken and cattle, taking their produce to Houston, where they would camp in Memorial Park, not far from the Reinermann place. Emil died in 1901 and was buried in the Hillendahl-Eggling cemetery on Langham Creek, to the east of Bear Creek community (item 17, Figure 6.18). His widow sold the property to Fred "Fritz" Pasche in 1911. Condemned by the Army Corps in the 1940s, the Brandt-Pasche farmhouse was ultimately sold and moved to another location, but the outbuildings were demolished in 1946–1947. All these buildings were photographed by the Corps prior to their demolition (Figure 6.23). They are classic examples of nineteenth-century German farm architecture.[112]

The Groschke, Hoffman and Moers families. Charlotte Henrietta Worg (1806–after 1870) was born in Prussia and married Ludwig (Louis) Groschke (1800–1853) in 1834 in Saxony. While living in Konigsburg, Hanover, Prussia, they had two sons, Carl Ernst (1835–1917) and Friedrich Emil (1836–1914), and a daughter, Albertine Marianne (1844–1909), all prior to emigrating to Texas in about 1847. They claimed three 160-acre pre-emption grants (homesteads) in 1855: one for Charlotte and one each for their adult sons, Carl and Emil. In 1850 the federal census of agriculture reported that Louis Groschke had cultivated ten of a total of 150 acres reported. He had three horses, two pairs of oxen, 10 milk cows, 15 beeves, and 19 hogs and harvested 125 bushels of corn (about two to three acres). His farm land was valued at $200, equipment at $60, and livestock at $250.

Louis died in 1853, and Charlotte sold her 160-tract to her daughter Marianne and her husband Frederick "Fritz" Hoffman (1840–1913), in 1870. The Hoffmans lived together on the property until 1910 (Figure 6.18, item 4). Their son Rudolph then operated the farm; he committed suicide in 1947 when the land was taken for the Addicks project. His widow moved those farm structures just north of the flood zone in the 1940s, thus saving them from demolition during construction of the Addicks Reservoir; it is not known whether they are still standing today.[113]

Henry Moers emigrated from Germany around 1878 and married Katie Hoffman, a sister of Rudolph Hoffman, in 1893. They purchased a northern part of the Charlotte Groschke tract in

Top left: Figure 6.24. Carl Ernst Groschke, daughter-in-law Katie, son George, and grandchildren, ca. 1916. Courtesy of Sondra C. Haltom. **Top right:** Figure 6.25. Dorothea Hillendahl Groschke, wife of Carl Ernst Groschke. Courtesy of Marie Neuman Gray. **Above:** Figure 6.26. The Carl Ernst Groschke farmstead as it appeared in 1944, shortly prior to demolition. Courtesy of Martha Doty Freeman and the U.S. Army Corps of Engineers.

1893 and established a home and farm (Figure 6.18, site 7). Their buildings were not condemned by the Corps but unfortunately burned in the late 1980s.

Carl Ernst Groschke (1835–1917; Figure 6.24) and Friedrich Emil Groschke (1836–1914), both children of Ludwig and Charlotte, received the other two Groschke tracts (Figure 6.18, sites 5 and 6), and at the time of the 1860 census both men and their wives were living at a home on Friedrich's tract. Both brothers served in the Confederacy, in the 4th Texas Field Battery, and later the 1st Texas Heavy Artillery Regiment; both survived the war.

Carl Ernst Groschke married Dorothea Hillendahl (1838–1915) in 1858 (Figure 6.25), and the couple had twelve children. After 1860 Carl built a home on his tract, where he lived until his death in

1917. The farm was passed on to Carl's son George Groschke (1873–1945), who continued to live in his parents' old home while he operated a dairy (Figure 6.26). George's son Lawrence Groschke (b. 1910) built a bungalow in 1930 and continued to work the family dairy. All buildings on the Groschke farm were destroyed by the Army Corps of Engineers in the 1940s. George Groschke committed suicide in 1945, depressed about both his health and the construction of Addicks Reservoir on his family's land. One remaining feature on the property is the family cemetery, where Carl and Dorothea and two sons are buried, along with other burials that are unmarked.[114]

Friedrich Emil Groschke married Catharine Koch (1842–1861), and they had a son, Fred Jr. Catherine died in 1861, and Friedrich then married Dorothea Feuerschutz (1844–1920) in 1862. They had nine children between 1866 and 1886. Friedrich had one of his feet amputated in 1911, after which time the farm declined. He died in 1914, and his widow moved to Houston. Before leaving, Dorothea sold the farm to their son, Walter Groschke, in exchange for caring for her for the rest of her life. His livestock included a dairy operation, cattle, and chickens. Walter died in 1924, and the farm was leased out for pasturage, its buildings rapidly deteriorating.[115]

Christian Meier. Christian Meier (1807–1875; also spelled Meyer) and his wife Dorothea Grobe (1814–1875) emigrated to Texas from Hanover, Germany, in 1848 along with a daughter, Dorothea (1840–1921), and by 1850 were farming in the Bear Creek community (Figure 6.18, site 8).[116] In 1849 Christian bought 100 acres of the Flournoy Hunt survey from John A. Block and acquired a 160-acre homestead grant from the state in that survey in 1860. In the 1850 federal census he is listed as living with his wife Dorothea and daughter Dorothea, age 10, and from the 1850 agricultural census records, they were barely making it. Christian had cultivated five of a total of thirty acres reportedly owned. He had one horse, no oxen, two milk cows, two beeves, and three hogs, and harvested 35 bushels of corn (probably less than an acre). His farm land

Figure 6.27. Annie Sophie Meier and Johann Heinrich (Henry) Addicks, 1870. Photo courtesy of Marie Neuman Gray.

was valued at $70, equipment at only $10, and livestock at $45. In 1855 the Meiers purchased 400 acres in the G. W. Toliver survey before receiving a preemption grant of 160 acres on the Flournoy Hunt grant, adjacent to the Striepe, Groschke and Brandt families.[117]

Their daughter Dorothea (1840–1921) married Frederick Kobs Jr. in 1858 (see Kobs family, later). In 1869 another daughter, Annie "Sophie" Meier (1852–1912), married German immigrant Johann "Heinrich" Addicks (1843–1879; also spelled Eidecks; Figure 6.27).[118] Heinrich, born in Oldenburg, Germany, came to Texas in 1852 with his parents and siblings on the bark Neptune; they settled in Cypress, northwestern Harris County. Annie and Heinrich purchased her parents' 160-acre homestead, and as part of the agreement Heinrich agreed to build Christian and Dorothea Meier a sixteen-by-eighteen-

Figure 6.28. Charles August Kunze, second husband of Sophie Meier, 1880. Photo courtesy of Marie Neuman Gray.

foot home for them to live in. In 1870, while Heinrich worked the farm with Sophie, 14 acres were being cultivated, with another 146 not improved. They owned 6 horses, 7 milk cows, 23 other cattle, and 8 hogs. They produced that year 300 bushels of Indian corn, 80 bushels of Irish potatoes, 20 bushels of sweet potatoes, 75 pounds of butter, and a ton of hay.

Heinrich was the first postmaster and namesake of Addicks, Texas, and went to Houston on horseback to get the mail. The town was laid out by the next postmaster, William "Uncle Billy" Shulz, and Shulz named it after Addicks, who died in 1879. After his death, Sophie married Charles August Kunze Jr. (1854–1935), of the Prussia-Silesian area of Germany, in 1880, and the couple raised seven children (Figure 6.28).[119]

Christian and Dorothea Meier were living in the home that Heinrich had built for them in 1875 when a large hurricane blew in; this same storm destroyed Indianola on the coast. Christian was sick in bed, and Dorothea went outside during the howling storm to rescue a calf; the calf shed collapsed on her, killing her. Christian died a week or so later. The main cemetery at the time was the Hillendahl-Eggling cemetery, but it was unreachable due to the remnant floodwaters, so they were interred in the Koch-Schmidt cemetery, of which more below.[120]

When Sophie Meier Addicks Kunze died in 1912, the original Christian Meier property was passed on to Sophie's children, Hilda and Winnie Kunze. The buildings were razed in the 1940s, when the property was condemned during the construction of Addicks Reservoir.

Johann Koch family. Johann Koch (1799–1854) and his wife Anna Elisabetha Naumann Koch (1806–1856) emigrated from Buchenau in the Hesse-Darmstadt Province of Germany on the Franziska in 1845, landing in Galveston on January 11, 1846. They brought with them their five surviving children: Joseph "Jost" (1829–1905), Marguerita (b. 1831), Johann (1834–1860), Ludwig (1838–1886), and Catherine (1841–1861). The seven members of the family are listed in the 1850 census. Johann bought 20 acres two miles from Houston in 1846 or 1847 and then bought 177 acres of land at Bear Creek, in the Christiana Williams labor, in 1848.[121] Their house (Figure 6.29) and later the family cemetery (Figure 6.30) were located on the latter plot; the site is now part of Cullen Park in Addicks Reservoir (Figure 6.18, item 9), where the cemetery is protected. The homestead was later owned by eldest son Joseph Koch.

Johann Koch's sons Joseph and Ludwig were conscripted into Confederate Army service during the Civil War (see Chapter 8), and after the war they bought a third of a league from Bartholomew Tuffy in 1870, east of Langham Creek. They divided the land between them, with Ludwig in the northern half and Joseph in the south (items 10 and 11, Figure 6.18). Joseph built a frame Greek Revival farmhouse on his part of the Tuffy land in about 1875 (Figure 6.31). Joseph married Susanna Matzke Koch (1832–1922; Figure 6.32) in 1851 they had one son, John (b. 1852), before they divorced in 1879. Within a month of the finalization of the divorce, Joseph married Elizabet "Lisette" Plessman (1840–1903), an immigrant from Saxony, Prussia. After the divorce Joseph continued to live at this property, which is within what is now Bear Creek Park, while Susannah moved back to the older Johann Koch place.[122] In 1879. In 1882 Susannah married Friedrich Schmidt (d. 1895).[123] Susannah's sister Dorothea Matzke Ankele (1834–1927) and her husband, Lutheran Minister David Ankele (1826–1895), lived at the

Top: Figure 6.29. Johann and Anna Koch's house, later the home of Susannah Matzke Schmidt, photographed prior to demolition, 1944. Courtesy of the U.S. Army Corps of Engineers and Marie Neuman Gray.
Above: Figure 6.30. The Koch-Schmidt family cemetery with its decorated graves, as it appeared in 1944 when the U.S. Army Corps of Engineers acquired the property. Courtesy of Martha Doty Freeman and U.S. Army Corps of Engineers.

Koch-Schmidt farm after they retired. According to Matzke descendant Marie Neuman Gray, Dorothea (Figure 6.33) wore a belt under her outer garments where she kept her savings of gold coins. These coins were later donated to a Houston Lutheran church to cover the academic expenses of any aspiring young minister. In the late twentieth century, after the vacant site of the former house became part of Addicks Reservoir, the site was reportedly covered with dirt to prevent vandals with metal detectors from tearing up the home site looking for those gold coins. After Susanna died, the old house went to her nephew Willie Matzke before being sold to D. W. Barnhill, prior to Addicks Reservoir construction.[124]

Top: Figure 6.31. Joseph Koch farm and home, ca. 1897. Built in 1875, the home was demolished during construction of the Addicks Reservoir in the 1940s. Courtesy of Marie Neuman Gray.
Above: Figure 6.32. Joseph and Susanna Koch. Photographs courtesy of Marie Neuman Gray.

Joseph Koch and his second wife, Lisette, left Bear Creek after 1888 and moved to Chaney Junction, a new subdivision near the Houston Heights. They were living at 1115 Dart Street at the time of the 1900 census. Lisette died in 1903 and Joseph Koch married a third time, to Albertina Polzin in 1904. After Joseph died in 1905, his niece, Susannah Koch Golbow (daughter of Ludwig and Sophia Koch; profiled next) and her husband Henry Golbow traded a place on Dairy Ashford Road for Joseph's house on the former Tuffy land; they already owned part of Ludwig and Sophia's adjacent farm, given to Susannah by her mother Sophia. The home was in the hands of family members until it

Figure 6.33. Dorothea Matzke Ankele with her chickens and an unknown man at her sister Susannah Matzke Koch Schmidt's home. Courtesy of Marie Neuman Gray.

was purchased and demolished by the Army Corps of Engineers in the 1940s as part of the construction of Addicks Reservoir.[124]

Joseph's brother Ludwig Koch (1838–1886), who owned the other part of the Tuffy land, married widow Sophia Addicks Eggling (1838–1923) in March 1863, during the war, and they had seven children between 1864 and 1879. Sophie also had three small children by her former husband William Eggling; the youngest was born in December 1862, only four months before she married Ludwig.[125] During the 1870 census, the Kochs were residing on the land bought from Tuffy and had 12 acres under cultivation, another 20 wooded, and 90 acres unimproved. Ludwig was running stock on the adjacent open range and owned 21 horses, 20 milk cows, 340 other cattle, 11 sheep, and seven hogs. He was trying his hand at cotton (one bale), and produced 25 bushels of Irish potatoes, 50 bushels of sweet potatoes, 70 pounds of butter, and a ton of hay.[126]

Sophia's grandson, Joe Golbow, told of his grandparents' early life in Bear Creek, when interviewed in 1982:

When they came over from Germany, they brought an old yellow umbrella [with them]. They had houses with straw roofs [at first]. That's all they had, so whenever the rains would get serious, they would get out this old umbrella and open it, and put it between them in the bed so they could stay dry. When they first came from Germany, things were very primitive, you see. Grandma Koch was always telling me about those times. . . . They would walk to town [Houston] and get their necessities, such as salt. They did not have horses and buggies yet. They used to take a "shucks basket" that had handles on each side. Grandma would be on one side, and Grandpa on the other. Main Street was down there at Allen's Landing; and it was the only street then. I guess it was about a half mile long at the very most at that time. . . . Then they would sleep on the ground at night—anywhere they could find a spot that was dry.

And when that age was past, they bought some oxen to get around from place to place. They would leave home and go by the straightest way into town. It would be very early in the morning, before day-

light. They would get there about dark. If the oxen were thirsty, and the weather was hot and dry, they would drive them over where Rice Hotel now stands and water them in the pond. There was just a water pond there at that time, you know. And the next morning they would water the oxen again, and after they got through with their shopping, they would get ready to go home the following day. So they would get their necessities and start back home. [They would] spend the night with whoever they knew that had a home along the way, like the Hillendahls. Oh, the ox cart had just two wheels.[127]

When a widowed Sophia deeded her farm to her son Ludwig Koch, she attached a few conditions in this agreement of September 10, 1894:

1) Provide a house in good dry living conditions and not more than 100 feet from the old living place;
2) Yearly: 20 lbs sausage, 20 lbs bacon, 2 dozen chickens (hens and roosters), 1 lamp oil, 30 lbs sugar, 6 lbs coffee, [and] so much chopped firewood as necessary.
3) Half yearly: 10 lb sack of German potatoes for winter, 10 lb sack of German potatoes for summer;
4) Monthly: 1 sack of the best flour;
5) Daily: 2 eggs.[128]

Golbow family. Carl Golbow (1821–1909; originally spelled Goldbaum) came alone from Lentzen, Prussia (Germany), in 1847. He married Dorothea Shulz (1829–1916) of Reckenthin, Germany, in 1853; she was living in Harris County with her parents, Christof and Elisabeth Shulz, who had emigrated from Germany with Dorothea (Figure 6.34). The two families were later neighbors. Carl bought 200 acres of the William Hardin survey in 1857 and had a home near what would later become the town of Addicks, south of the future Missouri, Kansas and Texas Railroad (Figure 6.18, item 12). He later had several other pieces of property in the area.[129] He and Dorothea had five children between 1854 and 1870; as earlier noted, their son Henry (b. 1867) married Susannah Koch and lived at the old Joseph Koch place.[130]

Schulz family. Johann Joachim Friedrich Schulz (ca. 1824–1900) and his wife (and first cousin) Sophie Schulz (1825–1900) were married in Germany in 1849 (Figure 6.35). They had six children between 1848 and 1866 while living in the town of Kletzke: Marie Emilie (1848–1925), Sophie Marie (1849–1927), Anna Marie Elizabeth (1852–1887), Carl Friedrich Wilhelm "Uncle Billy" (1857–1930), Augusta Louise (1860–1935), and Otto Adolph August (b. 1866). The family immigrated to Galveston in 1867 on the bark Anton Gunther and moved to Letitia, Texas, which was named for the daughter of Stafford Smith and was later renamed Addicks. By the time of the 1883 tax records they owned 50 acres, two horses, a cow and some personal property for a total of $635 in net worth (Figure 6.18, item 13). Sophie was killed in the 1900 storm, which nearly destroyed the town of Addicks. Johann died the next day due to the shock of his wife's death, and to exposure. They were buried in the Marks family burial ground and later moved to Memorial Oaks Cemetery in Houston.[131]

Their oldest daughter Marie Emilie Schulz (1848–1925; Figure 6.36) married William Addicks (d. ca. 1873); both were born in Germany. Three children were born to this marriage. William Addicks was dragged to death by a horse and was buried at the Hillendahl-Eggling cemetery. Marie then married Prussian-born Samuel Quade (1837–1895), and they had eight children between 1874 and 1887. According to Schulz family historian Maxine Sullivan,

Emile was a hard worker and raised her family the best she could. It is told that she could herd cattle and work the fields as well as any man, even though she was only five feet tall and heavy set. . . . She never rode a horse, but walked the fields with grass taller than she was. During that time it was known as open range. If a horse or cattle was loose and had no brand on it, she corralled it and branded it, and from then on it was hers.

She is buried at the Addicks Bear Creek Methodist Cemetery, where her headstone reads "She done what she could."[132]

Left: Figure 6.34. Dorothea Schulz Golbow and her husband Carl Golbow. Courtesy of the late Margaret H. Edwards.
Below: Figure 6.36. Marie Emilie Schulz. Courtesy of Andrea Burden and the late Maxine Sullivan.

Figure 6.35. Johann Joachim Friedrich Schulz and his wife Sophie Schulz, who lived in Addicks and died as a result of the 1900 Galveston storm. Courtesy of Marie Neuman Gray.

Johann and Sophie's second daughter, Sophie Marie Schulz (1849–1927), married German-born Friedrich Koennecke (1839–1916) in 1870; they settled in the Addicks area and had four children there between 1871 and 1883. Koennecke was a Confederate soldier (see Chapter 8); in later years he and Sophie moved to Rosenberg, Texas.[133] Friedrich is buried in St. Peter Church cemetery in Spring Branch. Another Schulz daughter, Elizabeth Schulz (1852–1887) married August Texas Marks, son of Gotthilf and Sophia Marks (profiled earlier). A Schulz son, William "Uncle Billy" Schulz Sr., began the first store in what would become Addicks, in 1881 or 1882, and laid out the town of Letitia (later Addicks); the Missouri, Kansas and Texas Railroad was built through there in 1893 (Chapter 11). He was postmaster for forty-seven years, and his son William Schulz Jr. and grandson Maynard Shulz operated the store well into the 1950s.[134]

Kobs family. Carl Frederick Wilhelm (Fritz) Kobs (1833–1905) was born in Kalbe an der Milda Province, Saxony-Anhalt, Germany, and emigrated to Galveston in 1848 with his parents, Frederick Kobs (b. 1798) and Fredericke Beckendorff (b. 1800), and his siblings.[135] Fritz lived with his family in Rose Hill, near modern Tomball in northwestern Harris County, until moving to Bear Creek to marry Dorothea Louise Meier (1840–1921; Figure 6.37) in 1858. Dorothea was the daughter of Christian and Dorothea Meier (profiled earlier). The Kobs settled east of Langham Creek (Figure 6.18, site 14).[136] Fritz served in the Confederate Army during the Civil War (see Chapter 8).

Fritz and Dorothea Kobs had nine children while living on the farm on Langham Creek between 1859 and 1876. Six survived to adulthood: Wilhelm Fritz (1861–1925), Hulda (1863–1916), Dorothea (1867–1934), Sophie (1870–1944), Gustav (1872–1939), and Charles Frederick (1874–1934). A photograph shows Fritz and Dorothea in front of their home about 1900 with sons Charles and Gustav and their wives (Figure 6.38). Their eldest son, Willhelm Fritz Kobs, later lived on that land with his wife Annie Marie Koim (1864–1946). They are shown in Figure 6.39, in front of their frame home and with

Figure 6.37. Dorothea Meier and Frederick Kobs in 1870. Courtesy of Marie Neuman Gray.

their four children, born between 1888 and 1898; the photograph was taken about 1901. Their second daughter Dorothea Kobs married Edward John Neuman, who was born in Washington County but settled in Austin County (later formed into Waller County) in 1871; some of their descendants live in Pattison.[137]

Fritz and Dorothea Kobs are buried at the Addicks Bear Creek Methodist Cemetery. The farm was passed on to their son Gustav (Gus) Kobs and then to Gus's son Harvey Kobs. Its buildings were destroyed during the construction of Addicks Reservoir.

Hillendahl family. Franz Ludwig "Louis" Hillendahl (1812–1880) was born in Fallersleben, Germany, and emigrated to Galveston in 1847. As we saw in the account of Spring Branch, he and his wife

Figure 6.38. Three Kobs couples in front of the Fritz Kobs home, ca. 1900. Left to right, Fritz and Dorothea Kobs, their son Charles and his wife Elizabeth, and their son Gustav and his wife Sabina. Photograph courtesy of Marie Neuman Gray.

Figure 6.39. Willhelm Fritz Kobs, his wife Annie Marie Koim, and their four children in front of their home, ca. 1901. Courtesy of Martha Doty Freeman.

Figure 6.40. A rear view of the home of George Hillendahl in 1944, showing the windmill, cistern and a machinery shop. The house was later moved to Addicks, where it still stands (see Chapter 12). Courtesy of Martha Doty Freeman and the U.S. Army Corps of Engineers.

Sophie Dorothea Schulz (1811–1881) originally settled in Spring Branch, but in 1860 they bought 507 acres of the Toliver survey in the Bear Creek area from Darius Gregg. Louis sold 234 acres of this land in 1871 to his son George Hillendahl (1847–1915), and George built a house on the property (Figure 6.18, site 15, and Figure 6.40).[138] That house later passed to George's unmarried children, his son Walter Hillendahl and his daughter Katie Marie Hillendahl, and was purchased in the 1940s by Joe Golbow and moved off the farm to nearby Addicks, to escape destruction when the Addicks Reservoir was built. It appears to be the only nineteenth-century building from Bear Creek still existing today (see Chapter 12).

Eggling and Grisbee families. Christian Eggling (ca. 1798–1849) and his second wife Maria Maehle Eggling (1821–1897) emigrated to the United States from Hanover, Germany, in 1847–1848, with their four children, Henry (ca. 1832–1867), William (ca. 1834–ca. 1863), Wilhelmina (ca. 1844–1871), and Henrietta (1847–1919). Almost immediately Christian died, and his widow married William Grisbee in Spring Branch in 1850. She had four more children with Grisbee, named Mary (1854–1900), John Henry (1857–1899), Lizzy (1859–1900), and George (1863–1900). They lived in the northeastern part of Bear Creek, near Langham Creek. Many of this extended family were buried in what became known as the Hillendahl-Eggling cemetery, near the original location of the Bear Creek Church on Langham Creek (see next section).[139]

There were other families at Bear Creek, of course, beyond those few profiled here. Some of their names include Ankele, Bachen, Beckendorff, Clay, Dopslauf, Grisbee, Hoffmeister, Liere, Otte, Weiman and Zorn.[140]

Community life. By 1876 a one-room schoolhouse was built and named for William Grisbee (Figure 6.41). A post office appeared in 1878, named for the Bear Creek community.

A Methodist church was established in 1879 with seven charter members; it met in members'

Figure 6.41. The 1876 Grisbee one-room schoolhouse, ca. 1890, located near the Grisbee farm, at modern Addicks Satsuma Road and Clay Road. Courtesy of Marie Neuman Gray.
Figure 6.42. Bear Creek German Methodist church, ca. 1890, when it was located on Langham Creek north of Patterson Road, near the Hillendahl cemetery. Photo courtesy of the Addicks United Methodist Church.

homes in early years. By 1890 a church had been built on the bank of nearby Langham Creek (Figures 6.42, and 6.43), next to the Hillendahl-Eggling family cemetery, which had been in use since at least 1875 (see map, Figure 6.18). The site was prone to flooding and to poor access when the creek was high, so the church was moved in 1903 onto three acres donated by Frederick and Catherine Brandt, at the intersection of Patterson Road and modern Highway 6. A new cemetery at the new church site was opened by 1904, and it is still an active burial site today, at the intersection of Highway 6 and Patterson Road. A parsonage was built in 1909 on land donated by William and Minnie Krauel. The original church building was destroyed by a hurricane in 1915, and a new church was built (Figure 6.44). Because the Army Corps of Engineers required the land for flood control use, this building was moved in the 1940s to nearby Addicks, where it is now known as the Addicks United Methodist Church.[141] The old Hillendahl-Eggling cemetery at the original church site (later called the "Blue Light" cemetery by the press, a term not favored by Bear Creek descendants; see discussion in Chapter 12)) was then aban-

Figure 6.43. The Bear Creek German Methodist congregation, ca. 1902, on the old church site on Langham Road. Photo courtesy of the late Margaret H. Edwards.

doned, and was nearly destroyed by looters and vandals in the late twentieth century; the site is now protected by the Army Corps of Engineers.

After the Bear Creek postmaster Heinrich Addicks died in 1879, and after the post office building burned down in 1885, the post office was moved south along the new Addicks-Satsuma road (now Highway 6; Figure 6.18). The town of Addicks that grew up there was named for the former postmaster. Upon the arrival of the Missouri, Kansas and Texas Railroad in 1893, with a stop at Addicks, the new town became a commercial center. That situation was to continue until the dissolution of the community in the 1940s with the construction of Addicks Reservoir.[142]

Addicks Reservoir and the destruction of Bear Creek. The growing city of Houston experienced disastrous floods in 1929 and especially 1935. The latter flood swept through residential areas and the commercial district, causing $2,538,000 in property losses. To protect the city, the Harris County Flood Control District was authorized by the State Legislature in 1937, and two dams along upper Buffalo Bayou were constructed. Barker Dam was completed in 1945 and Addicks in 1946. Farmland lying upstream of the dam walls was purchased by eminent domain, and buildings standing in the new reservoirs were either moved or destroyed.[143] Although much of the Barker Reservoir's land was only lightly settled, the building of Addicks Reservoir caused the destruction of most of the pioneer Bear Creek community.

By that time most of the families there had farmsteads dating back nearly a century, and their forced removal, although necessary and perhaps inevitable, was nonetheless a painful chapter in the area's history. Their descendants today are scattered throughout the Gulf Coast region. Other than a few cemeteries (see Chapter 12), there is now little to mark their former presence within Addicks Reservoir. Harris County's Bear Creek Park remembers the name, and several streets in one part of the park are named for former residents of the community. In the early 1990s broadcaster Ray Miller of the Eyes of Texas series on television, working with Precinct 3 County Commissioner Steve Radack, developed a plan to recreate some of the old farm buildings, homes, one-room schools and a dance hall, to be

Figure 6.44. Bear Creek Methodist Church (right) and parsonage (left), sometime after 1915. The dirt road is now Highway 6. The view is to the north, and the Bear Creek cemetery, still in existence at Highway 6 and Patterson Road, is visible beyond the church, right of the road. The church building was moved south to Addicks in 1948, just north of Interstate 10. Courtesy of Marie Neuman Gray.

placed along those named roads. Not supported by the Army Corps of Engineers, who operate the reservoir, the plan was scrapped. Today, the pioneer farmsteads of the Groschke, Brandt, Striepe and Hoffman families lie vacant and fallow, north of Groschke Road and west of Highway 6; they have largely been overtaken by invasive Chinese tallow and other trees. However, the natural area of their farms has not been churned under by development, and is now preserved by the U.S. Army Corps of Engineers as part of Addicks Reservoir.

White Oak Community

Early settlers. White Oak has had a number of colorful settlers, and its settlement started with a female innkeeper on the frontier wagon road to Washington-on-the-Brazos. She joined a list of hardy women farmer/innkeepers in pioneer times in this area, all widows who refused to give it up when their spouses died; Elizabeth Wheaton, Mary Silliman, and Harriet George have been previously discussed.

The first resident in what would become the general vicinity of the White Oak community was "Madame" Theresa Wolf, who settled along Washington Road by 1838 (item 17, Figure 6.2). She was born in about 1800, according to the 1850 census, in which she is shown living near the Christian Bethjes. She owned fifty acres of land purchased from D. H. Stover in September 1838, in the southwestern corner of the Henry Reinermann acreage; Stover had purchased the land from Reinermann the same year.[144] A German businessman and early visitor to Houston, Gustav Dresel (1818–1848), noted that Wolf had a traveler's inn on Washington Road in 1839, which he visited when traveling to and from Montgomery County:

> *Very next morning, I saddled and trotted along by myself the fifteen miles to Madam Wolf's, who here owned a posting establishment and kept an Inn. I knew her from my former stay in Houston and therefore found the best reception. Her description of the state of sickness in the capital [Houston's devastating yellow fever epidemic, Chapter 4] was horrifying.*[145]

He visited her again in January 1840, after a

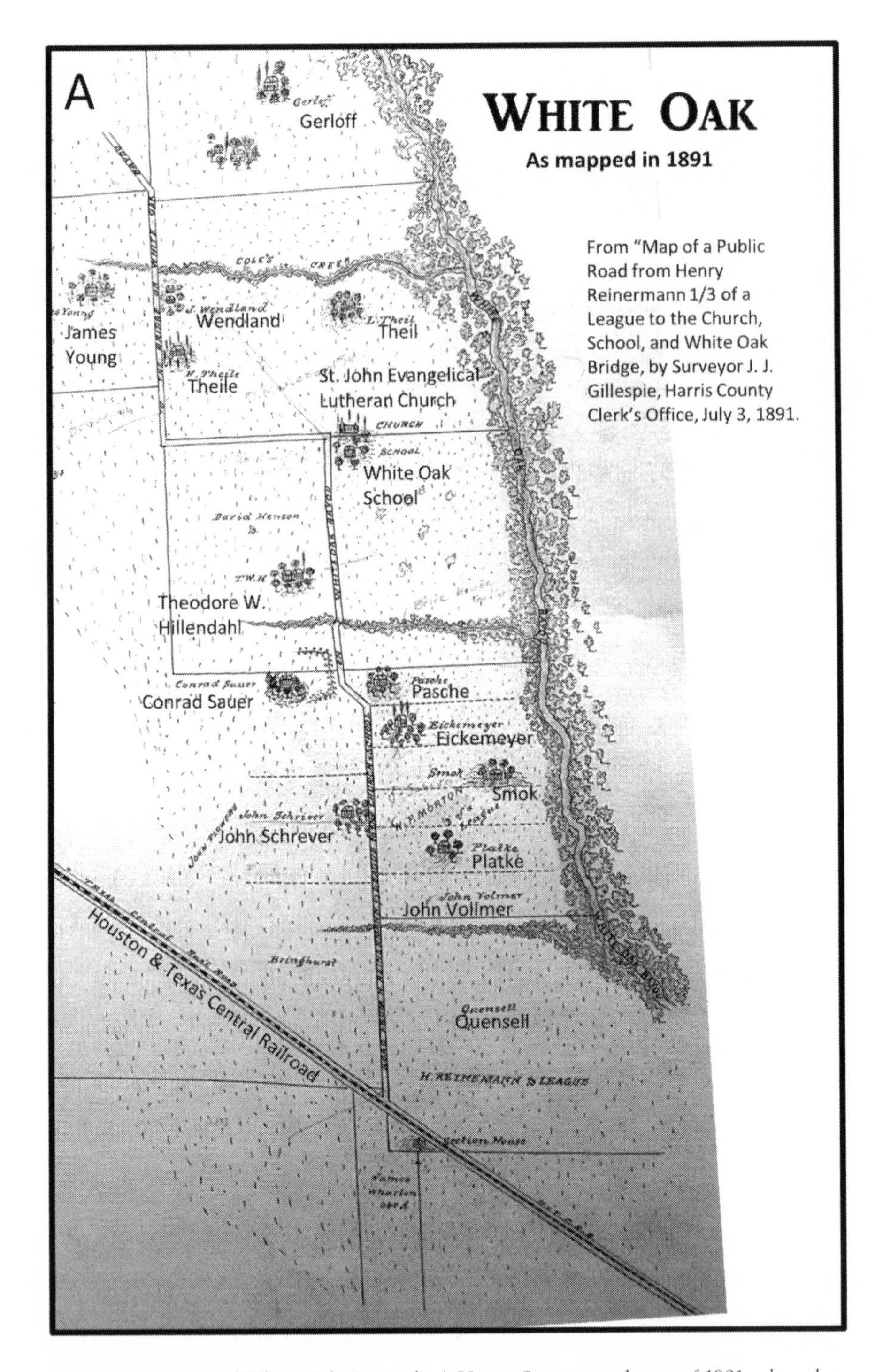

Figure 6.45. Maps of White Oak, Texas. **A:** A Harris County road map of 1891, when the "White Oak Road" (now Mangum Road) was improved. From "Map of a Public Road from Henry Reinermann 1/3 of a League to the Church, School, and White Oak Bridge," by Surveyor J. J. Gillespie, 1891, Harris County Clerk, Public Roads Maps, vol. 1.
B: Opposite Same features, plotted on a modern road map, courtesy of OpenStreetMap.

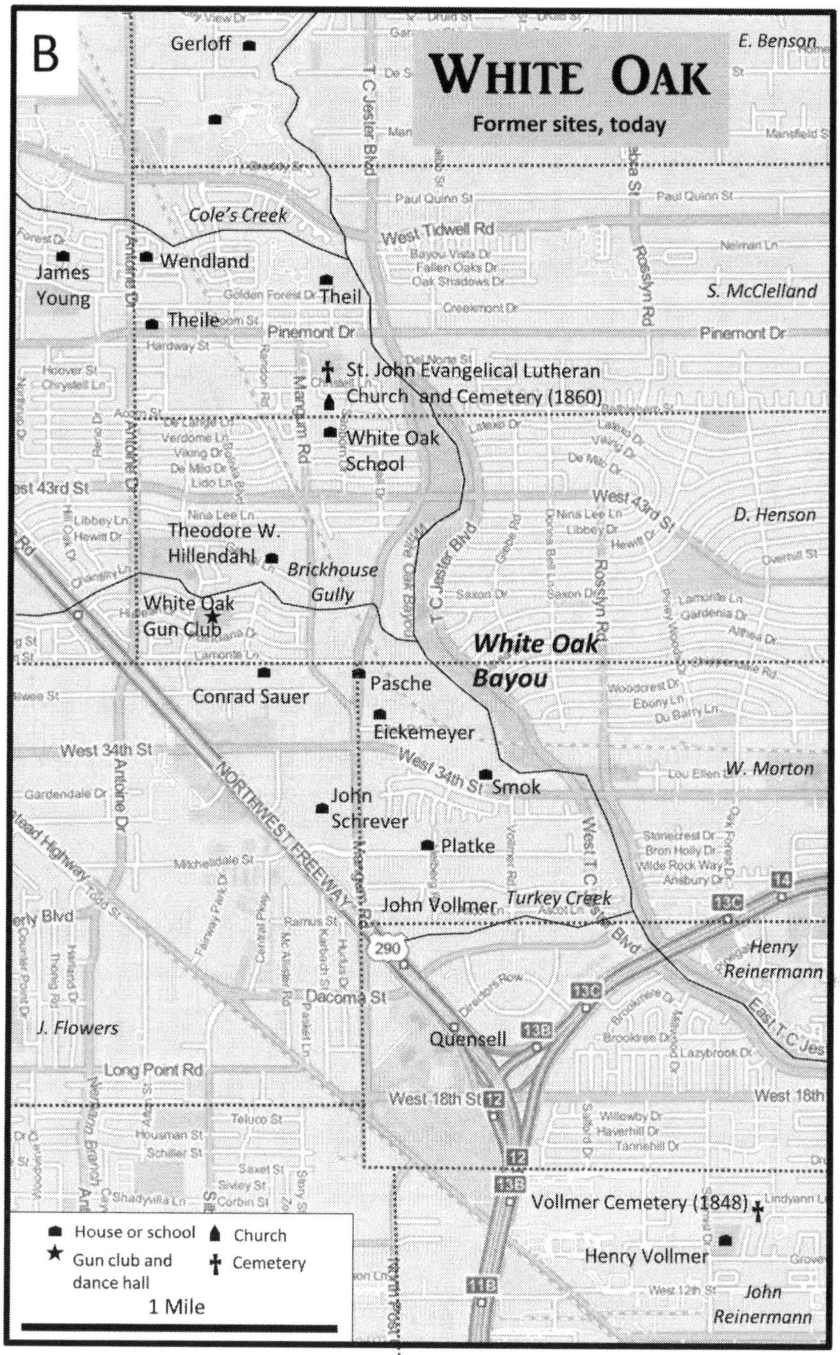

long ride through wintry rain, arriving at her inn after nightfall:

> *Good Madam Wolf was quite beside herself on seeing me in front of her with only one boot, my hair and clothes dripping with water. "Where, for God's sake, do you come from? No slave would be exposed to such weather at this hour! You will have the same experience as my late husband, who died a few weeks ago of such imprudence." All this was presented to me by my solicitous countrywoman when I poured a little glass of cognac into my stomach, which was sick and weakened by the cold, and I felt well by the fireside for the time being. Above all, I asked for clothes. Those of the late Mr. Wolf I did not want to have on my body [Wolf may have*

died of yellow fever, hence the reluctance]. Thus nothing remained but to compile my toilet from the garments of my kind hostess. When this was achieved, I resembled a female cook in dressing gown enough to deceive anyone, which vividly recalled the carnival joys of our old home country to our minds.

Soup, eggs, beefsteak, potatoes, sour pickles, and Madeira were dished up in turn by the active woman, everything well cooked, for she had served with high-class families in Germany for years and knew how to prepare something good out of the most ordinary foodstuffs, an accomplishment of which American women cannot boast. We chatted until two o'clock by a fire and wine.[146]

The name of her late spouse is not known. She soon married again, to John B. Glasgow on June 15, 1842.[147] But he appears to have left the scene by 1849, when her frontier business was described in the German-language Galveston Zeitung:

After passing from Houston through a little wood for a distance of four English miles, the traveler finds a very hospitable reception at Madam Wolf's farm. This German woman has been settled there for as long as eleven years and has gathered a wealth of experiences during that time. It is therefore highly interesting to listen to her stories about the past. She has transformed the surrounding prairie into fertile fields, and she directs the operation of her extensive domestic and agricultural possessions with the greatest energy and courage.[148]

In the 1850 census, the last look we have at her in the public record, she was living with three laborers and a cook, who no doubt were the hired help mentioned by the newspaper reporter. At the age of fifty, she had no husband or known descendants.

Soon after Madam Wolf moved to the area, two brothers emigrated from Hanover in Lower Saxony and settled not far away: Johann Heinrich (John) Ojemann (1814–1848) and Bernard Heinrich (Henry) Ojemann (b. 1812). The two came to Harris County, Texas, by 1842, where John married Catherine (Kate) Fenger (1820–1895) on December 9, 1842. Henry was married to Catherine Maria Kabbes Ojemann. The four are thought to have settled to the north of the John Reinermann tract. John and Kate Ojemann had two daughters, Nancy Ojemann (1845–1884) and Marie Henriette (Mary) Ojemann (1848–1912), before John died in 1848. His was the first burial in what became the Vollmer Cemetery, now behind a tall fence on Cindy Lane in the Timbergrove subdivision.[149]

A widow on the frontier, Kate Ojemann soon married German immigrant Henry Vollmer (1821–1878); they were married by the time of the 1850 federal census. Henry had purchased a 100-acre east-west elongated strip of land near the top of the Reinermann league, where he built a house. Kate brought her two young Ojemann daughters to this marriage, and the new couple soon added four more children: Katherine Vollmer Clay (1850–1916), John Vollmer (1855–1935), Henry Vollmer (1859–1891) and William Vollmer (1862–1940).[150] Henry prospered with his farm, and he invested in more land. This land went to his children, both natural and adopted. Son John Vollmer received a piece on the Morton tract (Figure 6.45 B). Step-daughter Nancy Ojemann received a piece on the Flowers tract and married German immigrant Conrad William Sauer (1843–1917) in 1871.[151] They had four children. Second step-daughter Mary Ojemann married Theodore W. Hillendahl (1844–1931), son of Spring Branch pioneer immigrants Louis and Dorthea Hillendahl, profiled earlier. Theodore was a Confederate veteran, and they married around 1869. They had seven children together. These three homesteads are listed on the White Oak map of 1891 (Figure 6.45 A) as those of John Vollmer, Conrad Sauer, and Theodore W. Hillendahl. The Hillendahl home was located where Scarborough High School is today.[152]

Meanwhile, John Ojemann's brother Henry and his wife Mary Ojemann had three children together: another Johann Heinrich Ojemann (1837–1921); Helene Margaretha Ojemann Stegemann O'Malley (1839–1908), who married Friedrich Wilhelm Stegemann (1827–1887) and later Bernard O'Malley (1843–1903); and Helena Catherine Ojemann Thiel

Top: Figure 6.46. The congregation of St. John Evangelical Lutheran Church at White Oak, Texas, ca. 1910. The church was built in 1891, on Mangum Road at its intersection with modern Trembling Oaks, where its cemetery still exists. This was the second church built by the congregation, which formed in 1860. It was moved in 1968 to Heritage Park in downtown Houston. Courtesy of the Heritage Society.

Above: Figure 6.47. The White Oak schoolhouse, formerly located across the street from the Lutheran church. Courtesy of Walker Richard "Sonny" Gray, Jr. and David Hornburg.

(1843–1882), who married Louis Thiel in 1868. The Thiels lived on the McClelland tract (Figure 6.45). Henry Ojemann died at some time after 1843, however, and Mary remarried, to German immigrant Hermann Friedrich Niemann (1823–1870) in 1847. They lived on a part of the northern Reinermann tract and had one child together, Henry Niemann (1852–1934).[153]

Vollmer and St. John cemeteries. The abovementioned pioneer German families formed the core of White Oak, and most are buried at Vollmer Cemetery on the John Reinermann tract (Figure 6.45 A). Other pioneers include Christoff Platke (1818–1900) of Brandenburg, Germany; Johann Christian Schmock (1818–1869) of Mecklenburg, Germany, who lived on the Morton tract; and Johann Steinhagen (1818–1889). These men and some family members are buried at the St. John Evangelical Lutheran Cemetery on Mangum Road, at the center of what was the White Oak community. They were joined by many other German families who arrived in the second and third waves of immigration to the area, in the 1850s to 1890s, as well as a number of Anglo families.[154]

White Oak community life. The early community was first named Vollmer, after the pioneer Vollmer family, but by 1860 became known as White Oak for its bayou. In 1866 a group of area families purchased two acres of land for a cemetery on a farm road that much later became Mangum Road, at its intersection with modern day Trembling Oaks. The church was formally established as the St. John German Lutheran Church in 1872, with Rev. Caspar Broun as pastor, and another six acres were purchased for a church building, which was forty by forty feet in size, functioning for many years as both church and school. A second, larger church building was erected in 1891 (Figures 6.45 B and 6.46).[155]

A school was built across the street from the church and is shown on the 1892 map of the area (Figure 6.45 B and 6.47). There was also a post office. In 1873 the White Oak *Schuetzen Verein* (gun club) was organized and placed on a small bit of leased land in the western part of the Henson tract; the club was at what is now Mangum Manor Park on Saxon Drive. These gun clubs—there were others in Spring Branch and Bear Creek—were popular among German farming folk in the late nineteenth century and are described in more detail in Chapter 11. In the 1880s the White Oak club was considered the premier club in the area and fielded fifty men for its shooting competitions.[156]

Decline and disappearance. The congregation of the Lutheran church diminished sharply in the early twentieth century, a victim of decline in the use of the German language, the growth of Houston into the area, and the setting up of a flood control district that condemned further growth in the White Oak flood plain. By 1918 only fifteen parishioners were left. The flood control district was later abandoned, and Oak Forest subdivision surrounded the church beginning in 1953.[157] The White Oak gun club was abandoned in the 1940s and razed in the 1950s. The 1891 church structure was moved to Sam Houston Park in 1968 for preservation, where it is today kept as a historic structure by the Heritage Society.[158] The post office was removed decades ago, and White Oak Road was renamed Mangum Road. Today the pioneer German community of White Oak is unknown to most urban dwellers in that area.

The Bering Family

The Berings were another early German immigrant family of the Houston area, arriving in 1846. They were primarily Houston dwellers and had a large retail lumber company and sash and door milling operation in Houston from the early 1850s. They had close personal relationships with both the Canfield/George and Morse families in the area south of Buffalo Bayou, and they owned land in the upper Buffalo Bayou area. Those relationships probably were an outgrowth of the purchasing of finished lumber from the sawmills operated on the upper bayou by those two families.

John Bering (1799–1848) was born in Hofgeismar, Hesse, Germany on April 24, 1799, and married Anna Margarette Reisse of Kassel, Hesse,

Germany. The couple had at least ten children, starting in 1829 and concluding just before they emigrated to Texas in 1846: Julius Cornelius (1829–1936), Conrad (1830–1915), Augustus (1827–1920), Louisa (1834–?), Theodore L. (1836–1911), Charles H. (1838–1931), Louis H. (1840–1891), Rosina (1842–?), Adolph (1844–1860), and Wilhelmina (1846–?). This family sailed for Texas in 1846 as part of a large group of German immigrants organized by the *Adelsverein,* known in Germany as the *Mainzer Adelsverein,* the "Society for the Protection of German Immigrants in Texas," founded in 1842. Prince Carl of Solms-Braunfels was appointed commissioner of the Adelsverein in May 1844, when the group acquired land grants at what would become New Braunfels. The large group that included the Bering family was emigrating to join the New Braunfels settlement. The group intended to land in Indianola and then travel by ox wagon to New Braunfels, but plans changed and they landed in Galveston instead, aboard the steamer *Spartan.*[159]

According to family legend, once the Berings landed in Galveston, they headed for New Braunfels, but their oxen "could not understand commands in German, and the cart broke down"—in Houston.[160] There may have been more to the story than that, however. Conditions at New Braunfels and Fredericksburg, colonies of the Adelsverein, were desperate and getting worse in the year before the Bering group arrived. At Indianola, their intended port, several hundred immigrants had died in the winter of 1845–1846, where they had been poorly housed and fed while waiting for transport to New Braunfels. Survivors among those earlier colonists could not get transport to their land inland even in 1846, because the American army bought all the available horses, so another two hundred died struggling to reach New Braunfels on foot. Their bleached bones marked the road to the colony. And disease awaited those who finally arrived, according to Moritz Tiling, who documented the history of the *German Element in Texas* in 1913:

The outlook was gloomy with every indication that both colonies of the Adelsverein were doomed to speedy extinction. While the scurvy epidemic was at its height, men and women became bereft of reason, all family ties were broken and the wretched people tried to forget their misery by dancing, carousing, and drinking. Dr. Koester, the only physician at New Braunfels, was powerless against the attacks of the disease, which only spent its force after one-third of the inhabitants had fallen victims to its deadly grip.[161]

Word got back to Germany around the time that the Berings left the country. Count Castell, of the Adelsverein in Bremen, wrote to his American Commissioner von Meusebach in Texas on June 10, 1846:

The letter of Mr. Klaener, addressed to the Mayor of Bremen, Mr. Schmidt, and published in the papers, has made the worst impression. It has been communicated to the governments, who now call for an explanation. It states that sickness and death prevail at Indianola and New Braunfels, and that the company does not come up to its promise to remove the immigrants upwards.[162]

Tiling gives a reason more compelling than a recalcitrant yoke of oxen for the Berings leaving the Adelsverein and heading for Houston:

Many of the immigrants coming in 1846 heard on board of the emigrant vessels of the piteous conditions of the colonists at New Braunfels, and those who had sufficient means for self support rather sacrificed their contract with the Adelsverein, than risking their lives in the infested colony of the Verein. Some, like J. Frederick, remained in Galveston; others, among them the families of Bering and Cabanis, came to Houston, while some went to Industry, Cat Spring and La Grange.[163]

The Berings traveled on the side-wheeler *Old San Jacinto* from Galveston to Houston. According to William Bammel,

The first home site was on the banks of the Little White Oak Bayou. John Bering was a cabinet maker and his son was an apprentice at the Thompson sash and door factory at Main and Capitol. John Bering later built their home at 1306 Louisiana Street, Houston, Texas, and two years later when August was only 19, his father John died of yellow fever. August and his brother Conrad started the first lumber business in Houston at the corner of Travis and Prairie. They then went into the sash and door business establishing the Bering Manufacturing Company.[164]

The firm started by Augustus and Conrad was called A. *Bering and Bro.* and was the first retail lumber yard and sash mill in the city. During the 1860s Conrad and Augustus are shown in the city directory living on Louisiana Street. At the same time, in the 1860 census, their mother Anna Bering was living in the Fourth Ward with sons Charles, listed as a carpenter, and Louis, listed as a clerk, plus two German young women, Sabine and Mente, also from Hesse (probably her daughters Rosina and Wilhelmina). They were living in a different neighborhood than Conrad and Augustus, and from their neighbors it appears it was a working-class area.

The Berings appear to have had business dealings with the Canfield/George family in Piney Point, and Theodore became an executor of Harriet George's estate when she died in 1892. In the late 1850s Louis and Theodore Bering became very close friends of the Rev. John Kell Morse family, who had a farm and a Methodist church ministry south of Buffalo Bayou on the western edge of the Agur Morse plantation (see Chapter 7). Louis Bering married the Morses' daughter Eugenia in 1861, just before he joined the Confederacy. When Eugenia's parents died of consumption in 1863-1864, Louis became executor of the estate, and Theodore Bering and his wife adopted Eugenia's young brother, George Edward Morse. Louis and Eugenia Bering purchased the old John Kell Morse 300-acre farm; modern day Bering Drive runs through the center of that former farm.

In the 1850s Theodore was running cattle on what was then an open range in the west Houston prairie. On December 22, 1858, Theodore Bering posted a notice in the *Houston Weekly Telegraph* that his five-year-old mare, which had been running with his livestock on his property seven miles from Houston, had been stolen. This notice (Figure 6.48), along with his absence from the 1860 census that listed the

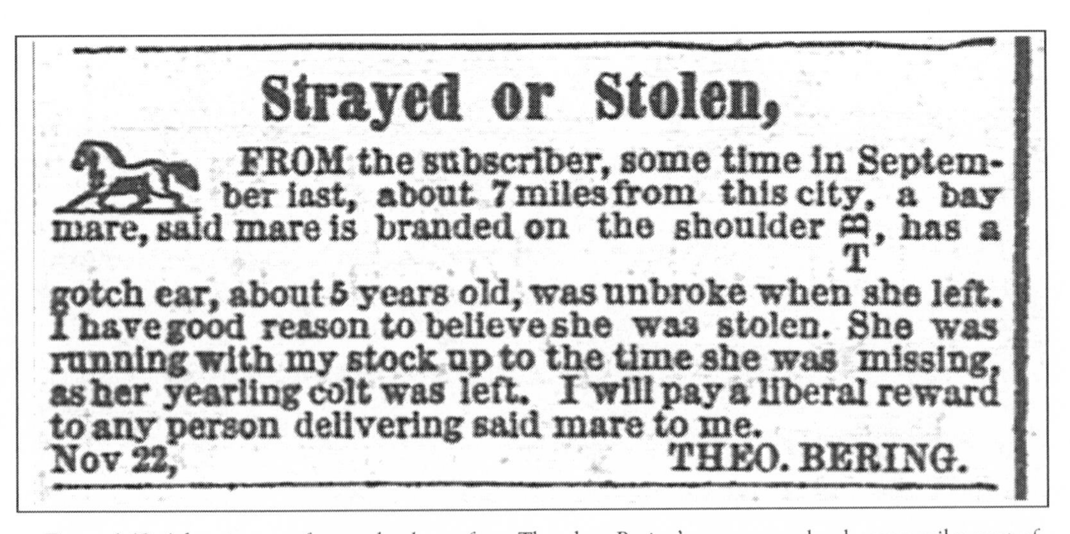

Strayed or Stolen,

FROM the subscriber, some time in September last, about 7 miles from this city, a bay mare, said mare is branded on the shoulder B T, has a gotch ear, about 5 years old, was unbroke when she left. I have good reason to believe she was stolen. She was running with my stock up to the time she was missing, as her yearling colt was left. I will pay a liberal reward to any person delivering said mare to me.

Nov 22, THEO. BERING.

Figure 6.48. Advertisement for a stolen horse from Theodore Bering's open range herd, seven miles west of Houston (near Piney Point). From the *Houston Weekly Telegraph*, December 22, 1858.

rest of the Bering family living in town in Houston, suggests that he might have been living in the area then, taking care of his livestock and perhaps buying lumber from local sawmills.

By 1862 Theodore was living in Houston, however. In the 1862 Harris County tax rolls, Theodore was listed as a retail seller living at 28 Hudson in Houston. By the 1870 census Theodore became a newspaper agent in the Fourth Ward, and by 1883 he was city circulator and collector for the Houston Post. Louis, after a stint in the Confederate army during the early 1860s, operated a hardware store in the city.

In 1886 and 1889 Conrad Bering purchased about 2,000 acres of timber and farmland in the Vince tract, which straddled Buffalo Bayou, adjacent to the former John Kell Morse farm then owned by Louis Bering.[165] He continued to live in town, however; this may have been a weekend place. Conrad Bering's grandson, also Conrad (1895–1984), owned land in Spring Branch, which was donated by the family in the 1950s to form Duchesne Academy, a Catholic girls' school, at the intersection of modern Memorial Drive and Chimney Rock. That property had formerly been the site of the Ahrenbeck sawmill, noted earlier in this chapter.

Legacy

These stories involve only a fraction of the pioneer Germans who flooded into the area in the 1840s and 1850s. By 1850 one-fifth of Texans were of German birth. In Harris and Galveston counties alone there were 6,000 Germans that year, split about equally between the two counties.[166] About 425 Germans lived in Houston town in 1850—about 18 percent of the town's population of 2,396—so another 2,500 or so were spread across the rural parts of the county, mostly north of Buffalo Bayou and along Spring and Cypress creeks in northern and northwestern Harris County. There were Kochs, Tegges, Kuhlmanns, Bodensteins, Beckendorffs, Appes, and hundreds of others, each with their own story. Their names can today be found on street signs across that part of Harris County and in the City of Houston.

At the same time that these pioneers were trudging alongside their ox carts as they headed to their new farms, another migration was happening south of the Bayou and across eastern Texas. A second wave of planters was coming in from worn-out lands in parts east, from the Old South, flowing in the footsteps of the Old 300 planters of the Brazos and Colorado plantations. One well-to-do planter among this new group, Agur Tomlinson Morse, was to build a large plantation in a very unlikely place, far from the fertile bottomlands of the Brazos and Colorado River valleys.

Figure 7.1. A southern cotton press and cotton gin. *From Frank Leslie's Illustrated Newspaper,* October 7, 1871.

SEVEN

The Morse Family of Pleasant Bend Plantation

I found that the agricultural resources of Harris County have been vastly underrated. A few years since Mr. A. T. Morse purchased a tract of land which by additions since made amounts now to 2100 acres. . . . On this tract of land Mr. M. has made 2/3 of a bale of cotton per acre. . . . He has realized fifty bushels of corn per acre on a portion of his farm. . . . He thinks his prairie land stands a drought better than the Brazos bottom lands. Now how many acres of land similar to those cultivated by Mr. Morse does Harris County contain? . . . Why expose our heads to be scalped by the Indians in search of good soil [in inland Texas], when we have it in such abundance in our own county? I found the lands in the vicinity of Mr. Morse are rapidly attracting occupants. The grazing facilities are superior. Farming and stock-raising can there be advantageously combined. A school is in demand.

—Reporter for the *Houston Weekly Telegraph*, May 25, 1859

IN 1851 Agur T. Morse and his wife Grace Morse arrived in this area from Lowndes County, Mississippi, where Agur had built a successful cotton plantation that was wiped out by a disastrous flood on the Tombigbee River. The cotton plantation that he established along the south side of Buffalo Bayou in 1851 marked an abrupt departure for what was then a frontier neighborhood with few settlers and fewer slaves. Before venturing into the story of the Morse family, however, it is appropriate to take a look at the upper Buffalo Bayou area west of Houston town at a time immediately preceding their arrival, from the view of John W. Bergin, the federal census taker (and city sexton of Houston), who spent a week there in January 1851 counting noses, working (a bit late) on the 1850 census.

Demographics of a thinly settled frontier, 1850

The census taker rode west from Houston along Washington Road on January 18 (see map, Figure 7.2), first listing the residents along that road. The first domicile noted the area west of modern Shepherd Drive was the Reinermann homestead, by 1850 under the ownership of Christian Ludwig Bethje

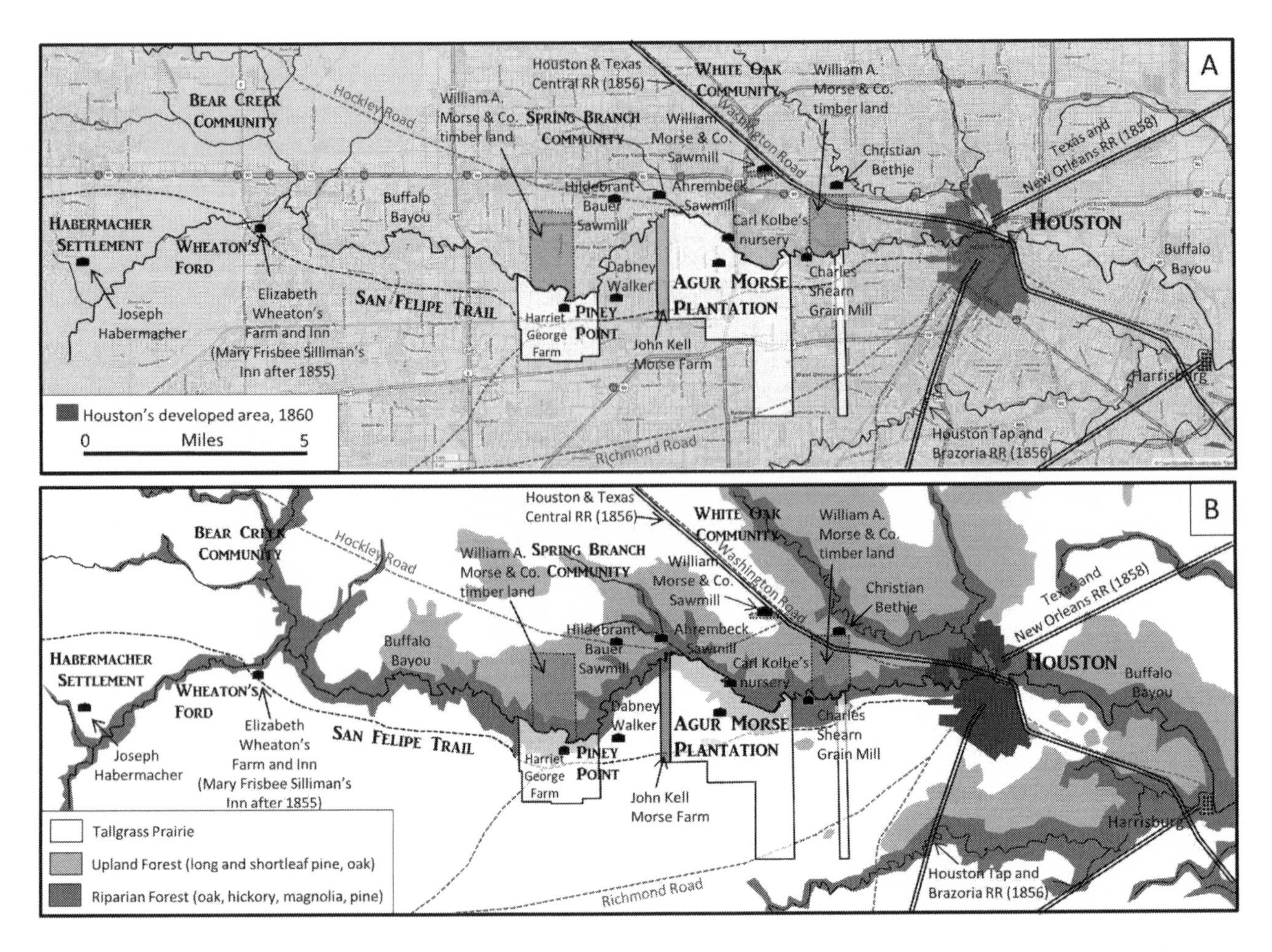

Fig. 7.2 Western Harris County, ca. 1860. Approximate routes of wagon roads are compiled from the de Cordova map of Texas of 1849, from surveyed points from land grants, and from an 1888 map of Harris County (see Chapter 11). Outline of the developed area of the city of Houston is approximated from the C. E. Wood maps of Houston of 1866 and 1869 as well as the map of Houston subdivisions in Dorothy Knox Houghton et al., *Houston's Forgotten Heritage* (Houston: Rice University Press, 1991). Areas of various landholdings of the Morse family are taken from Harris County Deed Records, courtesy of Harris County Clerk's Office. **A:** Features plotted on a modern base map, courtesy of OpenStreetMap. **B:** Version showing the extent of forest cover, as in Figure 1.2.

and his wife Louisa Schiermann. Louisa arrived in Texas in 1839 as a single mother, presumably a widow, with two children. In 1840 she married Henry Reinermann (John Reinermann's son, who owned a third of a league of land immediately north of the John Reinermann trace; see Chapter 6), and he died in 1844. After that, in 1845 she married Joseph Sandman, who died in 1846, and she then married Christian Bethje in 1847. Louisa had inherited the Reinermann property.[1]

After a day's rest back in Houston, Bergin then ventured into the area north of Buffalo Bayou. There were no established roads and very few fences except those around small vegetable plots. Other than the Reinermann place and James Crawford's farm, now owned by Karl Kolbe, every farm he encountered had been established in the last decade, and most of them only in the last two or three years. The cabins were made of logs, as there was not yet an active sawmill in the area north of the bayou. Bergin

Right: Figure 7.3. Population of upper Buffalo Bayou in 1850, by age and race (reflecting the study area between modern Shepherd and Fry roads, north and south of Buffalo Bayou). Compiled from federal census data.

Below: Figure 7.4. Birthplaces of adult pioneer settlers in the study area, as of the 1850. Compiled from federal census data.

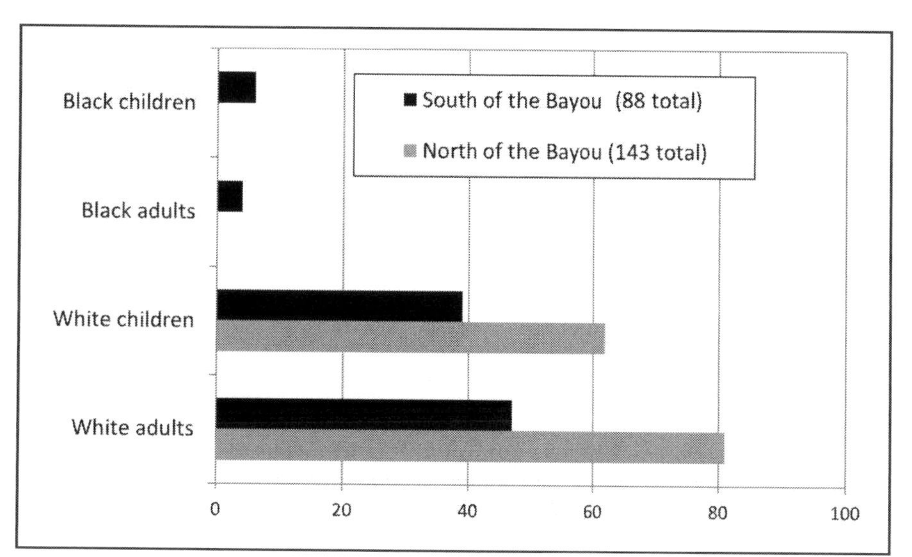

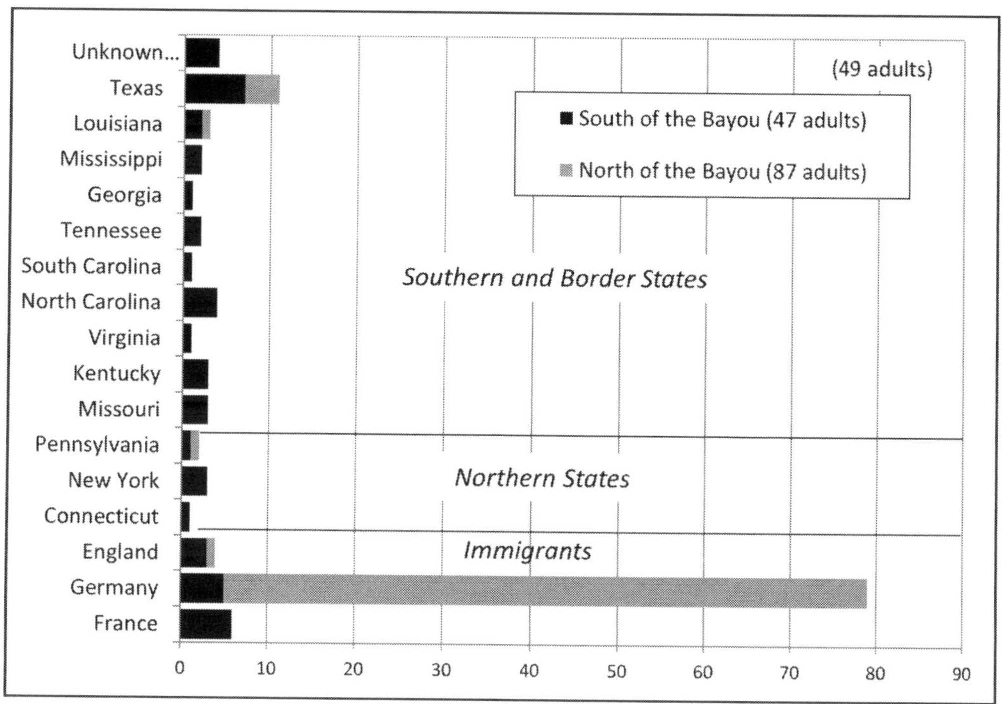

counted some 29 farms in the 100 or so square mile area north of the bayou, with 81 adults and 62 children (Figure 7.3). Remarkably, nearly all of the residents north of the bayou were German immigrants (Figure 7.4). The three Anglo families living north of the bayou were those of John Creagher, a wagoner and native Texan, and Caleb Clarkson, a hostler from England, both of whom had their businesses along Washington Road, and Hiram Lee, a stock raiser from Louisiana, who lived somewhere on the open range between German settlements at Spring Branch and Bear Creek.

Bernard Ahrenbeck and his sons William and Daniel were living along Spring Branch Creek (Figure 7.2). William and Daniel were operating a blacksmith's forge, and had not yet built their sawmill by the time of the census, but did so by the end of the decade. A next door neighbor, Henry Bertram, was a baker, suggesting that the Ahrenbecks had already built a water-powered grain mill where the sawmill

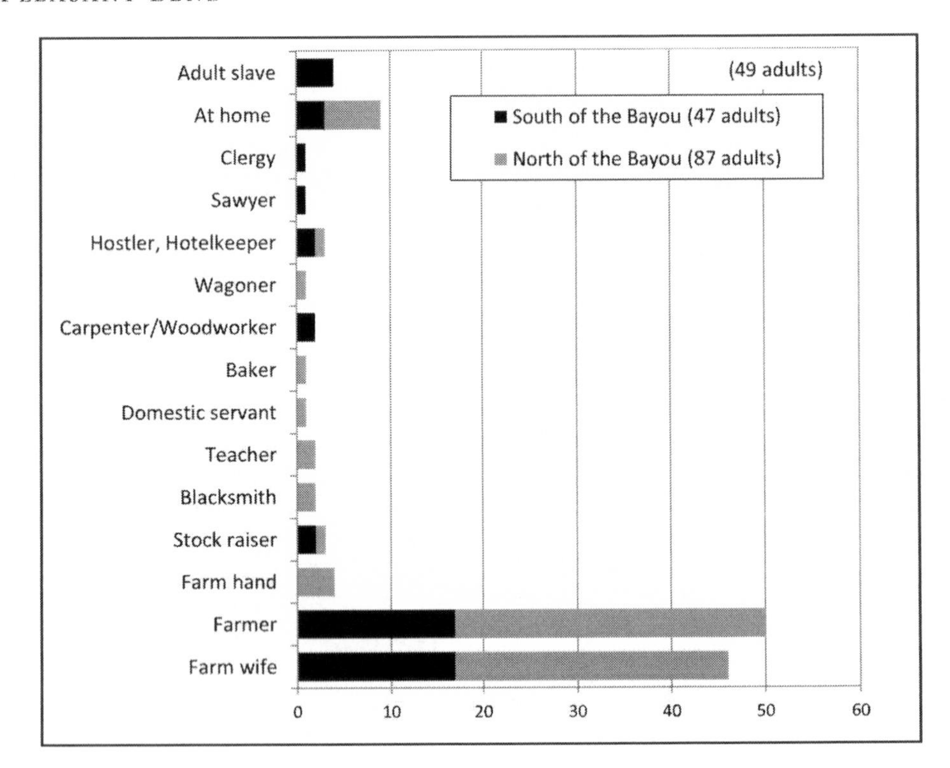

	South of the Bayou	North of the Bayou
Number of landowners	13	25
Total value of all holdings	$19,800	$8,700
Lowest value holding	$250	$50
Highest value holding	$10,000 (Charles Shearn's grain mill)	$5,250 (John Reinermann's land grant)
Average value per holding, except for highest value holding in each area (see text)	$817	$144

Left: Figur 7.5. Occupations of adult pioneer settlers in the study area, as of the 1850, when 136 adults were living in the area. Compiled from federal census data.

Below: Figure 7.6. Estimated value of landholdings north and south of Buffalo Bayou, as of the 1850 federal census. Total value of landholdings, and their average value, are much higher for the large parcels of the south relative to the German small farms in the north. On the north side of the bayou, the large value of the Reinermann place (including and larger than modern Memorial Park) dwarfed all the north side holdings, and the Shearn grain mill parcel in the south likewise dwarfed the next nearest southern holding. For that reason, those two outliers were removed from calculation of the average value of landholdings. The average Anglo farm was worth nearly six times the value of the average German farm.

was soon to be. There were also two teachers, but the vast majority of these pioneer German families were farmers and their wives, or hired farm hands; there were no slaves among them (Figure 7.5). Except for the relatively well-to-do Bethje-Reinermann clan, who lived on the late John Reinermann's large pre-independence league and labor of land at today's Memorial Park, most of these farms were small affairs of fifty to two hundred acres, much smaller than the larger farms of the Anglos south of the bayou (Figure 7.6).

After two and one half days spent counting and documenting these German families north of the bayou, Bergin crossed Buffalo Bayou at Wheaton's Ford and likely stayed at the inn that Elizabeth Wheaton and her two sons kept there. Nearby, J. L. Deliste also operated a hotel, likely also for travelers and wagon drivers carrying freight along the San Felipe road, who were often held up at the crossing for days and even weeks when the bayou rose during inclement weather. Also nearby were the James Brookshire family, who later moved to found Brookshire, Texas, west of Cane Island (later Katy).

From that point, the census taker headed east along the San Felipe wagon road, with a detour at each crossing track that led to a settler's home. The San Felipe Trail, then a commercial lifeline of the small town of Houston, was heavily used by ox carts laden with cotton heading east and supplies heading west. Other roads had been cut through the great prairie from Houston, including Washington Road (Figure 7.2), which was joined in 1856 by the Houston and Texas Central Railroad), and Richmond Road, which headed southwest to Fort Bend, by now called Richmond. These roads, too, brought cotton to Houston.

The area south of the bayou was very different from that to the north. It was more lightly settled, with only 17 farms populated by only 49 adults and 45 children in an area of about 100 square miles. Unlike the German area north of the bayou, this was a predominantly Anglo area, with most of the inhabitants having been born in and migrated from a mix of southern, border, and northern states; a few were native Texans (Figure 7.4). Those few who were immigrants from foreign lands were from England, Germany, or France in about equal amounts. There were no Hispanics documented as living in the upper Buffalo Bayou area in 1850, either north or south of the bayou.

Farming was the main occupation of Anglo and German settlers (Figure 7.5). There were a few stock raisers specifically listed, but nearly all these farmers also kept stock on the open range. There were only a smattering of craftsmen serving the farming communities; for example, the two German blacksmiths north of the bayou. The sawmill at the Harriet George place (Harriet was the widow of Buckman Canfield) employed a sawyer and a woodworker as well as one enslaved African American. Shearn's grain mill, east of what would soon become the Agur Morse Plantation, employed several child slaves, and the flour allowed a German baker to have a local business. There were a couple of primitive lodgings for travelers, one on either side of the bayou, and a wagoner (teamster) reflected the presence of the nearby wagon road. The one clergyman was temporarily living there (as a guest of the Shearn family), and there were two teachers from Germany, north of the bayou. There were no recorded teachers among the Anglo settlers south of the bayou; one would come to Morse's plantation later in the decade.

There were very few enslaved African Americans here at this time—four adults and six children—and all of them lived south of the bayou (Figure 7.3). Only the most prosperous farmers and ranchers had hired or enslaved help on their small farms; the Anglo settlers had a total of four slaves, whereas the German immigrants had four white hired hands. The enslaved African American population south of the bayou was to increase markedly later in the 1850s, but they were never commonly found on German family farms.

Half of the slaves listed in the census of the upper Buffalo Bayou area in 1850 were owned by Marvel McFarland (b. ca. 1814), Mary McFarland, and their apparent sharecropper Thomas Earl, who had a sizeable farm near the Habermachers in the western part of the area. By the time of the 1850 census Marvel McFarland appears to have been separated from his wife Mary, and the two are shown owning separate but adjacent farms. On the agricultural census he is credited with 1,280 acres, 17 of which are under cultivation; 19 horses, 40 milk cows, 135 beef cattle, 100 swine, and a corn crop of 60 bushels. He had arrived in the area only recently, having been a resident of Leon County in 1846.[2] By 1854 he remarried and moved to Jackson, Texas.[3]

The census taker recorded that the Habermacher family, consisting of the children of now deceased pioneer Thomas Habermacher, had spread out over the western prairie, where there were several farms in what would later be called the Habermacher Settlement, now in Barker Reservoir (Figure 7.2). They were French citizens from Alsace but were German speaking.

Harriet George and her family were still at Piney Point, eight miles west of Houston (see Chapter 5). Harriet was Buckman Canfield's widow and lived in 1850 with her sons William and John Canfield and daughter Hannah Canfield. She had married James Todd after Canfield's death in 1844 and they had a daughter, Mary. After James Todd died in 1846, Harriet married Benjamin George and had a final child, Edward, with him. She ran a farm and inn at the property. By this time her husband Benjamin George had deserted both her and his ingenious ox-powered sawmill, and her son William Canfield (by her previous marriage to Buckman Canfield) had taken over the role of sawyer. As we have seen, carpenter and cabinetmaker William Bethke was then living at the house and was at that time building her a new house. Harriet George owned three of the other African American slaves listed in the census, all children, and one of them, seventeen-year-old Maria, later married Bethke (Chapter 5).

Dabney Walker (b. 1800) and his wife Mary Binkley Walker (b. 1799) were also living at Piney Point at that time. According to the Walkers' great-granddaughter Cassie McFee Reeder,

> *Dabney Walker, wife Mary and children Faithy, Amy (grandmother of Cassie), and Dabney left Mt Airy North Carolina and came to Houston to [the place of] Constantine Buckley, Mary's boy [by a previous marriage] and Dabney's step son, in 1847. [They] settled about 6 miles west of Houston on Buffalo Bayou. . . . The family made the trip in a 2 horse wagon [and had] a dog. [They]came as far as Memphis Tennessee; there they sold their horses and wagon, and came by boat by way of Galveston to Houston to the Buckley's, and settled 6 miles west of Houston on then Buffalo Bayou.*[4]

Dabney Sr. is listed as a stock raiser in the 1850 census and undoubtedly kept livestock on the vast open range that extended south of the bayou. He was probably also either sharecropping or renting land from Harriet George.[5] Prior to moving to Harris County in the 1840s, Walker had been a stage driver, dry goods merchant, and sheriff in Mount Airy in Surry County, North Carolina.[6] A story has been recorded about his experience there as a stage driver.

> *The first stage in that direction [from Charlotte to Goldsboro, North Carolina] was inaugurated about the year 1828, by Thomas Wright of Mt. Airy. It had but three horses then, and Dabney Walker, who lived 6 miles above on the Ward's Gap road, near the Patrick line, Virginia . . . [was the driver]. Walker was a man of energy; and, as an illustration, I give the following story:*
>
> *The main leading road from this country to the West was by way of Ward's Gap and Poplar Camp; at the foot of the Ridge lived Mr. Mankin, who kept the stage breakfast house. Coming down the mountain the stage would get there a little after day light and breakfast would always be ready for the passengers. But old Mr. Mankin died and the house passed into other hands, and soon there was complaint that breakfast was not ready and the driver would only wait so long and then go on. One morning Walker was in the stage and expostulated in pretty strong terms with the landlord, who in turn told him to go to a warm place and get his breakfast. Walker replied, "that is the dearest speech you ever made," and he went to work and hired an engineer and some hands and spent three weeks prospecting up and down the mountain until he found a place where he could get a road, had it opened and built a breakfast house on top of the mountain, and gave it the name of "Good-Spur," and in six months the travel was completely turned away from the old road. Walker in turn sold out to "Bland & Dun" [Bland and Dunn Stagecoach line], and they kept up the route for many years.*[7]

Dabney Walker eventually purchased 88.5 acres from Harriet George's Taylor League (Piney Point) land in 1866.[8] After that, the public record on him and his wife is murky. Their daughter Amy later married Daniel Crump, who lived farther east along the bayou, and the Crumps' daughter Cecelia Walker Crump (1865–1930) married James and Cassandra McFee's son Lewis Lum McFee (of whom more later). Their son Dabney M. Walker lived in Sugar Land, where he was buried. According to McFee family history, Dabney Walker Sr. and Mary Walker were buried in the Piney Point cemetery, which was in the general vicinity of modern Piney Point Estates, but is now destroyed.[9]

Figure 7.7. Alexander McGowen, early businessman and mayor of Houston. His brother Thomas McGowen had a fifty-acre farm that was surrounded by the Morse Pleasant Bend Plantation.

Thomas McGowen. East of Piney Point, there were only two domiciles observed by census taker Bergin in January, 1851. Two miles to the east lay the small, recently settled fifty-acre farm of Thomas McGowen (Figure 7.2). Thomas's brother Alexander McGowen (1817–1893; Figure 7.7) had migrated to Texas from North Carolina, arriving in Houston in 1839. By the mid-1840s Alexander operated an iron foundry in Houston and purchased this fifty-acre plot in 1849 from Darius Gregg, on a part of a third of a league granted to Texas revolutionary war veteran William White in 1844. White, who never lived on the property, sold half of it to Gregg and the other half to another surveyor, George M. Patrick, within seven months of being awarded his grant. Gregg then sold fifty acres of his large parcel to Alexander McGowen. Alexander McGowen had been a delegate to the Constitutional Convention preparing Texas for statehood in 1845, and was later the mayor of Houston in 1858 and 1867–1868.

Alexander's purpose was not to live on the land but to have it managed by his brother Thomas McGowen (1800–after 1866), who apparently arrived in 1849. Thomas was a stock raiser, according to the 1850 census; like Dabney Walker, he raised cattle on the adjacent open range. The 1850 agricultural census reports that he had cultivated ten of his fifty acres, and owned one horse, 50 milk cows, 100 beeves but no swine; he also had raised 100 bushels of corn. He apparently was also raising corn and other vegetables for the Houston market as well as milk. The San Felipe Trail transected the southern part of McGowen's property, so there was ready access to the city.

When surveyor George Bringhurst was working in the area in February 1849, he noted that Thomas McGowen was already residing on the property.[10] Thomas McGowen and his family were very likely the first residents on the south side of the bayou between Piney Point and modern day River Oaks. He and his wife Elizabeth (b. ca. 1816) had eight children living on that farm in 1850, all but one of whom were girls: Eleonora (1), Julia (3), Eliza (6), Lucy (7), Frances (9), Elijah (10), Sarah (12), and Mary (15). The family had earlier been living in Alabama, and all the children were born in that state.

Charles Shearn. In 1850 the last farm to the east in the area concerned was that of Charles Shearn (1794–1877; Figure 7.8). Born in the small village of Midsomer Norton near Bath, England, Shearn married Mary Pode of Bath in 1818, and they emigrated to Texas in 1834. He signed the Goliad Declaration of Independence in 1835 and served in the Texian army under Captain Dimmitt during the Texas Revolution. Captured by Mexican General Urrea, he and his twelve-year-old son John Shearn were tied up to be shot when it was learned that they were as yet British subjects, and were released. Shearn and his family moved to Houston in 1837, where he operated a mercantile shop for a time. His first wife died, and he married Anna Maria Caldwell Waltmon (b. 1803) in 1844.[11]

By the late 1840s Shearn both farmed and operated a gristmill along Buffalo Bayou in the former Allen Reynolds tract (Figure 7.2). The mill was lo-

Figure 7.8. Charles Shearn. From Anonymous, *History of Texas, Together with a Biographical History of the Cities of Houston and Galveston* (Chicago: Lewis Publishing Company, 1895).

Figure 7.9. **Above right:** Mary Elizabeth Shearn House, the daughter of Charles Shearn. She married her father's business partner, T.W. House, in 1840. **Right:** Mary's husband, early Houston businessman Thomas William House.

Below: Figure 7.10. Four Mile Place, the former weekend home of T. W. House and his wife Mary Shearn House, ca. 1900. Courtesy of the Houston Metropolitan Research Center, Houston Public Library.

cated on the south side of the bayou near where the northernmost green of the River Oaks Country Club's golf course is today. Surveyor George Bringhurst, in his survey of 1846, mentioned Shearn's mill, which was at the site of the earlier Allen Reynolds mill (see Chapter 3).[12] The 1850 census notes that Charles Shearn lived there with his wife Anna Maria, Thomas Wesson (b. ca. 1783), and Church of England clergyman James Wesson (b. ca. 1819). He owned two African American slaves, a man and a woman, both thirty years old, who worked either in the mill or in their wheat and corn fields. Shearn also served as the City of Houston overseer of the San Felipe wagon road from Houston to Piney Point at this time.[13]

Shearn formed a business partnership of over a decade with his fellow English countryman Thomas William ("T. W. ") (1814-1880), a baker and confectioner who married Shearn's daughter Mary (1822-1870; Figure 7.9). It would seem that corn and perhaps wheat flour from the grist mill on Buffalo Bayou was Shearn's primary contribution to the partnership. By 1853 House owned the largest dry goods business in the state of Texas. House later became a blockade runner for the Confederacy, taking cotton to England, and became Mayor of Houston in 1862.[14]

Charles Shearn later became chief justice of Harris County for six years and was the founder of the Shearn Memorial (Methodist) Church in Houston.[15] After his death, the site of his old grain mill went to his daughter Mary, and she and her husband T. W. House had a country home there that they called "Four Mile Place," as it lay four miles from Houston (Figure 7.10). Their son T. W. House, Jr. later owned the place, and in 1923 he and Houston businessman Thomas H. Ball built the River Oaks Country Club there. They planned a residential development called Country Club Estates on an adjoining part of the property to the south of the club. The Country Club Estates land was sold soon after the opening of the country club and became the core of the larger River Oaks residential development of 1925.[16] Another son of T. W. House, Sr. and Mary Shearn, Edward House, was a key confidante of President Woodrow Wilson.

A new wave of Anglo planters migrates to Texas

Following the somewhat chaotic and uncertain years of the Texian Revolution, the Runaway Scrape, and the early years of the Republic, statehood—gained in 1845—brought a sense of stability and security that attracted a wave of new Anglo settlers from the Old South. These new Anglo settlers included both small farmers and ranchers—people like Marvel McFarland and Dabney Walker—and more wealthy southern planters. The planters were moneyed agricultural capitalists who invested heavily in slaves to break up and then cultivate the land. They were seemingly always on the march when new southern frontier lands opened up, because the fertility of their land played out under the heavy demands of cotton cultivation. When clearances of indigenous Indians opened up new lands in Mississippi and Alabama in the 1820s and 1830s, planters from worn out lands in the Carolinas headed westward to settle there. Now many of these same planter families needed fresh horizons again, and Texas beckoned both these planters as well as larger numbers of Southern small farmers, the latter mostly without slaves, with vast expanses of cheap land.

The first wave of planter capitalists had brought their slaves to Texas in the 1820s, and settled on the fertile bottomland soil along the Brazos, Colorado and San Bernard Rivers; these were the Old 300. There they built their plantations, located for the most part in the flood plains of the rivers. Slaves girdled and cut down trees, then planted and harvested cotton. The second wave of planters were to step beyond the bottomlands and experiment with raising cotton in the bald prairies, if for no other reason than that the best soil was already taken. As T. R. Fehrenbach noted in his history of the State, "in those [early] years it was not understood that the soils

Figure 7.11. A wagon train of Anglo emigrant farmers pauses in Jackson, Mississippi, en route to Texas from their worn-out southern farms. Drawing by J. Wells Champney, from Edward King, *The Great South: A Record of Journeys* (Hartford, Conn.: American Publishing Company, 1875).

of the prairies that opened up beyond the tree belts in Texas would grow cotton." One of the second wave was Agur Tomlinson Morse (1801–1865), who left behind a flooded plantation in Mississippi in 1851, and settled along the south bank of Buffalo Bayou.

The part of the great prairie adjacent to Houston and upper Buffalo Bayou was underlain by a Pleistocene clay-rich soil, familiar to most suburban dwellers of modern Houston as 'black gumbo' soil. Difficult to plow, even when wet, it had been almost completely overlooked by the early planters, excepting Allen Reynolds, who gave up on it after only a few years of effort. For that reason there were no early plantations to the west, south and north close to Houston; the nearest were along the Brazos River both to the north of San Felipe, and in the Richmond–Sugar Land area. Agur Morse was wary of bottomland floodplains anyway, having just been swept out of his former bottomland plantation in Mississippi by the great flood of the Tombigbee River in 1847. Perhaps for this reason, he was willing to experiment with trying to coax cotton and corn out of the prairie. He and his family would hedge their cotton bets, however, with timber operations along the Bayou, cattle ranching on the adjacent open range, and even a family-operated drugstore in growing Houston. By all accounts he was successful with the plantation he established, and a role model for those farmers who followed in farming the prairie, although the Civil War would ultimately bring his plantation and his life to an abrupt and tragic end.

Agur Morse's early years

Agur Tomlinson Morse was born in 1801 in New Haven, Connecticut, the second of eight children of Josiah Booth Morse (1775–c 1847) and Nancy Tomlinson (1783–c 1847). The Morse family had a very long history in New Haven. Agur's generation was the seventh in that city, where his immi-

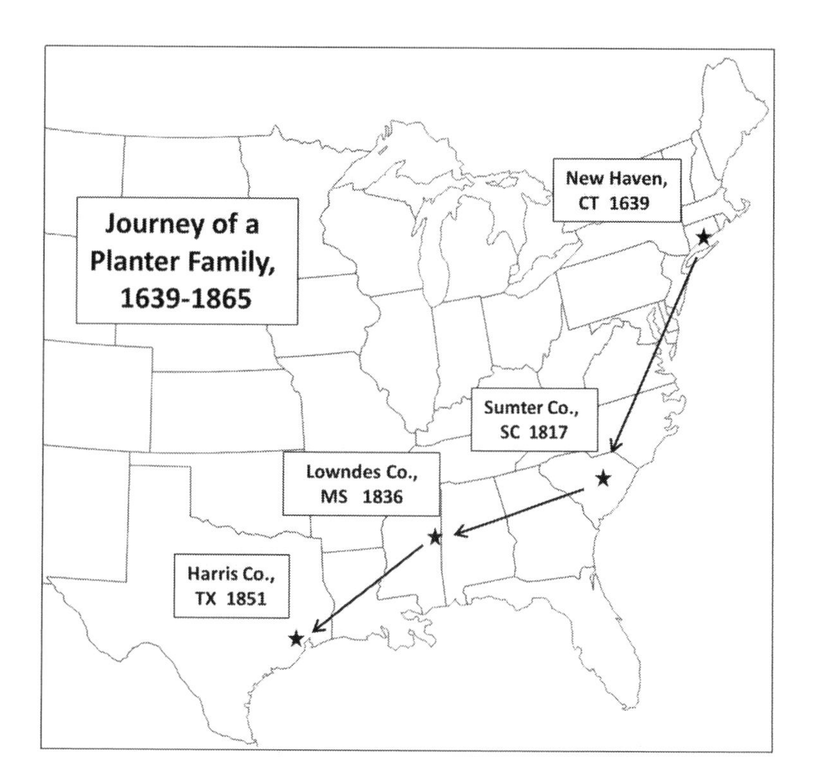

Figure 7.12. Morse family migration route, 1639–1851.

grant ancestor John Moss (1604–1707) had emigrated from England in 1639, one of the founders of the Planter's Associates of New Haven Colony.[17]

The life of a planter was deeply ingrained in members of the Morse family. Slavery had been practiced in Connecticut from at least 1639, and by the time of the Revolution, Connecticut had the largest number of slaves in New England (6,464). By 1774, all the principal families of Norwich, New Haven, and Hartford were said to have slaves, as did about half of the families of the professional class.[18] A gradual emancipation was enacted in 1784 that freed future children of existing slaves from bondage, but slaves continued to be counted in each federal census of that State until 1840. The practice of slavery was well known to the Morse family and others in their day.

New lands opening up for cultivation on the coastal plains of South Carolina beckoned Agur's parents, Josiah and Nancy Morse, and so that couple moved their family there, including their son Agur, first landing in Edgartown in 1817 and then purchasing land in Sumter County, where they were counted in the U.S. Census of 1820 (Figure 7.12). They established a cotton plantation, where they resided for twenty years. During that time Agur grew to manhood, and his earliest business venture outside of the plantation was his establishment of the Agur T. Morse Tavern, on the corner of Main Street and Liberty, sometime before 1825.[19] By 1829 he was also an innkeeper there, according to some letters of a neighborhood family.[20]

Even at this relatively early age, Agur was involved in the politics of the day. This was the time of John C. Calhoun's vice presidency, and the issue of the day was "nullification," the right of a state to nullify (veto) laws made by the federal government and to secede from the Union. The subject was a matter of great public debate in South Carolina and other southern states. The issue behind nullification was slavery, and the right of abolition-leaning northern states potentially to dictate solutions to southern states, an unsettled argument which ultimately led to Civil War a few decades later. Most planters at this time were conservatively unionist, hoping that the constitution would be sufficient to protect states' rights and that economically damaging conflict caused by hotheads could be thus avoided. In Sumter County the unionists, sometimes derisively termed "submission men," reportedly gathered at

Agur Morse's tavern, while the Calhoun-inspired nullifiers met at a tavern across the square.[21]

He married Grace Baldwin (1814–1890) in 1830 while living in South Carolina. Not much is known about Grace, except that she was from Connecticut, suggesting that he met her in his childhood or that they were acquainted through mutual family connections there.[22] The couple had their first two children while living in South Carolina: William Agur Morse (1831–1866), who was later to marry Harriet George's daughter Hannah Canfield in Piney Point, and Josiah B. Morse (1833–1889).

Meanwhile, Josiah and Nancy Morse continued working the family cotton plantation in Sumter County. Apparently, their returns were diminishing—a common occurrence when the land is intensely cultivation in an era without available fertilizers or much knowledge of field rotation. The Morses heard of new lands opening up for settlement in frontier northern Mississippi. The Chickasaw tribe was removed from their home along the west bank of the Tombigbee River by the congressional Indian Removal Act as well as by treaties of 1832 and 1834, whereby they ceded their lands east of the Mississippi River to the federal government. The Chickasaw were resettled in Oklahoma. The town of Colbert, Mississippi, in newly created Lowndes County on the west bank of the Tombigbee River, was platted in 1835, with town lots sold in 1836. At least by 1837, and probably a year earlier, both Josiah and his son Agur, along with their wives, children, servants and sixteen slaves (eight each owned by Josiah and Agur) had moved to Colbert, where they showed up on the county census of that year. Josiah had a white entourage (family and white servants) of seven, and Agur had nine. They settled in the rich bottomland around the river and began immediately to build homes and clear fields for planting. They reported no cotton production on their farms that first year.

The town of Colbert was well situated, with a ferry crossing at an important new east-west road that traversed the area between the more significant towns of Pontitoc and Columbus, as well as a port facility for river traffic to Mobile; the townspeople had big plans. By the following year, 1838, Agur and six other local men had founded the Colbert Male and Female Academy, no doubt looking to the education of their children in a frontier setting.[23] A militia was also formed that year. A cotton warehouse was soon built, where steamboats could take cotton bales down the river to Mobile.[24]

By the 1840 census both Agur and Josiah and their families were well into cotton production and town life. Agur and Grace had three more children while in Colbert: Elizabeth Adelaide Morse (1838–1920), Henry A. Morse (1840–1876), and George W. Morse (1845–1885). By 1847 both of Agur's parents passed away in unknown circumstances, which prompted Agur to rewrite his will, in which he hinted that all was not well after his father's death:

> *State of Mississippi*
> *Lowndes County*
>
> *Know all men by these presents that whereas I, Agur Morse of State and County above said, did make a will while living in South Carolina, making a division of my property to suit the then nature of the case, but those circumstances have changed. My parents are both dead and my brothers and sisters are grown up and able to provide for themselves and further the property I then possessed has by misfortune been swept away from me and I [am] compelled to begin the [illegible] anew to make something for my family of little children. I therefore deem it a duty I owe to them to prevent anything from disturbing them in their sight, of any property that I might leave them. I revoke the former will entirely, and [know] that the law in such cases makes a good division of man's estates. I hereby make this my last will and testament that whatever property may be left after paying my debts should be divided between my wife and children as the law usually directs.*
>
> *I make this knowing that the uncertainty of life and place it away in case I might at any time be*

suddenly cut off and not in a condition to make any disposition of my affairs.

In Testimony I hereby set my hand and seal this 25th May 1847.

Agur T Morse.[25]

The new settlers had chosen the rich bottomlands of the Tombigbee, but of course no one in Colbert knew of the flooding history of that river in this frontier region. Each year had brought higher and higher floods, and it would appear from Agur's comments about "property . . . has been swept away from me and I [am] compelled to begin . . . anew" that he had met with serious flood damage and that even his parents may have succumbed to the flooding.[26]

But the worst was yet to come. The end of that same year of 1847, in late December, there was a tremendous flood along the river that swept away not only most of Colbert but also the neighboring towns of Nashville, West Port, and parts of Aberdeen. Even though the town had been carefully placed twenty-seven feet above the river, the Tombigbee left its banks and "swept through the town, flooding homes, church, academy, stores and warehouses."[27] An eyewitness account tells the story of one town man's loss:

Towards the latter part of December A.D. 1847 the then town of Colbert was inundated by a freshet in the Tombigby River, and that besides several other houses being carried away by said freshet the office of J. M. Capshaw was also destroyed and when the bank of said river had caved so as to let said office down at one corner nearly to the ceiling so that it was considered dangerous to go into it, he further states that he in company with another went into said office, to rescue said Capshaw's desk containing his papers, that he found his desk floating in the water and endeavored to get it out but could not, we then procured an axe and broke open said desk, when it turned over and spilled all the papers in the water when with the exception of a few loose ones was immediately swept off by the current, very few of which I think was ever recovered.[28]

The town's residents decided to throw in the towel and seek still higher ground. They founded a new town to the north called Barton, and Colbert vanished nearly overnight. The ferry was initially moved to the north end of ruined Colbert, but by March 1848 Agur T. Morse and Hendley S. Bennett gained approval to establish a new ferry in Barton, and those two men became the major trustees for the stockholders of the new town. The ferry was of paramount importance; if the city lost control of the east-west route to Columbus, their town would soon become a complete backwater. It was apparently not altogether clear to Agur that the town would win that battle, and at any rate his rights to a ferry were soon taken away by rivals, who moved it to Jackson Springs.[29]

The loss of the Barton ferry was the beginning of the end for the new town of Barton; it was bypassed for the new railroad a few years later, and by the late 1850s was all but abandoned. The loss of the ferry was the last straw for Agur Morse, who by now had been cleaned out by at least two floods and now by the politics of ferry placement. Agur sold much of his Mississippi land in 1849, and although he and his family were counted in Lowndes County Mississippi by the US Census of 1850, later that same year they were Gone to Texas. Coming with them were six slaves counted in the 1850 Federal census Schedule of Slave Inhabitants: 3 men, two women, and one young girl.[30]

Building the Pleasant Bend Plantation

Like many other well-to-do southern planters who kept moving westward, ever in search of fresh soil or better circumstances, Agur and Grace Morse were not short of funds and used them to buy large amounts of relatively cheap land. By the time they arrived in Texas, however, the rich bottomland soil of the Brazos, Colorado and San Bernard rivers had long since been taken. To buy into existing plantations along those rivers would be too costly, and no doubt they were still recovering from financial losses incurred from the Tombigbee flood. The family focused their attention on the rapidly growing com-

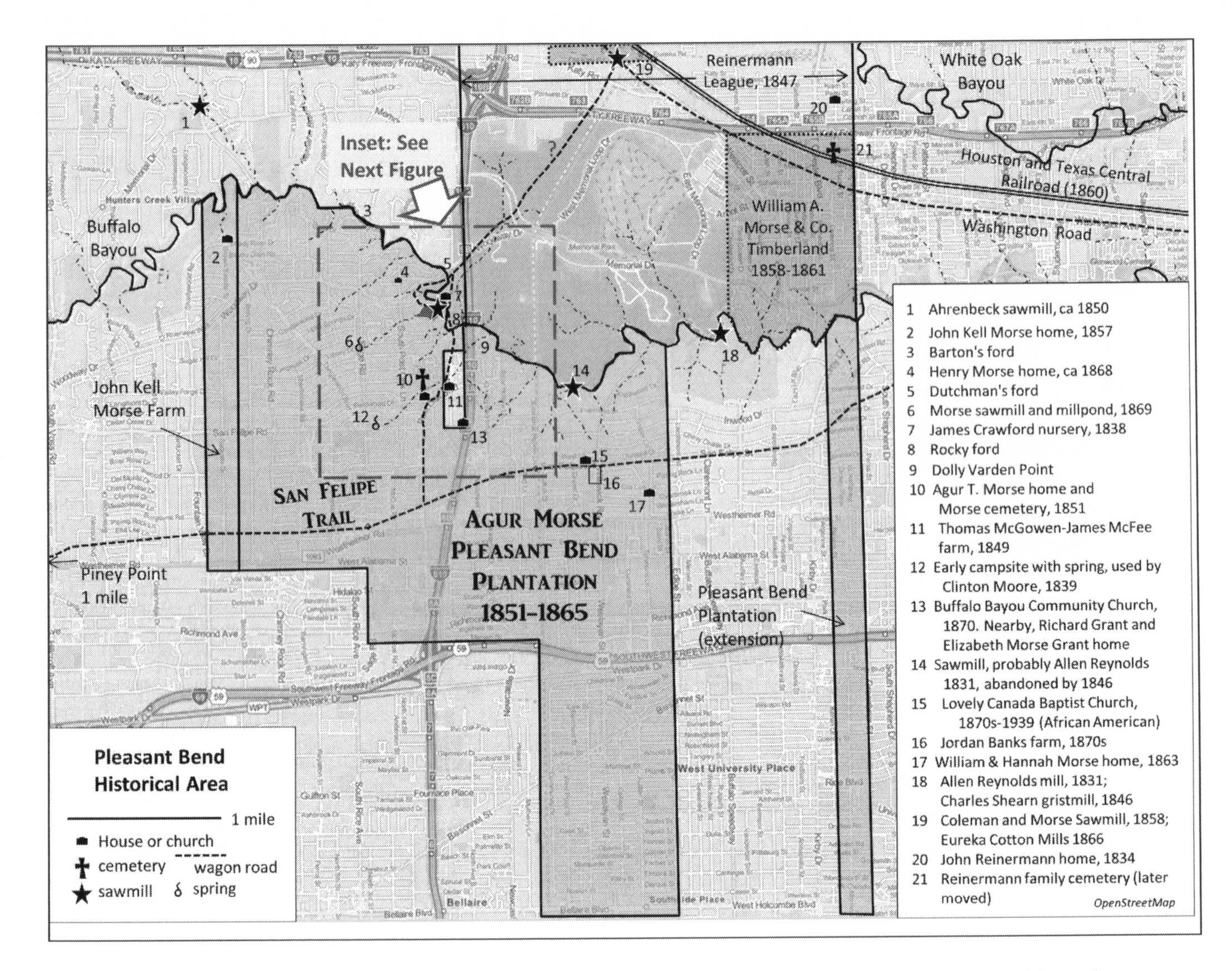

Figure 7.13. Map showing mid-nineteenth-century features of the Pleasant Bend area, with shading showing initial forested zone. Features are shown plotted on a modern road map, courtesy of OpenStreetMap.

mercial center of Houston. Agur and Grace Morse chose to buy land four to six miles west of the town, on the south side of Buffalo Bayou.

By 1850 it was clear that the new city of Houston was destined for prosperity, as it was well situated as a gathering and reshipping spot for Texas commerce. Ox wagons laden with cotton and sugar were arriving daily during harvest season, bound for the port of Houston along Buffalo Bayou. The city of Houston had more than doubled in size in the past decade. By the 1850 federal census the city had 2,397 inhabitants, of whom 527 (22 percent) were enslaved African Americans, and another 425 (18 percent) were recent German immigrants.[31] The non-German white population was made up mainly of Americans of English and Scots-Irish ancestry, the men either businessmen or tradesmen—often newly arrived from northern states—or, increasingly, southern planters searching for farmland.

Agur Morse started purchasing land in 1851 and his land eventually surrounded the small farm of Thomas McGowen, who arrived only two years earlier (Figure 7.13). Buffalo Bayou formed the northern boundary of the plantation, and the San Felipe Trail traversed its middle. The first piece that Morse purchased was 738 acres in the White third-of-a-league tract, bought from Josiah Cain Massie on December 26, 1851, for $1,400. Five months later he

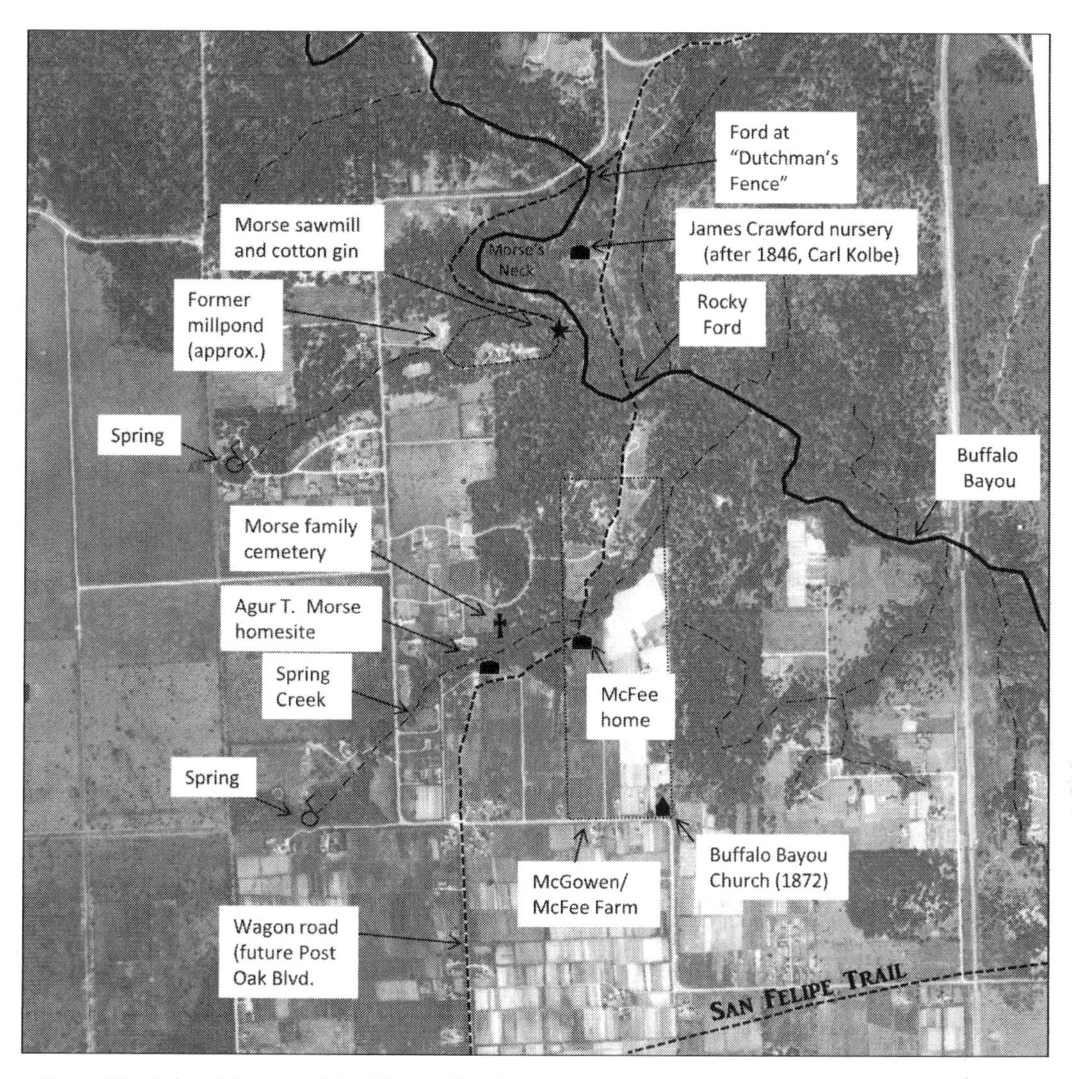

Figure 7.14.Cultural features of the Pleasant Bend area, mid- to late nineteenth century, superimposed on an aerial photograph of 1944, when the area was still relatively rural. Interpreted locations of nineteenth-century wagon roads shown in black dashed lines; other roads on the aerial photograph are mostly from the twentieth century. Buffalo Bayou and its tributaries are highlighted in black.

purchased another 160 acres from Darius Gregg, and in 1855 he purchased 1,476 acres of the Charles Sage tract immediately to the west. In 1856 he purchased 600 acres to the east in the Reynolds league, which included a mill and two homesteads. In 1860 Morse purchased 1,640 more acres in the Reynolds league as well as 150 more acres in the White survey and another 357 acres of the Reynolds league.[32] A survey adjustment on the Reynolds grant in 1863 (the "extension" shown on Figure 7.13) brought another 272 net acres.[33] At an eventual 5,243 acres, or more than eight square miles, the landholding was among the largest in Harris County, not an area known for large cotton plantations. In modern terms it contained all or most of present day Tanglewood, the Post Oak-Galleria area, River Oaks, and much of West University and Southside Place.

The basic natural features of the central core area of the plantation are shown in Figure 7.14, drawn on an aerial photograph of 1944, taken when the area was still rural—although it was by then traversed by a number of modern north-south and east-west roads that were not present in the mid-nineteenth century. Two prominent spring-fed creeks flowed northeastward into the bayou. The spring on the southernmost of the two creeks was the site of a campsite of wagon drivers along the nearby San Felipe wagon road, including Clinton

Moore in 1839 (see Chapter 3). Farther east along that creek, on its south bank, Agur Morse built a log home. The home was well sited, facing south into the prevailing breeze and yet within the edge of the riparian forest for shade. The spring provided a constant flow of water. Directly across the creek the family eventually installed a cemetery, now known as the Morse-Bragg cemetery and situated along modern South Wynden Drive off South Post Oak Lane. A north-south wagon track went from the San Felipe road, past the house, across the creek, and across the bayou at a sandstone outcrop called Rocky Ford. That wagon track continued through Karl Kolbe's farm and continued to the northeast; much of this road was later straightened and became known as North Post Oak Lane. That wagon track ultimately connected eastward to Washington Road and to modern day Memorial Park, north of which Agur's son William operated a sawmill in 1858 (Figure 7.13). Both that wagon track and the San Felipe Trail provided access to Houston, depending upon weather and road conditions. East of the Morse home was the small farm of Thomas McGowen, completely surrounded by the Morse plantation (Figure 7.14). It was later to be purchased by James and Cassandra McFee (discussed later).

The second, more northerly creek also flowed northeast into Buffalo Bayou. At some stage the Morse family had an earthen dam built across the creek, forming a millpond, and installed a grist mill, utilizing a thirty-foot drop from the dam to the water in Buffalo Bayou for water power. The spring provided a nearly continuous flow of water, and the millpond stored it to power the grist mill documented in Agur's probate of 1865. After the Civil War Agur's sons Henry and George would build a steam-powered sawmill at this site, in 1869, discussed much more fully in Chapter 9. As noted there, the pond that served to keep logs wet as they waited for sawing was located where the swimming pool and pond at the Omni Hotel are today, just off Woodway Drive.

A wagon track led northeast from the mill site to another sandstone outcrop and ford across Buffalo Bayou, at a place named "Dutchman's Fence" by surveryor George Bringhurst in 1846; that was a clear reference to German farmer Karl Kolbe, who then lived in the vicinity. That ford and its sandstone outcrop can be seen today from the modern Woodway Drive bridge at times of low water; the outcrop is perhaps two hundred feet south of the bridge. These sporadic soft sandstone outcrops were obvious locations for early fords, as the sandstone kept the wagon wheels from sinking into what would otherwise be mud. South of the ford and near the mill site, Buffalo Bayou makes a sharp bend. The resulting peninsula on the east bank was locally known as Morse's Neck, and the bend provided a name for the plantation and, eventually, the small community of Pleasant Bend.[34]

After his experience along the Tombigbee River, Agur Morse was careful to make his plantation as diverse in product as possible, and he seems to have been more than willing to experiment with a location away from the seasonal flooding of the big river bottomlands. The prairies to the south of the property were utilized mainly for raising cotton and corn, and the Morse family kept cattle and hogs on the open range stretching to the south. The pine trees that grew both along the bayou and in the forest to the north of it were used to make timber products that were likely sold to the Bering lumberyard in Houston and perhaps also exported. Agur Morse's probate inventory of 1865 shows additional production of hogs, sugar, tobacco, potatoes, and hay. At his death he had a grist mill, sugar mill, five cast mills, and a cotton gin and press.[35]

Because of his experiment in plantation farming on the prairie rather than on river bottomlands, Agur seems to have been on the cutting edge of Harris County farming, as seen in this *Houston Weekly Telegraph* article of August 18, 1858:

> *The "mean Houston prairies" are a byword and reproach. But they have been proved productive. Whitmarsh, of the Union Press [a cotton press and warehouse in Houston], in this city yesterday, finished bailing seventeen bales raised by* A. T. Morse,

Esq., on the bald Houston prairies last year, at about two-thirds of a bale per acre. This was good cropping for that year anywhere. The fact is, nearly every acre of Harris County prairies may be made to produce first rate crops of cotton by cultivation. The proximity of these lands to market, ought to make them valuable if nothing else, and when their capabilities are fully tested, we shall see a population upon them that will astonish old settlers.[36]

There was yet more praise in the Weekly Telegraph of May 25, 1859. This article reflects upon the conundrum that arriving immigrants were then heading west in large numbers to settle in dangerous central Texas Indian lands, when Agur Morse was demonstrating that there was plenty of good, fertile and inexpensive farm land to be had in safe, peaceful Harris County, on the open prairie:

For the Telegraph,
RAMBLES THROUGH HARRIS CO., No. 1.

According to your request I will sketch for your paper such matters as I think may interest your readers, and conduce to the wealth of our county, during my perambulations through its limits. Thus far my explorations have not extended more than six miles from Houston, but even within that distance I have found much to interest me. . . .

I found that the agricultural resources of Harris County have been vastly underrated. A few years since Mr. A. T. Morse purchased a tract of land which by addition since made amounts now to 2100 acres. The average cost of the whole tract was about one dollar per acre. It is situated some six miles south-west of Houston, near Buffalo Bayou. On this tract of land Mr. M. has made 2/3 of a bale of cotton per acre, planted 8th and 9th April. He has realized fifty bushels of corn per acre on a portion of his farm. He planted corn one season 7th and 8th of April and had no rain, worth mentioning, until the crop was matured and yet that season he realized from thirty to fifty bushel per acre. Mr. M. says he needs nothing but to have his ground thoroughly broken up during winter to ensure a good crop of corn. He thinks his prairie land stands a drought better than the Brazos bottom lands.

Now how many acres of land similar to those cultivated by Mr. Morse does Harris County contain? Will someone—some of our county surveyors—present or former—inform your readers? Why expose our heads to be scalped by the Indians in search of good soil [farther inland in Texas], when we have it in such abundance in our own county? I found the lands in the vicinity of Mr. Morse are rapidly attracting occupants. The grazing facilities are superior. Farming and stock-raising can there be advantageously combined. A school is in demand. A good teacher could make a support now with a prospect of doing better.[37]

This piece makes clear what many others in the second wave of Anglo planters were to experience at their new lands on the Texas prairie, in places farther inland like the blackland prairie and even in the East Texas pineywoods: in Texas, it was not necessary to own bottomland soil to farm cotton and corn.

African American slavery at Pleasant Bend

The farm labor at Pleasant Bend was largely based on the work of African American slaves. Agur owned six slaves in Mississippi in 1850, including three men, two women and one eight-year-old girl.[38] When Agur first shows up on the Harris County tax records in 1854, he still owned six slaves, as he did in 1856. By the 1857 tax season he had added a seventh slave, and that was the number that he owned during 1859, the last year for which we have any record (1860–1864 county tax records were lost during the Civil War, and by 1865, after Emancipation, slavery no longer existed). These slaves are unnamed in the tax records. Near the Morse plantation in 1856, his next door neighbor James McFee owned three, Charles Shearn used four at his milling operation, and the Canfield/George family at Piney Point owned four.[39] Overall, only about half of Texas farmers in the coastal prairies had slaves.[40]

Academic historians typically define "planter" as

Figure 7.15. Scene on a cotton plantation, Alabama. Drawing by J. Wells Champney, from King, *The Great South*.

"a landholding farmer of substantial means."[41] Agur Morse certainly met that criterion, with landholdings at his death in 1865 of 7,116 acres in Harris County and another 1,600 acres in other counties (see inventory, Chapter 9). An average Texas farmer in 1850 had only a thousand acres of unimproved pastures and woodlands—of which seventy-five acres were improved cropland—and eight slaves.[42] In that era most large planters in the bottomlands of the Brazos and Colorado rivers had twenty or more slaves. In 1850 only 6 percent of slave owners met this definition, and 80 percent, like Agur Morse, owned fewer than ten.[43] Morse, however, was both the largest landowner and the owner of the most slaves among the Anglo settlers south of the bayou. It would appear that he was growing his landholdings and experimenting with crop raising on the prairie soil until the Civil War intervened, ending his plantation effort.

As noted in a newspaper account already mentioned, Agur Morse and his slaves produced 17 bales of cotton in 1858, which at two-thirds of a bale per acre would mean that he cultivated about 25 acres in cotton. Typically, most planters realized two bales per slave owned, and with seven slaves one would expect about 14 bales; Agur may have had some hired help with the remaining three bales. Corn, sugar, potatoes and tobacco were also grown, likely for consumption on the plantation rather than for sale. Sweet potatoes were one of the main staple foods for slaves, along with corn.

Tax data show that slaves constituted the single most valuable portion of Agur Morse's wealth. In 1859 his 2,376 acres of Harris County land plus another 1,080 acres of investment property in Milam County were together worth $3,655, his 100 head of cattle were worth $600, and his two wagons and ox teams were worth $300. His seven slaves, however, were taxed at a value of $4,300. This is completely consistent with the 1860 observation of Texas visitor, horticulturalist and agriculturalist Thomas Affleck that "a planter's almost sole wealth consists in negroes; his land is comparatively valueless."[44] Affleck toured the South and lectured on the matter of soil fertility; he observed that planters were quick to move when soil played out under the demands of cotton production and were drawn to Texas by abundant and relatively inexpensive land. The means of production on the Morse and other plantations rested solely on the backs of the slaves, and the slaves were valued accordingly.

Political talk in Texas throughout the 1850s centered on the slave question in national politics. Many planters like Agur Morse had initially come from the northern states and had lived through the last stages of the gradual emancipation of slaves in those northern states in the early nineteenth century. As T. R. Fehrenbach pointed out, whereas by the middle of the nineteenth century northern capitalism was based on industrial growth, "The Texas capitalist had two ingredients to work with, fresh lands and negro slaves. Out of this land and forced labor he created new capital, which almost universally was reinvested in more land and more slaves."[45] By the census of 1860 the assessed value of all slaves in Texas was $106,688,920, which was 20 percent more than the value of all cultivated lands in the state.[46]

Family life at Pleasant Bend

By the middle to late 1850s Pleasant Bend was a large agricultural operation. Besides Agur Morse and his wife Grace, they had five sons who were either engaged at plantation work or in business ventures in nearby Houston. William Agur Morse (1831–1866) was the oldest son of Agur and Grace Morse, and was already twenty when he and his family arrived in Texas in 1851. William married Hannah Putnam Canfield (1835–1894) of nearby Piney Point in 1854 (Figure 7.16). She was the daughter of Buckman Canfield and Harriet Putnam Canfield (later Harriet George; Chapter 6). William and Han-

Figure 7.16. William Agur Morse and his wife, Hannah Putnam Canfield.
Courtesy of Kathy Monahan Phillips.

nah had five children: Charles Canfield Morse (1855–1905), Willie Morse (1855–1870), Mary Ella Morse (1857–1889), Edwin George Morse (1858–1863), and Hattie Louisa Morse (1860–1863). William Morse's first business venture off the plantation appears to have been a hardware store on Main Street in Houston that was advertised in the *Houston Weekly Telegraph* of February 20, 1856, and in succeeding weeks and months. Later that same year, however, William began to become interested in the timber business and formed a timber company, William A. Morse & Company (discussed later).

A second adult son, Josiah Booth Morse (1833–1889), became a merchant in Houston, where he married Mary Ellen Rowley in 1860. In 1856 he operated the Houston Boot, Shoe, Leather and Finding Store, and he later teamed up with Charles Holmes in a grocery and auction business, advertised in the *Weekly Telegraph* of August 19, 1857.[47] By 1858 he was managing the bookstore owned by Lovett Taft's brother, Joseph Strong Taft, of whom more later.[48] After his father died in 1865, Josiah Morse ran a drugstore purchased by his father during the Civil War.

Three other sons were boys at the start of plantation operations and grew to manhood at Pleasant Bend. In 1860 Henry Morse (1840–1876) married Celia A. Hough (1839–1896; probably a relative and perhaps a sister of neighbor Cassandra Hough McFee, discussed later). George W. Morse (1845–1885) married Anna Dowd after the Civil War. Frederick Morse (1855–1874) was the only child of the Morses who was born at the Pleasant Bend Plantation; he died as a teenager.

Agur and Grace had one daughter, Elizabeth (1838–1920), who married a young Houston businessman, Lovett Taft Jr. (1828–1864) in 1857. Lovett and his older brother, Joseph Strong Taft (1808–1896), were born in Sheffield, Berkshire County, Massachusetts. Their parents were Lovett D. Taft (1784–1853) and Betsey Strong (1787–1869), both buried at Hewins Cemetery in Sheffield.[49] Lovett Taft Sr. was a brother of Alonso Taft, who was the father of President William Howard Taft.[50] Joseph Taft and his wife Caroline Baldwin moved to Houston in the 1840s, and at least by the time of the 1850 federal census he operated what he claimed was the oldest (and perhaps the first) bookstore in Texas (more on this later).

Elizabeth and Lovett Taft Jr., who lived in Houston's Fourth Ward near Lovett's work rather than on the plantation, had four children between 1858 and 1865: Henry Chauncey, Lovett Jr., Grace and George. Lovett Taft Jr. died of typhoid fever in 1864 and was buried in the Morse family cemetery on the plantation. Elizabeth then married Houston businessman Richard A. Grant (b. 1838).

The William A. Morse & Company Timber Company

In 1856, while running his hardware company in Houston, William Morse saw another business opportunity in the large stands of virgin pine in the upland forest that extended along the north side of Buffalo Bayou west of Houston (Figure 7.2). That same year he bought 842 acres of forested timber land in the northern half of the Taylor League at Piney Point, just north of his mother-in-law Harriet George's place at Piney Point. This land, including lots 5 and 6, was part of the John Taylor tract that went to Stephen F. Austin after Taylor left that land, and it was later owned by S. S. Perry.[51]

William formed a company of like-minded sawyers and investors and named it William A. Morse & Company. His co-owners included Abraham Groesbeck, Appleton H. Coleman, and David H. Paige; all were Texans except for Paige, a New York businessman. Besides Morse's 842 acres of timber, the group added another 394 acres of the Taylor tract in lot 7, adjacent to the Morse tracts (bought by Groesbeck); and 883 acres in the southeastern part of the Reinermann league (due east of modern Memorial Park; see Figure 7.2), conveyed to the group by G. S. Hardcastle in February 1858.[52] They then bought another 150 acres in the Reinermann tract, from S. K. McIlhenny.[53] Those purchases brought the timber company up to 2,269 acres of forest land.

Top: Figure 7.17. Loggers at work in virgin pine forest, East Texas, 1907. Courtesy of Texas A&M University Forest Service.
Above: Figure 7.18. Logging "bull team" hauling logs, East Texas, 1944. Courtesy of Texas A&M University Forest Service.

Figure 7.19. A lumber mill on the Houston and Texas Central Railroad, 1891. From M. F. Sweetser, King's *Handbook of the United States* (Buffalo, N.Y.: Moses King, 1891).

For a location for their steam engine and milling, they purchased 66 acres in the Reinermann tract, from William P. and Martha Rogers.[54] This land was immediately adjacent to the new Houston and Texas Central Railway. Track laying began in Houston in July 1856 and reached Cypress by September. That railroad reached 81 miles to Millican, between Navasota and College Station, by the time the Civil War started, when construction ceased. After the war it was extended to Dallas and to Red River City, in 1873, where it joined the Missouri, Kansas and Texas Railroad.[55] The location of the William Morse & Company sawmill on the railroad allowed it to ship finished lumber to Houston and Galveston, with an option to ship it to inland locations, and perhaps even out of state, in the future.

An 1861 inventory of the company included the above property plus "the steam saw mill situated on the sixty acres of land purchased from Wm P & M L Rogers and heretofore described, together with all the engines, machinery, implements and tools. . . . Also all the horses, mules, oxen, wagons, carry logs, blacksmith and carpenter tools, cordwood, and between seventy and ninety head of cattle."[56]

The upland forest north of Buffalo Bayou was the southernmost part of the vast East Texas Piney Woods, and was the first part of the Piney Woods to undergo logging. John Richardson Harris had begun construction of a sawmill at Harrisburg in 1829, which was operated by his brothers David, Samuel, and William Harris after his death that year.[57] There was an operating sawmill at Houston by 1838, a sawmill at Piney Point by about 1850 (Chapter 5), and several operating sawmills in the Spring Branch area by the middle of the 1850s, including a steam sawmill operated by Daniel and William Ahrenbeck (Chapter 6). These early mills were mainly located along Buffalo Bayou and its tributaries. With the advent of the railroad, vast areas of upland forest were opened to timbering, and the Morse & Company sawmill was among the first to head north into the vast Piney Woods. Virgin pine logs measured as much as five feet in diameter, dwarfing the men who cut them by hand (Figure 7.17). Oxen were used to drag cut trees in the forest and to haul sections of logs to the mill by wagon (Figure 7.18). As the timber lands purchased by the group were divested of timber, they were divided into smaller parcels of land and sold.[58] At the sawmill, limbs and smaller or otherwise unusable trees were burned for power. Finished lumber was loaded onto railroad cars for shipment to Houston, where the company had an office. There was a ready market as the city grew rapidly northward, enveloping the near-city railroad tracks of both the Houston and Texas Central to the northwest and the Texas and New Orleans railroad to the northeast, both begun in the late 1850s (Figure 7.2).

Despite a propitious first few years, current events were to go against the partnership. With the attack on Fort Sumter in Charleston harbor on April 12, 1861, war fever hit Texas, and the partners of William Morse & Company dissolved the partnership in late June 1861.[59] The partners may have realized that with the war, there would be other demands upon their manpower, and other demands as well on their own time. There may have been other internal or external reasons. For his portion of the partnership, William Morse obtained $1,000. By 1863 Harris County deed records show that William and Hannah were living on the Pleasant Bend Plantation just to the northeast of the modern intersection of Westheimer at Willowick, near a tree "island" in what was then open prairie, just south of the San Felipe wagon road (Figure 7.13). During the war he joined Lawrence's Company D, First Infantry Regiment, Texas State Troops, and served most of his time in that unit within Texas, patrolling the Indian frontier and guarding prisoners of war (Chapter 8).

David Paige assumed control of the bulk of the land of the former Morse & Company, and after the war was over he sold the sawmill tract and the rights to cut timber on the 883 acres in the southeastern Reinermann league to Sylvester S. Munger (1820–1901), a Connecticut-born Texan who built the Eureka Cotton Mills on the old sawmill tract in 1866 while he continued to cut and process timber there (Chapter 9).[60]

John and Caroline Morse join the plantation

By 1856 or 1857 Agur was joined by his brother Rev. John Kell Morse (1808–1863) with his wife, Caroline A. Jones (1820–1864). That couple left their home in South Carolina and bought a 300-acre farm that lay along the western edge of the Pleasant Bend Plantation.

Like Agur Morse, John Kell Morse was born in New Haven, Connecticut, the son of Josiah Booth Morse and his wife, Nancy Tomlinson. John, Agur and the rest of the family had moved to South Carolina in 1817, where they operated a plantation when John was a boy. His parents as well as his brother Agur remained there until about 1837, when his parents and Agur left for Lowndes County, Mississippi, to start a new plantation there.

By the time that his parents and brother Agur left South Carolina, John Kell Morse had long since reached adulthood and had become a Methodist preacher. He was admitted as a preacher "on trial" in the Methodist Episcopal church in 1831 in Darlington, South Carolina.[61] He was "received into full connection" (ordained as a preacher) in 1832 and became a traveling preacher for several years.[62] Morse was stationed in Laurensville, Charleston and Congaree in 1834, was stationed in 1835 in Morgantown, and was stationed in Barnwell in 1836, all in South Carolina.[63]

In 1836 Rev. Morse moved to Houston County, Georgia, where he married Caroline Ann Jones (1820–1864), who was born in Orangeburg County, South Carolina, on December 21, 1836. Their first child, Mary, was born in 1838. From the 1840 census it seems likely that they were living in Houston County with Caroline's parents, Donald Bruce Jones (1792–1853) and Mary Elvira (Polly) Rumpf (1796–1854).[64]

Rev. John Kell Morse and Caroline Ann Jones Morse were certainly a couple with an impressive American ancestry. John's (and his brother Agur's) fifth great-grandfather was Corporal John Moss (1604–1707), who emigrated from England in 1637 on board the ship Hector and was one of the earliest settlers in New Haven Colony, Connecticut. He was a member of the 1st General Court of that colony in 1639 and later was one of the founders of Wallingford, Connecticut. John Moss married Mary (Abigail) Charles (1606–1656), another early English immigrant, in 1638 in Hartford, Connecticut.[65] Caroline Jones's fifth great-grandfather, Lewis Jones

(1605–1684), a Puritan, emigrated from Wales to Watertown, Massachusetts, in about 1630. Her fourth great-grandfather, Captain Josiah Jones (1643–1714), Lewis's son, was a captain in the local militia and served in King Phillip's War of 1675–1676, in which Puritan colonists battled Metacomet, chief of the Wampanoags, known to the Puritans as King Phillip.[66] It was a desperate war of survival for both sides, with about 2,600 colonists and perhaps three times as many Indians perishing. Caroline's maternal grandfather, Captain (later General) Jacob Rumpf (1752–1812) was born in Orangeburg, South Carolina, of Swiss immigrant parents. He commanded a troop of cavalry under General Francis Marion (the "Swamp Fox") during the American Revolution and was renowned for a series of encounters with British redcoats.[67]

By 1843 John and Caroline were living in Dooley County, Georgia, where three more children were born: Eugenia M. (1843–1866), Donald Bruce (1848–aft 1850), and George Edward (ca. 1853–1901, born in Oglethorpe County, Georgia). John was listed as a tailor on the 1850 census and may temporarily have given up being a traveling preacher to better provide for his family.

By 1857 they had moved to Texas. On July 28, 1857, as he was moving to Texas, John Kell Morse and his wife sold a slave woman named Bella and her three children for $1,700 in Georgia, probably so as not to break up a family, and they purchased a slave named Moses, thirty-five years old, for $1,000. They brought Moses with them to Texas. When they arrived, Agur Morse sold 300 acres of the western edge of the Sage survey to his brother John (Figure 7.13) and at the same time sold a slave named Harriet to Caroline.[68] John resumed his career as a preacher and held Methodist services at Pleasant Bend, according to this account from the Weekly Telegraph of June 30, 1858:

> *PLEASANT BEND. This beautiful place, which is situated about eight miles from this city, is one of the most pleasant places in Harris County. Several extensive improvements have lately gone up. A. T. Morse has lately erected a large Gin House [for processing cotton], also several new farms have been laid out. Crops look exceedingly well in this neighborhood. The neighbors meet every other Sunday, and have preaching by the Rev. J. Morse.*[69]

Rev. Morse officiated at the 1859 Harris County wedding of Daniel Crump and Amy Walker, according to an announcement in the *Houston Weekly Telegraph*.[70] Ms. Walker was the daughter of Dabney Walker in Piney Point, their nearest neighbor to the west. No doubt Morse also officiated at the wedding of his daughter Eugenia, who married Louis Bering (1840–1891) on June 12, 1861. Louis had immigrated to Texas from his native Germany in 1846 along with his parents, Johann Bering and Anna Margaret Reisse, and a number of siblings. As described in Chapter 6, the Bering family operated a lumber company in Houston and probably were customers of William Morse's sawmill operation. Louis's brother Theodore kept livestock on the adjacent open range in the neighborhood during the late 1850s.[71] Louis's family were founders in 1848 of the First German Methodist Church (later Bering Methodist Church) in Houston, coincidentally members of the same religion as Rev. John Morse.[72]

The McFee family at Pleasant Bend

James McFee (1814–1903) and his wife Cassandra Hough (1824–1890) came to Harris County from Mississippi (Figure 7.20). James was born in Delaware of Scottish and Irish immigrant parents and lived in Louisiana for a number of years. Cassandra was from Mississippi and married James in Natchez in 1848. They arrived in Texas about 1852, after the birth of their son John Hough McFee (1852–1888) in Mississippi that year. Cassandra purchased Thomas McGowen's fifty-acre farm on July 19, 1853, purchasing it from G. H. Fisher, who had purchased it from (probably Alexander) McGowen. Apparently Thomas McGowen continued to live on the farm as a sharecropper and stock raiser.[73] They had at least four other children, born in Harris County, Texas: Joseph Adam McFee (1853–1874), Hugh Cecil McFee (1855–1887), Lewis Lum McFee

Figure 7.20. James McFee and his wife Cassandra Hough. Courtesy of Matilda Reeder.

(1861–1947) and Annie Cecelia McFee (1863–1941).

James McFee was a carpenter and carriage maker. He also farmed, and county tax records for 1859 show that he owned three slaves. They would live on this site until 1866, when the land was sold to Sophronia Parker. In the 1880s the family returned to live at Piney Point (Chapter 11), where their son Lewis married Cecelia Walker Crump, granddaughter of Dabney Walker. James and Cassandra McFee and McFee sons John, Joseph and Hugh were all buried on Pleasant Bend Plantation at the Morse family burial plot, now known as the Morse-Bragg cemetery (Chapter 9).

A young visitor becomes a plantation schoolteacher

Like many early Texas settlers, the Morse family left few written records and no photographs of life on their plantation. In December 1859 the Agur Morse family received an unlikely visitor who has left a written record, albeit brief, of life there. William H. Keeling, who according to the 1860 census was a native of Vermont, was sailing on board the brig Renshan from the Bahama Islands to Galveston in 1859, apparently without funds or a plan. On December 4 of that year the ship rounded Havana, and on the evening of December 9 it arrived offshore of Galveston. Keeling disembarked at Galveston on December 11, was in Houston December 13, and somehow, by pure chance, he met Grace Morse on December 14 in Houston. He was a penniless stranger, and she invited him to visit the Morse plantation. Grace and Agur took in the young man, giving him a place to stay as well as a job teaching the children of the plantation. At that time, Agur's son Frederick was 5, George W. Morse was 15, and Henry was 20. George Edward Morse (John Kell Morse's son) was 7, and his sister Eugenia was 16. The McFees and probably others had school age children as well, so there was no shortage of potential pupils.

Two weeks later, a lonely William briefly described his Christmas day there as well as that of the plantation's African American slaves:

> *Sunday December 25, 1859. I am among strangers, alone and lonely, cannot keep from my mind the poetry commencing with "It is not that my lot is low,["] and well does "I weep [for] thee, I am all alone" cross with my feelings now, for I am with those that have not known [me], and as they know nothing of me, more than I have told them. It is strange that with some there should be a distant feeling exhibited, but taking all into consideration they are all very kind to me.*
>
> *The family that I am stopping with—that of Mr. A. T. Morse—I like very much. They consist of Mr. & Mrs. [Agur and Grace] Morse, Henry*

Morse, George Morse, Freddy Morse; a niece and nephew of Mrs. Morse, Emmett and Emma Frasee; a Mr. Wells and Dr. Duvalare stopping here; [and] a hired man by the name of Stewart. I know not how many servants. Mrs. Morse is a very fine lady. They have a son in Houston, Josiah B. [Morse]. She advised me to come here.

Christmas in the South is a great time for frolicking and visiting, and in which time the n____rs look forward with great delight as they have their holidays, and spend what little they made and saved from time to time either in drinking and frolicking or in decking themselves off as gaudily as possible, of which they are excessively fond and put on airs to kill.

Yesterday was a most beautiful day, warm and pleasant. Today wasn't, but cloudy and some occasional slight showers. The family are mostly gone, and this afternoon have spent in my chamber, reading and writing.[74]

Keeling intended his stay at the plantation to be but temporary, and he hoped to land a more permanent position as soon as possible. Meanwhile, he made the best of his situation with the Morse family:

Wednesday December 28, 1859. The boys have not returned from their Christmas visit in town so am yet at leisure. . . . I hardly know what will yet be my occupation here but do know that [I] can do something that will in the end be a paying business. If I cannot get such a situation as I would like to have, I must [have] such as I can get. . . .

Thursday December 29th 1859. The boys have come back so that it does not seem quite so dull as it has [been] for the past few days. Sent letters to the office by Henry Morse and do hope that he will bring some home, as I do want to hear from some of my friends, for all here are strangers and a letter from some friend would be gladly welcomed. . . .

Monday Jan'y 2d 1860. Another new year commences and finds me far from where I was the first of the last year and, I need say, much differently situated. But I'm not [whining] or complaining.

It has been very cold for the past few days, and last night it froze some and had a very heavy frost. This morning it is very pleasant and so cold that a fire feels quite comfortable and in fact is necessary for any degree of comfort. . . . I did not get any letters last week.

At this time, Keeling began to do some surveying work for William Morse, who was in the midst of acquiring timber property in the northern part of the Taylor League, just north of his mother-in-law Harriet George's home in Piney Point. Such property acquisitions were necessary to keep the sawmill supplied with new timber. Keeler tells of Henry Morse's unannounced wedding to Celia Hough, who was perhaps the sister or niece of the Morse's neighbor Cassandra Hough McFee:

Sunday Jan'y 8th 1860. Yesterday I traced out some old lines for William Morse.

When I came home I found that Henry was married, which took me entirely by surprise, though I had known he was paying his attention to Miss Cecelia Hough, but I did not once dream of his marrying so soon. But I do think he has done the right thing for himself. From what his mother says, he has secured for a companion one of the best of women, and though I have seen but little of her that has gone to confirm it, and though I have had but a short acquaintance with Henry, I do think him well worthy of such a lady, and may they enjoy life to its fullest.

It was a fortuitous marriage for family history, because Cecelia Hough Morse (informally called "Celia" in passages to follow) was to begin a diary during the absence of her new husband in the Civil War (Chapter 8). Keeling continued: "Josiah B. Morse has been here today, and says there is a prospect of an opening for me in their store." At this time Josiah Morse was managing the bookstore of Joseph Strong Taft (1808–1896), a merchant of the town and brother of Lovett Taft Jr., who had married

Josiah's sister (and Agur Morse's daughter) Elizabeth Morse in 1857. The *Houston Weekly Telegraph* carried a piece about that store on March 24, 1858, which also mentions J. S. Taft's son, Joseph Baldwin Taft (1839–1863):

> *We are indebted to Mr. J. B. Morse, the gentlemanly manager of J. S. Taft's branch bookstore, a few doors above the post office for some reprints of standard novels. A great variety of books of all kinds, as well as stationery, fancy goods, &c., may be seen at this establishment gratis, and bought cheap for cash. Call around.*

Keeling surveyed again for William Morse:

> *Sunday Jan'y 15 1860. I have been surveying for William Morse again today. Went to Houston Tuesday. Am to go to Mr. Taft's soon, as his son goes east.*

Joseph B. Taft (Joseph S. Taft's son) left his management position at the store and headed to New York, probably for schooling. Joseph. Jr. was later to join the U.S. Army in the coming Civil War; he died in battle in Tennessee (Chapter 8).[75]

Keeling continues:

> *Monday Jan'y 16 1860. Have been to Houston this afternoon. They have had a fire there. A cotton warehouse belonging to Whitmarsh & Co. was burnt to the ground, loss about $200,000.00, no insurance. . . .*
>
> *Mr. Morse returned from Austin this evening. [He] succeeded in getting the Buckley tract of land for Messrs Holstein & Brown. There is about 1300 [acres] vs they are to pay $3500 which I think is reasonable for it, is it is well timbered as I am told.*

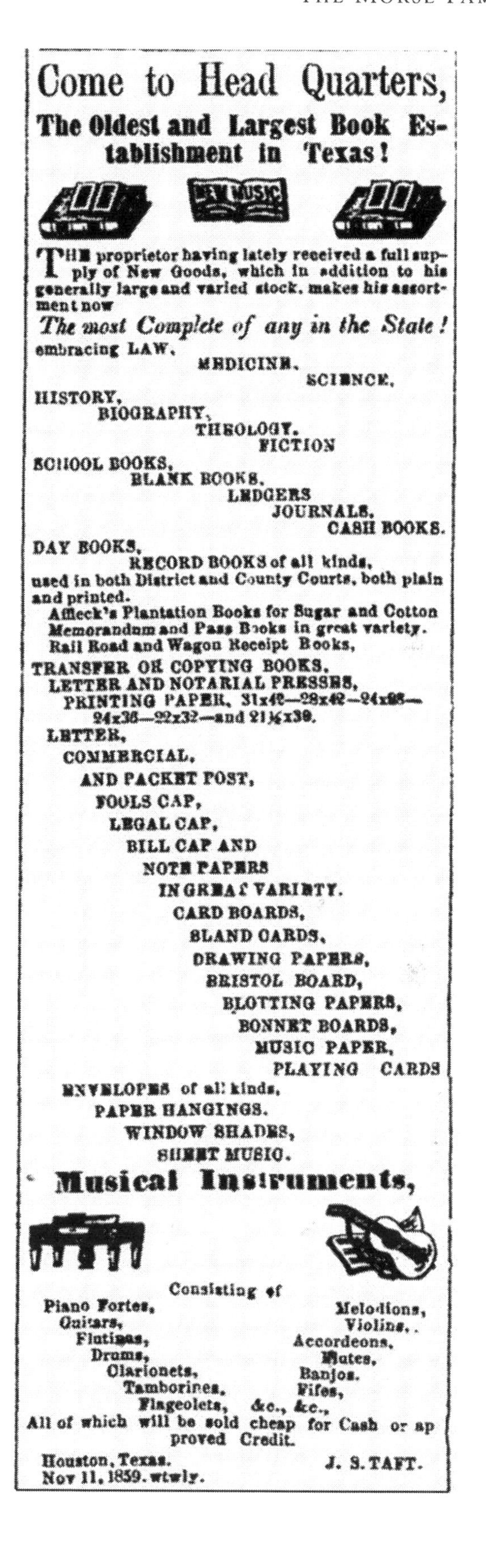

Right: Figure 7.21. Advertisement for Joseph S. Taft's bookstore, which claimed to be the oldest in the state. *Houston Daily Telegraph*, May 8, 1860.

The job in Joseph Taft's shop finally became vacant, and Keeling worried about whether to take it, because he had been working as a schoolteacher for the Morse family. But within days he had made up his mind, and within a couple of weeks he was well ensconced in his new job:

Tuesday Jan'y 17 1860. Mr. Morse went to town today. I expect as Joseph Taft is to leave today that they will send for me, but I feel under obligation to Mr. Morse's family and the children. [They are] just beginning to learn well, and I am getting interested in them and want them to succeed in their studies. I do like Mr. and Mrs. Morse and think them to be the best of people, and I hope to be able to repay them [for] their kindness to me, who was a total stranger to them.

Mr. and Mrs. Henry Morse have been here the past week. I like them still better the more I become acquainted with them. They are to settle here on a farm.

Pleasant Bend, Texas, Friday Jan'y 20, 1860. I have been expecting Mr. Taft would send for me, but he has not done so. I shall go see him tomorrow and expect to commence with him if nothing happens, next Monday. Mr. and Mrs. Morse want me to remain here, but if I do not accept this offer I do not know as I will have another opportunity of getting into business in Houston, and I am well satisfied that it is one of the best places for it that I have ever been, and if I am not successful in this, I think there will be no doubt but that there will be a chance at something else.

Houston, February 5th 1860. I have been with Mr. [J. S.] Taft since Monday the 23rd. I like it so far, very well. He is a very quiet man [and] says but very little, and I don't know whether I am suiting him. . . . J. B. Morse is clerking here, too. I like him very well. He is quite a pleasant person.

Business is some days good and others very dull. Sales will average, since I have been here, eighty dollars a day, and the profits are all of fifty percent. Am boarding with Mr. Taft.

William Morse is going to lay off a town at his new place.

William Morse's new place was the tract of land he had purchased near Piney Point. With the events of the Civil War soon to unfold, he was never able to complete that dream. One last entry into Keeling's diary mentioned how pleased he was to have paid off some debts in Kansas, but that his store job had come to an end:

Houston July 8, 1860. My journal has been a long time neglected, for I have not felt like writing . . . for the past few months, as I have had no convenience for writing in my room.

My employer J. S. Taft was burned out the 10th of March. . . . I have been to Mr. Morse's frequently since coming here.

I have disposed of my Kansas claims so that I am now rid of that, and they can claim no more from me. . . .

W. K. Keeling, Esq.
St. Louis.

This is the last entry by Keeling in his diary. He appears to have died abruptly, perhaps from yellow fever, typhoid fever or a similar ailment, and is thought to have been buried at the Morse-Bragg cemetery.[76] His diary was left behind, and Henry Morse's wife, Celia Hough Morse, took it up as her own diary from that time; it became her journal during the tumultuous war years to come.

The fire Keeling mentioned in his diary that burned Joseph S. Taft's bookstore was the largest in the city to that time and destroyed a two-block area around the intersection of Main and Congress.[77] Taft received an insurance payment and was off to New York to purchase new stock, as reported in the *Telegraph* of March 27. By April 1860 he was back in business, but within a year and the advent of the Civil War, Joseph Taft, Sr. closed the shop and returned to the North, where his son had joined the U. S. Army.

Legacy

The 1850s were, without doubt, an idyllic decade for the Morse family, who according to the *Telegraph* lived in "one of the most pleasant places in Harris County." With impressive success at growing cotton on the prairie as well as in the construction of both a cotton gin and a grist mill, a steam sawmill started by his son William, and the continued aggressive acquisition of local land, Agur's plantation had been much more successful than one would have thought, given its location outside the normal bottomland soil of the Brazos and Colorado rivers. From a cultural standpoint, the church services of Rev. John Morse as well as the growth in the number of residents in the area meant that a new community of Pleasant Bend had been created. It was a time of the last hurrah for the plantation system and its forced slave labor. Events would soon unfold across the South to alter this landscape dramatically and forever.

Figure 8.1. Confederate dead in front of Dunker church at Antietam battlefield, September 17, 1862. Here the Fifth Texas Infantry, in which Henry and George Morse served, suffered 60% casualties.
Courtesy of the Library of Congress.

EIGHT

The Civil War Years

Mr. Morrison told me he had just seen a letter from the Bayou City Guards and they had just been in a fight and one skirmish but one or two had been killed. What fate our loved ones share we do not know. . . . Oh, how I long for a letter, just one more . . . but Providence rules all things and to Him we entrust ourselves and feel that all will be well. . . . How my heart does ache. I am so afraid when news does reach us it will be of sorrow, and God knows what will become of us if this present state of things exists long. Our families are broken up and our homes left desolate and all is broken up.

—Diary of Celia Hough Morse, wife of Henry A. Morse, July 6, 1862

THE STORM CLOUDS had been gathering in Texas for decades. When Stephen F. Austin began his colony in 1821, it was initially settled not so much by family farmers intent on subsistence farming as by well-to-do planters of both northern and southern origins, most of whom had run cotton plantations in the South before migrating to Texas. They were agricultural capitalists and slave owners, looking for large amounts of cheap land that had not yet been exhausted by cotton cultivation. While Spain (and later Mexico) forbade slavery, an under-the-table compromise would soon be reached: the planters would bring their forced, unpaid servants as "indentured servants," not as slaves. Slavery was fully allowed by the Republic of Texas government after 1836, which brought the system into the open. When Texas entered the United States in 1845, it did so as an established slave state.

In the late 1840s southeastern Texas saw a great number of newly arriving southern planters like Agur Morse, who filled in many of the vacancies in arable places in the humid eastern part of the state, where earlier planters had not settled. Most arriving German immigrants and most Anglo small farmers did not practice slavery, operating small farms where manual labor was provided by the farmer, his family, and perhaps a hired hand or two. Nonetheless, the majority of whites supported the institution, both from a sense of insecurity against rumored slave insurrections in the South—where enormous numbers of African Americans lived in close proximity to whites—and from a general opposition to Negro equality, especially among small farmers.[1]

In November 1860 Abraham Lincoln, an abolitionist, was elected president of the United States, and that event sent shock waves throughout Texas.

To southerners and Texans of the 1850s, slavery was an economic necessity, and they feared the social and economic upheavals that would be brought about if slavery were to be abolished. Sentiment within the majority of the state's white population, dominated by small farmers, tilted dramatically toward secession after Lincoln's election. In northern states there was a growing equation of slavery with sin, in a population that was proud of its efforts in previous decades to remove earlier slavery in most of its area.

Governor Sam Houston, who only fifteen years previously had helped guide Texas into the United States, was against secession. He had an abiding belief in the Constitution, thinking it would protect southern interests and that such legal protections within the Union would be preferable to any radical changes. Although himself an owner of twelve slaves, Houston had long been known as an opponent of the institution of slavery. While representing Texas as a U.S. senator (1846–1859), he alone among southern senators voted against the Kansas-Nebraska Act of 1854, which would have opened up the western territories to slavery. Although there were calls for his resignation throughout Texas after that vote, Houston stayed in place.[2] In 1859 Texans voted him governor regardless of his stance on that Act, a vote that was no doubt shaped by his lasting image with Texans as the hero of San Jacinto.

Slave-owning planters, many of them old-time Whigs and Constitutionalists, were initially anti-secession as well; mostly conservative in outlook, they feared a secession into uncharted waters. Following John Brown's raid at Harper's Ferry in late 1859, and Lincoln's election in 1860, populist pro-secession sentiment grew to fever pitch, and most Texas planters fell into line.[3]

Harris County and Houston move toward secession and war

When the governors of several other southern states came out for secession in late 1860, Governor Houston refused to give his support to it, so citizens in various Texas towns and counties began to petition for a special legislative session to decide on the issue, in effect circumventing the governor. In Houston a Harris County mass meeting was held on December 1, 1860, to consider the matter. It was a serious business, with much on the line for the citizens of the county. At the meeting, on the motion of Thomas Lubbock, a former Texas Ranger and secessionist, a committee of twenty-two prominent Harris County and Houston citizens was formed to draft a petition for the governor. Among them was Agur Morse, along with other prominent citizens, such as cotton factor and northern transplant William Marsh Rice, and railroad magnate and later Houston mayor William R. Baker. Their report stated:

> *That danger is imminent, and that our social institutions are doomed to ultimate destruction under the domination of Black Republicanism, either by the strong arm of power or by a sure process undermining them, is too apparent to be questioned. Resistance in some shape is a necessity; without it we cannot reasonably hope for a settlement of the conflict—with it we may secure our future peace and safety, and liberty. Whether in the Union, or out of it as a separate nation, the march of events may determine. In either case it becomes the people of the State to consult together, and take such action as may best secure their rights.*[4]

The committee recommended a plan to elect delegates for a state convention, and further recommended that the statewide convention be held in late January 1861, in order to decide the state's immediate course of action. Those recommendations were echoed in much of the state, and the arguments won support in the legislature over the objections of Sam Houston. At the convention on February 1, the delegates voted to secede. Sam Houston was forced out of office on March 16 for refusing to take an oath of loyalty to the Confederacy.[5] By that time seven other states had already seceded.

War began on April 12, 1861. Sam Houston had predicted well before the presidential election of 1856 that such a conflict between North and South would bring disaster to his beloved Texas:

Each section, in blindness and ignorance of the other, will rush madly into war, each anticipating an easy victory. But alas! alas! Oh what fields of blood, what scenes of horror, what mighty cities in smoke and ruins—it is brother murdering brother, it is Greek meeting Greek. . . . I see my beloved South go down in the unequal contest, in a sea of blood and smoking ruin.[6]

Houston's vision was correct at all levels: across the South, across Texas, and across the small part of the state that surrounded upper Buffalo Bayou.

Among the many attendees at the Harris County public meeting in December 1860 were Agur Morse and his son-in-law Lovett Taft Jr., along with Taft's brother-in-law (and bookstore owner) Joseph S. Taft. Joseph also brought his son Joseph B. Taft, who had been sent to New York for schooling but had reappeared in Houston, perhaps for this meeting.[7] Raised in New York, the Taft brothers were about to be split apart in the coming storm. Joseph S. Taft, although an owner of four slaves, was anti-secession, and Lovett allied himself with his wife's pro-secession plantation family.[8] Lovett was among a list of donors to the city's home-grown contribution to the Confederate Army of Northern Virginia, the Bayou City Guards, in August 1861.[9] There is no record of his war service. We last see Joseph S. Taft before the war in a brief *Telegraph* story of May 27, 1861, when he and a number of merchants allowed their young male employees to participate in military preparedness drills every afternoon. Soon after that Joseph S. Taft appears to have left the scene for the North, where his son Joseph B. Taft had joined the Union Army in New York.

The upper Buffalo Bayou neighborhood goes to war

Out in Spring Branch, north of Buffalo Bayou, the small immigrant German community had seen war before, most of its adult residents having fled Germany only a dozen years earlier during the lead-up to the Revolution of 1848. Many of the men had left Europe precisely to avoid being impressed into the Prussian army, and their wives and parents knew first-hand the economic chaos that accompanied the carnage of war. The reaction of Carolina Bauer Rummel (1816–1899) to the coming Civil War in her new home of Texas is hardly surprising. In the words of her grandson:

[When] the Civil War broke out she . . . salted her savings and buried it in the ground. She packed all the silver and coins and wrapped them in heavy paper and then a large stone jar. They pulled up the floor in the log cabin, dug a deep hole in the ground, and after the stone jar was well sealed with bees wax they buried it, and no one knew but Grandpa and their two oldest sons, William and Herman.[10]

By August 1861 ten full Confederate companies of eager volunteers had been raised in Harris County. These Harris County volunteers represented fully 12 percent of the white population of the county (24 percent of the white males).[11] These volunteers were not to prove enough, however, to backfill the ranks of Confederate soldiers who were falling in battle or disabled by sickness, captured by Federal troops, freed from service when terms of volunteer enlistment expired, or—especially later in the war—lost to desertion. The Confederate Congress passed an act of conscription in early 1862, which applied to all males between the ages of eighteen and thirty-five, unless a substitute was provided. After 1863 even the system of substitution was abolished; every adult male from eighteen and thirty-five had to serve, except for those in specified service occupations (teachers, government workers, ministers, etc.) and those involved in essential heavy industry like mining.[12]

In a rural area like western Harris County, most of the free men were either farmers or stock raisers, and thus neither conscription-exempt nor wealthy enough to hire substitutes. Available records for the area from Wheaton's Ford, Piney Point and Pleasant Bend on the south side of Buffalo Bayou, and for the German settlements of Bear Creek, Spring Branch, and White Oak north of the bayou, show that nearly all male residents of an age eligible for service took part in the war. Some men in the neighborhood volunteered in 1861, like Agur Morse's sons George W. and Henry A. Morse, and Mary Silliman's son Harris Watson Silliman, but most enlisted later, in 1862, 1863 or even 1864, when conscription forced the issue.

Most men who were married with children, like Agur's older son William, or several of the Habermacher men, found a way to enlist in the Texas State Troops, which served as a defense force at home, protecting settlers on the frontier from continuing raids by Comanche and Kiowa Indians. It was a much safer alternative for those older men with families and an honorable alternative for those who followed Sam Houston's thinking on secession.

Men in the Texas State Troops typically served in cavalry units, which were much to the liking of Texans, who disdained walking anywhere. Others who joined cavalry units in the regular Confederate Army sometimes had rueful surprises awaiting them. John Wesley Thornton, Mary Silliman's son-in-law from Wheaton's Ford, joined such a cavalry unit (Texas 24th Cavalry, Granbury's Brigade) that was later sent to the front in Arkansas, Tennessee and Georgia. That unit, like several other cavalry units from Texas, was almost immediately dismounted by the Confederacy war department, and its troops were required to serve as infantrymen, much to their displeasure.

Younger single men typically found themselves in infantry and cavalry units of the regular Confederate Army at the battle front, like George and Henry Morse, Harris and Issac Benson Silliman of Wheaton's Ford, William and John Canfield of Piney Point, William Rogers of White Oak, and Frederick Reinermann of the Reinermann/Bethje family. This was a much more dangerous proposition, and of the seventeen men from the neighborhood south of the Bayou who served in this manner, seven never returned, and one other was maimed. On the other hand, all the known neighborhood men who served with the Texas State Troops survived the war.

Older men in their fifties and sixties, too old to serve in battle, usually joined Home Guard units. These were typically volunteer outfits, designed to be the last line of local defense. Especially later in the war, many of these units also rounded up runaway slaves and deserters who fled from the horrors of the war in the East. Agur Morse, at age sixty, volunteered to organize and lead the Beauregard Cavalry, one of several such Home Guard units in Houston by August 1861.[13] Few in these patriotic volunteer home guard units, and few of those who volunteered for the regular army in 1861, imagined the length and the extent of the carnage of the war to come. Many of these home guard units were to keep the peace for four years in towns where the police forces were decimated by volunteerism.

A rural area of only twelve by twenty miles, with a population of only a few hundred, the sons of the upper Buffalo Bayou area experienced the full gamut of the Civil War, from service in the Indian War at the western edge of the Confederacy, to the war in the Trans-Mississippi and Vicksburg, to service in Lee's Army of Northern Virginia in the most iconic battles of the war. Their service ranged from the heroic to the tragic and the senseless, from stunning victories to capture as prisoners of war, from idealism and heroism to desertion, and from the very beginning of the conflict to its very last engagement. The men from each of the various rural neighborhoods surrounding Buffalo Bayou were to see slightly different aspects of the war.

Census, property and military records are available for some thirty-nine men of service age from the rural upper Buffalo Bayou neighborhood (see box). The list is almost certainly incomplete. Of these, twenty-five were German- or Alsatian-born immigrants, most of them either from north of the bayou (Bear Creek and Spring Branch communities) or from the Habermacher settlement, and another fourteen were Anglos, most from the less populous Anglo settlements at Wheaton's Ford, Piney Point and Pleasant Bend. Of the twenty-five Germans, some served in Texas State Troops or coastal defense

Known Civil War Soldiers from Upper Buffalo Bayou

Legend: * seriously injured or maimed + died in service

Bear Creek and Habermacher Settlement

Brandt, Frederick / Texas State Troops
Groschke, Carl Ernst / Haldeman's Battery, 1st Brigade, Walker's Texas Division, Texas 1st Heavy Artillery, Cook's Reg't., Co.C
Groschke, Friedrich Emil / Haldeman's Battery, 1st Brigade, Walker's Texas Division, Texas 1st Heavy Artillery, Cook's Reg't., Co.C
Habermacher, Lawrence / Texas First State Troops,Sheldon's Co. B
Habermacher, Stephen / Texas Cav, Ragsdale's Batteries, Co. C
Habermacher, Thomas M. + / Pennsylvania 23rd and 82d Inf, Birney Zouaves
Habermacher, Casper / Texas State Troops 23rd Brigade, Co. F
Kobs, Frederick (Fritz / Texas, Waul's Legion, Co. F
Koch, Jacob / Texas, Waul's Legion, Co. F
Koch, Joseph / Texas, Waul's Legion, Co. F
Koch, Ludwig (Louis) / Texas 1st Heavy Artillery, Cook's Reg't., Co.C
Marks, Albert / Texas, Waul's Legion, Co. C
Marks, August / Texas, Waul's Legion, Co. C
Marks, Hilf + / Texas, Waul's Legion, Co. C

Spring Branch, White Oak and the Reinermann League

Beinhorn, Christian / 4th Field Battery, Texas Light Artillery (van Dorn's)
Beutel, Ernst / Texas 1st Heavy Artillery, Co. E
Hillendahl, Theodore W. / Texas 1st Heavy Artillery, Cook's Reg't., Co.C, 4th Co., 4th Field Artillery Battery, Tx Light Artillery (Haldeman's)
Hillendahl, Ludwig "Louis", Jr. / 4th Field Battery, Texas Light Artillery (van Dorn's)
Matzke, Gottlieb / Texas State Troops, 1st Inf., Co. F
Matzke, Christian, Jr. / Texas, Waul's Legion, Co. F
Rummel, William / Texas, Waul's Legion, Co. F
Koennecke, Friederich (Fritz) / Texas, Waul's Legion, Co. B
Reinermann, Frederick + / 2d Texas Infantry, Co. B
Rogers, William P. + / Colonel, 2nd Texas Infantry
Schroeder, Henry / 4th Field Battery, Texas Light Artillery (van Dorn's)

Wheaton's Ford and Piney Point

Canfield, John Dewitt + / Texas, Waul's Legion, Co. D
Canfield, William Byron + / Texas, Waul's Legion, Co. D
Silliman, Harris Warson + / Terry's Texas Rangers, 8th Cav., Co. H
Silliman, Abram Frisby / 16th Brigade, Texas State Troops
Silliman, Isaac Benson + / Texas, Waul's Legion, Co. D
Thornton, John Wesley / Texas 24th Cavalry (Granbury's Brigade), Co. F

Pleasant Bend and vicinity

Bering, Louis / 13th Texas Volunteers (Bates' Texas Infantry), 2d Company A, 26th Texas Cavalry, Co. A
Holmes, Robert J. / Texas 35th (Brown's) Cavalry Regiment
McFee, James / Texas Infantry, First State Troops, Sheldon's Co. B
Morse, Agur T. / Beauregard's Cavalry (Houston Home Guard)
Morse, George W. / Co. D, 1st Texas Heavy Artillery, 5th Texas Infantry, Co. A (Bayou City Guards), Capt. O. G. Jones' Battery, Texas Light Artillery
Morse, Henry A. * / 5th Texas Infantry, Co. A (Bayou City Guards)
Morse, Josiah B. / Co. A, Terry's Regiment, Texas Cavalry,
Morse, William A. / Texas First State Troops, Capt. J.W. Lawrence's Co. D, 1st Inf., Bourland's Regi ment Texas Cavalry, Co. C

units, and others served in the regular Confederate Army (most of the latter served in Waul's Legion). One of the Alsatian families in Habermacher's settlement left for Pennsylvania during the war and had a son killed in a Pennsylvania regiment. Two of the Germans of the upper bayou area died during the war, including a soldier in Waul's Legion and another in the 2nd Texas Infantry, and another two deserted, but the rest returned more or less in good form. Of the fourteen Anglo-Texans, only two served in Texas State Troops, and twelve were in the regular Confederate Army. Five of the latter died during their service. For at least two other known neighborhood men there are no records of service. Following is fuller detail about the service of all these men from the neighborhood.

Wheaton's Ford and Piney Point

The old Wheaton place–including the inn along the San Felipe Trail at the ford on Buffalo Bayou–had been purchased in 1855 by the widow Mary Frisby Silliman (1808–1864). She had moved there from an earlier home near the old Thomas Habermacher place along the bayou to the east, and began operating the old Wheaton inn that year (Chapter 3). Mary Frisby Silliman had four sons and one married daughter, and of these, three sons–Abram, Harris and Isaac Silliman–and a son-in-law–John Wesley Thornton, married to her daughter Mary Jarvis Silliman–would serve. There is no service record for her fourth son, James Monroe Silliman (1840–1875). He worked as a clerk in Fort Bend County at the time of the 1860 census, and survived the war years, marrying Lucy Foster in 1867.

Elizabeth Wheaton's son James Perry Wheaton (b. 1830) was still living in the area at the start of the war, and subject to conscription, but there is no record of his wartime service either. In the 1860 census he is listed as a farmer, probably on an unsold part of his father's Wheaton tract. He lived there with his wife M. J., two children aged one and three, and three more apparently adopted children aged two through eight. It may be that he had an exemption, or that he served and the record is lost (not uncommon, especially for those who served in the Texas State Troops).

At the age of thirty-seven when the conscription law was passed, Mary Silliman's eldest son Abram Frisby Silliman (1825–1891) was exempt and would not have been compelled to serve in the early days of the conflict. Nonetheless, he did serve, although in a brief way with no combat experience. By the time of the war he was living in Fort Bend County, according to the 1860 census. In December 1862 he signed up with the Fort Bend Scouts (Captain Patrick Terry's Texas Local Defense), which does not appear to have engaged in much activity. His occupation was listed as "mechanic and wheelwright." He signed up with 16th Brigade of the Texas State Troops in July 1863 for six months and appears to have served in place.[14] At his age, it was probably deemed enough.

First to fall. Mary Frisby Silliman's second son, Harris Warson Silliman (1836–1861), volunteered in September 1861, before conscription, joining Company H of Terry's Texas Rangers, 8th Cavalry, as a private reporting to Captain John T Holt.[15]

In the early part of the war, the Confederate government thought the war would be of short duration, as did most citizens. In March 1861, in the euphoric days following the secession of Texas, Benjamin Terry, Thomas Lubbock and John Wharton planned to raise a regiment of Texas cavalry to aid the war effort but were initially rebuffed by the Confederate War Department. Distant Texas was considered too far from the front, and the expense of transporting Texas soldiers to the East was considered too costly. The scale and carnage of the First Battle of Bull Run (Manassas) soon shocked the department into reality, and the Texas cavalry unit was approved. Four thousand volunteers flocked to Houston, where in September 1,176 men were sworn in, including Harris Silliman, who resided with his mother at Wheaton's Ford.[16] The early optimism of these troops was soon to be replaced by the sobering realities of the war and perhaps its main danger, disease. Harris Silliman was to be an early victim.

The new unit marched without horses to New Iberia, Louisiana, many falling ill along the way. They then traveled by boat to New Orleans, and by train to Nashville and then Bowling Green, Kentucky, in October or November, where they received mounts. According to one account:

> *The late fall and winter of 1861, in Kentucky, was both wet and cold. Camp sanitation among Confederates about Bowling Green was as bad as imperfect medical knowledge and lax discipline could make it. Epidemic outbreaks began early and continued through the winter, scourging the Rangers with the rest. Men to whom the war had been an unprecedented lark were now sobered as comrades died with measles, camp fevers and respiratory infections. Hospital facilities, irregularly organized and staffed, were inadequate, and the sick overflowed into private homes in Kentucky and Tennessee. Others were transported by rail to hospitals at Nashville. According to a contemporary newspaper account penned by Ranger Chaplain Robert F. Bunting, by the end of January, 1862, eighty four Rangers had died, only five from enemy action. At no time during the winter months were more than half the Rangers available for duty.*[17]

Ranger Chaplain Bunting reported that Harris Silliman died of disease in December 1861 during this time of sickness.[18] His compiled service record states that he died "at hospital in Nashville."[19]

Terry's Texas Rangers were to go on to build up an impressive and lengthy war record, at Shiloh, Murfreesboro, Chickamauga and elsewhere. Between disease and attrition by combat, the losses were staggering, however. By the end, when the Rangers surrendered in North Carolina on April 26, 1865, only 90 members remained of the 1,176 sworn in three and a half years earlier in Houston.[20]

Freezing and starving with Waul's Legion. Harris Silliman's death was only the first personal tragedy for Mary Frisby Silliman, back at Wheaton's Ford. Her son Isaac Benson Silliman (1842–1863), the youngest of her family, would join two sons of Harriet George of Piney Point in a company formed in Brenham, Texas, destined for Vicksburg, Mississippi. None of the three neighborhood men was to survive the experience. Isaac joined Company A of Waul's Legion, mustered at Camp Waul near Brenham in July 1862, not long after the Conscription Act was passed.[21] Also mustered into the same Company of Waul's Legion were Harriet George's sons from Piney Point, John Dewitt Canfield (1842–1863), in May 1862, and William Byron Canfield (1832–1862) in April. All were unmarried.

Waul's Legion, under the leadership of General Thomas Neville Waul, was sworn in at the Glenblythe Plantation near Gay Hill in Washington County, not far from Brenham. Two thousand men joined cavalry, infantry and artillery units, including a number of German Texans from Bear Creek and Spring Branch (more on them later). After training, they left camp on foot on August 17, 1862, to join the lengthy campaign to defend Vicksburg, Mississippi, the strategic fortress town that was key to General Grant's strategy to divide the South by taking control of the Mississippi River. The Texans arrived at the Sabine River on September 11 and at Vicksburg on September 30. They moved by train to Holly Springs, Mississippi, on October 8, after being paid 10 cents per mile for the long walk from Brenham.[22] There they joined the Army of Western Tennessee, which was in retreat from a recent defeat at Corinth, Mississippi. Waul's Legion soldiers were issued Springfield muskets and ammunition, and their first task was to cover the army's retreat. To this end they were ordered to Coldwater River to block General Grant's advance, and then were redeployed to Salem, east of Holly Springs. After some days there, the soldier ranks were full of rumors that they were being encircled by the Union Army, and they beat a hasty and disastrous winter retreat.[23] It was bitterly cold and raining incessantly, and in the hasty retreat

Figure 8.2 **A.** William Canfield (1832–1862), son of Buckman Canfield and Harriet George, operated the Canfield sawmill at Piney Point in the 1850s. **B.** John Dewitt Canfield (1842-1863), William's brother. Both were killed in the lengthy Vicksburg military campaign. Courtesy of Kathy Monaghan Phillips.

on December 1 the army had to destroy most of its stores. By December 3 all their tents, tables, and much of their baggage had been lost, and still the icy rain continued. Soldiers were weakened with hunger, and men searched fields for corn cobs to roast in the fire. There were significant skirmishes on December 4 at Waterville and on December 5 at Coffeeville. They were marching to Grenada, still in the cold rain, from December 6 to 7.[24]

According to the diary of a German-born Texas soldier in Waul's Legion, "in battle not any more men would have been lost than did during the retreat with those dying from great physical exertion from the cold, rain, and mud of this winter month."[25] On December 7, 1862, thirty-year-old William Byron Canfield, the sawyer at his mother's sawmill back in Piney Point (Figure 8.2 A), died at Grenada, Mississippi. Available records do not give the cause of death. No skirmishes were recorded that day, and it seems likely that he was one of the many who died from the long exposure to inclement winter weather, without shelter on the winter retreat.

By January 25, 1863, the Legion moved again, ultimately arriving below Greenwood, Mississippi, thirty miles northeast of Yazoo City, where they built Fort Pemberton to protect Confederate troops at Vicksburg from an enemy advance coming down the Yazoo River; at this they were successful.

By May all but one company of Waul's Legion were on the move to Vicksburg.[26] On May 22 Waul's men were centrally involved in the defense of the city from a frontal assault by Grant's forces (Figure 8.3). Seeing a breach at Forth Hill, two companies were ordered to retake it, which was done in a valiant effort "amidst smoke, blood, the stench of death and the deafening sound of cannon balls," and the Union forces were repelled.[27] This third attempt to take Vicksburg by assault was Grant's last, and he resorted to retaking the city by a siege that lasted forty-seven days, in which Waul's men and other Confederate forces there were cut off from food and supplies.[28]

Figure 8.3. Confederate troops defend Vicksburg from a frontal attack, May 1863. Courtesy of the National Park Service.

The Confederate forces surrendered on July 4, 1863, and most men were paroled by July 10. They evacuated Vicksburg on July 12, and although they were supposed to go to Demopolis, Alabama, to await exchange, vast numbers deserted at this time and made their way home.[29] Not among them were Isaac Benson Silliman, who died on July 5, 1863, a day after surrender, and John Dewitt Canfield (Figure 8.2 B), who died on July 12. There are no available records to state the means by which they died, but either starvation or disease, contracted during the long stay in the trenches surrounding the city, seems a reasonable guess. It is not known where either is buried, and the death dates come solely from family diaries. Mary Frisby Silliman and Harriet George, both widows, had each lost two sons by the middle of 1863, halfway into the war. Each also had a daughter who was married to a Confederate soldier, so their long ordeal was not yet over. Hannah Canfield had married Agur Morse's son William A. Morse, and Mary Jarvis Silliman had married John Wesley Thornton, both from the neighborhood.

Thornton's war, from Arkansas to Georgia. John Wesley Thornton (1832–1918) married Mary

Figure 8.4. John Wesley Thornton and his wife Mary Jarvis Silliman. From the author's collection.

Frisby Silliman's daughter, Mary Jarvis Silliman (ca. 1833–1871) in 1853 (Figure 8.4), and the couple lived for some time with Mary's mother at the inn she had operated at Wheaton's Ford since 1855. By 1860 the couple lived in now-forgotten Pittsville, Texas, three miles north of Fulshear, where John was a stock raiser. By the beginning of the war they had three young children, aged three to seven. Two more were born during the war, and one two years after the war's end. His wife Mary's brothers Isaac Benson Silliman and Harris Silliman were to die in the war, as already mentioned.

Thornton mustered into Company F, Texas 24th Cavalry on April 15, 1862. Methodist minister George Washington Carter had the idea of forming three "Lancers" cavalry units of soldiers, the 21st, 24th and 25th Cavalry, armed with lances, mounted on their own horses, and armed with their own guns. Cavalrymen tended to be older than infantrymen, and acted more independently. The idea of fighting on horseback greatly appealed to most rural Texan men, many of them ranchers who generally disdained walking. Confederate brass grumbled, though, at the idea of these new cavalry units, as what they needed were infantrymen in great numbers.[30] When the Lancers units arrived in Arkansas in May, their leaders were ordered to dismount the troops, including the 24th Cavalry. This extremely unpopular decision led to terrible morale and mass desertions, especially since the mounts were the property of the soldiers and were essentially confiscated.

In late 1862 the troops were sent to the small town of Arkansas Post, where they built a fort to defend the Arkansas River from General Grant's Union forces, who considered the fort a threat to their lines of communications in the Vicksburg campaign. About 6,000 Confederates were initially stationed there, with a number of naval guns. On January 9, Union Major General John McClernand advanced on the fort with 6,000 men and three gunboats, and the gunboats opened fire the following

Figure 8.5. The Confederate surrender at Arkansas Post, January 9, 1862. General Stephen G. Burbridge is planting the Union flag after the capture of the post. The white flags were raised by Texas troops, who mistakenly surrendered due to miscommunication and perhaps panic. Sketch from *Battles and Commanders of the Civil War*, by General Marcus F. Wright of the War Department, 1907.

day. The Confederate guns were put out of commission, and the infantry were under saturation bombardment. At this time, in the panic of the moment, a cry rang out among the 24th Cavalry to "Raise the white flag, by order of General Churchill; pass the order up the line." There was no official order to do so, and in the confusion the Federals stepped into the breach to accept the surrender. The Confederates by this time had no choice but to surrender (Figure 8.5). It has been said that the low morale of the dismounted Texan troops was partly to blame for the miss-step, which was a Confederate blunder of very large proportions.[31]

Surrendered soldiers, including Private John Wesley Thornton, were sent up north as prisoners of war; many others simply escaped and deserted. After four months of incarceration at Camp Butler, Illinois, Thornton was exchanged at City Point, Virginia. His fragmented regiment was consolidated with other such remnants and became Granbury's Consolidated Texas Brigade. After that he was

> *sent to the Tennessee Army, where he fought at Harrison's Crossing of the Tennessee River and at Chickamauga in September 1863. So many men were killed [that the remaining] fragment was sent to Bragg's Regiment. John was furloughed for 60 days on March 4, 1864, when he went home. On returning [to the front], he was under Hood and fought in battles at Ringgold and Dalton, Georgia, Kennesaw Mountain, and four or five battles around Atlanta. He saw the fall of Atlanta, September 2, 1864.*[32]

It was at this time, during the battle for Atlanta in September 1864, that John Thornton wrote to his

Figure 8.6. Brothers John Wesley Thornton and Thomas Henry Clay Thornton, after the war. From Mrs. Arch B. Marshall, *Forebears and Descendants of an Early Houston Family* (Houston: Privately published, 1975).

brother Thomas Henry Clay Thornton (Figure 8.6). Thomas was born at some time after 1842 and was enlisted elsewhere in the Confederate Army; family notes written by John Thornton's daughter Florence indicate that Thomas was severely wounded in the Second Battle of Bull Run (Manassas) on August 30, 1862; after recovering, he rejoined. The letter from John to Thomas is a poignant reminder of the depth of the many sacrifices made, not only at the front but at home:

> *September 11, 1864*
> *Jonesborough, Georgia*
> *Dear brother,*
>
> *As I have an opportunity of sending a letter across the Mississippi River, I embrace it in writing you a few lines. I am quite well at present and have passed through the campaign thus far unhurt. You no doubt have heard of the protracted campaign that appears to have closed for a short while and terminated so unfavorable to our cause. Atlanta has fallen and we have sustained quite a loss. Besides though while our loss is great, that of the enemy has greatly exceeded ours. We have had a hard time of it ever since my return and have come in for a double share of the fighting, a detailed account of which from me would be uninteresting and I presume you are well informed of it as I am, although I have been present all the while. A private soldier here knows but little except what he sees and feels. It is rumored in camps that there is an armistice for ten days between Generals Hood and Sherman. At least it appears so to us, for we have had a few days quiet unaccompanied with bullets and bomb shells, a thing that has not been since the first of May. Our command has had some of the hardest fighting that we have had during the war. There has been four killed and seven wounded in my old Company since my return to the command, leaving but eight of us.*
>
> *Brother, I have not received a line from you since I parted with you. I have looked anxiously for a letter and would be very glad to receive one soon. I have not heard from my wife and children since I left and I am so anxious to hear from them. I received a letter from sister Mollie a short time ago, they had not heard from you since I saw you, they were very uneasy and anxious to hear from you. . . . Mollie wrote all were well except some of sister's children. They were doing well and had an abundance of fruit and melons, a thing I so much desire. I have not tasted but one melon this season, and that I paid ten dollars for. Such luxuries are impossible to get here, but God grant this hard and cruel war may end soon and we may yet enjoy more of the beautiful blessings of nature. Brother, we have considerable talk of peace in the army here. Whether or not we have any good reasons to expect it is more than I can at present tell. I [p]resume the events that will transpire at the north during the*

Figure 8.7. "Texas Settlers Pursuing the Indians," from the *New York Illustrated News,* April 13, 1861.

next few months will decide whether or not the war will continue next year.

Dear brother, I must close this with the request that you immediately write to your affectionate brother,

J. W. Thornton[33]

Later in 1864 Thornton fought again at Lovejoy Station and at Franklin, Tennessee:

After being repulsed at Nashville in December, 1864, he was sent to [General] J. E. Johnson in North Carolina. His last engagement was at Bentonville, North Carolina, on March 19, 1865, where he said, "All was lost, save honor." In May, 1865, John signed the amnesty and was paroled to go home.[34]

Thornton was one of the lucky ones, surviving numerous battles over the course of three years. His wife, Mary Jarvis Silliman, died in 1871, and he eventually remarried, later to start a new ranch in Sweetwater, Texas. His daughter Mary Luna (Mollie) Thornton (1861–1898) was to marry George Edward Morse, the son of Rev. John Kell Morse and his wife Caroline at Pleasant Bend.

William A. Morse and a second war on the frontier. Harriet George's daughter Hannah Canfield Morse (1835–ca. 1894) married William Agur Morse (1831–1866) in 1854. As has been discussed, William was Agur Morse's eldest son (Figure 7.16), and by the beginning of the war he was a part owner of the William A. Morse & Company sawmill. At the beginning of the war the couple had five children ranging from one to six years of age.

We often forget that Texas fought two wars concurrently in the 1860s: the Civil War to the east, and the Indian War on its northwestern frontier, which by 1860 consisted of a string of United States cavalry forts stretching from approximately Del Rio to Wichita Falls. The U.S. Army had been actively engaged in frontier defense in Texas since the Mexican-American War of 1848, but the "depredations" of Comanche and Kiowa Indians along the frontier actually increased in 1859–1860 relative to previous years (Figure 8.7). These activities, which comprised a last-ditch effort by the native Americans to defend their lands, included brutally killing settlers, stealing and slaughtering livestock, and stealing horses along the entire northwestern frontier. At the start of the Civil War in 1861, the frontier settlements—which had already long been suffering these attacks—received a double hit. U.S. Army cavalry units, which included some three thousand troops by 1861, were forced to withdraw upon the state's secession from the Union in early 1861, leaving the Texas frontier essentially unguarded. The second hit came from the exodus of young men from Texas into Confederate ranks, just when they were needed for frontier defense.[35] Thomas Lubbock formed a frontier regiment of Texas Rangers in 1862 to deal with this threat and attempted unsuccessfully to have the Confederate government adopt and fund it. By 1863 it was called the Mounted Regiment of Texas State Troops, and then, after December 1863, it was reorganized as the Frontier Organization, part of the Confederate government forces.[36]

Our first record of William Morse's service is with Lawrence's Company D, First Infantry Regiment, Texas State Troops, in which he served from September 1863 to February 1864. It is possible he served earlier, as records are incomplete. The local prominence of his father, who by this time had organized a Houston Home Guard, and who among neighborhood residents had the most to lose in the war because of his ownership of a number of slaves, would certainly have been an added incentive to volunteer, as his younger brothers did.

Not all service in the Texas State Troops was active or heroic. In 1863 Lawrence's Company guarded prisoners of war at Tyler, Texas, and there is no record of the unit having been in any battle engagements. But by November 1864 William was a private in Company C, Bourland's Regiment, Texas Cavalry. This regiment was organized under James Bourland in early 1863 and was fully occupied in northern Texas, from headquarters at Gainesville, in guarding the northwestern frontier against Indian raids. It was also called the Border Regiment, because they occasionally confronted Federals in the adjacent Indian Territory.

James Bourland's reputation had become severely tainted by an 1862 episode called the "Great Hanging" at Gainesville, where forty Unionist sympathizers were summarily hanged. Confederate brass had overlooked this in giving him command of the cavalry regiment.[37] Such disturbing leadership behavior on Bourland's part was to recur. By late 1864 hundreds of deserters from Confederate service were crossing Texas, trying to escape to California; others were trying to get to Union lines across the Red River. James Bourland's troops attempted, only partially successfully, to ferret them out. Bourland himself dealt harshly with those captured, murdering some of them in the brush, without a trial. Many of his own men, including five of his captains, turned against him for a court martial, but Bourland remained in charge until Confederate surrender.[38]

We have no additional details of William Morse's service on the Texas frontier. By the end of the war he was back at Pleasant Bend Plantation with his wife Hannah Canfield Morse. He was included in a list of registered voters of Harris County in the *Houston Tri-Weekly Telegraph* of October 13, 1865, and the Masonic Lodge of Houston noted his passing on July 23, 1866. The young age of his demise suggests either that he had been wounded in service or that he contracted some sort of fatal disease. His wife Hannah was to marry twice more, finally to Abram Frisby Silliman of Wheaton's Ford, who had lost two younger brothers in the war.

An unwelcome war comes to the German settlers along the Bayou

German immigrants in Texas did not generally practice slavery, and most were against it. The economic model of German settlers, exemplified by the early farms of the Habermacher family in western Harris County as well as those of the German settlers of the Bear Creek community, was to farm small acreage very efficiently, using the labor of large families rather than of slaves. Because Germans were on the whole not slave keepers—and some were vocally against the practice—they lived somewhat apart from the Anglo settlers. In some parts of the state, especially in central Texas where Germans were in the majority, pro-Union sentiment was high; many had left Germany precisely to escape the folly of war. But the German settlers were nevertheless subject to conscription. Most loyally served out their duty to their new home, but some enrolled and then deserted,

Figure 8.8. Corporal Thomas M. Habermacher, Pennsylvania Infantry, who died at the battle of Winchester, Virginia, in 1864.
Courtesy of the late William H. Plageman.

and still others left the state. All these reactions were seen in the Buffalo Bayou neighborhood.[39] War service was especially hard on German families, because the father was a crucial part of the labor force on their small-acreage farms. There were no slaves to fall back on for providing basic food needs.

Habermachers: a family divided. Because of their family history, the Habermachers were even more conflicted and divided in their loyalties than were other Texas German families. As we have seen, the Habermachers had lived for years in Pennsylvania before coming to Texas in 1841. When most of the Habermacher family left Pennsylvania for Texas, Thomas Habermacher's son Joseph stayed behind. He had married a Pennsylvania woman, Petronilla Rutler, and they had four children born in that state between 1836 and 1844 before finally joining the rest of the Thomas Habermacher family in Texas in 1846, where their last child was born in 1847. It would appear that with Civil War looming, Joseph and his wife Petronilla returned to Pennsylvania during the war, as she died there on March 19, 1861. Joseph's oldest son, Corporal Thomas M. Habermacher (1836–1864), became a Union soldier, serving in both the 23rd and 82nd Pennsylvania Infantry, the Birney Zouaves, and was killed at the battle of Winchester, Virginia, in 1864 (Figure 8.8). His other son, Texas-born John Charles (1847–1923), was too young to serve and was enrolled at a Pennsylvania Catholic College.[40]

Thomas Habermacher's two youngest sons, Thomas (1828–after 1910) and Peter (1831–after 1884), had been born in Pennsylvania, and there is no record of their service. It seems possible that they may have traveled there with their brother Joseph for the duration of the war.[41]

At the same time, two of Thomas's sons served in the Confederate military. Stephen Habermacher (1814–after 1880) served in Company C, Ragsdale's Batteries, Texas Cavalry, and Lawrence Habermacher (1822–1895) served in Sheldon's Company B, 1st State Troops of the Texas Infantry (the same regiment as William Morse, profiled earlier). Both these units were part of the Frontier Regiment, mostly involved in Indian fighting and the rounding up of deserters. Such work kept the men close to home and away from killing Union soldiers. Given the divided loyalties of the family, it was probably a good compromise. Lawrence deserted in 1864, as did a large number of State Troops late in the war.[42]

Casper Habermacher (1820–1883) was also in the Frontier force but apparently only very briefly. He served as a private in Company F, 23rd Brigade, Texas State Troops, reporting to General J. R. Sayles. He enlisted on January 5, 1863, but apparently the experience was not to his liking. Like his brother Lawrence, he was reported absent without leave by January 13.[43] There are no other service records for him. Casper, Stephen, and Lawrence Habermacher all survived their service in the Texas State Troops.

In summary, the Habermacher family was split in two over the Civil War, which is not surprising given their relatively short residency in Texas before the war, their family ties to and presence in Pennsylvania, and their non-ownership of slaves.

War and the Bear Creek and Spring Branch communities. Most of the founding families of the Bear Creek community had been in place for little over a decade when the Civil War broke out: the Marks family arrived in 1843, and the Koch, Meier, Brandt, Kobs, and Groschke families arrived between 1847 and 1850. These families were all small farmers and stock raisers, and none appear to have owned slaves. Nonetheless, every able-bodied male of service age in these families served in the Confederacy.

This war service came at a high cost for their families, as many of these men had wives and young children who had to fend for their farms in their absence. The women had not only the vegetable gardens and corn fields to tend but cattle to mind. At that time cattle were raised in the open range, and one had to venture out on the range to find an appropriate cow to slaughter, cut it out from the herd, drive it home, and butcher it—quite a task for a woman rearing small children. In practice, most cattle were left wild over the war years. Wild game and hogs, also significant parts of the diet, were typically gathered and butchered by men, and most women and children had to do without in their absence. Cash crops like cotton tended to be dropped.

The Marks family, the first to have arrived in the area, sent three sons to the Confederate forces. Albert (1842–1910), August (1843–1891), and Hilf Marks (1843–c1863) joined Waul's Legion, the same unit in which Isaac Silliman and John and William Canfield had perished. They mustered into Company C of that unit at Brenham in April 1862.[44] Like the Silliman and Canfield men from south of the bayou, they may have been drafted. Only Albert and August were to return; Hilf went missing and was presumed dead during the Vicksburg campaign.[45] From the experience of the Canfield and Silliman boys in Waul's Legion, one can speculate on the causes: exposure from a winter retreat without shelter, disease, starvation from the Vicksburg siege, and of course the violence of warfare itself.

During the war, in 1862, their widowed mother Sophia finally received a homestead grant for the 160-acre farm along Bear Creek on which they had

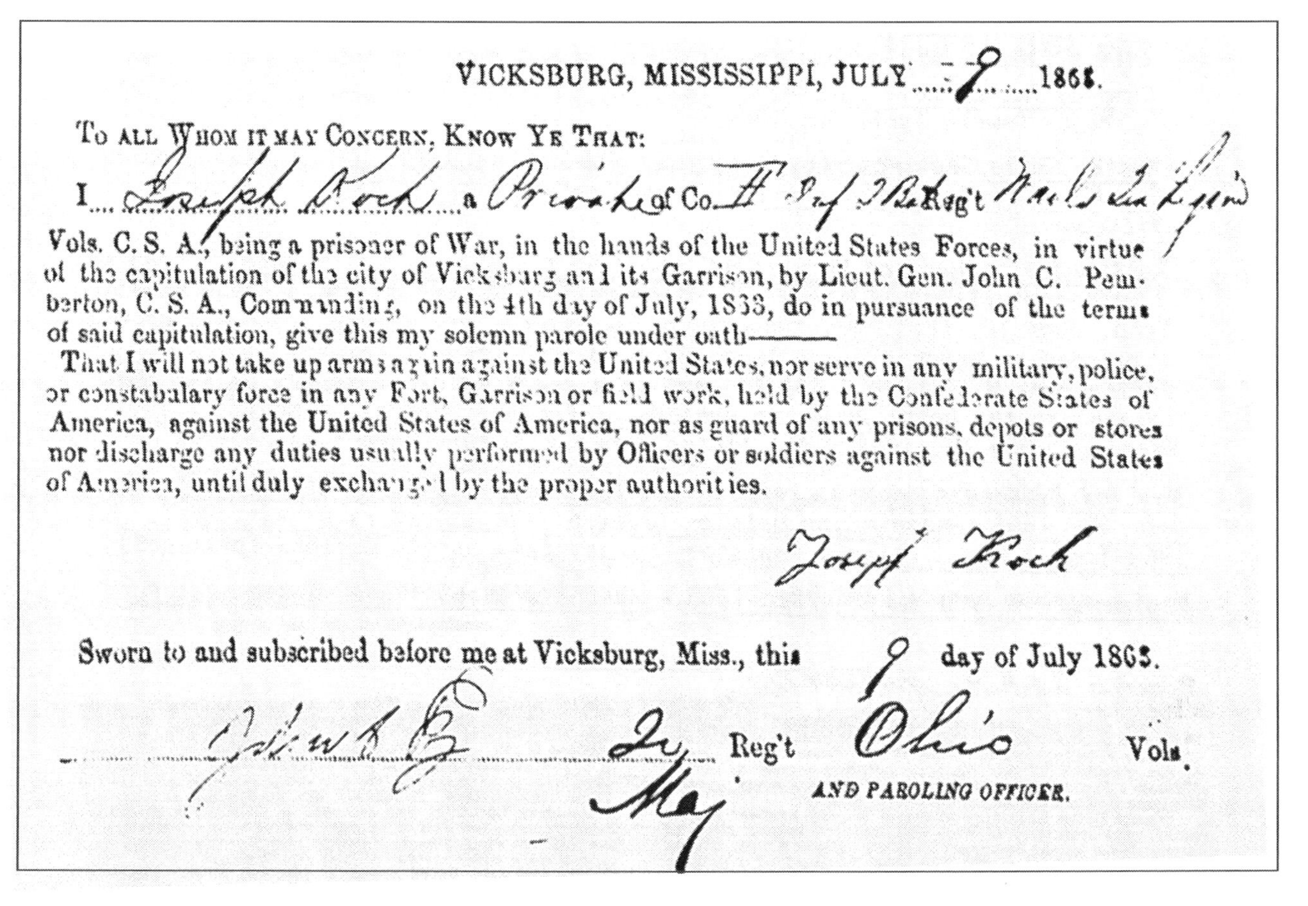

VICKSBURG, MISSISSIPPI, JULY 9 1863.

To all Whom it may Concern, Know Ye That:

I Joseph Koch a Private of Co. F Inf 1 Bat Reg't Waul's Tex Legion Vols. C. S. A., being a prisoner of War, in the hands of the United States Forces, in virtue of the capitulation of the city of Vicksburg and its Garrison, by Lieut. Gen. John C. Pemberton, C. S. A., Commanding, on the 4th day of July, 1863, do in pursuance of the terms of said capitulation, give this my solemn parole under oath—

That I will not take up arms again against the United States, nor serve in any military, police, or constabulary force in any Fort, Garrison or field work, held by the Confederate States of America, against the United States of America, nor as guard of any prisons, depots or stores nor discharge any duties usually performed by Officers or soldiers against the United States of America, until duly exchanged by the proper authorities.

Joseph Koch

Sworn to and subscribed before me at Vicksburg, Miss., this 9 day of July 1863.

[illegible] 2y Reg't Ohio Vols.

May

AND PAROLING OFFICER.

Figure 8.9. Joseph Koch's parole, signed after he and his unit were captured at Vicksburg in July 1863. Courtesy Marie Neuman Gray and the late Margaret H. Edwards.

been living for over a decade. She owned a single-barreled muzzle-loading rifle during that time, which according to her grandson E. H. Marks, she used during the war, perhaps after losing her son Hilf: "There were seven notches on the stock, and she never would tell us what they were for. But if they were for deer, she would have told us."[46]

Besides Hilf Marks, a number of other Bear Creek men were to join Waul's Legion. Joseph Koch (b. 1829) and his cousin Jacob Koch (b. ca. 1837) both joined. Joseph enlisted in Houston on May 26, 1862, joining Company F, and received a bounty of $2.10. He was thirty-two years old, married (to Susanna Matzke, in 1851) and had a son, John, born in 1852 (Chapter 7). Somehow, Joseph Koch survived the winter retreat near Holly Springs, Mississippi, in December 1862 that killed William Byron Canfield and possibly Hilf Marks, and was captured with the rest of Waul's Legion on July 4, 1863. He signed a parole on July 9, 1863, which effectively ended his wartime service (Figure 8.9). Jacob Koch was also in Company F and was employed as a scout during the Vicksburg campaign. He was captured by June 9, when he appears on a list of Confederate prisoners. His regiment declared him "absent without leave." Jacob signed a United States fealty oath on September 23, 1863, declaring that he "was conscripted into the Rebel service at Galveston, Texas on the 20th day of May 1862."[47] It is not known how Jacob spent the rest of the war, but it was not likely that he saw any more service in the Confederate Army. Frederich Kobs Jr. (1833–1905) also joined

Company F of the legion. He was married to Dorothea Meier (1840–1921), the immigrant daughter of the Bear Creek Christian Meier family, and the couple had a small child at the time of his enlistment. Frederich joined the unit in June 1862 and left on a three-day parole, when he was forcibly conscripted into a sappers and miners group within the Texas State Troops, serving in the construction of fortifications along the southeast Texas coast. He was paroled from that unit on June 27, 1865.[48]

In Spring Branch, pioneer settler Carl Wilhelm Rummel (1812–1867) and four others from the Spring Branch area were visiting Houston during the early days of the war when they were arrested and placed in jail for being disloyal to the Confederacy. His wife Carolina (Bauer) Rummel (1816–1899), using a writ of habeus corpus, had them quickly tried in open court; nothing could be proven, and they were released.[49] Their son, Carl William ("William") Rummel, Jr. (1837–1915), and Friederich Koennecke (1839–1916)—who after the war was to marry Sophie Marie Schulz of the Bear Creek community—joined the Bear Creek men already mentioned in Waul's Legion. William Rummel served in Company F, bringing with him the knowledge of his mother's buried coins back at their log cabin; he survived the war. He wrote of his war experiences in his diary:

> *1862, I was assigned to Waul's Legion and sent to the Instruction Camp at Brenham. In August the last of us marched to the Mississippi. When I left I was sick with malaria which grew worse and worse and they sent me home on 30 days furlough which was extended to six months when the fever ran into typhoid. When rheumatism disabled me altogether I was given a discharge for one year which was a great surprise. On the 24th of April, 1864, I was called again and sent to Houston for instruction in woodwork and in making tools which was good training. In May 1865, the Confederation came to an end and there was much looting in Houston.*[50]

Koennecke, a native of Sueldfeld, Hanover, Germany, was in Company B. He was captured at Vicksburg, and was moved to a prisoner's camp at Gettysburg, Pennsylvania, for the duration of the war. When he was released in 1865 he had to walk back to Texas. According to Schulz family biographers Maxine Sullivan and Annette M. Parker, "He told the story that the only food he could find [on that walk] was in the fields alongside of the road, and not much of that, as it had been destroyed by the Yankees."[51] Koennecke is buried at St. Peter's Church in Spring Branch.

Other men from Bear Creek and Spring Branch were fortunate to find their way to the Texas State Troops, which kept them closer to their homes. Frederick Brandt (1837–1923) was married with three children at the start of conflict and reportedly had little desire to go to war. He enlisted in the Texas State Troops, where he found service as a wagon maker and repairer. Carl Ernst Groshke (1835–1917) and his brother Friedrich Emil Groschke (1836–1942) of Bear Creek enlisted in Haldeman's Battery of the First Brigade, Walker's Texas Division.[52] That unit was employed in the Western Theater of the war, in a support role, seeing action at Milliken's Bend and Young's Point, Louisiana, in the Vicksburg campaign of 1863, and at the battles of Mansfield and Pleasant Hill in the Red River campaign in 1864, both of which were victories for the Confederates.[53] The Groschkes were transferred to Company C of the 1st Texas Heavy Artillery Regiment, also known as Cook's Regiment, in 1864, where Carl rose to the rank of sergeant.[54] Both men were discharged in 1865 and returned home to their wives (and in Carl's case, also to two children).

Ernst Beutel of Spring Branch and Theodore Hillendahl of White Oak were in the 1st Texas Heavy Artillery Regiment too, and spent their time on coastal Texas defense duties.[55] Ernst Beutel (1836-1912) had only arrived in Houston from Hannover, Germany, in 1860, and was wearing Confederate grey within two years. He survived the war, and married Sophia Kruse (1846-1923) in 1866; they had seven children between 1875 and 1890 while he farmed in the area; the couple were buried at St. Peter Church in Spring Branch.[56]

Louis Hillendahl Jr., Christian Beinhorn (1833-

1905), and Henry Schroeder (b. 1837), all of Spring Branch, enlisted in the 4th Field Battery, Texas Light Artillery (Van Dorn's), one of twenty-six Texas-organized batteries of field artillery.[57] The unit, organized on July 1, 1861, served under Capt. William T. Mechling in Arkansas and Louisiana and surrendered at Arkansas Post in January 1863—the same surrender in which John Thornton took part, as described earlier. It is not known whether Hillendahl and Beinhorn were sent north to a prison camp or whether they escaped and deserted, as some did. In November 1864 that artillery unit was designated as the 4th Field Artillery Battery under Captain Hardeman; the battery was armed with two 12-pound Howitzers and two 12-pound Napoleons. Louis's brother Theodore W. Hillendahl transferred into the unit around that time, where he served for the rest of the war. Theodore had earlier been in Cook's Regiment of Heavy Artillery, where the Groschke brothers were.[58] After the war Theodore moved to White Oak, and Louis Hillendahl, Henry Schroeder and Christian Beinhorn all returned to Spring Branch.

A family story tells of how Christan Beinhorn came by his wife during the war. His future wife, Mary Mueller (1848-1925), related the story to a daughter, who passed it on:

> *Before Christian went into the service, a party was given in his honor and of other volunteers from Spring Branch, who were probably Louis Hillendahl and Ernest Beutel. He saw little 14-year-old Marie Meuller with her long black braids and taking her on his knee, told her how pretty she was. He promised that when he got back, he would marry her. We don't know how serious he was about that at the time, but when he returned, she reminded him of it. Apparently he had forgotten his promise when she tugged at his sleeve for attention. She repeated his words, adding "and I waited for you."*[59]

The couple (Figure 8.10) married in Spring Branch in 1866, and had nine children from 1867 to 1881. A farmer, he succumbed to a spider bite in 1905.

Gottlieb Matzke (1827–1865) of Spring Branch, brother of Susannah Matzke Koch Schmidt at Bear Creek, was born in Silesia, Poland, and arrived in Texas in 1846 with his parents Christian and Jo-

Figure 8.10. A promise kept: Johann Heinrich "Christian" Beinhorn and his wife Marie Mueller.

Figure 8.11. Confederate land forces retake Galveston, January 1, 1863, while a naval battle occurs offshore. From *Harpers Weekly Illustrated,* January 31, 1863.

hanna Matzke. He spent the war in the Texas State Troops, in Company F of the First Infantry.[60] Little is known of his service, but his death on June 30, 1865, only a little over a month after Appomattox, suggests that he may have had a difficult transition back to civilian life in Spring Branch. His younger brother, Christian Matzke Jr., also served, enlisting in Company F of Waul's Legion in 1862. He must not have found the war to his liking; he was noted as absent without leave on four separate occasions in 1862–1863.[61]

Ludwig Koch (1838–1886) joined the Confederate service on November 1, 1861, and served for the duration of the war. A single man, aged twenty-two, his immigrant parents were both dead by this time and buried at the Koch-Schmidt family cemetery in Bear Creek (Chapter 6). Ludwig was in Company C of Col. Cook's Regiment, Texas Heavy Artillery.[62] His regiment manned the defense of the port of Galveston.[63] In May 1862 he came down with "Dysenteria Cholera" but recovered after a week at a local boarding house. He reenlisted for two more years in June 1862, with Lt. Col. Manly, remaining in Galveston. During that stint of duty he took part in the Battle of Galveston.[64] A northern navy squadron captured Galveston in October, but on New Year's Day 1863, forces under General John B. Magruder sailed two cottonclads to the city and engaged a force of six Union ships, while a land force attempted to retake the town (Figure 8.11). The Confederates captured one ship, the *USS Harriet Lee*, and another, the *USS Westfield*, was grounded on a sand bar. Union troops blew up the latter ship, and their compatriots on shore took that as a sign that their ships were surrendering and followed suit. The remaining Union ships retreated, and the engagement was a major Confederate victory.

Galveston remained in Confederate hands for the remainder of the war, which suited Ludwig Koch. On March 21, 1863, he married a widow in Bear Creek named Sophie Addicks Eggling (1838–1923) but remained in service at Galveston. Sophie had a three small children by her former husband William Eggling; the youngest was born in December 1862, only four months before she married Ludwig. A one-week furlough to Harris County granted to Ludwig provided a welcome relief in February 1864, perhaps due to an injury, because on March 21, 1864, he was given a medical release from active duty because of a hernia. On July 7, 1864, that release was again certified by the assistant surgeon of Cook's Regiment, who found an "inguinal hernia of the right side which prevents his lifting of heavy objects. I recommend that he be detailed for light duty." Ludwig Koch then became involved in procuring leather for the war effort. A letter of July 14, 1864, from Allen and Poole Government Contractors to his commanding officer requested the "detail of Ludwig Koch, Co. C, Cook's Regiment, a farmer, his service being necessary to carry out the contract for leather which we have entered into with the Clothing Bureau. . . . [We] are under contract for the delivery of 24,000 lbs. of leather to this department." Koch served in this capacity until war's end in April 1865; he was paroled on June 27.[65] No doubt this procurement activity allowed him to visit his family and friends in Bear Creek, many if not all of whom kept cattle.

Except for Hilf Marks, all the Bear Creek men were to return safely, and they resumed life on their family farms much as before the war. In 1874 Sophia Striepe (widow of Gotthilf Marks, and Hilf's mother) sold her 160-acre farm to her returning son Albert for $350 and a lifetime supply of corn:

> *The Twenty Five Brls. of Corn to be given yearly to Mrs. Sophia Striepe by Albert Marks, during her life until her death, must be of a good sound and merchantable Quality and deliverable in the proper season of the year . . . [deliverable] at the time of the general and usual harvesting of corn in Harris County.*[66]

Albert married Mina Walter, then eighteen, and they raised a family in the Bear Creek community. Sophia's third son, August Marks, had his eye on stock raising (Chapter 10).

The war and the Reinermann league. As we learned in Chapter 6, Louisa Schiermann (1813–1867) was twice married in Germany before she came to Texas, where she met and married Henry Reinermann (1808–ca. 1844), son of the immigrant family patriarch John Reinermann (1775–ca. 1836). She had two children prior to marrying Henry Reinermann, Anna Marie Louisa Gerding (1836–1916) and Frederick Hobein (ca. 1838–1862). Henry adopted these two children so that they would be able to inherit his headright one third league of land, just north of the John Reinermann league. Both children changed their surnames to Reinermann. Frederick Reinermann grew to adulthood near Houston, where he became a bartender for Peter Gabel and John Wagner.[67]

Frederick Reinermann, aged twenty-two at the war's outbreak, joined Company B, 2nd Regiment, Texas Infantry, on August 7, 1861, at the rank of private.[68] That unit was organized by John C. Moore in Galveston, with most of its men coming from Houston and Galveston. In its early days the unit served in Texas, but they soon moved to Tennessee, joining with General Albert Sydney Johnston.[69] There Frederick took part in, survived and wrote about one of the great battles of the war, at Shiloh, Tennessee (also called the Battle of Pittsburg Landing), on April 6–7, 1861. His letter was written to William Quesnell (1829–1890), a half-brother of Frederick's step-father Christian Bethje and the husband of Frederick's sister Anna Marie.[70]

> *Corinth, Mississippi April the 23rd, 1862*
> *Honored brother-in-law,*
> *I take the opportunity of writing you a few lines, so you may see that I am well. We landed here on the first of April, after a tidious jurney of twenty days; one hundred and eighty five miles by land to Gilse-ander [?], there we took the boat, to the Mississippi river where we changed boats. Our orders where to go to Arkansas, but the river was so overflowing that we could not find dry land in Napolion [Napoleon, below Memphis], from there we would have to stop and wait for smaller boats. So we came*

to Memphis. There the orders where that we should stay there, for there would be a fight soon. On the second we were marched on to Montera [?] Tenessee, about eighteen miles from there towards the enemy.

The fight came the next day, on April 6. General Johnston's army attacked the Union forces under General Ulysses S. Grant from the south, and in the first day's fighting drove the Yankees out of their camp toward Pittsburg Landing on the Tennessee River. After an exhausting and very bloody day of fighting, the Confederates rested at the former Union camp, among large amounts of captured supplies and thousands of captured Union soldiers. Confederate General Johnston had been killed.[71] But it appeared to be somewhat of a Confederate victory:

On the 6 we attacked the enemy on four places in their tents. This is on the Tennessee river, Petersburg [Pittsburg] landing. We drove them back to the river by hard fighting. We fought all day. We killed a great meny of them, we took 6,000 prisoners and 28 pieces of artillery. They where so clost to [the] river that when we had driven them back They would throw their bombshells from their gun boats and make us go back.

Overnight, the exhausted men of both armies listened to the cries of dying and wounded soldiers left on the battlefield after what had been the bloodiest battle in American history to that point. Grant's beleaguered position was reinforced in the wee hours of the early morning by the arrival of one of his divisions as well as the army of General Don Carlos Buell. That was enough to turn the tide on the second day, and the Confederates were forced to retreat:

But the next day they landed new reinforcements. They made us fall back to Montera. There we still hold our possision. It is supposed that the enemy will leave there. We got rite smart of provision in the fight. We had bad chance of giting it a way for the roads where so bad.

Our Regement has completely broke down, for we had no rest in the day we [were] run from one place to another. At night it rained so we had no sleep, we had no tents, this lasted five days that we [were] run. We lost our knapsacks and some little clothing. Some we left in our tents, blankets [were] all lost.

We had five killed three wounded and six missen out of our company. I had two holes shot through my coat, I was not hurt.

There I must close my little letter. There is not ink to be had. We lost all our ink an paper. There is none to be had for love nor money.

Private F R
2 Regt Tex Volunteer
Co B
J. C. More [Moore] Curnel [Colonel]

My best respects to all. I wrote to Father [Christian Bethje, his step-father] twice, I do not know whether they got them or not.

Respectfully yours, F. Reinermann[72]

Little more than a month later, on May 29, 1862, Frederick Reinermann was sent to the "General Hospital" in the hospital town of Columbus, Mississippi, where he died on July 1, 1862.[73] It has been reported that he died of pneumonia.[74] No doubt this would have been the result of the exposure that he and his unit suffered after losing their tents and gear at Shiloh, and their having to sleep in the rain for many nights—not unlike Piney Point soldier William Canfield's death in Grenada, Mississippi, seven months later. Frederick's burial place is unknown but is likely in the area around Columbus.

Death of a Confederate hero. Frederick was not the only one to serve from the rural area surrounding the Reinermann league. William Peleg Rogers (1819–1862; Figure 8.12) and his wife Martha Lucinda Halbert Rogers (1824–1880) came to Texas from Alabama by way of Mississippi, where he began

Figure 8.12. Colonel William P. Rogers, C.S.A. From *Century Illustrated Magazine,* October 1886.

practicing law in 1842. He served in the Mexican American War, as captain in command of the "Mississippi Rifles" under Col. Jefferson Davis. After that war, he served for a time as United States counsel at the port of Veracruz and came to Texas in 1851, where he was both a practicing attorney and a professor at Baylor University in Independence. He, Martha and a growing family moved to Houston in 1859, where he established a law practice.[75]

William and Martha bought a tract of land in the Reinermann league, where they had a home. In 1860 they sold a part of their property, a 66-acre tract, to William Morse and a group of investors, who built a sawmill on the land near their home (Chapter 7). The Rogers family then lived in Houston's Fourth Ward and were noted there at the time of the federal census of 1860. William Rogers was an ardent secessionist and a Harris County delegate to the Texas secession convention.

When the Civil War began, Rogers at the age of forty-one enlisted at the rank of lieutenant colonel in the Houston City Battery, Texas State Troops.[76] He eventually became a lieutenant colonel of the 2nd Texas Infantry, under Col. John C. Moore—the same unit in which young Frederick Reinermann served as a private. Rogers was in the same contingent as Reinermann, arriving in Tennessee just before the battle of Shiloh. The 2nd Texas Infantry was lauded for its bravery in that battle but lost more than one third of its men in casualties.[77] Rogers described the battle and its aftermath in a letter to his wife on April 18:

> *The battle of Shiloh was fought on the 6th and 7th and only now do I sit down to write to you. . . . Our exposure during the battle was very great and our sick list in the Reg. is over 400 this morning—the sickness is slight however and in ten more days with rest the bloody 2nd will be ready to fight again.*
>
> *On the morning of the 6th of April at 6 a.m. I reached the battlefield, inquired for my Regiment. . . . The boys greeted me with a shout and [in] ten minutes we advanced upon the enemy. We swept the Yankees before us and took a camp. After a short delay we were ordered to move on and in a few minutes again encountered the enemy and again drove him before us. Later in the day we took another camp, a battery and a stand of colors. . . . We slept on the field without tents or food except such as we took from the Yankees. In the morning I was the commander of the Reg. During the day we had several bloody skirmishes. At night our troops were exhausted and we moved several miles and camped in the rain without food or tents.*

In a letter of May 18 he continued:

> *For four nights after the battle we were exposed to rain without tents and with little food. This produced a great deal of sickness—I have been here for 10 days on sick furlough. Am now much better and will go up in a few days.*[78]

It may have been this same sickness that felled young Reinermann, one of Rogers's troops.

In the fall of 1862 what was left of the 2nd Texas Infantry was part of the effort to remove an en-

Figure 8.13. Death of Colonel William P. Rogers as he carried the regimental colors up the Union parapet at Battery Robinett, Corinth, Mississippi, October 4, 1862. From *Century Illustrated Magazine,* October 1886.

trenched Union army at the railroad hub of Corinth, Mississippi. On October 4 Rogers led the vanguard in a desperate assault on Battery Robinett, at the center of the Union line. Rogers led on horseback, at the front of his men, as they were repulsed. On a second charge the Confederates reached the deep trench in front of the battery, where the color guard was killed–the fourth that day. Rogers dismounted and picked up the colors himself and, armed with a pistol, climbed the parapet, where he saw a sea of Yankee reinforcements surging toward them on two sides. He shouted, "Men, save yourselves or sell your lives as dearly as possible," and was killed by a volley of bullets, along with a great many of his comrades (Figures 8.13 and 8.14).[79]

The day was lost, but Union General Rosencrans witnessed Rogers's extraordinary act of personal bravery and leadership, and he commented about Rogers to his victorious Yankee troops after the battle: "He was one of the bravest men that ever led a charge. Bury him with military honors and mark his grave, so his friends can claim him. The time will come when there will be a monument here to commemorate his bravery."[80] Rosencrans was as good as his word. His men buried Rogers with full honors, and erected an iron fence around his grave. A large obelisk stands over his gravesite at the battlefield today, dedicated to Rogers in 1912 by the Daughters of the Confederacy.

William Rogers's widow, Martha, returned after his death to their country home near Houston, on their land within the old Reinermann league, and was noted there at the time of the 1870 federal census. Her home was adjacent to the 66-acre lot that she and William had sold to William Morse in 1858 (later the site of Eureka Cotton Mills).[81] Frederick

Figure 8.14. Confederate dead lay gathered at the bottom of the parapet of Battery Robinett on the day after the Battle of Corinth. The body of Col. William P. Rogers lies at far left. Courtesy of the Library of Congress.

Reinermann's grieving mother, Louisa Bethje, continued living nearby, also on the old John Reinermann grant, and both women no doubt looked forward to the peace brought by the end of the war in April 1865. Both, however, were about to endure one more violent incident brought on by Union troops only a few months after the war's end, in August 1865.

A midnight gunfight. The beginning of Reconstruction in Houston had been fairly peaceful, for the most part. The city had not been the site of any Civil War battles, and occupying federal soldiers, finding little use for their peacekeeping, left the town along with their provost marshal in November 1865.[82] Nonetheless, there were isolated outbreaks of violence, such as the nighttime home invasion by Union soldiers at the Christian and Louisa Bethje country home in modern day Cottage Grove near Memorial Park, then a rural area. This home had been built in the 1850s to replace the log home built by Louisa's father-in-law John Reinermann (see Chapter 6 and Figure 6.5).

The Texas First Cavalry (Union) was involved in the fracas. They were one of two regiments that Texas had contributed to the Union cause and consisted of Union loyalists from the state. Organized in New Orleans in 1862, the unit saw action in Louisiana and at Brownsville, Texas, during the war, mainly engaged in patrolling and reconnaissance duties. They were at Vidalia, Louisiana, just after the war's end, in May and June 1865, whereupon they were ordered to Texas.[83] While waiting to be mustered out of service (which was not to happen until November 1865), some idle members managed to get into trouble near Houston. The *Houston Tri-Weekly Telegraph* of August 25 carried the story:

Daring Attempt at Robbery
One of the Robbers Killed and Two Wounded
On Tuesday night last, Mr. Bethje, a German, residing on the Central Railroad, about 3½ miles from town, was aroused, about one o'clock, by the barking of his dogs. He went out on the gallery and saw a party of some six or eight men coming into the yard and toward the house. He hailed them, told them to stop, and demanded what they wanted. He received for reply several pistol shots—as he says "the balls rained around me from their revolvers." He ran into the house for his rifle, and while in, Mrs. Bethje, who was aroused and frightened by the reports of firearms, ran out into the hall, and was seized by the robbers, who it appears by this time effected an entrance into the house. Mr. B, hearing his wife's screams, ran out into the hall, gun in hand, and seeing one of the robbers holding his wife by the hair, leveled his gun and fired, the shot taking effect and putting this robber hors du combat.

By this time Mr. Bethje's son came to the rescue of his parents with a revolver, and the father ordered him to fire on the rest of the party in the hall, which he did, and it is believed wounded two of them. The robbers then ran out of the house; but in a few minutes made another attempt to re-enter. Mr. Bathje had by this time armed himself with a sabre, and as the foremost robber stepped into the door, Mr. B. struck him across the face with the sabre, inflicting he thinks a serious wound. The robbers then skedaddled, leaving the one who was first wounded in the house. This man died of his wound at about 3 o'clock. In the morning Mr. Bathje came into town and surrendered himself to the Provost Marshal, making oath to the above facts, and that the robbers were United States soldiers. Suspicion fell upon the 1stt Texas Cavalry, camped near town, and several officers of the regiment went out to Mr. Bathje's house to see the dead man, in whom they recognized a member of their regiment. Upon learning this, the Provost Marshal ordered a strict investigation into the affair, the result of which we have not yet learned. . . .

A lady, whose name we could not learn, residing in the neighborhood of Mr. Bathje's was robbed the same night, and doubtless by the same party.[84]

That lady was Martha Rogers, the widow of the Colonel William P. Rogers, gallant hero of the Battle of Corinth. The robbers visited her first at her home near the former William Morse & Company sawmill, and articles taken from her were found on the body of the dead soldier, Francisco Terres. The rest of her stolen property was found with four other captured robbers, all men of the First Texas Cavalry (Union), who were brought to justice by their officers, ashamed at the disgrace that had befallen their unit.[85]

The war years at Pleasant Bend

Of all the people along the south side of Buffalo Bayou in western Harris County, one might expect that the Morse family of Pleasant Bend Plantation would be the most supportive of the war effort, because as the only major slave holders in this rural area, they had the most to lose. The family was indeed very proactive, with all the adult males involved in the war effort. That support started at the top with the family patriarch Agur Morse, aged sixty, volunteering to organize and lead a Houston Home Guard unit, the Beauregard Cavalry; that unit was active by at least August 1861.[86] As noted, such units were organized to keep public order on the home front and to round up deserters and runaway slaves, many of whom were in desperate straits and thus often involved in crimes against persons and property. A good general description of a Home Guard effort led and staffed by senior men, written from the admittedly limited perspective of a young eyewitness in New Orleans, gives a picture of such a unit in an urban setting:

Every afternoon found us [young boys] around in Coliseum Place, standing or lying on the grass watching the dress parade of the Confederate Guards. Most of us had fathers or uncles in the long, spotless, gray, white-gloved ranks that stretched in such faultless alignment down the hard, harsh turf of our old ball-ground. This was . . . the home guard. The merchants, bankers, underwriters, judges, real-estate owners, and capitalists of the Anglo-American part of the city were all present or accounted for in that long line. . . . Here and there among them were individuals who, unaided, had clothed and armed companies, squadrons, battalions, and sent them to the Cumberland and the Potomac. A good three-fourths of them had sons on distant battlefields, some living, some dead. . . . And they really served for much. [As] a gendarmerie they relieve . . . many Confederate soldiers of police duty . . . and enabled them to man forts and breastworks.[87]

After Texas had seceded and three days before the war began on April 12, 1861, Agur Morse made a strategic investment. Five months previously he had participated in discussions with a group of Houston leaders who had recommended the state convention that had led to secession, as earlier described. He had no doubt considered the warning of Sam Houston that the South would be ruined by the conflict and that emancipation would ensue. Agur had been ruined by natural disaster before, in the Tombigbee River flood of 1847, and seems to have been a careful planner where his family's safety and future were concerned. He and all other plantation owners knew full well that emancipation would mean the end of their way of life. While fully supportive of the Confederate cause, he hedged his bets slightly on April 9, 1861, when he and a partner named A. J. Hay bought the drugstore of the late A. D. McGowan, located on Preston Street near Main Street in Houston (Figure 8.15).[88] If all was lost in terms of the future of slavery, this drugstore could provide for the family. As events were to unfold, by 1865 the investment was proven a sound one; the family was to lose nearly everything else that they owned, except their land.

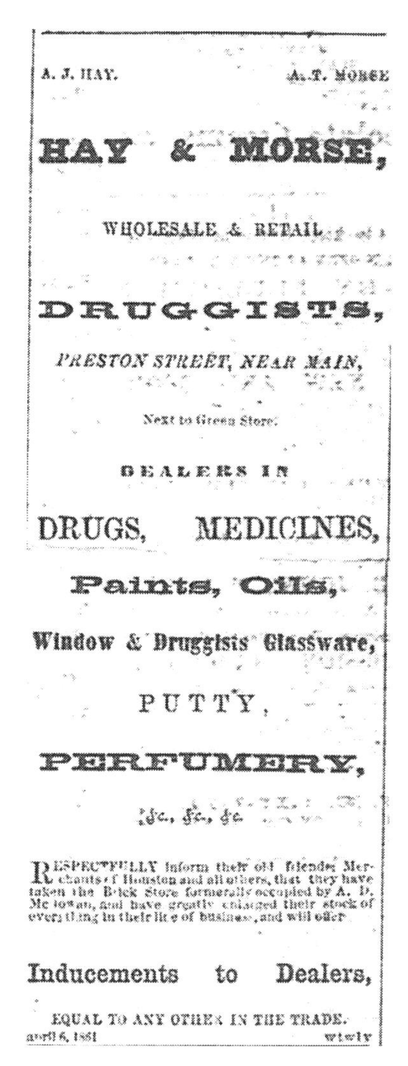

Figure 8.15. Advertisement for the Hay and (Agur) Morse Drugstore. From the *Houston Weekly Telegraph*, April 9, 1861.

The Bayou City Guards. Even before secession, militia units were forming throughout the state. In the city of Houston the Washington Light Guards and the Milam Rifles were formed in 1855. By 1861 five members of the Light Guards were part of a reorganized company called the Bayou City Guards, under Captain W. B. Botts, a Houston lawyer from Virginia.[89] This company was ultimately to be assigned to the Fifth Texas Infantry, later to be known as the famous "Bloody Fifth," part of the Texas Brigade led by General Hood in Lee's Army of Northern Virginia. The Fifth saw some of the toughest fighting and highest casualties of any unit on either side in the Civil War, and saw action at such battles as Second Battle of Manassas, Sharpsburg (Antietam), Fredericksburg, Gettysburg, Chickamauga, Chattanooga, Knoxville, the Wilderness, Cold Harbor, the sieges of Richmond and Petersburg, and Appomattox. It was into this brigade, as part of the Bayou City Guards, that seventeen-year-old George W. Morse (1845–1885) and his twenty-two-year-old older brother Henry Augustus Morse (1840–1876) enlisted on March 27, 1862.

The Bayou City Guards, proudly named for their home city, initially mustered in Houston on July 19, 1861. George W. Morse no doubt would have liked to join at that time, but he was just sixteen years of age, and instead went into the First Texas Heavy Artillery on September 17, 1861. He remained there for only about three months and was perhaps booted out because of his young age.

Meanwhile, the Bayou City Guards trained on Galveston Island in September and returned to Houston in early October, as noted in the *Galveston Daily News*:

> *The Bayou City Guards, Capt. Botts, returned to Houston on this morning's train. They were escorted to the depot by Capt. Conrad's Artillery Company and the Galveston Rifles, Lieut. Yard; and, as they passed through the streets, the general remark was that it would be difficult to get together three better looking or better drilled companies. The Guards were the guests of the Rifles during their brief sojourn here, which was the cause of much pleasant feeling and cheerful social intercourse. Their uniform, of blue and white, is simple, neat and handsome; their marching faultless and their band very good.*[90]

In the unbridled optimism of those early days, a recruit in the Bayou City Guards wrote their battle anthem, patterned after Dixie:

From Houston city and Brazos bottom
From selling goods and making cotton,
Away, Away, Away, Away!
We go to meet our country's foe,
To win or die in freedom's cause;
Away, Away, Away, Away!

Chorus
We're going to Old Virginia, Hooray, Hooray!
To Join the Fight for Southern rights—
We'll live or die for Davis, Hooray, Hooray!
We'll live or die for Davis.

You've heard of Abe, the gay deceiver,
Who sent to Sumter to relieve her;
Away, Away, Away, Away!
"Sumter's ours and must be taken!"
Away, Away, Away, Away!

Our country calls for volunteers,
And Texas boys reply with cheers—
The "Henderson Guards" and "Leon Hunters,"
Friends in peace—in war like panthers.

The "Tom Green Rifles" and "Lone Star Guards,"
In a cause that is just, nothing retards;
The "Echo Company," and all the brave "Five Shooters,"
Will deal out death to all freebooters.

The "Liberty Invincibles" and the "Hardeman Texans"
can wallop ten to one, whether Yanks or Mexicans
From the "Waverly Confederates" and the "Dixie Blues,"
And the "Bayou City Guards" you can expect good news.[91]

The Guards became Company A of the Fifth Texas Infantry in early October and were issued their arms in November. They soon left for Virginia, partly marching along rain-swept muddy roads, and partly traveling in open railroad cars. They soon learned the realities of a harsh winter in camp, living in tents with much illness and hardship, and enduring horrific losses in battle.

Signing up. Back in Houston, a second recruitment effort was made for the company to replace the first year's heavy casualties, and this time young George Morse was not to be denied, although in the companionship of his older brother, Henry Morse. The two enlisted as privates in the Bayou City Guards on March 27, 1862. At just seventeen years old, George was the youngest in the group. The Houston newspaper reported the new additions to the company on March 26, the new recruits just managing to replace the losses to the company in the first few months of fighting:

> *The Bayou City Guards in Virginia numbered 97 men when they left here, of which 70 were from this city. Within a few days past 30 new recruits have been enrolled by the representative of the company now here. Total, 100.*[92]

The new recruits left on April 2 for the front. At this time the stark reality of their situation started to become clear, at least to their loved ones back home. Henry's wife Celia Hough Morse (1839–1896) began a diary the same day that the recruits and her new husband left Houston, using the same diary book that had been left behind by the late William Keeling at the plantation a few years earlier (Chapter 7):

> *April 2 1862. I have often thought that I would begin a journal as it is instructive as well as interesting. This has been the longest and saddest day I have spent since the death of our little boy January the 22d, 1861. Our boys started for the War today and [there is] no specified time for return. Oh, it is so hard to give them up, but to Him who doeth all things will I [en]trust them. I have felt as if they were lost forever. . . . Last night I stayed [in Houston] at Miss Taft's and at 4 o'clock went to Bettie's [Elizabeth Morse Taft, her sister in law] where all assembled and prepared to go. Words are poor substitutes to express the heart's deepest feeling, and now I feel like one that travels life's dreary road alone. Why am I so [sad] and is there no help for this suffering?*[93]

Celia lived with Grace Morse at the Pleasant Bend Plantation house throughout the war. It was a good arrangement for both women, as Agur was in away Houston much of the time, attending to Home Guard business as well as to his new drugstore. Celia Hough Morse was most likely a close relative of the Morse's neighbor Cassandra Hough McFee (1824–1890), who lived with her husband James McFee (1814–1903) on the fifty-acre farm that had been encircled by the plantation. James McFee was a carriagemaker, carpenter, and farmer who later in the war would join a Texas State unit as a carpenter.

> *April 5, 1862. This morning Ma and I rose early and after cleaning the house I finished her dress this afternoon. . . . Mrs. H and Ma and I went over to see Cass [Cassandra Hough McFee] and all was glad to see us. Mr. Mc [James McFee] had just finished [building] a gallery; everything looks nice now. How much I wish our loved ones were home to participate in our pleasures. . . .*
>
> *April 13, 1862. I think of my dear husband and wonder if God in His infinite mercy has and will spared him to return to his little family once again. It is hard, very hard for us to be separated and I spend many very lonely hours. But I suppose it is all for his country's good. . . . I have heard nothing from him yet. Lewis B [Louis Bering, husband of Eugenia Morse, Henry's cousin] was here yesterday and seemed to regret very much that Henry had gone.*

Celia Morse was a worrier. Henry's absence seems always to have been on her mind; she seemed to stay in a perpetually depressed state over it, and not without reason. Within days of arriving at Richmond, Virginia, on April 24, fully 20 percent of the new recruits were sick.[94] Camp diseases were virulent and included dysentery, measles, influenza, typhoid, and nearly anything else that could be spread by troops in close, rough quarters. Disease was to be

Figure 8.16. Members of the First Texas Infantry, Hood's Texas Brigade, in camp near Dumfries, Virginia, during the winter of 1861–1862. Courtesy of the Library of Congress.

one of the main causes of casualties for this unit, and indeed for most Confederate units, throughout the war. The worrying and depression took a toll on Celia and others as they read of casualties at the front:

> *July 6, 1862. Mr. Morrison told me he had just seen a letter from the Bayou City Guards and they had just been in a fight and one skirmish but one or two had been killed. What fate our loved ones share we do not know. God hope for the best. We can hear nothing from them [in the way of official pronouncements], only occasional answers, and generally speaking they are false and not worth reflecting. Oh, how I long for a letter, just one more . . . but Providence rules all things and to Him we entrust ourselves and feel that all will be well. . . . Oh, are our friends to come back to us safe and sound or [has] God ordered them to be of that number that will never return? My little darling [son Emmett] is just six months old and very interesting indeed. Would to God his Pa could see him. . . . How my heart does ache. I am so afraid when news does reach us it will be of sorrow, and God knows what will become of us if this present state of things exists long. Our families are broken up and our homes left desolate and all is broken up.*

In June Henry had written home to Celia of his experiences to date, which included some skirmishes in which his unit had taken part. Any initial sense of optimism and jingoism was gone, according to

Celia's account, written after she finally received his letter in July:

July 29, 1862. I received a letter from Henry. He has been in two fights and feels very low spirited because he has not heard from home yet. He writes as though it would be some time before the war was over. This letter was dated June 12. They have been in two fights. Thank God . . . [they were not] hurt as we know of. George has been sick ever since he has been there. Henry says if he is spared he will try to get a transfer to some company in Texas, but I am most afraid to have him [do that], for fear he will be sent to some other place worse than Virginia. . . . God grant me this one [wish], that they may all live to bless home once again.

George's first large battle was at Gaines's Mill on June 27, a bloody battle that was won by the Confederates. The man who had recruited the brothers in Houston, Lt. J. E. Clute, was shot through the heart, among heavy casualties for both their company and the Texas Brigade. Henry was in the hospital at Richmond for a four-day stay during the battle, the first of many stays at that hospital for the two brothers and for many others, as camp illnesses took their toll. Celia wrote that:

2d of August, 1862. I had another letter from Henry. It was after the fight since I dared to open it, but glad it was to hear [that] no one was hurt. Henry was sick and had been sent to the rear, and was going down to the sick company that night after he wrote. . . . George was still there. Henry said it was a bloody battle; a good many Texians were killed, none that I knew. God has been merciful to us so far, He has spared our friends.

Next was the Second Battle of Manassas, August 28–30, where the unit earned its name, the "Bloody Fifth." Letters from the front written to the newspaper and published on October 3, well after the battle, highlight the positives:

The 5th carried the Lone Star Flag in the battle of Manassas. It had 28 shots through it and two through the staff. The regiment took three stands of colors and 12 pieces of artillery. We met the celebrated Zouaves 800 strong, and whipped them in five minutes, completely routing them and killing over four hundred in the field. The Texas Brigade covered itself with additional glory, sustaining the Lone Star fully. Our victory was complete. . . . The strength of our regiment today is 238.

J.B. Robertson, Col. Commanding 5th Texas[95]

Another letter, catering to Houston readers, said that "None of Major Morse's boys were hurt. Will McGowan is all ok." The casualty list for the Bayou City Guards, published from a letter in the Houston Weekly Telegraph of September 29th, could hardly have comforted many in Houston:

Orderly Searg't E. A. Noble, wounded, thigh; Searg. John McMurtry, wounded, thigh; Searg. B. C. Simpson, wounded, arm; Private J. Heffron, do. jaw; W. Patton, leg and foot; Sam Bailey, side (dead); Dempsey Walker, breast, mortally; John DeYoung, hip; J. Angell, thigh, mortally; Owen O'Malley, thigh; John Delesdernier, shoulder; J.W. Kelly, hip and finger; J. Massenburg, thigh; S. Hands, thigh and foot; R. Campbell, below knee; C.B. Gardner, hip; Has Sanger, neck; R. Morrise, side; John Leverton, hand; A. Wolfe, leg; John Garrison, thigh; T.W. Fitzgerald, knee; Corp. John Bell, neck.

Total, 23 killed and wounded [in the Texas Regiment as a whole]. There was not a dozen men in the regiment whose clothes were not riddled or struck by the balls. All fought bravely and deserve the greatest praise. The brigade travelled so fast that the supports could not keep up, and their General said: "Boys, you are too fast, we can't keep up."...

P.S. The Telegraph was represented. Two from the office were wounded.[96]

The Guards suffered 38 percent casualties in the two day battle.[97] The New York Zouaves, in their colorful uniforms, sustained over 60 percent casualties from the Texas Fifth, the highest of any Federal unit in the war for a single engagement. These details were not yet known in Houston or at Pleasant Bend when Celia wrote:

> *September the 8th, 1862. Ma [her mother-in-law, Grace Morse] and I ironed all day. She is going to town today and to church tomorrow. We have had another battle in Virginia and a report says we whipped [them]. Am afraid the boys were in it, but hope they were not. Every battle has so much terror attached to it that I dread to hear. . . .I spent the day up to Mrs George. She is going to send for us soon to help quilt...*

Harriet George, at Piney Point, had her two Canfield sons at Vicksburg at that time, and Celia's visit was likely intended mainly to commiserate.

> *Pa killed a beef today and I expect it will spoil as he has not cut it up. They are putting salt on it. Hannah [Canfield Morse] went to town yesterday. Ma said Mrs. Taft [Mother of Lovett Taft, Elizabeth Morse's husband] felt very blue and wanted me to come in. They have just had a letter from Mr. Smith. He had seen Henry and the boys. . . . The baby has gone to sleep. How much I wish I could get a letter, but none has come as yet. If Henry only knew how glad and how often I wanted to hear he would write every day.*

Within weeks of the Second Battle of Manassas, the Fifth Texas Infantry was at Sharpsburg (Antietam), where casualties were even higher, at 60 percent for the regiment (Figure 8.1). Four Guards were wounded, and one later died. There were others lost through sickness, some were captured, and six deserted, even before the battle started.[98] The unit saw little action at Fredericksburg (December 13–15) and soon went into winter quarters, in log huts that they constructed. By year's end Company A (the Guards) had had 12 casualties to enemy fire (two deaths) for the year, but 24 were discharged for medical reasons, and there had been 18 desertions (11 from the group with whom Henry and George had gone in March).[99]

The absence of the men, and the sporadic nature of letters home, continued to be intensely wearing on their wives and families. Celia wrote in her diary:

> *Wednesday the 22d (October) 1862. I wrote to Henry today, sent it by Bob Hermon. Heard Mr. Steward was wounded in the foot. That is two out of the number. I am afraid our boys will catch it next. But I pray God they will escape. Bettie [Elizabeth Morse] is expected tomorrow. Hope she will come. Time flies very heavy indeed. . . . We have had two letters from George, he is writing [from] the sick [bay]. Mr. Patton is taken a prisoner which is not very pleasant. Ma had a letter from Henry Friday. He says they have had very hard times. Since days [they] do not have anything but green corn to eat, and lay on their arms for days together. I think he might have written to me, but expect he knows his own business best.*

On December 7, 1862, Harriet George's son William Canfield died in Mississippi, likely of exposure on a winter march. There is no mention of it in Celia's diary, which was focused on Henry's absence and trials.

George Morse went into Richmond, sick yet again, on December 18. By January 30, 1863, he was still doing poorly and was sent home to Texas on furlough. George remained on the Guards' sick roster throughout 1863 and early 1864. Henry was left to soldier on without a brother at the front.

In Houston, times were hard for many families, especially those on small family farms, where the husbands—now at the front—were the main breadwinners. In February 1863 the *Houston Tri-Weekly Telegraph* observed that Agur Morse was donating corn meal from his plantation for the destitute in Houston.[100] The Morse family and the George family also took in boarders, some of whom were wives or mothers of soldiers. Those soldiers were breadwinners absent from their farms, leaving their wives in difficult straits:

> *August 12, 1862. Mrs. Holmes has gone to Mrs. George's to live; left here last week. [She] thought Pa charged too much, but I don't think she can live for less. . . . Mrs. Holmes sent me word that she was going to come to see us today. Mrs. Holmes came down, and I wrote to Robert and her brother for her. Mary has troubled her shameful but she will be repaid for all this.*

John Kell Morse's daughter, Mary E. Morse (1838–1900) married Robert J. Holmes (d. ca. 1873) in 1861 in Houston; "Mrs. Holmes" was probably his mother. Robert was a member of the 35th (Brown's) Cavalry Regiment, organized with 927 men in October 1863 by consolidating two earlier Texas Cavalry battalions. The unit served in the Trans-Mississippi Department and was primarily engaged in scouting duty along the coast. Robert's aging mother, with no breadwinning son at home, was reduced to boarding first with the Agur Morses and then with Harriet George. Whatever Mary Morse's tiff with her mother-in-law was, the marriage of Mary and Robert was to survive the war, as was Robert. The couple had three children from 1865 to 1870 and lived by 1880 in Piney Point, not far from Harriet George and also near John Morse's son George Edward Morse, who moved there in about 1880. According to George's daughter Jeannette,

> *Papa's oldest sister, Mary, married Robert Holmes and they lived in this community and later, when their eldest son Charlie married, he lived near Papa. . . . When Robert Holmes died, Mary married a man named James L. Mallette.*[101]

Another boarder with the Morse family during the war was Emma Frazee Bachelder, whose brother Emmett Frazee was in the Bayou City Guards, and whose husband Edmund Bachelder was likely also a soldier. Emma was reportedly a niece of Grace Morse and had been mentioned in William Keeling's diary of the late 1850s. Celia mentions Emma in her diary entry of August 12:

> *I had another letter from Henry dated August the 20th. They were not well. . . . Mr. George came from there about two months ago and said they looked badly and had not been well since the battle, poor fellows. They wanted to come home very much indeed. . . . I have been sick all day . . . my baby fretted a good while last night [and] Emma took him a time in the night. I am going to let him sleep with her and see if it will get any better.*
>
> *Mr. George has been gone one week today with our letters and I hope it won't be long before I can get an answer to mine. We had a letter from Emmett [Frazee]. He was not well but could write. He said George and Henry were well. I am so anxious to hear from them. . . . I wrote to Henry tonight for I felt lonely and could not feel right until I had written. Emma has gone up to Mrs. George today [and] is coming home tomorrow.*

"Mr. George" appears to be Harriet George's former husband, Benjamin Moore George (1804–before 1880), who had deserted Harriet and her children after building the ox-driven sawmill at Piney Point in the 1850s. He seems to have been acting as a courier, taking family letters to the front.

During this time, when all but one of the Morse family adult men were engaged in the war effort, day to day operations of the large plantation fell to Grace Morse and her African American slaves. In Celia's diary entry of March 5, 1865, on a day when Agur and Grace Morse were in town, she wrote that "There was not a white person on the place all day. It seemed to me the longest dreary day I ever spent for I was sick." Pleasant Bend slaves kept working throughout the war, which allowed Agur to donate corn to the local war effort.

In July 1863 the Bayou City Guards were with the Texas Fifth Infantry and the rest of the Texas

Figure 8.17. The 'Slaughter Pen' between Round Top and Little Round Top, Gettysburg, where the city of Houston's Bayou City Guards, including Henry Morse, spent a grueling day of battle, July 3, 1863. The Guards suffered 50% casualties in that single battle. Courtesy of the Library of Congress.

Brigade at Gettysburg, a very bloody battle that represented the "high tide of the Confederacy." On the day of battle, July 3, the Fourth and Fifth Texas were sent to take Little Round Top, adjacent to Devil's Den, where the First Texas and Fourth Arkansas were engaged. The Fifth Texas troops encountered fire from behind a stone fence, but overcame the Federals, who retreated up Little Round Top. The Texans then were caught in murderous fire in a saddle between Little and Big Round Top, in a place that was to be called the "Slaughter Pen" (Figure 8.17). They made several brave but unsuccessful attempts to dislodge the Federals, who had higher ground. During this same afternoon, the 15th Alabama was having their celebrated fight with Col. Joshua Chamberlain's 20th Maine on the other side of the hill.[102]

The day's fighting was extremely intense against higher numbers of Federals, and Confederate losses were very high. The Houston newspaper reported that soldiers in the Texas Brigade numbered 342 before the battle, and afterward only 150 were still fit for service. The Bayou City Guards (Company A) had 38 men in the battle, of whom two were killed and 17 wounded or captured, for a casualty rate of 50 percent in one engagement. The Confederate army retreated to Fredericksburg, Virginia, where the Texans stayed until they were moved to Tennessee to support General Braxton Bragg.[103]

The Texas Brigade remnants then faced battles

at Chickamauga and Chattanooga in September, with more casualties. Unbeknownst to Henry Morse, the opposing Union Army of the Tennessee contained Lt. Joseph Baldwin Taft, First Brigade, Second Division, 11th Army Corps (143rd New York Infantry), the son of former Houston bookstore owner Joseph S. Taft. Both father and son had left Houston following the vote for secession, the father leaving at some time after May 1861. Henry Morse's sister Elizabeth was married to Lieutenant Taft's uncle Lovett Taft, who remained in Houston during the war and supported the Confederate cause.

In November 1863 the Bayou City Guards left to lay siege to Federals in Knoxville, while Confederate General Bragg remained with the rest of his forces at Missionary Ridge and Lookout Mountain, promontories where they were soon to engage with Union General Grant. Grant attacked Missionary Ridge and overran Bragg's Confederates. Among the dead was Lieutenant Taft, of whom his commanding officer wrote:

> *At about noon, November 25, the brigade received orders to assist a brigade of the Fifteenth Corps. In compliance with this order this regiment, under the command of Lieut. Col. J. B. Taft, formed in line of battle, advanced at double-quick and at a bayonet charge, under a very destructive cross-fire from the enemy's batteries and musketry, dislodged a strong force of the enemy from log huts at the foot of Tunnel Hill, occupied the same, and twice repulsed the enemy, who endeavored to outflank us. A line of battle, in attempting to gain the summit of Tunnel Hill, being broken and our ammunition being entirely exhausted, the enemy succeeded in surrounding us, thereby capturing 8 officers and 91 enlisted men; many of the latter are supposed to be wounded. During the action we lost our noble commander, Lieut. Col. J. B. Taft, and 14 enlisted men, besides 3 other brave officers, who were mortally wounded . . . and 55 enlisted men wounded.*[104]

Taft is buried beneath an imposing marble obelisk at Chattanooga National Cemetery, surrounded by a circle of the tombstones of his fellow soldiers. It is not known when or how the news of his death reached the Morse and Taft families at Pleasant Bend.

Following the siege at Knoxville, the Bayou City Guards went to winter quarters in Morrisburg, Tennessee. By the end of 1863 the Guards were down to just seventeen men. More men had deserted the unit in the year 1863 (nine) than were killed in action (four). Six had been captured, seven discharged for wounds, and one died from disease. Total losses from all sources had reached 75 percent from the beginning of the war.[105] Henry Morse, apparently in good health after some bouts of illness during 1863, continued service with his remaining fellow Bayou City Guards, who were by this time seasoned and battle-hardened soldiers.

A tragic 1863 at home. There is no existing report on Gettysburg from Celia; the entire year of 1863 went unobserved in her diary. There was little to cheer about. After the fall of Vicksburg in July 1863, mail service to Texas from the troops in the Army of Northern Virginia was all but cut off, except by pricey couriers. Such news as was arriving was not good. Celia's friend Harriet George's son John D. Canfield died at Vicksburg on July 14, 1863, the second of Harriet George's sons to perish in the war, and as we have seen, their neighbor Mary Frisby Silliman at Wheaton's Ford lost her son Isaac Benson on July 5, also at Vicksburg.

Meanwhile, there was more bad news at home on the Pleasant Bend Plantation that same year. Agur's brother Rev. John Kell Morse died in November, 1863, following a long illness that was probably consumption (tuberculosis), and his wife Caroline died in October 1864, likely of the same disease. Executor of Caroline Morse's estate was her daughter Eugenia's husband, Louis Bering (1840–1891). Louis was one of several brothers who, with their parents, had emigrated from Germany and founded a number of sawmill, lumber and hardware establishments in 1860s Houston.

The estate left by Reverend Morse and his wife was modest. It included their 300 acres of land in Harris County, valued at $1,500; some "old" Confederate notes in the amount of $533.24; and three slaves, Ike (45 years of age, valued at $400), Harriet (50 years, valued at $100; she had been purchased from Agur Morse in 1857 for $600), and Moses (45 years; valuation not given, but in 1857 he had been purchased for $1,000). In the ensuing 1864 probate, daughters Mary E. Morse Holmes and Eugenia Morse Bering bought the slaves, and Eugenia Bering purchased the 300-acre farm from the estate executor, Eugenia's husband Louis. The couple moved into the former Morse home on the edge of the bayou, on the western edge of Pleasant Bend Plantation (Figure 8.3).[106] In modern Houston, Bering drive runs down the axis of the former John Kell Morse farm; the road was named for Louis Bering, who died in 1891.

Caroline's death left her ten-year-old son George Edward Morse an orphan, to be raised initially by the Theodore Bering family (Theodore was the brother of Louis Bering). After an initial few years living with the Berings, and after his sister Eugenia died of yellow fever in 1867, George found a permanent home with Harriet George at Piney Point by the time of the 1870 census, where he and his future family were to live for the rest of the century (Chapter 12).

Other Pleasant Bend community soldiers. The war was less tragic for some other Pleasant Bend men. Louis Bering, Eugenia Morse's husband, enlisted in 2nd Company A, 13th Texas Volunteers, on May 6, 1862, in Houston. This unit was also known as the Bates's Texas Infantry Battalion. Initially a Trans-Mississippi unit based in Velasco, Texas, it moved to Houston in October 1862 serving garrison and fatigue duty; it had no major engagements during the war. Louis later enlisted as a private in Company A, 26th Texas Cavalry, by May 1863, serving in the Quartermaster's Department and later as a detective in Houston. He was thus close by when his father-in-law died in November and available to execute the estate. Louis was paroled from the 26th Texas Cavalry on June 22, 1865. He owned a hardware store in Houston after the War. His wife, Eugenia Morse Bering, died of yellow fever in 1867, and he remarried twice after Eugenia's death.

Another neighborhood son who was able to stay close to home was James McFee (1814–1903), who had a fifty-acre farm that was enveloped by the Morse plantation at Pleasant Bend. Although thirty-eight years of age, generally considered too old for conscription, he enrolled as a corporal in Sheldon's Company B, First State Troops, Texas Infantry, on August 7, 1863, in Harris County. By November 1863 he was in Company B, 16th Battalion Texas State Troops, and worked in the quartermaster's office in Houston as a carpenter. After the war he continued to work in Houston as a carpenter. His son John (1852–1888) was employed as a laborer in the Morse family sawmill in the early 1870s.

Another year of loss and hardship. In 1864 Celia Morse resumed her diary:

> *January 10, 1864. Another New Year has dawned upon us and still this war is raging. Seems without any indication of stopping or even letting the poor wearied Soldier have a moment's rest. God is said to be gracious to all both high and low, and to me I find he has been very kind there for sparing one who is everything in the world to me, and without him this world would be but a dreary waste. . . . We were married 4 years last Thursday and two years has been passed nearly enough. Our dear little boy is now two years old and can talk and walk everywhere. He often speaks of his Pa and it does me good to hear him speak of him. I sincerely trust in God that this time next year he will be with us.*

By early 1864 a member of the Guards, William P. McGowan, was promoted to first lieutenant and made a permanent regimental adjutant in the Texas Brigade.[107] His uncle Thomas McGowen had sharecropped and raised livestock at the fifty-acre farm that was enveloped by the Morse plantation, and his father ran an iron foundry in Houston.

In May, the Texas Brigade faced the Battle of the Wilderness in a stretch of dense woodland between Fredericksburg and Orange Court House, Virginia (Figure 8.18). The Texans reached the area on the second day of the battle, May 6. The fighting was fe-

Figure 8.18. Union troops firing on Confederates through dense tree cover at the Battle of the Wilderness, May 6, 1864. From *Harper's Weekly Illustrated Newspaper*, June 4, 1864.

rocious at close quarters, with high casualties; the brigade lost 445 casualties (from about 800 at the start of battle), and the by now tiny Guard lost one killed and several wounded. By May 8 they were fighting at Spotsylvania Court House, where the Guard lost two more original members, one captured and another killed. After only a slight participation in the Battle of Cold Harbor on June 3, they left by train for Petersburg, then on to the defense of Richmond in late July.

At home, the long wait for Henry's return continued. Celia wrote:

> *October 16, 1864. Months have passed along and I find that I have not fulfilled my vow to thee my Journal, although I cannot write such that is cheering. . . . I have heard nothing from the absent and loved one and . . . my heart is still sad and lonely. . . . Our family has been sorely afflicted. All have been sick and it has been nothing but nurse all summer long.*

George W. Morse had been on a sixty-day sick furlough to Texas since January 30, 1863—over a year and a half—and it became increasingly clear that he was not going to return to the unending horrors of the war in the east, at least not by choice. Probably it was only the continued and loyal presence of his brother Henry within the Guards that prevented him from being listed as a deserter. Celia continues in her letter of October 16:

> *Less Turner has returned [from the front] and says that he will be obliged to take George and all back*

with him, and thinks Henry stands as good a chance as anybody to come home this winter. I hope so and still hope this unholy war soon will close and let all come home that wishes to do so.

By this time George found an honorable way to stay in Texas. He had transferred as private to Captain O. G. Jones's Battery, Light Artillery, on August 25, 1864, and the transfer was noted in the books of the Texas Regiment. He remained in this unit until the end of the war.

For Celia, a galling occurrence happened to her after Turner's visit: "[Henry] wrote to me by Captain Turner, but unfortunately Josiah, on one of his drinking scapes, lost it." Josiah was Josiah B. Morse (1833–1889), Agur's second eldest son, who had left home over a decade earlier to live in Houston, where he was recorded in the 1860 census as clerking in Joseph S. Taft's store. He married Mary Ellen Rowley in November 1860 in Houston. Josiah enlisted in Company A, David A. Terry's Regiment, Texas Cavalry on April 18, 1864. Nothing is known of any earlier service. Terry's unit began in April 1864, mustering at Camp Jacinto in Montgomery County (it is not the same unit as the more famous Terry's Eighth Texas Cavalry). It was assigned to southwestern Louisiana and then on to Arkansas, to oppose Federal General Sterling Price in his invasion of Missouri. The unit saw action on several occasions in Louisiana and Arkansas during May through mid-November, 1864, after which it returned to Texas for commissary duty.[108]

It is clear from Celia's diary that Josiah was at home in Houston in late 1864, and that he was drinking heavily. Following the death of his father in 1865, Josiah took sole ownership of his father's drugstore and operated it until his death in 1889.[109]

There was another family death in 1864, as Celia wrote in late October:

Many evil and dreary changes has taken place since last I [communicated] with you, my dear Journal. Death with her witness head has been amongst our happy little band and culled one of our chosen members. Poor Lovett [Taft, Jr., Elizabeth Morse Taft's husband], after a brief illness of 10 days, breathed his last on Tuesday the 25th October [1864]. Oh, what a severe and sad trial to give up one we love so well . . . his poor weeping widow will find this world that used to seem so bright and happy now a desolate waste. . . . He died . . . leaving four fatherless little ones, [and] that troubled him. . . . Bettie says she will go back to town to live.

Lovett Taft died of typhoid fever, according to the *Weekly Telegraph*.[110] They laid Lovett Taft in the Morse family burial ground on the plantation, across a small spring creek from the Morse plantation house. That family cemetery, now called the Morse-Bragg cemetery, is on South Wynden Drive in the Post Oak area of Houston, just outside Interstate 610. A stone marker at his grave was in the process of being removed by vandals in the 1990s when a neighbor saved it. It has now been returned to the restored cemetery.

Last Sunday the 23rd Captain Farmer was out here and Ma was sick all day long and my little Emmett had three spasms and I thought him dead. . . .Mrs. Anderson and Eugenia [Morse Bering, daughter of the late John and Caroline] are here with us from yellow fever . . . Ma and Pa here [have] been sick all summer.

"Captain Farmer" was Captain D.C. Farmer of the Bayou City Guards, who had been wounded in the right leg at Gettysburg. He recovered and became major of the regiment on October 8, 1863. He was wounded in the hip at the Battle of the Wilderness and was briefly the acting commander of the Texas Fifth Regiment until he left for Texas on a recruiting trip in August 1864. He was unable to return due to deteriorating conditions late in the war. After the war he became deputy clerk for Harris County.[111]

Henry Morse's war finally ends. Back in Virginia, the dwindling numbers of men in the Texas Brigade fought in a number of skirmishes in the area surrounding Richmond in August, September and

Figure 8.19. A Union battery at the Battle of Darbytown and Newmarket Roads, October 7, 1866, from Harper's *Weekly Illustrated Newspaper*, October 29, 1864. After breaking past Union cavalry at Darbytown Road, the Confederates advanced through the jumble of tree stumps and felled timber at the right toward the fortified Union line of defense in the foreground, to great casualties. Henry Morse was among the wounded.

October, in which there were many more wounded, killed, and captured and who deserted.[112] One of those skirmishes was the Battle of Darbytown and New Market Roads, on October 7, 1864 (Figure 8.19). The Confederates had dislodged Union cavalry troops from Darbytown Road, only to be faced by well-entrenched Union defensive lines on the Newmarket Road. According to a Fourth Texas soldier who was wounded that day among the many other casualties, "it was a desperate attack by a small force upon well-manned earthworks, approachable only through open ground, and protected by a *chevaux-de-frise* made of felled timber."[113] Another said:

> *Every tree of the many lying on the ground over which we charged, pointed its sharpened branches at our eyes, faces, and clothing. No sooner was a fellow out of the detaining clutch of one, than another presented itself, and taking hold of flesh or clothing, held him captive for awhile. There was no staying in line, and could be none.*[114]

The Confederates were repulsed with high losses. Among those wounded was Henry Morse, severely wounded in the upper arm. He had survived nearly every major battle in the eastern theatre of the war—the most harrowing and deadly string of battles in American history—but his war was now over. He was evacuated to Richmond, and then sent on to Mobile, Alabama, on November 4, 1864 to convalesce.

After the operations around Richmond, the Texas Brigade limped into winter camp. The Bayou City Guards were now down to only ten able-bodied soldiers, a total casualty rate of 87 percent for the war. Rations where short, as was fuel for fires. Men sheltered in makeshift hovels, where they remained until April 1865. They, General Robert E. Lee, and the rest of the Army of Northern Virginia were in retreat in early April and surrendered on April 9, 1865. Only 602 survivors of the Texas Brigade were left standing to surrender at Appomattox, out of about 4,400 near the start of the war, for a 61 percent casualty rate. The City of Houston's Bayou City

Guards (Company A) were left with only nine standing members at Appomattox, eight of whom were original recruits. Their long war was finally over.[115]

The news of Henry's wounding in October slowly made its way back to Celia:

> *November 15, 1864. I have just received a letter from B. Y. Fuller stating [that] Henry was wounded on the 7th of October 1864 in the arm where the shoulder and arm joint [meet]. This was sad and startling news to me. I feel harried and tried to think someone near and dear to me should be in a land afar suffering from wounds and no one near to sooth and cheer his lonely heart.*

By December there was news of another loved one who had gone missing from Henry's company, the Guards. Emma Frazee Bachelder, a niece of Grace Morse, had been living with the Agur Morse family off and on since the 1850s and was noted by William Keeling in his diary. She was almost certainly the sister of Emmett Frazee, another private in the Bayou City Guards. He had been with the Guards since at least early 1863, and had been slightly wounded at Gettysburg, returning to duty on August 8 of that year. At the evacuation of Chattanooga in early November, he fell to the rear, sick, and was taken by Federal forces or possibly deserted, according to James Moore's history of the Guards.[116] Celia had heard from him on December 23, 1864, at a time when her sister-in-law, Elizabeth, was still mourning for her husband Lovett Taft:

> *Poor Bettie she is badly afflicted. This year has been a sad one to her. . . . I feel truly sorry for her and wish it [were] in my power to bring him back. . . . I am a little disappointed tonight Ma [Grace Morse] went in to stay with Bettie and I thought Emma would come home but she had a bad headache and could not come. I hope she will come home tomorrow night. . . . Yesterday we have at last heard from Emmett. He has been in East Tennessee all this time, sick, and is at last recovering. I hope that he will be able to return to us before long for I love him as a brother. We are looking for George every day and do not know what detains him. I hope our little band will once more meet again, to part no more.*
>
> *January 1, 1864. . . . Ma has been in town almost two weeks and has not returned yet. I have been all alone ever since she left. I thought Emma would come out and stay with me, but she did not. You cannot expect a girl to love a country life and the severity of the married (such is life).*

Emma appears to have been single during this period, and married Edmund J. H. Bachelder (1840–1872) after the war. They lived in Houston's Fourth Ward, and she attended Houston's First Presbyterian Church with Grace Morse and Elizabeth Morse Taft. She died in 1871 and is buried at the Morse-Bragg cemetery; Edmund died a year later and was buried at Glenwood Cemetery.

Henry returns home. By January Henry had finally made it home. He had been paroled on June 8, 1865, in Mobile, where he was recuperating, and it took him another seven months to make it home. Celia recorded the homecoming and was circumspect in the matter of his injured arm:

> *January 26, 1865. Henry has come home at last. [He] had changed little in looks. Three years will make changes in most everyone. I wish there was no change and all things would be as they once were. I know there is not a happier person in Houston than me. . . .*
>
> *February 28, 1865. 'Tis the last day of February 1865 and I feel quite elated. My spirits and health are never better, and while Henry is at home it should not be otherwise. I see others around me that are sad and those whom the rough and rugged hand of affliction has been laid heavily upon. I feel deeply for [them].*

Agur Morse's war experience

There is little written information regarding Agur Morse over the war period, when most of his sons were in service. At the beginning of the war he was active in setting the political foundation for secession, participating along with other Houston leaders in the Harris County mass meeting of December 1860. He had raised a unit called the Beauregard Cavalry in early 1861, for the purposes of Home Guard; but there are few mentions of it in the local papers after its foundation. The only references to it seem to be on two occasions in the *Houston Tri-Weekly Telegraph*. First, he was referred to as "Major" Morse in a letter from the front of October 3, 1862, describing the Second Battle of Manassas; the correspondent said: "None of Major Morse's boys were hurt." Another indication of his continued activity in the Home Guard role came in a *Tri-Weekly Telegraph* advertisement of January 22, 1864, where he reported that his horse had been stolen:

> *Strayed or stolen from, in front of the Theatre, Wednesday evening, a bay horse without shoes; had on at the time he was left, a light McLellan saddle, with brass stirrups; also a light grey hair rope bridle. Any information of the same will be gladly received and rewarded by Lieut. A. Morse, Room 33, Fannin House.*[117]

That he signed the advertisement as "Lieutenant" Morse, and was riding a military McLellan saddle (not favored by stock raisers), indicate that he was on an active war footing. He was staying often in Houston, as Celia Morse's diary makes clear. This would have been partly because of his service in the Home Guard and partly because of his drugstore, which by 1863 was being called "Morse's drugstore."[118]

The *Tri-weekly Telegraph* newspaper records that Agur Morse was paid by the Houston City Council at several intervals during the war, specifically on May 21, 1862 ($200), July 28, 1862 ($9.75), and March 23, 1863 ($60). We do not know precisely what those payments were for, because Houston's city council records of 1848–1865 were destroyed by Federal troops when the soldiers were quartered in the council chambers upon their arrival in the city in June 1865.[119] The payments may have been for medicines, as he was noted as selling $53.50 in medicines, apparently for the troops, in the *Tri-Weekly* of July 7, 1862. He was reported as donating corn meal for relief of the poor on February 25, 1863.[120]

As the war came to a close in late 1864 and early 1865, the work of the Houston Home Guard became increasingly difficult in ever more trying circumstances as the economy worsened, the public mood darkened, and Confederate desertions increased. In most cases, captured deserters faced return to the front, and in some cases even death, so they were not to be captured easily. By early 1865 the news from the front grew yet more dire and the city of Houston began to experience civil unrest, as streams of deserters from the east passed through the city, and as citizens began to revolt against rampant private and government fraud and corruption. People started pointing fingers, questioning why local and state government officials had not done more to confront corruption that harmed the overall war effort. District Court Judge William P. Hill, serving the Eastern Texas District, formed a "Grand Jury of the Confederate Court" to deal with the worsening situation, hoping to speed up the process of ferreting out wrongdoers of all stripes before public confidence in government institutions eroded further. On January 20, 1865, a panel of nineteen prominent Harris County citizens was formed, including Agur Morse as well as George W. Frazer, T. M. Bagby, and Andrew Crawford. Of this group, the Tri-Weekly Telegraph stated:

> *It will be seen that the gentlemen composing this Grand Jury are all men of character, and in whom the public will not fail to have the utmost confidence. . . . We have good ground to hope that the present session of the court will have an important bearing on the respect of the people and their servants for the laws of the Confederacy.*[121]

The Grand Jury reported out on March 6, 1865, having served a great number of indictments on "vast and various" crimes to the District Court. Among these crimes, they especially singled out speculation in Confederate currency by government workers. With regard to the larger issue of the overall state of the Confederacy in Harris County, they were upbeat—in retrospect, they seemed to be in denial of current events. Only one month before the surrender of Lee's army at Appomattox, the Grand Jury reported:

> *In the conditions and prospects of our cause and country, we are unable to perceive any cause for discouragement, or an abatement of confidence. Revolution implies a condition of gloom and suffering. When the storm rages, we hardly expect sunshine, and if it comes at all it is only in glimpses. With some reverses and defeats our progress is onward, and our success only a problem of time. . . . For a while, some talked of reconstruction, but the moral and patriotic sentiment of the people has been so shocked at the suggestion that it is now only to be mentioned to be denounced.*[122]

Such unreasonably upbeat reports in the face of torrents of horrifically bad news from the front were typical of the press of Houston and other Texas cities at the time, and the Tri-Weekly Telegraph served up weekly helpings of jingoistic optimism up until nearly the day that the victorious Federals arrived in Houston in June.

In the tumult of the last few days and weeks of the Confederacy, Agur Morse contracted typhoid fever and died on April 10, 1865, only a day after Lee's surrender at Appomattox. His obituary, published in the *Galveston Daily News* of April 13, reads as follows:

> *Died at his residence, near this city, April 10th, 1865, of typhoid fever, Captain A. T. Morse, of the firm of A. T. & J. B. Morse, Druggists, of Houston. Capt. Morse was born in the city of New Haven, Conn., October 1801, but was raised in South Carolina; thence the family emigrated to Alabama; thence to Mississippi. The last thirteen years of his life have been spent in Texas, where he has earned and enjoyed the confidence and esteem of all who knew him, as an honest man and an honorable gentleman. The community have lost a most valuable citizen and patriot; the Presbyterian Church a firm friend and supporter; and the bereaved family the gentle, noble and loving guardian. Peace to his ashes.*
>
> —T.C.
>
> *Alabama, Mississippi and South Carolina papers please copy.*[123]

Grace Morse, three of Agur's four sons, and his daughter Elizabeth laid him to rest in the Morse family cemetery, just across the creek from his plantation home, where he had died.

Confederate soldiers in Houston looted government warehouses on May 23, and the postal system crashed in early June. Trade was all but halted as all awaited the arrival of Federal troops. As one newsman commented, "Business is at a standstill, the machinery is out of gear, and every one appears to be waiting for the crack of the whip which is to start us—God knows where." That waiting came to an end on June 20, 1865, when Federal troops from Ohio and Iowa arrived by train from Galveston.[124]

The last war involvement by the Morse family was by Agur's son George W. Morse. He likely missed his father's funeral, as he was still engaged in fighting the Federals down in South Texas at the end of the war. Following a long convalescence after his service in the Bayou City Guards in Virginia, he was temporarily assigned to Captain O. G. Jones's Battery of the Texas Light Artillery in August 1863, by special order of Lt. Gen. E. Kirby Smith. This unit traversed the Texas coast from Sabine Pass to Galveston to Brownsville. George's new unit played a leading role in the last battle of the Civil War at Palmetto Ranch, near Brownsville, Texas, on May 12–13, 1865; the Confederates won the skirmish.

General Kirby Smith surrendered the Army of the Trans-Mississippi, which included the Texan troops at Palmetto Ranch, on May 26. George W. Morse was paroled in Houston on July 3, 1865, and rejoined his mother and surviving brothers at Pleasant Bend. In his youthful idealistic patriotism, he had been the first in the Pleasant Bend–Piney Point neighborhood to volunteer, and he was the last to lay down his arms.

Peace Returns to the Upper Buffalo Bayou neighborhood

Back in Spring Branch, north of Buffalo Bayou, Carolina Bauer Rummel welcomed home her returning son William, and the family dug up the jar of coins—the family's savings—that they had buried underneath the floorboards of their log cabin in 1861. Christiane's grandson recalled:

> *Four years later when the war was over, they dug up their treasure, but it was no longer neatly wrapped in paper. The twenty dollar gold pieces were mixed with ones, fives, and tens. They claimed [that] severe lightning and thunder caused the paper wrapping to break and mix the coins; there wasn't any missing. Then after the Civil War was over they built their first frame house.*[125]

Carolina Rummel's careful prudence had paid off. Money of any sort was to be short in supply during the Reconstruction to come.

Figure 9.1. Enslaved African Americans returning from cotton fields, near Charleston, ca. 1860. Photograph by George N. Barnard, courtesy of the New York Historical Society.

NINE

Reconstruction and African-American Migration

The people of Texas are informed that, in accordance with a Proclamation from the Executive of the United States, all slaves are free. This involves an absolute equality of personal rights and rights of property between former masters and slaves, and the connection heretofore existing between them becomes that between employer and hired labor.

–Major-General Gordon Granger's Executive Order Number 3, Galveston, June 19, 1865[1]

They travel mostly on foot, bearing heavy burthens of clothing, blankets, etc., on their heads—a long and weary journey. They arrive tired, footsore and hungry.

–*Houston Tri-Weekly Telegraph*, June 30, 1865, on freed slaves arriving in Houston

African American migration to upper Buffalo Bayou

GENERAL GRANGER issued his famous proclamation upon arriving in Galveston, a day before he arrived in Houston. That date of the delivery of the news of their emancipation, June 19th, has been celebrated ever since as "Juneteenth" by persons in Texas of African American descent. The news spread fast; most slaves heard about the change of affairs from their former masters. In an instant their freedom had finally come, but with it came the uncertainties of living in an extremely difficult and unpredictable new postwar world, in which most formerly enslaved people who left the plantations were homeless and illiterate, with few financial resources and few friends in the white communities to which they migrated. As T. R. Fehrenbach noted in his history of Texas,

> *Now, more than 200,000 [Texas] Negroes were cast adrift in one of the greatest social revolutions of all time. The first instinct of the plantation slave was to pick up and go. But he had nowhere to go. Thousands jammed the roads and trails, wandering from county to county. . . . They were naturally eu-*

phoric, and expected to be led into some new Promised Land. But nothing like a red dawn appeared in the state, or in the South. . . . They left the land, and thousands of plantations fell into disrepair and disuse.[2]

Houston was the second largest city in Texas at that time (Galveston was the largest), and many headed to the Bayou City, looking for employment. The San Felipe Trail and the Washington and Richmond wagon roads became the prime routes for the freedmen's exodus from plantations along the Brazos and Colorado rivers. Others headed back to the deep South from whence they had come in the 1820s to 1850s, searching for long lost relatives. Still others settled on white-owned rural farmland that surrounded the city, and began to work for food and shelter. Most of this latter group became sharecroppers, and those who settled along the San Felipe Trail would completely change the fabric of the rural area along the south bank of upper Buffalo Bayou. In less than five years these freed African Americans were to become the dominant ethnic group along the San Felipe road.

Meanwhile, the plantation system, which had relied on unpaid slave labor, was finished. For planters, a major asset vanished with Emancipation: the monetary value of their slaves evaporated. Many of the plantations and large farms of Texas and across the South were soon to be broken up and either sold or rented out as much smaller farms that could be worked by a farmer, his family, and perhaps a hired hand or two. Such was the case locally at the Morse family's Pleasant Bend Plantation, and in time at Harriet George's large farm at Piney Point. Times were difficult for everyone, black and white, but also full of promise. In this chapter, I examine the effects of the tumultuous aftermath of the war on rural upper Buffalo Bayou, beginning with the newly arriving African American freedmen.

The Emancipation migration of 1865 and the founding of Freedmantown

The issuance of emancipation orders by General Granger fell on despairing and hardened hearts among Texas' white community:

Although our fellow citizens of this State have been prepared for it, . . . yet the order of Gen. Granger, published yesterday, at once severing the connections between masters and servants all over the State, and placing them on an equality, so far as rights of person and property are concerned, will, we doubt not, cause a sensation of sorrow and humiliation not to be described. . . . It will bear harder on the feelings of the slaveholders of Texas than those of any other State. In the other States, they were somewhat prepared, practically, by the presence of invading armies, and by the escape or impressment of many of their negroes. But Texas has never been over-run by armies; the fiat for a new order of things finds her with the old order of things undisturbed, and operating precisely as it did before the war. . . . To wake up some morning and find it their duty to tell all their servants that they are free, that they no longer have any legal claim on their time and labor . . . will be a hard, unhappy trial. . . . But as it has been with the people of all the other Southern States, so it is with them; the necessity is upon them, and it must be done.

—Houston Tri-Weekly Telegraph, *June 23, 1865*

Freed slaves immediately left their places of servitude by the thousands, walking the roads toward cities where they would try to find work. Houston was a principal destination for those who lived in the area of Austin's old colony. Large numbers of freed slaves left the Brazos and Colorado plantations and walked east on the San Felipe Trail, headed to Houston, where they gathered on the fringe of town along the San Felipe Road (now West Dallas Street) at what became known as Freedmantown in the Fourth Ward, just outside the city limits of that time (Figure 9.2).[3] Others came from Brazos plantations farther north, traveling along Washington Road, and from the San Jacinto River plantations to the northeast of Houston, settling in the Fifth Ward. Still others came from Brazos plantations farther south, traveling along Richmond road, and settled in the Third Ward. The *Houston Tri-weekly Telegraph* described the freedmen's migration only two weeks after Granger's decree and suggested that the migrating African Americans return to their plantations:

> *A trip to Houston is quite a fashionable excursion with the freedmen of the Brazos and Trinity. They travel mostly on foot, bearing heavy burthens of clothing, blankets, etc., on their heads,—a long and weary journey. They arrive tired, footsore and hungry, only to learn what they were told before they left, that they were better off at home and that they had better go back again. Some are returning, some go to the public negro quarter here and take such [fare] as they can get. Some hire out, people generally taking them conditioned on the consent of their late masters. Those who stay at home will do best. Those who go home, next best, while, as a general thing, those who "go it alone" will become triflers and vagabonds. Those who are in the hands of the government will be taken care of as well as in the power of the officers, but it is quite another thing from the comfortable homes many have left behind.*
>
> —Houston Tri-Weekly Telegraph,
> *June 30, 1865*

Those arriving in Houston were to experience a difficult transition over the next few years, made all the more difficult by the reaction of a sizeable number of embittered white Houstonians. Many were still in mourning for lost soldiers, in shock at the war's outcome, and—especially some of those who had owned slaves—in denial of the new order of things that was brought on by the federal emancipation decree and Reconstruction.

Arriving blacks found accommodation in overcrowded vacant buildings, warehouses, and stables. Many came expecting help from the occupying Union army, and local officials such as Colonel G. W. Clark, post commandant of Houston and colonel of the 34th Iowa Volunteer Infantry, provided what help they could.[4] But the government was soon overwhelmed with the numbers of arriving supplicants.[5] Freedmen took what work they could find, as house servants and common laborers. Those remaining unemployed were treated harshly, as this notice of September makes clear:

> *Another improvement instituted by the military authorities of this city, requires all negroes to obtain a certificate from their employer showing that they obtain an honest living. If they cannot do this they are immediately sent to the Hotel d'Afrique and forced to work on the street to pay for Uncle Sam's grub they eat. Houston is a poor place for negro vagrants.*
>
> —Houston Tri-Weekly Telegraph,
> *September 6, 1865*

White workers, whose ranks were already swelled by returning former Confederate soldiers, feared loss of jobs as a result of the flood of African American workers from the plantations. This resulted in the beginning of a virtual lockout of skilled black "mechanics" (tradesmen such as carpenters, blacksmiths and the like):

> *We do not wish to say anything that shall prevent enterprising freedmen from getting an honest living, but we must tell them that they are bringing their eggs to a poor market when they bring them to Houston. The breaking up of the war has left thousands of industrious white men out of employment. The disposition of the people is to give them employment in preference to anybody else. The rush of negroes here has also lowered the prices of that class of labor, until good negro men can now be hired at a less cost than the actual cost of keeping them decently clothed. . . . There is a universal disposition on the part of the white mechanics to exclude negroes from plying their trades among them. They will not work on the same bench, or admit to the same level the black so long as they can help it. Exclusive unions of this kind are being formed now.*
>
> — Houston Tri-Weekly Telegraph,
> *July 14, 1865*

It is perhaps not surprising that burglaries and petty theft were on the rise during these first postwar

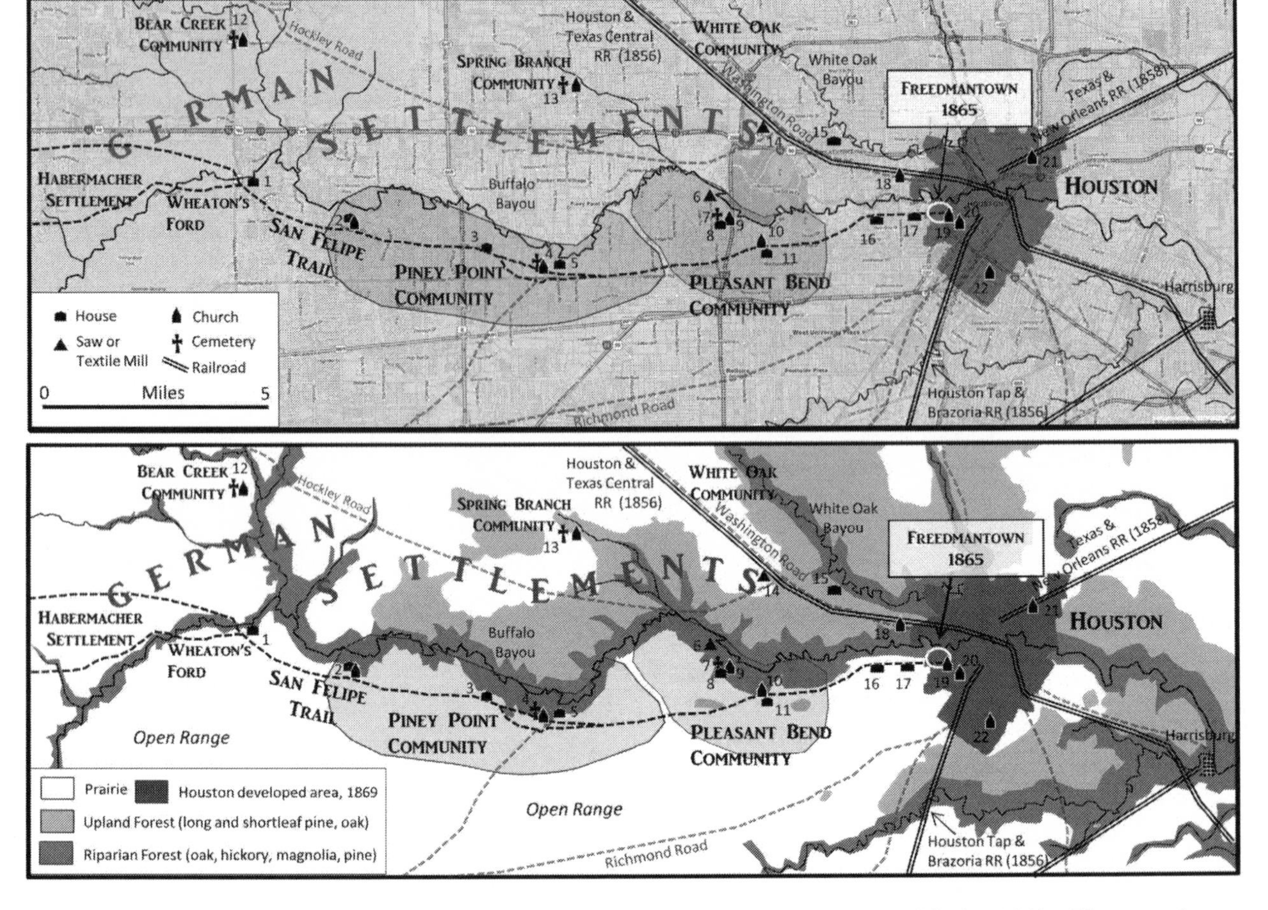

Figure 9.2. Upper Buffalo Bayou during Reconstruction and the African American migration of the late 1860s. The upper figure is drawn on a modern road map, courtesy of OpenStreetMap. Lower figure depicts natural features of the time (as in Figure 1.2). Houston's developed area of 1869 is shaded dark gray. Legend for numbered sites (* marks African American sites):

1. William Habermacher, 1871 (formerly the inn at Wheaton's Ford, 1831)
2. David McGee, 1869, and McGee church and school, 1876*
3. James Normand
4. Rufus Wilkins*
5. Pilgrim Rest Baptist Church, ca. 1865 (original location), with cemetery*
6. Harriet George (formerly Harriet Canfield), 1838
7. Henry and George Morse sawmill, 1869
8. Morse family cemetery
9. Grace Morse home, 1851
10. Buffalo Bayou Community Church, 1870
11. Lovely Canada Baptist Church, 1876*
12. Jordan and Rachel Banks, 1875*
13. Bear Creek German Methodist Church, 1879 (original location)
14. St. Peter Church, 1864
15. Eureka Cotton Mill, 1866 (formerly William Morse sawmill)
16. Christian Bethje home
17. Allen Coward and George Butler homes, 1867
18. George Baker home, 1845

The five earliest African American churches in Houston:

19. Damascus Baptist Church, 1865*
20. Antioch Baptist Church, 1866 (in Freedmantown)*
21. Trinity United Methodist Church, 1865 (original location)*
22. Mt. Vernon United Methodist Church, 1865*
23. Mt. Zion Baptist Church, 1866*

Anglo and German churches of the Reconstruction era are not highlighted within the Houston developed area.

Figure 9.3. Reconstruction era African American families, northwest of Houston. Drawing by J. Wells Champney, from Edward King, *The Great South: A Record of Journeys* (Hartford, Conn.: American Publishing Company, 1875).

months, and African Americans showed up with regularity on court dockets. But most newly arriving blacks settled in quickly and peacefully, as this reporter begrudgingly observed in August, less than two months after Emancipation:

> *The freed men and women behave themselves very well in this city now. We will do them justice to report this fact. The thieving black scoundrels are the cause of giving all the honest colored people a bad name. We hope the honest ones will aid the authorities in securing the arrest of all the thieved and burglars among the colored people.*
>
> —Houston Tri-Weekly Telegraph, *August 9, 1865*

Freedmen may have been excluded from some jobs, but they had a few new powers of their own after Emancipation, a principal one being the right to choose their employers, as the following example shows:

> *We have been a good deal amused lately, by the experience of our friends in servant hunting and hiring. The case of one of them was one of peculiar hardship. Some six weeks ago, being in want of a servant, a friend sent him two (mother and daughter), just from the Brazos. They were clothed in rags, and he bought goods and clothed them decently. Ten days ago his wife was taken very ill, and while she was confined to bed, someone offered his*

servants one dollar a month more than he was paying them. This was last Sunday afternoon, and the servants left his house Monday morning. . . . For three days he and his children have done all his housework, including cooking and cow-milking.

— Houston Tri-Weekly Telegraph, *August 11, 1865*

Freedmen in Houston were helped by the formation of the Bureau of Refugees, Freedmen, and Abandoned Lands in March 1865; this national branch of the U.S. Army became known as the Freedmen's Bureau. Among many duties, the bureau concentrated on two tasks: protecting a system of free labor for freedmen by way of legally binding labor contracts with employers, and starting a system of schools for African Americans.[6] The labor contracts attempted to provide fair remuneration, choice of employers, and freedom from abusive overseers. A first school for Houston's African American children opened in 1865, followed by the Freedmen's Academy to educate black teachers (soon renamed the Gregory Institute, in honor of the bureau's first director, General Edgar M. Gregory).[7]

The Freedmen's Bureau was not popular among white Texans and Houstonians; the bureau's Texas commissioner in 1867, Charles Griffin, wrote to his national director, Otis Howard: "The majority of the inhabitants of this state are as hostile today as they were in [18]62 + 3."[8] That hostility toward freed African Americans was to be felt for a long time. However, Reconstruction brought the rule of reform-minded Republicans and black suffrage. At this time Houston city government included several black alderman, and in 1869 former slave Richard Allen became the first black person elected to the Texas House of Representatives, representing Harris and Montgomery counties.[9] Reconstruction in Texas ended in 1873–1874 with the Democratic Party's takeover of the Texas legislature, and was followed by many decades of harsh Jim Crow segregation.[10]

Freedmantown, on the west side of Houston adjacent to San Felipe Road (as the San Felipe Trail was known in settled Houston), developed as the principal area for African Americans living in Houston. Arriving freedmen and their families at first settled in vacant and rented dwellings in the existing Castanie, Seneschal and Hopson subdivisions; Castanie lay adjacent to the city's cemetery, and a rural area of cattle pens with a slaughterhouse lay just to the west (Figure 9.4 A); the cattle pens were at that time involved in the shipment of cattle up the Chisholm Trail, as is discussed in Chapter 10. With the press of arriving African American families, the new Hardcastle subdivision was laid out and occupied in 1866.[11]

The Castanie subdivision of 1848, named for the Louisiana Frenchman Jules Castanie who bought the land in that year, was a working-class area even before the arrival of the migrating African Americans. Rows of small cottages housed German immigrants, such as Charles Engelhard, who bought the Acadian-style house pictured at the center of Figure 9.5 in 1858 from Castanie. By the 1880s the house had been inhabited by a succession of African American and occasional Italian residents. It was moved to Houston's Heritage Park in 2002 for preservation.[12] A bird's-eye view of Houston prepared in 1891 (Figure 9.6) shows the entirety of Freedmantown, which was still at the western fringe of the city. The rows of small cottages and shotgun houses are clearly visible, their diminutive size apparent in comparison to the more substantial homes of adjacent Houston. The railroad at the western edge (right) in this view was the Galveston, Harrisburg & San Antonio Railroad; modern Montrose Street was laid out on its defunct right-of-way in the twentieth century. San Felipe Road, at the heart of Freedmantown, projects westward (to the right) into then-rural farmland and forest of western Harris County.

Important and immediate additions to the social and cultural life of Houston's African American community at this time were a number of churches, five of them started within a year of the Emancipation migration (Figure 9.2). The first of these was Trinity United Methodist. Some of its members had been part of an earlier African Mission Church that met at a frame structure on Milam Street, but in 1865 they decided to build their own sanctuary at 1410 Travis and affiliate with the Methodist Episco-

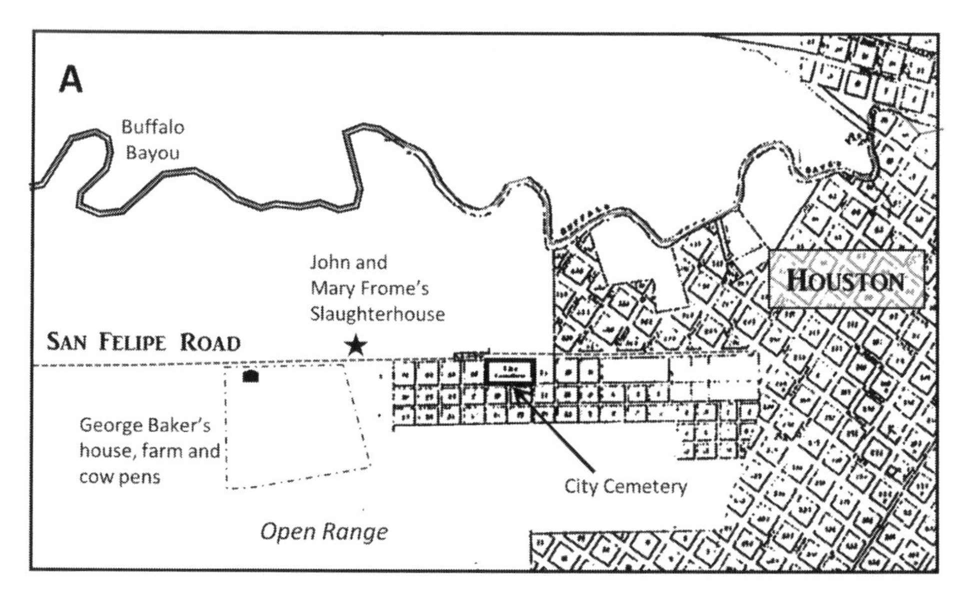

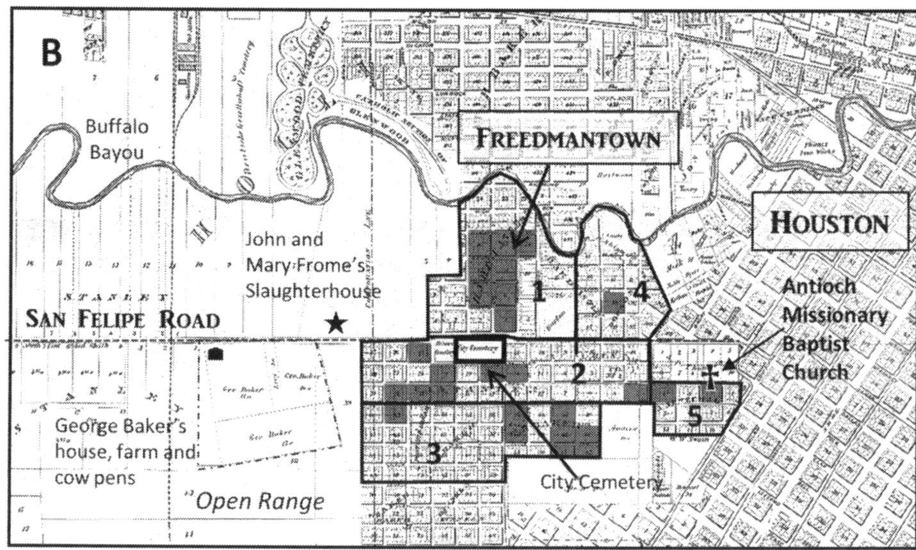

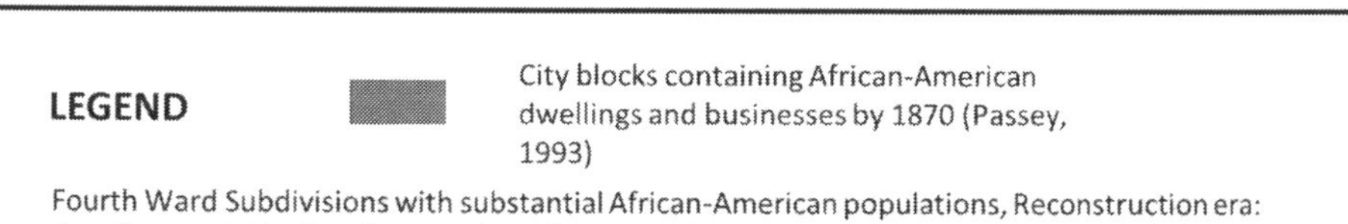

Figure 9.4. The development of Freedmantown. **A:** The developed area of western Houston at the end of the Civil War.Features west of Houston are superimposed on part of a map of Houston by C. E. Wood, 1866. **B:** Areas ofAfrican American settlement of Freedmantown by ca. 1870 superimposed on a map of the city of Houston of 1895, by Whitty and Stott.Both base maps are courtesy of the Houston Metropolitan Research Center, Houston Public Library. Subdivision data are from Mary Louise Passey, *Freedmantown: The Evolution of a Black Neighborhood in Houston,* 1865–1880, M.A. thesis, Rice University, 1993.

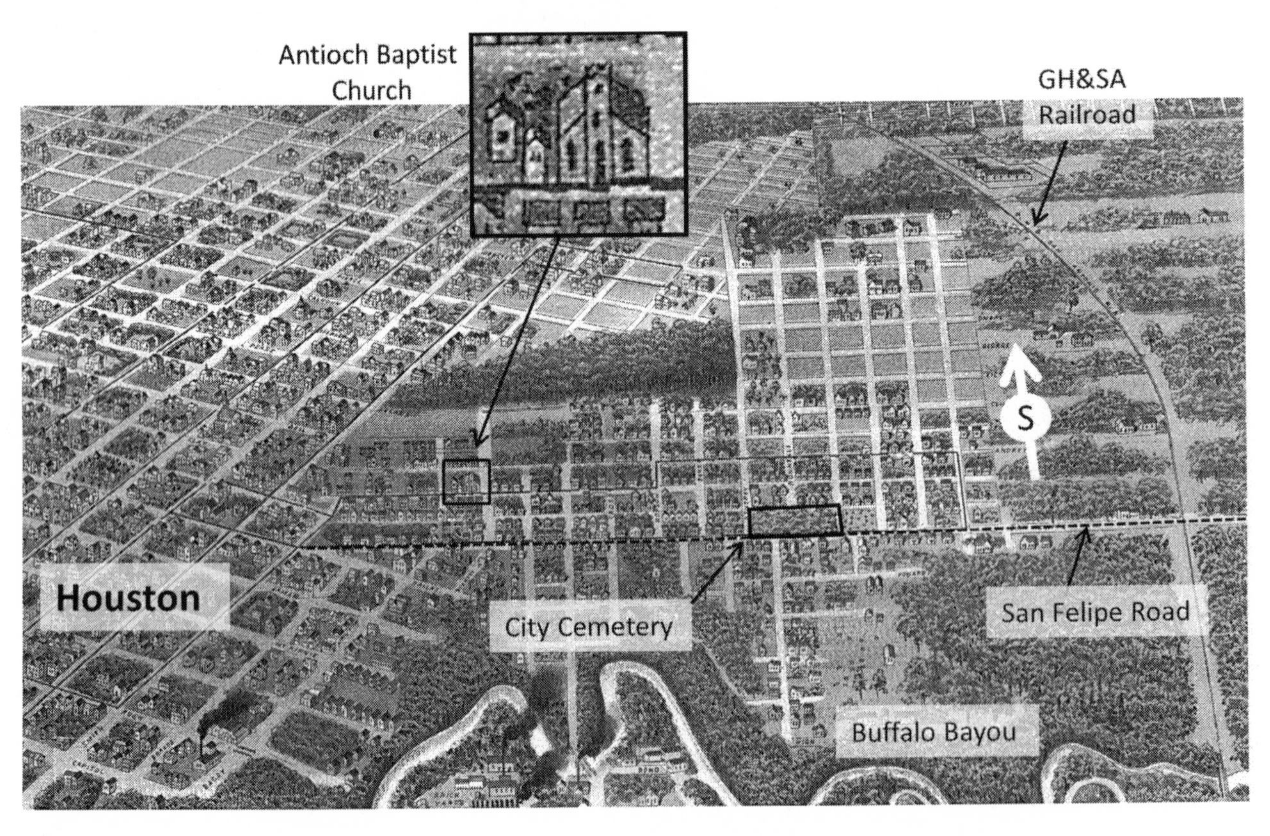
Antioch Baptist Church
GH&SA Railroad
S
Houston
City Cemetery
San Felipe Road
Buffalo Bayou

Figure 9.7. Antioch Baptist Church as it appeared in 1915. From Anonymous, *The Red Book of Houston:* A Compendium of Social, Professional, Religious, Educational and Industrial Interests of Houston's Colored Population (Houston: SoTex Publishing Company, 1915).

pal Church.[13] Rev. Elias Dibble was pastor for the new Trinity United Methodist in its early years.

The first church within Freedmantown was Antioch Baptist Church, at 311 Robin Street (now renamed 500 Clay Street), organized in January 1866 (Figures 9.6 and 9.7). By August that year Rev. I. S. Campbell was pastor, to be succeeded by Rev. Jack Yates in 1868. Prior to the completion of its present brick building in 1879 (the first brick church building owned by African Americans in Houston), the congregation met at "Baptist Hill" on Rusk at Bagby.[14] The three other early churches were Damascus Baptist Church (1865), Mt. Vernon United Methodist Church (1865), and Mt. Zion Baptist Church (1866; see Figure 9.2). By the end of the century, there were a number of others, including Good Hope Missionary Baptist Church (1872), St. James United Methodist Church, Bebee Tabernacle CME Church (1879), and Bethel Missionary Baptist Church (1891). The latter four churches were all located in Freedmantown.[15]

Opposite Top: Figure 9.5. A row of cottages on the 800 block of Robin Street, in Freedmantown, as they looked in 1988. The building in the center, thought to have been built by immigrant farmer Jules Castanie as early as the late 1840s, has since been moved to Houston's Heritage Park for preservation. Photo (c) Gerald Moorhead FAIA.

Opposite: Figure 9.6. A portion of an 1891 bird's-eye view of Houston, Texas, looking south, focusing on the portion showing Freedmantown, Fourth Ward. The railroad to the right (west) of Freedmantown is the Galveston, Harrisburg and San Antonio Railroad; modern Montrose was laid out on its defunct right-of-way. Note the position of San Felipe Road, which at its western extremity (to the right) projects into then rural farmland and forest of western Harris County. A copy of this map is at the Houston Metropolitan Research Center, Houston Public Library.

Figure 9.8. A group of elderly African Americans—all formerly enslaved—photographed in Harris County, 1915. From Anonymous, *The Red Book of Houston*..

The migration of African Americans from Texas plantations following Emancipation was to alter the demographics of the city of Houston substantially. Whereas in both 1850 and 1860 the black population of the city comprised 22 percent of the total population (totals were 2,396 in 1850 and 4,845 in 1860), by 1870 the arrival of freedmen brought the black population to 3,691 out of a total of 9,382 persons, or 39.3 percent of the total (Figure 9.9 A). This was the highest ratio of African Americans to whites in the city's history to the present date.[16] The ward with the highest overall number and percentage of African Americans in 1870 was the Fourth Ward near San Felipe Road, where 1,314 blacks made up fully 43 percent of the population. That percentage, high as it was, increased abruptly to the west, in areas lying along San Felipe Road in rural upper Buffalo Bayou.

Freedmen in rural upper Buffalo Bayou

Not all freed slaves arriving in Houston found work there, and many knew little else than the agricultural tasks that they had performed on the plantations. With few other options, many headed out to the small farms outside Houston, where things were rapidly changing. As the large landholdings of an earlier era were broken up into smaller parcels—the Canfield-George Piney Point estate and the Agur Morse Pleasant Bend Plantation to its east (both discussed later in this chapter) are two good examples—new small farmers moved in, most of whom, initially, were white. As the freed African Americans wandered toward or away from Houston to seek their fortune, some stayed along the San Felipe Trail—by now usually called the San Felipe Road—to become farm laborers or sharecroppers. Sharecropping was a dif-

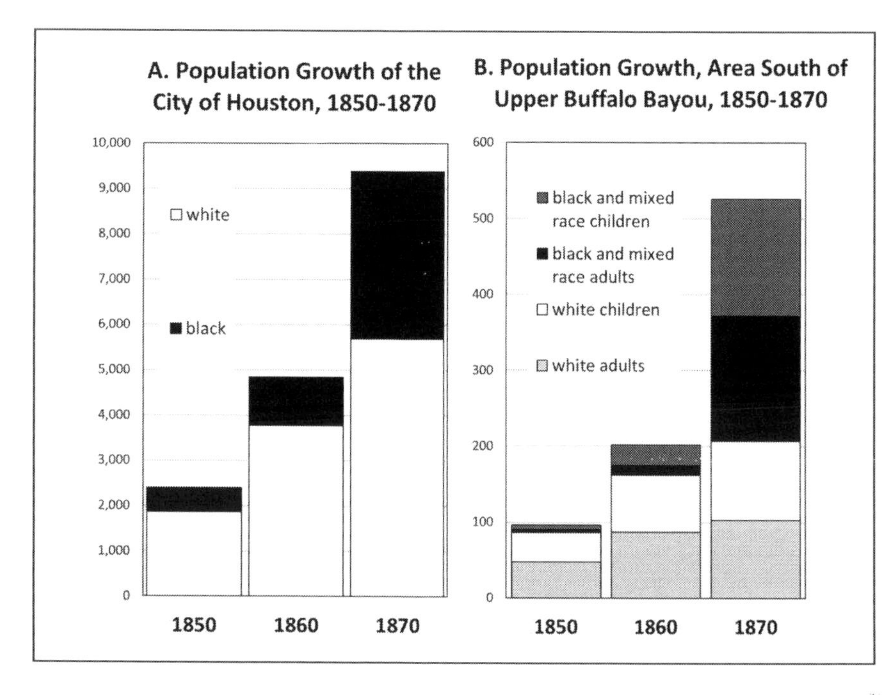

Figure 9.9. Demographics of the city of Houston (A) and the rural areas south of upper Buffalo Bayou (B), 1850–1870. Compiled from U.S. federal census data of 1850, 1860, and 1870.

ficult way to make a living, but was a useful first step for many, and the new immigrants were typically welcome for the extra income that they brought to white-owned farms—a situation unlike that found in the city of Houston, where migrating African American men were looked upon by whites as competitors for scarce jobs. Many of the small farms in the post-plantation period were still several hundred acres in size. A white farmer with his mule working such a tract of land could perhaps keep up with 20 or 30 cultivated acres in an era before mechanical farm implements, and the rest was left as unimproved prairie or woodland and utilized for open range cattle raising. By renting out or sharecropping some of this land to arriving African Americans, the farmer got a return on acreage that he otherwise could not cultivate.

Rural demographics. In 1850, federal census data show that there were only 10 African Americans in the rural region south of Buffalo Bayou from Fry Road (Katy) to Shepherd Drive, out of a total of 96 persons (10 percent; see Figure 9.9 B). Most of the few farmers and cattle ranchers living in that frontier zone did not use slaves at that time, as there were no Brazos-style cotton plantations on the open prairie. By 1860 that number had risen to 40 black slaves out of 202 total persons (20 percent), mostly a result of experiments in prairie cotton production begun in the 1850s by Agur Morse and another planter named K. Halston. However, as a result of the floods of migrant freedmen following Emancipation, the black population of this area in 1870 reached 319 persons out of a total of 526 residents, or 61 percent of the population. It was a notable development for what had heretofore been a mostly Anglo-American frontier area (as we have seen, most immigrant Germans lived north of the Bayou).

These new black residents had come from Brazos and Colorado cotton plantations where they had been brought in the previous three or four decades from other southern states. Few had been born in Texas (Figure 9.11), which underscores the relative newness of slavery in Texas in the decades before the Civil War. Cultivation of cotton depleted nutrients from the soil in a relatively short time, which was a serious shortcoming in the days before artificial fertilizer. Planters made up for this problem by moving their operations to areas with fresh soil, and the early history of the lower South is one of a repetitive ever-westward opening of new Indian lands, each zone then settled by planters. For example, the Agur T. Morse family initially had plantations in Connecticut in colonial times, and moved to South Carolina in 1817. When that soil was spent they moved to Mis-

Figure 9.10. Rural African American home near Houston, ca. 1889.
Courtesy of the Metropolitan Research Center, Houston Public Library.

sissippi in 1836, and to Texas in 1851 (see Figure 7.12). By such a process, repeated in the migration history of scores of planter families, Texas slaves had come from nearly all of the southern states.

As mentioned, by far the largest numbers of this influx of freedmen were employed in farming (Figure 9.12). The local farming landscape was changing quickly. Several of the established large landowners of the area, such as the Morse and Canfield/George families, sold tracts of land as small farms for newly arriving white farmers. Most newly arriving freedmen had no savings for such investments. With the ready availability of black labor, many if not most white farmers employed black farm hands to help work their acreage. Other farmers began to rent out parts of their acreage to freedmen for a share of the crops or for a rent payment. Among the black population, the 1870 census counted 12 laborers (unspecified) and 40 farm laborers, and only one farmer who owned his land. By 1880 the census breakdown was more specific, showing 4 laborers, 23 farmers on rented or sharecropped land, and 11 farmers who owned their land. In a decade, a significant number of freedmen had been able to buy their land. In 1870, only 8 percent of black farmers owned land, versus 58 percent of whites. By 1880, 38 percent of black farmers owned their own land, versus 79 percent of white farmers; black farmers had more than quadrupled their share of local farms in just a decade.

Other significant means of employment in the area in 1870 lay in the Morse family sawmill on the grounds of the former plantation (discussed later in this chapter) as well as the cattle ranching and stock-

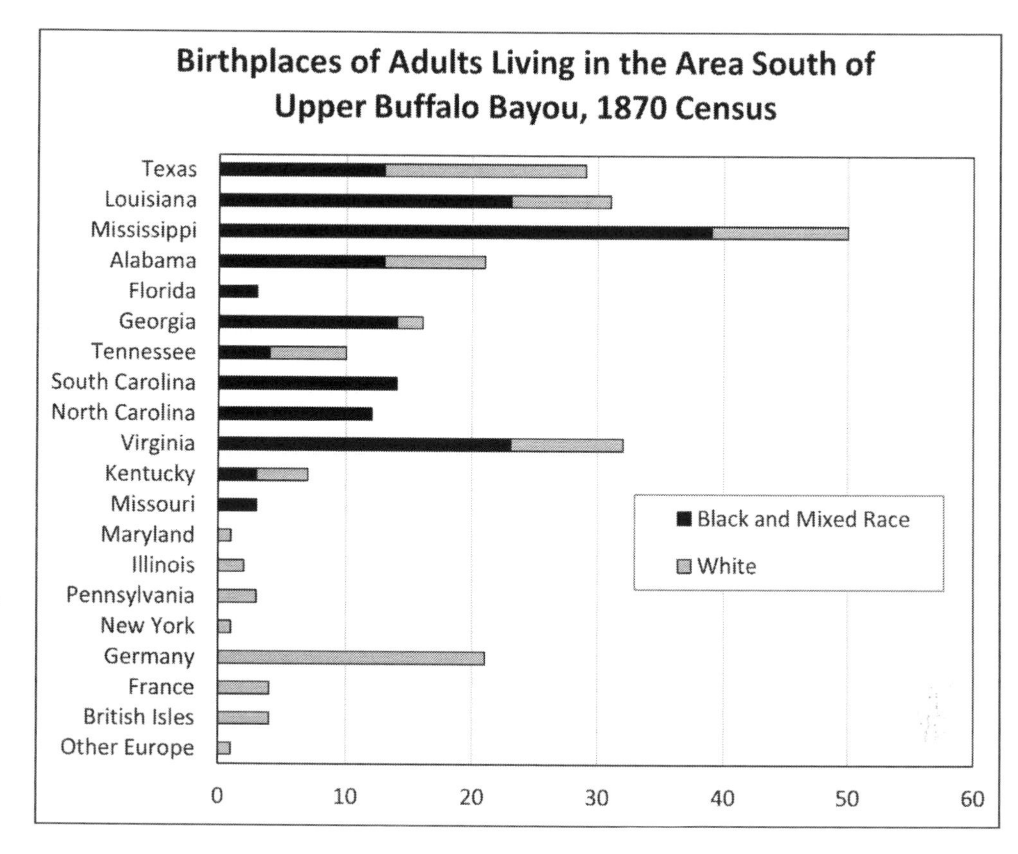

Figure 9.11. Birthplaces of adults living in the area south of upper Buffalo Bayou, 1870. Compiled from U.S. federal census data of 1870.

yards owned by George Baker that lay along the San Felipe Road near present day Shepherd Drive (Chapter 10). The Morse sawmill in particular employed large numbers of freedmen, but it closed before 1880, leading to a reduction in the local African American population.

Pilgrim Rest Church and the new African American residents of Piney Point. A number of newly arriving African Americans settled in what became somewhat loosely defined as the community of Piney Point. Although it was centered around the southern salient of Buffalo Bayou, where Harriet George still owned her farm from pioneer days, the rural community extended for a couple of miles in either direction (Figure 9.2). Almost all these freedmen were illiterate in 1870, working as farm laborers on land owned by others, but many had plans for the improvement of their lot. Like their city neighbors ten miles to the east in Houston's Freedmantown, African American families of this rural area wanted their own churches, which replaced their previous plantation-centered social life. They knew they needed to establish schools for their children, and while they had few resources, they began to work toward their future.

A large and partly inter-related group of these arriving African American families lived on the west side of Piney Point, in between the farms of immigrant English immigrant James Normand and (by 1880) African American Rufus Wilkins (Figure 9.2). This group included the families of Thomas and Harriet Amos, Adam and Ellen Blackstock, Phillip and Richey Blackstock, Strong and Davanah Blackstock, Moses and Jane Blackstock, Richard and Alina Patterson, Fanny Williams, Mac and Catherine Austin, Washington and Sallie McGee, Thomas and Hannah Erasmus, and Roscoe and Rosetta Wilkins. In 1865, near the former farm of the Canfields at Piney Point, this group as well as other black families living in the eastern half of Piney Point formed the first new African American church in the rural area west of Houston. Its founders included Hannah Rasmus (b. ca. 1832) and Max Austin (b. ca. 1835). Hannah Rasmus was an ex-slave born in Mississippi,

Adult Male Employment, South Side of Upper Buffalo Bayou

		1870		1880	
		African American	White	African American	White
Agriculture	Gardener				1
	Laborer (unspecified)	12		4	
	Farmer, owns farm	1	11	11	21
	Farm laborer, renter or sharecropper	40	8	23	9
Ranching	Butcher		8		
	Teamster		2		
	Stock Driver	2*	1		1
	Stock Raiser		5		4
Lumber	Wood merchant		3		
	Sawmill Co-owner		3		
	Sawmill Worker	4	2		
	Teamster	9			
	Wood chopper	14			
Craftsmen	Shoemaker		1		
	Blacksmith				1
	Wagonmaker		1		
	Carpenter	1	2		
Other	Retired	1	2		
	Domestic Servant	1		3	
	Teacher			1	
	Minister	1			
	Barkeeper		1		

*note: does not include two African-American teenage cattle drivers

Figure 9.12. Employment of adult males in the area south of upper Buffalo Bayou, 1870 and 1880. Compiled from U.S. federal census data.

whose parents were from North Carolina. The 1870 census shows Hannah (b. 1830), living with husband Thomas "Erastmus," born ca. 1830, a farm laborer originally from Virginia. They did not own land, and were probably sharecropping; Hannah is listed as a farmworker on the 1870 census. They had a ten-year-old son Adam and an eight-year-old son Howard. The 1880 census records this family as "James" and Hannah "Rasmos," born ca. 1832 and 1839, respectively. In 1900 "Tomas" and Hanna Rasmus are shown with birthdates of May 1836 and July 1844, respectively; by 1910 Hanna Rasmus (b. ca. 1839) was widowed. The death certificate of their son Adam gives his parents' names as Tomas Rasmus and Hannah "Bockstaf." Hannah's maiden name may have been Blackstock, in which case she was likely closely related to the four Blackstock families of their group. Max (Mac) Austin (b. ca. 1835) was a farm laborer from North Carolina, and like Hannah was very likely an ex-slave. His wife Catherine (b. ca. 1837), from Virginia, was listed as a housekeeper. They had four children at the 1870 census: Maggie aged 11, Elijah 13, Ora 8, and Mac Jr. 3.

Max Austin became the pastor of the new church, which members named Pilgrim Rest Missionary Baptist Church. In the early years they met at one another's homes, but in 1884 they purchased one acre of land from Harriet George for twenty dollars, built a church, and established a cemetery.[17] The church and cemetery lay to the east of what is now a home at 26 East Shady Lane, about a quarter mile north of Westheimer Road (Figure 9.2, item 4).[18] That congregation has moved over the years and is now located about one mile to the south, at 3401 Jeanetta Street, just south of Richmond Avenue.

Many of the Piney Point African American men exercised their right to vote in the heady days of Reconstruction; the 1867 voters rolls of Harris County show the participation of Thomas Amos, Thomas Erasmus, Mac Austin, and Roscoe Wilkins of Piney Point, and Jordan Banks of nearby Pleasant Bend.[19]

These families also saved their money. By 1880 Mac Austin had property worth $200, and by 1890 Rufus Wilkins had purchased a small farm north of Westheimer Road, west of modern Rivercrest Drive (Figure 9.2, item 3, and Chapter 11). Others of these early Piney Point families found farm land elsewhere. The families of Thomas Amos, Phillip Blackstock, Richard Patterson, and Willis Woods made money from both farming and fence building in the area as well as from making charcoal. With their savings in hand, the Woods and Blackstock families bought land in 1873 along Cypress Creek in northwest Harris County, in what was called "The Bottoms," near the modern day intersection of Louetta Road and Highway 290, where they all were living by 1880. Willis Woods, who had purchased 310 acres in The Bottoms, gave land to the new community for a church, a school and a Farmers Improvement Hall. The church they established there was named Pilgrim Branch Baptist Church, because they considered it a branch of the mother church (Pilgrim Rest) in Piney Point; the two churches have remained close cousins to this day.[20] Phillip Blackstock became an early pastor of Pilgrim Branch, and J. Blackstock was a later pastor of Pilgrim Rest, from 1870 to 1900.[21] The Cypress families also established a cemetery called "The Bottoms," near modern day Lakewood Forest Country Club. The area was prone to flooding, and the community was moved to the nearby area around the intersection of modern day Spring-Cypress and Kohrville-Huffsmith roads, where the church was moved in 1897. Thomas Amos owned land there and donated an acre for a cemetery, across from the church. Named Amos Cemetery, it and the church both remain there today. A new school was built nearby, and Thomas Amos—a former slave who according to census records remained illiterate during his lifetime—lived to see his sons Amos Jr. and Isaac become the earliest teachers at the new school.[22]

Among the other African Americans living in the Piney Point vicinity in 1870, when the first census to include now free African Americans was taken, were Washington McGee (b. ca. 1833 in Mississippi) and his wife Sallie (b. ca. 1849 in Mississippi) and two children, and Roscoe Wilkins (b. ca. 1825 in North Carolina) and his wife Rosetta (b. ca. 1825, also in North Carolina) and five children, of whom the eldest was Rufus Wilkins, aged twenty-one, who had been born in Mississippi. The McGee, Wilkins, Erasmus and Austin adults were all illiterate, according to the census, and it is probable that all were ex-slaves from Brazos River plantations. None of them owned land in 1870 except McGee, who owned a small tract worth $175.

There are still a substantial number of African American families living in the Piney Point area today. Pilgrim Rest Baptist Church celebrated its 150th anniversary in 2015.[23] A Houston city park adjacent to Piney Point Elementary School and a couple of blocks from the present church is named for Hannah Rasmus's grandson, Walter Rasmus Sr. (1882–1977).

David McGee and the McGee church and school. A few miles to the west of Piney Point, along the San Felipe Trail, was the small African American "McGee Settlement," founded in 1869. David

Figure 9.13. Fannie McGee Williams and her husband Doc Williams, among the founders of McGee Chapel Baptist Church. Fannie was David McGee's daughter. Courtesy of Pastor Walter K. Berry, McGee Chapel.

McGee (1820-1890) was born in Choctaw County, Mississippi, and married Violet (born 1821 in Virginia) while living in that state; both were slaves during their early life. According to the 1870 federal census, they had five children while living in Mississippi and North Carolina before the Civil War (Albert, Floretta, Emilie, Lucian and Fannie); the youngest of these, Fannie, was born in 1856. The McGee family moved to Texas in 1862, perhaps part of the temporary resettlement of African American slaves westward to Texas by their deep South slave owners during the Civil War. At war's end, in 1865, they were living in Harris County, where they had one more child, Sandy, born in 1869. David McGee voted when given the opportunity, in 1867.[24]

David McGee was a blacksmith during slavery times, and like many skilled African American tradesmen was allowed to work at times for himself. In the years after Emancipation, he continued his trade and saved his money, and in 1869 he purchased about 370 acres of prairie land on the Joel Wheaton survey, just south of the San Felipe Trail (Figure 9.2), from John Perry.[25] Here he built his home and farm. The federal census of 1870 stated that his property was worth $560 and his farm equipment was worth another $160, which made him the wealthiest of the African Americans then living in the upper Buffalo Bayou area. That year he owned four horses, 2 milch cows, and two pigs, and raised 300 bushels of corn. At that time they were also caring for five non-McGee children ranging from three to sixteen years of age. It would seem that he and his wife were caring for these non-McGee, Texas-born children out of charity.

In 1870, the McGees were the only African American family for miles around; to the north were the Bear Creek German settlers, to the west and southwest were the Habermachers, and to the east were the Normands and Beelers. The nearest African American community was in Piney Point, five miles to the east. David McGee made his land available for other family, friends, and farm laborers to settle, and the land became known as the McGee Settlement. The small congregation of homes was just south of old Goar Road, which was slightly relocated and straightened into modern Briar Forest. The group of homes that was the settlement was centered about where Auto Check is today at 13424 Briar Forest, west of Eldridge; the area was urbanized in the 1980s. There is no marker there that indicates its prior history.

By the time of the 1880 federal census, McGee Settlement families included those of Doc and Melissa Richards, Guy and Cora Williams, Samuel and Lizzie Williams, David's adult son Albert McGee and his wife Flora McGee, and Doc Williams and his wife Fannie McGee Williams (Figure 9.13). Fannie, born a slave in Mississippi in 1856, was David McGee's daughter. By 1870, the settlement had 25 people, including children. The men were all farmers or farm laborers. David McGee's children were given some of the land, others eventually purchased some of it, and still others worked for McGee.

McGee had sold down his own acreage to a total of ninety acres by 1880, but according to the agricultural census it was a much more substantial farm than it had been ten years earlier. He had twenty acres tilled, ten acres in orchard, ten in woodland, and fifty were unimproved. His farm was valued at $1,000 for its land, $116 in equipment, and $500 in livestock. He paid $400 in wages to hired hands during the year, and made $800 in farm production. He had twenty milch cows, twenty other cattle, ten calves,. and forty swine. He harvested five acres of corn (200 bushels) and twelve acres of cotton (8 bales).[26] He had done well.

In the 1870 census David McGee and his wife were both listed as illiterate, as were most ex-slaves at this time. They set aside some of their land for a school for the settlement's children. Census records indicate that the children of the McGee and Williams families were in school by at least 1880. A school building was erected, and the school was shown on U. S. Geological Survey topographic maps of 1915 and 1919.

A church was started when settlement's families began praying at each other's homes. By 1876, they founded a formal church, which in time was named the McGee Chapel Missionary Baptist Church. Founding members were J. H. Grady, Doc and Fannie Williams, Lucius McGee (David's son), and Fanny Johnson. David McGee's son, Prince Albert McGee (1847-1925), was the first pastor. A permanent church building was constructed in 1912, on prairie land near Goar Road that was isolated and muddy during wet spells. For that reason, the congregation moved the church in 1919 to its present location on State Highway 6 between Westheimer and Briar Forest, where it is called McGee Chapel, now in its 140th year.[27]

Lovely Canada Church and the new African American residents of Pleasant Bend. There was a large influx of African Americans into the area of the former Agur T. Morse Pleasant Bend Plantation, the land of which was being sold off as small farms following the probate of Agur Morse (Figure 9.2). Besides the availability of vacant land for sharecropping, a draw to black families was employment opportunities provided by the Morse sawmill, described later. In 1870 about 220 African American men, women and children were living in the rural area extending from the Morse sawmill to the farm of J. M. Dozier (in modern times, from about Post Oak Boulevard to River Oaks Boulevard). Like their neighbors in Piney Point, these were mostly illiterate ex-slaves from plantations on the Brazos River, as the Morse family owned relatively few slaves (eight by the time of the Civil War, according to tax records).[28]

Among this group was the family of Jordan and Rachel Banks. Jordan Banks (ca. 1847–1933) was born in Virginia and arrived in Harris County in about 1860.[29] Because of his close ties to the Morse family after the Civil War, it seems likely that he entered Texas in 1860 as a slave of that family. After the war he worked for the Morse family; the diary of Celia Morse (wife of Henry Morse) mentions him as a family servant in an entry of June 27, 1869. The 1910 and 1930 federal census records show that he claimed to have given service to the Confederacy, although he was a young teenager when the war broke out; many Texas slaves were put on Confederate work details during the war. At some time in the 1860s he married Rachel Davis (ca. 1845–1919) from Louisiana. By the time of the 1870 census Jordan and Rachel Banks were living next door to Henry Morse, and Jordan Banks was working at the Morse sawmill, listed in the census as a "sawmill laborer." At that time the couple had three children, Maria (ca. 1865), James (ca. 1868–1927) and Fred (b. 1870). Jordan was able to save some of his mill wages, and in August 1875 he purchased an eight-acre plot along San Felipe Road, on part of the former plantation (Figure 9.2, item 11).[30] Rachel eventually bore fifteen children from 1865 to 1893 while they lived on that small farm. Three of those children, James Banks (ca. 1868–1927), Sadie Banks Scott (ca. 1881–1927) and Laura Banks Koontz (ca. 1872–1928) are buried with their mother Rachel Banks in the Morse family cemetery. Jordan Banks, the family patriarch, outlived those family members and was buried in Houston's Oak Park Cemetery (now known as Golden Gate Cemetery) in northeast Houston in 1933, according to his death certificate.

Banks was to be instrumental in building a church for the Pleasant Bend African American community. An African American Baptist minister already lived in the community: Samuel Francis, age twenty-eight, from Texas, who lived with his wife Amy Francis, thirty-eight, from Mississippi. Both were illiterate and most likely were freed slaves. The location of their meeting house, if they had one, is unknown. However, on January 29, 1876, Jordan Banks and two other men, Jack Alfred and Quince Oliver, acting as trustees, purchased one acre of land directly across San Felipe Road from the Banks farm (Figures 9.2 and 7.13) for the purpose of building a church, which was to become known as the Lovely Canada Baptist Church. Elder S. H. Francis was the first pastor of that church.[31] One fifth of that land was purchased by Harris County when the county widened San Felipe Road in 1898, at which time the trustees of the Lovely Canada Baptist Church included Alena Allen, Allen Williams and Jerry Oliver.[32] The African American neighborhood around the church became known as Lovely Canada, which is listed as the city or address of residence on the death certificates of Rachel Banks, her daughter Sadie Banks Scott, and another daughter, Julie Banks Robinson.

That church and its black neighborhood fell to the suburban encroachment of Houston in the middle of the twentieth century. In 1938 the River Oaks Corporation, as part of the expansion of the exclusive River Oaks subdivision, bought the church land and sold the church a larger plot farther away, on the southwest corner of modern Timmons Lane at Westheimer.[33] By 1953 the church appears to have been demolished at that latter site, according to historic aerial photos on Google Earth. The old neighborhood names of Pleasant Bend and Lovely Canada are today virtually unknown in that area.

The church appears to have had a small cemetery, even though on a very small lot at its original site. The Texas death certificate of Julie Banks Robinson (ca. 1873–1918), daughter of Jordan and Rachel Banks, lists her place of burial as Lovely Canada. However, as mentioned earlier, most of the Banks family were buried at the Morse family cemetery in Pleasant Bend, now known as the Morse-Bragg cemetery. There is a likelihood that a number of other African American members of the Lovely Canada Baptist Church and neighborhood are buried at Morse-Bragg.

Reconstruction at Piney Point

Reconstruction at Piney Point was a time of great transformation. Besides the large influx of African American families already described, the area grew from the large farm of Harriet George to a small village, complete with a number of shops that appear to have been spread out along the two strands of the old San Felipe road now present south of the George home (Figure 9.2). The shopkeepers at the time of the 1870 census included German wagon makers William Schmidt and his son Emil, German carpenter William Heise, a French butcher named Charles Louis, a New York State shoemaker named William Bohle, and a wood merchant from Germany named William Guy. There was also a saloon owned by G. W. Gregar from Pennsylvania and his English-born wife E. C., who had one child born in New York. Gregar's prosperous saloon business was valued at $5,000, which is double the value of Henry Morse's owner's portion of the nearby Morse sawmill property. Also living at the Gregars' saloon-home were three single white females ages sixteen to twenty-one, two of whom were from Louisiana and the third from Switzerland. From their last names they were apparently unrelated to each other or to the Gregars. Because they lived at the saloon it seems likely that they were employed there, either as barkeepers or dance hall girls. This was the only known saloon between Houston and San Felipe and was within easy horseback distance for local farmers, sawmill workers, and the cowboys and meatpackers of the nearby Butler, Coward, and Baker cattle yards and slaughterhouses to the east (Chapter 10).

At her farm in Piney Point, Harriet George—Buckman Canfield's widow, James Todd's widow,

Figure 9.14. "Cow-boys," an illustration for "Through Texas," which appeared in *Harper's New Monthly Magazine*, October, 1879.

and by 1860 separated from her third husband, Benjamin George—was in mourning for the loss of her two sons, William and John DeWitt Canfield, both of whom had died in the extended military operations of the Vicksburg campaign. Her daughter Hannah, who by the late 1860s was also living at Piney Point, was also in shock, having lost two children to disease in 1863, and her husband, William A. Morse, to cholera in July 1866. As a result of all these deaths, by the time of the 1870 census the residents at the old Canfield-George farm consisted only of Harriet, Hannah, and Hannah's remaining children Charles Canfield Morse (1855–1905) and Mary Ella Morse (1857–1889). Hannah's other son Willie B. Morse (b. 1855) had left home by 1870.

After her husband William Morse's death, Hannah Canfield Morse married J. T. Hurtt in 1867. But that marriage was short-lived, as he appears to have died soon after the wedding. They had no children. At the age of forty-one in 1874, she married a third time, to Abram Frisby Silliman (1825–1891)[35] The son of Mary Frisby Silliman, Abram had grown up at nearby Wheaton's Ford. Hannah was his fourth wife, the others all having passed away. Hannah and Abram (Figure 9.15) each had two brothers killed in the war. By the 1880 census they were living in San Felipe with five children from his previous marriages, ranging in age from seven to twenty-two years, as well as Hannah's twenty-three-year-old daughter Ella.[36] Harriet sold part of the old Taylor Reserve property at Piney Point to Hannah and Abram in 1884.[37]

Harriet's other daughter, Mary Elizabeth George (born Mary Elizabeth Todd in 1845, but adopted by Benjamin George after Todd's death), married Ben Smalley in 1867, and Harriet deeded them a 200-acre farm just to the east of the Canfield/George Piney Point farm, which became known as the "Smalley Place"; they had two children.[38]

Figure 9.15. Hannah Putnam (Canfield) Morse and her new husband Abram Frisbee Silliman at their wedding in 1874. Courtesy of the late Mrs. Arch B. Marshall.

Another resident listed in the 1870 census, George Edward Morse (1853–1901), had been adopted during the Civil War by Harriet George. He was the son of Rev. John Kell Morse (1808–1863) and Caroline A. Jones Morse (1820–1864), who owned a 300-acre farm along modern day Bering Drive a mile or two to the east of Piney Point, adjacent to Agur T. Morse's plantation. John was Agur's brother.[39] Both John and Caroline Morse died during the Civil War years, of consumption. George, who had been orphaned at the age of ten by these deaths, was initially adopted by Mr. and Mrs. Theodore Bering, German immigrants living in Houston. George's sister Eugenia Morse (1843–1866) had married Theodore's brother Louis Bering in 1861. Louis was the executor of Caroline Morse's estate, so he held some sway on what happened to orphaned young George.[40] Louis and Eugenia purchased the old John Kell Morse farm from Caroline's estate, but Eugenia died of cholera in 1866, and Louis soon sold the farm. George, by then living in Houston with the Theodore Berings, was bereft of close relatives and no doubt homesick. He went to live with Harriet and Hannah in Piney Point (Hannah was the widow of his first cousin, William Morse). Harriet George effectively adopted George, eventually writing him into her will as one of her own children. All these people—Harriet, Hannah, and George—were heartsick from multiple tragic family events during the war and its immediate aftermath.

Like many other large landholders of the time, Harriet George began to sell portions of the old farm, since there were no longer either family menfolk or slaves to work it. She retained the core area with the family home, however. By the time of the 1880 census Harriet was living at Piney Point with her grandson Charles Morse only, but with extended family all around her.

Reconstruction in the Pleasant Bend Community

Grace Morse and the war's aftermath at Pleasant Bend Plantation. The wealthiest of the Anglo families south of the bayou before the war was the Morse family, but times had changed, and the events that immediately transpired mirrored the stories of many former plantation owners across the South. The Agur T. Morse family had been all in for the Confederacy, with Agur heading the local home guard and four sons in Confederate military service. It fell to Grace Morse, still in mourning for her husband Agur's death in April 1865, to deliver the news of their freedom to the former slaves at Pleasant Bend Plantation. This ended a two-hundred-year period in which the Morse family had operated plan-

Inventory and appraisement of the community property belonging to the estate of A.T. Morse, deceased, and Grace Morse, his surviving wife

January 30, 1866; Sterling Fisher, Clerk

Lands in Harris County

1176 acres Charles Sage Abst 493	$2800.00
910 acres, Wm White Abst 573	$2250.00
150 acres, Wm White Abstract 573	$450.00
320 acres, William Lewis Abstract	$750.00
2000 acres, N.C. Reynolds	$4000.00
640 acres, H.T.R.R. Company	$640.00
640 acres, H.T.R.R. Company	$640.00
640 acres, H.T.R.R. Company	$640.00
640 acres, H.T.R.R. Company	$640.00

Out of county lands

640 Acres, Hunt County	$640.00
320 Acres, Marcaro (sic) County	$320.00
640 acres, McLelland County	$640.00

Household goods

2 sofa and lounge	$30.00
Side board	$25.00
5 bedsteads	$20.00
1 clock	$10.00
1 pair balances	$5.00
1 gun and mop	$7.00
2 gin stands	$300.00
5 mattresses, 3 feather beds	$125.00
Bowls	$5.00
3 wash stands	$9.00

Farm inventory

Livestock

One hundred head of cattle	$400.00
60 hogs	$100.00
4 yoke oxen	$80.00
2 horses	$40.00
7 mules	$280.00

Agricultural produce

500 lbs tobacco	$150.00
60,000 pounds hay	$130.00
20 bushels potatoes	$12.00

Farm equipment

3 old wagons	$120.00
1 cart and harness	$40.00
Old buggy	$20.00
4 sets mule harnesses	$20.00
grist mill and gearing	$50.00
2 cast pots	$23.00
5 cast mills	$25.00
sugar mill	$4.00
1 cotton press	$200.00
old iron and steel tools	$60.00
14 ploughs	$75.00
2 cross saws	$4.00
hay machine and rack	$100.00
6 pitchforks	$6.00

Other

The interest in a drug store in the City of Houston owned jointly with J.B. Morse, undivided and unascertained.

Totals (except drug store)

Land
$14,410.00

Farm implements and produce $2,251.00

Household items
$224.00

Reference:

Harris County, Minutes January Term 1866, Book E, p. 296. Estate, page 447-449.

Figure 9.16. Grace Morse's silver tea strainer, all that is left of the Agur Morse family's silver. It is monogrammed "ATM." Courtesy of John Kell Morse descendant Kathleen Riffe.

tations with slave labor, from the early days of the New Haven Colony in Connecticut to South Carolina, Mississippi, and Harris County, Texas. Grace was also left to deal with the grim tally of the war's aftermath for the family. First and foremost, she had lost the family patriarch, Agur. Her son Henry was maimed at a battle in Virginia, late in the war. Her son-in-law Lovett Taft was dead, and her son William would be dead within a year.[41] Agur's brother Rev. John Kell Morse and his wife Caroline were both dead; their daughter Eugenia would soon die too. Besides land, the portion of the family's wealth that had not been invested in now-freed slaves was in worthless Confederate notes. Loss of the slaves left the economic base of their plantation in ruins, as there was no one to work the crops. Still worse, cotton prices fell precipitously in 1866, making it difficult to try to recover.[42]

Grace applied to become the executor of her husband's estate, which was not automatic for a woman in those days. The situation of the Agur Morse family is made clear by examining the inventory of that estate, taken on January 30, 1866 (see box). Several items are worth noting. Most striking is how limited their household possessions are, for such large landowners. It is clear from Celia Morse's diary that Agur and his wife lived quite modestly. Remarkably absent is any silver service, in contrast to the long list of such items in the inventory of Buckman Canfield's estate in 1844 (Chapter 5). The family silver had likely been donated to the Confederate war effort; such donations were considered a patriotic duty during the long war. A single small piece of Morse silver remains today (Figure 9.16), a tea strainer with the monogram ATM, passed down to grand-niece Annie Maie Morse Worrall. There is no cash mentioned in the estate inventory. Their money had likely been kept in Confederate notes, which were now no longer legal tender, so their cash reserves had been wiped out. The family's largest prewar means of wealth production, their slaves, emancipated only months earlier, are not listed in his inventory.

The crops raised at Pleasant Bend Plantation can be surmised from the inventory, and included cotton and corn with (probably) smaller amounts of sugar, tobacco, and potatoes. Large amounts of hay were harvested for the farm animals, which included mules, horses, oxen, cattle, and hogs. A sawmill is not mentioned (his sons Henry and George built and operated a sawmill on the property later, by 1869), but Agur had owned a grist mill, sugar mill, and cotton press.

Of most value were Agur Morse's listed landholdings of 8,716 acres: the plantation and other properties scattered in Harris and other Texas counties. The holdings were large (nearly 14 square miles), but their value was modest at an average of $1.65 per acre. Strapped for cash, Grace began to dismantle the plantation, selling some pieces of land and passing on other pieces to her children as required under the terms of Agur's will, which she administered.[43] Grace retained half of the Morse land, and her children or their estates received equal shares of the re-

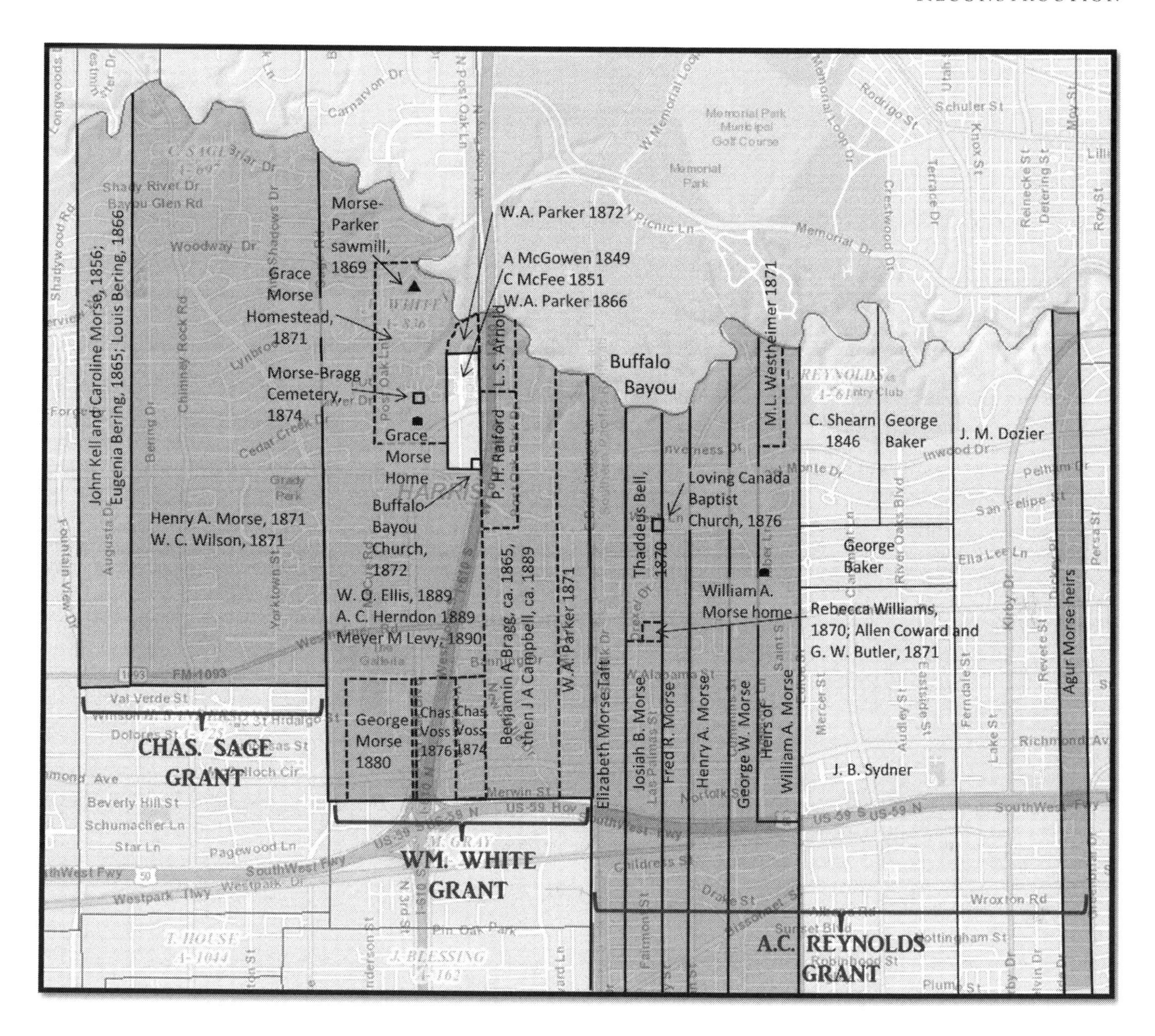

Figure 9.17. Map highlighting the property exchanges that resulted from the dismantling of the Pleasant Bend Plantation, post-1865. Modern base map courtesy of OpenStreetMap

mainder. By 1869 these heirs included William Morse's remarried widow, Hannah P. Hurt, Josiah B. Morse, George W. Morse, Henry Morse, Elizabeth Morse Taft, and Grace's youngest son Frederick Morse, still a minor.[44] Grace Morse applied for a partition of the remaining Agur Morse plantation land in 1869, and that partition was completed and surveyed by January 1870. She retained 750 acres of the western William White tract in this partition, 150 acres in the eastern White tract, plus a 200-acre homestead, also in the White tract.[45] The Morse children received six parcels in the Reynolds survey as their inheritance, which each nearly immediately began to sell off.[46]

Grace appears also to have retained the remaining 1,176 acres of the Sage survey (the other 300 acres had been sold to John Kell Morse back in the early 1850s). She sold this remainder to her son Henry in March 1871 for $1,000. Henry flipped that property the same day to W. C. Wilson for a $300 profit.[47] Grace then sold a tract of 150 acres in the eastern White survey to Wylie A. and Sophronia R. Parker, who had become neighbors earlier in 1866 by buying the McGowen-McFee 50-acre plot next door to the Morses.[48] She began selling off other remaining parts of the White tract, selling 43 and then 50 acres to Charles Voss in 1874 and 1876.[49] In 1879–1880 her son George W. Morse swapped his land in the Reynolds survey for a 100-acre tract in the William White third of a league, closer to his mother's house.[50]

Figure 9.17 shows the distribution of the various Morse parcels (shaded with solid boundaries), plus a few of the ensuing sales to others (dashed lines). These transaction mirror those of many other large Texas landholdings of that era, as the old plantations were broken up into small farms. The Morse deeds of sale contain some interesting items of local interest. Two of Grace Morse's sales in the White grant, to Charles Voss in 1876 and George Morse in 1880, leave out a "farm lane" in between the parcels that was part of the preexisting plantation. That farm lane is today the location of Houston's elegant Post Oak Boulevard, which got its start in antebellum days as a north-south farm lane emanating from the Agur T. Morse plantation home. The north side of those two tracts faced the right-of-way of the Texas Western Railroad, built in 1875 (see Chapter 11). Josiah sold 285 acres of his inheritance to Thaddeus C. Bell (1822-1871), an Old 300 settler from Columbia, Texas, who had been superintendent of Texas prisons after the war (more on him later). Bell sold 50 acres of his tract to Rebecca Williams, who sold it on to cattlemen and local residents Allen Coward and George Butler. Butler was in the business of buying area cattle and taking them up the Chisholm Trail in the years immediately after the Civil War, and he and a German butcher named Charles Schiebler operated a slaughterhouse on this tract for animals unfit for the rigors of the Chisholm Trail (discussed more fully in Chapter 10). The tract faced Westheimer Road, this part of which must have been another farm lane at the time. Almost all this land was still unfenced open range during Reconstruction and thus ideal for that cattle enterprise.

Activities of the Morse family. William A. Morse, Grace's eldest son, was living with his wife Hannah Canfield and five children on the eastern part of the old plantation land at the end of the war (Figure 9.17). These children included Charles Canfield Morse (1855–1905), Willie B. Morse (b. 1855), and Mary Ella Morse (1857–1889). A son, Edwin George Morse (1858–1863), and a daughter, Hattie Louisa (1860–1863) died during the war. William Morse died in 1866 of cholera and was buried next to his father and two children at the Morse family cemetery. His widow, Hannah, then went back to Piney Point with her three remaining children to live with her mother, Harriet George.

Meanwhile, Grace's son Josiah kept the family drugstore operating, and no doubt she received some portion of its income. Initially Josiah entertained the idea of selling it, and ran an advertisement to that effect in the Galveston News of December 3, 1865, but he eventually found a way to keep it going. In later years Josiah was known affectionately as "Professor Morse" due to his pharmacy experience. He died in 1889 after being run over by a horse-drawn streetcar in Houston.[51]

Grace Morse and her youngest son Frederick (1855–1874) moved in with her daughter Elizabeth shortly after Agur's death at the end of the war, immediately sensing that plantation life in the country was not to be her future. Elizabeth had married Richard A. Grant in 1870, following the death of her first husband Lovett Taft during the war; the Grants lived in Houston. Freddie died as a teenager in 1874. In 1887 Grace Morse sold one of the last remaining large parcels of the old plantation, which included her homestead and the Morse plantation house, to her daughter Elizabeth Grant. This plot of some 750 acres consisted of all of the third of a League of the William White survey that had not already been conveyed to others. In return, Elizabeth was required to "pay over to me [Grace] monthly the sum of Fifteen dollars and shall provide me at her home with lodging and board as a member of her family free of cost and charge."[52]

Elizabeth and her husband had a country home built near the old plantation house, on what was then San Felipe Street, just west of present day Loop 610. The Grants eventually moved to San Antonio, where both Grace and Elizabeth ended their days. In later years their former country home was reportedly moved a few blocks and used as the restaurant Ma Maison; both the house and the restaurant are now gone. Elizabeth died in San Antonio in 1920.[53]

The deceased Lovett Taft's brother Joseph S. Taft, early Houston bookseller and an ardent Unionist throughout the war, had left Texas for the North during the conflict, and his son Joseph B. Taft died in the service of the Union Army in 1863. Returning to Houston soon after the end of hostilities in 1865, Joseph S. Taft became postmaster during Reconstruction.[54] The *Houston Tri-Weekly Telegraph* paid him grudging respect:

> *We are glad to see the appointment of Mr. Taft as Postmaster of this city. Mr. Taft has, as all our citizens well know, been a consistent Unionist during the whole war. We recognize and acquiesce cheerfully in the necessity that men of this stamp should hold all Federal offices when honest men can be found for the purpose. There is no man in Houston we would rather see in the position than him. While we have waged all opposition in our power to his views, the logic of events has destroyed the ground of opposition. We always believed him honest, and respected his persistency.*[55]

The postwar city may have seemed lonely and perhaps even alien to Joseph Taft without his son and without his brother Lovett. Federal census data show that he was living in St. Louis by 1870 and that by 1880 he moved to Waco, Texas. Later still he moved to Seattle, Washington, where he died in 1896.[56]

The Morse-Parker sawmill. The largest single employer in the rural upper Buffalo Bayou neighborhood during the Reconstruction years was the Morse-Parker sawmill, which operated on a retained piece of Pleasant Bend plantation land north of the old Agur T. Morse home. After receiving their paroles at the end of the war, Henry and George Morse returned home and started up this sawmill with partner Wylie A. Parker (b. ca. 1847). Parker had been born in Alabama of an English-born father and an Alabama-born mother and was living with his parents in Houston during the 1860 census. By the 1870 census he was living near Henry Morse's home and near the sawmill, with his wife S. E. Parker, their two young children, and boarder John McFee, son of Morse neighbor James McFee. Henry and George Morse had likely learned the sawyer trade by working with their older brother, William Morse, at his sawmill in the Reinermann league in the late 1850s (Chapter 7).

In 1869 the partners bought the engine and machinery of a sawmill that had formerly been at James McLeod's plantation. Wylie A. Parker made his payment in sawn lumber.[57] By at least 1869 the trio had the sawmill in operation, and they are listed in the 1870 federal census as co-owners. It is thought to have been located where a northeast-trending spring-fed stream spilled into Buffalo Bayou (Figures 9.2 and 9.18). A dam was built below the spring, making a millpond. The spring assured a fairly constant supply of water, and the millpond kept logs wet while they waited for cutting. It is possible that the millpond was built in the plantation era, to power Agur Morse's grist mill and cotton press. The partners installed a 15-horsepower McGovern stationary steam engine to power a circular saw. The Schedule of Industry of the 1870 federal census states that they directly employed 10 mill workers, who the previous year had sawn 4,320 pine logs, turning that $864 worth of raw material into 432,000 board feet of lumber intended for building purposes, worth a total of $6,480. It and the Bering sawmill, located in central Houston, were the two largest sawmills in operation in Harris County at the time, each having produced 432,000 board feet of lumber in 1870. There were another eight sawmills in operation in Harris County in 1870, with production ranging from 50,000 board feet up to nearly that of the Morse-Parker and Bering mills.[58]

The pine logs probably came mostly from the part of the upland pine forest that occupied the up-

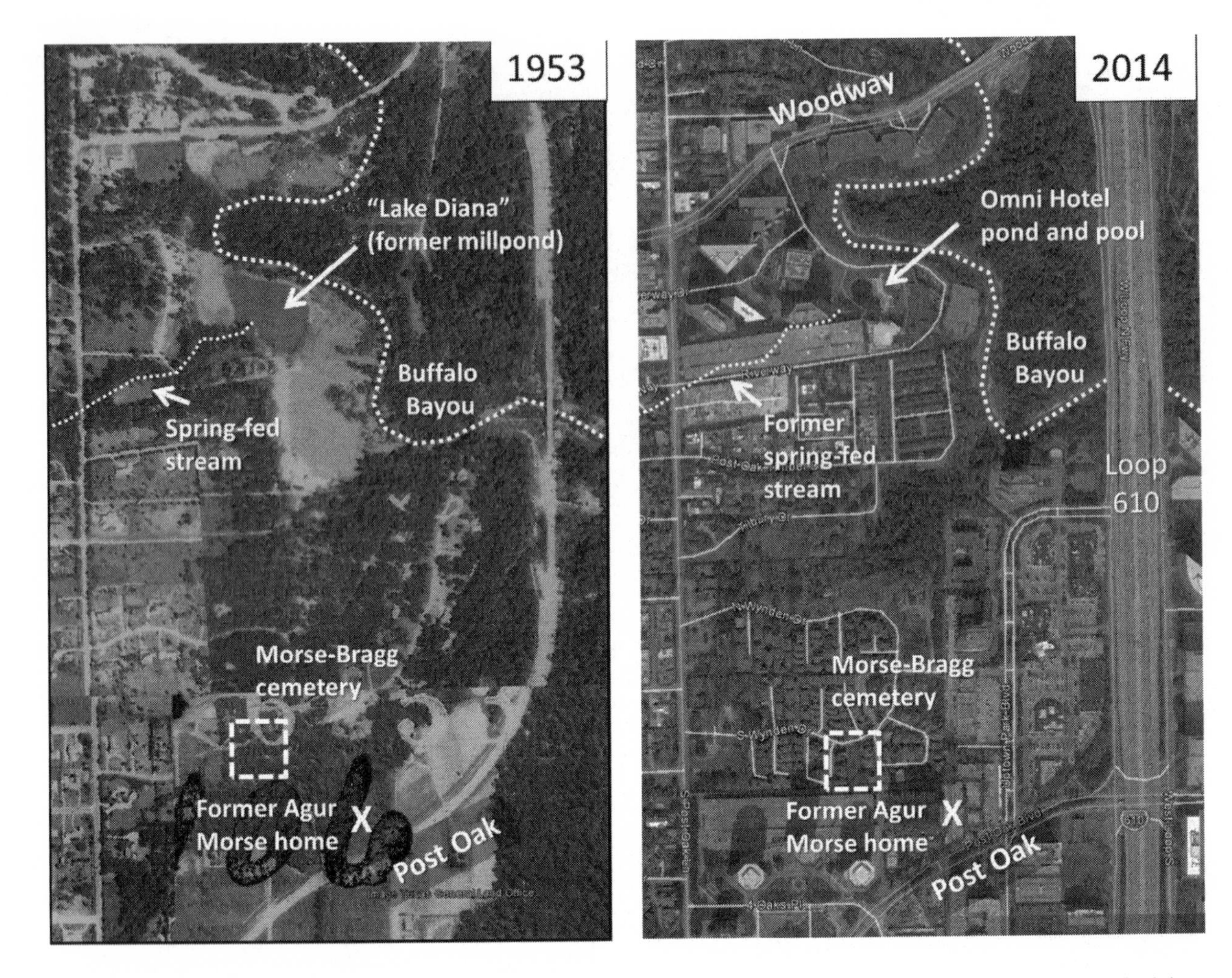

Figure 9.18. Aerial photographs showing the site of the former millpond at the Morse sawmill, in 1953 (left) and 2014 (right). Photos courtesy of the Texas Resources Information System, Austin.

lands to the north of Buffalo Bayou, or from within the riparian forest along the bayou. Timber land would have been locally purchased or leased. William Morse had purchased timber properties to the north of the bayou in the Taylor league in 1860, north of the old Canfield place, but that timber may have already been sawn at the William A. Morse & Company mill before the war (Chapter 7).

A rural community grew up near the Morse-Parker sawmill, and the federal census of 1870 gives us a clear view of its extent (see box). The mill community numbered a total of 126 persons, including the men employed at the mill plus their families. The sawmill itself was operated by six sawmill workers and the three owners, and its machinery was provided wood by a small army of fourteen woodchoppers, nine teamsters with ox wagons, and three timber merchants; most of these were probably independent subcontractors not directly employed by the mill. All lived in the immediate vicinity of the mill.

The mill's employees were a diverse mix of ex-Confederate soldiers and other Anglo settlers, German immigrants, and African Americans. All but

Employees and Contractors at the Morse-Parker Sawmill, Harris County, as listed in the 1870 federal census

Terms are as used in the census

Sawmill part owners

Henry A Morse, 29, white, Mississippi, with wife and 3 children
George W. Morse, 25, white, Mississippi, no family, lived with Henry
W A Parker, 30, white, Mississippi, with wife and 2 children

Sawmill Laborers

Jordan Banks, 23, black, Virginia, with wife and 3 children
Jefferson Brown, 25, black, South Carolina, with wife and 2 children
John McFee, 20, white, Mississippi, no family. Son of James McFee
D Meyers, 28 white, Mississippi, with wife and 5 children
Lewis Silas, 23, black, Alabama, with wife
Ephesius Greene, 34, black, Mississippi, with wife and two children

Wood merchants and dealers

Fritz Engel, 35, white, Germany (Prussia), with wife and 2 children
E H Harrington, 35, white, Texas
William Guy, 41, white, Germany, with wife, 1 child, and parent

Teamsters

Taylor Meyers, 24, black, Mississippi, no family, probable relative of Jury Meyers
James Collins, 40, 'mulatto,' Georgia with wife and 4 children
James Brown, 35, black, Alabama, with wife and 3 children
Stephen Roberts, 24, black, Texas
Edward Axle, 22, black, Virginia, with wife (?) and 1 child
Sam Axle, 22, black, Virginia, with wife or sister
Leonas Thomas, 19, black, Texas, no family
Jerry Maxwell, 24, 'mulatto', Mississippi, with wife and 1 child
John Edmond, 24, black, Alabama, single

Woodchoppers

Shade Thomas, 24, black, Georgia, with wife and 1 child
Joseph Hodon, 22, black, Louisiana, no family
Thomas Bryan, 24, black, Georgia, no family
William Edwards, 22, black, Georgia, no family
Harry Shields, 45, black, Virginia, with wife and 2 children
Peter Thomas, 35, black, Georgia, with wife and 1 child
Edmond Graye, 50, black, Georgia with wife
Abraham Powell, 24, black, Mississippi, with wife and 1 child
Henry Matthew, 49, black, Louisiana with wife and 1 child
Sandy Cornstone, 55, black, Louisiana, with wife
Alford Hardin, 50, black, Mississippi, with wife and 2 children
Benjamin Thomas, 34, black, Alabama, with wife and 2 children
Dempsey Jones, 40, black, Tennessee, with wife and 3 children
Samuel Jourdan, 38, black, South Carolina, with wife and 2 children

Wagon makers

William Schmidt, 47, white, Germany with wife and 5 children
Enid Schmidt, 17, white, Texas, son of William Schmidt

Carpenters

Jury Meyers, 80, black, Georgia, probable relative (father?) of David Meyers
William Hesse, 54, white, Germany, with wife

House Servants to Morse family

Andrew Wheaton, 30, black, Alabama, no family

two of the mill laborers were African Americans, as were all of the woodchoppers, teamsters, and one house servant. Two of them, Jordan Banks and Andrew Wheaton, can be tied by records to the Morse family of Pleasant Bend during or immediately after the Civil War; the rest had likely migrated from Brazos River plantations. The wood merchants were all white; two were German and one was an Anglo-Texan. Two local wagon makers were German, as was the one white carpenter; a second carpenter was an eighty-year old African American.

Part owner Henry Morse and his family lived near the mill, and according to the census lived next door to African American Jordan Banks and his family. Henry lived in a new frame house built from lumber freshly cut at the mill. His wife Celia described in her diary her delight with the new home as well as her lack of satisfaction at living so far out in the country:

> *April 19, 1869. Well dear Journal it has been three years since I penned a line to you. This is a beautiful day, not a leaf stirring. We have moved down on the bayou in a sweet little frame house, all of Henry's work, and began life as it were. I am doing my own cooking and everything. I don't know how long I will continue to do it. . . . I have been [working] with my stove considerable today. The pipe all came down which was full of soot, and that was the cause of its not burning better. Andrew [Wheaton, a black house servant] and Joe have been working on the fence for a cowpen and yard. We are living right in the woods but our home is a very pretty place. . . . I had a note from Ma last night. Her hand is troubling her very much. She wants to come out this week to have a picnic.*
>
> *June 19, 1869. Ma and Taith [?] went into town yesterday with Henry. I let [son] Julian go in with him, and kept [son] Lovett with me. Julian seemed perfectly delighted with his trip, [and] brought Lovett some candy. Henry brought me a barrel of flour, I find it very dark, yet it is sweet. Also some sugar and coffee. It is quite lonely now . . . the house seems lost. I expect it will rain as it looks very much like it. I would [like] to attend church today very much, and it is a great affliction living in the country. One cannot [make] public worship. . . . [I] read the bible and think of a better world than this.*

Her son Emmett George Morse, born in 1862 while Henry was away at war, and who had been sick so much of the time during the war, died in 1866. Those pages dealing with his death were missing from Celia's diary, and that death no doubt caused her much grief.

Henry Morse died of smallpox in 1876, and he was laid to rest near young Emmett at the Morse family cemetery.[59] His widow Celia finally got her wish to move downtown, living at 218 Louisiana, at the corner of Polk, by the 1880s with her four boys, Julian (1866–1919), Lovett (1867–1890), Edward (1870–1909) and Henry D. (1872–1938) as well as her nephew, Lovett Taft III. Her daughter Elizabeth Cecelia Morse (1874–1949) married L. D. Williams in 1894. Celia died in 1896 and is buried in the old Washington cemetery, now part of Glenwood Cemetery. Her son Henry D. Morse (1872–1938) became a Houston civic leader and realtor, and his son, Robert Emmett Morse (1897–1957), became speaker of the Texas House of Representatives in Austin during the 1930s, where he was instrumental in the passage of Harris County Flood Control District legislation in the aftermath of the devastating 1935 Houston flood.

By the 1880 census the sawmill had disappeared, probably because local timber resources were tapped out. The mill, woodchoppers, teamsters and wood merchants, the saloon at nearby Piney Point with its young ladies, the shoemaker and wagon makers were all gone, as if they were all part of a circus that had left town. With the advent of a more extensive railroad network in the 1880s there was a general migration of timbering operations from Buffalo Bayou to East Texas, which had seemingly limitless virgin stands of tall pines that needed only steam rail transport to make them economically viable for timbering. The old Morse sawmill site was reclaimed by the Buffalo Bayou forest and forgotten. Its millpond dam was repaired in the 1940s and was called Lake

Diana by the neighborhood children in the 1950s. Today the pond and swimming pool of the Omni Four Seasons Hotel, off Woodway Drive, are located where the millpond once was; the spring and its small stream have been buried by urban development (Figure 9.18).

George W. Morse lived alone near the mill until he married Annie M. Dowd in 1873; they had one child, Willie Morse (1877–1887), who died in childhood. Annie died in 1877, and George married Mary Eugenia (Cassaway) Anderson (1847–ca. 1905). George died in about 1885, and his widow became a dressmaker, living first at 150 Capital, then 1012 Rusk, and finally 509 Crawford, where she died about 1905.

The Morse-Bragg cemetery. After Grace Morse had parceled off various pieces of the plantation land to her children and some buyers, she turned her attention to the family graveyard, not wanting to see it lost in all the selling. In 1874 she set aside one acre of her homestead, leaving it to the relatives of the deceased Agur T. Morse, "including the family burial ground for the Morse family, and to be used exclusively for a burial ground for the Morse Family and their decedents and other neighbors of the surrounding neighborhood."[60] An additional adjoining third of acre was sold to neighbor Benjamin A. Bragg, "to be used only and exclusively as a burial ground for B. A.Bragg, his family and descendants."[61] The graveyard, which had been used from the 1850s by the Morse family and their neighbors, was located on a small rise north of a spring-fed creek, about 500 feet to the north of the Morse home, across the (now underground) creek (Figure 7.13).

The most complete historical research of burials at the site was done by J. K. Wagner & Company in 1993–1995.[62] Records came from the Harris County archives and other historical resources as well as a 1975 genealogical study by Marie Marshall of the Morse family.[63] Table 1 is based upon Wagner's work, with a few additions and deletions based upon sources recently found by the present author.

Research to date has identified thirty-four individuals buried in the Morse-Bragg cemetery from 1857 to 1928 (see box). Most are members of the Morse, McFee, Bragg, and Banks families that lived in the Pleasant Bend neighborhood. Five are African Americans, one of whom was formerly enslaved; one was a member of Stephen F. Austin's Old Three Hundred; and seven were Confederate veterans. There are undoubtedly others buried here for whom no definitive records have been found, especially among people who died in the mid-nineteenth century, when the area was very rural and death certificates did not yet exist.

Houston and parts of rural Harris County along Buffalo Bayou were dangerous places to live in the middle of the nineteenth century. Many of the early settlers lived along the edge of the bayou in the shade of the riparian forest trees, which left them especially vulnerable to mosquito-borne diseases. Yellow fever was a significant killer at the Pleasant Bend Plantation, as can be seen from the list of burials.[64] The risk of yellow fever was especially high after overflows of the bayou during flooding left behind breeding ponds for mosquitoes. At that time the connection between yellow fever and the mosquitoes that spread it had not yet been made, and window screens were not yet in use. There are historical records of Houston yellow fever epidemics in 1838–1839, 1845, 1847, 1853, 1855 (quarantine), 1856 and 1857 (sporadic), 1858 and 1859 (quarantine), 1863, 1867, 1871 (sporadic) and 1897.[65] Some of the burials in the Morse-Bragg cemetery relate to these epidemics, for example the death of Mary Ellen Rowley Morse in 1867.

Other killers were cholera and typhoid fever, spread by contaminated water. In the earliest days, settlers drank from Buffalo Bayou or the spring creeks that fed it; these surface sources were easily contaminated by livestock and humans. Many pioneer settlers began to dig open wells, usually ten to thirty feet in depth; these too were susceptible to contamination if livestock or humans lived close by. There were cholera epidemics in Houston in 1845–1846 and 1866 (when Houstonians endured a quarantine).[66] Eugenia Morse Bering and William A. Morse were felled by the cholera epidemic of 1866. Typhoid fever, another disease spread by contami-

Interments in the Morse-Bragg Cemetery

AGUR TOMLINSON MORSE FAMILY

Agur Tomlinson Morse (1801-1865). Pioneer settler from New Haven, Connecticut via South Carolina and Mississippi; his widow Grace Morse protected the family burial ground by deed in 1874. Died of typhoid fever.

William A. Morse (1831-1866). Son of Agur Morse; thought to have died from cholera. His wife, Hannah Putnam Canfield, married twice more.

Henry Augustus Morse (1840-1876). Son of Agur Morse; died of smallpox. His wife Celia Morse kept a Civil War diary of life on the Pleasant Bend Plantation.

Infant Morse (1861). Child of Henry and Celia Morse.

George W. Morse (1845-ca. 1885). Son of Agur Morse.

Anna M. Dowd Morse (ca. 1852-1877). First wife of George W. Morse

Willie D. Morse (after 1873-1887). Child of George W. Morse and Anna M. Dowd.

Mary E. Morse (ca. 1847-1898). Second wife of George W. Morse. After George's death, she became a dressmaker, living in Houston.

Frederick Morse (1855-1874). Son of Agur Morse. Never married.

Lovett A. Taft , Jr. (1828-1864). Native of Sheffield, Berkshire County, Massachusetts; died of typhoid fever. First husband of Agur Morse's only daughter, Elizabeth A. Morse Grant (1838-1920). His son Lovett A. Taft III (ca. 1861–1889) is buried in Glenwood Cemetery, in section C-1, Lot 122, in the same lot where his grandmother, Grace Morse, and uncle, Josiah B. Morse, are buried.

Mary Ellen Rowley Morse (ca. 1833–1867) Wife of Agur Morse's son Josiah B. Morse, who is buried at Glenwood Cemetery. Yellow fever.

Infant Morse (1863). Child of Mary Ellen Rowley and Josiah B. Morse.

Mollie E. Morse (1861-1864). Child of Mary Ellen Rowley and Josiah B. Morse.

Infant Morse (1867). Child of Mary Ellen Rowley and Josiah B. Morse. Possibly yellow fever.

Emma Frazer Bachelder (ca. 1852-1871). Niece of Grace Morse and wife of Edmund J. H. Bachelder (1840-1872). Edmund J. H. Bachelder (1840–1872), was buried at Glenwood Cemetary, section West Avenue, lot 260.

JOHN KELL MORSE FAMILY

Rev. John Kell Morse (1808-1863). Pioneer settler from New Haven, Connecticut, via South Carolina; Cause of death probably consumption. Brother of Agur T. Morse.

Caroline A. Jones Morse (1820-1864). Pioneer settler from South Carolina. Wife of Rev. John Kell Morse. Cause of death probably consumption.

Eugenia Morse Bering (1843-1866). Daughter of John and Caroline Morse; wife of Louis Bering. Cholera.

Louis Bering (1840-1891). Pioneer German settler; died of paralysis. Husband of Eugenia Morse Bering. He remarried twice after Eugenia's death.

JAMES McFEE FAMILY

James McFee (1814-1903). Pioneer settler of Pleasant Bend and Piney Point; born in Delaware of Scots-Irish parents; died in old age. See McFee family detail later in text.

Cassandra Hough McFee (1824-1890). Pioneer settler, Pleasant Bend and Piney Point; died of stroke. Wife of James McFee. Stroke.

John H McFee (1852-1888). Son of James McFee and Cassandra Hough; caught pneumonia and died after a hunting trip on Buffalo Bayou.

Joseph S. McFee (1853-1874). Son of James McFee and Cassandra Hough.

Hugh Cecil McFee (1855-1887). Son of James McFee and Cassandra Hough. Died of accidental gunshot in Piney Point.

Aaron Truitt Reeder (1915). Infant child of Cassie McFee Reeder, and great grandson of James McFee. Reportedly removed to Piney Point Cemetery in 1915.

JORDAN BANKS FAMILY

Rachel Davis Banks (ca. 1845-1919).* Wife of Jordan Banks, daughter of Spencer Davis of Louisiana, Rachel Banks was probably brought to Texas as a slave. Domestic servant and mother of fifteen (or perhaps nineteen) children. Died of pneumonia.

James Banks (ca. 1868-1927).* Son of Jordan Banks and Rachel Banks. Died of "apoplexy."

Sadie Banks Scott (ca. 1881-1927).* Daughter of Jordan Banks and Rachel Banks, and husband of Pleasant Scott. Died of "apoplexy."

Laura Banks Koontz (ca. 1872-1928).* Daughter of Jordan Banks and Rachel Banks. Died of cirrhosis of the liver.

BENJAMIN BRAGG FAMILY

Mary Bragg (1822-1873). Born in Vermont; wife of Benjamin A. Bragg.

Benjamin A. Bragg (1818-1886). Born in Vermont; husband of Mary Bragg. Co-founder of Morse-Bragg Cemetery, via purchase of 1/3 adjoining acre from Grace Morse.

OTHER NEIGHBORHOOD BURIALS

Thaddeus Constantine Bell (1822-1871). "Old 300" settler; reportedly the first male child born in Stephen F. Austin's colony. Superintendent of Texas prisons after the Civil War. Kidney cancer.

William H. Keeling (died 1862). Schoolteacher on Pleasant Bend Plantation; kept a diary of antebellum plantation life with the Morse family.

Patsy Thomas (ca. 1872-1910).* Listed amongst Morse-Bragg decedents in the above-mentioned 1929 lawsuit. African American, daughter of Sidney Sullivan and Celia Francis Sullivan, who lived next door to Jordan Banks at the time of the 1880 Federal census. Wife of teamster John Thomas.

* = African-American Burial

nated drink and food, was sporadically present and was the cause of death of Lovett Taft Jr. in 1864 and Agur Morse in 1865. With his position in the Home Guard, Agur was traveling and was especially vulnerable to such an ailment. Another killer was smallpox, which killed Civil War veteran Henry Morse in 1874, when the Houston newspapers mentioned that the disease was afflicting the city. There was another smallpox epidemic in Houston in 1890.[67]

Grace Morse, who dedicated the cemetery, died of malaria in 1890 and was buried at Glenwood Cemetery in Houston. By the time of her death she was living with her daughter Elizabeth Morse (Taft) Grant in Houston, and because the plantation land was virtually all sold by this time, Elizabeth had her buried in Houston in what was and still is a perpetual care cemetery. Elizabeth soon moved to San Antonio, and the old plantation cemetery began to slip into neglect. The burial of George W. Morse's second wife Mary E. Morse in 1898 was probably the last time the Morse family used the cemetery for a burial.

An 'Old 300' settler's grave. Of particular interest among the graves at this cemetery is that of Thaddeus Constantine Bell (1822-1871). He was born near old Washington, in Washington County, on October 4, 1822. He was reportedly the first male Anglo-Texan child born in Stephen F. Austin's colonies in Texas, and the second Anglo-Texan child born in the State (after Jane Long's daughter, born on Bolivar Island in December 1821).[68]

Thaddeus (Figure 9.19) was the third of eight children of Josiah Hughes Bell (1791-1838) and Mary Evaline McKenzie Bell (1799-1856), who had married in Kentucky in 1818. Josiah Bell brought his family and slaves with him to join Stephen Austin in 1821, and the family settled on New Year Creek, near old Washington. From 1822 to 1823, Josiah Bell was Austin's Alcalde at San Felipe, when Austin was in Mexico. Josiah and his family moved downriver on the Brazos in 1824 to what is now Brazoria County and established a plantation. Over the next few years Josiah Bell founded what became the towns of East Columbia and West Columbia, where he died in 1838.[69]

Figure 9.19. Thaddeus Constantine Bell (1822-1871), an Old 300 settler and the first male child born in Stephen F. Austin's colony. Photo courtesy of the Brazoria County Historical Museum.

In 1837, Josiah Bell took young Thaddeus and his siblings, Lucinda and James, to Bardstown, Kentucky for schooling. Upon returning in 1840 at age 18, Thaddeus took over his widowed mother's farms and business. He married Elizabeth Hodge Cayce in 1847, and they had six children during the period 1848-1864. Thaddeus had the life of a successful cotton planter until the Civil War intervened. According to his son-in-law, Andrew Phelps McCormick (1832-1916), Bell:

> *...continued to devote himself to the business of a cotton planter until the close of the Civil War brought even to Texas [June 19, 1865] the actual emancipation of the slaves. He voted against the ordinance of secession. He believed that it was impolitic to the degree of madness and unpatriotic in the highest degree. He, however, submitted to the powers that be and rendered such service as was required of him by the Confederate and State authorities.*[70]

Thaddeus Bell eventually enrolled as a matter of duty, and became a Private, Company C, Brazoria County, Volunteer Cavalry, 16th Brigade, Texas State Troops.

Thaddeus Bell's wife died in 1864, during the War. In 1867, he moved with some of his children to Huntsville, where he was superintendant of the state penitentiary. While there, he married Cornelia McKinney (1844-c1900). After his term finished, he moved to Harris County, to the neighborhood around the Morse sawmill along Buffalo Bayou, where he appears in the 1870 census with his new wife and a daughter by his previous marriage, Sophronia Lucinda Bell (1855-1925). They joined the First Presbyterian Church in Houston – the same church that Grace Morse and her daughter Elizabeth Taft had also joined in 1868, following the deaths of their respective husbands during the War.[71] Thaddeus purchased land in the Reynolds survey (Figure 9.17) and began a farm. That farm was not to last, as he died of kidney cancer on May 22, 1871, not long after the birth of his last son, John Randolph Bell (1871-1945).[72] First Presbyterian Church records show that Thaddeus was "interred near the Morse place." Those records also show that Grace Morse's niece, Emma Frazier Bachelder, was also interred at the Morse cemetery, the same year.[73]

There is a granite 1936 Texas Centennial marker[74] dedicated to Thaddeus Bell and his first wife Elizabeth Hodges Cayce Bell at the old Columbia Cemetery in Brazoria County, where Elizabeth and her father-in-law, Josiah Hughes Bell, are buried. There appears to be no documentation showing that he was buried there, however,[75] and abundant documentation and biographical information that places him in Harris County at the end of his life, and interred in the Morse-Bragg Cemetery.

The Parkers and the Buffalo Bayou Church. Although Rev. John Kell Morse held Methodist church services on the Pleasant Bend plantation in antebellum times, the first Anglo-American church building south of the bayou in then rural west Houston was erected in 1871, on land donated by Wylie and Sophronia Parker. In 1866 Cassandra McFee, wife of James McFee, sold their fifty-acre farm—formerly the Thomas McGowen farm (Figure 9.17) and adjacent to Grace Morse's homestead—to Sophronia Cayce Parker (1837–1924), the wife of Wylie A. Parker.[76] Wylie, as we have seen, sold the machinery to Henry and George Morse for their sawmill. The McFee family then moved to Sugar Land, where they resided until moving back to the area in the 1880s, to Piney Point. The Parkers moved onto the farm and by the 1870 census had four children, all born in Texas: Hannah, 10 years of age; Anna, 5; Robert, 3; and William, an infant. In 1872 Grace Morse sold Wylie Parker an additional eleven and one third acres to the north of their property, so that their farm reached all the way to Buffalo Bayou.[77]

This rural area had lacked regular church services ever since the death of Rev. John Kell Morse in 1863. Celia Morse remarked several times in her diary about the lack of a church and how either Grace or she but not both could go to church service on any given Sunday. By 1871 Grace Morse had moved into Houston with her daughter Elizabeth, and those two and Emma Bachelder had joined Houston's First Presbyterian Church. The remaining Pleasant Bend community, however, including those working at the Morse sawmill, still had no church, and Houston remained a long six-mile wagon ride away.

On September 13, 1872, Wylie and Sophronia Parker, along with Grace Morse, donated three quarters of an acre from the southeast corner of the Parker property for the building of a church to be named the Buffalo Bayou Church (Figure 9.17). The trustees included Grace Morse's neighbor Benjamin A. Bragg (who was to purchase a small piece of land at the Morse cemetery two years later), Henry Morse, and James W. Dozier, a neighbor living nearby on the Reynolds tract.[78] That church faced south to the "new" San Felipe Road, oriented east-west along the southern edge of the McFee farm, transecting the former Morse plantation—effectively replacing a part of the original San Felipe Trail of 1830, which was then locally abandoned. That segment of the "new" San Felipe Road of the 1870s is now called Hallmark Drive.

The new church held a fundraiser for the church building in 1872, at Dolly Varden Point, a well-known local picnic ground of that time located on a green, shaded peninsula on the south bank of Buffalo Bayou (see Figure 7.13; the modern site is just east of West Loop 610, and just east of the parking lot of the Gulf Coast Veterinary Specialists Hospital). On September 12, 1872, they raised sixty dollars at a barbecue for the "little church near Dolly Varden Point," with the next picnic planned for October 17.[79] The name Dolly Varden refers to the elaborate women's fashion in Britain and the United States of the period from 1869 to 1875, which looked back to fashions of the 1770s and 1780s; Dolly Varden was a character in Charles Dickens's novel Barnaby Ridge, set in 1780. A Dolly Varden hat was a straw hat bedecked with flowers and ribbons.[80]

The church used nearby Buffalo Bayou at that picnic ground to baptize their members during revivals, as is clear from the autobiography of Cassie McFee Reeder (granddaughter of James McFee of the Pleasant Bend community). In 1895 the McFee family traveled to Baptist revivals at Clodine, Richmond, and Missouri City and to a baptism and picnic at the Buffalo Bayou Church:

> *A [Baptist] preacher named Brother J. W. Anderson . . . preached at Hodge Bend school house and Clodine, a meeting that lasted about three weeks. Everyone went. Summertime, Aunt Sallie, Aunt Daisy, and Uncle Pat were Baptized on Sunday in the Buffalo Bayou. . . . I remember when we came across the prairie that there were buggies coming from every direction. [There was a] church dinner on [the] ground, and Baptizing [in the] afternoon. Charlie Voss was baptized, then we went home and to church every night to the meeting at Clodine, and*

the next Sunday we all went back to Buffalo Bayou church under the trees, dinner on the ground, and Baptizing, Aunt Dora, Uncle George, and others were baptized.

This same summer we went to Missouri City to a Baptist Children's Day. We took our dinner in a box in the back of the buggy, but the Pastor wanted us to eat dinner with them and we did. We were the only family from our neighborhood. . . .

That same summer several families would take their dinner and go to Richmond to church under a brush arbor in the middle of town. I remember they sang "When the Roll Is Called Up Yonder I'll Be There," first time I ever heard it. We all ate our dinner under the big trees by the Brazos River, just south of the big bridge, this side of the river.[81]

Aerial photographs from 1953 show that the Buffalo Bayou Church was still standing in the 1950s, but it was torn down about the time adjacent West Loop 610 was built in the 1960s. A newly constructed condominium tower is on that site today, but a few of the old oak trees remain on its perimeter. A part of the picnic and baptizing ground at nearby Dolly Varden point is still undeveloped, though obscured by buildings and parking lots in all directions.

Reconstruction at the Reinermann League

The Eureka Cotton Mills. The citizens of Houston and Texas experimented with many types of new industries during the Reconstruction years, as they worked to resurrect the local economy. The site of the sawmill of the former William A. Morse & Company, disbanded at the start of the Civil War (Chapter 7), was used for the location of a cotton mill. This was something quite new, as most cotton mills had been located in northern states before the war. The mill was built in 1866 at the old sawmill site along the Houston and Texas Central Railroad by the Eureka Manufacturing Company, owned by Judge Sylvester S. Munger (1820–1901). He was a Connecticut native who had moved to San Felipe, Texas, in 1838, fought in the Mexican War, and become a judge in Fayette County in 1855. During the Civil War, with cloth for soldiers' clothes in short supply, he was one of a group of men who imported cotton milling machinery from Mexico and set up a cotton manufacturing plant in Bastrop, Texas, which operated until the close of the war.[82] There must have been some encouragement from that enterprise, because he moved to Houston after the Civil War to establish his Eureka Mills factory, one of several cotton mills established in the state at that time by enterprising individuals looking to profit from the proximity of Texas cotton to railroads.

Munger purchased the mill property from David H. Paige, one of the partners of the former William A. Morse sawmill company.[83] The mill was located on the northwest corner of the modern intersection of Old Katy Road and Hempstead Highway (Figure 9.2); it was immediately adjacent to the Houston and Texas Central Railroad track. The *Houston Tri-Weekly Telegraph* of May 2, 1866, tells the story of the mill's construction:

We had the pleasure of a most delightful drive the other evening with Judge Munger, out to the grounds where he is establishing his cotton and woolen factory, to be known by the name of "Eureka Mills." They are about four miles and a half from Houston, immediately on the Central Railroad, on a beautiful site most aptly chosen. The work is being pushed forward with rapidity, and will be completed by the first of September or earlier. At the time the factory is ready to begin operations, some fifty thousand dollars will have been invested in the enterprise.

The [steam] engine is already in position. It is a most powerful one, from the most approved foundries in the country, capable of driving fully fifty looms with over two thousand spindles. The work of manufacturing will be begun with forty looms and 1,584 spindles. The construction of a house for the machinery is progressing. It is two hundred and twenty-five feet in length and forty-

five in width, besides which there will be an extensive engine-house adjoining. A number of neat little cottages will be erected near the factory, to be used as dwellings for the operatives and their families.

Judge Munger intends to devote his personal care and supervision to the mills. He has already completed a handsome residence on the grounds, in which he himself will abide. He has secured, however, the services of a skillful superintendent, of many years experience in one of the best factories of the North. We left the grounds thoroughly convinced that the enterprise so properly undertaken and vigorously pushed forward, will be not only a complete success, but a credit to the State and a thing of incalculable advantage. It is through men of the public spirit and enterprising character of Judge Munger that the South is to be again enriched, and secure more than its former power in the Union.[84]

Glowing prose notwithstanding, it was a typical southern cotton mill of its day. There were a handful of experienced men in the managerial and mechanical positions, and a large number of children, teenagers and young adults doing the bulk of the milling, spinning and weaving. The mill grew to a full complement of forty-five staff by 1870, when its employees were listed by a federal census taker (see box). The mill workers were mostly from Texas, Louisiana and other parts of the South and ranged as young as ten years of age. All but one, a fireman, were white. The superintendent, Mr. Taylor, had been brought in from Munger's previous Civil War–era mill at New Braunfels.[85]

Production at the mill included cotton and wool "sheetings, shirtings, drillings, denims, cottonades, stripes, ticking, apron checks, ginghams, linseys, kerseys, Kentucky jeans, and all of the staple cotton and woolen goods required in this market." The company also continued to operate the old Morse sawmill that had existed at the site prior to 1866.[86] By 1867 it was reported:

The Eureka Mills in this city are now turning out 1200 yards a day of splendid 7¼ oz. osnaburgs,

Eureka Cotton Mill Staff,
as listed in the 1870 U.S. Federal Census

Superintendent of Cotton Mill: M. Taylor, 61, Scotland
Bookkeeper: J.P. Cramer, 54, Prussia
Weaving Boss: John Rosenbusch, 35, Bavaria

Weavers:
Nancy Basinger, 23, Tennessee
Josephine Basinger, 21, Tennessee
Albertine Basinger, 19, Tennessee
Jennie Basinger, 17, Tennessee
Charlotta Basinger, 14, Tennessee
Spinner:
Richard Riggs, 11, England
Cotton Mill Workers:
Adolph Schneider, 16, Prussia
Minford Davis, 24, Mississippi
Ellen Coldiver, 43, Tennessee
Elizabeth Williams, 16, Tennessee
Susan Williams, 14, Texas
Mary Dunn, 13, Texas
Mary McPeters, 19, Texas
Samuel McPeters, 16, Texas
Martha McPeters, 14, Texas
William McPeters, 12, Texas
Benjamin Blackman, 18, Louisiana
Louisa Blackman, 24, Louisiana
Joseph Blackman, 18, Louisiana
Benjamin Blackman, 16, Louisiana
Peter Blackman, 12, Texas
Jacob Blackman, 10, Texas
Kenney Blackman, 14, Louisiana
Samuel Ellis, 25, Texas
Martha Ryan, 17, Texas
Pricilla Ryan, 15, Texas
James Ryan 14, Texas
Jacob Arndt, 56, Pennsylvania
Mary Bevins, 24, Texas
John Scappard, 24, Texas
A.T. Belk, 21, Alabama
Thomas Gammon, 25, England
Harriett Dickey, 55, Mississippi
Jane Dickey, 16, Mississippi

Figure 9.20. Spooling yarn at the Dallas Cotton Mills, Dallas, Texas, 1905. Courtesy of the Boston Public Library.

which they are selling by the bale at 17 cents, gold. Their domestics, 34-inch, of fine quality, almost up to State A, they sell at 16½ c, currency. They have demonstrated that they can, on all heavy goods, make a good profit and undersell the New England factories. Labor is about the same as in New England, living is cheaper, and cotton costs six cents less per pound here than there, to say nothing of the cost of getting the goods back. It will be wonderful if a little more demonstration of this sort does not turn us into a manufacturing people. Indeed, the Eureka Mills are now increasing their productive capacity to 2000 yards per day.[87]

All was not rosy, however. By the time the staffing list was compiled by the federal census in 1870, the mill had already endured at least two major crises, so it is very likely that its staff numbers in the late 1860s had been higher. In late 1867 the same yellow fever epidemic that killed 492 persons in nearby Houston—and probably took the lives of Louisa Bethje and her son Joseph on the nearby Bethje farm (see Chapter 6)—raged through the plant. Fully thirty-five of the workers caught the fever. Probably because of new and aggressive nursing techniques ("evacuate the stomach and bowels, and keep up a gently perspiration, by foot baths and teas"), only three died.[88] Nonetheless, operations at the plant must have come to a standstill for a time.

Another serious work stoppage came in 1868, with a cause hinted at in a newspaper piece about the company's stock:

In stocks we hear of very little movement. There is not much on the marker, except as such as are greatly below par. We hear of some sales of Eureka at 20c. currency, which we believe is about as much as it would command, since the mills have been stopped and some time yet must elapse before work is resumed, more money having yet to be raised for the purchase of machinery. We doubt whether such a large amount could be sold at these figures.[89]

The expensive mechanical problems suggest a

faulty engine. The engine was a 100-horsepower engine that, with its machinery, had cost forty thousand dollars and had been shipped from New York in 1866. [90]

Problems notwithstanding, the Eureka Mills succeeded in winning more top prizes at the Third Annual State Fair of Texas in 1872 (in Houston) than any other textile mill in the state, including: "Best piece of jeans, Texas made; Best three pieces of cottonade, Texas made; Best two pieces of woolen tweeds, Texas made; Best bunch wool knitting yarns; Best three pieces of ticking, Texas made; Best cotton knitting yarn, Texas made (honorable mention); Best piece of brown stripes; Best three pieces of cotton tweed, Texas made; Best bundle mixed colors, cotton yarn; Best piece hickory stripes; Best display of bed ticking."[91]

Despite the high quality of the mill's products, financial problems persisted and were exacerbated by the global financial panic of 1873, the impact of which was felt all over the United States for decades. Production ceased in summer 1874 at both Eureka Mills and Harris County's other cotton mill, Houston City Mills, and work stoppage was followed by a sale of Eureka company equipment and property in 1875.[92] Houston City Mills, which had been erected in 1872 in the city's Second Ward, burned to the ground in 1875, a total uninsured loss. From that time forward no cotton mills were attempted in Houston until 1903.[93]

Reinermann community. Martha Lucinda Halbert Rogers was the widow of the celebrated Confederate war hero Colonel William P. Rogers (1819–1862), the woman who had survived the robbery of rogue Yankee troops in the weeks immediately following the end of the war (Chapter 8). She was noted in the 1870 federal census as living in this vicinity with her grown son Joshua Halbert Rogers (b. 1845), daughter Maggie (b. 1855) and youngest son Timothy L. Rogers (b. 1858). She and her late husband had sold the mill property to William Morse & Company in the late 1850s, who in turn sold it to Sylvester Munger. Once those children grew up and left the house, she moved to Wharton to live with her daughter Mary Eliza Rogers Bolton (1849–1939), according to the 1880 census. Martha died in 1880 and was buried in Oleander Cemetery in Galveston.[94]

Henry Reinermann's widow, the by now twice remarried Louisa (Schiermann) Reinermann Sandman Bethje (see Chapters 6 and 8), died in 1867, leaving behind her husband Christian Bethje (who died in 1876) and children Louisa Reinermann Quesnell, Bertha Bethje, and Eliza Bethje. She, her former husband Joseph Sandman and their twin children, and some other members of the family were interred in a family cemetery located at what is now 5217 Inker Street. The remaining family land in the old Reinermann league was sold by family heirs in 1910 and became the Cottage Grove subdivision. At that time the bodies of Louisa and other family members were moved from the old rural family cemetery to Glenwood and Washington cemeteries, allowing the land to be developed. Christian Bethje and two of the Bethje children were also reinterred at Glenwood in 1910.[95]

Reconstruction at Wheaton's Ford

At what had once been Wheaton's Ford, in the far west of the upper Buffalo Bayou area, things would never be the same after the war. Mary Frisby Silliman, who had operated the old Wheaton inn along the San Felipe Trail since 1855, had lost two of her youngest sons in that war: Harris Silliman died in the Nashville campaign in 1861, and Isaac Silliman died at Vickburg on July 5, 1863. The shock must have been too much for the widow; she passed away on September 13, 1864, not long after Isaac's death. The surviving children and heirs were Abram Frisby Silliman, who by this time was living in San Felipe (discussed earlier), James Monroe Silliman, who was living in Fort Bend County, and Mary Jarvis Silliman Thornton and her husband, Confederate veteran John Wesley Thornton (Chapter 8). After living for a while with Mary Silliman at Wheaton's Ford, the Thorntons had obtained a farm and timber property on uppermost Buffalo

Above: Figure 9.21. John Wesley Thornton's ox wagon laden with Buffalo Bayou timber, ca. 1895. Courtesy of the late Mrs. Arch B. Marshall.

Left: Figure 9.22. Daughters of John Wesley Thornton and Mary Jarvis Silliman Thornton, ca. 1872. From left to right: Lelia Olivia, Florence Genevera, Mary Luna (Mollie – later to marry George Edward Morse), and Nancy Caroline Thornton. Courtesy of the late Mrs. Arch B. Marshall.

Bayou, just a few miles west of the ford and due south of modern Katy; a photo from around 1895 shows John Wesley Thornton and an African American wagon driver with a load of timber on an ox wagon (Figure 9.21). That couple had four girls and a son who reached adulthood; the four girls are shown in a ca. 1872 photograph in Figure 9.22.

After the death of Mary Frisby Silliman and two of her sons, her surviving children surveyed the situation at the old Wheaton (now Silliman) home and inn at the ford across Buffalo Bayou. Mary had purchased the property in 1855 for $1,000 from the heirs of Elizabeth Wheaton, who had established the inn at the ford on the San Felipe Trail in 1831 with her husband, Joel Wheaton. Mary Silliman had operated it from 1855 until her death.[96] Mary had operated a tavern at the inn, which was once a major waystation for ox teams and stagecoaches traveling to the interior. Traffic on the old San Felipe wagon road was much reduced by the 1870s, due to the effects of two railroads that had been built just before the war. These railroads—the Houston and Texas Central that went to Washington County and beyond, and the Buffalo Bayou, Brazos and Colorado that had reached Alleyton before the war and Columbus in 1867[97]—had siphoned off much of the cotton shipment that until then had been carried in ox wagons on the San Felipe Trail, past the inn. There was clearly no prosperous commercial future at the old ford. A bridge over the ford would not be built until the early twentieth century.

On May 22, 1868, Mary Frisby Silliman's children and heirs sold the first piece, a 200-acre parcel, to William Bluik of Harris County. Then on April 14, 1869, the main property, consisting of 1,500 acres plus the improvements, was sold to August Texas Marks (1847–1891) of Harris County, for $500. The drop in value relative to the $1,000 price Mary Silliman had paid for it fourteen years previously reflected the reality of hard times in Texas after the war; land prices nearly everywhere had fallen.

August Marks was born on an immigrant ship off Galveston in 1843. His German mother, Sophia Marks, had raised August and three other siblings in the Bear Creek community (Chapter 6). When Confederate soldiers and brothers Albert and August Marks returned to Bear Creek after the Civil War, Albert bought his mother Sophia's 160-acre farm at Bear Creek. August Marks became a local cowboy who participated in some of the great trail drives after the Civil War (Chapter 10).[98]

August Marks did not own the Wheaton-Silliman property for long, and he does not seem to have lived on it, as no residents are noted there in the 1870 federal census. Operating an inn was not part of the ranching that August Marks had in mind, and he reportedly regretted his purchase of it, saying, "I wish I could sell this old flak land. I'd take eight hundred dollars for it." William J. "Billy" Habermacher Sr., a grandson of German immigrant Thomas Habermacher, purchased the property in 1871 and moved in with his family. His granddaughter was still living there—at what became known as the Habermacher house—nearly a century later.[99] That house lay a few feet east of modern Highway 6, on the south bank of Buffalo Bayou (see Figure 3.11). During Habermacher ownership the house was a family home, and no longer an inn and tavern. They also closed the ford and that part of the San Felipe Trail, which now used a more southerly route to areas west of the old ford (Figure 9.2).

By 1870 August Marks had married Anna Marie Schultz. After selling the Silliman property, he purchased a 260-acre spread between Wheaton's Ford and the Bear Creek community in what was twenty years later to become the town of Addicks. Then, with his father-in-law's help, he bought another 120 acres from Adolph and Emma Brandt.[100] His son Emil H. Marks remembered an idyllic childhood there:

> *We had too much turkey, prairie chicken, deer, ducks, and geese in my days. We always had plenty of wild game. My folks never would eat a rabbit or a 'coon or a possum. We never had that on the table, from the time I was a boy. We raised our*

Figure 9.23. A southern plough team of the 1870s, a fixture on small Texas farms during Reconstruction. Drawing by J. Wells Champney, from Edward King, *The Great South: A Record of Journeys* (Hartford, Conn.: American Publishing Company, 1875).

sweet potatoes and killed our meat. We had plenty of meat in the summer and pork in the winter. We had wild hogs running in the woods, and the acorn crop was lots better than it is now, you know.

We raised our potatoes and we always had lots of turnips and we ground our own corn and made our own molasses, so we didn't have much to buy, just flour and sugar. We had cornbread all week. We didn't make flour bread, but we had cornbread for breakfast every morning and good homemade syrup. We raised peaches and plums and apples by the bushels. We had five acres in an orchard when I was a boy.[101]

Those happy times were not to last. August's wife Elizabeth Marks died in childbirth at the age of thirty-five in 1887, and August died of smallpox four years later, leaving five orphans, including Emil Marks, who was raised by two different sets of uncles and aunts. By 1917 Emil had learned the cattle business and become a rancher in his own right, founding the LH7 Ranch in Barker, not far from Addicks. By the early 1930s he had amassed some 36,000 acres, an unimaginable amount of land from the perspective of his immigrant father and grandfather. He founded the first rodeo in Houston out at his ranch, was one of the founders of the Saltgrass Trail Ride at the Houston Livestock Show and Rodeo, and belonged to one of the seven ranching families that saved the longhorn from extinction and got it formally established as a breed.

Legacy

In the decade following the Civil War much of the area south of Buffalo Bayou in western Harris County changed considerably. The two largest landholdings, those of the Canfield and Morse families, had been or were being broken up into smaller family farms. Population of the area increased accordingly, as the new farmers arrived. African Americans, newly released from bondage, spread out across the prairie in an unprecedented migration, finding work as sharecroppers, hired hands on white farms, and sawmill workers; considerable numbers were eventually able to buy their own land. Least changed were the German areas north of the bayou, where small family farms of the immigrants continued much as before.

To the east, the city of Houston made it through Reconstruction without a lengthy military occupation, but was plagued by institutional corruption.[102] It continued to grow rapidly, however, reachinga population of 9,382 by 1870 and 16,513 by 1880. It became a regional center for railroad transportation, although those railroads did not yet reach into rural western Harris County. Houston's rapid growth began to have a larger impact on the rural area to its west, typified by the Morse sawmill on Buffalo Bayou and the Eureka Cotton Mills near the tracks of the Houston and Texas Central Railroad. Neither of these industries survived the Reconstruction years, however, and the vast area west of Houston remained predominantly rural.

Western Harris County by 1875 was no longer frontier, but it was still pretty rough. Other than the San Felipe Trail (by now more usually termed the San Felipe Road), the Washington and Richmond roads, and a few other barely improved mud tracks across the prairie, there was still no formal road system linking up the emerging small farms. Landholdings were still unfenced, except for fences protecting crop areas; the open range still held sway. People moving from point A to point B, in an area not served by one of the few main roads, would simply point their horse or wagon across the prairie. That open range allowed another important industry to thrive in the rural area west of Houston during the Reconstruction years: the gathering of semi-wild Texas cattle for shipment up the Chisholm Trail.

Figure 10.1. "The Texas Cattle Trade—Guarding the Herd," from *Harper's Weekly,* March 24, 1874.

TEN

A Cattle Kingdom along the Bayou

Outside of money making, a cow-hunt possessed a fascination for me.
It had many of the features of a soldier's life—the living out in the open air,
the sky for a roof and the grassy sod for a pillow; the eager appetite for the simple meal;
the story and merriment around the campfire with friends; plenty of excitement,
combined with a touch of danger, and considerable generalship
in controlling large herds of cattle.

– Francis R. Lubbock, early Houstonian, Harris County rancher and Governor of Texas[1]

AS WE HAVE SEEN, the city of Houston developed first and foremost as a point of trans-shipment of cotton from the San Felipe Trail–and somewhat later from a myriad of newer roads and railroads–to waterborne transport along Buffalo Bayou. Lumber was another important early export. Often overlooked, however, is the importance of cattle, both to the early city of Houston and to Harris County. A popular Houston newspaper columnist recently wrote that despite the enthusiasm Houstonians show each year in honoring Houston's cowboy heritage at the annual Houston Livestock Show and Rodeo, "Houston doesn't have a cowboy past . . . no saloons . . . no cattle drives . . . no gunfights." He underscored his argument with an interview of a local academic historian, who said that "The cattle kingdom was not part of Houston's background. . . . No cattle drives went through Houston. Most Texans adopted a Western style [of dress] in the early and mid-20th century preferring that legacy of rugged individualism to one of slavery."[2] Memories in Houston can sometimes be a bit short, even in academia. In this chapter I examine the role of cattle husbandry in the upper Buffalo Bayou area. There was a significant local cattle industry and a slaughterhouse west of Houston from the beginning of the city in the late 1830s, involving cattle raised on the open range by local farmers and ranchers. During Reconstruction, there was also a large cattle operation run from an area along the eastern part of the San Felipe Trail (modern West Dallas Street, between Shepherd Drive and the old Fourth Ward). This operation involved the buying, rounding up, and driving of thousands of cattle up the famed Chisholm Trail from Houston, using African American cowboys. Houstonians come by the mystique of things western honestly, and many are descended from people who worked cattle in the area.

Background

The coastal prairie of Harris and adjoining coastal counties abounded in early times with longhorn cattle and wild horses, animals that descended from Spanish stock of the missions in South and East Texas. They adapted well to the abundant tall grass of area prairies (Chapter 1). Early Texans could capture and domesticate wild cattle, either for their own use or for marketing. Before the Texas Revolution, marketing opportunities were few, as there were few large towns needing meat. In 1828, in what was arguably the first recorded long distance cattle drive in Anglo Texas, Nicholas, Joseph and Edward Clopper and a few others drove thirty head of cattle from San Felipe to San Antonio to sell them. It was a horrific trip during which Edward died, and nearly all in the party became deathly ill, but they made it to San Antonio with the beeves (Chapter 2).[3]

From colonial times, settlers claimed ownership of wild cattle and horses in the open range in their vicinity by branding them. Land-owning persons could keep cattle by registering a brand and using it on their stock. During the year, cattle in the area would run wild, with the cattle of various owners comingled. When a farmer needed some fresh meat, he would venture out into the prairie to find his branded cattle and retrieve them. Celia Morse was thinking of this process when she wrote, on March 22, 1869: "Henry has gone on the prairie to look for cows. Hope he will find one."[4]

Each spring, cattle would be rounded up and separated so that ranchers could brand their new calves. Cassie McFee Reeder (1886–1979), who grew up in the 1890s in the Piney Point community when it was surrounded by unfenced open range with free-roaming cattle, described the family ranch activities at that time:

> *We had open range—no fence for miles and miles in front of our house. . . . When my parents married, my mother had stock in her brand . . . a forked C. I would always worry and wish there were no branding days. The cows would bellow, calves moan, and little colts would fight, but the men roped them [and] held them down . . . the hot fire, burning close, by would heat the iron rod with [the brand] on it. . . . [It would be applied] to the right hip of the animal to be branded, it would smell, days later it would peel off and leave the pretty brand, and everyone would know the animal was McFee's. If it got lost we could prove it to be ours . . . . We always sold the calves in June, then we had money.*[5]

The unfenced open range that underpinned this system of cattle management existed in areas as far east as modern Montrose Drive during the early 1870s. A railroad investor named N. A Taylor rode westward from Houston on horseback along the right-of-way of the then new Texas Western Railroad in 1876 (see Chapter 11); this railroad was close to the San Felipe Trail, more or less parallel with it, and he was writing about the area near modern day Westheimer at Loop 610:

> *About four miles from Houston the last vestige of human habitation disappears, and I ride upon a prairie which to the westward appears boundless. It is dead of winter, but it smiles with a green luxuriance upon which ten, nay, fifty thousand cattle are feeding, and some are basking in the sunshine, chewing the cud with a lazy air of contentment. To the right and left, ten miles apart, are dark lines of forest, which mark the sleepy course of Buffalo Bayou on the one hand, and Bray's Bayou on the other. This prairie is as smooth as a billiard table, with scarcely perceptible inclination to either bayou. . . . Numerous farms are seen in the distance along the bayous, but not one intrudes upon the prairie. Why should such an expanse of fertile lands be left in nature's wildness? Why should this rich heiress not be plucked? Simply because the Texan will hug the forest and the stream. There he builds his home and tills his field, and this [prairie] he leaves to his cattle to roam upon at will.*[6]

By the time of the founding of Houston in 1836, there were already a number of rural settlers along

San Felipe Trail who were keeping cattle, like Joel Wheaton and Joseph Habermacher. Buckman Canfield, arriving at Piney Point in 1838, kept cattle, and when an infantry company from Houston marched through his farm in 1840 headed for Indian wars farther west, he was able to supply them swiftly with 575 pounds of beef for their provisions (Chapter 5). By the time of the 1850 federal agriculture census, his widow Harriet George had 175 head of cattle ("milch cows" and other cattle). As documented in that same census, Thomas McGowen kept 150, Elizabeth Wheaton 100, and Casper Habermacher 100. There were many others with lesser numbers of cattle. These were farmers equally interested in beeves as in crops. Typically, they would slaughter some cattle for their own domestic use and market the rest. At the McFee farm, cattle were brought in from the range and slaughtered as needed. Cassie McFee Reeder describes the process:

> *In summer when papa killed a beef, mama would take some of it and cut it into thin slices, put it on a white sheet on top of the barn to dry, and [she] would turn it over once in a while. It was cured (in sunshine) and we ate it. Some papa would put in a big barrel with water and plenty of salt, and put a weight on top of the meat to hold the meat below the brine. There was no refrigerator, or any way to save food. Hog meat was made into sausage. It and [beef] meat were hung at the top of the smoke house and a fire was kept smoking under the meat. After so long a time, it was cured.*[7]

The McFees also kept horses on the open range, a practice that extended back to the earliest days of Spanish Texas:

> *We had a herd of horses and their colts, wild in the prairie. Sometimes one or two of our horses would stray away and get with someone else's stock, but papa would keep a watch for them. Sometimes when we went to [visit] the Fort Bend kinfolks, we would go across the prairie in the buggy. [There was] no road; if there was a pond of water, we would go around it. We would see a bunch of stock, ride by and see a new colt, and we [children] would say this one is going to be mine. We all had claims on ponies.*
>
> *Once in a while a man would buy a wild horse from us. Then papa would have to go pen the pony, rope him, ride him, gentle him for the man. They would bridle the horse, blindfold him, pat him gently on the neck, put a thin blanket on his back. The saddle would be fixed with a little roll made of blanket tied on each side, just behind the pommel of the saddle, so it would keep the man in the saddle. The saddle had two girts, one under the horses stomach behind the front legs, and a girt under his stomach near the back legs. It would take some time to get it all fixed. Another man on another horse would be by the horse, [with] a rope from the pommel of the saddle to the wild horse's bridle, so he could help. We would all be standing by. Mama would say "This is the last wild horse you are going to ride." Everything was quiet; horses didn't like noises. Then papa would get into the saddle, someone would pull the blind off [the horse's] eyes. [Papa would keep his] feet in the stirrup, hold his head up, so he can't get his head down. If he gets his head down, he will throw you. Some horses give up easier than others. Sometimes they pitch every time you ride for weeks, when you least expect it. Sometimes papa would be so shook up, it wasn't funny. Papa was never fat, so he was a good rider.*[8]

The aforementioned N. A. Taylor stayed overnight at a cattle ranch near modern-day Pattison in 1876, just west of Bear Creek, where he interviewed a rancher on raising open-range cattle in the Texas manner. The rancher, like others in the area, regularly drove cattle into Houston to market them:

A Talk About Cattle-Raising

> *After supper the [rancher] sat by me on the gallery, and we smoked, I a clay pipe and he a cob one. The night was so bland that I could hardly think of it as winter. While he spake his legs were thrown over the railing of the gallery, and his feet projected a considerable distance above his head. I asked him*

with what rapidity his cattle increased. His reply was: "That, sir, I can hardly tell you. I keep no books. They say you can calculate on an increase of twenty-five to thirty-three per cent a year, and that might be so if none were stolen and none strayed away. About all I know of it is that they increase fast enough to keep me pretty busy, what with branding calves and chasing the runaways back from the ends of creation. It is a business that you must watch closely, else you may start this year with a thousand head and in a few years find yourself with none."

"What will become of them?"

"Other people will brand your calves, while the old ones will die or stray away. After a calf has become a year old without a brand, it is the custom to look upon him as public property. He belongs to the first one who will catch and brand him. I know men who have accumulated large stocks in this way. A man must be up and doing, sir, and if he cannot make up his mind to do this he had better let the cattle business alone. I am so continually in the saddle that I don't feel right elsewhere."

"Do you find ready sale for your beeves?"

"No trouble about that. When I find myself running short of pocket change, I gather a few head and drive them to Houston, where they will sell readily at fifteen to twenty-five dollars a head. Beeves are like cotton—ready sale in any market in the world."

"You never feed your cattle?"

"Oh, no, but I am thinking of starting a little farm near Houston, where I shall raise corn, and always keep a few corn-fed beeves on hand. Such cattle will bring fancy prices."

He was totally unable to tell me how many cattle he had, but evidently supposed that he had several thousand.[9]

The early ranching industry in Harris County

Earlier ranches in Harris County extended far out on the open prairie and were typically much larger than the McFee farm at Piney Point. Francis Lubbock (1815–1905) moved to Texas in 1836 from South Carolina and became governor of Texas during the Civil War. His account of his ranching experiences in Harris County is among the most detailed from a pre–Civil War cowman. As a young man Lubbock operated a general store in Houston in 1837, then became district clerk of Harris County. With money scarce, he decided in 1846 to try cattle ranching and bought 400 acres on the south side of Sims Bayou, in what is now the Sunnyside area of South Houston, a mile or two south of Interstate 610.[10] He hired a stockman, and by the time of the 1850 federal census of agriculture he owned 750 milk cows and 1,500 head of cattle. That number of animals would not of course fit onto his 400-acre ranch; like others, he utilized the free open range, gathering wild cattle and branding them. He described participating in the classic annual roundups on the open range:

> *Outside of money making, a cow-hunt possessed a fascination for me. It had many of the features of a soldier's life—the living out in the open air, the sky for a roof and the grassy sod for a pillow; the eager appetite for the simple meal; the story and merriment around the campfire with friends; plenty of excitement, combined with a touch of danger, and considerable generalship in controlling large herds of cattle.*[11]
>
> *The cattle being without any restraint during the winter would drift freely from the ranches of their respective owners. So it became necessary early in the spring to hunt them up and drive them back preparatory to the branding of the calves. In order to do this the ranchers who wished to have the same range assembled with from five to twenty men, as circumstances required. Each household would have its own pack mule and provisions, consisting of biscuit, . . . hard tack, bacon, coffee in great abundance, sugar and molasses. When the drive was expected to be long continued a wagon with a pair of mules would be taken for transportation. According to the extent of the range the time*

of the hunt would be determined; three to eight days would make up a drive when not going very far from home, and a larger scope of country would demand sometimes as much as thirty days.[12]

Lubbock's trips ranged at least as far east as San Jacinto, south of Clear Creek well into Brazoria County, and west into western Harris County and beyond. This was antebellum Texas, and he utilized African American slaves for cowhands:

I had a number of negroes, good men and efficient workers. In Osborn and William I owned two boys very valuable both for their honesty and intelligence with cattle and horses. After they became free they were employed by stockmen, receiving high wages. But my best cowboy and most expert rider and horse-breaker was Willis, or Cy. Brought up by a Louisiana stockman who gave him many privileges, he had a brand of his own and possessed a small number of horses and a good herd of cattle. For some cause or another he had been sold and he was not satisfied with his next owner, who had none besides him. . . . So not satisfied, he took to the woods and stayed there. By some means he sent a message asking me to buy him; that he was a good stockman and would render me valuable service. I said that I would like to have him, and his owner having heard it, sold him to me . . . he had a great desire to be free, so he could manage his stock to suit himself. I sold him his freedom, he paying me a portion of the money. Subsequently he interceded with me to assist him in purchasing for himself his children and wife. . . . He paid part down, and I guaranteed the balance.[13]

The cattle had to be driven to market. In a world of small towns and large distances, opportunities were limited, and cattle were usually sold for hides and tallow rather than for meat:

The marketing of cattle when I was a ranchman was a different thing from the present time [1900]. In 1845 and for several years afterwards, Galveston and Houston, then small towns, consumed but few cattle, and had a large scope of country well stocked to draw their supplies from. . . . At Houston there was an establishment for the slaughtering of cattle for the hide and tallow. They would give from one to one and one-quarter cents per pound net weight . . . it took a pretty good Texas three-year-old to bring you four dollars and a real good beef to bring you five dollars. The butcher gave a little better price, but consumption [in Houston] was so small that the stock people had to sell to the tallow company.[14]

That slaughterhouse had been operating on the San Felipe Trail just west of Houston (Figure 10.2) since at least 1838, when John Hunter Herndon visited it (Chapter 4), as noted in his diary: "Returned by the slaughterhouse where I saw upwards of two hundred beeve's heads, a little further and I saw a pretty girl—how great the contrast?"[15] The slaughterhouse was located on the north side of the road, near Sam Houston's old ranch. It had been owned by George H. Meyer and Samuel S. Betts, who sold it to Hiram McCleaster in 1840. McCleaster operated it through 1850. John Boercher and George Baker had cattle pens on the south side of the road in the 1840s and sold cattle to the slaughterhouse (more on them below).

Lubbock and other ranchers drove cattle to Galveston as well, loading them into small sailboats to get them to the island, ferrying three to seven cattle per trip. They also drove them overland to New Orleans, along what became known as the Opelousas Trail. Eventually they began to drive their cattle to Buffalo Bayou near Harrisburg and load them on barges bound for Galveston, then using steamers to take them to New Orleans. Lubbock utilized this route with S. W. Allen, another prosperous early rancher, from eastern Harris County.[16]

Texas cattlemen drove cattle eastward to Louisiana during the Civil War to support the Confederate war effort. But after the South was cut in two with the fall of Vicksburg and the loss of control of the Mississippi River in 1863, demand for local beef plummeted, as did its value. Meanwhile, women who ran the small farms and plantations while their

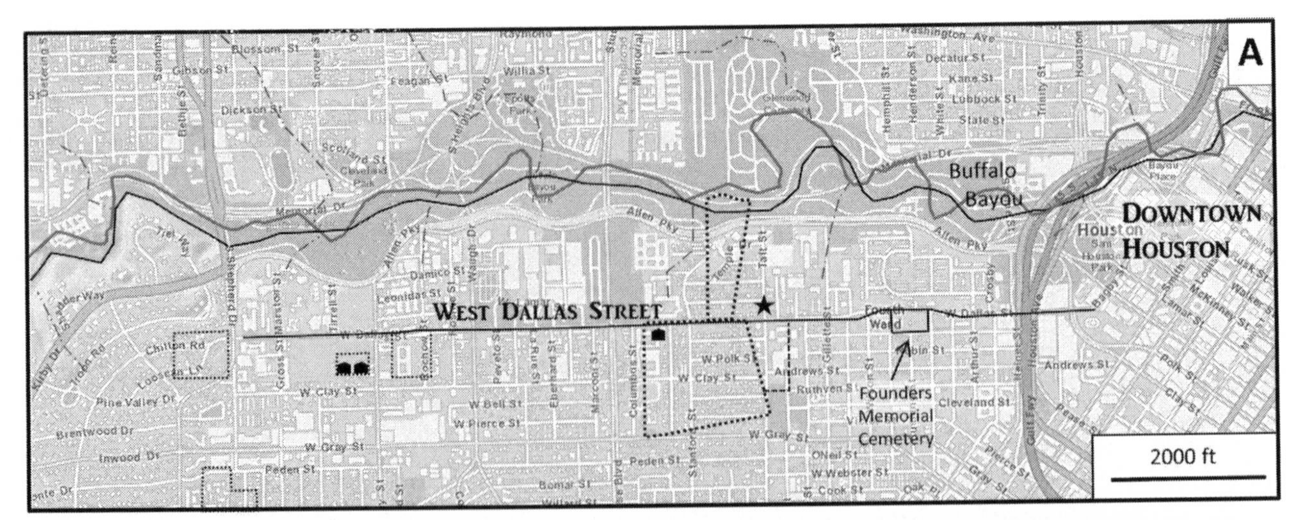

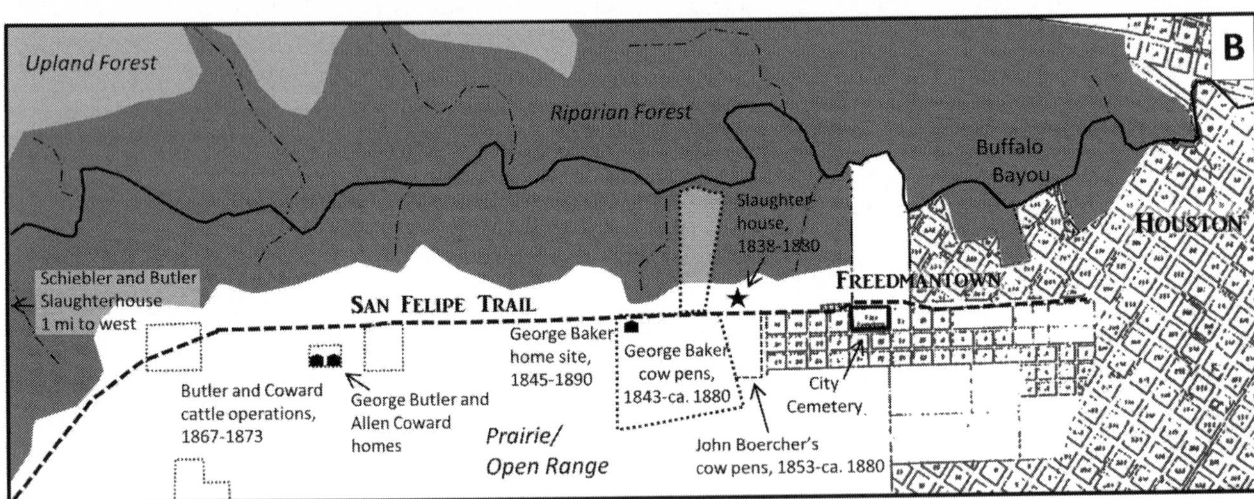

Figure 10.2. Elements of the cattle trade along eastern San Felipe Trail, upper Buffalo Bayou, during the period 1866–1873. **A:** Locations of interest plotted on a modern road map, courtesy of OpenStreetMap. The modern position of Buffalo Bayou and its tributaries is shown in black, and its late nineteenth century position is shown in light gray. **B:** The area as it looked circa 1867. The developed area of Houston is from the 1866 map of Houston by C. E. Wood, courtesy of the Texas Room, Houston Public Library, and from Mary Louise Passey, *Freedmantown: The Evolution of a Black Neighborhood in Houston, 1865–1880,* M.A. thesis, Rice University, 1993. Edge of forest cover is as discussed in Figure 1.2.

men were in Confederate service were often unable to keep up with their open range cattle during the war, and the cattle reproduced and multiplied in the open prairie, unbranded. This situation presented a business opportunity for returning Texas soldiers, many of whom went into the cattle business during the difficult years of Reconstruction. One of these new ranchers was the aforementioned August Texas Marks (1843–1891), who had been raised in the Bear Creek German community in western Harris County (Chapter 6) and whose son, rancher E. H. Marks (1881–1969), later recounted the tale:

> *The Longhorn was the salvation of Texas. In the Civil War when all the men went off to the army, the women folks couldn't find any cattle. They [the cattle] ran off and they didn't have a brand on them. The women couldn't take care of them. But the Longhorns could take care of themselves. Then when the men came back, why, there was a lot of*

wild cattle. Everybody that had cattle when they went to the army could brand all the unbranded cattle they could find.[17]

August Marks preferred the life of a cowboy to farming and participated in many trail drives on the famed Chisholm Trail, taking cattle north to the railhead in Kansas. Those trail drives helped him get a financial start. In 1869 he used his earnings to purchase the prairie land with the old inn at Wheaton's Ford from the heirs of Mary Frisby Silliman, as we saw in the previous chapter.

The cattle empire of the Coward, Perkins and Butler families

Twenty miles east of Wheaton's Ford, along the San Felipe Trail in the neighborhood that once held Sam Houston's and Mirabeau B. Lamar's country retreats, two men were to run a large cattle business after the Civil War. Their outfit drove cattle northward from Harris and surrounding counties along the Chisholm Trail. Allen Coward (1808–1891) and his nephew George Washington Butler (1845–1921; Figure 10.3) were part of a closely inter-related clan of pastoral families named Coward, Perkins and Butler, whose ancestors had been herding cattle since at least the Revolutionary War, starting in North Carolina. Those families began to drift westward with their herds of cattle and horses, and by the late eighteenth century they reached the saltgrass prairies of southern Louisiana. Here they first met and absorbed Spanish cattle-raising traditions (Louisiana was under Spanish rule from 1762 to 1802). Their clan and others like them began to migrate into Texas in the early nineteenth century, raising large herds of cattle in the lush coastal saltgrass. Historian Alecya Gallaway has researched this fascinating and often overlooked aspect of early Texas cattle history.[18]

Figure 10.3. George Washington Butler. Courtesy of Helen Hall Library, League City, Texas.

James Taylor White (1789–1852) was among the earliest of Anglo-Texan cowboys. Born in Louisiana, where his parents had migrated from the Carolinas, he took his cattle herd into Spanish Texas in 1828, settling in Southeast Texas along Turtle Bayou in what is now Chambers County, where his cattle grazed on the coastal saltgrass.[19] The traveler Fiske, who passed through and reported on Texas in 1831, visited White in his log home near Anahuac. White already had "three to four thousand" head of cattle. Fiske witnessed the process of lassoing wild mustangs, the annual cattle roundup on the open range, branding cattle, and other foundational elements of Texas cattle culture.[20]

The Coward, Perkins and Butler families followed a similar route to Texas. The Cowards were from North Carolina, from where Isaac Harry (or Hardy) Coward (1778–1844) migrated to Branwell

County, South Carolina by 1799, and Amite Valley, Mississippi, by 1811. The patronym "Coward" is interchangeable with the old English "Cowherd," and indeed some federal census entries for the family use this spelling. While in Mississippi they lived close to Rees Perkins (1774–1846) and his family, who had migrated there from South Carolina in 1810. Both families were keeping cattle in the newly opened Creek Indian lands in that state. Hardy Coward and Rees Perkins and their families and slaves migrated to the Calcasieu River area of southwest Louisiana in 1824, where they continued to raise cattle on the open prairie. The families lived together, and their children intermarried. At that time an orphan named George "Willis" Butler (1802–1870) lived nearby, and he married Rees Perkins's daughter Hepsibah Perkins, which drew him into the clan. Hardy Coward died in 1844 and Rees Perkins in 1846, at which time the combined Coward, Perkins and Butler families considered moving to Texas, where vast amounts of open land were to be had following Texan statehood.[21]

Hardy's son Allen Coward married Rees Perkins's daughter Margaret Perkins (1805–1895) in 1829 in St. Landry Parish, Louisiana. The first of the clan to move to Texas, probably in the late 1840s, that couple settled on the creek that later bore their name, Cowart's (Coward's) Bayou, where it joined Clear Creek, in modern day Friendswood, Texas (FM 518 crosses Cowart's Bayou just south of that road's intersection with Whispering Pines Avenue, not far from Stevenson's Park). They brought their slaves and their cattle. The 1850 federal census reports them with real estate worth $2,600; Allen Coward's name was spelled "Cowherd." Allen continued his ranching activities and reportedly took two cattle drives to New Orleans on the Opelousas Trail before 1854. The rest of the combined Coward, Perkins and Butler clan left Louisiana in a wagon train containing 101 individuals including those three families and their slaves, arriving at Clear Creek in 1854.[22]

Willis Butler and his wife Hebsibah Perkins settled near where Chigger Creek drains into the larger Clear Creek, also in modern day Friendswood Texas and just a mile or so south of the Cowards on Cowart's Bayou. That area can roughly be described as lying within the triangle formed by the intersections of modern day FM 528 (East Parkwood Drive), FM 518 (S. Friendswood Drive) and Bay Area Boulevard. In a late twentieth century subdivision there, a road called Butler Drive recalls the Butlers' presence there. The Perkins family settled along Magnolia Bayou (or Magnolia Creek, a short distance east of the Butlers, in modern day League City. Cowart's Bayou, Chigger Creek, and Magnolia Bayou are all small waterways that empty into larger Clear Creek.

The 1860 census gives a pre-Civil War snapshot of the combined families who all lived near Clear Creek at this time (Figure 10.4). The combined Cow-

Name	Age	Spouse's Name	No. of Children in Household	Value of Real Estate, inc. spouse's	Value of Personal Estate	No. of Slaves	No. of Improved Acres	No. of Unimproved Acres	Cattle (inc. milk cows and oxen)	Bushels of corn
Richard Coward	54	Harriet B. Smith Coward	7	$2,000	$12,000	12	120	795	240	600
Willis Butler	56	Hepsibah Perkins Butler	5	$500	$3,500	1	30	71	428	500
Margaret Perkins	80	Rees Perkins (deceased)	0	$150	$3,000		-	-	-	-
Allen Coward	52	Margaret Perkins Coward	0	$4,350	$47,000	28	140	285	1743	800
Neadham Coward	45	Eliza A. Perkins Coward	6	$0	$4,000	9	60	240	411	600
Rebecca Perkins	36	unknown (prob. deceased)	9	$4,840	$20,138	36	75	850	1670	500
M. M. Butler		unknown	-	-	-	15	150	2216	236	300
Austin Coward	33	Sarah	3	$0	$137	0	-	-	-	-
TOTAL			**30**	**$11,840**	**$89,775**	**101**	**575**	**4457**	**4728**	**3300**

Figure 10.4. The assets of the Coward-Perkins-Butler clan on Clear Creek in Galveston County, Texas, in 1860. Data compiled from the U.S. federal census of 1860, including the Slave Schedule and Agricultural Schedule; and Alecya Gallaway's "Saltgrass Cattlemen" (unpublished manuscript), 2003, archives, League City Public Library. "M.M. Butler" appears in the Slave Schedule as a slaveholder, but not in the federal census, so his or her identity is unknown.

ard, Perkins and Butler clan consisted of 13 adults and 30 children, and they had 101 slaves (men, women and children). They owned more than 5,000 acres of land and had access to many thousands of acres of surrounding unfenced prairie. They were primarily involved in cattle ranching, with nearly 5,000 head of cattle; they grew some 3,300 bushels of corn but had no other reported crops. Their combined total wealth (land and personal property) reached $101,615, a huge figure for the time. Over half of that figure, $51,350, resided with Allen Coward and his wife. They owned only a few hundred acres at that time, and most of their wealth lay in their 28 slaves. Rebecca Perkins, the second wealthiest of the group, owned 36 slaves. Among these African American slaves were the cowboys who worked the Coward, Perkins and Butler ranches; more on them later.

Willis and Hepsibah Butler had three sons: Richard (1836–1904), Green (1843–1872), and George Washington Butler (1845–1921). George, the youngest, was nine years old when they arrived in Texas. Because their uncle Allen Coward was childless, the three young men began to work cattle for Coward. The three made a cattle drive on the Opelousas Trail to New Orleans with their uncle Allen before the Civil War, and George and Green also made a cattle drive to Madison County for Richard, who moved there.[23] These experiences prepared them well for the Chisholm Trail drives that came later.

During the war most of the men of the Coward, Perkins and Butler clan joined the Confederate army. Their sympathies with regard to secession were similar to those of the planters; their livelihoods as ranchers depended upon the African American slaves who worked their cattle herds. They joined the Magnolia Rangers, Company D, 1st Brigade of the Texas Cavalry, Texas State Militia, in January, 1861. Of that unit's 68 men, fully 12 were from the Coward, Perkins and Butler clan, all of them descendants of Rees Perkins. Allen Coward and his brothers Needham and Hardy were in the unit, as were Willis Butler and his sons Richard, Green, and George Washington Butler. Their unit stayed mainly in Texas and Louisiana and took part in the Battle of Galveston (January, 1863) as well as the Red River Campaign in Louisiana (Battles of Mansfield and Pleasant Hill, April, 1864).[24] George Butler was wounded in a skirmish at Spanish Town on April 7, 1864, taking a minnie ball in his shoulder. He was taken to Lands End Plantation near Shreveport, Louisiana, where he was nursed to health by Elizabeth "Litza" Frierson, a daughter of the plantation's owners, who volunteered there as a nurse for wounded Confederate soldiers. George married her later that year, before returning to Texas.[25]

Partly recovered, George Butler was placed in charge of a labor containment camp on Clear Creek in northern Galveston County in late 1864. These camps were places where male slaves, freedmen, and captured escaped slaves were impressed into work details to support the Confederate war effort. Many of the Coward, Perkins and Butler clan's slaves were there. At this time, Allen Coward was awarded a contract to drive cattle east to feed Confederate soldiers. George Washington Butler took charge of driving those cattle, using the labor of some of his family's black slaves from the camp.[26] Litza joined him at the containment camp but died in childbirth a year later.[27]

The Chisholm Trail beckons

Allen Coward and the rest of the Coward, Perkins and Butler clan lost their slaves to Emancipation at the end of the war, losing a source of much of their wealth. They still had their land, cattle, and experience, however. They employed a number of their former slaves as free cowboys and looked northward for their financial future.

Texas cattle, worth only a few dollars a head locally, were worth ten times as much in faraway northern markets. In 1867 the Kansas Pacific Railroad reached central Kansas, and Illinois stock dealer Joseph G. McCoy conceived the idea of herding Texas cattle overland to Kansas, whence they could be taken by rail to markets in the East. The first Texas herds reached Abilene, Kansas, in September

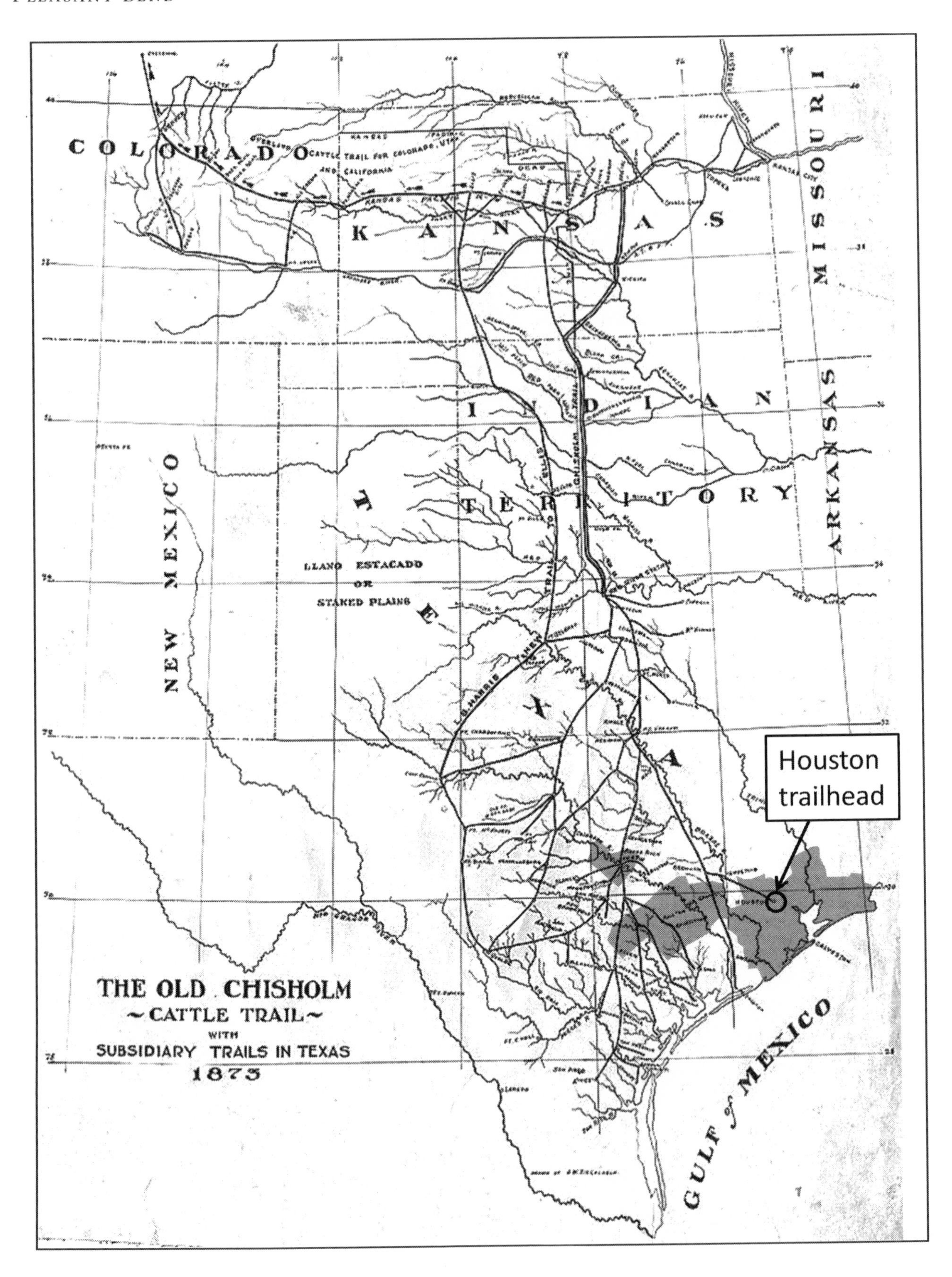
COLORADO
KANSAS
MISSOURI
INDIAN TERRITORY
ARKANSAS
NEW MEXICO
LLANO ESTACADO OR STAKED PLAINS
TEXAS
GULF of MEXICO
Houston trailhead
THE OLD CHISHOLM ~CATTLE TRAIL~ WITH SUBSIDIARY TRAILS IN TEXAS 1873

1867. Thirty-six thousand head, or about 1 percent of the Texas supply, arrived in the first season.[28] The preferred route became the Chisholm Trail. Cattle herds from various parts of southwestern, southern and southeastern Texas converged at a crossing on the Red River, from which they moved north to Abilene and other railheads in Kansas. The southeastern-most part of the collection area in Texas included the lush, cattle-rich coastal prairies that lay between Houston and the Gulf of Mexico. An arm of the trail headed from Houston to Hempstead, then to Brenham, before heading in a more northerly direction to the Red River crossing and ultimately Kansas (Figure 10.5).

Following the end of the war, Allen Coward and his nephew George Butler moved to Houston to build a regional cattle business there. Butler bought a house lot north of Buffalo Bayou in January 1867,[29] and Coward set up shop in an office at Franklin Street at West Broadway, according to the Houston City Directory of 1867–1868. Here Coward managed his cattle interests, at first consisting of his large herd along Clear Creek. Allen Coward was on the Texas voter registration lists for Harris County that year.[30] In February, 1867 Coward bought twenty-two acres along the by-then straightened San Felipe Road in the rural area west of Houston, and then bought a four-acre tract a short distance away, where he built a home; both tracts were in block 48 of the Obedience Smith survey (Figure 10.2).[31] As we have seen, this still largely unfenced rural area opened up into the vast open range prairies south and west of the town, essential for moving large numbers of cattle. Coward's property was also close to the cattle operation of cattleman and butcher George Baker (of whom more later) and to the slaughterhouse that had been operating since at least 1837 near the City Cemetery, supplying beef to the small town of Houston. George's brother Green Butler worked Coward's cattle down on Clear Creek while George worked directly with Coward.

Coward and George W. Butler went to Victoria in 1867, buying a cattle herd from a Mr. Owen.[32] Also in 1867, the three Butler brothers (George, Green, and Richard) made a deal to purchase a large stock of cattle belonging to a number of Gonzales County cattlemen, consisting of 82 brands belonging to the twelve cattlemen. Lead drover N. T. Moeller had driven cattle to Kansas before, and the Butlers learned how to travel the Chisholm Trail on this trip. Six of the Coward, Perkins and Butler clan's former slaves, now free men and skilled cowhands, also made the trip. They left in April 1868.[33]

With that first Chisholm Trail experience behind him, and flush with new cash, George Butler set his eye on moving cattle from closer to home. He entered into a partnership with a German immigrant from Prussia named Charles Schiebler (b. ca. 1838). Together, these two partners bought thousands of cattle for taking up the trail, but not all of the cattle were fit for that long and taxing journey. The culls went to a slaughterhouse and local butcher market owned by the partnership and operated by Schiebler. Small-town Houston's needs for beef were relatively modest, but the partners also harvested hides that were salted down for shipping, tallow for candlemaking, hooves for glue, bones for fertilizer and for refining sugar, and horns for making small plastic-like items of all sorts (such as buttons). At the time of the 1870 federal census, Schiebler and his Prussian-born wife Mary Schiebler (b. ca. 1847) and a young child lived near the homes of George Butler and Allen Coward, who by that time were both living in houses west of Houston and just south of San Felipe Road (Figure 10.2). Schiebler is listed as a butcher in the census, along with three other German-born butchers who also lived in the Schiebler

Opposite: Figure 10.5. Map of the Chisholm Trail, with its subsidiary trails in Texas, 1873. Note the position of Houston at a southeastern terminus of the trail. Gray shading has been added to represent the thirteen counties in which Butler and Coward purchased cattle during the period 1867-1874. Map courtesy of Wikimedia Commons and the Kansas Historical Society.

Figure 10.6. "A Drove of Texas Cattle Crossing a Stream," sketch by A. R. Ward, from *Harper's Weekly*, October 19, 1867.

domicile: Charles Weber, Hermann Buisse, and Charles Buisse. Schiebler marketed fresh beef from the slaughterhouse at stall number 33 in Houston's City Market, listed in the 1870–1871 Houston City Directory.

The Schiebler-Butler slaughterhouse appears to have been located on land previously belonging to Rebecca Williams, and before her to Thaddeus Bell, and before him to Josiah Morse, in the Reynolds survey about a mile west of where the partners were living (Figure 9.16).[34] The slaughterhouse faced a wagon road that later became known as Westheimer Road, near its modern day intersection with Drexel Drive; that site is now a Central Market grocery. Trail-weary cowboys did not have far to go to wet their whistles after bringing cattle either to the slaughterhouse or to the Coward and Butler pens on the prairie near modern day Shepherd Drive. A saloon complete with several young barmaids was at Piney Point, a short ride from there (Chapter 9).

Butler and Schiebler continued to work closely with Allen Coward throughout the Chisholm Trail years of 1867–1873, even though Allen was too old to take the annual Chisholm drive. With San Felipe Road as a home base, they bought cattle and assembled herds to drive northward. Butler bought 40 head of cattle from J. T. Matthews in Harris County in June 1870, and in October, 1870 he purchased herds from J. T. Gross and L. S. Betts in Austin County.[35] Earlier that year, in March, Coward and Butler purchased from T. C. Sparks a large herd that was spread across the open range of Harris and three nearby counties, paid by a bond agreement valued at $2,000, in which the responsibility of collecting

Figure 10.7. Mary Matilda Baker Butler and grandchildren. Courtesy of Helen Hall Library, League City, Texas.

the cattle fell to Coward and Butler. The agreement gives an idea of what was involved in buying cattle for these drives, noting that it required gathering

> *all the cattle branded by [image of several brands] running in Austin, Fort Bend, Harris and Montgomery Counties. Now if the said Coward and Butler shall will and faithfully gather all the cattle in the above bounds within twelve months from the date hereof, then the bond and all herein contained to be null and void, otherwise to remain in full force & effect should the parties hereto be unable to agree whether or not the said Coward and Butler have gathered the cattle well, then the matter will be referred to Church Collins, John Grier, Louis Brookshire and John Thornton, and three of which shall determine whether or not the said Coward and Butler have faithfully performed their part of the contract.*[36]

Butler bought a herd in Austin County from Joseph Greer in February 1872, paying $3,653 in gold for cattle at a price of $6.50 per head; the 562 cattle were gathered up all over that county in six months of work. In October 1872, he bought two hundred cattle from Patsey Jiron in Jefferson County, for which she was paid $1,400 in gold.[37] These cattle were taken up the trail in 1873.

There were other such contracts, and Butler kept meticulous records of the brands he purchased; these records are now in the archives of the Butler Longhorn Museum in League City, Texas.[38] Other cattle came from the Coward herd along Clear Creek, which numbered in the low tens of thousands of animals. In all, the combined Butler, Schiebler and

Coward operations purchased cattle in thirteen counties for their trail drives of 1868-1874.[39] There were two groupings of the counties in which they operated. One set (Austin, Fayette, Lavaca, Travis, Colorado, and Gonzales) lies to the west, surrounding the open range of the first group of cattle purchased in 1868, from Gonzales County cattlemen. The second group (Harris, Galveston, Chambers, Jefferson, Liberty, Brazoria, and Fort Bend Counties) are coastal southeastern counties that included vast amounts of open range that was the home ground of the Coward, Perkins and Butler clan. Most cattle in this latter area would have been driven northward through the area of the Butler-Schiebler slaughterhouse operations – where culls would be processed – and then would have been driven across Buffalo Bayou to the old Washington Road (now Hempstead Highway), thence to Brenham and on to Kansas (Figure 10.5).

As mentioned earlier, both Coward and Butler were living along San Felipe Road west of Houston by the time of the federal census of 1870, and Butler built a house there, on an acre of land he purchased from Coward (Figure 10.2).[40] He lived there with his new wife Alice Tyson Beatty (1847–1871), whom he had married in 1868; her name was spelled "Ellis" in the 1870 census.[41] The couple had a daughter before Alice died in early 1871. Later that same year Butler married Mary Matilda Baker (1850–1936; Figure 10.7), daughter of Houston neighbor and fellow cattleman George Baker, of whom more later.[42] It was to be George Butler's last and longest-lasting marriage; they would have seven children together.

The federal census of 1870 captures the growing Reconstruction-era wealth of Coward and Butler, which was due in no small part to their cattle operations. Allen Coward, aged 61, had $2,000 in property and $10,000 in personal estate. George W. Butler, aged only 24, owned property worth $2,500 and a personal estate of $500. Neither of these men shows up in the Harris County agricultural schedule for that year, probably because they were cattle brokers in that county rather than cattle raisers (their breeding stock was in Galveston County). Also living nearby west of Houston in 1870 were James Coward, 22, and F. W. Allen, 28; both listed as stock raisers. These two and their families were living at the same domicile. James was likely another nephew of Allen Coward.

African American cowboys. During their cattle drives to Kansas, the Butlers hired many of their clan's former African American slaves, who were now skilled herders as free men. Most had been slaves at the Clear Creek containment camp during the war, and worked cattle with George Butler at that time, including Thomas Britton, Willie Britton, Alfred Perkins Sr., Alfred Perkins Jr., and Calvin Bell. Thomas Britton (1851–1917) was a slave of Martha Perkins, as were his father Kneeland Britton (1810-ca. 1875) and his brother Willie Britton (b. ca. 1845). Alfred Perkins and his son were also Perkins slaves; in later years Alfred Jr. later was a butcher on the Butler ranch, and his descendants owned the former, well-known Perkins Barbecue establishment in Texas City. Calvin Bell, Sr. (1833–1920; Figure 10.8) was the only one of this group who was not a slave of the Coward, Perkins and Butler clan; he had been a slave of Colonel William McCrea of Jasper, Texas before coming to the containment camp. Accounting skills that Bell had earned from McCrea, an accountant, were useful on the trail drives, where Bell kept track of cattle and brand counts, a difficult task in a moving herd.

On the first Butler trail drive from Gonzales County in 1868, drover N. T. Mueller took along Willie Britton, "Big Tom" Britton, "Cal" Bell, "Al" Perkins, and two others who had not been at the containment camp, Seaborn Lyons and Thomas Caldwell. Seaborn Lyons (b. 1845), who had been a slave of George Butler, traveled with and assisted Butler during the Civil War. Seaborn and George were born during the same year and had grown up together, riding and herding. Thomas Caldwell (1851–1942; Figure 10.8) had been a slave at the plantation in Louisiana where George Butler had recovered from his wound during the Civil War. When Butler proposed to Litza Frierson at that plantation, Litza was at first reluctant to leave her family and her Louisiana plantation home. Caldwell, then a boy of nine years, was "given" to Litza Frierson so

Figure 10.8. **Left:** Calvin Bell, Sr. (1833-1920). **Right:** Thomas Caldwell (1851-1942). These African American men drove cattle on the Chisholm Trail for the Butlers. Photos courtesy of Bell descendant Vera Bell Gary.

that she would be less homesick, and he came to Texas with Litza and George.[43] One other cowboy of the Butler trail drives was David Hobgood (1848-1910), an ex-slave from Alabama, who was employed by Butler from the early 1870s. All of these men took part in the Butler cattle drives up the Chisholm Trail.[44]

Beginning in 1867, many of these men began purchasing land from Judge William J. Jones in an area near the Coward and Butler landholdings, founding the "Settlement," now a National Register historic district in Texas City. The first to buy ten acres of land there was Thomas Britton. Britton married the Butler Ranch's English-born camp cook, Mollie Whittington (1846-1918), and took part of his Butler ranch pay in cattle, thereby establishing his own herd. In 1870, Calvin Bell married Eunistine "Katie" LaBlunt Johnston (1834-1908), a German-born widow of a Confederate soldier, who became a schoolteacher at the Settlement. Bell's cattle brand, U, honored his wife, and is now on display at the Smithsonian's new National Museum of African American History and Culture in Washington, D.C. David Hobgood and his wife Ellen Bell Hobgood (1852-1928) moved to the Settlement in the 1880s.[45] The Calvin Bell home, at 117 S. Bell Drive in Texas City, has been restored and is at the core of the Settlement historic district. Many of these early African American cowboys and their families are buried nearby at Phillips Memorial Cemetery, Texas City.[46]

Peak and decline of Chisholm Trail activity. Activity on the Chisholm Trail peaked in 1871, when nearly one million cattle reached Kansas. The Butler and Coward drive that year was their largest. After that date, although activity on the trail continued, railroads began to better connect Texas with northern and midwestern markets, providing a cheaper way to ship cattle.[47] In 1871, perhaps sensing that the end of the trail business was coming, or perhaps because he was now sixty-three and ready to hang up his chaps, Allen Coward sold his remaining interest in his Galveston County cattle business to George Butler and Charles Schiebler, for $10,000. That sale included cattle in "Galveston and adjoining counties branded OT marked with a crop and under half crop

Figure 10.9 Texas longhorn cattle on the trail in Kansas. From Joseph G. McCoy, *Historic Sketches of the Cattle Trade of the West and Southwest* (Kansas City: Ramsey, Millet & Hudson, 1874).

in each ear, all horses and mares that are broken to ride with the same brand, reserving out of said stock four milch cows and two two-year old heifers of said mark and brand."[48] The purchase price was shared by Butler and Schiebler, indicating the amount of wealth the two were accumulating from trail drives and from their local slaughterhouse business.

As business on the Chisholm Trail slowed, barbed wire made its appearance in Texas, causing tension among cattle ranchers accustomed to open ranges. In 1872 another Harris County rancher named Sam Allen, who had partnered with another famed local rancher named Shanghai Pierce, began using barbed wire fencing to enclose areas of the previously open range, inevitably leading to friction between the Butler and Allen ranching interests, which overlapped in southeastern Harris County. In May, 1872, George Butler's brother Green was murdered by two of Sam Allen's cowboys.[49] The killers were caught, but the process of obtaining justice dragged on for years, resulting in yet more tension. A shootout nearly erupted in 1878 in Wallisville but instead resulted somewhat surprisingly in the end of the feud. As reported in the *Galveston Daily News*:

> *One of the Butler party came running down the street, stopped within ten feet of the foe (Autry), threw up his hat in the air, caught it on his left heel, kicked it into the air again and caught it on his head, turned a back double somersault, fell full face to the enemy, and, with drawn pistols announced*

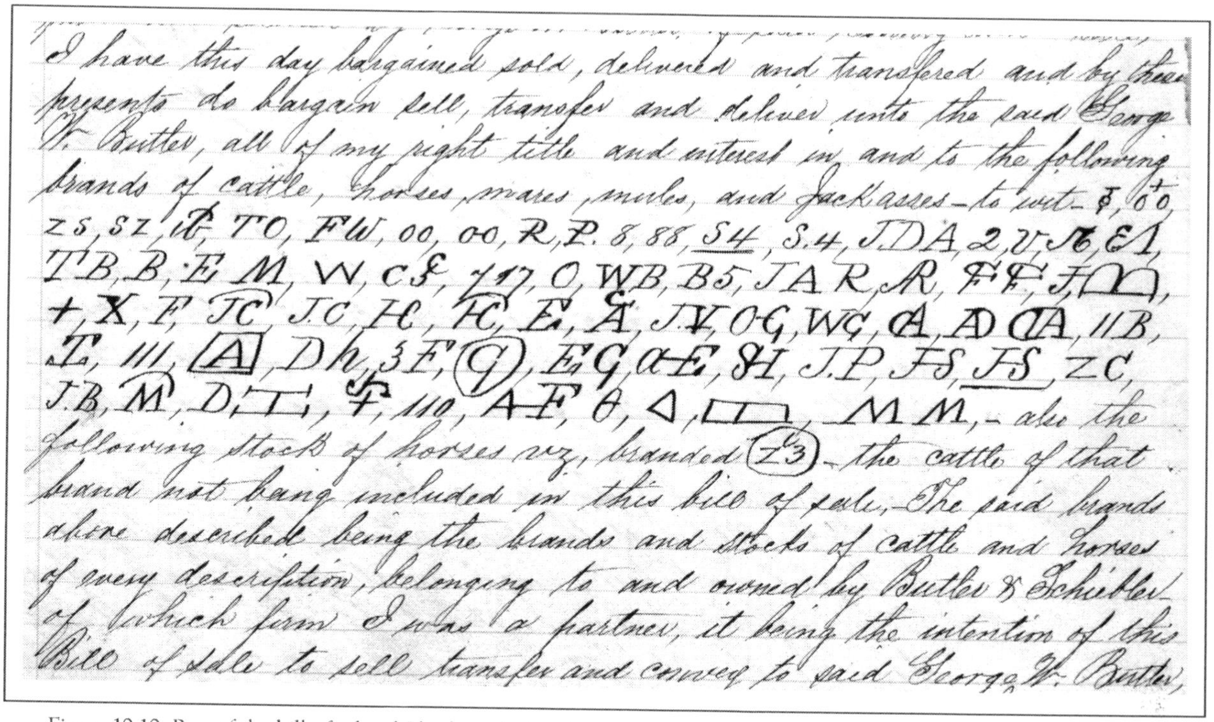

I have this day bargained sold, delivered and transfered and by these presents do bargain sell, transfer and deliver unto the said George W. Butler, all of my right title and interest in, and to the following brands of cattle, horses, mares, mules, and Jack asses – to wit – [illegible], ZS, SZ, [illegible], TO, FW, OO, OO, R, P. 8, 88, S4, S.4, JDA, 2V, [illegible], EA, TB, B, EM, W, CF, 717, O, WB, B5, JAR, R, [illegible], +, X, F, JC, J.C, HC, FC, E, A, JV, OG, WG, [illegible], 11B, T, 111, (A), Dh, 3F, (Q), EG, [illegible], SH, J.P, FS, FS, ZC, J.B, M, D, [illegible], 110, AF, [illegible], MM, – also the following stock of horses viz, branded (Z3) – the cattle of that brand not being included in this bill of sale. – The said brands above described being the brands and stocks of cattle and horses of every description, belonging to and owned by Butler & Schiebler of which firm I was a partner, it being the intention of this Bill of Sale to sell transfer and convey to said George W. Butler,

Figure 10.10. Part of the bill of sale of Charles Schiebler's interest in his partnership with George W. Butler, March 1873. It includes a listing of the various brands used in the Texas herds they purchased, gathered, and guided up the Chisholm Trail from 1868 to 1873. Harris County Deed Records 11:942, courtesy of Harris County Clerk's Office.

Figure 10.11. George W. Butler's ranch in League City, 1907. **Left to right:** Milby Butler, Burel Dismuke, Henry G. Butler, and George W. Butler. Milby and Henry were sons of George Butler, and Burel Dismuke was an African American cowboy working for Butler. Courtesy of the Helen Hall Library, League City.

himself ready. This act so amused both parties that they closed all hostile demonstrations and put away their arms.[50]

In 1872, preparing for the post-trail future, George Butler bought 30 acres of land adjoining the Galveston, Houston and Henderson Railroad from Col. Henry B. Andrews, an investor in the railroad. That land was located near the intersection of modern day Railroad Avenue and East Main Street in what became the core of League City. This new cattle station was about 5 miles east of his former home on Chigger Creek, but his railroad siding there would do away with the need to drive cattle for long distances. Butler was moving with the times, sensing that cattle ranching in the future was to be done on private fenced land.

In 1873, Butler discontinued his partnership with Charles Schiebler, signaling an intent to leave the trail business and move operations to his new ranch headquarters. He bought from Schiebler the jointly owned land (the slaughterhouse where Schiebler had worked) for $500, as well as Schiebler's portion of their livestock, valued at $16,000.[51] A listing of brands that changed hands during that sale provides a glimpse of the numbers of local cattle herds that they had purchased, rounded up, and driven up the Chisholm Trail in those years (Figure 10.10). The rise in wealth of Butler over the Chisholm Trail years is impressive; their total partnership, now solely Butler's, was worth over $32,000—not bad for an ex-Confederate cowboy, with few resources after the Civil War except his family connections and knowledge of cattle. Butler and his crew of African American cowboys took their last herd of cattle up the Chisholm trail in 1874.

George Butler's new railway station and ranch headquarters later became the site of modern League City, Texas, where Butler continued to ranch for the rest of his life (Figure 10.11).[52] He now concentrated on acquiring land and improving the genetics of his cattle by cross-breeding with imported Brahma stock. He loaded his cattle on railway cars for transport to Galveston, where the cattle were sold on to markets served by that port, as far away as Cuba. George W. Butler passed away in 1921 and was buried at Magnolia Creek Cemetery in League City. Today's Butler Longhorn Museum in that city tells the story of this pioneer rancher and his son, Milby Butler (1889–1971), who was to help preserve the old Texas longhorn breed for posterity.[53] Pioneer Louisiana and Texas rancher Allen Coward continued to live in

Figure 10.12. Headstone for Allen Coward and Margaret Perkins Coward at Magnolia Cemetery, 816 Montrose Boulevard at West Dallas, Houston.

Houston until his death in 1891; he and his wife Margaret Perkins Coward were buried in Magnolia Cemetery not far from their home on the former San Felipe Road (now West Dallas).

George Baker

There were other early cattlemen in the upper Buffalo bayou area, chief among them George F. Baker (1812–1890; Figure 10.13). He was born in Baden-Baden, Germany, and immigrated to Pennsylvania at an early age with his parents. He learned the trade of butchering in Harrisburg, Pennsylvania, then moved to New Orleans for a few years. He came to Houston in 1838 and became active as a butcher.[54]

At that time the active slaughterhouse in the town was out on San Felipe Road, just west of the cemetery, as earlier noted (Figure 10.2). It is probable that he worked in that slaughterhouse for a time. As also noted, that place of business was purchased in 1840 from original owners George H. Meyer and Samuel S. Betts by Hiram McCleaster, who operated it through 1850.[55] Baker is listed as a butcher in the 1850 federal census.

George Baker bought part of the old Sam Houston ranch property in 1843, which included Sam Houston's old log cabin and a quit claim deed from Houston (Chapter 4).[56] The property was situated along the south side of the San Felipe Trail, just west of the slaughterhouse (Figures 4.4 and 10.2). The 1843 quit claim from Sam Houston was in conflict with Mrs. Obedience Smith's title to the land, and in 1845 Baker received from Smith a quit claim deed for 11 acres—the western, major part of the old Houston Ranch; the deed mentions that Baker was already residing on the land at that time.[57] The address of Baker's home was much later noted as 2101 San Felipe Road (later West Dallas), and he lived at that home for the remainder of his life.[58] He married Rebecca Stringer Spottell in LaGrange in 1839, and the couple had ten children.

Also in 1845 Baker purchased another three-acre piece of the old Sam Houston ranch from Louis

Figure 10.13. George F. Baker. Photo from Anonymous, *History of Texas, Together with a Biographical History of the Cities of Houston and Galveston* (Chicago: Lewis Publishing Company, 1895), courtesy of Harris County Archives.

Levi, who had earlier purchased it via a quit claim in 1843.[59] Baker purchased three other parcels of land in and near the old ranch from 1849 and 1855, which brought the boundaries of his property into conformity with the north-south blocks of an 1860 subdivision of the Obedience Smith survey. He also bought a thirteen-acre plot north of the road (Figure 10.2).[60] From his property along the San Felipe Trail, Baker set up cattle pens that fed the local slaughterhouse operation and began to farm as well as buy and sell cattle. His son George A. Baker (b. ca. 1847), became a butcher like his father, according to the 1870 federal census, and George Sr. was listed as a butcher with stall number 54 at the Houston market house in the 1867–1868 *Houston City Directory*.

In the 1850s another German immigrant arrived, named John Boercher (also spelled Beecher). The 1850 census lists him as a butcher, living with his wife Wilhelmina Seiling. John Boercher bought the old slaughterhouse premises in 1850 and operated the business until 1859, when he sold it to John

Figure 10.14. George Baker's Greek Revival brick building, constructed in 1870 at 315 Travis Street, near Market Square, Houston. It has been used as the home of Treebeard's Restaurant for over thirty years.

and Mary Frome. Boercher also bought some land south of the slaughterhouse in 1853, which he used as a cattle pen operation (Figure 10.2).[61]

Besides running his cattle pen and butchering enterprises, Baker was also a farmer. In the agricultural census of 1870 his agricultural activities look like those of many of the other farmers along the San Felipe road to the west. He owned 70 improved and no unimproved acres, worth $2,500, and he had invested $100 in machinery. He owned 20 horses, two mules, two milk cows and 100 cattle. However, the value of his livestock, $9,000, was the largest value by far for livestock around this rural neighborhood (Butler and Coward do not show up in the 1870 agricultural census). This large value reflected the sales of livestock sold and/or butchered during the year that were not on hand when the census was taken; clearly Baker was buying cattle from local farmers and either shipping them north on the Chisholm Trail or butchering them.

Also in 1870, Baker constructed a Greek Revival brick commercial building on 315 Travis Street that still exists today, now occupied by Treebeard's Restaurant (Figure 10.14). Because both George Baker and his son George Baker were butchers as recently as 1867–1868, and because George Baker shows up as a butcher as late as 1873 in the Houston City Directory, it is reasonable to assume that this building served as a meat market, although documentation for the building's 2010 designation as a historic structure suggests that it may have been a feed store.[62]

By 1880 Baker had turned to other interests. In 1880 he purchased the old slaughterhouse premises, by then defunct, and merged the property with his brickworks next door. In the 1882–1883 City Directory he is no longer listed as a butcher but as a "brick manufacturer," with a yard and residence along San Felipe Road. His expanding interests also included investments in real estate; he became one of the wealthiest landholders in Harris County by the time of his death in 1890.[63] He is buried alongside his wife Rebecca Baker (1819–1905) at Glenwood Cemetery in Houston, beneath a marble obelisk capped by a statue of an angel.

The end of the trail

The demise during the 1870s of the slaughterhouses and the cattle buying and selling operations of George Baker, Allen Coward, George Butler and Charles Schiebler along the eastern section of San Felipe Road was brought on by a number of factors. Certainly the growing ability of railroads to deliver cattle played a major role in the closure of the Chisholm Trail. Another factor was the arrival of barbed wire, first demonstrated in Texas in 1876 by Illinois manufacturer John Warne Gates, to a crowd of skeptical but soon convinced Texans in San Antonio's Alamo plaza.[64] Fences began to chop up pieces of the old open range in much of Harris County in the 1870s, compromising the overland movement of cattle, especially in the rural near west side of Houston, which was being actively subdivided for acreage lots by the 1870s. A competing slaughterhouse and meat packing plant with ice-making facilities was established on Buffalo Bayou to the east of Houston by 1869, no doubt contributing to the demise of the thirty-year-old slaughterhouse on San Felipe Road. That newer meat packing plant failed in 1873, but its equipment was reused in a newer packing plant opened in 1875. The meat packing industry thus moved permanently to the east side of Houston, and by the 1890s both Swift and Armour operated meat packing businesses there.[65]

Although the cattle drive and local slaughterhouse business on eastern San Felipe Road were in decline, there were still small farmers in the 1870s in the rest of the upper Buffalo Bayou area, both north and south of the bayou, who continued to keep cattle on the open range. Most kept only a few animals, enough for their immediate needs and a little extra for the occasional sale. Wylie Parker, who was mostly engrossed by his lumber business with the Morse brothers in the early 1870s, nonetheless found time to keep 20 cattle in 1870. Robert McCorkle owned 57, and James Dozier, one of the new farmers on the old Morse plantation land, kept just 6. The most significant cattle raiser along the road to the west of George Baker was the aging Harriet George on her large farm at Piney Point, who owned 176 cattle in 1870.[66]

With the continued division of large antebellum landholdings in the area into small farms, and increasing use of barbed wire on those small farms, the open range was to disappear from Piney Point by the end of the nineteenth century. It existed a little longer farther west in the area around modern day Barker Reservoir. There Emil Marks (1881–1969), son of Chisholm Trail cowboy and German immigrant August Marks (1843–1891), founded the LH7 Ranch in 1917, which by the 1930s covered some 36,000 acres, most of it open range not owned by Marks. The headquarters of that ranch lay adjacent to what is now Barker Reservoir along Barker Clodine Road. The roots of the Houston Livestock Show and Rodeo are there: in the 1930s Emil and his family held rodeos for years for Houston folks who trekked out to the bald prairie at branding time. Marks was later one of the founders of the Salt Grass Trail.[67] After his death in 1969, his ranch's vacant headquarters buildings lasted until the summer of 2015, when they were demolished to make room for apartments.

With that, the last vestige of the old cattle culture along the San Felipe Trail in Harris County was gone. While cattle raising continues in some pockets of Harris County today, it is easy to forget that the urban streets of the city of Houston and its suburbs rest on vast amounts of formerly lush prairie grassland, home to a rich heritage of early Texas ranching.

Figure 11.1. *Fin de siècle* farming scenes in the upper Buffalo Bayou region. **A:** Canning day at Theodore Hillendahl's farm in White Oak, ca. 1895. Photo courtesy of Kay Howard and Walker Richard "Sonny" Gray Jr. B-D: Scenes on the Carl Frederick Kobs farm, Bear Creek community, ca. 1900, courtesy of Martha Doty Freeman: **B:** Satsuma orange orchard, with house in the background. **C:** Dairy herd. **D:** Feeding the poultry. **E:** Harvesting operations northwest of Houston, 1904. MSS 114-904 and MSS 114-905, courtesy of the Houston Metropolitan Research Center, Houston Public Library.

ELEVEN

A Transition to Modern Time

Papa built our family home facing the railroad track and Westheimer Road . . .
[On] the north tract thirty acres were reserved for a garden, an orchard, and corn
and grain sorghum. He planted peach trees that lived long enough to bear a few times,
and then they died of leaf curl. Fig trees planted around the home site grew large,
and the figs were sweet. . . . One of the fig trees growing between the smokehouse
and the stock pen was the favorite of all of us children for climbing and we were never denied
the joy and privilege of picking any figs within our reach.
There was always enough for the family table and for preserving.
I can still remember quart glass jars being sterilized by upending them
on the white picket fence in the sun
to dry after being washed.

—Jeannette Morse Hollady (1890–1975), on her childhood home in Piney Point[1]

THE LAST QUARTER of the nineteenth century marked a transition in the upper Buffalo Bayou area, from frontier and Civil War days, when the area was still rough around the edges, to a time when the first harbingers of modernity began to arrive, as the city of Houston began its inevitable westward expansion. In many ways it was an idyllic time. The children and grandchildren of the hardy pioneers reaped the benefits of their settled rural life, with mature farms and orchards all around them. There was time to enjoy new social institutions like the German Shuetzen Verein (gun club) gatherings with dances and songfests north of the bayou, and the open-air platform dances, religious revivals, and barbecues to the south, near the tracks of the upper bayou area's first railroad.

At the same time, there were still vestiges of the old frontier setting. In 1875, when travelers in most of western Harris County could still traverse the open prairie, the area remained enough of a frontier that the Alabama-Coushatta Indians, by then settled in East Texas, could follow old trails to favored hunting and fishing spots, as an old resident remembered:

The Indians came in large numbers and camped near Buffalo Bayou near the Habermacher Crossing [Wheaton's Ford]. In 1875 they suffered from a severe winter and many died. This was the last time that a large tribe ever came.[2]

Demographics. The area north of the bayou had perhaps been least changed by the after-effects of the Civil War. The tabulations of the 1880 federal census show that it was still heavily German—certainly there had been more small farms there in each decade since 1850—and that there were still few African Americans in that vicinity. Many of the aging German pioneers and their children, now adults with their own families, continued to farm there: the Rummels, Bauers, Groshkes, Brandts, Kochs, Hillendahls, and others in the farming communities of Bear Creek, Spring Branch and White Oak. In the far west of the area, Adolph Marks was ranching in what was still open range.

The largest demographic changes had taken place south of the bayou, which in the course of a decade following the Civil War had moved from a landscape of plantations and large landholders to one of relatively small farms of a few hundred acres. Whereas before the war it had had a mostly white rural population, by 1870 and 1880 it was majority African American, the result of the freed slaves from the Brazos plantations settling in the area to become sharecroppers (Chapter 9). Increasingly, these African Americans owned their own farms.

There were 258 people living south of the bayou along San Felipe Road between modern Addicks Reservoir and modern Shepherd Drive at the time of the 1880 census.[3] Of these, 104 were white (39 percent), and 158 were black or mixed race (61 percent). The ratio of black to white residents had stabilized and was essentially the same in 1880 as it was in 1870. In 1880 this area was still overwhelmingly a farming area (Figure 11.2), with a few stock raisers, who by now mostly resided in the central and western zones. Lumbering had effectively ceased with the closure of the Canfield sawmill during the Civil War and the Morse sawmill at some time in the 1870s. The Eureka Cotton Mills, employees of which were listed in the 1870 census, closed down in 1875, and the bulk of the millworkers left the area.

By 1880 at least 38 percent of black farmers owned their own farms (up from 8 percent in 1870), an impressive feat given the fact that in all probability nearly every one of these farmers had been enslaved only fifteen years before (Figure 11.3). Black owner-farmers included the families of Joseph Black, Frank Nash, James Rasmus (whose wife, Hanna Rasmus, had started the Pilgrim Rest Missionary Baptist Church in 1865), Guy Williams, Doc Williams, Albert McGee, Edmund Francis, and Alexander Alfred. Jordan Banks, who had been an employee of the Morse sawmill (defunct by 1880), is not listed in the census as a property owner, but he had purchased an eight-acre plot along San Felipe Road in August 1875, on part of the former plantation. The deed was not filed until 1896.[4] Black sharecroppers included Stephen Davis, Harrison Chainey, David Groves, Henry Mason, Roscoe Wilkins, David Sullivan and Sidney Sullivan. Samuel Francis and Arthur Essacks rented their farms for a fixed rent rather than a share of the crops. Farm ownership among black families continued to rise during the last quarter of the nineteenth century, and by 1890 sharecropper Roscoe Wilkins's son Rufus owned his own farm.

White owned-farms included those of the families of Benjamin Bragg, Charlie Voss, James Mallette (husband of Mary Morse), George Graves, William Abell, Harriet George of Piney Point, George W. Morse (who by this time had closed the sawmill he had operated in 1870 with his now deceased brother Henry Morse), George Edward Morse, Charles Smith, Amile Smith, Charles Schneider, J. B. Normand, Lawrence Habermacher, Joseph Habermacher, and William Wright. Renters included C. M. Bullock, Irish immigrant John McCue, and J. C. Redding. The sole sharecropper was Charles O'Neal, a second generation Irish American from New York.

Because the census was taken house by house along fairly linear roads, a sense can be gained of how closely together white and black populations were living and working in 1880 (Figure 11.4). This rural neighborhood was closely integrated at this

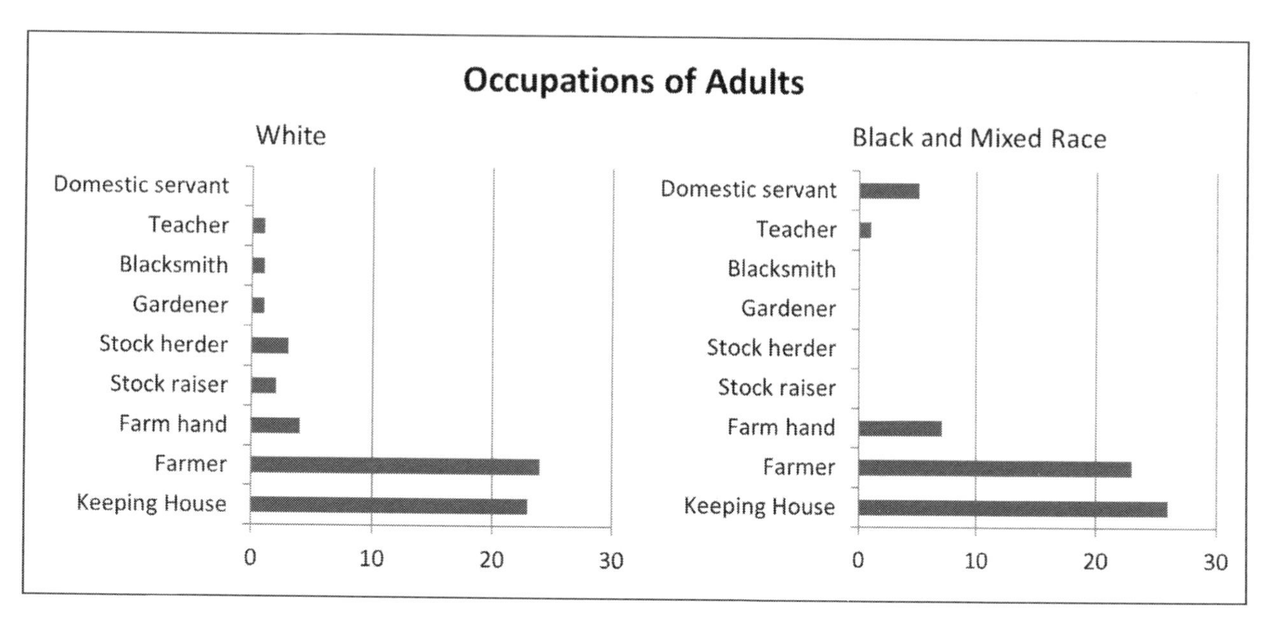

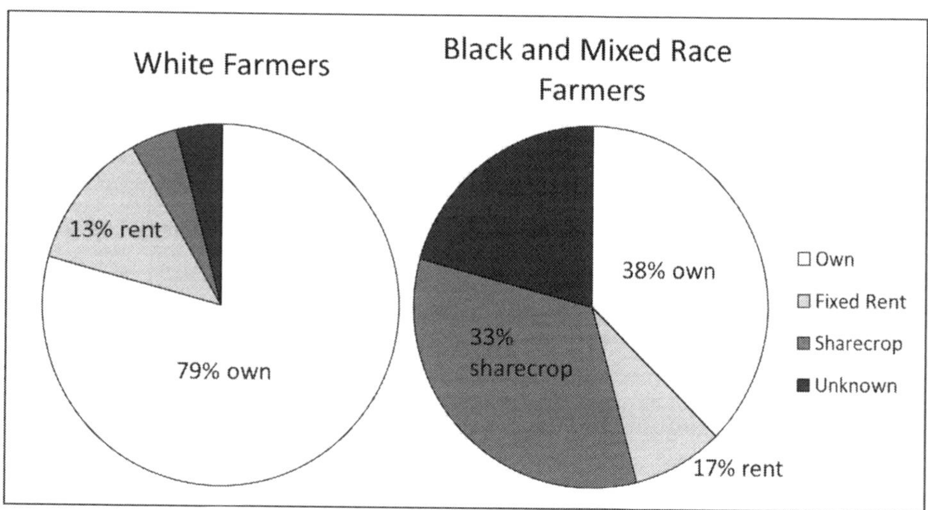

Top: Figure 11.2. Occupations of adults in the rural neighborhood south of Buffalo Bayou, 1880, from U.S. federal census data. "Keeping house" is a census term for housewife; in this rural area these women also took part in farming activities.
Above: Figure 11.3. Farm ownership south of the bayou, 1880, from U.S. federal census data (Agricultural Schedule).

time, with black families living next door to and, in some cases, at the same domicile as white families. This integration was not necessarily a sign of mature and harmonious race relationships, however, as it grew out of the practice of sharecropping. Subsistence farms at this time, for both races, consisted of only ten to thirty cultivated acres, regardless of the size of the farm acreage as a whole, because there were limits to the amount of land one man and a mule could cultivate.[5] During Reconstruction white farmers found that they could increase their overall yield by allowing a black family to settle and sharecrop, and 1870 census data show that most blacks were either sharecropping on white-owned farms or working as farm laborers. By 1880 many blacks owned farms, and the pattern of mixing continued. This pattern was quite different from that which was to come in the twentieth century, when all farms of

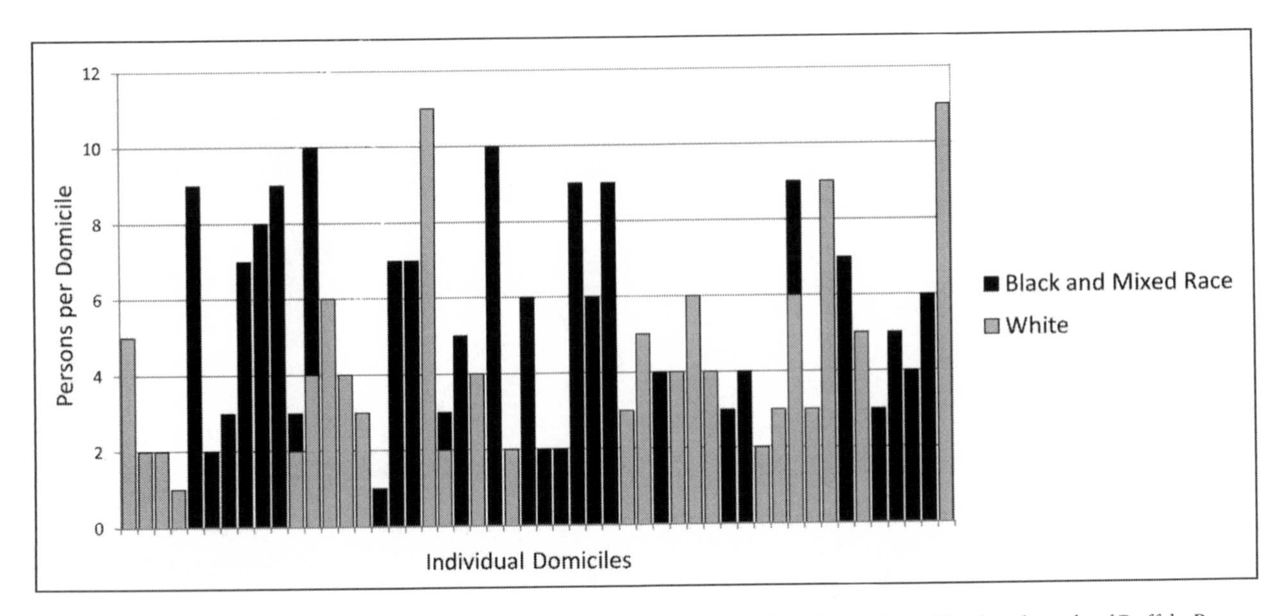

Figure 11.4. Residents, shown by race, of domiciles (individual dwelling places) in the rural neighborhood south of Buffalo Bayou, 1880 U.S. federal census. The census was taken more or less linearly along roads, so that the apparent racial integration of the neighborhood is mostly real.

the area were lost to suburbanization; at that time the area became much more racially segregated, as farm families resettled in other areas.[6]

In 1850 this frontier area had two hotelkeepers south of the bayou and one to its north.[7] By 1880 the occupation of hotelkeeper no longer appeared in census records (Figure 11.2), indicating that the San Felipe Trail was no longer an important route for long-distance travelers and that distances to Houston were shrinking. Inns were no longer needed this close to a growing Houston. This dramatic change—one that moved this area from a settled frontier before the Civil War to a rural area flanking a rapidly growing city by the end of the century—was due partly to the coming of the railroads.

The Texas Western Narrow Gauge Railroad

A big change in the rural west of Harris County came with the construction of the Texas Western Narrow Gauge Railroad (TWNG). It was planned as a route from Houston to San Antonio and ultimately to the Gulf of California.[8] The TWNG left Houston bearing due west across the prairie, its right-of-way within what was one day to become the western part of Westheimer Road (Figures 11.5 to 11.7). The first ten miles of track were completed in 1875, from Houston to Piney Point, and another ten miles were completed the following year; by 1882 it reached Sealy, Texas. The railroad was built in some haste, and it was only in 1881 that the many landowners along its route, for example Grace Morse, and Elizabeth Morse Grant and her husband Richard A. Grant, were officially to sign deeds granting a one-hundred-foot right-of-way to the company.[9]

The Texas Western Narrow Gauge Railroad had two official stops in the area, one at Piney Point and one farther west at Habermacher settlement, within what is now Barker Reservoir and George Bush County Park (Figure 11.6).[10] People used the train not only for shipping cotton but for pleasure excursions. City folks would get off in the open prairie to hunt, fish, pick berries or just picnic, and then flag down the train for their return. People could flag down a train anywhere on the prairie. In the beginning the train moved at a stately 15 miles per hour, but as the equipment aged, it slowed down to

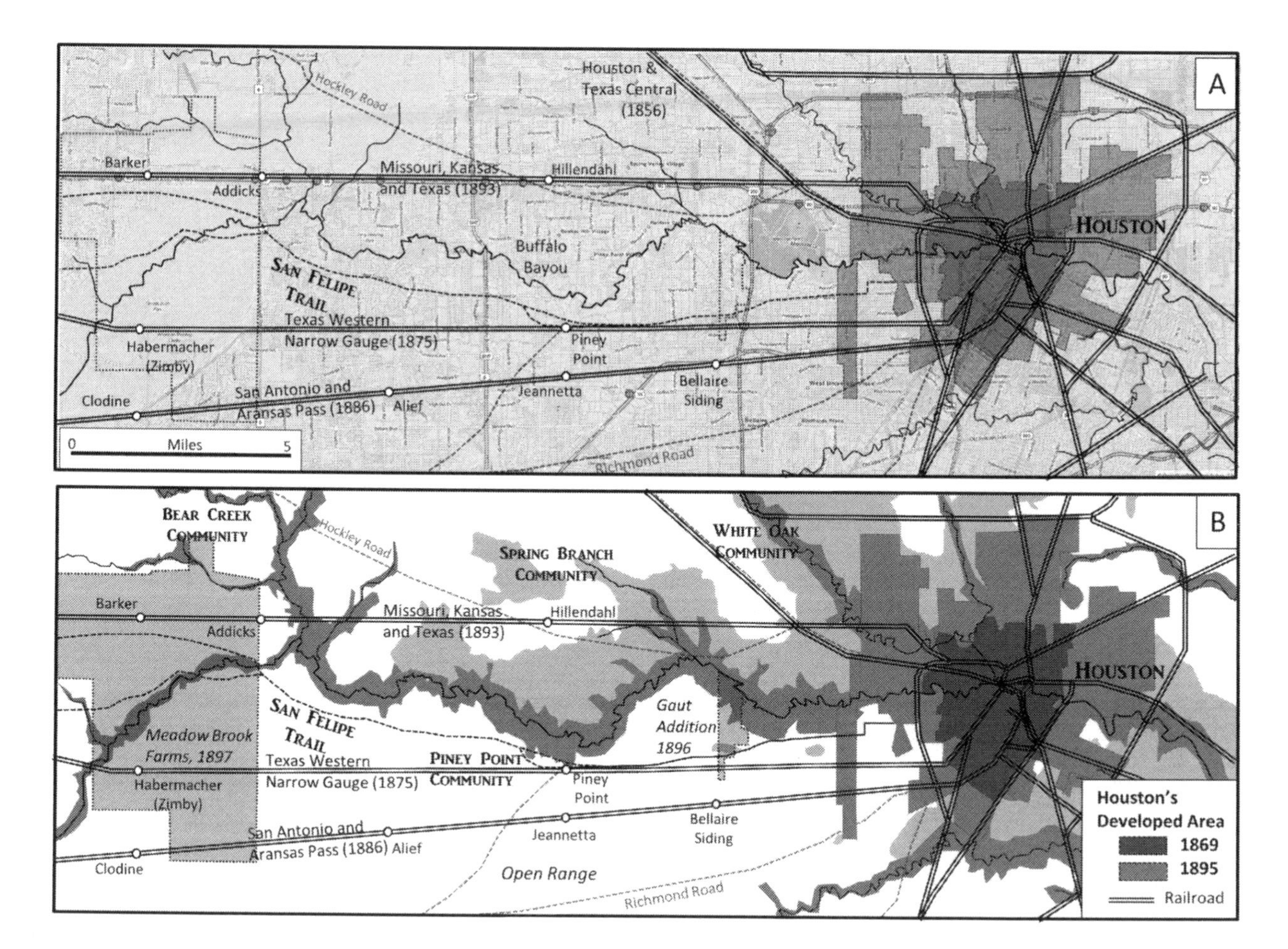

Figure 11.5 Late nineteenth-century railroads of western Harris County, including some of the prominent railway stops. **A:** Features shown on modern road map base, courtesy of OpenStreetMap. **B:** With natural features shown. Railroad locations are taken from the 1915 U.S. Geological Survey topographic map of the area and an 1888 map of Harris County (see Figure 11.6). The outline of the City of Houston's developed area in 1869 is taken from the city map of that year by C. E. Wood, and that of 1895 is taken from the Whitty and Stott map of Houston of 1895. The rural Meadow Brook Farms and the Gaut subdivisions of the 1890s are highlighted. Also shown are the major surviving wagon roads of western Harris County in 1885, which were still included on area maps of that era.

5 mph and could easily be outrun by a horse.[11] A resident of the area recalled that "to ride the narrow gauge then, a passenger could leave Habermacher Station at 10 a.m. and reach Houston by 4 p.m. Stories are told of thirsty cowboys riding up along the side of the engine, with an accommodating fireman handing them cups of water."[12]

A train moving slowly enough to pass cups of water to cowboys on horseback was not something that would satisfy those craving speed and punctuality, but such was not the goal of at least one of the railroad's investors, N. A. Taylor, who wrote in the 1870s of riding horseback along the line and of the intended (but never attained) western extension of the narrow gauge railroad to the silver mines at Presidio:

> *The gauge of this road is three feet—a system upon which I believe most of the railroads of the future will be built. Perhaps in the general railroad system as it is, too much of that has been sacrificed to speed which had been better given to transportation. We can afford to live slower when by that we live better and cheaper; and what is saved will increase the comforts of those from whose toils the cities are made and the waters of the oceans are white with rich argosies.*[13]

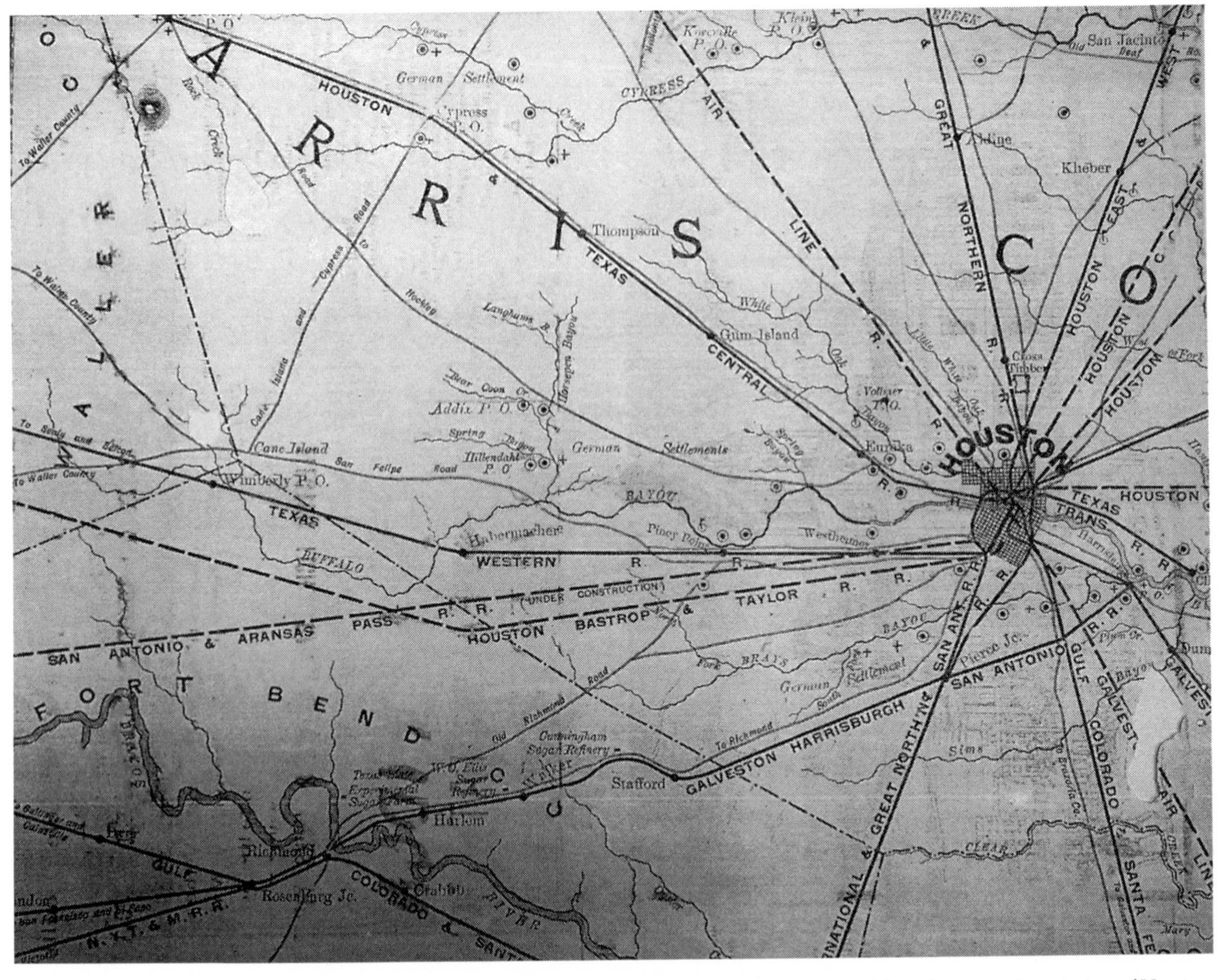

Figure 11.6. A portion of a map of Harris County published in 1888 by the Immigration and Development Association of Harris County, as part of a "Home-Seekers' Journal." The San Antonio and Aransas Pass Railroad was under construction at the time this map was printed. The Houston Bastrop and Taylor Railroad, shown as "planned," was never built into Houston but merged with the later Missouri, Kansas and Texas Railroad of 1893 (not shown). Of particular interest on this map are the county's old wagon roads, about to be replaced by the new railroads. Note the designation "Cane Island" where Katy was soon to be, and the "German Settlements" north of Buffalo Bayou. Courtesy of the late Charles Kruse and of Christine Brown, U.S. Army Corps of Engineers.

Perhaps so, but the railroad was not the hit for which its investors had hoped. After it was extended forty-two miles to Pattison, it ran into financial trouble. Reorganized with former President Ulysses S. Grant's son Frederick D. Grant in charge, it bridged the Brazos and reached Sealy in 1882, where it connected, imperfectly, with the Gulf, Colorado and Santa Fe Railroad, which had a standard gauge track.[14] The standard gauge Missouri, Kansas and Texas Railroad was built to Sealy in 1893, which ultimately led to abandonment of the Texas Western Narrow Gauge in 1899. All rails were removed the following year.[15]

Despite its short tenure of twenty-five years, the Texas Western had a major impact on the rural communities of western Harris County, giving instant relief to residents who had previously headed to Houston on the muddy and sometimes impassable San Felipe Trail. In addition, the railroad became the transport of choice for cotton merchants bringing bales of cotton from the Brazos River at San Felipe.

The Texas Western joined two other early Houston area railroads. In 1856 construction had begun on the Houston and Texas Central Railroad, heading northwest out of Houston (Figures 11.5 and

Figure 11.7. The Texas Western Narrow Gauge Railroad at the San Felipe Station, 1890s. Courtesy of the Katy Heritage Society.

11.8), and by 1861 it had tapped into the upper Brazos cotton traffic at Millican, near Navasota. Also in 1856 the Houston Tap and Brazoria Railroad was constructed to tap into the cotton and sugar trade carried by the new Buffalo Bayou, Brazos and Colorado Railroad. It was extended to Columbia in 1860.[16] Both these lines cut deeply into cotton traffic on the San Felipe Trail, but it was the Texas Western that administered a coup de grâce. No more was the San Felipe wagon road choked with ox wagons, and no longer could freight be held up for weeks by flooded conditions.

Westheimer and other new roads replace the old San Felipe wagon road

An 1890 Harris County road surveyor's map of the "Old San Felipe Road" in the Piney Point area shows dramatic changes in land use, partly as a result of the railroad (Figure 11.10).[17] Part of the old San Felipe wagon road that had existed slightly south of the railroad had already been abandoned and is not shown on that map; the replaced part of the old road is shown parallel to and just to the north of the Texas Western railroad tracks (along its right of way), along with a newer cutoff road that had developed parallel to it but farther north. North of the railroad track, a series of pastures is shown enclosed by fences that extend north-south from the railroad to the bayou. Barbed wire came into common use in Texas after it was successfully demonstrated by Illinois manufacturer John Wayne Gates to some ranchers in San Antonio in 1874.[18] By 1880 long fences were easy to construct in a way that they had not been in frontier times. This fencing signaled the end of the open range in the zone immediately north of the railroad at Piney Point; the fences surrounding the

Top: Figure 11.8. A cotton train at the Galveston depot of the Galveston, Houston and Henderson Railroad, ca. 1874. Drawing by J. Wells Champney, from Edward King, *The Great South: A Record of Journeys* (Hartford, Conn.: American Publishing Company, 1875), made from a photograph now at the Lawrence Jones III photo collection, Southern Methodist University.
Above: Figure 11.9. A bustling railroad passenger depot in Houston, 1874. Drawing by J. Wells Champney, from King, *The Great South.*

James McFee farm provide an example. Vast other areas, especially to the south and west, were still open range as late as the 1880s and 1890s, according to accounts by the McFee and Marks families.[19]

Those barbed wire fences had a particularly devastating effect on what remained of the San Felipe Trail. Where the old road traversed the prairie away from the railroad (see west side of Figure 11.10), the fenced pastures required a series of gates that were a nuisance for travelers. At Wheaton's Ford crossing of Buffalo Bayou a few miles to the west, where William J. Habermacher had purchased the Silliman/Wheaton house and property in 1871, he closed off the part of the San Felipe wagon road at the ford, causing the road traffic to be shifted elsewhere, and turned the old traveler's inn into a pri-

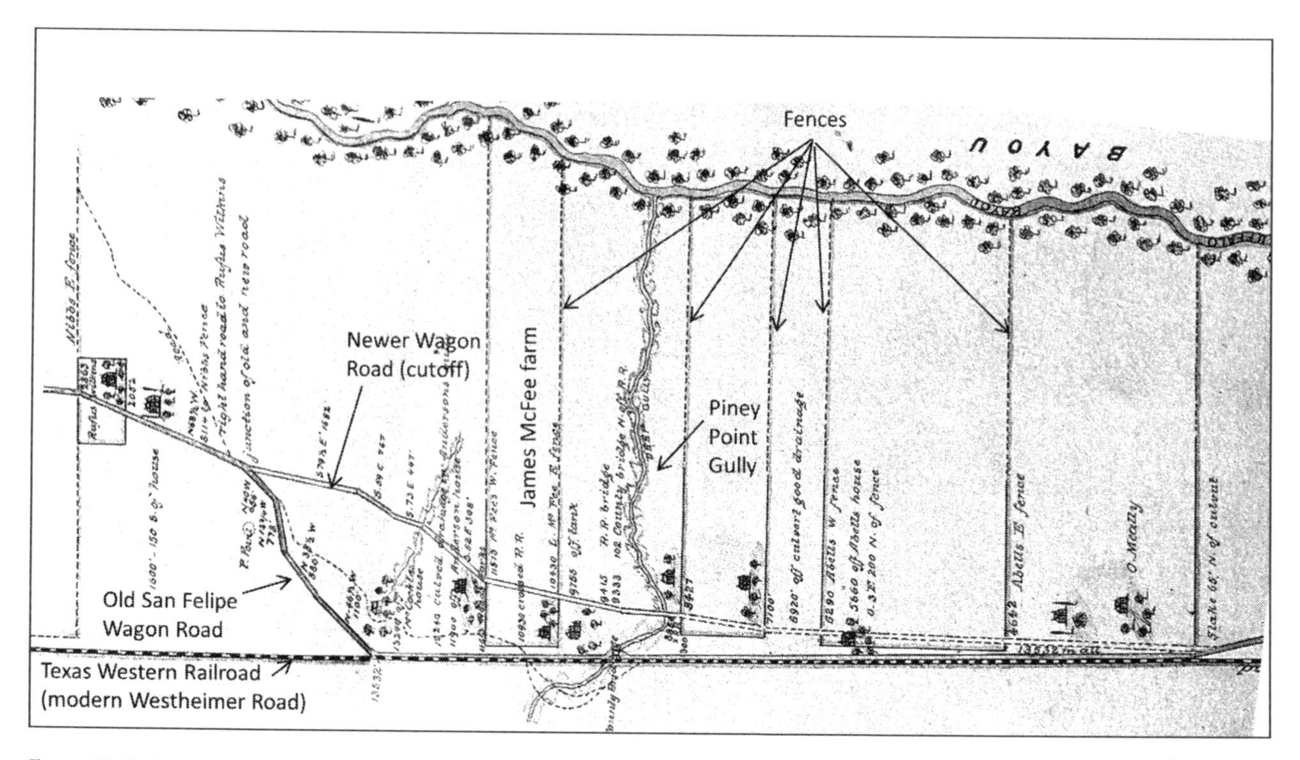

Figure 11.10. Piney Point segment from a "Map of the Old San Felipe Road," ca. 1890, courtesy of the Harris County Clerk's Office, Public Roads Maps, vol. 1. Buffalo Bayou was only schematically included on this map and it is not shown to scale relative to the roads. This map segment has been integrated into a redrawn compilation of the Piney Point area, shown in Figure 11.13.

vate home.[20] The 1890 Harris County map of the "Old San Felipe Road" leaves off the original road, showing a newer spur (Figure 11.11). That spur is likewise shown on an 1893 Harris County sketch map; the spur heads to the Joseph Habermacher house, the site of which is now part of Barker Reservoir (Figure 11.12). The original location of the western part of the road was shown as late as 1888 on maps of the area (Figure 11.6). For reference, both the old and new locations of the western part of the San Felipe Trail are shown in Figure 11.5. All western parts of the pioneer San Felipe Trail fell rapidly into disuse, and the road does not appear on the 1915 U.S. Geological Survey topographic map of the region. The old trail simply faded away from disuse.

Part of its local replacement near Piney Point after gates compromised the old San Felipe Trail was an unnamed dirt track following the north side of the Texas Western Narrow Gauge right-of-way, later to become Westheimer Road (Figure 11.13). Already by 1890, when the county road map shown in Figure 11.10 was prepared, a southernmost part of the old San Felipe Trail was abandoned, and travel shifted to the railroad right-of-way, which included a useful bridge over the steep banks of Piney Point Gully. This dirt road along the railroad right-of-way continued to expand eastward along the north side of the railroad track toward Houston, until the dirt track diverged from the railroad right-of-way just east of the modern intersection of Chimney Rock Road and Westheimer. At this point the railroad continued due east into Houston, passing the farm of Mitchell Westheimer. That eastern segment of the dirt road was first officially known as "New San Felipe Road," as mapped on a Harris County road map of 1889.[21] New San Felipe Road and the aforementioned road to the west that occupied part of the railroad right-of-way (Figure 11.13) became joined and were jointly known as Westheimer Road by 1900, after the Texas Western Narrow Gauge Railroad had been abandoned and its tracks had been removed. East of the point near modern Chimney Rock where New San Felipe Road diverged from the railroad tracks, the abandoned tracks became Alabama Street, and New San Felipe became Westheimer. The area in between the diverged road and railroad is now occupied by the Galleria shopping complex.

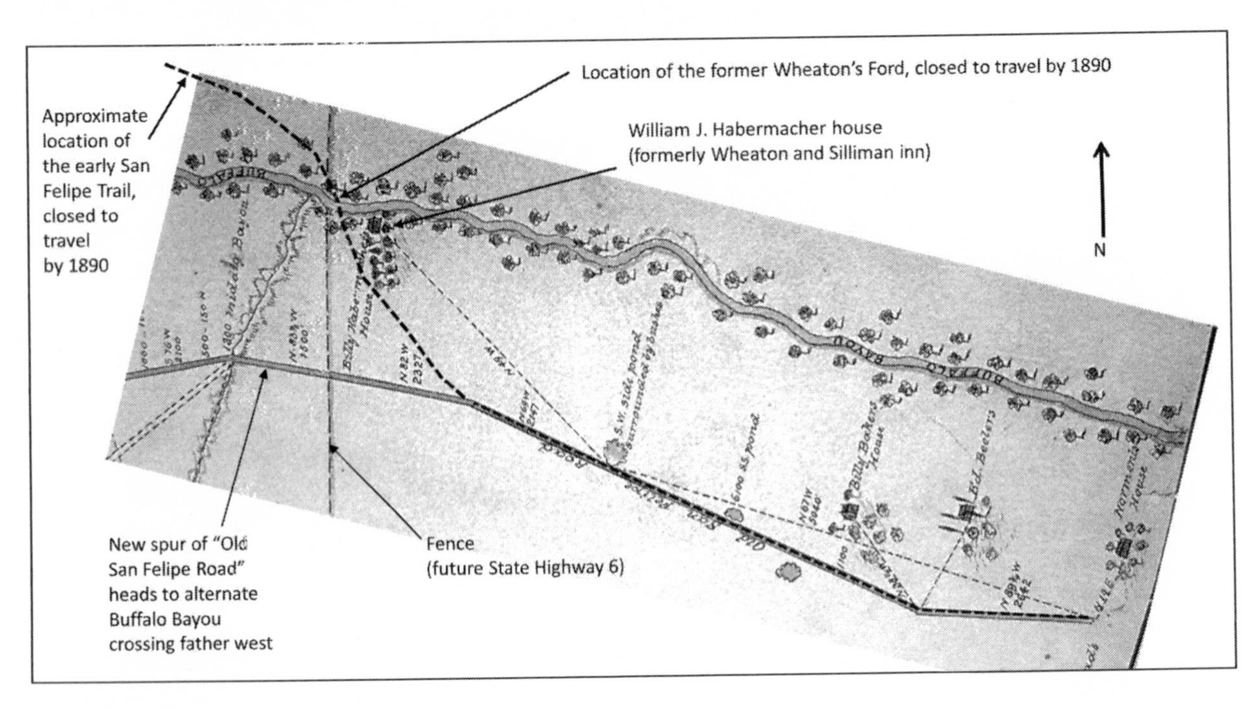

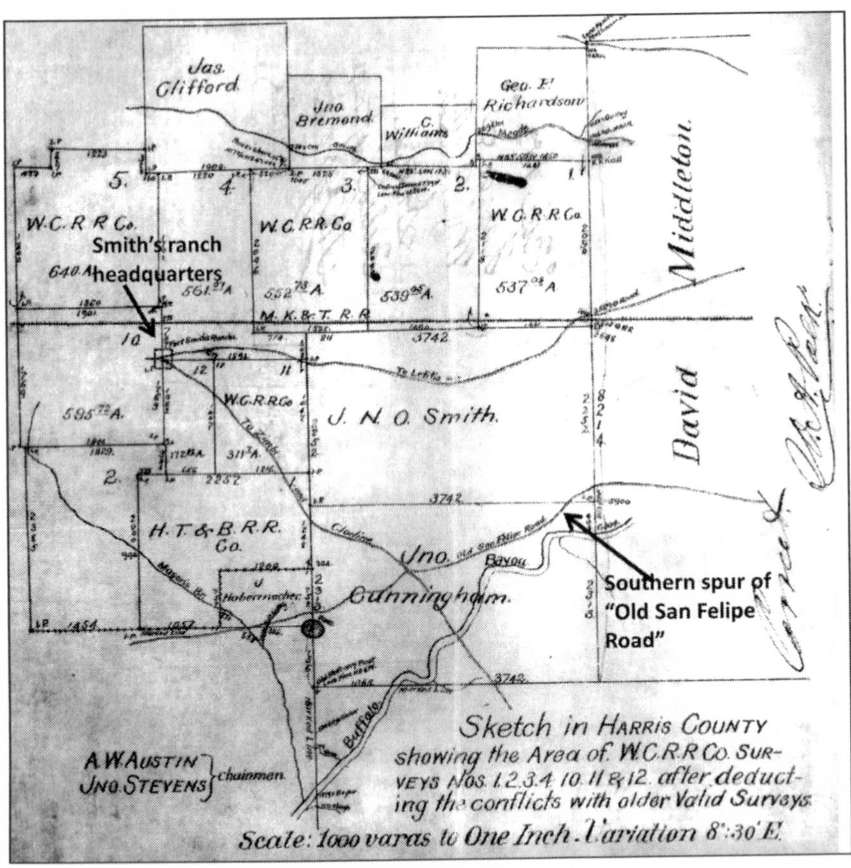

Top: Figure 11.11. "Map of the Old San Felipe Road," ca. 1890, in the vicinity of modern State Highway 6. It includes the locations of Billy (W. J.) Habermacher's house and the Baker, Beeler and Norments (Norman) houses. Buffalo Bayou was only schematically included on this map and it is not shown to scale relative to the road. In the 1830s and 1840s, the W. J. Habermacher home was owned by the Wheaton family, and after 1855, by Mary Silliman. By around 1890, the original ford and the San Felipe Trail in that vicinity (the added heavy black dashed line) had been abandoned and was not shown on the 1890 map. Courtesy of the Harris County Clerk's Office.

Above: Figure 11.12. Sketch map of 1893 showing the land west of old Wheaton's Ford, and the newer southern spur of the San Felipe Road that was then in use (it transects the Jno. Cunningham tract). That southern spur is also shown in Figure 11.5. Also shown is the location of Ben Fort Smith's ranch headquarters in the west-central part of the map, with roads extending from it to the Habermacher Station (then called Zimba) and to Letitia (later called Addicks). Map courtesy of Harris County Clerk's Office.

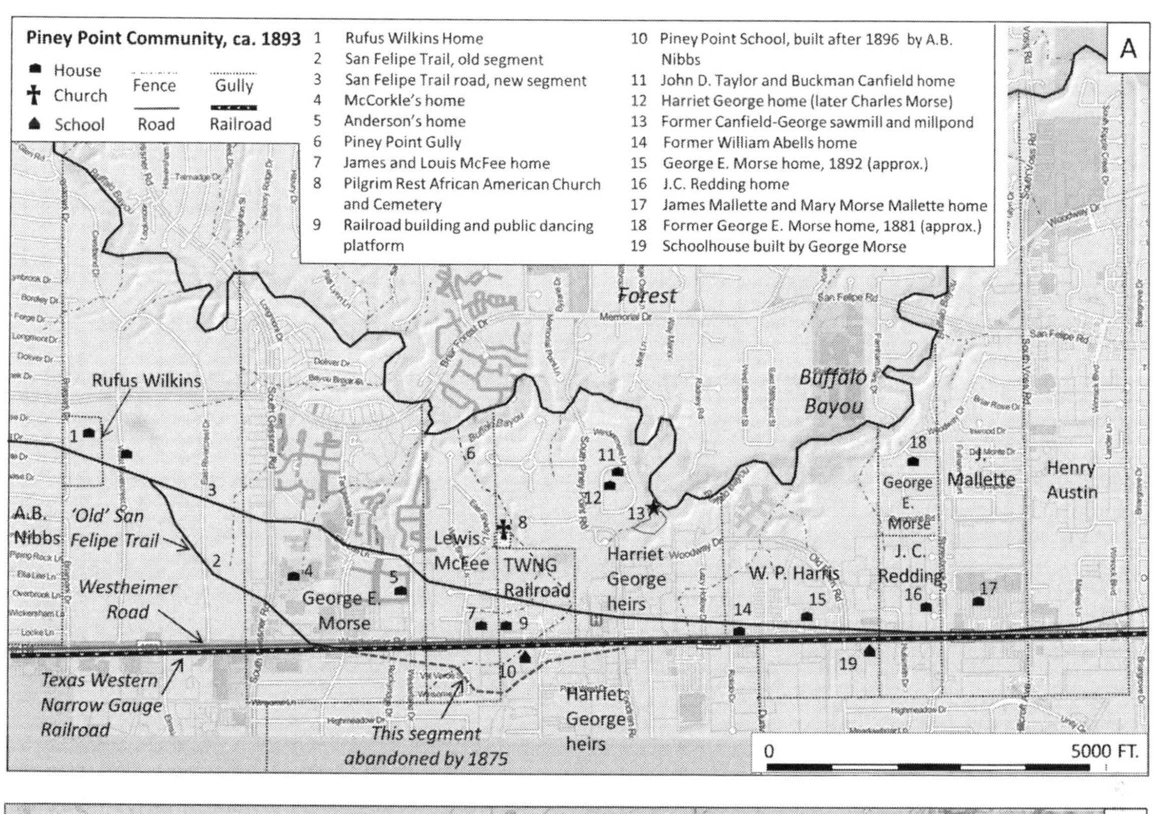

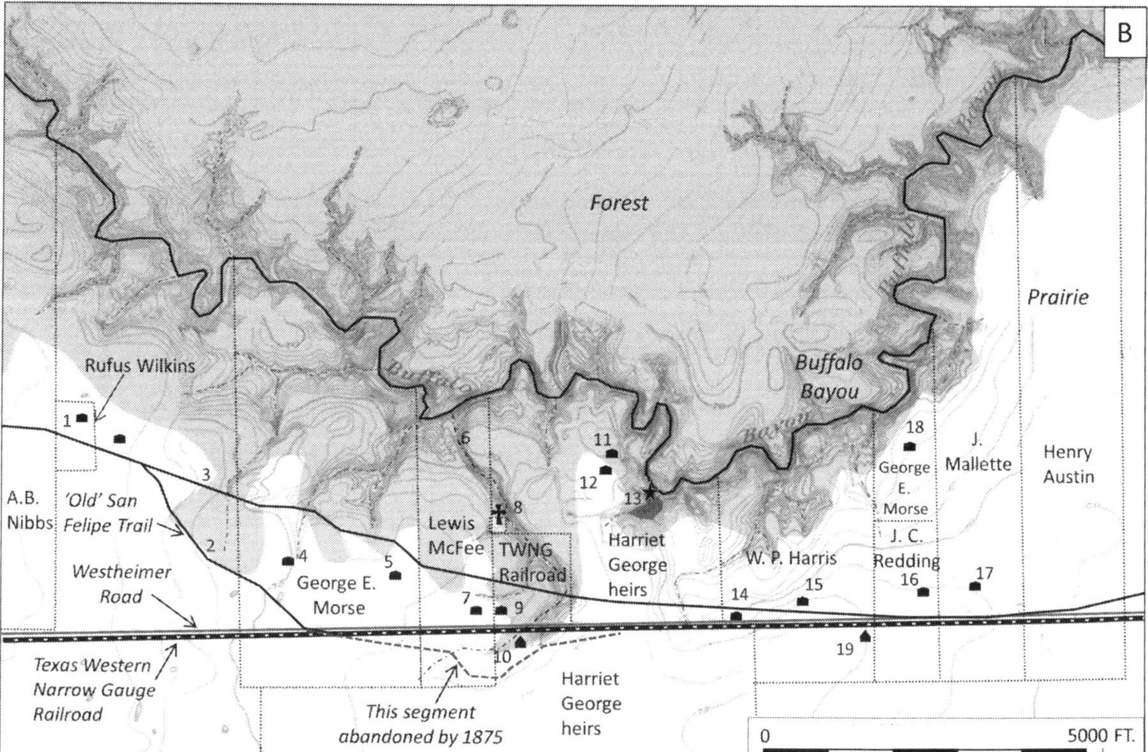

Figure 11.13. The Piney Point community in 1893. **A:** Property outlines and roads superimposed on a modern base map, courtesy OpenStreetMap. **B:** Same area, but overlying a topographic map of 1915 from the U.S. Geological Survey. Shading on B represents areas of forest cover, as shown on the 1915 map.

Mitchell Louis Westheimer (1831–1905) was a German immigrant who moved to Texas in the 1850s.[22] He and his wife Bessie owned a 640-acre farm with a home that was near the intersection of modern Claremont and Westheimer roads, where Lamar High School is today.[23] There he operated a free public school for his sixteen children (eight of his own, three orphans, and five nephews) as well as those of the neighborhood. By the 1870s he is said to have built a road to Houston from his property, which for a time was called New San Felipe Road—the same road mentioned that, farther west, joined the dirt track along the railroad right-of-way.[24] Both the western road, along the right-of-way, and the eastern road, past Mitchell Westheimer's place, were colloquially known as Westheimer Road long before the county mapmakers finally gave up on using the name New San Felipe here.

Westheimer Road, then little more than a dirt path, was only marginally better than the old San Felipe Trail; there were frequent stoppages during inclement weather. The James and (later) Lewis McFee family had a farm to the north of the railroad tracks in Piney Point (Figures 11.10 and 11.13 A). Cassie McFee Reeder described travel on new Westheimer Road in about 1890 or 1891:

> *I said in the beginning that we always had horses. When my mother's sister, Sissie Barnhill, was at the point of death in Houston, they sent word [from] ten miles to come at once. Papa was not at home; he had gone to town. So [Mama] left Lillian and me with Violet [hired help] and grandpa [James McFee], and took Jim, the baby. The [h]ired man drove the single buggy. It had been raining for days, was still raining, and the dirt road was mud, deep mud. They [were] nearly hub deep on Westheimer Road, drove for a while and then rested the horse. Finally the horse gave out. They stopped near Mr. Westheimer's house. She told the hired man to tell Mr. Westheimer that Lewis McFee's wife needed a horse, that her sister was at the point of death, and her horse was given out. He came out and told his man to get the best buggy horse he had and hitch him to her buggy, and put her horse in the stable, so she went on to Houston. She told me years after [that] little did she know, with all the horses she had, that they would be so badly in need to borrow a horse. She stayed and the hired man came back, changed horses and [headed] home. Aunt Sissie died. Papa took Lillian and me back to Houston. I remember my Aunt Daisy lifting me up and me looking into the casket. She was holding a song book in her hand.*

So much for convenient travel from Piney Point to Houston. The muddy emergency run that Cassie McFee Reeder described making from the McFee home to the Westheimer home was about six miles in length.

Heading west at this time, the prairie was still unfenced open range. In the late 1880s Cassie and her family headed southwest from their farm into Fort Bend County:

> *About this time we made a trip to the Brazos in Fort Bend County, all of us in the buggy. We drove this high spirited horse named Duke. We were proud of him, and people envied us. Well, we did fine until we got to Bray's Bayou (the one where all the houses get under water now—fashionable Houston!—but then only prairie, no road). Well, this was a flat place where we could cross. When we got to the middle, Duke just lay down and began splashing water, harness and all. I was afraid, and papa was mad. He climbed over the dash board of the buggy and out on the shaft, and into the water ahead of Duke. The bayou wasn't very wide, but he got wet. He pulled [Duke's] head up and made him walk out. We all told all about it to Aunt Faithey, John, Uncle Dabney and Aunt Sallie.*

Westheimer Road and the Texas Western railroad quickly became the focus of new housing construction in the still rural area. In the preceding pioneer era, nearly all settlers placed their homes near the bayou, in the shade of large trees. Connecting paths would be made to the San Felipe or other significant east-west roads. By 1890 houses were being built close to and facing the railroad and Westheimer in the new era of smaller, more numerous farms (Figure 11.10).

Two of these new groups of settlers at that time were the McFee family and the George Edward Morse family (Figure 11.13A). Both families had deep roots in the area of the former Pleasant Bend Plantation.

The McFee farm at Piney Point

As was discussed in Chapter 7, James McFee (1814–1903) and his wife Cassandra Hough McFee (1824–1890) moved to Texas in 1853 to a fifty-acre farm that was surrounded by land of the old Pleasant Bend Plantation. After the Civil War and during the ensuing depression years of Reconstruction, the James McFees sold that farm in 1866 and moved to Fort Bend County, and in 1876 moved again, to Waco. In March 1886 James's son Lewis Lum McFee (1861–1947) married Celia Walker Crump (1865–1930; Figure 11.14) and moved to Piney Point with his new wife. James McFee along with his wife and a single son, John, came into an inheritance, and thus left Waco and bought a farm near his son Lewis's new farm at Piney Point. James and Cassandra McFee and McFee sons John, Joseph and Hugh were all buried at the Morse family plot on Pleasant Bend (now the Morse-Bragg cemetery, located on South Wynden Drive, off South Post Oak Lane, where there is a Harris County historical marker (Chapter 9).

Toward the end of her life Cassie McFee Reeder (1886–1986; Figure 11.15), daughter of Lewis Lum McFee, wrote an autobiography that is rich with detail on life on a small farm in Piney Point at this time, in the final two decades of the nineteenth century. She was born in the then new home there of her grandparents, James and Cassandra McFee, a place she remembered fondly (Figure 11.16). It was located approximately where Chuy's Restaurant sits today, on the north side of Westheimer Road at modern Shady Lane. The portion of their farm that was north of Westheimer Road had more or less the same boundaries as the modern Piney Point Estates subdivision (Figure 11.13 A):

Figure 11.14. Lewis Lum McFee and his wife Celia Walker Crump McFee. Courtesy of Matilda Reeder.

Figure 11.15. Cassie McFee Reeder, ca. 1908. Courtesy of Matilda Reeder.

Right: Figure 11.16. Lewis Lum McFee, Celia Walker Crump McFee, and (probably) John Hough McFee, standing in front of the James McFee home in Piney Point, ca. 1886. Courtesy of Matilda Reeder.

Below: Figure 11.17. Lewis Lum McFee with children Jim and Annie Mazie at the McFee Piney Point farm, ca. 1896. Courtesy of Mark Parmenter.

Papa owned a place at the Piney Point on Westheimer Road near the Western Narrow Gauge. It was a two room house. . . . In June 1886 my [McFee grandparents] . . . came and bought a trac[t] of land adjoining my father's, and built a seven room house. . . . [In] the fall of 1886 papa sold his place off and bought a place in Fort Bend County near uncle Dabney [Walker]. . . . They moved into it, but thought it best to go back to grandma's big house until after I was born, so I was born at Piney Point, [at what is now] Piney Point Estates, Westheimer Road. The Doctor was a midwife that lived on the other side of the bayou, a Mrs. Schroeder. She was the Doctor for all my mother's five children and a good one. . . There were so many kin to hold until I was spoilt, and gave them plenty to think about.[25]

Mrs. Schroeder, the midwife, was very probably Dorathe Bleker Schroeder (1842–1919), wife of Fritz Schroeder. They lived in the heavily German north side of Buffalo Bayou in what is today Piney Point Village (Chapter 6).

Lewis Lum McFee, Cassie's father, was one of five children born to James and Cassandra McFee. The other three sons were John Hough McFee (1852–1888; Figure 11.16), Joseph Adam McFee (1853–1874) and Hugh Cecil McFee (1855–1887), and their fifth child was Annie Cecelia McFee (1863–1941). Cassie was the oldest of Lewis and Celia McFee's five children, the others being Lillian (1888–1895), James Ivie (1890–1956), Annie Mazie (1892–1980; Figure 11.17) and Cecelia Estelle (1893–1894).

House and home. Cassie told about life in the late 1880s, when unmarried uncles John and Hugh lived with her parents and grandparents at Piney Point:

Our house was a big house. One front room was grandpa's room. The furniture was just like grandma had it when she died. The high wooden bed [stood with] the head of it across the west window. The room was sixteen by sixteen feet and had five windows and a fireplace. There was a washstand, on it was a pretty water set, pitcher and washbowl . . . soap dish, chamber [pot] with lid, all had pretty pink flowers on them. I guess it all must have cost plenty. . . . There was a dresser with some little square shelves on each side of the mirror. A big old-fashioned wardrobe, and two trunks. . . . Mama's room was the same size as grandpa's except it had four windows, and it also had a chimney. The wallpaper was pink roses. Grandpa's was green leaves and flowers. Behind mama's room was our room; [it was] smaller, with two windows and a door onto the back porch. It had dark paper. Next to our room was a sitting room painted pink, then the dining room. Then the big kitchen, twenty feet long, with painted walls and a big pantry with a big window and shelves. And a barrel of flour with a rolling pin and a big dough board on top.

We always cooked enough pie and cake at Christmas to last two weeks, and when someone came they were served coffee and cake or pie. I remember hearing mama say one day that she and the colored woman had made twenty-one pies that day. They were green apple, raisin, currents, dried peach, sweet potato custard, and egg custard . . . the mincemeat came in yellow buckets about a gallon size. The raisins and currants came in paper sacks . . . nothing was in packages.

We had a big wood cookstove and plenty of wood, but it had to be cut to fit the stove, about two feet long. Sometimes when the men didn't cut the wood, mama would go to the woodpile. The woodpile was a pile of wood of all lengths that had been cut down in the woods and hauled to the house and piled down, and then a good solid short big log was kept for a chopping block. Then the long piece was put on it and an ax cut two feet off, two feet off until it was gone, then another. . . . .

Our hall was about eight feet by sixteen feet, and the walls were sealed with about four inch boards . . . running cross ways, painted white and looked real nice.

When it rained day after day, we stayed in the house and looked out the window at the water. The house was built [next to] a pond, because grandpa

Figure 11.18. Charles Canfield Morse and his wife Abby Ivie ("Joy") Beeler. Courtesy of Leilani Morse Cross.

wanted it there because of the pretty trees. Uncle John had said he had killed wild ducks in the pond, years before the house was built. . . .

We had colored help . . . cooks. One was named Violet [and she] stayed two years; one named Rhena, a good cook. But the place was big and lots of cleaning to do. [There were] sixty trees in the yard, water oaks, lots of leaves.

The farm buildings: *When it was real dry weather, we played all over the yard, lot, pasture, in the big barn, the buggy house. The big barn had two sixteen foot by sixteen foot rooms, one on each side of the drive hallway in the middle. Each was filled with hay and other feed. There was a little door on either end, high up, so the wagons of hay could drive up on the outside and put the hay in from the top. Other feed was put in by the door. The chickens would have their nests in this hay, and we would go high to find them. We were never allowed in the lot if there were any stock in it, but when they branded their calves and colts, we looked through the fence or sat on top of the fence. All fences were made of six inch planks, running long ways, and we could see through the spaces between the planks.*

The fence was fastened to the barn. The barn had a big roof. It covered the two hay cribs and hallway, and all across was a shed for the cows (about 42 by 8 feet), and the same across the front for horses' stalls.

The neighborhood. *Our neighbors were the Howards. . . . Mr. Wash Howard [was] papa's best friend. They had three boys and then a girl named Eva, my age. . . . They all had the whooping cough, and their baby little Dave died with it. . . . Mr. Charlie Morse and family lived right across the gully in a big two story house. . . . The Charlie Morse family had several children when their mother died, Mrs. Ivie Morse, leaving husband, Willie, Hattie, Ella, and Ivy. The Holmes family lived about three miles from us. The Arseneaux family, and another named Cosmos, and the George Morse family.*

Charlie Morse was the son of Hannah Canfield and William Morse and the grandson of Agur Morse. Charlie and his wife Abby Ivie Beeler Morse (Figure 11.18) lived with his grandmother, Harriet George, until Harriet died in 1894. Mrs. Holmes was Mary E. Morse, daughter of Rev. John Kell Morse, and sister of George Edward Morse. Many of the locations of their residences are shown in Figure 11.13.

Elizabeth Morse and her husband Richard Grant lived on Rusk Street in Houston with their children and with Elizabeth's mother Grace Morse (Agur Morse's widow), but they had a weekend home on a remnant piece of the old Pleasant Bend Plantation that she inherited. The Grants moved to San Antonio after her mother Grace Morse's death in 1890. By the time Grace died, the next generation of the Agur Morse and John Kell Morse families lived either at Piney Point (Charlie Morse, George E. Morse, Mary Morse Holmes Mallette) or in Houston (Josiah Morse and George W. Morse); none lived on the old Pleasant Bend Plantation grounds.

The Lewis McFee family moves to West Texas, in 1890

Farming was a difficult, unpredictable and often unprofitable occupation, at a time when subsistence farming was nearly the only source of income on a small family farm. In his effort to provide for his growing family, Cassie's father moved the family around quite a bit, to Fort Bend County in 1886 for six months, to San Angelo in Tom Green County in 1890–1891 for ten months, to a spot on the Brazos River in Fort Bend County in 1895, and to the Bauer and Norman homes along Westheimer Road east of Piney Point, also in 1895. Each seems to have been a move to what he hoped would be a better life, and in nearly every case they seem to have been disappointed, and returned for a time to her grandfather James McFee's house to regroup or recharge. These moves were made in covered wagons and buggies. Here is her description of one of those adventures, the move from Piney Point to San Angelo in 1890, when she was four years old; she drew the accompanying illustration (Figure 11.19):

> *My father and Charlie Bodeen the German man were on horseback with the stock, in the lead. The two wagons were driven by Jim and George Nast, and mama was in the buggy with Lillian, me and Jim, last. Quite a procession, going west to get rich. . . .*
>
> *The two wagons had wagon sheets tied down over the wooden bows, with our household goods and plows, rakes, hoes, etc. inside. [There was] a wagon seat for the colored man who drove to sit on. The back end gate had a troft made on the outside for to feed two horses at a time. In the daytime, things were put in the trofts. . . . Water jugs . . . were crockery jugs with a cork stopper, or if lost, we put corn cobs for stoppers. [We] kissed our grandfather goodbye, and he wished for us all the good luck. I often wondered if he thought it was a good move. The roads were rough and rocky, sandy trails. Someone told papa to draw a line to San Angelo and follow that line. Whether he did or not, they went through little towns, big ones . . . Fluellen's Gin, Fulshear, Brookshire, Columbus, La Grange, Bastrop, Austin, Llano, Fields Creek, Brady, Eden, to San Angelo, and fifteen miles on*

Figure 11.19. Cassie McFee Reeder's drawing of the Lewis McFee family moving from Piney Point to San Angelo in 1890. Lewis and a German hired man, Charlie Bodeen, were on horseback, driving the family herd in front of the procession. African American hired men Jim and George Nast drove the two wagons, and Celia McFee drove the buggy. Lightly retouched. Courtesy of Matilda Reeder.

the other side. . . . It was August and hot weather...no rain anytime, and no one was sick during the trip. They made only a few miles a day, probably 25 or 30 miles. At night they had to cook, cooked biscuits in a big iron skillet. Mama said that the colored man did most of the cooking. [He made] the fire first, took the coals and put them under the long legged skillet, put the bread in the skillet, and put the iron lid on it. The skillet lid had a hook on top in the middle, and the lid was sunk in around the hook. This was to hold the coals of fire so the biscuits could cook. They were good. [We had] bacon, eggs, Irish potatoes, steak, when they could buy it. They had some wild game—birds, I guess rabbits. They stopped at noon for lunch and feed and rest the horses. [We would] sleep in a tent at night. Charlie slept under one wagon and the colored men under the other wagon. . . .

Dry weather and high climate, sunburn, thirsty, hot, tired. Jim [her baby brother] would go to sleep and mama made him a bed in the foot of the buggy at her feet. He was there asleep one day when we came to a creek, and before we or she thought we were fording the creek, and it was deeper than she thought, and the water touched the bottom of the wagon bed, she had to drive but she wondered what if the water could wash out the bottom and the baby, but it didn't.

My papa had a violin wrapped up in a flour sack, and at night some time he would play. Us and the colored men were his audience. Well, one day the wagon went over a big rock and the violin fell out, and under the wheel. When George picked it up, it sounded like a sack of bones. Well, the music ceased for awhile. When we got to San Angelo, papa sent to New York for another violin. . . .

There were no negroes in these counties, and everyone would say, "Where are you going, we don't have negroes in this county." Papa would say, "We are going through the country. I will send them back to Houston when I have reached my destination." The negroes were afraid, and papa would say, "I won't let you get hurt."

Papa would buy corn along the way. One time we were in a German settlement. He asked to buy corn, and they said "don't understand," so he didn't get anywhere. Finally he told Charlie the German boy, "It is up to you to speak German." Charlie had always said "I don't know German, I don't understanding their jabbering." But papa had to have the corn, so he gave Charlie the money. He didn't want to go, but he did, and how he made them understand [I don't know], but we got the corn. Charlie had two Bibles in German, and mama was keeping them in a safe place for him.

On we went, it was so dry, until water was a problem, especially for the herd. I guess they only got water when we came to creeks, where there were springs. One day it was nearly night. We all stoped in front of a farm house, we were all thirsty, to get a drink, but the lady said, "I don't have any water to give you, and she held up a pitcher, only about half a gallon, and said, "This is all I have for my family to drink, but there is a good creek with plenty of springs water seven miles down the road." So we went the seven miles, and it was after night when we got there. When the woman [there] said she didn't have any water, mama said that I said, Let's go back to grandpa's house, there's plenty of water in his well." On Sunday we got to a creek, and stayed over. Mama washed Jim's diapers on Sunday. She said the "ox was in the ditch," but that she had never done washing on Sunday before.

Well, we finally got to San Angelo . . . papa went to the Court House to see about his land. . . . Well, we went to our new land, fifteen miles west of San Angelo. It was a pretty place, grass, mesquite trees, prairie dogs. Everywhere [were] holes and the dogs would just fall in their holes when you chase them. They barked, barked. There were rocks, colored rocks, all kinds of cactus—some flat, some tall, all had stickers. . . . We needed a pen for the work horses, so the men would cut mesquite tops and made a pen, round with an opening for a gate. . . . No fence, no house, so papa unloaded the wagons of everything, and we camped. No sign of rain. We went into town, bought enough lumber for our house, and the men built it in a few days. A sixteen by sixteen foot one room, boxed house. We didn't have a well, so we brought a big barrel, made a slide, and hauled water from the Concho Creek, one mile away from a spring in the creek. Mama always kept a tin cup hanging on the side of the barrel, so when the Mexicans travelling along the road stopped for a drink, it was always ready. . . .

Well after we had been in Tom Green County about ten months, they decided to move back to Piney Point, not in wagons this time, but by train. [They] put all the furniture and farming equipment on a box car, all stock in a stock car, and old Frank the dog had to be put in a crated box labeled "Feed and water this dog." . . . I had never ridden on a train, so I was excited about everything, especially the water cooler and its faucet. I had never seen a faucet before, so I proceeded to turn it, and with my tin cup I brought water for mama, Jim, Lillian and myself. When I got to papa, he said, "If you don't leave that faucet alone and sit down, I'll whip you!" So I sat down.[26]

Death and cotton. The life of a small farmer was hardscrabble at best, and death was a frequent visitor to homes that still had unscreened windows and open water well shafts. The following passage tells of the death of Cassie's younger sister, Lillian, at age seven in 1895—and how even Lillian had worked in the family's cotton fields at Piney Point.

We looked out [one day] and there was Uncle Dabney [Walker] and Dab Barnhill . . . both on horseback. [They] had come some twelve miles, looking for stock, and came by to see us. . . . After we had an early supper, and our kinfolks left for home, we went to bed. The next morning, Lillian had a fever, and Jim was already sick. By Friday Lillian was much worse, and we had Dr. Hample to see both of them. Lillian became unconscious, fever higher and higher. They took Jim into another room. One of the neighbors, Mrs. Annie Strubing, came on horseback and stayed all night. . . . They began bathing her head with cold water. Her hair seemed to be in the way, so they cut some of it away. She would draw her feet backwards until they would almost touch her back of her head. . . . . She would have spasms [that] lasted about twenty minutes. . . I didn't sleep anytime that night. When I would get close to the room, I could hear papa crying, and mama praying as Mrs. Strubing and they did all they could for her. But the next day . . . my little sister Lizzie Lillian aged 7 years and 3 months and about 20 days passed away. . . . The neighbors laid Lillian out. Mrs. Ed Beeler made a white lawn dress for her. One of the men went to Houston in a single top buggy to get the casket. . . . Mr. Ed Beeler went horseback the twelve miles to the Brazos to tell Aunt Daisy and Pat, Uncle Dabney, to have the grave dug beside Estell. It was very hot weather. I remember Aunt Daisy and Uncle Pat came in their one-seated buggy, and their colored hired hand in the big wagon. Mr. Wash Howard that lived at grandfather's came in a nice new spring wagon. Late in the afternoon, nearly night we left to go to the Brazos. Jim was still very sick. Mr. Howard and Uncle Pat went in his spring wagon and took the remains. Mama wrapped Jim (he was 5 years old) in a quilt and she, Jim and Aunt Daisy went in the buggy. Papa and the negro man sat on the seat of the wagon, and Annie May and I sat on some quilts on the floor in the back of the wagon. I held her in my lap. I stayed awake a long time. . . .

The next morning was Sunday. . . . At 10 a.m. we went to the White Lake cemetery [Hodge's Bend Cemetery, in modern Sugar Land], two miles from Aunt Sallie's. . . . Uncle Dabney [related to Cassie's mother] stayed at the house with Jim. . . . The neighbors sang "When the Tree of Life is Blooming Meet me There." It was very hot weather. While we were at the grave, Annie May took a high fever and she lay down under the shade of a tree. Mama said that Lillian and Estell both died of Congestion [malaria]. A lot of sick people that year. . . .

Monday morning Mr. Howard took us home. . . . We sat, all five of us, under the trees in the front yard before we went into the house. The wagon had cotton in it. We took the sacks of cotton out of the wagon. We hadn't picked much cotton, but mama had put strings on the flour sacks to put over our shoulders. Lillian's had a colored string, with about two pounds of cotton in it. Sad indeed. We had picked it when we were well. Her little hands had handled this very cotton only a week before. I remembered Papa crying and so crushed. Finally mama said, "We must not take it so hard on account of the children." The days that followed were almost unbearable. Everywhere we looked, we saw something of her.

July 20 1887. My uncle John Hough McFee, 32 years old, was single and living with his mother and father in the big house at Piney Point. [He] had many friends [and would] go out of his way to make more friends, drove a good horse and buggy, came to Houston often. Liked by everyone. He and the negro hand were going to kill a beef at 5 a.m. and his pistol jammed, and did not fire; he threw the pistol down, it turned over, and fired, hitting Hugh in the side . . . [they] sent for a Doctor. He lived until 3 am next morning. My mother said it was a moonshiny night, and that the night he was sick the house was full of people and that every post around the place had a buggy and horse tied to it, many from Houston 10 miles away, but no one could save him. His last words [were] "I hate to leave my mother." He was buried by his brother Joe and great grandparents in Morse cemetery 6 miles west of Houston. They sold one of his horses and bought a nice tombstone (it is there now).

Well, his parents needed someone to tend the ranch, run the cattle. My father was the only one, so in a few weeks my father and mother moved into the big house with my grandparents. My first remembrance was to carry my grandmother a drink of water down a long back porch and spilling half of it before I reached her.

The area was still half wild, and hunting was still a necessary pastime:

The days came and went [that] summer, and . . . the roses seemed to me now that they were always in bloom, but in the fall death called again. My papa and uncle John went hunting on the Bayou, spent the night sleeping on damp ground, didn't hurt papa but uncle John caught Pneumonia and died in a few days leaving his wife, 2 girls and expecting another baby. . . . John was buried by the side of Hough McFee and Joe in the Morse cemetery 6 miles from Houston.

These McFee family burials at the Morse cemetery at the former Pleasant Bend Plantation began in 1874 with the death of her uncle Joe, the same year Grace Morse opened the burial ground up to the public. The McFee family had been close neighbors throughout the 1850s and 1860s, so it was only natural to bury Joe and the others there.

The George Edward Morse family and farm, Piney Point

George Edward Morse (1853–1901; Figure 11.20 A) came to Texas as a toddler in the 1850s with his parents, Rev. John Kell Morse (1808–1863) and Caroline A. Jones Morse (1820–1864), as we saw in Chapter 7. They settled on the west edge of Agur Morse's Pleasant Bend Plantation, where John Kell Morse was a Methodist preacher and small farmer. John Kell Morse was Agur's brother. George Edward Morse was orphaned at a young age when his parents died of consumption in 1863–1864, and he went to live first with Houston sawmill operator and hardware merchant Theodore Bering and his wife. By the 1870 census George had moved in with Buckman Canfield's widow, Harriet George, and her daughter Hannah Canfield (widow of his uncle, William Morse) at the old Canfield estate at Piney Point. Harriet adopted him as one of her own.

In 1879 George married Mary Luna (Mollie) Thornton (1861–1898). Mollie (Figure 11.20 B) was the daughter of Mary Jarvis Silliman and John Wesley Thornton, a Civil War veteran and a stock raiser in Pittsville, south of modern Katy in Fort Bend County. Mollie Thornton Morse's grandmother, Mary Frisbee Silliman, had run the inn at Wheaton's Ford in the 1850s and early 1860s. Mollie was probably born there, only a few miles west of Piney Point. The couple had five children who survived to adulthood (Figure 11.21): Lena Ethelyn (1881–1947), Annie Maie (1884–1960), Jeannette Oliver (1890–1975), George Edward Jr. (1891–1921), and Martha "Mattie" Florence (1897–1967).

Figure 11.20. George Edward Morse and his wife Mary Luna "Mollie" Thornton.
Courtesy of the late Mrs. Arch B. Marshall.

Figure 11.21. Children of George Edward Morse and his wife Mary Luna "Mollie" Thornton, ca. 1900.
Left to right: George Edward Jr., Mattie Florence, Annie Maie, Lena Ethelyn, and Jeannette Oliver.
Courtesy of the late Mrs. Arch B. Marshall.

In 1880 George Edward Morse bought the first of two homes he would own in Piney Point, on a tract called the Smalley Place. Harriet George's only daughter by her second husband James Todd was Mary Elizabeth Todd (also called Mary George), who had married Benjamin Smalley (b. 1841) in 1867. In 1868 Harriet deeded the couple a 200-acre tract east of the Canfield-George home that became known as the Smalley Place. It is not clear whether the Smalleys ever lived there. Smalley, born in Illinois, came to Texas as a young child and served in Waul's Texas Legion during the Civil War. After the war he settled in Waller and later Austin and Galveston counties, where he pursued a career in timber production and stock raising.[27] After Smalley's wife Mary died, Charles Morse obtained the tract, and then sold the north part of it to George Morse. The south side was obtained by J. C. Redding; both owners are shown on the east side of the map in Figure 11.13 A.[28]

George Morse's daughter, Jeannette Morse Holladay (1890–1975), recalled that house:

> *After Papa . . . married, he brought his bride . . . to an area about twelve miles west of the then very small town of Houston, where they lived in a two-story house in a clearing in front of deep woods close to Buffalo Bayou. This old two-story house much later was sold to a German family by the name of Timm [Timme] and became known as the Timm place. It was in this house that Lena Ethelyn (Sister), John, who died at two months, and Annie Maie were born. Papa's oldest sister, Mary, married Robert Holmes and they lived in this community and later, when their eldest son Charlie married, he lived near Papa and had a daughter named Gertrude. . . . While living at that home, when the family wanted game for the table, Papa would go in the woods and bring back turkey, deer, prairie chickens, doves or quail. Whatever was easiest. There was never any lack of game, as he was a good marksman.*[29]

The family moved into Houston in about 1889, seeking an easier life, and built a house at the corner of Smith and Hadley, where their children Jeannette and George Edward Jr. were born. But three years later Harriet George died, and left her Piney Point property to be divided among Ennis and Myra Smalley (her two grandchildren by her daughter Mary), her grandson Charles Canfield Morse, and George Edward Morse.[30] George then moved back into the community, on acreage purchased from W. P. Harris (west side of Figure 11.13 A). His cousin Charles Canfield Morse lived nearby, in Charles's mother Harriet George's old house. Jeannette remembered her life at their new Piney Point home and its surrounding farm, where the last two of the family's children, Nancy and Mattie Florence were born. The farm varied only in details from the small farm of their McFee neighbors:

> *This land was divided by the narrow gauge railroad plying between Houston and Sealy, Texas, and said road was paralleled by a farm road that later was designated Westheimer Road. Papa built our last family home facing the railroad track and Westheimer Road and fenced both tracts. On the north tract thirty acres were reserved for a garden, an orchard and corn and grain sorghum. He planted peach trees that lived long enough to bear fruit a few times, and then they died of leaf curl. Fig trees planted around the home site grew large, and the figs were sweet. On the avenue in front of the house, hackberry trees were planted for shade, and in the back of the house cottonwood trees grew tall and furnished lots of shade.*
>
> *This white-painted home consisted of six rooms divided by a wide, long enclosed hall, which served as a combination hall and sitting room. The hall was furnished with an upright piano, chairs, and a lounge that served as a bed at night. The hall opened onto a large, long back porch from which three steps led down to the backyard. There were no screens on the house then. On the west side of the hall was Mama and Papa's bedroom; next was a big dining room; and then a large kitchen with a wood-burning range. This was where on Saturdays a huge galvanized tub was brought in for the family*

baths as there was no indoor plumbing at this time. In front on the east side was the parlor and two bedrooms with plenty of sleeping facilities for all of us. We had no clothes closets then, only big armoires in each bedroom. . . . Each bedroom had a large dresser with deep drawers, a wash stand (Mama's had a marble top), and open ends on each side of the middle enclosure where our shoes were placed, and we had plenty of chairs.

To furnish water for the house, we had a grand water well, with a hand pump set up on a big five foot square platform. A wooden trough led from the pump to a large tank for the livestock. Located in front of the pump under the shade trees was the dairy room, which did have a screened window and door. The big milk pans, curd cups and large churn sat on stout shelves on the wall. North of the pump was a thirty foot square smokehouse with heavy timbers supporting the roof, and bare rafters for hanging links of sausage and hams to be hickory smoked after curing. Only a few barrels of salt pork were made. I well remember the rendering of the lard and its being poured into ten-gallon cans, later dubbed Silver Leaf Lard cans. Here Papa again raised cattle, horses, and hogs.

One of the fig trees growing between the smokehouse and the stock pen was the favorite of all of us children for climbing, and we were never denied the pleasure of picking any figs within our reach. There was always enough for the family table and for preserving. I can still remember quart glass jars being sterilized by upending them on the white picket fence in the sun to dry after being washed.[31]

What is clear from this description is that the small farms in the area were quickly being all but completely fenced in, marking the end of the open range north of the railroad, at least at Piney Point and points east. Also clear is a marked change in the standard of living; the amount of household furniture and improvements—though still not modern, and still with no indoor plumbing—were vastly ahead of those that had been listed in the probate inventory of George's uncle Agur T. Morse only thirty years earlier, or of those in Buckman Canfield's inventory fifty years earlier.

All was not roses. While living at this farm George and Mary Luna ("Mollie") dealt with the tragic early death of a child to disease, just as had their neighbors, the McFees. Following the death of her infant daughter Nancy Thornton Morse, Mollie wrote to her sister Nancy Thornton, for whom the baby was named:

Piney Point
May 10th, 1895

My darling sister,
I hardly know what to say, for my heart is breaking. I reckon you have gotten the word on this. The last was written to be sent as a telegram. We sent two in by Charlie M [Morse]. . . . My darling had fever so I had the Dr. to prescribe for her on Saturday last. She seemed to be doing well, was up all day Sunday & Monday until 3 o'clock p.m. when she took a cramp in her stomach. I worked with her & got her easy but felt uneasy so stayed up all night with her and sent for the Dr. the next morning, Tuesday. He came & gave more medicine & stayed quite a while. She seemed to be doing as well as could be expected until Wednesday 2 o'clock p.m. when she took another cramp as I thought. But there were several there who heard she was sick & happened in just at the moment when she took worse, & they thought that it surely was a congestive chill as she passed away so quick & so easy. Not a struggle. She left us at half past 4 Wednesday evening. I will be so glad when your school is out & you can come. We are so lonely. Mr. Shea sent a basket of flowers (pansies) and a sweet note. Several friends from town came out; our friends seemed to be many. But there is nothing that anyone can say that will ease the pain. Good night, darling sister. I can't see to write any more. Do write to me.
Your loving sister,
MLM[32]

Schools

The federal census of 1880 lists as a teacher Harriet Wright, aged twenty-eight, from England; she lived near Wheaton's Ford (by then called the Habermachers' place). It is not known precisely where her schoolhouse was, if indeed she had one. There was also an African American schoolteacher named Henry Turpin, from Haiti. The location of his schoolhouse is also not known. According to the census he lived near the Alfred family, who worked for the Morses, so it is likely that his instruction took place in Piney Point.

The first known permanent school in the area was near the southwest corner of modern Jeanetta Street at Westheimer Road, in Piney Point. The schoolhouse lay next to the wooded Piney Point Gully, which has since been filled in south of Westheimer and covered with concrete. Jeannette Morse Hollady, daughter of George Edward Morse, had this to say of it about 1893:

> *Occasionally, on the week-end, Papa would go to Houston to get a preacher to preach on Sunday in the one-room school house he had built on the corner of the east end of the south side tract of our land. This was the only schoolhouse for many miles outside of Houston. The preacher stayed with us and occupied a bed placed for him in the parlor. Also, during the summer months, the parlor was turned into a bedroom for the teacher, and I assume she paid a minimum amount for the board. She, Lena Ethelyn and Annie Maie were taken in a buggy to school during very bad weather; otherwise they walked. I was much too young, and brother younger still.*[33]

By about 1905 there was new and apparently improved schoolhouse just a mile to the west, and it appears on the U.S. Geological Survey topographic map of 1915. There is now an automotive safety inspection station on that site, at the southwest corner of Jeanetta Street at Westheimer Road. Jeannette Hollady writes about this later schoolhouse as having been built by a Colonel A. B. Nibbs, who purchased the old Harriet George home and its surrounding 200 acres from Sam and Josephine Bongio in 1899; the Bongios had bought it in 1896 from Charles Canfield Morse:[34]

> *Col. Nibbs had built a fairly large one-room schoolhouse on the corner of the land on Westheimer Road, adjoining our land, and Mollie [Nibbs's daughter] and I, being the same age, became good friends. Col. Nibbs had two daughters, maybe three. One, when I knew her, was the widow of a Judge Means; one was Mrs. Roy Kinkaid of Houston. The latter established the second private grade school in Houston . . . where only the wealthiest families sent their children.*
>
> *Our teacher, old Professor Wakefield, the country schoolteacher, boarded with the Nibbs. He taught all the grades. I was then in second year high school, and Latin, English and history were my loves. He was a dear old man and a wonderful teacher.*[35]

Hard times for have-nots: African Americans, Arab travelers, and wanderers

Times were exceedingly hard for many African Americans in the area in the late nineteenth century. Those who remained in the countryside and who were not farm owners or sharecroppers found low-paying jobs as farm workers, day laborers, and domestic servants on white small farms. Even a struggling farm family like that of James and Cassandra McFee could afford to employ several black farm hands; their granddaughter Cassie McFee Reeder (1886–1979) wrote that they employed two women domestic servants and two male hired hands in the early 1890s.[36]

A perhaps rather idealized view of the life of African American servants at the time can be found in the childhood memories of Jeannette Hollady, speaking of her father George Edward Morse's farm in Piney Point:

East and about fifty feet from our house was a two-room cabin built by Papa for the colored boys working for Papa, who paid them the going wage plus their food, same food as our family ate and all they wanted. Papa was known as a good provider and never lacked for adequate help. At night the three colored boys, Ed Sullivan sixteen years old, Henry Alford about eighteen years old, and Tommy Alford about twenty years old would eat their supper on a big table in the kitchen and then wash the dishes. There was an ample supply of milk, both sweet and buttermilk, plus Jersey butter for everyone. About dusk in the summer, the family gathered on the big front veranda running the full width of the house. The colored boys sat on hard pan ground, leaning against hackberry tree trunks and all would sing, with the exception of Tommy Alford, whose humming sounded like a violin. Henry had a beautiful voice and Ed played the jew's harp, pronounced as if "juice-harp." We children would listen until the sandman took over.[37]

Cassie McFee Reeder painted a bleaker portrait of the world that black workers inhabited in the neighborhood. Writing of 1893, she remembered:

It was hard times for the colored folks in the neighborhood. When we hired a colored woman for a day or two, they brought sometimes two little children with them to play in the yard while she worked, and when they started home, the woman would ask mama for some of the leftovers from our dinner for the family. I remember mama telling papa about it, and they said "Well, we can't see them go hungry" and would give them groceries.

Times were hard for others as well. Cassie noted a number of itinerant people wandering the roads at the time, both white "tramps" and even some rather exotic traveling Arab families:

Papa began building our [new] house on the Brazos and was gone. Tramps came in by day to ask for food. [Mama] would fix a handout for them, but it was very often, through the years, [that] she was afraid of them. Late one evening we saw one coming. She told the hired man [Willie, an African American] to say. . . they couldn't keep him, and that there was a house just up the road. Sure enough, the tramp asked, and Willie told him. When Willie told mama, she said, "Yes, but I know they won't let him stay and we will have him back here." Sure, he hollowed "Hello" and Willie went out to see him, so mama told him to sleep in the buggy house and not to smoke. That was the reason she didn't like people sleeping there. Then she let Willie sleep in our hall; it was about 10 o'clock by now, but I was still awake. Mama didn't sleep at all. Next morning, the tramp thanked Willie for letting him sleep in the buggy house, and our dog just played with the tramp.

Early that year [1893] in the summer Arab women—with little baskets with jewelry, beads, fans, whistles, combs, hair pins—would start from Houston and about get the ten miles by night. Sometimes one; one night there were two and before night there were three more, so all five of them stayed all night, and mama gave them our room and we slept on the floor in mama's room. They kneeled down in the middle of the floor and prayed. We couldn't understand them, but they sold us some goods the next morning. When they ate at the table they held their bread in their laps and pinched it off part at a time.[38]

Socializing out in the country

The neighborhood south of the bayou was close-knit, and there were many opportunities for socializing. One gathering place was a large wooden platform constructed by the Texas Western railroad at its forty-acre Piney Point facilities, which were located in between the McFee farm and the Canfield-George place, east of the McFee farm and north of the railroad tracks (Figure 11.13 A).[39] That outdoor platform was used for dances and religious revival meetings. Cassie McFee Reeder, who lived nearby, described it:

Near our house at Piney Point, there was a platform (pavilion) that belonged to the Railroad Company. It was built when the railroad came through and was back in the woods, but it was railroad land and their property.

The colored people had dances on the old platform . . . east of our place in the pretty woods. Whites had dances there, too, and picnics. Later, my mother would get Brother J. W. Anderson—a Baptist preacher who spent many nights at our house on his way to preaching at places—she would get him to preach a week meeting on this platform. She and pa would carry lights (lantern and kerosene lamp; wind sometimes blew out the lamp), pitcher of water and glass, anything else that was needed. [We would] invite the neighbors to church. We all would go. Brother Anderson would preach "the unchurchable [unsearchable] riches of Jesus the Savior of the world." [They were the] only sermons some people ever heard. We all would sing. My papa would sing bass. The preacher sang "Railroad to Heaven."[40]

Cassie's grandfather James McFee's farm was close to the African American Pilgrim Rest Missionary Baptist Church (see Chapter 9), and she tells of the salvation of one of its members after an epic dancing contest at that open-air platform. The woman who was saved was Rhena, a favorite African American servant of the McFee family during Cassie's childhood in the late 1880s and early 1890s:

We had a colored girl from Fort Bend County named Rhena. She was a worker. She would hitch up the mules to the wagons, and go to the woods and get wood for the fires. Rhena liked to play with us children, she was a real maid. I remember she would take us for a walk. . . . One day we went out to the big road, crossed the road, crossed the railroad, down the hill, to the gully . . . a long wide thick board (I can see it now) was a bridge. . . . Rhena put me across first, then she took Lillian. Lillian had on a starched blue bonnet. It fell off in the water, the stream was swift, and Rhena couldn't catch it, so we went home without the bonnet. When Rhena told my mama, [mama] just hugged Lillian and said, "Just so you didn't lose my little girl." Rhena went away just as happy [as she could be]. Mama said maybe some little girl will find it who needed it worse than you do.

Rhena could dance. Well, Rhena went to the dances. Some of the white men would go sometimes and watch them dance. We always heard about it from Rhena anyway. I used to hear papa tell about it long years afterward that one night there was a little negro girl from town, out there, and she was one of the best, or supposed to be the best. Well, she did her best, it was fine. . . . but Rhena was a good-sized woman, and you know how they dance; [they] cut so many shines. Finally, Rhena sauntered out to the middle of the floor and held her dress on each side with her hands and really danced all over the place and took the cake. Papa laughed about it at home, to Rhena. Mama didn't like so much [papa] bragging about the dance.

Not long after that, the colored people had a revival in the little country church just behind our house (about eight city blocks, [but] this was country). Rhena was gloriously converted, and never would dance anymore. I know now [that] my mama was praying for her.[41]

In 1893 seven-year-old Cassie tasted her first ice cream at a picnic at the platform:

At a picnic I saw my first ice cream. Cousin Charlie Redding had a big ice cream freezer, about 2 gallons. We were at a picnic at the platform. He had bought the ice in Houston in one big piece, about three feet high and two feet through. It was in a grass sack with sawdust between the ice and sack. While they were grinding the ice cream freezer, I asked, "What are you doing?" They said this is ice cream, and it is good, and it is black. So I was looking for black ice cream!

At that time Houstonians would take a day trip on the narrow gauge train out to Piney Point to picnic on the sandy beaches of Buffalo Bayou and swim in its then clear water. Catfish and "buffalo fish" caught in the bayou were the focal point of many a fish fry among the German communities north of the bayou.[42] July 4 brought barbecues and dances, as Cassie described:

> *One July 4, we all went to Fort Bend to a barbecue, all day and supper also, dancing at night. We went in the wagon, and Miss Lena Morse and Annie Maie Morse went with us. Another year, we went in the wagon, and papa put up the wagon sheet, to a barbecue, all day and dance that night. Charlie Dodson and her aunt Mrs. Patterson went with us.*[43]

Interrelationships

The farmers in the rural upper Buffalo Bayou neighborhood along the southern bank of the bayou were almost all inter-related by the late nineteenth century, as they were the children of the old pioneers at Wheaton's Ford, Piney Point, and Pleasant Bend, and they had all grown up knowing one another. As mentioned earlier, for example, Elizabeth Wheaton's daughter, Amanda Jane Wheaton, had married German immigrant Thomas Habermacher's son Lawrence Habermacher around 1850. At Piney Point, Harriet (Canfield) George's daughter Hannah Canfield had first married William Morse of Pleasant Bend, but after his death in 1866 and the death of her second husband, Thomas Hurt, she married Abram Frisby Silliman in 1874. Abram was a son of Mary Frisby Silliman, previous owner of Wheaton's Ford. Abram Silliman's sister, Mary Jarvis Silliman, married John Wesley Thornton, which made Hannah an aunt by marriage of the Thornton's children. Their daughter Mary Luna ("Mollie") Thornton married George Morse in 1879. By the end of the

Figure 11.22. The former home of Hannah Canfield (Morse) Silliman and her husband, Abram Frisby Silliman, in San Felipe, Texas. The home had a number of earlier owners before the Sillimans moved there in about 1880, and was later named the Hill House for residents who purchased it in 1899.

century, everyone seem to be related to everyone else in that rural world, just as the German settlers north of the bayou were inter-related.

Abram and Hannah moved to San Felipe, Texas, in about 1880, to a house that is now called Hill House, on modern Park Road 38 (Figure 11.22).[44] The couple were in their twilight years in February 1891. Abram would die later that year, resulting in Hannah moving back to Piney Point to nurse her aged mother, Harriet George. Harriet and Hannah would both be dead before the end of 1894. But before all that came to pass, Nancy Thornton came for a visit in 1891, and she wrote to her sister Florence Thornton from the Silliman home. The letter shows the complex family ties binding this former pioneer community on Buffalo Bayou—children and grandchildren of Agur Morse and John Kell Morse at Pleasant Bend, Buckman Canfield and Harriet George of Piney Point, and the Sillimans and Thorntons of Wheaton's Ford, Sealy, and San Felipe:

> *San Felipe, Texas*
> *Feb. 21st, 1891*
> *Dear Florence,*
> *I am spending a few days with Aunt Hannah, while Uncle Abe is away, and this is a splendid place to write letters, so I will reply to yours of recent date. I cannot begin to tell what a pleasant time I am having. So peaceful and restful. At first I was somewhat lonely, because there are so few here in this great large house compared to what it used to be. But you know Aunt H is lively company, and Elias is a model boy—almost a man. Now he seems melancholy at times, on account of Piercey's death, which of course he feels very much. Abie and Lizzie are quite a cozy couple. I spent one afternoon with them.*
>
> *Aunt Hannah gave me a beautiful book that was Miss Ella's as a keepsake. I scarcely know how to phrase my appreciation of such a treasured memento of one whose influence was so precious and who was never [tempted] to wander from the path of duty and love. We miss her, but I feel at times that she is present.*
>
> *San Felipe is almost like a deserted village, but I find too much pleasure here among books, and music to long for social success. I suppose I will go back to Houston next week. All were well at Pa's when I left on Tuesday last. . . . Little Sis and babies have suffered all ills that human flesh is heir to. They now have whooping cough. Aunt Hannah sends her love and says think of her sometimes.*
> *Good bye,*
> *Nannie*[45]

"Little Sis" was their sister Mary Luna ("Mollie") Thornton Morse (1861–1898), wife of George Edward Morse (1853–1901). At the time she had four children to care for at their home in Piney Point. "Miss Ella" was the daughter of Hannah and her first husband William Morse's daughter Mary Ella G. Morse (1858–1889), who had just died two years earlier.

Wheaton's Ford and the Beeler neighborhood

As mentioned earlier, William J. Habermacher (1851–1919) purchased the old inn at Wheaton's Ford in 1871 and converted it to a private home. He married Kathrene Cole (1855–1933) in 1874, and lived there with his family until his death in 1919. His granddaughter Kate Habermacher (1874-1957), who was born in that house and never married, lived there as late as 1949 (Figures 11.23), when a reporter stopped by to interview her. He described the old house, which Mary Frisby Silliman had occupied in 1855–1864 and, unbeknownst to the reporter, Elizabeth and Joel Wheaton had lived in from the 1830s:

> *Timber for building material in the house was all cut and hand planed on the place. The walls are pine and the sills hewed oak. Mrs. W. J. Habermacher's nephew, Jack Birtchet . . . said: "I have been in the attic and tried nailing into the old rafters—but they are just too hard." In the original rooms, two fireplaces are still usable. The bricks used in*

Right: Figure 11.23. Mrs. Kate Habermacher, granddaughter of William J. Habermacher, in the living room of the Habermacher (former Wheaton and Silliman) home. Courtesy of the *Houston Chronicle,* February 13, 1949.
Below: Figure 11.24. Habermacher home at Wheaton's Ford, as it appeared ca. 1950. The home, built in the 1830s, was destroyed by fire in 1956. Courtesy Marie Neuman Gray and Mrs. Janet Habermacher Bobbit.

the chimneys were fired in the backyard by slaves. The clay was carried from a clay bank about 500 yards from the house, Miss Kate said. A large kitchen which originally was set out from the main house was torn down and the timber used in adding the three new rooms to the old house.

Many interesting stories unfold as visitors sit and chat in the Habermacher living room—stories about the past with its Indians, the event of the railroad's arrival and other developments that made the area less of a wilderness. . . . It used to be that a wagon road . . . forded the bayou just back of the Habermacher hog pen. Today, as in days more than a century ago, travelers still cross Buffalo Bayou in the same place, and some visit the old inn. Hospitality reigns in the Habermacher house.[46]

A photograph from the 1940s, made before the home burned in 1956, still shows the dual entrances of the old inn: one for the owners, and one for the visitors (Figure 11.24).

Beeler neighborhood. In the 1880s and 1890s, just a mile east of Wheaton's Ford (the William Habermacher house) was the Beeler neighborhood, named for the family of James Arlie Beeler (1827–1888) and his wife Amanda Frances Milam (1832–1914), who moved there in the late 1870s. They were from Kentucky, where they were married in 1857. James appears to have had a previous marriage and had several sons, among them Milam (1854–1944), William (1855–1934), and Edward (1856–1953). After the marriage of James and Amanda, they lived in Bonnieville, Hart County, Kentucky, where Abby Ivie Beeler (1861–1896) was born. James and Amanda settled in Louisiana at the time of the Civil War, where several more children were born between 1861 and 1876: Ida, William, Kate, Daisie, and Robert. By the 1880 census the family of eight (including the parents, children borne by Amanda, and their son Edward) were living south of Buffalo Bayou. James was a farmer, aided by his son Ed. Another son, William Beeler, tended cattle on the open range. Harris County tax assessment rolls for 1880 note that the family owned 250 acres in the Wheaton survey and another 24 in the adjacent Hardin survey; they owned 35 cattle, four horses, and a carriage, among other farm equipment. By 1890, when a map was made of the old San Felipe Trail, James had passed away, and his son Ed was shown as the owner (Figure 11.11).

Cassie McFee Reeder told of moving into the Beeler neighborhood for a short time in 1895, in one of her family's many moves of those decades. They eventually moved into a home purchased by Lewis McFee a few years earlier from English settlers J. B. and Eliza Normand, both of whom were born about 1815, according to both the 1870 and 1880 census, which record their stay here. The 1880 tax rolls show that J. B. Normand owned fifty acres in the Hardin survey; their house is also shown on the 1890 map (Figure 11.11). Cassie recalled the Beelers as follows:

About February 1895 we moved to the Beeler neighborhood, 16 miles up the Bayou from Houston, to our Norman[d] place, but it had to be repaired. So we rented a place from Mr. Ed Beeler for several months until our house was ready. . . . The Bauer place was about 1/4 mile from our place. This place had a high fence around the house, china trees . . . the blooms were beautiful and sweet. . . . When spring came the yard was full of all kinds of roses, bridle wreath, lilies, and annual flowers. There was an ash hopper in the backyard where they had made lye for their soap. We had two rooms, and another room in back where mama cooked. . . . We lived in the edge of the woods, and there were three big old oak trees that had fallen down or [were] cut down some time before...[with] clean bleached limbs and we played on these a lot.

We never were across the Bayou, but big children on horseback came every day for their cows from the other side. It was all open prairie, no fences. One was a boy about twelve years old. He got sick and died, the girl said he ate green grapes. We missed him after that.

The biggest snow ever in this country was while we lived here. Papa went to Houston on horseback, and was after dark getting home. When he came back in the house he had snow on his coat.

Figure 11.25. Grave marker at Beeler cemetery for James Arlie Beeler. This cemetery is a Harris County pocket park on Enclave Parkway.

> *other Mrs. Milam Beeler had one boy, then grandma Beeler lived close by with her single girl, Daisy, and a single boy, Jim.*
>
> *Miss Daisy Beeler married at Mr. Ed Beeler's house (Ed was her brother). [She] married Mr. Hillendahl. Everyone from miles around was invited; we went. I remember they took out the partition and had a big long room where the wedding took place. It was summer or spring. Out in the yard at one end, the table was about 100 feet long, with all kinds of food. . . . The bride was in white and a bridal veil.*

Today the old Beeler neighborhood is marked only by the Beeler cemetery that Cassie mentioned, now conserved as a Harris County pocket park on Enclave Parkway. James and Amada Beeler and their son Milam are buried in that graveyard (Figure 11.25). Ed and Bertha left the neighborhood at some time after 1895 and are buried in Humble, Texas; he was a retired rancher at the time of his death. Daisy Beeler married Charles Hillendahl, from north of the bayou, in 1895. James and Amanda's daughter Abby Ivie married Charles Canfield Morse, son of Hannah and William Morse, in 1881, as discussed earlier, and that couple lived at nearby Piney Point on the Canfield estate with Harriet George.

Twilight of the Morses, Canfields and McFees at Piney Point

The time of the pioneer Canfield, Morse, Silliman and McFee families at Pleasant Bend, Piney Point and Wheaton's Ford drew to a close by the end of the century, as death claimed the last of the old pioneers and their children moved on to other places.

Deaths of Mollie and George Morse. Mary Luna ("Mollie") Morse died at the age of thirty-seven on July 12, 1898, of causes that were not recorded but likely were related to disease. Mollie Morse, according to her daughter Jeannette Hollady, was:

> *buried in the cemetery on land which belonged to Grandma George. She (Grandma George) may be buried there also, as I am sure Charlie Morse's wife Joy was. I do remember there was an iron fence around it; it's probably long since rusted down. I do hope the present day owners of all that old property have not destroyed all trace of the graveyard. I have no way of knowing if the grant by Grandma George was ever recorded as a cemetery. If not, it is sad.*[47]

The "Grandma George" Jeannette refers to is Harriet George, Buckman Canfield's widow and essentially George Edward Morse's mother by adoption. That cemetery is very likely the same one mentioned as a second "Morse cemetery" by Trevia Beverly in her book on Houston cemeteries.[48] It was located behind the former Rosewood Hospital, currently St. Michael's Emergency Room, 9000 Westheimer, and appears to have been paved over by apartments. Harriet's son, Charles Canfield Morse, is also thought to have been buried there, with his wife Joy.

George Edward Morse was now left to care for the farm and his family by himself, including infant Mattie Florence ("Patsy"), 7-year-old George Jr., 8-year-old Jeannette, 11-year-old Annie Maie, and 17-year-old Lena Ethelyn (Figure 12.25), as well as tend to the farm. Jeannette recalled: "He had worked many long hours daily to give a good home to his wife and children, and now he was left to cope with two teenage daughters, Brother, Patsy and me. His health failed quickly and steadily, and within two and one-half years he joined Mollie in death, on June 4, 1901."[49] George Edward Morse was buried in Magnolia Cemetery in Houston.

The children were left, as he had once been, as orphans on a farm in the country. Lena Ethelyn married in 1900:

> *When my eldest sister was nineteen, my first school teacher, Miss Grace McPherson, who lived at our house, introduced my sister to Arch Levin Marshall, a divorced widower forty-one years old, who immediately began courtship, and she, never having a beau, thought by marrying it would give us smaller children plus herself a home.*

They lived in the new Houston Heights.

> *My younger sister, Mattie Florence, and I lived with Sister and our guardian paid $5.00 a month each for room and board, and gave them two of Papa's milk cows and what furniture I do not know. . . . Aunt Florence Thornton came and with the consent of her guardian took Mattie Florence (Patsy) with her to old Mexico, where she had been teaching school for six years at the University.*

Lena and her husband and siblings eventually moved back to the old Morse homestead in Piney Point, but the marriage ended in a divorce in 1905; Lena then married Peyton Griffith in 1909. Meanwhile, Annie Maie Morse (Figure 11.26) had moved to Houston, boarding with a Mrs. Archer, and learned a trade. By 1903 she was a stenographer with the Houston Business League, the forerunner of the Houston Chamber of Commerce. By 1905 she was assistant secretary for that organization—its first woman member—and took in her younger siblings Patsy and Jeannette following Lena's divorce.[50] She later became secretary of the Houston Business League, working with her organization on promoting the planned Houston Ship Channel and helping to organize the annual No-Tsu-Oh carnival. In 1910 she married a railroad freight agent and later insurance agent named John Griggs Worrall. The couple had two children before John died in the nationwide flu epidemic of 1918–1919. With the grit of one who had seen adversity before, Annie Maie took over the insurance company and managed it herself. She died in 1960.

The old farm in Piney Point was sold in the first decade of the twentieth century, and with that, none of the descendants of the Houston Morse family—which had been an agricultural family for many generations, going back in time to colonial Connecticut and beyond that to rural England—were directly engaged in agriculture.

Final days of the Canfield-George house and farm. The construction of Harriet George's new house in 1849–1850 involved a love-struck carpenter building it in exchange for the freedom of the slave woman whom he later married (described in Chapter 6). Harriet lived there until her death in 1892, according to the Putnam family Bible.[51] She was probably buried in the Canfield family graveyard at Piney Point.[52] Her obituary appeared in the *Galveston Daily News* of January 6, 1892:

> *This evening, news reached here of the death of*

Figure 11.26. Sisters Jeanette Morse Hollady and Annie Maie Morse Worrall, ca. 1905.

Mrs. Harriett George, one of the earliest settlers of this section. She came here early in the thirties and died after having passed the eightieth mile-post of life. She was a most estimable lady and leaves four grandchildren, all grown, a daughter having died about a year ago. Her death occurred at Piney Point, where she owned large land interests. There are only half a dozen people now living in this section who were here when she came.[53]

Hannah (Canfield) Morse Silliman, whose last husband Abram Silliman had passed away in 1891, had moved back into the Piney Point home to be with her mother in her final months. Hannah died in 1894 and is buried in Glenwood Cemetery in Houston.

Harriet's grandson Charles Morse (1855–1906), the son of Hannah Canfield and William Morse, inherited Harriet's house. He lived at the old house with his wife Abby Ivie Beeler between 1882 and 1896, and while living at Piney Point the couple had seven children: Hattie, Willie, Edith, Bessie, Ella May, Ivie, Daniel, and Clarence. Abby Ivie and her last child, Clarence, both died following complications from childbirth in 1896. According to Jeannette Hollady (1890–1975), Abby Ivie (whom Jeannette called "Joy") was buried in the former Canfield-Morse family cemetery at Piney Point.[54]

The interesting story of the construction of Harriet George's home was addressed in Chapter 5, but certain aspects of that story – those that bear on the building's ultimate demise – bear repeating here. The George home was sold in 1896 after Joy's death, along with 200 acres.[55] Jeannette Morse Hollady, a Morse cousin of Hannah Canfield's husband William Morse, and a niece of Nancy Thornton Eatwell, described the old house that the German carpenter William Bethke had built to win his lover's freedom:

Grandma George's land [Grandma George being her name for Harriet] . . . had a large white colonial house on it built from lumber and heavy timbers that had been milled on the place with machinery she had hauled by ox team from Alabama. Later, this home was inherited by Charlie Morse, whose wife was Joy and they had a daughter named Hattie. . . . Charlie Morse sold Grandma George's home to Sam Bongio, an Italian immigrant.

Sam Bongio . . . sold the Grandma George estate to Colonel A. B. Nibbs, who ostentatiously lived the old-type Southern aristocratic life with his son, Alan B. Nibbs. Young Mrs. Nibbs and daughter, Mollie lived there. Col. Nibbs had built a fairly large one-room school house on the corner of the land on Westheimer Road, adjoining our land, and Mollie and I, being of the same age, became good friends. . . . As Mollie's and my friendship grew, I had the rare privilege of spending many hours in Grandma George's magnificent home, now Col. Nibbs'. Both of Mollie's aunts furnished a grand library with a wealth of the finest literature. . . .

Col. Nibbs died and the Grandma George place was then sold to young Tom C. Dunn, Jr. He took his bride there, furnished it extravagantly, so we were told, as I never was there after the Col. Nibbs family left. But young Mr. Dunn and his wife didn't like the country. The house and all contents burned to the ground to the consternation and regret of all around. The colored help said there was plenty of time and they could have saved much if not all of the furnishings, but Tom Dunn Jr. wouldn't permit anyone to even try. The home and the furnishings were insured.[56]

According to Albert C. Timme (1906–2001), a neighbor who watched the fire as a small boy in January 1912, the pipes had frozen, and the hired help were using lighted hay to try to defrost them when the old home caught on fire. Timme remembered that the house was square in shape, with two stories and a "widow's walk" on the roof (a small high deck with porch railings), typical of Greek Revival southern homes of the mid-nineteenth century.[57] The Houston Daily Post, writing about the fire, described it as a "two-story, twelve-room structure . . . built on the Southern colonial style, and [it] was one of the historical landmarks of Harris County." The house and its contents were valued at $25,000, according to the *Post*.[58] Its position was likely to the northwest of the sawmill on the small rise not far from where the original Taylor/Canfield house had been. That site, obliterated by sand removal operations in the 1950s, is now part of the Windermere subdivision.

The nearby millpond to the Canfield sawmill was beautifully kept into the new millennium as the backdrop of Vargo's Restaurant, but that site was sold by heirs to developers in 2014 and is currently the location of dense, high rise residential construction. The pond has been retained.

Death of James McFee. James McFee's wife Cassandra had died at Piney Point in 1890, after a ten-month stint recovering from a stroke. After her death James lived on in the house at Piney Point. In his golden years, Cassie remarked:

My grandpa was old, and I would undress him at night, and dress him in the morning. He would talk to me of his home in Delaware. He reads all day. . . . He lived in New Orleans many years. He had yellow fever there, and his brother, 21 years old, died of the fever. My grandfather was a little man with a strong voice. . . . He had been a carpenter contractor, building all the [cotton] gins in the Brazos Bottom. For years, there were houses he built.

By 1903 Cassie and her parents and siblings were living in the Houston Heights, with their grandfather. Her grandfather became ill:

In 1903, my grandpa got sick in the summer. He did not get better. He wanted to go back to Piney Point, so we took him back. We still had the place in town. I sat up one night and papa the next with him. . . . I was so worried about him, we all loved him so. . . . On November 9, 1903 he died, in his room at Piney Point Texas. He lacked two months of being 89 years old. Mr. Dodson and someone else laid him out. We buried him in the old Morse burying Ground. . . . His three sons, his wife's grandmother and grandfather and his wife were all buried there, and years later my baby was buried there. Brother Evanda Ammons, a Baptist preacher, preached the funeral. Mrs. Timme brought the prettiest flowers. . . . We missed him so much, even the cat. His cat would go through the house and mew.

James McFee was perhaps the last of his generation of early pioneer settlers of the area south of the bayou to go. Lewis McFee and his family returned to their new home in the Houston Heights, where he was elected city marshall in 1917.[60]

Two more railroads shorten distances to rural western Harris County

As the old pioneers were passing on, the city of Houston was knocking on the door. Two more east-west railroads that erased distances from the city into this area and allowed streams of new families to settle in parts of what had once been open range on the great prairie.

The San Antonio and Aransas Pass Railroad, better known at the time as the "SAP," was built in 1886 to connect San Antonio with a port on the coast at Aransas Pass. That line was eventually extended as far as Kerrville. A 176-mile eastern segment that served Houston, connecting with the main line at Kenedy, was completed in 1889. That segment had stops at Jeannetta station, a mile south of Piney Point, and at Clodine, just west of the Harris County line in Fort Bend County (Figure 11.5). Commuters could leave Jeannetta station and be in Houston in the amazingly short time of 28 minutes, replacing what had been a half day horse and buggy ride.

An intermediate freight stop at Alief led to a post office there in 1895, operated by Alief Ozelda Magee. She and her husband Dr. John S. Magee had moved there the previous year. The town was at first named Dairy, but was renamed Alief after Mrs. Magee, when the name Dairy was deemed by the railroad as potentially confusing with another stop named Daisy. The small town of Alief came about only because of the influence of the railroad, and although there had been farms in the area since the 1860s, much of the surrounding prairie was open range until the arrival of the railroad. In the twentieth century Alief was to grow rapidly under the influence of the automobile.[61]

The SAP was plagued by the poor quality of its track, laid too quickly, which led to a number of wrecks. It went into receivership in 1890 and was taken over in 1892 by the Southern Pacific Railroad, which kept parts of it in operation as late as 1998. Tracks of the Harris and Fort Bend County portions were removed in 2001. Part of the former railroad's right-of-way became the Westpark Tollway.[62]

The Missouri, Kansas and Texas (MKT) Railroad began in Kansas and crossed the Red River into Texas in 1872. The part extending through Fort Bend and Harris counties was built in 1893, and service began in 1895. The railroad was called the "Katy," and the new town of Katy, which grew up along the tracks, was named after it. The town of Katy grew where an old canebrake along upper Buffalo Bayou once was. The canebrake was gone by 1880, and only the old-timers remembered the sparsely populated rural community of Cane Island that had preceded the town of Katy (see map, Figure 11.6, published before construction of the MKT).

The MKT effectively put the struggling Texas Western Narrow Gauge Railroad of 1875 out of business. It stimulated growth all along its course in western Harris County, especially at a small town that was originally named Letitia but soon became known as Addicks. That small town grew at the railroad stop for the Bear Creek community, which lay just a few miles to the north of the track (Figure 11.5). That community had a post office on Addicks-Satsuma Road north of the current Addicks Dam. The post office had been named for the community's first postmaster, Henry Addicks, and by about 1890 was being run by William Schultz. Part post office and part general store, it became a social and commercial center for the Bear Creek community. With the coming of the MKT Railroad, Schultz

Figure 11.27. The Addicks cotton gin, ca. 1898. Courtesy of Andrea Burden and the late Jerry Davis.

moved the post office and store a mile south, to form the new town of Addicks at the railroad stop.[63] The railroad and its stop at Addicks had a huge impact on the nearby Bear Creek community, eliminating what had been a one-and-a-half-day-long wagon ride into Houston for local farmers. A cotton gin was constructed by the early 1890s (Figure 11.27). Eventually a new school at Addicks replaced the small one-room schoolhouses at the Bear Creek community.[64]

The MKT east of Katy was abandoned and its tracks were removed in 1998; its right-of-way became part of the expansion of the Katy Freeway (Interstate 10) in the early twenty-first century.[65] Much of the former town of Addicks was consumed in the various enlargements of that highway and in growth of the offices and residential suburbs of Houston's Energy Corridor.

Life in the German settlements

As the frontier era became a memory held by the aging pioneers of the German communities north of Buffalo Bayou, churches and clubs stitched together the fabric of the widespread rural settlements, and post offices and school buildings began to appear (Chapter 6). Many farms prospered, times grew easier, and people had more leisure time.

The Schuetzen Verein. A staple of country life in northern Harris County German communities at this time was the Schuetzen Verein, or gun club. These organizations held picnics, dances, and shooting competitions for their local members, to which members of the other gun clubs were invited, serving to knit together the widespread German communities. In Harris County some of the main clubs were at White Oak, Spring Branch, and Bear Creek (Figure 6.2) as well as others at Cypress, in Houston and at Bray's Bayou. These clubs began to be popular after the Civil War, when formal club buildings replaced what the informal neighborhood gatherings of frontier times.

The White Oak gun club was established in 1873 and was located near modern day Mangum Manor Park, at Saxon Drive and Costa Rica Road, between Antoine Drive and Mangum Road. A badge from that club, which belonged to founding member Theodore Hillendahl (1844–1931), has survived (Figure 11.28). An ex-Confederate soldier, Hillendahl was a crack shot and was at one time the "King" (champion shooter) of the club.

The Spring Branch gun club was organized in 1876. On December 21 of that year the "Spring Branch Schutzen Company," with its president Louis Clay and vice president Hermann Bauer, leased a 450- by 400-foot parcel of land adjacent to Henry Shaper's farm, in the Hoskins survey (Figure 6.2), for a term of fifty years. The lease was granted "Provided that said Spring Branch Schutzen Company shall not use the ground so to them leased . . . for any other purpose than for a place of peaceable Amusement, not Offensive to the laws of the State of Texas, such as social & peaceable Meetings, Drilling, dancing, shooting at a Mark, Theatre, Concert or the holding of Fairs and such."[66] A photograph taken during one of their festival shoots, Figure 11.29, shows a row of kneeling men with rifles next to a keg of beer. A flag at the rear of the photo says "Spring Branch Schuetzen Verein, 1876."

Figure 11.28. Badge of the White Oak Schuetzen Verein that belonged to Theodore Hillendahl, a former "King" for that social club. Courtesy of David Hornburg and Hillendahl descendant Kay Howard.

The Bear Creek community built their Schuetzen Verein in 1883. The first building was located on Patterson Road near the early Methodist church and Hillendahl cemetery, where they also had an outdoor dancing platform (Figure 11.30) like that of their neighbors south of the bayou. The club was moved around 1900 to a location on South Mayde Creek, on land leased from Albert Marks by the club's trustees Emil Groschke, George Hillendahl, William Schultz, and August Marks (Figure 6.2).[67] There the community built an octagonal dance hall ("Turnverein;" Figure 11.31). Dances were held weekly on a circuit that included other German communities at nearby Spring Branch, White Oak, and Cypress.[68] By the 1940s, in addition to the dance hall and dining room, the new site had a barbecue shed and pit, a shooting stand, a concession stand, and various outbuildings.[69]

At the German community of Cypress in northwestern Harris County a gun club was organized as early as 1878, and after a disastrous fire, a large dance hall and shooting range were built in 1889. Tin Hall, as it was known, had a 4,000-square-foot upstairs dance hall and lasted into modern times as a country western dance hall; it closed in January 2016. Finally the victim of suburban sprawl, it was sold for a housing development, and its contents were auctioned off.[70]

A description of a gala shooting competition at the White Oak Shuetzen Verein published in the Houston Post in 1887 captures the essence of gun club activities of the day:

> *The White Oak Shoot*
> *The shoot of the Whiteoak Gun club tomorrow (Sunday) at Whiteoak, bids fair to be an event of considerable importance. The following shooting bodies will be present in force: Bray's Bayou club, composed of 30 men; Spring Branch club, 46 men; Bear Creek club, 35 men; Houston club, 90 men; and Whiteoak club, 50 men. From each of these clubs ten crack shots will be selected, who will contest for prizes in different ways. Each team can win a prize, which will be owned by the club. After the club contests, the Whiteoak club will hold its interesting and novel King shoot. The member of the club making the best score will be declared king.*

Above: Figure 11.29. The Spring Branch Scheutzen Verein (Gun Club), ca. 1890. The photo includes men from both Spring Branch and Bear Creek. The man with the gavel is William Shulz Sr. Standing at far left is Arnold Hillendahl Sr., next to Albert Bauer. Standing at extreme right is Louis Golbow. In the middle row, Albert Bienhorn is at left, and Louis Hillendahl is fourth from left. Henry Kolbe is kneeling at right. The flag reads "Spring Branch Schuetzen Verein, 1876" (the year of its founding). Courtesy of Nelda Blackshere Reynolds and Marie Neuman Gray.

Below: Figure 11.30. The outdoor dancing platform at the old Bear Creek Schuetzen Verein (Gun Club), ca. 1897. The back of this photo reads "on Patterson Road." Courtesy of Andrea Burden and the late Elva Weiman.

Figure 11.31. The octagonal dance hall at the newer Bear Creek Scheutzen Verein (Gun Club), ca. 1914. Courtesy of Marie Neuman Gray.

After this declaration he will be placed in a procession, headed by music, and paraded over the grounds, and finally to the grandstand, where the old monarch will abdicate and crown him king, which position he will hold until the next annual contest. In the midst of this royal scene there will also be speaking and drinking of foaming bumpers to the new ruler of the club. At the close of the crowning ceremonies the general prize shoot will take place. It will be open for all, and will end the gun matches.

During the day a grand barbecue will be spread, comprising beef, pig, poultry and viands of the season. This can be enjoyed for the small sum of 25 cents. At dark dancing will commence in the pavilion. For this privilege 50 cents will be charged, which will give the ticket-holder the privilege of dancing until the stars pale and cease winking in the morning.

The shooting range extends 127 yards, and is in a most eligible location in the woods, on the banks of Whiteoak bayou. The club, the crack one of all the clubs here, has done much toward making their grounds very fine in all respects. Henry Nieman is now king and Fritz Jechow president. It is probable that the attendance to-morrow on the festivities of this club will be very large, as many citizens of Houston are now making preparations to go, and the attendance of the neighborhood people is generally extremely large.

These shooting clubs lasted well into the twentieth century, until encroaching suburban developments dispersed the farm people who supported them, and newer generations found amusements other than country dances.

Hillendahl. With the coming of the Missouri, Kansas and Texas Railroad, commercial activity in Spring Branch moved south to meet it, just as Bear Creek effectively moved its activity south to Addicks. By 1890 a railroad siding just west of Bunker Hill Road was named Hillendahl, for local pioneers Louis and Henry Hillendahl and their families (Figure 11.5). The community had a post office from 1885 to 1912 and a school, which was located on modern day Witte Road a few hundred feet north of the railroad.[71]

In 1892 the grandchildren of hardy old area pioneers wrote letters to the Houston Post from their schoolhouse in Hillendahl. These letters recall both the pioneer names of the Spring Branch area as well as the still rural farm life there. All are marked "Hillendahl Texas, June 16":

Dear Post: I read the children's letters every week and they are very interesting. We live about ten miles from Houston in the piney woods, where papa has a saw-mill. We often have an excursion ride on the tramroad. It is about one and one-half miles long and it crosses the Missouri, Kansas and Texas railroad track. Mamma has a nice flower yard with four nicely trimmed cedar trees in it and some pot plants. Charlie Bauer

Dear Post: I go to school every day. I am in the Fourth reader. I study spelling, arithmetic, geography and history. My teacher's name is Mr. B. H. Heithaus. I have two pet chickens. I feed them out of my hand. I have a pet horse. I get the cattle every night. I have one brother, younger than I am. He plays with the dogs and chickens. Fritz Sauer

Dear Post: I have one little brother. I have a pet dog; his name is Tip. I play with him all the time, and if I throw a stick in the pond he gets it back. I have to hunt eggs in the evening and have to get the cattle every night. Fred Hillendahl

Dear Post: I am a little country girl. I have a few pets. The pets are eight little geese. I had ten, but the old Missouri, Kansas and Texas killed two of them. We had a very good rain last Friday. I have a little pet dog; his name is Jack. This is the first letter I have written to The Post and I hope it will not reach the waste basket. Dora Beinhorn[72]

Suburban developments reached Hillendahl in the mid-twentieth century, and the village did not survive the transition. The local name Hillendahl lives on as a branch of the Houston Public Library and as a community health clinic.

Benjamin Fort Smith and the promotion of Meadow Brook Farms

Concurrent with the development of the MKT Railroad and the town of Addicks was the beginning of the town of Barker, part of an ambitious real estate promotion by Ben Fort Smith (1857–1919; Figure 11.32), a great-grandson of early Houstonian Obedience Smith (1771–1847). His father was Benjamin Josiah Smith (1831–1886), but he was named for a grand-uncle Ben Fort Smith (1796–1841), soldier of both the War of 1812 and the Texas Revolution. The elder Ben Fort Smith brought his mother Obedience to Texas just before the Texas Revolution (Chapter 4).

The mother of the younger Ben Fort Smith (hereafter Ben Fort Smith) was Laura Celeste Stafford (1835–1885), a member of the ranching family for which the modern town of Stafford. By the early 1880s Ben Fort Smith along with two brothers, Joseph Stafford Smith and Clinton Terry Smith, and with his uncles Howard K. Stafford and Josiah S. Stafford and his wife Nannie Brooks Stafford, began to buy up property surrounding the old Joseph Habermacher place in the modern day Barker Reservoir. Within a few years they had amassed a large holding of some 13,000 acres, including most or all of the Middleton, Cunningham, J.N.O. Smith, Jesse Sitton, Blas Herrera, Washington County Railroad Company, and Houston Tap and Brazoria Railroad Company surveys. This enormous parcel was used as ranch land, and they enclosed it with a barbed wire fence, the eastern border of which ran along modern Highway 6, which did not yet exist. Smith's daughter Laura Krey recalled that the ranch in the 1890s was situated on a bald prairie with wildflowers. Cattle were shipped to San Antonio on the MKT Railroad.[73] The location of the ranch headquarters is depicted on Figure 11.12.

Smith's attention turned to real estate development toward the end of the century. In 1895 he platted the town of Barker along the MKT Railroad a few miles west of Addicks, named for the track-laying contractor, Ed Barker.[74] In 1897 he designed and filed a subdivision of most of the Smith-Stafford ranch property into 100- to 200-acre blocks and named it Meadow Brook Farms (Figures 11.33 and

11.5). The land was promoted as ideal for rice cultivation, and many of the purchasers were midwestern farmers moving to Texas.[75] One of those residents was a Mrs. Fisher, who moved to the Barker area from Kansas with her father around 1900. She recalled that the "old Southerners" in the area did not care for the midwestern newcomers and especially disliked their fences, which broke up the old open prairie and ended open range cattle raising.[76]

Although rice was grown on these lots for a number of years, by about World War I it became apparent that underground water resources feeding artesian wells were being depleted. Many of the midwestern rice farmers then abandoned the area; Mrs. Fisher recalled that they were "just like blackbirds; when one moved, they all moved."[77] Much of this land then reverted to cattle ranching. Ben Fort Smith continued to raise rice and cotton near the town of Barker that he had begun, but his efforts at farming were less than prosperous. At the time of his death in 1919 he still held about 2,000 acres.[78]

Emil Marks and the LH7 Ranch. In the bust that followed the Meadow Brook Farms land boom, Emil Henry Marks (1881–1969), son of August Marks and Anna Marie Schulz of Bear Creek, and grandson of German immigrants Gotthilf and Sophia Marks, picked up four lots (640 acres) in Meadow Brook Farms in 1917. By this time an accomplished cowman, Emil and his wife Maud May Smith (1897–1970) raised thousands of cattle both on this land, named the LH7 Ranch, and on thousands of acres of leased land to the north. Cattle were butchered on site and the meat was shipped to nearby Houston.[79] Marks actively collected good examples of old-time Texas longhorn cattle, helping to preserve the breed, while raising and selling Brahman cattle for beef. An annual rodeo that he held at his LH7 ranch at branding time in the 1920s and 1930s later became the inspiration for the Houston Livestock Show and Rodeo. In 1952 Marks was one of the founders of the Salt Grass Trail ride associated with that rodeo.[80]

The construction of the Barker Reservoir in the 1940s by the U.S. Army Corps of Engineers required much of his land, ending the last large cattle ranch in the area. A remaining portion of the ranch included numerous headquarters buildings, and his daughter Maudeen Marks applied for a registration of the property as a State Archeological Landmark, which was granted in 1985. After her death her heirs petitioned for removal of the designation in 2010.[81] The buildings were destroyed in 2014, and the headquarters site on Barker Clodine Road is now occupied by a new apartment complex.

Figure 11.32. Ben Fort Smith, ca. 1890.
Courtesy of Martha Doty Freeman.

Meyer Levy and the Gaut Subdivision

The old Morse plantation lands, by the end of the century long since divided into small farms and sold, had one remaining large parcel: the 700 acres of Grace Morse's homestead and surrounding land in the western part of the William White third of a league. It was purchased in 1889 for an acreage subdivision, the first of its type in the rural area near

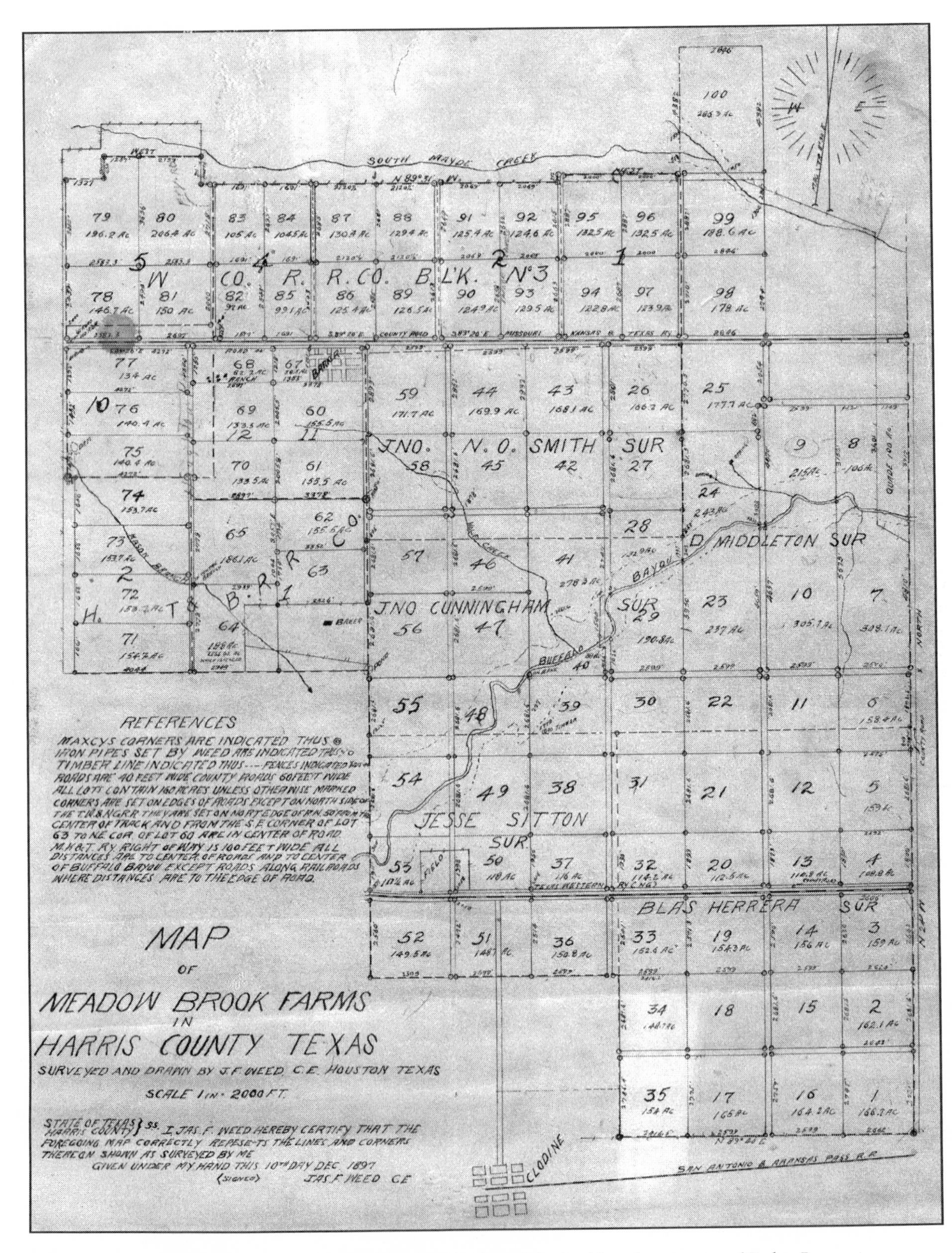

Figure 11.33. Map of Meadow Brook Farms, 1897. Most of this land later became part of Barker Reservoir. Courtesy of the Harris County Clerk's Office, Map Records vol. 1, p.6.

present day Loop 610.

An aged Grace Morse, within a year of her death, along with her daughter Elizabeth Grant and Elizabeth's husband Richard A. Grant, sold the property for $7,000 to W. O. Ellis on October 10, 1889; Ellis then flipped it to A. C. Herndon on the same day for $8,500. Only a few months later, on March 19, 1890, Herndon sold the property to Meyer M. Levy of Galveston for $11,200—thus making a tidy profit.[82] Meyer M. Levy (1843–1928) was born in New York to immigrant English Jewish parents. He moved to Galveston to pursue a variety of business interests and married Louisiana-born Houstonian Julia Kiam in 1877. They had four children between 1878 and 1890, while living in Galveston at a Victorian house on 1227 Winnie, which still stands today.[83]

Levy hired surveyor William Gaut to subdivide the large parcel into 20-acre lots, separated by streets; this subdivision survey was dedicated in 1896 (Figure 11.34).[84] The tract was transected by three existing east-west roads: the Texas Western Railroad (later to become Alabama Street in this vicinity), Westheimer, and San Felipe Road. The latter road was straightened into a rectilinear east-west confirmation from its earlier rambling frontier status; the earlier trail is also marked on the survey map and was soon to be forgotten. An existing country lane that had once extended from the San Felipe Trail to the former Morse home (see Figure 7.13 and discussion, Chapter 9), became Post Oak Road and later, Post Oak Boulevard. In the twentieth century the area was to become Houston's premier luxury shopping destination, but for now the lots were sold primarily to Italian truck farmers. Later, wealthy Houstonians began to buy lots for weekend homes, now that distances to Houston were growing ever shorter.

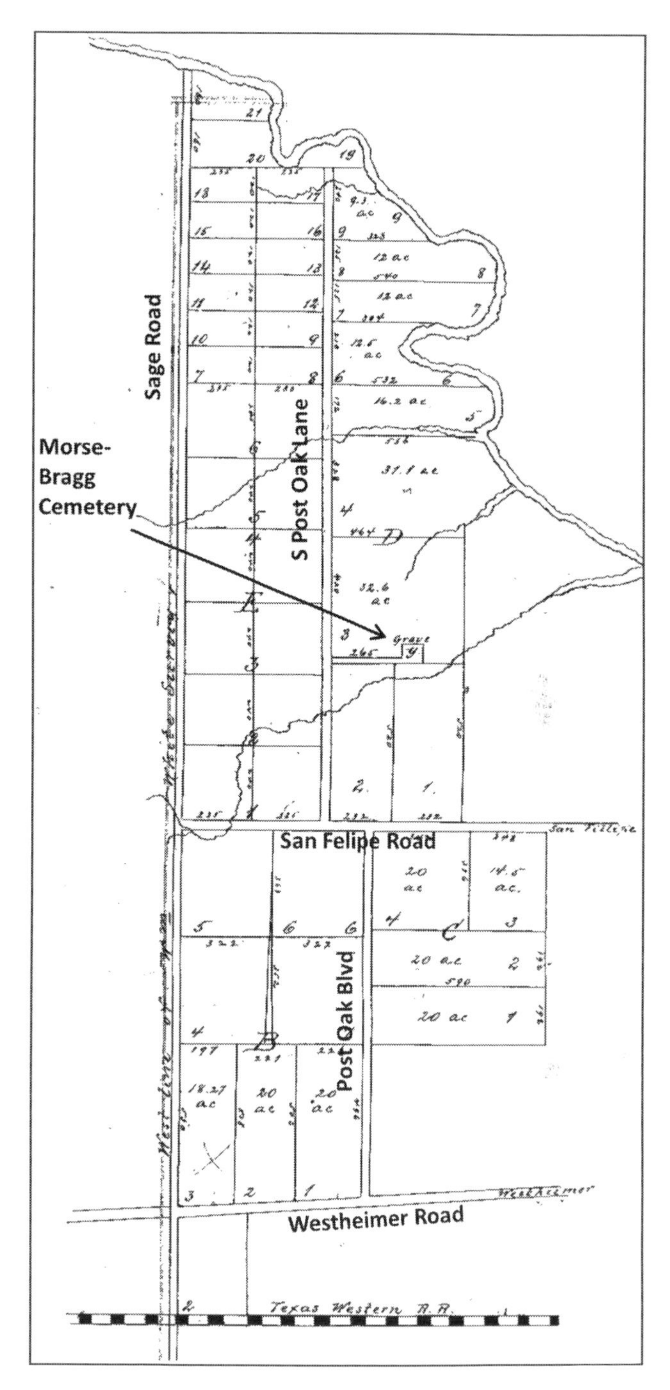

Figure 11.34. The survey of the Gaut subdivision of 1896, from Harris County Deed Records, courtesy of Harris County Clerk's Office. Note the position of the Morse-Bragg cemetery.

The Galveston Storm, and the twilight of an era

By the end of the nineteenth century much of the upper Buffalo Bayou neighborhood was a rural eden of reasonably prosperous small farms (Figure

Figure 11.35. Theodore W. Hillendahl and family at their home in White Oak, ca. 1900. Theodore is standing at center, with beard. This home was located where modern Scarbrough High School now stands, on Mangum Road at Georgi Road; it was demolished in the mid-1950s. Photo courtesy of Hillendahl descendants Kay Howard and Walker Richard "Sonny" Gray Jr.

11.35). The children of the old German pioneers built new frame houses to replace most of the old frontier farmhouses, and they had fenced pastures containing dairy cattle, orange orchards and crops of cotton and corn (Figure 11.1). This bucolic setting began to disappear at the beginning of the new century, the result of rapid western growth of the city of Houston—growth that was spurred on by the economic results of a storm and a discovery. Within little more than a half century most of these farms, both north and south of Buffalo Bayou, were to vanish.

On September 8, 1900, a massive hurricane swept much of Galveston off the map, killing over 6,000 people on that island. The direct effects of that storm were felt as far inland as Addicks, where the building housing the post office and general store was destroyed, along with most of the rest of the town.[85] At one home the roof had blown off, killing rancher Emil Marks's grandmother Sophie Schultz, which in turn caused the death by shock of her husband Johann Shulz, among the last of the original German immigrants of Bear Creek.[86]

At Piney Point the damage was less severe. Cassie McFee Reeder reported:

> *Grandpa was ok, but the front door and two panel windows beside the door were blown into the hall. . . . The top of the front porch . . . had blown off and must have blown over the top of the house. We found it rolled up against the field fence, about five city blocks from the house. The big barn and the*

buggy house . . . were blown down.

At the brand new railroad town of Alief, the Methodist Episcopal Church was destroyed, along with most of the corn and cotton crop, devastating the rural farming neighborhood there. Twenty-four of the town's thirty families left, leaving only a general store and farmlands that soon reverted to prairie. Wolves were reportedly seen in the town in the daytime.[87]

The impact of the storm on upper Buffalo Bayou neighborhoods was to be much greater than this transient inland storm damage, however. The city of Galveston soon lost to Houston its primacy in shipping, especially after the Houston Ship Channel was completed in 1915. This shift caused a boom in early twentieth-century Houston that would send residential and commercial growth surging westward, bringing an end to an agrarian economy and rural lifestyle that had lasted since the days of Austin's Colony. The discovery of oil at Spindletop in 1901 only added fuel to that rapid growth, as the city of Houston became the center of a dynamic U. S. petroleum industry. Within fifty years the entire area from the old Pleasant Bend Plantation lands near modern Loop 610 out to Bear Creek and Wheaton's Ford would be transformed into either suburbia or exurbia and, by the turn of the twenty-first century, into a thoroughly urban landscape.

Figure 12.1. Buffalo Bayou west of Houston. Undated photograph, MSS 157-73, courtesy of the Houston Metropolitan Research Center, Houston Public Library.

TWELVE

Epilogue

Taxes of $200 an acre had made a family farm untenable. . . . He and Etta . . .
raised the white flag, gave up the farm and moved a few miles west. . . .
Two century-old barns were razed, along with the workshop, smokehouse, hog pens
and chicken coops. A storm cellar and an old well, dug by hand and pumping for a century,
was covered over. Developers turned what was left of the Hillendahl family farm
into a shopping center, anchored by an 88,000-square foot Kmart. . . . A sea of concrete
was poured, hardening over what once were fields of beets and onions, cabbage
and collards, turnips, tomatoes, beans and peas. The only trace remaining,
besides a street named for the family, was the cemetery.

—*Houston Chronicle*, August 8, 1999

THE NATURAL LANDSCAPE and frontier settlements that surround Upper Buffalo Bayou have figured in nearly all the major episodes of Texas history. From the founding of the frontier San Felipe Trail during the Mexican colonial period to the days of the ox-wagon-drawn cotton trade that helped build the early city of Houston, to the German immigration and settlement of the republic period, the antebellum period and its Old South plantation economy, the trials of the Civil War and the great Emancipation migration that followed it, the gathering and shipment of thousands of cattle up the Chisholm Trail from west of Houston, and the coming of the railroads—this relatively small area of the upper bayou has seen much. What are we to make of this history?

The most remarkable thing about the specifics of this local history is how little of it is commonly remembered today. Had this area been located perhaps fifty miles farther west, its history would have been recorded by small town historians, and everyday people would know something of their local history from statues and plaques in the town square. However, stories about the former rural communities of the upper Buffalo Bayou area have been almost completely overshadowed by those of the giant metropolis of Houston. As mentioned at the outset of this work, most published histories of the region address Houston's birth and growth. The Battle of San Jacinto, the Allen brothers, the Ship Channel, Spindletop, Space City and the Astrodome are the pillars of Houston history, and historians may be forgiven if they leave out what happened in the former rural communities of Piney Point, Bear Creek and the like. The histories of such small settlements could not be expected to figure prominently in the story of Texas' largest city.

There is a more salient reason that the history of the area is so scantily documented: the rapid expansion of urban and suburban Houston has done much to destroy the formerly rural area's cultural institutions and scatter its storytellers. The nineteenth-century rural farmlands and communities of upper Buffalo Bayou were to be steamrolled by the rapid sprawl of suburban Houston in the twentieth century, and those old communities were replaced—for better or worse—by subdivisions and homes, highways and roads, shopping malls and parking lots. Beyond the radical alteration of the physical landscape and its ecology, the rapid growth of Houston deeply affected cultural memory by displacing the former residents of the area.

In exploring the cultural and ecological results of that rapid growth, and enumerating the very few physical, cultural and natural relics that survive from pre-urban times, it is easy to draw negative conclusions about the extent of destruction of the historical landscape. However, those of us with deep roots in that history also have deep roots in the metropolis that enveloped and smothered that rural world. The vibrant metropolis of greater Houston provides our jobs and feeds our families, and has done so for generations. My aim in this chapter is to document what happened to this rural world as the metropolis expanded, and then consider issues of historical, cultural and natural preservation in those areas where small remnants of that earlier world persist.

Westward urban and suburban expansion in the twentieth century

By 1895 the developed area of greater Houston had reached the area of Shepherd and Kirby drives (Figure 12.2 A), and exurban and suburban homes began to replace what had been open range only twenty-five years earlier. By the first decade of twentieth century the automobile age had begun, and with it came a boom in road building that has never ceased. Unlike the pioneer-era wagon roads and dirt tracks that twisted and turned around natural barriers like creeks, wetlands, and riparian forests, these new automobile roads tended to be laid out in straight east-west or north-south directions, as an examination of any map of modern west Houston shows. This was partly the result of the advent of inexpensive barbed wire fencing; by the end of the nineteenth century, farmers could and did ring their property boundaries—which had always been surveyed along rectilinear lines—with boundary fences. These rectilinear boundaries then guided new east-west and north-south roads. The boundary fences spelled the final end of the old San Felipe Trail, which had been declining for decades. The unused dirt road was rendered all but inaccessible by the fences (opening and closing a series of boundary gates was a nuisance), and the former trail was quickly forgotten. Its name continued in San Felipe Road, but west of Loop 610 the location of that newer east-west road does not even approximately overlie the original. The easternmost part of the trail, once straightened, was rechristened West Dallas Street by 1935.[1] Only a stone marker erected by the Daughters of the American Revolution at the entrance of Founders Memorial Park at 1217 West Dallas, and another on River Oaks Boulevard at San Felipe Road, recall the trail's former location in Houston.

The West University Place development, begun in 1917, and the River Oaks housing development, begun in 1922, were the first of many new housing developments west of Shepherd Drive. By the mid-1950s Houston's city limit stretched as far west as the modern Sam Houston Tollway, and previously lightly settled areas of pine forest north of old Piney Point were converted into the residential cities of Piney Point Village, Hunter's Creek Village, and Hedwig Village. By the 1960s and 1970s, suburban housing developments sprang up throughout West Memorial, Dairy Ashford and West Bellaire areas. By the 1980s suburban growth had reached a natural barrier at the Addicks and Barker reservoirs, but jumped across those reservoirs, reaching Katy (for-

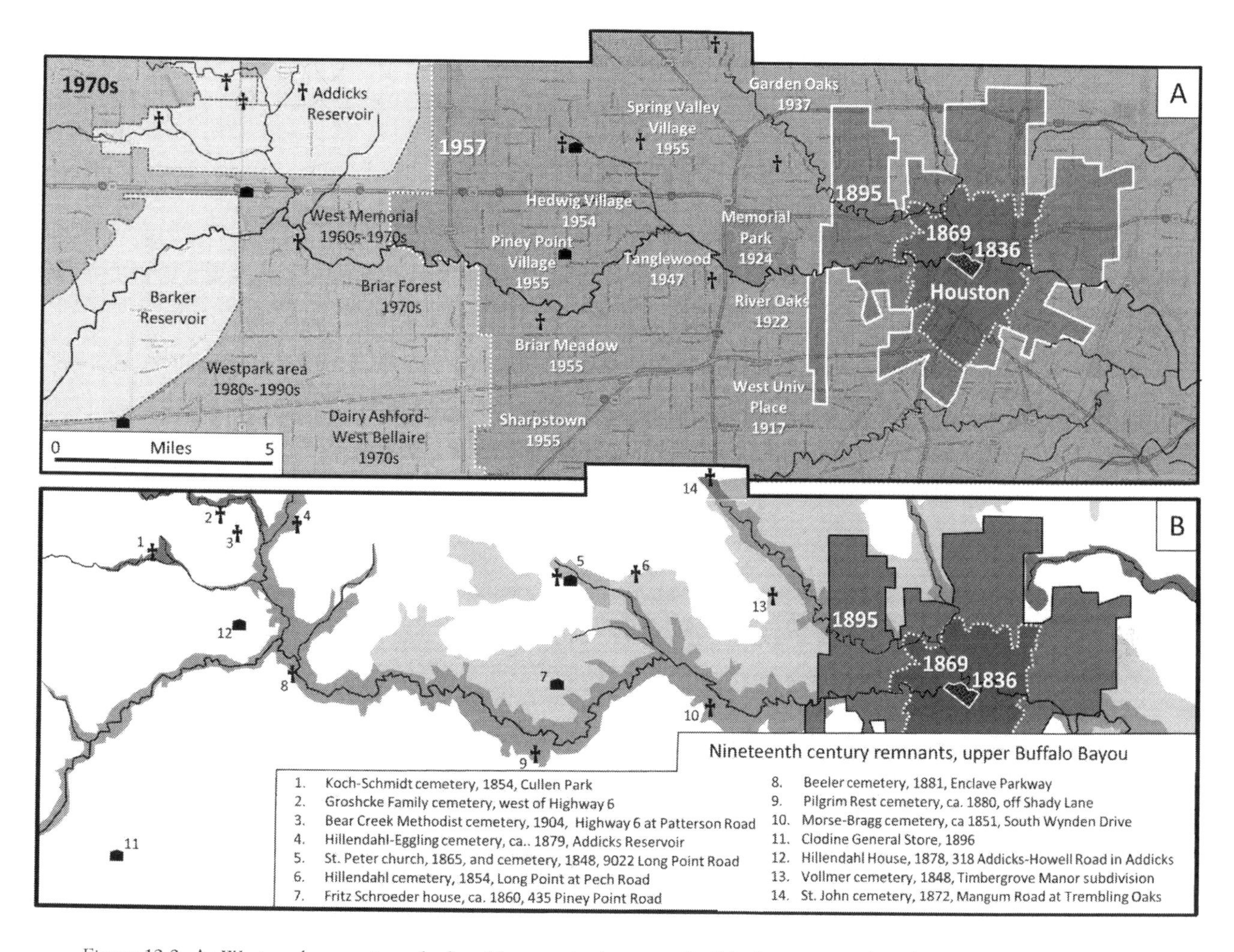

Figure 12.2. **A:** Westward expansion of urban Houston in the upper Buffalo Bayou area, plotted over a modern road map courtesy of OpenStreetMap. **B:** Locations of nineteenth-century historical remnants.

merly Cane Island) by the end of the century. By 2016, the only large, relatively undeveloped parts of the upper Buffalo Bayou area consisted of the very large Barker and Addicks reservoirs (Figure 12.2 A). Even there, however, the wrecking ball held sway. Nearly the entire pioneer German settlement of Bear Creek was condemned, purchased, and then razed for flood control purposes in the 1940s, as the Addicks Reservoir was built.

The staggering scale of Houston's growth is best seen in satellite imagery, from which a map of the contiguous developed area of greater Houston was compiled (Figure 12.3). This depiction shows the full area of dense suburban, urban and industrial development that is contiguous with the central city of Houston (not including a wide rim of exurban small, non-working farms). Developed greater Houston is an enormous area, eighty miles from north to south, and fifty miles from east to west. A more historical perspective on all that urban growth can be had by placing the map of greater Houston's developed area over a map of the location of early Texas Old 300 settlements (Figure 12.4). In antebellum days an ox wagon would take three days to get to the Brazos River at Fort Bend (modern Richmond), where the river was closest to Houston. A mid-nineteenth-century person, magically transported to the present, would have extreme difficulty accepting the fact that

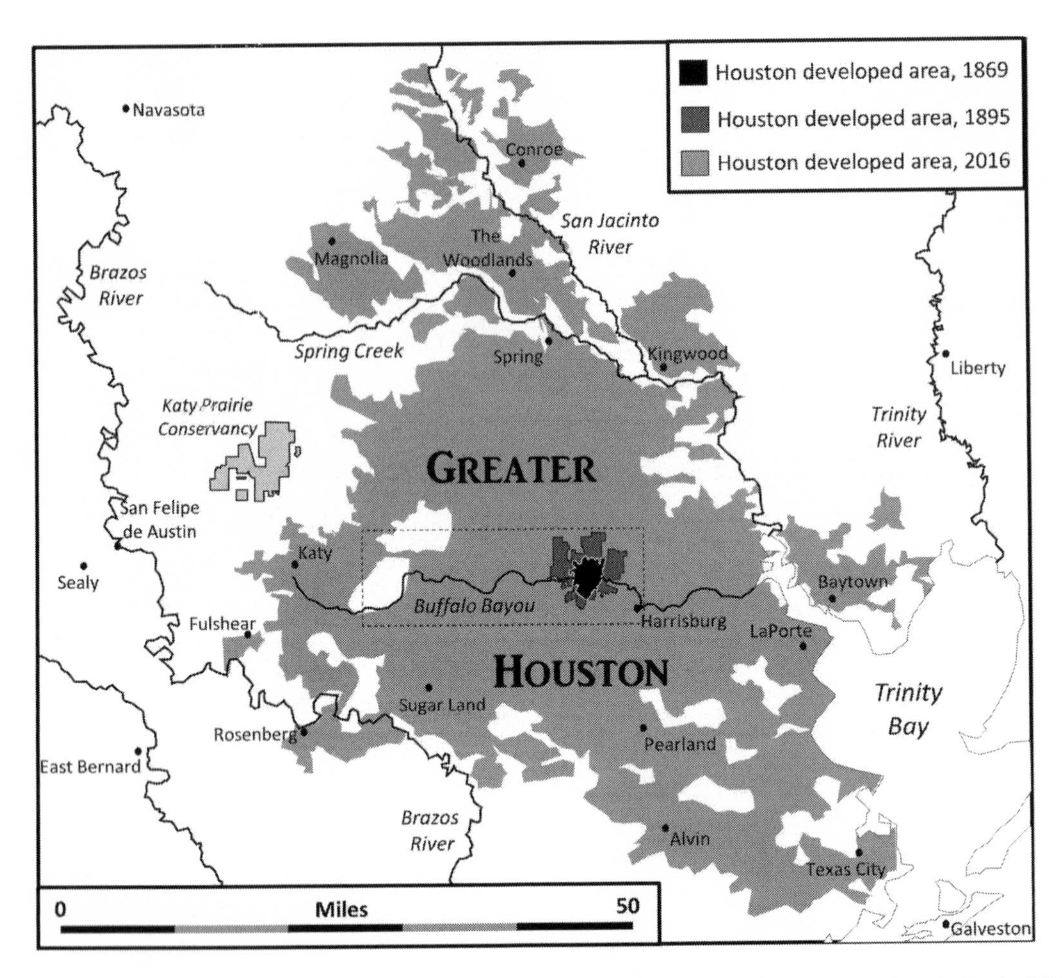

Figure 12.3 The extent of modern day Greater Houston, compiled from aerial photographs in Google Earth, 2016. The shaded area depicts the urban areas and industrial zones of the City of Houston and its (more or less) contiguous suburbs. Insets show the approximate developed area of Houston in 1869 and 1895, as well as the current preserved area of the Katy Prairie Conservancy. A dashed rectangle outlines the focus area of this book.

the developed area of greater Houston not only stretches all the way to the Brazos River but locally spills over to the other side, as it does in the Richmond area.

When suburban development arrives, it is not typically a matter of slow, gradual settlement of new people within an existing social fabric. Urbanization hits like a tsunami, sweeping away landscape, buildings, culture and people, replacing them all with a manufactured new world. At this stage, a sense of history is often lost. At the outer periphery of this growing metropolis, the cutting edge where pasture land is converted into subdivisions, the ecological costs are most evident and staggeringly well-defined. In 2016 the western part of that edge was located to the west of Katy at the nineteenth-century town of Fulshear (Figure 12.3). The dense new suburban developments that are racing across the prairie replace prairie and pasture grasses, shrubs and wildflowers—some native, some imported—with a monoculture of St. Augustine or Bermuda turf. Outside the cutting edge are coyotes, bobcats, opossums, wild hogs, land-roving box turtles and the occasional white-tailed deer or red fox. Inside the cutting edge, in densely packed brand new housing estates of upper middle-class homes, there are domestic dogs, cats, and a few squirrels, with vanishingly small numbers of native animals living only near the periphery or along

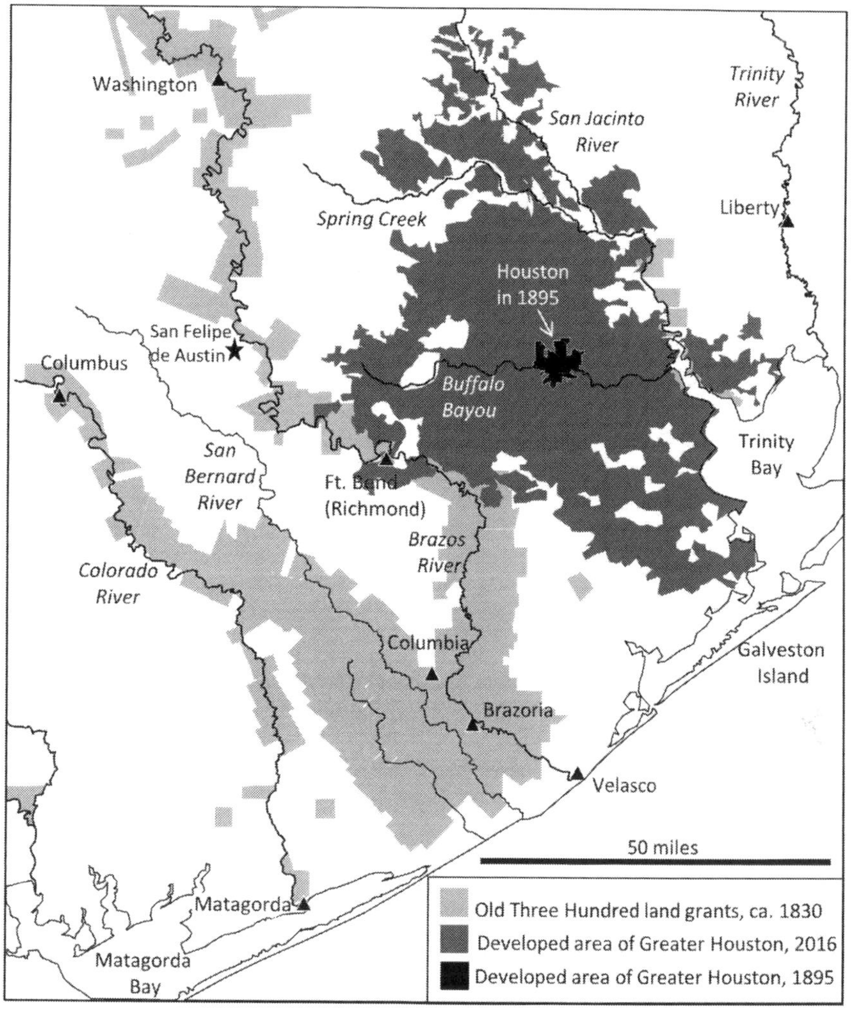

Figure 12.4. The developed area of modern Houston (dark gray) and locations of the earliest land grants of the Old 300 settlers, ca. 1830 (pale gray). Locations of the early land grants are taken from the General Land Office, Austin, and were compiled and retraced from local area compilations in von Maszewski's *Austin's Old Three Hundred* (Waco: Eakin Press, 2011).

wooded waterways. Just west of the edge are bobwhite quail, scissortail flycatchers, white-tailed kites, meadowlarks, and even the occasional roseate spoonbill. These avian species are typically absent more than a mile inside the edge, except where there are sizeable remnant pockets of grassland. West of suburbanization's knife-sharp edge one may find swarms of fireflies on a summer night, but they are rare indeed in the mosquito-controlled developed zone. When dense planned communities come, the green tree frogs and other amphibians that provide the sound track of a summer night all but vanish.

In many of the new suburban planned communities, lakes–typically manufactured as holding ponds for flooding–are a big selling point, but they are typically lined, devoid of vegetation, and often sterile; activities like boating, fishing and swimming are often disallowed. West of the cutting edge, natural streams and ponds are brimming with life. In a small town, for example Sealy or Brenham, Texas, such loss of habitat with growth is easily accepted, as those towns are geographically small and surrounded by farmland. But the explosive and unchecked growth of the city of Houston is breathtaking in scale and acceleration, and one wonders how much larger the city may become in this century.

Even farm families that were resolute in their desire not to be uprooted could not resist the tidal wave of growth. In Spring Branch, urbanization came in the late 1950s. There, farmer Arnold Hillendahl Jr. (1893–1976) and his wife Henrietta "Etta" Williams (1894–1983), grandchildren of German pioneers, held out against urbanization as long as they could. However, as the *Houston Chronicle* later reported:

> *Taxes of $200 an acre had made a family farm untenable. He [Arnold Hillendahl] gave 5-acre parcels to each of his four kids, Rosie, Arnold, Herb*

and Ruth, and all but 12 acres went into Monarch Oaks [subdivision]. He and Etta farmed those last 12 acres until, surrounded, the couple raised the white flag, gave up the farm and moved a few miles west. . . . When they moved, they took the farmhouse, a couple of magnolia trees and Rock, their 21-year-old mule, with them. Two century-old barns were razed, along with the workshop, smokehouse, hog pens and chicken coops. A storm cellar and an old well, dug by hand and pumping for a century, was covered over. Developers turned what was left of the Hillendahl family farm into a shopping center, anchored by an 88,000-square foot Kmart. . . . A sea of concrete was poured, hardening over what once were fields of beets and onions, cabbage and collards, turnips, tomatoes, beans and peas. The only trace remaining, besides a street named for the family, was the cemetery.[2]

By 1999, when a Houston Chronicle reporter visited the area, the cemetery (of which more later) was surrounded by

the cityscape of Houston. There are strip centers, pawn shops, flea markets, apartments, auto repair shops. Kolache stands, barbecue joints and taquerias. Places for wiring money back to Guatemala. Places to rent living room furniture or shoot pool. Places to eat Vietnamese pho noodle soup, Thai spring rolls, Korean kimchi. At some spots, construction pocks the roadway, narrowing traffic's progress to a crawl . . . a drive down Long Point reveals a landscape almost as alien [to Arnold Hillendahl's children] as would a cruise of the moon.[3]

Loss of cultural institutions

As the city closed in around the Hillendahl farm, the community's venerable church also felt a chilling side effect of urbanization. St. Peter Church was founded with a service of thanksgiving in 1848, as the new immigrants arrived at their wilderness destination. Each year thereafter, the families of that church held a turkey feast in the Autumn to remember, give thanks, and celebrate. In a pattern repeated in countless country churches across rural Texas, the families cooked the meals at home, and brought their homemade goodies to the public feast. At some time after the City of Houston annexed the area in the 1950s, an edict was given by the City Health Department that all food had to be cooked on the premises, for health safety concerns.[4] A church and community tradition for well over a century – part of the fabric that wove the community together – disappeared, as the church members could not, or would not, comply.

Cultural institutions of former rural communities surrounding upper Buffalo Bayou crumbled in the face of urbanization. As farms were sold to advancing developers, or were condemned for use in flood control projects, farm families typically resettled elsewhere. Land acquisition and regulations connected to Houston-related flood control efforts in still rural White Oak in the early twentieth century caused attendance at St. John German Lutheran church (organized in 1866) to drop precipitously.[5] When suburban Oak Forest surrounded the property in the 1960s, the unused shell of the 1891 church building was moved to Heritage Park in downtown Houston for preservation.[6] South of the bayou, the Buffalo Bayou Church, founded by Anglo families in 1872, fell to highway construction and suburbanization in the Post Oak–Loop 610 area in the 1960s. Nearby to the east, the land beneath the African American Lovely Canada Baptist Church, founded by ex-slaves in 1876, had been purchased by River Oaks Corporation in 1938 for subdivision expansion. The church building was moved to another location, where it was demolished by 1953, as "gentrification" set in and black families left the area.[7]

Besides churches, other rural cultural institutions also fell. The nineteenth-century German Schuetzen Verein gun clubs and their Turnverein dancing pavilions at White Oak, Spring Branch, and Bear Creek (Chapter 9) were all gone by the middle of the twentieth century; White Oak and Spring Branch fell to suburbanization, and Bear Creek to flood control. As we saw in the preceding chapter, the German gun club at Cypress in northwest Harris County fared somewhat better, and its 1889 dance hall, Tin Hall, survived until January 2016 as a country western dance place. But by then the previous multi-generational gatherings of the German American community at the hall were only a memory, as urbanization had displaced many of the original families. When the owner of Tin Hall was asked in 2012 about placing a historical marker there, he replied: "I purposely did not certify [Tin Hall] as a historical structure because if I make it a marker I will never be able to sell it. It's a great idea, but once you think it all the way through, it's like ordering a big fat steak that you can't eat and you can't sell." The forty acres remaining of the old gun club were recently sold for a housing development.[8] Time did not "move on" for these social gathering places and churches; the institutions were destroyed by the process of urbanization itself.

Local town governments are strongly altered in this process. In Fulshear, the leading edge of today's westward urbanization, the small town (its population was 716 at the time of the 2000 federal census) is now host to several large new suburban developments that have arrived in the last five to ten years. By 2013 the population reached five thousand,[9] and according to town planning officials it is on track to reach 50,000 within a decade. The previous town population included a substantial African American minority, heirs to a proud heritage that dates back to the time of Old 300 settler Churchill Fulshear's plantation on the nearby Brazos River. For many years there had been a representation of one or two African Americans on the elected town council, which consists of five council members and a mayor. In the 2016 election the newly elected slate was all white, elected by the numerically dominant new suburban arrivals, in their thousands. The change seems not racially motivated, as long time white members were similarly affected: only one of the six newly elected officials has any deep roots in the area. Old-time area representatives have been voted out by a tidal wave of new residents. Urbanization brings high population densities that radically alter any rural community.

In addition to the loss of religious and cultural institutions, cultural memory itself is decimated in the process of urbanization. The development of the area of modern Uptown Houston in neighborhoods surrounding Post Oak Boulevard over the past century and a half provides a good example. The old Morse plantation in which Uptown was to develop was parceled off into small farms by the 1870s, then some of these farms were broken up and sold as exurban twenty-acre lots in the late 1890s, purchased for truck farms or for elegant country retreats for Houstonians. By the late 1940s and early 1950s these exurban properties were turned into subdivisions with half-acre lots, which by the 1980s were being broken up yet again for townhouses on lots of a small fraction of an acre. In recent decades the area has seen the development of elegant high rise towers, as population density continues to climb along with the area's prosperity.

Each transaction in this continuum of successive real estate transactions witnessed a change in ownership, and with each change, cultural memory faded. A survey of known Morse, McFee and Banks family descendants, made in 2014 as part of an effort to save the Morse-Bragg cemetery from development, found no descendants living in the area of Pleasant Bend and Piney Point today.[10] Of the four children of the aforementioned Arnold and Etta Hillendahl in Spring Branch, descendants of immigrant German pioneers Wilhelm Heinrich and Maria Hillendahl and the last of their family to grow up on the family farm, only one remained on the area of the old farm by 1999.[11] The others had long since left for other parts of Houston, Katy, and Weimar. None of them farmed for their primary living.[12]

Former area residents like the Hillendahls or the Morses and McFees lived in a low-population rural setting. When displaced by farmland purchase, even those few who might remain in suburban homes became a tiny minority in the high population density suburbs and urban areas that followed—the pattern seen in modern Fulshear. For this reason, there are few familial or cultural reasons for ensuing generations to linger in the area. As a result, few to none are left to remember the area's history. Today, in the small Windermere subdivision of Piney Point Village, few residents will know that the first log cabin in a vast frontier stretching from the mouth of Buffalo Bayou to San Felipe was built in their midst in 1824. Few residents of Smithdale Estates will know that their homes were on the farm of pioneer resident Fritz Schroeder, or that his antebellum home still exists only a short distance away, where it is used as the office of a water works. And probably no residents of Vargos on the Lake apartments will know that the small lake that their dwellings overlook was once a spring-fed millpond for a water-powered sawmill of the Canfield family–and that there are forgotten graves of millworkers around its periphery. In contrast, in a small town like Cat Spring or Fayetteville or Brazoria, it would be much less common to find a resident today who knew so little about his or her local history.

Remaining buildings

Given the simple fact that urbanization strongly alters the natural and cultural landscape, one might well ask what small physical samples have been saved of the pioneer world that preceded us in west Houston and western Harris County. In the 200-square-mile area surrounding upper Buffalo Bayou described in preceding chapters—extending roughly from Shepherd Drive in Houston to Fry Road in eastern Katy—only two nineteenth-century buildings are known to have survived in more or less their original settings (see map, Figure 12.2 B). An additional three were saved by moving them to new locations.

St. Peter Church. St. Peter United Church of Christ, at 9022 Long Point Road in Spring Branch (Figure 12.5), was built in 1864 to replace an 1854 log cabin church. It is one of the oldest church buildings still in use in Harris County, and its adjoining cemetery dates from 1848 (Figure 12.6). The church building has been carefully maintained to its original appearance, and has its original pews. An exhibit of the photographs and artifacts of its pioneer German families adorns a wall in the interior. As of 2002, about a fifth of its then current membership of 125 had roots in the area.[13]

Clodine General Store. Just west of the Harris County line, in Fort Bend County, lies the Clodine General Store. It was built in 1896 at the Clodine stop on the San Antonio and Aransas Pass Railroad. That railroad's tracks were later removed, and the Westpark tollway now occupies its right-of-way. The building was moved slightly to its present location, at the corner of FM 1464 and the Westpark Tollway (Figure 12.7).[14] Another general store of similar vintage was the Barker General Store of 1898 in Barker, Texas. Originally located in that small town, it had been relocated within a cluster of early twentieth-century buildings at the early twentieth-century Emil Marks LH7 Ranch headquarters on Barker-Clodine Road, but the headquarters buildings were demolished in 2014 to make way for an apartment complex. The current whereabouts of the general store is unknown, but it does not appear to have survived anywhere near its original site.

The following three survivors from the nineteenth century have been substantially moved from their original sites.

The Fritz Schroeder home. The oldest remaining house in the study area is that of Fritz Schroeder, dating from about 1860 (Figure 12.8). It originally lay on land Schroeder purchased in 1859 (Chapter 6), and was located a few hundred feet north of Smithdale Road, near the cul de sac of modern Wexford Court. It was slated for demolition by developers in the early 1990s, but was donated to the Memorial Villages Water Authority, and moved a few blocks to their property at 435 Piney Point, where it rests today. The single-story six room clapboard house contained cypress logs in its ceiling, and was likely constructed with sawn timber from the nearby Rummel-Hildebrandt-Bauer sawmill.[15] It has been very well maintained, but its restoration introduced several features, including a protruding front deck and spindle railings, that are not particularly appropriate for its era. It is today nearly certainly the oldest remaining home in west Houston, west of Shepherd Drive. Despite being on public property, there are no public signs indicating its location or history.

Hillendahl house. In Addicks, at 318 Addicks-Howell Road at Griggsby, is a small house that was

Figure 12.5. St. Peter United Church of Christ, on Long Point Road in Spring Branch. It is one of the oldest church buildings still in use in Harris County. This and the other surviving entities that follow were all photographed by the author.

Figure 12.6. St. Peter Church cemetery in Spring Branch, established in 1848.

Figure 12.7. The Clodine General Store of 1896.

Figure 12.8. Fritz Schroeder home, 435 Piney Point Road. The home, built in or after 1859, was originally located north of Smithdale Road in Piney Point Village. It has been extensively altered.

Figure 12.9. The George Hillendahl house, 318 Addicks-Howell Road in Addicks. Built in 1878, the house was moved to this site in about 1944 to escape destruction within the Addicks Reservoir.

built in 1878 by German immigrant George Hillendahl. His father, Franz Ludwig "Louis" Hillendahl, emigrated with his wife Sophie Dorothea Schulz from Hanover, Germany in 1847 when George was an infant.[16] Louis bought a farm east of Highway 6 on the Toliver survey in the Bear Creek community in about 1860, and George built his house on part of that land. In 1943 the Army Corps of Engineers purchased the family's land to become part of the Addicks Reservoir, and the house was to be demolished. Former Bear Creek resident Joe Golbow purchased the Hillendahl home and moved it a few miles to its present location, where he used it as a rental house. Today it is the location of a roofing company (Figure 12.9).[17] It is perhaps the only remaining farmhouse from the Bear Creek community.

St. John Church. As noted in Chapter 6, the St. John German Lutheran Church building in White Oak (1891) was moved to Heritage Park in downtown Houston for preservation by the Heritage Society.

In summary, in the upper Bayou area west of Shepherd Drive, just five buildings appear to be survivors from the nineteenth century—St. Peter Church, the Clodine store, the Fritz Schroeder home, the Hillendahl home, and St. John Lutheran Church. If there are others, they are not known to the author. The rest of the early pioneer farmhouses and inns that have featured in this narrative are all gone. The pioneer Fred Brandt home of about 1850, like many other homes and farms in the Bear Creek community, succumbed in the 1940s to flood control activities in the Barker and Addicks reservoir areas. The nearby Wheaton/Silliman/Habermacher house at Wheaton's Ford, which dated from the 1830s, survived straightening of the bayou but was lost to fire in 1956. Harriet George's historic old home of the 1850s fell to fire in the early twentieth century, and its site was mined for sand and gravel before a subdivision blanketed the home site in the 1950s. The Agur T. Morse home at Pleasant Bend seems to have disappeared at about the same time.

The record of preservation of nineteenth century buildings is better in early urban sectors of the city of Houston; there are a number of early buildings downtown, such as George Baker's brick building of 1870 on Old Market Square (Chapter 10). Freedmantown in Houston's Fourth Ward, east of Shepherd Drive and geographically part of nineteenth-century Houston, contains a number of nineteenth-century buildings and churches (Chapter 9). The survival of historical artifacts is significantly enhanced in areas that start as urban centers.

Cemeteries

Traditionally, cemeteries are the places where the past is preserved in an urban environment, and here the record of preservation of the area's frontier past is a bit better. Ten surviving nineteenth-century cemeteries are located on the map shown in Figure 12.2 B.

St. Peter cemetery. Perhaps the oldest cemetery in the area is the one attached to St. Peter United Church of Christ, on Long Point Road in Spring Branch, a cemetery founded in 1848 (Figure 12.6). Burials include pioneers Jacob Schroeder (ca. 1804–1880); Carl Wilhelm Rummel (1812–1867) and his wife Christiane Caroline Rummel (1816–1899); Franz Ludwig "Louis" Hillendahl (1812–1874) and his wife Sophie Dorothea Schulz (1811–1881), along with their son Louis Hillendahl (1840–1921), who served in the Texas Light Artillery of the Confederate Army; Wilhelm Ludwig Schulz (1827–1886); Heinrich Daniel Telge (1808–1864); Wilhelmine Feurscheutz (1856–1893); Friedrich Koenneke (1839–1916), who served in Company C, Waul's Texas Legion, during the Civil War; Frederich Brandt (1818–1878) and his wife Henriette Pfeiffen (1811-1875; this Brandt couple is different from the Frederick Brandts of Bear Creek); and members of many other early Spring Branch families. There is also a plaque dedicated to Rev. B. M. Hailfinger and other yellow fever victims of his congregation.

Vollmer cemetery. Equally old is the Vollmer (or Vollmer-Nieman) cemetery at 6618 Cindy Lane in the Timbergrove subdivision inside Loop 610, north of Interstate 10. The cemetery is located on part of the John Reinermann league, and its oldest burial is that of Johann Heinrich Ojemann (1814–1848), born in Hanover, Germany, and thought to be related to the Reinermann family. Others interred include members of the Vollmer, Hillendahl, Clay, Niemann, Sauer, Thiel and Hilton families. The cemetery was in sporadic use until 1985 but is now behind a locked wooden fence in a private residential area.[18] It is unmarked.

Hillendahl cemetery. The small Hillendahl cemetery at 8325 Long Point at Pech Road, mentioned earlier, was founded in 1854 on the 130-acre farm of pioneer German immigrant Wilhelm Heinrich Hillendahl (1814–1870) and his second wife Maria Schmidt (1828–1907), both of whom are buried in the cemetery. The family still maintains it as a small graveyard, adjacent to the parking lot of an auto service facility (Figure 12.10). There are nineteen burials of other family members there, including their daughter Elizabeth Hillendahl, who died in 1854 and was the first burial there, and their son Arnold C. Hillendahl (1855–1939) and his wife Marie Schneider (1857-1929). It is marked with a State Historical Marker.

Hillendahl-Eggling cemetery. Another Hillendahl family cemetery is off War Memorial Drive in Bear Creek Park within the Addicks Reservoir, in an unmarked setting behind a high chain link fence. This was the Hillendahl-Eggling cemetery along Langham Creek, at the site of the first location of the Bear Creek Church (Chapter 6). The cemetery was almost completely destroyed by vandals and motorcycle gangs in the late twentieth century, when it was known as the "Blue Light" cemetery for the dull glow emitted by the labradorite-bearing gray granite used for headstones. Many stones were removed or kicked over, and some graves were unearthed by grave robbers looking for gold rings and the like.[19] There were about twenty burials, including pioneers John H. Grisbee (1857–1899) and his brother George H. Grisbee (1866–1895); George Hillendahl

Figure 12.10. Hillendahl family cemetery, Long Point at Pech Road, Spring Branch, established in 1854.

(1847–1915); Rev. Fred Ries (1832–1884), Dena H. Sauer (1850–1899), E. Thompson (1840–1880), and Samuel Quade (1837–1895). Some of the burials were moved to the Bear Creek Methodist cemetery for protection. What remains of the former cemetery is now is protected by a high chain link fence.

Bear Creek Methodist cemetery. The largest cemetery in the Bear Creek area is the Bear Creek Methodist cemetery on Highway 6 at Patterson Road (Figure 12.11). The Methodist church was first located near Langham Creek, near the Hillendahl–Eggling cemetery, but was moved to this site in 1902 before being moved again to its present site at Highway 6 just north of I-10. Its cemetery dates from 1904, and contains the burials of many area pioneers. It is still in active use. Some of the pioneer burials include Fred Brandt (1829–1923) and his step-daughter Henrietta Schur Brant (1853–1942); Dorothea Feuerschutz (1820–1907), Dorothea Schultz Golbow (1829–1916), Ernest A. Gummert (1850–1922) and his wife Christine Feuerschitz Gummert (1853–1926), Frederick "Fritz" Kobs (1833–1905), Dorothea Meyer Kobs (1840–1921), Henry Kruse (1850–1931), Charles A. Kunze (1854–1935), Herman Liere (1856–1940), Albert Marks (1842–1910) and Minnie Marks (1857–1957), and Charles Otte (1834–1912).

Koch-Schmidt cemetery. The Koch-Schmidt cemetery, located within Cullen Park on Groschke Road (Figure 12.12), is the oldest within the former Bear Creek German community and is only slightly younger than the cemetery at St. Peter's Church in Spring Branch. Its oldest burial is that of John Koch (1799–1854), who emigrated from the Hesse-Darmstadt area of Germany in 1846 and purchased a 177-acre tract that includes this cemetery in 1847. To preserve the cemetery, its land was deeded by his daughter-in-law Susanna Matzke Koch and his grandson John Koch in 1901. Susanna is buried there, along with Heinrich Addicks, the first postmaster for whom Addicks town was named. Other pioneers buried there include Anna Elizabeth Koch (1806–1856; John Koch's wife); Ludwig von Koch (1838–1886, John's son) and his wife Sophie (1837–1923); Sophie Marks (1817–1882), Rev. David Ankele (1826–1895) and his wife Dorothea; Christian and

Figure 12.11 Bear Creek Methodist cemetery, on Highway 6 at Patterson Road, saw its first burial in 1904, but contains the graves of several notable pioneer Bear Creek families. Some of the graves from the nearby Hillendahl-Eggling cemetery were moved here after that cemetery was nearly destroyed by vandals.

Figure 12.12. The Koch-Smith cemetery, lying within Cullen Park and Addicks Reservoir, was established in 1854.

Figure 12.13. The pioneer Beeler cemetery, along Enclave Parkway, is now maintained as a Harris County pocket park.

Dorothea Meier; Henry Otte (1824–1900) and his wife Fredericka Moers Otte (1831–1904), and others, many unmarked. The plot has been protected by a high chain link fence installed by the Addicks Reservoir branch of the Army Corps of Engineers, and it is a beautiful place, nicely kept within in a peaceful forest setting. A marker there tells of its history.

Groschke cemetery. The Groschke family had a cemetery on their farm, off Pine Forest Road in Addicks Reservoir.[20] The U.S. Army Corps of Engineers purchased the Groschke farm, including this site, for the Addicks flood control reservoir in the 1940s. There were a small number of family burials at that site, including pioneer immigrants Carl Ernst Groschke (1835–1917) and his wife Doris Hillendahl Groschke (1838–1915), and children Gustav Groschke (1877–1903), Ernest Groschke (1860–1922), and August Groschke (1877–1903), and some unmarked graves. It is protected by a high chain link fence.[21]

Two smaller cemeteries in the Bear Creek area are probably lost. The Christian-Eggling cemetery on Redhaw Road, near I-10 and on the edge of the levee, had no markers on it in the 1990s. A small cemetery next to the railroad track north of the I-10 feeder had the gravestone of pioneer Oscar Abstein (1846–1884).[22] His grave and two others were removed to Washington Cemetery, at 2911 Washington Avenue in Houston, in 2003 by the Texas Department of Transportation. Washington Cemetery was originally founded in 1887 as the German Society Cemetery and changed its name in July 1918.

Beeler cemetery. In the Anglo and African American communities to the south of the bayou there are fewer preserved cemeteries and no nineteenth-century buildings. The Beeler cemetery on Enclave Parkway (Chapter 11), was saved by action of Harris County Precinct 3 Commissioner Steve Radack, who "adopted" it in 2003 on behalf of the county as a historic cemetery site. The county maintains it as a pocket park, and the grounds are attractively kept in a verdant, peaceful setting (Figure 12.13). The graves date from 1881 and include those of the pioneer family of James A. Beeler (1829–1888) and his wife Amanda Beeler (1832–1914), discussed in Chapter 11, as well as of F. P. Mapps (1855–1934) and Kate Mapps (1857–1931).

Pilgrim Rest Baptist cemetery. An African American cemetery associated with the first site of the Pilgrim Rest Baptist Church is undeveloped but threatened. The cemetery was established upon the purchase of the one-acre property by the church from Harriet George in 1884.[23] It may have been used as a burial ground on the Canfield-George farm before that deed; the church's history dates back as far as 1865.[24] The cemetery was marked on a 1915 topographic map of the U.S. Geological Survey, and was shown on as a "private cemetery" on the initial plat of the Piney Point Estates subdivision in the 1950s, east of Shady Lane, east of lot 23, and west of Piney Point Gully (Figure 11.13). According to Trevia Beverly's book about the cemeteries of Harris County, all the markers except one have been removed, and the land is no longer on the "exempt" list on the county tax rolls.[25] It is an endangered remnant, surrounded by very valuable real estate, and unmarked.

Morse-Bragg cemetery. The most prominent antebellum cemetery south of the Bayou was located on the grounds of the Morse family's Pleasant Bend Plantation, now located on South Wynden Drive east of South Post Oak Lane. It was used from about 1856 by the Agur T. Morse and John Kell Morse families and the James McFee family as well as the African American family of Rachel Banks, an ex-slave (Chapters 9 and 11). Nearly destroyed by activities related to surrounding suburban and urban development in the late twentieth and early twenty-first century, it has recently been transferred to Harris County, where Precinct 3 Commissioner Steve Radack is preserving it as a Harris County pocket park. Area descendants of the Morse, McFee, and Bell families have erected an obelisk, a Harris County Historical Marker, and a few historical display panels (Figure 12.14).

Canfield-Morse and Canfield sawmill cemeteries. There was a Canfield-Morse family cemetery near the Pilgrim Rest cemetery, probably associated with Charles Morse, which contained the graves of Charles Canfield Morse (1855–1905), his wife Abby Ivie Beeler Morse (1861–1896), Dabney M. Walker (b. ca. 1800) and his wife Mary Binkley Walker (b. 1799), and Mary Luna Thornton Morse (1861–1898), among others (see discussion, Chapter 11). It has been lost and the land developed; it was reportedly located behind the Rosewood Medical Building, north of 9000 Westheimer Road.[26] Also, a small cemetery seems to have existed next to the millpond at the old Canfield sawmill, east of Fondren Road south of the bayou. When landscaping operations were underway in the 1960s at the Vargo's restaurant, which incorporated the old millpond as a scenic backdrop, a groundskeeper reportedly ran into several graves in an area by the pond, one of which was marked simply as the grave of "Noah Cambeaux, New Iberia Parish, La., 1861."[27] That gravesite was not one used by the Canfield/George family, who used the Canfield-Morse cemetery for their burials. It would seem reasonable to conclude that Noah Cambeaux was a millworker, buried near the mill site. The Canfields used slaves to work their sawmill, and it is likely that he was one of them.

Besides these few cemeteries and four buildings, there is little physical evidence left of the pioneer settlers of the upper Buffalo Bayou area. A concerted effort was made in the early 1990s by the late television newsman Ray Miller and Precinct 3 Commissioner Steve Radack to place a reconstructed group of German pioneer farm and commercial buildings on the land of Bear Creek Park within Addicks Reservoir. Architectural plans were made, and roads named for German pioneers were laid out for that purpose, but the project was disallowed by the U.S. Army Corps of Engineers because of wetlands concerns as well as concerns over proximity to the foundations of a former nineteenth-century farm building.[28] That former building was one of those purchased and destroyed by the Corps in the 1940s during reservoir construction.

Remnant natural areas

Most city and county parks have manicured, closely cropped lawns for the comfort of visitors and their families. In this section, we consider instead the preservation of significant pieces of natural environment—Houston's original setting of bayou, forest and prairie. What has been preserved? In a metropolis as geographically large as greater Houston, public open spaces are at a premium. There are three large, partly natural open spaces in upper Buf-

Figure 12.14. The Morse-Bragg cemetery on South Wynden Drive, now maintained as a Harris County pocket park.

falo Bayou west of Shepherd Drive: the narrow gully of Buffalo Bayou itself with its locally accompanying parks, Memorial Park, and—by far the largest open space anywhere within Houston's city limits—the reservoirs at Addicks and Barker.

The courses of many of upper Buffalo Bayou's tributaries have been channelized with concrete (e.g., White Oak Bayou, Little White Oak Bayou and Spring Branch), but Buffalo Bayou itself is still remarkably intact within its cut bank walls, where kayakers can enjoy a natural setting deep within the city. That feeling is somewhat illusory, however, as development in nearly all areas has extended all the way to the bayou's cut bank edge, except within Memorial Park and Terry Hershey Park (and east of Shepherd Drive, within the new Buffalo Bayou Park), where some adjacent open space has been preserved. Memorial Park includes at its western and southern fringe the riparian forest along parts of Buffalo Bayou. It is the largest of Houston's city parks at 1,466 acres, but nearly half of its expanse is used for the closely managed landscapes of a golf course, athletic fields, Memorial Drive and a railroad track. A very positive recent development in western Houston has been the formulation of a new Memorial Park Master Plan.[29] A sensitive restoration of the park's ecology is envisioned, aimed at having most athletic fields and the golf course coalesce in the north of the park and attempting to reestablish a "wild" character in the park's southern and western portions. The proposed restoration includes an effort to rid the forest and prairie remnants of invasive woody species. Such restoration will add much to the popularity of the hiking trails among Houston families and may provide places to contemplate the area's wilderness beginnings.

Barker and Addicks reservoirs. Such sensitivity to the natural and cultural landscape is relatively new and very welcome to Houston. Less than fifty years ago, David McComb was to observe in his 1969 book, Houston: A History:

> *Nature is oppressive in the Bayou City and not especially attractive. Houston lacks such natural vistas as the mountains of Denver, or the bay of San Francisco. This may explain why there is no effort to preserve open space or reserve land for parks. The sights worth looking at were all created by humans. As such they fall apart, age, and people are willing to replace them. As George Luhn, an architect, noted: "There is really no sense of history felt in the city. So everything is bright and shiny and new."* [30]

Such attitudes were once common in this city and account for the relative paucity of open space, and especially wild space, within the city limits. Two key exceptions are the large Barker and Addicks reservoirs, which were set aside in the 1930s, built in the 1940s, and are operated by the U.S. Army Corps of Engineers in order to prevent flooding downstream in central Houston (Figure 12.2). Here Buffalo Bayou and its tributaries, and large portions of the surrounding prairie, are still undeveloped in a vast urban wilderness of nearly 26,000 acres (Figure 12.15 A), roughly 18 times the size of Memorial Park and about 31 times the size of New York's Central Park.

There is much of historical interest in the reservoir areas, including the site of a portion of the San Felipe Trail of 1830 (Figure 9.2), a critical lifeline for Austin's colony and later for Harrisburg and Houston in the republic era and early statehood times. The bridge of adjacent State Highway 6 is at the site of Wheaton's Ford, a prominent crossing of the bayou and the site of an inn built in 1831. Most of the sites of the early German farmsteads in the former Bear Creek community, dating from 1848 and razed during reservoir development in the 1940s, lie within Addicks Reservoir, as do several pioneer German cemeteries mentioned earlier. The 1851 Joseph Habermacher farm was located in Barker. The Emil Marks ranch headquarters of 1917 was just outside Barker Reservoir; as noted, it was destroyed for apartment construction in 2014, but the location of Houston's first rodeo grounds, a part of that former ranch, lies within Barker Reservoir.

Except for some well-used and well-maintained Harris County and City of Houston recreational parks within the two reservoirs, and a number of hike and bike trails, the bulk of this enormous urban wilderness is little visited. Much of the reason lies with the large and dense swaths of invasive trees that now cloak the once open prairie. When the land for the reservoirs was purchased by the federal government in the 1940s, it contained mostly ranching land and rice pasture, with a riparian forest along Buffalo Bayou and its tributaries. As late as the 1980s, large expanses of grass-filled (although partly degraded) prairies were evident. Those prairies are now largely covered with enormous areas of trees and brush, including invasive Chinese tallow, salt cedar, and McCartney rose; native mesquite and yaupon; and many other species. These invaders are visible in the 2015 airphoto of Figure 12.15 A as a dark zone covering most of each reservoir. An airphoto of the area taken in 1953, less than ten years after the reservoirs were constructed, shows a strong contrast with the 2015 airphoto; the original prairie and the riparian forest were still sharply defined in the 1950s through 1970s (Figure 12.15 B). The contrast between the two images is striking and records the disappearance of open prairie and pastureland during the seventy years since reservoir construction.

The reservoirs were built in the 1940s as a response to disastrous Houston flooding in 1935. In contrast to popular perception, these are "dry" reservoirs, usually mostly empty of water but available when needed to capture a surge of runoff; heavy rains of historic dimensions in early 2016 temporarily filled large parts of both reservoirs. The U.S. Army Corps of Engineers, which operates the reservoirs, states:

> *Under normal conditions, the gated structures at both Addicks and Barker Dams are set to allow the unimpeded passage of low water flow down Buffalo Bayou. This will prevent the unnecessary impoundment of water behind the dams. If severe weather is predicted that could cause excessive flows in Buffalo Bayou downstream of the dams, the dams will be closed until the threat of flooding has passed . . . [when] the dams will be opened to allow any impounded waters to pass down Buffalo Bayou . . . in a controlled manner.*[31]

This policy means that flooding is infrequent over most of the reservoirs, and is fairly quick to dissipate in most parts of the reservoirs when it does occur. According to maps in the U.S. Army Corps of Engineers' 2009 master plan, only about 20 percent of the area of the reservoirs floods as frequently as every two years, and in about 40 percent of the reservoirs, intervals between floods can stretch from every 25 to 100 years or more (Figure 12.15 C).[32] For this reason, these two reservoirs create a huge resource of natural, albeit degraded, prairie and riparian forest environment within the city limits of Houston, including large undeveloped portions of upper Buffalo Bayou.

In pre-colonial days this land was part of the great Texas coastal prairie, and in colonial times it was described by Fiske, among others:

> *An unbroken surface of grass, intermingled here and there with beautiful flowers, extended on every side of us a great distance: in some places bounded by a distant grove or range of trees. . . . I had never been at all prepared for the indescribable beauty of a Texas Prairie. . . . [The flowers] were often spread around us in the utmost profusion, and in wonderful variety.*[33]

The prairie, twinned with the riparian forest of the Buffalo Bayou waterway, is the core from which Houston grew. This dual habitat provided for the first timbering and open range ranching, for cotton cultivation and bayou transport in the antebellum and post-war periods, and for the small family farms of German, African American and Anglo farmers of the mid- to late nineteenth century. In greater Houston, this prairie ecosystem has been built over with houses, roads, parking lots, offices, and apartments by the thousands of acres for many decades without being given much of a second thought. The only large-scale efforts to preserve parts of this primeval habitat are those of the Katy Prairie Conservancy, which is working to conserve parcels of prairie land in Waller and northwest Harris counties, amounting to some 20,000 acres to date.[34] Their current holdings are outlined on Figure 12.3. Their lands are a fair distance outside of Houston, however, and they have recently been planting tiny pocket prairies within various parts of Houston, in order to entice both schoolchildren and the general public to better understand and get involved in preserving this key habitat, before it is lost to continued urban sprawl.[35]

Houston and Harris County, however, already have in Barker and Addicks reservoirs an enormous piece of rare undeveloped and government-owned prairie land, parts of which could replicate the scene observed by early Texas visitors, if only the reservoirs were rid of invasive woody species that have compromised the prairie habitat. Prairie ecological management, however, is not the budgeted remit of the U.S. Army Corps of Engineers that manages the site. Their primary goal—successfully reached for decades—is to prevent catastrophic flooding of the city of Houston, not to preserve nineteenth-century ecosystems.

Opportunities for Philanthropy, at All Scales

Given the near-total disappearance of all traces of pristine frontier ecosystems within the upper Buffalo Bayou area, as well as the disappearance of nearly all physical reminders in this area of our frontier cultural past, what things might be done to restore a better sense of history and natural place in

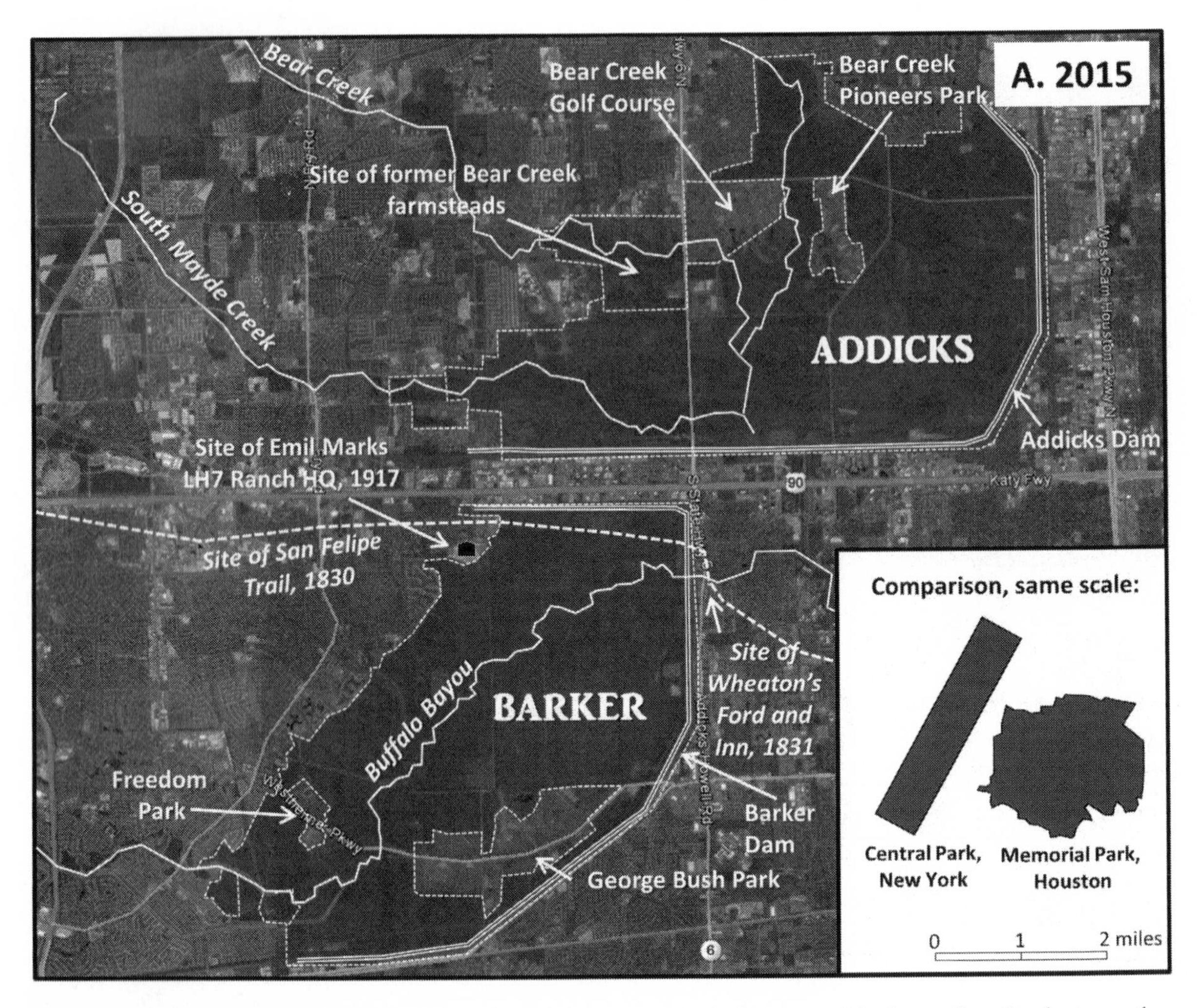

Figure 12.15. The Addicks and Barker Reservoirs. **A:** Aerial photo, 2014. The locations of the former Bear Creek pioneer farmsteads as well as the former San Felipe Trail are highlighted. Extensive dark areas are due to the widespread expansion of invasive trees into former prairie zones. **B:** Aerial photo, 1953. Note the dark, narrow strips of riparian forest that follow the streams, with lighter surrounding prairie, which contrasts greatly with the reservoirs current state. Aerial photographs are courtesy of the Texas Natural Resources Information System, Austin. **C:** Maps of the frequency of flooding, generalized from the U.S. Army Corps of Engineers Master Plan for the two reservoirs, 2014. Base map from OpenStreetMap.

this intensely urban area? To be certain, significant steps have already taken by Houston citizens as well as philanthropic and governmental organizations in recent years to renew and restore the bayous that are at the heart of Houston: Buffalo Bayou Park, Terry Hershey Park, and the Spring Creek Greenway are all examples. From this report, it might be imagined that, in addition to restoring bayou space, we could do more for our prairie greenspace as well as our pioneer cultural heritage. On these counts, there is a role for action and philanthropy at all scales, from that of individual neighborhood citizens to charitable foundations and government entities.

Historical markers. The placement of historical markers at appropriate sites within neighborhoods and public spaces helps connect current residents with their area's historical past. Generous area citizens have long supported county and state markers, but relatively few adorn the area of west Houston (upper Buffalo Bayou).

The Harris County Historical Commission (HCHC) has an active program for documenting his-

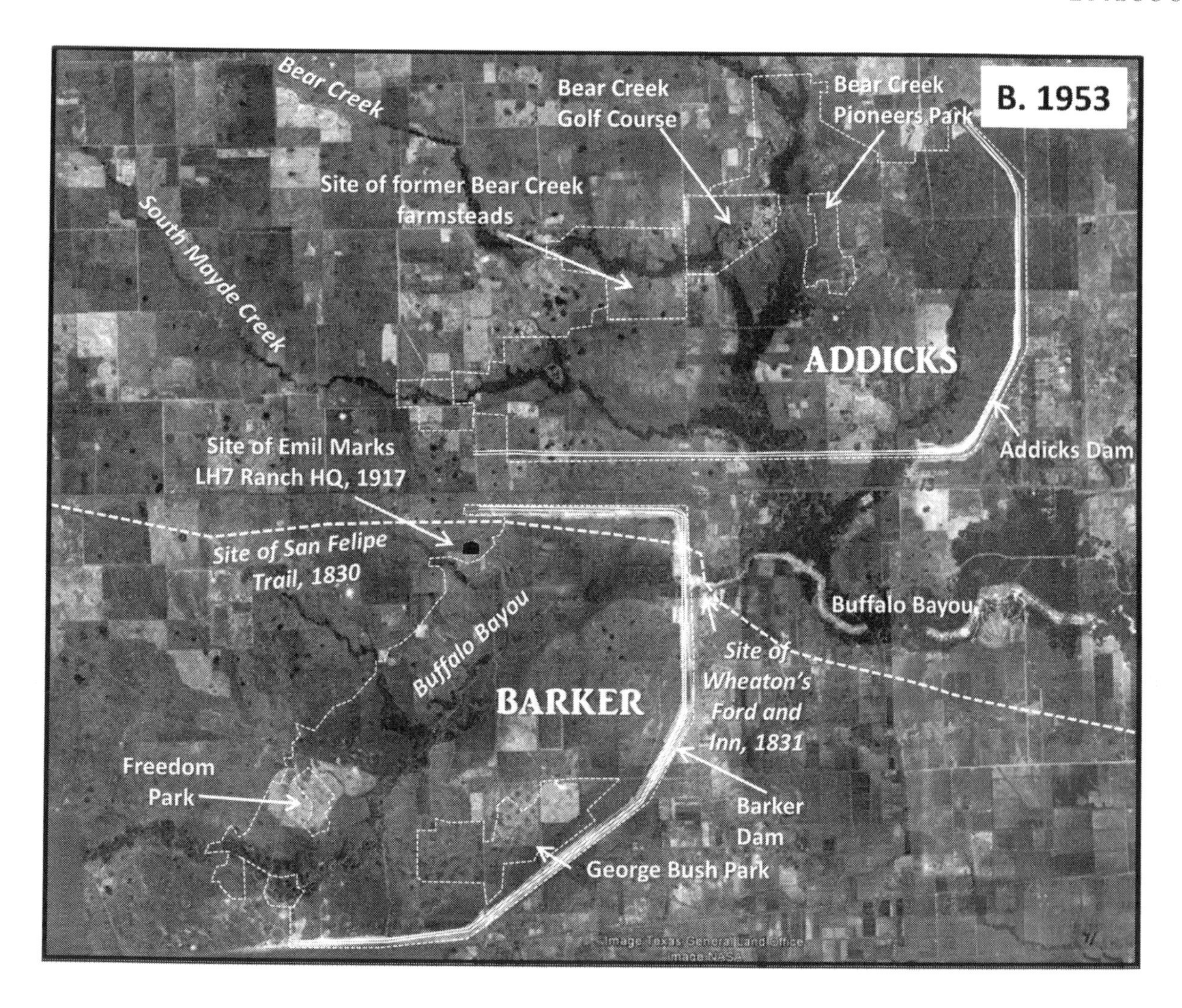

torical sites and placing Harris County Historical Markers, and the Texas Historical Commission (THC) sponsors a similar program (also operated locally under the umbrella of the HCHC).[36] County markers are relatively inexpensive, at about $2,200 each. Each marker must be funded by donations, because neither the all-volunteer HCHC nor the THC funds the markers themselves. All that is needed is appropriate documentation, which an HCHC volunteer sponsor can help provide (along with the documentation in this study), as well as permission from a landowner at an appropriate site. There are many potential sites for historical markers shown on the various maps included in this report, for example: locations of the San Felipe Trail of 1830; the 1865 African American walk to freedom that occurred along that trail; the 1875 Texas Western Narrow Gauge Railroad; the millponds for several old area sawmills; Charles Shearn's grain mill of 1846; the site of numerous pioneer farmsteads in the German north side of the bayou; the site of Butler cattle operations that connected to Chisholm trail drives; the sites of African American and Anglo churches that were started immediately after the Civil War. The potential list is nearly endless.

Recently, the residents of the small Arrowwood subdivision in Piney Point Village collected money door to door for a Harris County Historical Marker for the nearby site of John D. Taylor's 1824 log cabin, the earliest home in this area. In addition, descendants of area pioneers south of the bayou recently collected funds for a historical marker, historical dis-

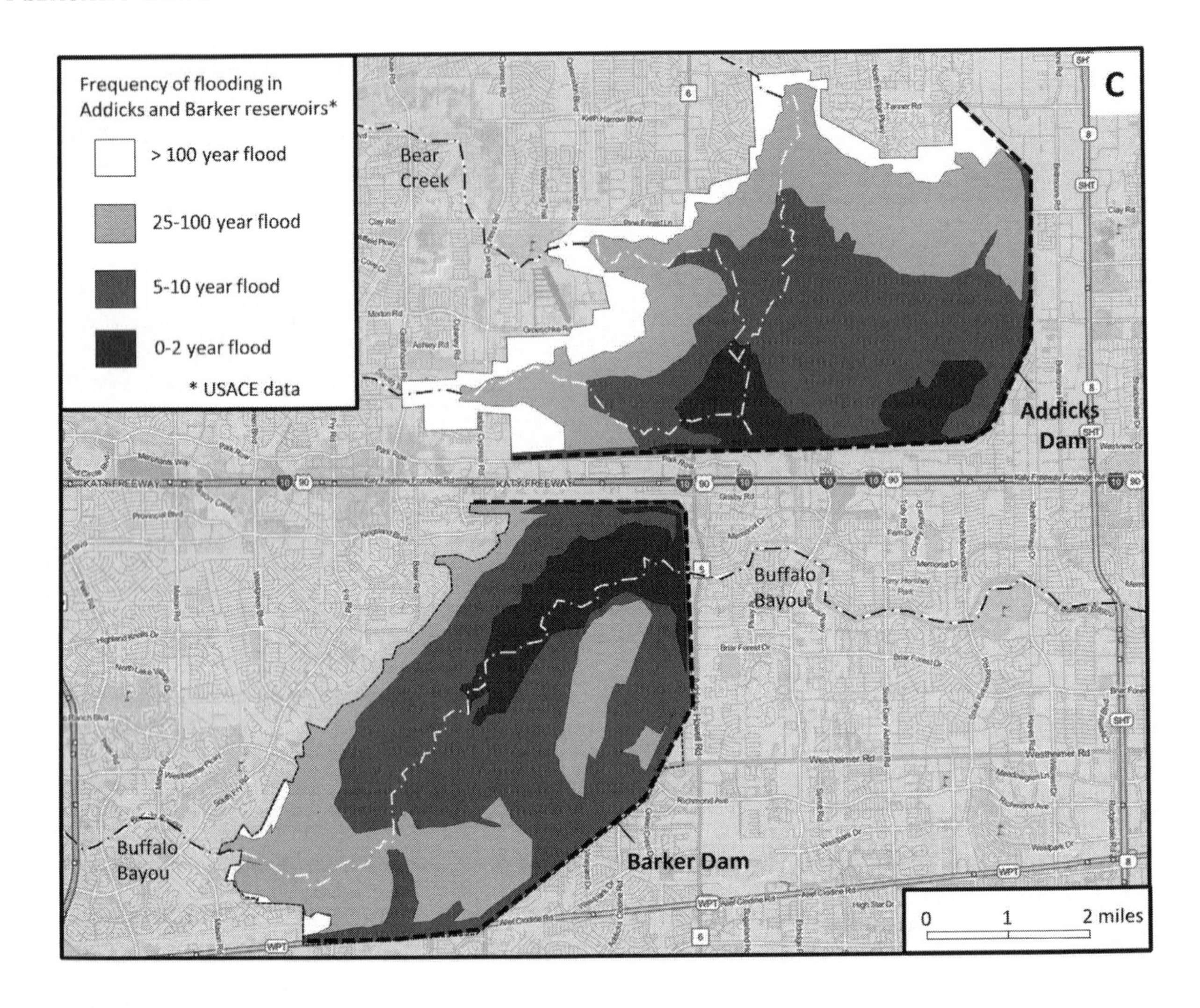

plays, and restored monuments at the Morse-Bragg cemetery in the Uptown area, and Harris County as well as the Uptown Houston District have stepped forward to help maintain the site.

Historical sites. The restoration of existing historical sites presents a different set of challenges. The earlier-mentioned ca. 1860 home of Fritz Schroeder on 435 Piney Point Road, within the Village of Piney Point, provides an example. That historic farmstead, the oldest remaining home in the area west of the inner city, lies all but forgotten on public land of the Memorial Villages Water Authority, a water conservation and reclamation district of the State of Texas. With some philanthropy, that building might be graced with an historical marker, and its front portion restored to its earlier appearance, perhaps to be used as a public meeting place or even a small village museum. The same could be said of the 1875 farmhouse of Bear Creek immigrant George Hillendahl, in the former townsite of Addicks. Now owned and operated by a commercial firm, perhaps someday it might be purchased, moved to a public space, and restored as a museum dedicated to the Bear Creek pioneers.

A significantly larger project, with larger historical and cultural significance, would include the grounds of St. Peter Church on Long Point. This Spring Branch site was the first stopping point of pioneer German immigrants in 1847-1848. The 1864 church building is the perhaps the oldest in Houston. It is still in use, as is its historic cemetery, but the portion of its modest membership with German heritage continues to decline. The potential property, much of which still lies in a natural state, fronts on Long Point and is bounded on the west by the 1864 chapel, including the church's holdings west of Spring Branch Creek. It notionally could extend eastward along Long Point across the creek to the intersection of Spring Branch Drive, a total parcel of about ten acres. The eastern segment is privately owned and vacant, and still in a natural state. The large oak trees that were mentioned and enjoyed by the early immigrants still exist, both at the cemetery and in the segment across Spring Branch Creek.

This historic property is hugely significant in ways that should resonate with all groups of Houstonians today. In many ways, it is Houston's Jamestown, where newly arriving pioneer immigrants gave thanks at their safe arrival, but then underwent their own "starving time," when the German settlers were wracked by multiple diseases and by hunger; they buried their dead in mass graves (Chapter 6). These hardy folk persevered, and ultimately prospered. Could this area be re-envisioned as a public historical park, where the Church and its cemetery continued to operate but where the rest of the site is taken back to its original appearance? San Antonio has taken active Spanish mission churches and incorporated them into public parks; could this 170 year old site become a State historic site? The drive and funding for such a thing could perhaps only be undertaken by the private sector.

Prairie greenspace. Although a complete restoration of the Addicks and Barker reservoirs to an open, native landscape is seemingly too large to contemplate, consider that there are smaller pieces that would make wonderful natural and historical parks. Here are two to consider, both on public land.

At the spillway for Buffalo Bayou, in front of Barker Dam and west of State Highway 6, lies a six acre grassy area managed by the Army Corps of Engineers. It is graced with bicycle paths that connect the trail system of Terry Hershey Park to the east with a system of trails within and around Barker Reservoir. The 1831 San Felipe Trail once passed directly through that site, and Joel Wheaton's wagon ford over Buffalo Bayou was located where the adjacent bridge of State Highway 6 lies today. The large open space is largely featureless, its surface closely mown as lawn grass with few adornments. If replanted with native prairie grasses, this public site could provide a pocket prairie reserve through which hundreds of bicyclists, hikers and runners pass each day. A reconstruction of Joel Wheaton's Inn there—there are existing photographs to guide the way—might provide a bicyclists' and hikers' watering hole, where exhibits could be placed that describe both local history as well as Harris County flood control operations. This area is being extensively reworked at present—the Army Corps of Engineers is re-routing the Buffalo Bayou spillway—and when things are put back together, a bicycle path could be routed precisely over the former site of the historical San Felipe Trail, taking bicyclists across a restored prairie. The dam provides an attractive green backstop to the site, giving one an illusion of a rural setting, and the bayou provides a soundtrack of rushing water. A row of trees installed along the adjacent highway would do much to lower the level of traffic noise. As the site is in front of Barker Dam, it is not flood prone. Such a natural/historical park could be managed by either the county or the city; both entities already manage recreational parks in the two reservoirs. Private philanthropy would be needed to provide funds.

The northwestern part of Addicks Reservoir is its highest in elevation, and hence its most flood-resistant part. It is in just this specific area that the German pioneers settled, along Bear Creek (see highlighted area, Figure 12.15 A and B). This area of perhaps 800 undeveloped acres would provide a perfect place to restore a good-sized piece of Houston's native prairie, complete with a through-going tributary of Buffalo Bayou and its riparian forest—yet within the urbanized confines of Houston. There are still some open areas within that property that are not yet totally clogged with china tallow trees, so a prairie foothold is already there. Such a space of restored native prairie grasses would present a profoundly different experience to the visitor than that of existing City and County parks in Addicks and Barker reservoirs, which typically consist of closely mown lawns for recreational purposes. Bear Creek, a tributary of Buffalo Bayou that is still largely in its natural state at this site, cuts through the prairie there and would give the visitor a superb view of the primeval landscape that existed before our city and county were founded. If a recreated German farmstead were added to a portion of the restored prairie—thus reviving a small part of newsman Ray Miller's vision from three decades ago—and a network of nearby bicycle trails were routed through it, the whole package would provide Houston and Harris County residents with a wonderful public place to celebrate the area's natural and cultural beginnings.

During the historic floods of April, 2016, the eastern part of this tract was underwater, like most of Addicks and its other parks, but the upper, western part did not. That experience could be used in planning any physical additions, although the main goal of such a project would be to emphasize prairie and woodland landscape, with a few added hiking and biking trails.

This latter prairie greenspace site is somewhat large in scale, but the culture of philanthropy in the city of Houston is large, too. The significant recent projects at Buffalo Bayou Park and Discovery Green, coupled with the vision of Bayou Greenways 2020 and the Memorial Park Conservancy give great hope for the future. If public vision could be widened a bit more to include the importance of preserving significantly large parts of the original prairie ecosystem, in addition to ongoing efforts to preserve and restore the area's wooded bayous, there can be great hope for the future.

Postscript

If you ever find yourself traveling westward on Westheimer Road outside Loop 610, passing the endless array of strip shopping centers and filling stations, keep an eye out for the intersection of Jeanetta Street, just after the Fondren intersection. Turn right at Jeanetta, and on your immediate right is a small half-acre green space associated with the entrance of the adjacent Marquis of Piney Point apartment complex. Find a parking place, and stroll over to the green space. You will see a steep gully that projects southwestward into a culvert that is buried beneath ultra-busy Westheimer. You are standing at what was once called Pine or Piney Point, the southernmost part of the riparian forest that once extended north from here to Buffalo Bayou. In front of you is Piney Point Gully, and because in pioneer days its forested banks were too steep for ox wagons to negotiate, the east-west San Felipe Trail skirted the gully just south of this point, a hundred feet or so south of modern Westheimer.

If you look closely at the trees in this manicured green space, you can begin to read their secrets. Some are non-native palms planted by the apartment owners to beautify an otherwise undevelopable plot along the steep gully. Interspersed among the palms, however, are a precious few tall pines, surrounded in all directions by the concrete prairie of urban Houston. Those are special pines; they are the last remnants of the tall pines at this site that beckoned early pioneers heading west from Harrisburg and later Houston. They and this half-acre site are all that is left of the old frontier natural landmark called Piney Point. Just a half mile north of here, a frontiersman and his wife built a log cabin in the wilderness. That occurred in 1824, years before Houston was even a collection of tents and cabins in the prairie mud.

From the 1830s to 1850s, thousands of ox wagons creaked eastward along the San Felipe Trail past this point bearing heavy loads of cotton that had been picked by enslaved African Americans on Brazos River plantations, turning Houston into an early Texas commercial powerhouse. During the Texas Revolution, many Texian families fled past this site in the great Runaway Scrape, trying desperately to stay in front of Santa Anna's advancing army. In the 1840s, thousands of German immigrants labored westward past this site with heavily laden ox carts, headed for pioneer settlements at Bear Creek, Cat Spring, Fayetteville, and La Grange. Near the old frontiersman's cabin, in the early 1850s, an immigrant German carpenter built an elegant house to gain the freedom of the slave girl that he loved and later married. Immediately after the end of the Civil War, thousands of African Americans, newly freed from their forced servitude on Brazos plantations, trekked past here on foot. Carrying their belongings in blanket-wrapped bundles, they headed east for Houston and freedom.

After Reconstruction a bridge was built across Piney Point Gully where Westheimer is today, and a narrow gauge steam railroad arrived. This was the site of the Piney Point stop on that railroad, and the railroad company owned forty acres where the adjacent apartment complex is today. The company built a simple wooden outdoor platform there where farm people, white and black, could enjoy dances on a summer's evening or listen to a country preacher attempt to save their souls. Just across Westheimer from this site, where a small state auto inspection shop now stands, residents of the neighborhood built a one-room schoolhouse.

There is now no general public memory of the many events that took place here. This small site is a focal point for far too much history to place on a simple historical marker. But it is in just such small, forgotten places all over the city and county that our frontier beginnings may be recalled and cherished.

ACKNOWLEDGMENTS

I HAVE HAD THE ADVICE, support, and critical thoughts of many historians, scholars, genealogists, family and friends in producing this book, for which I am very grateful. Janet Wagner, chair of the Harris County Historical Commission, has provided invaluable information and support through her previous research into the history of Harris County, especially that of the Agur Morse plantation and its vicinity, including the Morse-Bragg Cemetery, as well as the early history of parts of the Fourth Ward.

The staff of the Harris County Archives, the General Land Office in Austin, the Texas Room of the Houston Public Library, the Clayton Library Center for Genealogical Research, and the Texas Heritage Museum in Hillsboro have provided valued assistance. The late Marie Marshall's 1975 book on the Morse family, Forebears and Descendants of an Early Houston Family, was enormously helpful, as was the autobiography of Cassie McFee Reeder, a manuscript generously made available by her granddaughter Matilda Reeder. Matilda and her sister, April Reeder Wiggins, also made available a number of family photographs of the pioneer McFee family. La Quencis Gibbs Scott shared information about her ancestor Allen C. Reynolds, including several useful files and illustrations. Barbara Bullard and Pastor Walter K. Barry of the McGee Chapel Missionary Baptist Church helped provide insights into their church's history.

I am greatly indebted to amateur genealogists, many but not all of them in my extended family, who have helped research the descendants of those interred in the Morse-Bragg Cemetery. That information helped not only in the effort to save the cemetery but also in connecting me with stories of long-lost distant relatives and neighbors in the old Pleasant Bend, Piney Point and Wheaton's Ford neighborhoods. These helpful family and friends especially included my sister Nancy Worrall Peterson; cousin Terry Patterson; distant cousins Leilani Morse Cross, Linda Dianis, Kathy Monahan Philips and her father Earl Monahan; and Allyne Reeder. A thesis by James Orville Moore at the University of Houston at Clear Lake was very useful in following two Morse sons through their adventures in the Civil War. Jo Petty of the Houston First Presbyterian Church kindly shared access to her church's archives.

Several historians were of great help in teaching me about the now lost pioneer German settlement of Bear Creek and the history of the Barker and Addicks reservoirs. Martha Doty Freeman shared her extensive knowledge of the old settlement and her collection of old photographs of its buildings, which date from the time when she researched and prepared cultural assessments of the Addicks and Barker reservoirs in the 1980s. Marie Neuman Gray shared her extensive archives of material on the people in the Bear Creek settlement, some of whom were her ancestors. The family history books of the late Margaret Hopkins Edwards were full of insight on the lives of these frontier families. Kristine Brown of the Addicks office of the U.S. Army Corps of Engineers shared her extensive collection of historical documents on the reservoirs and helped introduce me to the work of Freeman and Neuman Gray. I am also indebted to Andrea Renee (Stahman) Burden for a very useful history of the Bear Creek community, which formed part of her 2004 master's thesis at Texas A&M University, as well as access to a number of illustrations and stories. I thank Edward Matzke of the Addicks United Methodist Church, who shared information regarding that congregation's history and allowed access to some of their old images.

Nelda Blackshere Reynolds, Evelyn Schroeder Kingsley and Ruth Hillendahl Plumb very kindly shared information, stories and photographs of their

Spring Branch ancestors. The process of finding and compiling the stories of the pioneer Reinermann clan and their descendants—the initial settlers of the Memorial Park area—and the story of the Reconstruc-tion-era Eureka Cotton Mills was enormously helped by the careful research of David Hornburg, Louis Aulbach, and Bernice Mistrot. I learned the history of the adjacent White Oak German settlement with the gracious help of area Hillendahl and Ojemann descendants Kay Houston and Walker R. "Sonny" Gray Jr.

The forgotten story of some important post–Civil War cattlemen who brought Harris County cattle up the Chisholm Trail could not have been told without information and assistance from Galveston County historian Alecya Gallaway and from Anita Butler, a granddaughter of early Texas cattleman George W. Butler. Likewise very helpful were the staff of the Helen Hall Library and the Butler Longhorn Museum, both in League City, Texas, as well as Floyd Martin and Melody Hauch of the Galveston County Historical Society. Vera Bell Gary, of League City, graciously shared images of her forebears who rode the Chisholm Trail.

Harris County officials have played and continue to play a leadership role in preserving pieces of the area's history. In particular, County Judge Ed Emmett and Precinct 3 Commissioner Steve Radack adopted the Beeler pioneer cemetery for preservation and maintenance as a county pocket park some years ago, and they recently stepped forward to protect the pioneer Morse-Bragg cemetery in similar fashion. In the 1960s Harris County set aside part of Addicks Reservoir as Bear Creek Pioneers Park, a memorial to the old German families who first settled there and whose descendants were uprooted by the needs of Greater Houston for the flood control reservoirs that were built there in the 1940s.

The Harris County Historical Commission is spearheading an effort to place more historical markers commemorating significant parts of the county's development, some of which are in the area of this study. Parts of the present work were used to document proposed new markers, and several members of the commission kindly helped correct and extend that documentation, including Bernice Mistrot, Barbara Eaves, Janet K. Wagner, Dr. Gayle Davies, Sarah Canby Jackson, Mike Vance, Ann Becker, and Debra Blacklock-Sloan. Bernice Mistrot also helped me research the Jordan Banks family and other early African American families in the Pleasant Bend area as well as the long-gone Lovely Canada Baptist Church. Her meticulous editing comments on parts of the text were extremely valuable.

I also thank my fellow pioneer descendants and many other friends who have helped in various ways to preserve the history of their families and of their city, county and state: Drew Patterson, Steven Loy Jr. and Steven Loy Sr., David H. Burrow, Justin Burrow, Jim Worrall, John Worrall, Rita White, Kathleen Riffe, Susan Lacy, Tom Morse, Gail Anderson, Robert Arnold, Joe Hudson, Steve and Mary Judson, Ruth Taft Judson Knapik, Mary Page Judson Kruse, Mary Lundgren, Bob and Roberta Martin, Sarah Mendell, James Dudley Morse, Don Reeder, Sandi Wade-Janik, Pamela Wagner, David Wallace, Scott and Kendra Williams, and Gary E. White.

Sally E. Antrobus of Seabrook, Texas helped enormously by copy-editing my fractured English, and I am equally indebted to Barbara M. Whitehead of Austin, for both the beautiful cover illustration as well as the book design and layout. It is wonderful to be able to rely on such talented and creative people for their highly skilled help.

I would be greatly remiss if I didn't thank several mentors from my earlier days who instilled in me a love for both natural history and for technical research and writing: Sig Snelson, Albert W. Bally, Richard L. Nicholas, and the late Professor John C. Maxwell. And finally, my wife Mary Ryan Worrall has put up with my history and cemetery preservation activities beyond all measure; her support and counsel was, as always, essential.

NOTES

Introduction

1. Bill Fulton, *"Growth and Development Trends in Metro Houston,"* presentation, National Federation of Municipal Analysts' conference, Houston, January 22, 2015, online at kinder.rice.edu/presentations, accessed May 2016.

1. The Grand Prairie

1. Joseph C. Clopper, "J. C. Clopper's Journal and Book of Memoranda for 1828," *Quarterly of the Texas State Historical Association* 13 (July 1909): 57–58, online at Portal to Texas History, http://texashistory.unt.edu (hereafter Clopper, "Journal").

2. Donald E. Chipman, *Spanish Texas, 1519-1821* (Austin, Texas: University off Texas Press, 1992).

3. James M. Day, Review of *A Visit to Texas: Being the Journal of a Traveller through Those Parts Most Interesting to American Settlers, Journal of the Southwest* 18, no. 3 (1976): 302–304.

4. Anonymous ["M. Fiske"], *A Visit to Texas: Being the Journal of a Traveller through Those Parts Most Interesting to American Settlers* (New York: Goodrich and Wiley, 1834), 18. A second edition was published in 1836 (New York: Van Nostrand Dwight) and a version edited by Robert S. Gray was reprinted in 1975 (Houston: Cordovan Press). Although the author is unknown, it is here attributed to "M. Fiske" (see note in text). A copy is available in the Harris County Archives.

5. Ibid., 186.

6. Ibid., 158–159.

7. Clopper, *"Journal,"* 57–58.

8. Glen E. Lich, "Postl, Carl Anton," *Handbook of Texas Online*, Texas State Historical Association, uploaded June 15, 2010.

9. Adele B. Looscan, "Extracts from an Historical Sketch of Harris County, 1822–1845," *Southwestern Historical Quarterly* 18 (1915): 205.

10. Charles Sealsfield, *The Cabin Book, or Sketches of Life in Texas*, trans. from German by Prof. C. F. Mersch (New York: J. Winchester, 1844), 10–13, online at the Portal to Texas History, www.texashistory.unt.edu.

11. Ferdinand Roemer, *Texas, Mit besonderer Rücksicht auf deutsche Auswanderung imd die physischen Verhältnisse des Landes nach eigener Beobachtung geschildert* (Bonn, Germany: Adolph Marcus, 1849), 168 pp. Translated by Oswald Mueller (San Antonio: Standard Printing Company, 1935) and republished as *Roemer's Texas* (Austin: Eakin, 1995; Mockingbird Books, 2012).

12. Anonymous ["M. Fiske"], *A Visit to Texas*, 88.

13. J. Frank Dobie, *The Longhorns* (New York: Grosset and Dunlap, 1941), 7.

14. Paul J. Foik, trans., *Captain Diego Ramón's Diary of His Expedition into Texas in 1716* (Austin, Tex.: 1935), 17, as quoted by Dobie.

15. H. E. Bolton, *Athanase de Mézières and the Louisiana-Texas Frontier, 1768–1780* (Cleveland, Ohio: Arthur H. Clark, 1914), 2 vols., 2:187–188.

16. Anonymous ["M. Fiske"], *A Visit to Texas*, 47.

17. Writer's Program of the Works Progress Administration in the State of Texas, *Houston: A History and a Guide* (Houston: Anson Jones Press, 1942), 43.

18. W. C. Moore, "How Buffalo Bayou was Named," *Frontier Times* 18, no. 2 (1940): 50–52.

19. Anonymous ["M. Fiske"], *A Visit to Texas*, 189.

20. Ibid., 58.

21. Dilue Rose Harris, "Reminiscences of Mrs. Dilue Harris," *Southwestern Historical Quarterly* 4 (1900).

22. Clopper, "Journal," 52.

23. George W. Bonnell, *Topographical Description of Texas, to which is Added an Account of the Indian Tribes* (1840; repr. Waco, Tex.: Texian Press, 1964), 28.

24. Moore, "How Buffalo Bayou was Named."

25. Anonymous ["M. Fiske"], *A Visit to Texas* , 40–41.

26. Ibid., 191–192.

27. Carol Adams, *Historic Katy: An Illustrated History* (San Antonio, Tex.: HPNbooks, 2012), 6.

28. Harry H. Weinman (1904–1994), *The History of Katy and Vicinity* (unpublished manuscript, undated), Katy Public Library.

29. Lawrence Aten, *Indians of the Upper Texas Coast* (New York: Academic Press, 1983).

30. "Tonkawa Tribal History," Tonkawa Tribe Official Website, www.tonkawatribe.com, accessed March 2016.

31. Carol A. Lipscomb, "Karankawa Indians," *Handbook of Texas Online*, Texas State Historical Association, http://www.tshaonline.org/handbook/online/articles/bmk05, uploaded June 15, 2010, accessed March 29, 2016.

32. John R. Swanton, *The Indian Tribes of North America, Bureau of Ethnology Bulletin 145* (Washington, D.C.: Smithsonian Institution, 1953), 198.

33. John C. Ewers, editor, *The Indians of Texas in 1830*, by Jean Louis Berlandier: (Washington D.C.: Smithsonian Institution Press, 1969), 139, footnote 205.

34. Robert A. Ricklis, "The Prehistory of the Texas Coastal Zone: 10,000 Years of Changing Environment and Culture,"

Texas Beyond History, University of Texas at Austin, www.texasbeyondhistory.net/coast/prehistory, accessed September 6, 2014.

35. *The Journey of Alvar Nuñez Cabeza de Vaca and His Companions from Florida to the Pacific 1528–1536*, trans. Fanny Bandelier (New York: A. S. Barnes & Company, 1905). Also Enrique Pupo-Walker, ed., *Castaways: The Narrative of Alvar Núñez Cabeza de Vaca* (Berkeley, University of California Press, 1993), 26–27.

36. Carly Whelan, "El Orcoquisac," *Texas Beyond History*, University of Texas at Austin, www.texasbeyondhistory.net/coast/images/he2.html, accessed September 6, 2014.

37. Louis Leclerc Milfort, Memoirs, or A Quick Glance at My Various Travels and My Sojourn in the Creek Nation, chap. 15, Rootsweb Homepages.

38. Donald E. Chipman, *Spanish Texas, 1519–1821* (Austin: University of Texas Press, 1992), 164–168.

39. Ibid., 200–201.

40. Andrew J. Torget, *Seeds of Empire: Cotton, Slavery and the Transformation of the Texas Borderlands, 1800-1850* (University of North Carolina Press Chapel Hill, 2015), Introduction.

41. Juan N. Almonte, 1833, "Statistical Report on Texas," in *Southwestern Historical Quarterly* 28:212, 1925.

42. Andrew Torget, 2015.

43. Stephen F. Austin to Josiah H. Bell, August 6, 1823, *Austin Papers* 2, pt. 1: 682, Eugene C. Barker Texas History Center, as quoted in Bob Arnold, First in Texas: Three Texans and Their Contributions to Texas History, 1821–1978 (privately published, 2011), 34.

44. *The Narrative of Robert Hancock Hunter* (manuscript), 1860, Texas State Archives, Austin, online at http://www.tamu.edu/faculty/ccbn/dewitt/hunternarrative.htm

45. Lipscomb, "Karankawa Indians," *Handbook of Texas Online*, accessed September 04, 2014.

46. *Handbook of North American Indians, vol. 14: Southeast*, ed. William C. Sturtevant and Raymond D. Fogelson(Washington D.C.: Smithsonian Institution, 2004), 661. Also see Atakapa people, en.wikipedia.org/wiki/Atakapa_people.

47. Susan Dial and Steve Black, ed., "Native Peoples of the Coastal Prairies and Marshlands in Early Historic Times," *Texas Beyond History, University of Texas at Austin*, www.texasbeyondhistory.net/coast/peoples/index.html, accessed August 2015.

48. Jerry Withers, *The Tonkawan Indians of Texas*, online at www.tamu.edu/faculty/ccbn/dewitt/adp/history/mission_period /valero/indian/tonkawa.html. Also see "The Tonkawa Story," Manataka American Indian Council, www.manataka.org, and "Tonkawa Tribal History," Tonkawa Tribe Official Website, www.tonkawatribe.com, accessed March 2016.

49. *Narrative of Robert Hancock Hunter* (manuscript), 1860, Texas State Archives, Austin.

50. Benjamin H. Carroll, *Standard History of Houston, Texas, from a Study of the Original Sources*, (Knoxville, Tenn.: H. W. Crew & Company, 1912), chap. 3. Electronic version, Electronic Resources Center, Fondren Library, Rice University.

51. Obituary of Ida Hoehmann, *Houston Chronicle*, 1961, as quoted by Andrea R. Stahman, *Bear Creek: A Case Study in Locating Historic Site Remains in Southeast Texas*, MA thesis, Graduate School of Texas A&M University, 2004, 48–49.

52. (probably Herman Charles Rummel), *History of Spring Branch, 1837–1937* (Houston: Privately published, 1937), Archives of Clayton Library, Houston Public Library.

53. "Saga of West Harris Revealed at 75th Birthday of Addicks Resident [Henrietta Bleick]," *Houston Chronicle*, February 13, 1949, as quoted in Stahman, Bear Creek.

54. Joe Ben Wheat, *River Basin Surveys Papers, No. 4, An Archeological Survey of the Addicks Dam Basin, Southeast Texas Bureau of American Ethnology Bulletin* 154 (Washington, D.C.: Smithsonian Institution, 1947).

55. Melissa M. Peterson, ed., *The Road to Piney Point* (Houston: Piney Point Village Historic Committee, 1994), 3.

56. Robert A. Ricklis and Steve Black, "Mitchell Ridge, Camp and Burial Ground on Galveston Island," *Texas Beyond History, University of Texas at Austin*, online at http://www.texasbeyondhistory.net/mitchell/.

2. Dreams of a Commercial Empire

1. Edward Nicholas Clopper, *An American Family: Its Ups and Downs through Eight Generations in New Amsterdam, New York, Pennsylvania, Maryland, Ohio, and Texas, from 1650 to 1880* (Cincinnati: Standard Print and Publishing Company, 1950), 127–129.

2. Donald E. Chipman, *Spanish Texas, 1519–1821* (Austin: University of Texas Press, 1992), 231, 241.

3. Ibid., 233–239.

4. David B. Gracy II, "Moses Austin," *Handbook of Texas Online*, Texas State Historical Association, accessed November 13, 2013.

5. Christopher Long, "Old Three Hundred" *Handbook of Texas Online*; Wolfram M. Von-Maszewski, ed., *Austin's Old Three HHundred: The First Anglo Colony in Texas* (Waco: Eakin Press, 2011), 163.

6. Von-Maszewski, *Austin's Old Three Hundred*, x.

7. Adele B. Looscan, "Harris County, 1822–1845," *Southwestern Historical Quarterly* 18 (1915):197.

8. Merle Weir, "Phelps, James Aeneas E."; Gladys E. Clark, "Frostown, Tc"; Deolece M. Parmelee, "Wilkins, Jane Mason," all in *Handbook of Texas Online*.

9. Looscan, "Harris County, 1822–1845," 196–197.

10. Ibid., 197.

11. Harris Gaylord Warren, "Long Expedition," *Handbook of Texas Online*, http://www.tshaonline.org/handbook/online/articles/qyl01, accessed September 08, 2014.

12. "Austin, John," *Handbook of Texas Online*, http://www.tshaonline.org/handbook/online/articles/fau09, accessed September 08, 2014.

13. Looscan, "Harris County, 1822–1845," 197.

14. "Austin, John," *Handbook of Texas Online.*

15. Boyse House, "An Incident at Velasco, 1832," *Southwestern Historical Quarterly* 64, no. 1 (1960): 92–95.

16. "Austin, John Punderson," *Handbook of Texas Online*, http://www.tshaonline.org/handbook/online/articles/fau10.

17. Looscan, "Harris County, 1822–1845," 197.

18. Melissa M. Peterson, ed., *The Road to Piney Point* (Houston: Piney Point Village Historic Committee, 1994), 9.

19. Diana J. Kleiner, "Taylor, John D.," *Handbook of Texas Online*, http://www.tshaonline.org/handbook /online/articles/fta21, accessed September 07, 2014.

20. Peterson, *The Road to Piney Point*, 17–18.

21. Karl von Sommer, *Bericht über meine Reise nach Texas im Jahre 1846 (The story of my trip to Texas in 1846)*, (Bremen, Germany: Johann Georg Hesse, 1847). Available at Göttingen State and University Library, Germany; translation by the author.

22. Comer Clay, "The Colorado River Raft," *Southwestern Historical Quarterly* 52 (April 1949), 410-426, online at Portal to Texas History, http://texashistory.unt.edu.

23. Harold W. Hyde, *Soil Survey of Matagorda County, Texas*, United States Department of Agriculture, Natural Resources Conservation Service, 1993, 9.

24. Joseph C. Clopper, "J. C. Clopper's Journal and Book of Memoranda for 1828," *Quarterly of the Texas State Historical Association* 13 (July 1909), 58, online at Portal to Texas History, http://texashistory.unt.edu.

25. Wesley N. Laing, "Ariel," *Handbook of Texas Online*, accessed April 04, 2016.

26. Jean L. Epperson, "Cayuga," *Handbook of Texas Online*, accessed April 04, 2016.

27. Lois Wood Burkhalter, "Yellow Stone," Handbook of Texas Online, accessed April 04, 2016.

28. Leonard Kubiak, "History of Steamboats in Texas," www.forttumbleweed.com, accessed April 2016.

29. Andrew Forest Muir, "The Destiny of Buffalo Bayou," *Southwestern Historical Quarterly* 47 (October 1947), 98, online at Portal to Texas History: https://texashistory.unt.edu/ark:/67531/metapth146054/m1/109/

30. James V. Woodrick, *Bernardo: Crossroads, Social Center and Agricultural Showcase of Early Texas* (CreateSpace 2011), 191.

31. Muir, "Destiny of Buffalo Bayou," 95.

32. J. C. Clopper, "Journal," 52.

33. Andrew Forest Muir, 1943, "The Destiny of Buffalo Bayou," 97–98.

34. Looscan, "Harris County, 1822–1845," 199–200.

35. J. C. Clopper, "Journal," 52.

36. Julia Beazley, "Harris, John Richardson," *Handbook of Texas Online*, http://www.tshaonline.org/handbook/online/articles/fha85, accessed September 09, 2014.

37. Anonymous ["M. Fiske"], *A Visit to Texas: Being the Journal of a Traveller through Those Parts Most Interesting to American Settlers* (New York: Goodrich and Wiley, 1834; repr. New York: Van Nostrand Dwight, 1836; ed. Robert S. Gray, Houston: Cordovan Press, 1975), 18.

38. Looscan, "Harris County, 1822–1845," 200–201.

39. Diana J. Kleiner, "Moore, Luke," *Handbook of Texas Online.*

40. "Brown, John," *Handbook of Texas Online.*

41. Marilyn M. Sibley, "Clopper, Nicholas," *Handbook of Texas Online.*

42. Edward Nicholas Clopper, *An American Family*, 593.

43. Ibid., 109–110.

44. Ibid., 127–129.

45. San Felipe de Austin State Historic Site, Texas Historic Commission, 2D Map Tour, accessed 2015 online at www.visitsanfelipedeaustin.com.

46. *The Narrative of Robert Hancock Hunter* (manuscript), 1860, Texas State Archives, Austin, online at www.tamu.edu.

47. Edward Clopper, *An American Family*, 152.

48. Ibid., 167.

49. Ibid., 154–155.

50. Ibid., 181.

51. Ibid., 186–192.

52. Ibid., 202.

53. Ibid., 225.

54. Ibid., 225–229.

55. Abstract 16, Matagorda County, General Land Office, Austin. Also see Edward Clopper, *An American Family*, 320–325.

56. Sibley, "Clopper, Nicholas," *Handbook of Texas Online.*

3. The San Felipe Trail in Colonial Times

1. Ferdinand Roemer, *Texas, with Particular Reference to German Immigration and the Physical Appearance of the Country*, trans. Oswald Mueller (San Antonio: Standard Printing Company, 1935; repr. Austin: Eakin Press, 1995), 71.

2. Eugene C. Barker, "Minutes of the Ayuntamiento of San Felipe de Austin, 1828–1832, Part I," *Southwestern Historical Quarterly* 21, no. 3 (1918):299–326, online at Portal to Texas History, http://texashistory.unt.edu.

3. Noah Smithwick, *The Evolution of a State* (Austin, Tex.: Gammel Book Company, 1900), online at Google Books, 57.

4. Barker, "Minutes of the Ayuntamiento," 183, 189. Also see previous mention, *Southwestern Historical Quarterly* 22 (July 1918): 79.

5. *Roemer, Texas*, 66.

6. Map of Texas with Parts of the Adjoining States, com-

piled by Stephen F. Austin, online at Portal to Texas History, http://texashistory.unt.edu.

7. http://www.houstontx.gov/parks/founderscemetery.html.

8. "Map of the Old San Felipe Road, from B. A. Bragg's Farm to Waller County Line at Cane Island," ca. 1890, Harris County Archives.

9. Stephen F. Austin, *Register of Families, General Land Office,* Austin, vol. 1, 66.

10. Plan and Division of Joel Wheaton's League and a Labor, map and field notes by George Bringhurst, February 9, 1849, Harris County Archives.

11. Rosa Kleberg, "Some of My Early Experiences in Texas," *Quarterly of the Texas State Historical Association* 1 (July 1897–April 1898): 298–299.

12. Harris County Clerk's Office, Harris County Probate Papers, Old Case Papers, W-71. Also see Janet K. Wagner and Danny K. Reed, February 1992,"Habermacher Cemetery Study," 3D/Environmental Services, Inc., Houston, Texas.

13. Harris County Clerk's Office, Harris County Probate Records, 1839, vol. H, p. 234.

14. Harris County Marriage Records, number 168.

15. Republic Claims, Texas State Library and Archives Commission, claim # 8945, Elizabeth Wheaton, reel 113, 226.

16. Miles S. Bennet, "Experiences on the Western Frontier, Republic of Texas, 1838–1842," from a series of articles in the Cuero Star and Houston Post in 1898 constructed from Bennet's diary and titled *The Bennett Scrapbook,* online at www.tamu.edu/faculty/ccbn/dewitt/bennetscrap.htm, accessed September 2014.

17. *The Narrative Diary of Miles Squier Bennett,* DeWitt Colony Diaries, The Bennet Family, online at www.tamu.edu/faculty/ccbn.dewitt/bennetscrap.htm, accessed April 2016.

18. *Roemer, Texas,* 73.

19. Harris County Marriage Records, number 302.

20. Argive Wheaton, probate papers of November 4, 1845, Harris County Probate, Old Case Papers, S-61.

21. *David Normand, Nathan Brookshire, 1786–1853* (unpublished manuscript, 1996), in possession of Marie Neumann, Pattison, Texas.

22. Wheaton family tree, www.ancestry.com.

23. St. Vincent's Church Marriage Records, pp. 4, 13; also Harris County Probate Records, vol. H-2.

24. Harris County Deed Records, vol. S, 177.

25. Harris County Deed Records, Book P, 465, 1855.

26. Mrs. Arch B. Marshall, *Forebears and Descendants of an Early Houston Family* (Houston: Privately published, 1975), 66–67, 166, copy at Clayton Library, Houston Public Library.

27. Marshall, *Forebears and Descendants,* 67.

28. Ibid., 68.

29. Harris County Deed Records, Book 7, 407.

30. Mrs. Glen T. Bundick, "Oldest Buffalo Bayou Home Rich in History," *Houston Chronicle,* February 13, 1949.

31. The photograph is from Anonymous, *A History of Addicks High School, the Area and the People, West Harris County, Texas* (N.p., n.d.), 11.

32. Bundick, "Oldest Buffalo Bayou Home."

33. Anonymous, *History of Addicks High School,* 4.

34. Ibid., 4.

35. La Quencis Gibbs Scott, "Reynolds, Allen C.," *Handbook of Texas Online,* Texas State Historical Association, http://www.tshaonline.org/handbook/online/articles/frels, accessed September 18, 2014.

36. Reynolds family Bible, owned by Joseph David Crawford; a page from that Bible was posted by susiakc under the entry for Allen C. Reynolds, www.ancestry.com, July 2010.

37. Register of Families, Austin Colony: Texas General Land Office, Austin, pp. 93-94.

38. Abstract 61, Spanish Collection, Texas General Land Office, Austin, file no. 102853.

39. Scott, "Reynolds, Allen C.".

40. Janet Wagner, personal communication, 2015.

41. Sarah H. Emmott, *Memorial Park, a Priceless Legacy* (Houston: Herring Press, 1992), p. 10.

42. Scott suggested that the house may have been in the prairie north of the intersection of modern day Weslayan Street and Highway 59, based upon proximity to an early race track and horse market, although such a location seems a long distance from his mill and from trees and water. See Scott, "Reynolds, Allen C."

43. Original documents in the personal collection of La Quencis Gibbs Scott. Also see Dorothy Knox Howe Houghton and others, *Houston's Forgotten Heritage* (College Station: Texas A&M University Press, 1991), pp. 266-267.

44. Inflation data from Historical Statistics of the United States (Washington, D.C.: U.S. Government Printing Office, 1975).

45. La Quencis Gibbs Scott, personal communication, 2016.

46. Scott, "Reynolds, Allen C."

47. Ibid.

48. William Bledsoe Hardin and Sarah Looney, biography posted by family members, www.ancestry.com, November 1, 2010.

49. Henry K. Lewis land grants, Spanish Collection 26:68, 14:39, and 13:16, General Land Office, Austin.

50. George Lyman Bellows, in Knee-Troke-Brown-Dyke family tree, www.ancestry.com.

51. C. David Pomeroy, entries on Robert Vince and William Vince, www.earlytexashistory.com, accessed September 2014. Also see "Vince, Robert," *Handbook of Texas Online,* www.tshaonline.org/handbook/online/articles/fvi10, accessed September 28, 2014.

52. Texas General Land Office, Register of Families, entry for Charles Sage, appeared February 6, 1836, p. 93. General Land Office, Austin, http://www.glo.texas.gov/history/

archives/land-grants/registeroffamilies.cfm?intID=1987.

53. Charles Sage grant of 1/3 league, Abstract Number 697, Patent Date March 18, 1845, http://www.glo.texas.gov/ncu/SCANDOCS/archives_webfiles/arcmaps/webfiles/land-grants/PDFs/2/3/2/232613.pdf.

54. Work Projects Administration, Transcript of Passenger Lists of Vessels Arriving at New Orleans, Louisiana, 1813–1849, Accessed at www.ancestry.com, microfilm series M2009, roll 1.

55. J. R. Edmondson, *The Alamo Story: From Early History to Current Conflicts* (Plano, Tex.: Republic of Texas Press, 2000), 80–81.

56. Martha Menchaca, *Recovering History, Constructing Race: The Indian, Black, and White Roots of Mexican Americans.* Joe R. and Teresa Lozano Long Series in Latin American and Latino Art and Culture (Austin: University of Texas Press, 2001), 200.

57. William C. Davis, *Lone Star Rising* (College Station: Texas A&M University Press, 2006), 89–95.

58. Stephen Hardin, *The Alamo 1836: Santa Anna's Texas Campaign* (Westport, Conn.: Osprey Publishing, 2004), 102.

59. T. R. Fehrenbach, *Lone Star: A History of Texas and the Texans* (1968; Cambridge, Mass.: Da Capo Press, 2000), 227.

60. William DeWees and Emaretta C. Kimball, *Letters from Early Settler of Texas to a Friend* (Morton and Griswold, 1852), 203–204.

61. Ibid., 201.

62. Rosa Kleberg, "Some of My Experiences in Texas," *Quarterly of the Texas State Historical Association* 1 (July 1897–April 1898): 300–301.

63. Herbert H. Lang, "Harris, Dilue Rose," *Handbook of Texas Online,* accessed January 04, 2016.

64. Dilue Rose Harris, "Reminiscences of Mrs. Dilue Harris," *Southwestern Historical Quarterly* 4 (1901): 162–166.

65. Dr. O. F. Allen, *The City of Houston: From Wilderness to Wonder* (Temple Tex.: Privately published, 1936), 54, online at Portal to Texas History, http://texashistory.unt.edu.

66. James V. Woodrick, *Bernardo: Crossroads, Social Center and Agricultural Showcase of Early Texas* (CreateSpace, 2011) 128–134.

67. Charles Christopher Jackson, "San Felipe de Austin, Tx.," *Handbook of Texas Online,* accessed January 6, 2016.

68. Stephen L. Moore, *Eighteen Minutes: The Battle of San Jacinto and the Texas Independence Campaign.* (Plano: Republic of Texas Press, 2004), 194.

69. Hardin, *The Alamo 1836,* 191.

70. Ibid., 190–193.

71. Moore, *Eighteen Minutes,* 209–210.

72. Treaties of Velasco, Texas State Library and Archives Commission website: https://www.tsl.texas.gov/treasures/republic/velasco-01.html, accessed July 2016.

73. Dilue Rose Harris, "Reminiscences," 168.

74. Ibid., 172–173.

75. Kleberg, "Some of My Experiences," 302.

4. The Town of Houston and the San Felipe Trail after Independence

1. David G. McComb, *Houston: A History* (Austin: University of Texas Press, 1969), 11–12.

2. Sam Houston to Robert A. Irion, April 28, 187, in *Sam Houston, The Writings of Sam Houston, 1813–1863,* ed. Amelia W. Williams and Eugene C. Barker (Austin: University of Texas Press, 1938–43), vol. 4, 29.

3. Gustav Dresel, *Gustav Dresel's Houston Journal: Adventures in North America and Texas, 1837–1841,* ed. Max Freund (Austin: University of Texas Press, 1954), 36–37.

4. Dresel, *Houston Journal,* 78–79.

5. Marguerite Johnston, *Houston, the Unknown City, 1836-1946* (College Station: Texas A&M University Press, 1991), 45.

6. Audrey B. Cook, *Obedience Smith (1771–1847), Pioneer of Three American Frontiers, Her Ancestors and Descendants* (Houston: Early Publishing Company, 2008).

7. Cook, *Obedience Smith,* 97–125.

8. Cook, *Obedience Smith,* 268–271.

9. Ibid., 266.

10. General Land Office, Austin, File 000070, Harris County, Abstract 696.

11. Cook, *Obedience Smith,* 126.

12. Ibid., 260.

13. Benjamin H. Carroll, *Standard History of Houston, Texas, from a Study of Original Sources* (Knoxville, Tenn.: H. W. Crew & Company, 1912), 43–45, electronic version, Electronic Resources Center, Fondren Library, Rice University.

14. Cook, *Obedience Smith,* 151.

15. Cook, *Obedience Smith,* 177.

16. Carroll, *Standard History of Houston,* 442.

17. Ed Rider, "Breath of History Lingers over Houston's Byways," *Houston Chronicle,* July 27, 1930.

18. Harris County Deed Records, vol. K, no. 202.

19. The homes are shown on an 1889 map in Harris County Archives entitled Map of New San Felipe Road from Webster Street to Lamar Place, and Northwest Corner of Mrs. Bragg's Farm.

20. Cook, *Obedience Smith,* 160.

21. Ibid.,178.

22. Herbert Gambrell, "Lamar, Mirabeau Buonaparte," *Handbook of Texas Online,* Texas State Historical Association, accessed January 7, 2016.

23. See Cook, *Obedience Smith,* 241–242.

24. Giles family tree, www.ancestry.com; and see entry by Julie Karen Hancock in 2004 on Rev. John Woodruff on Findagrave.com, Founders Memorial Park, Houston.

25. Cook, *Obedience Smith,* 178.

26. Ibid., 498, footnote 179.

27. Richard L. Himmel, "Jones, Mary Smith," *Handbook of*

Texas Online, accessed January 07, 2016. Also see entries on Rev. John Woodruff and Sarah Pevehouse Smith Woodruff on Findagrave.com, Founders Memorial Park, Houston.

28. Cook, *Obedience Smith,* 212–215.

29. Cook, *Obedience Smith,* 215. Also see discussion of Allen Reynolds in Chapter 3 of this work.

30. Cook, *Obedience Smith,* 216–217.

31. John H. Herndon is described in Anonymous, *History of Texas, Together With a Biographical History of the Cities of Houston and Galveston* (Chicago: Lewis Publishing Company, 1896), 601–662.

32. Andrew Forest Muir, ed., "Diary of a Young Man in Houston, 1838," *Southwestern Historical Quarterly* 53 (July 1949–April 1950): 294–303.

33. Herndon, in *History of Texas,* 601–662.

34. Founders Memorial Park cemetery (Old City Cemetery), Daughters of the American Revolution, online at http://www.dar.org/national-society/historic-sites-and-properties.

35. Findagrave.com, Founders Memorial Park cemetery.

36. Andrew Forest Muir, "The Destiny of Buffalo Bayou," *Southwestern Historical Quarterly*47 (1943): 101–102, online at Portal to Texas History, http://texashistory.unt.edu.

37. Friedrich Wilhelm von Wrede, *Sketches of Life in the United States of North America and Texas,* comp. Emil Drescher, trans. Chester W. Geue (1844; Waco: Texian Press, 1970).

38. Larry and Kathryn Priest, eds., *The Diary of Clinton Harrison Moore,* first published 1904, online at files.usgwarchives.net/tx/history/moore.txt, accessed October 2014.

39. Ferdinand Roemer, *Texas, with Particular Reference to German Immigration and the Physical Appearance of the Country* (German, 1849; English 1935; repr. Ingleside, Tex.: Copano Bay Press, 2011) , 69–70.

40. Karl von Sommer, *Bericht über meine Reise nach Texas im Jahre 1846 (The story of my trip to Texas in 1846),* (Bremen, Germany: Johann Georg Hesse, 1847. Available at Göttingen State and University Library, Germany; translation by the author.

41. Harry H. Weinman, *The History of Katy and Vicinity* (unpublished manuscript, undated), Katy Public Library, 2. Also Carol Adams, *Historic Katy: An Illustrated History* (San Antonio, Tex.: HPNbooks, 2012), 7.

42. "Proceedings of the Board of Roads and Revenues of Harris County, January 17, 1844," *Telegraph and Texas Register* (Houston), February 14, 1844, 1.

43. Anonymous, "Houston–Its History etc.," in *Houston City Directory,* 1866, 99.

44. Jesse A. Ziegler, *Wave of the Gulf: Ziegler's Scrapbook of the Texas Gulf Coast* (San Antonio: Naylor Company, 1938), 53–56.

45. Ibid., 56.

46. McComb, *Houston: A History,* 26–29.

47. Texas State Library and Archives Commission, *Hazardous Business: The Railroads Come to Texas,* www.tsl.texas.gov.

48. Ordinance Granting Bounties of Land to Volunteers, *Telegraph and Texas Register* (Harrisburg), April 14, 1836, 147, repr. San Felipe de Austin State Historical Park, Texas Historical Commission.

49. Anonymous, "Notes on Texas," chap. V, in *The Hesperian, A Monthly Miscellany of General Literature,* (Cincinnati, Ohio) 1, (1838); 432.

50. "Categories of Land Grants in Texas," unpublished file, General Land Office, Austin, Texas, online at http://www.glo.texas.gov/history/archives/forms/files/categories-of-land-grants.pdf.

51. John Reinerman, entry in the "Register of Texas Families" of 1831, Spanish Collection, General Land Office, Austin.

52. John Reinerman, Harris County Abstracts 642 and 649, General Land Office, Austin.

53. Harris County Deed Records, vol. J, 350, 357.

54. Darius Gregg, Harris County Historical Marker, Glenwood Cemetery, Houston, erected 1973.

55. Wolfram M. Von-Maszewski, ed., *Austin's Old Three Hundred: The First Anglo Colony in Texas* (Waco, Tex.: Eakin Press, 2011), 124. Also, Shahan-Wyatt Family Tree, ancestry.com; and *Handbook of Texas Online*, Margaret Swett Henson, "White, Amy Comstock."

56. Harris County Abstract 761, General Land Office, Austin.

57. File of David Middleton, Abstract 535, General Land Office, Austin.

58. Adolph Casias Herrera, "Herrera, Blas María," *Handbook of Texas Online.*

59. File of Blas Herrera, Abstracts 320 and 321, General Land Office, Austin.

60. Aragorn Storm Miller, "Smith, John N. O.," *Handbook of Texas Online;* file of John N. O. Smith, Abstract 691, General Land Office, Austin.

61. File of John Cunningham, Abstract 193 and Register of Families, General Land Office, Austin.

62. Thomas W. Cutrer, "Booker, Shields," *Handbook of Texas Online.*

63. Jack R. McKinney, "Redfield, Henry Prentice," *Handbook of Texas Online*

64. File of Jesse Sitton, Abstract 689, General Land Office, Austin.

5. The Canfield - George Family of Piney Point

1. Alvin Sorgel, *Sojourn in Texas, 1846–47* (Austin: German-Texas Heritage Society, 1993), 38.

2. Melissa Peterson, *The Road to Piney Point* (Houston: Piney Point Village Historic Committee, 1994), 17–24.

3. Canfield Family Tree, www.ancestry.com.

4. Connecticut Town Birth Records, pre-1870 (Barbour Collection), www.ancestry.com.

5. Linda Dianis family tree, www.ancestry.com. Dianis is a

descendant of Harriet George and Buckman Canfield. Also see the "Betty Jim Lot Family Tree" prepared by Kathy Monaghan Phillips, www.ancestry.com.

6. Report and Manifest for a Ship or Vessel of the United States from a Foreign Port, ship's manifest for the Schooner *Helen Mar*, bound for New Orleans from Brazoria, Texas, June 25, 1833, www.ancestry.com.

7. Gifford E. White, *They Also Served: Texas Service Records from Headright Certificates* (Nacogdoches, Tex.: Ericson Books, 1991).

8. A very useful compilation of Buckman Canfield's land purchases is to be found in Peterson, *The Road to Piney Point,* 23–24. Also see Mrs. Arch B. Marshall, *Forebears and Descendants of an Early Houston Family* (Houston: Privately published, 1975), L.O.C. number 75-36340, p. 277, copy at Clayton LIbrary, Houston Public Library.

9. Canfield Family Bible belonging to Arthur Earl Monaghan, Katy, Texas.

10. Stephen L. Moore, *Savage Frontier Volume III: Rangers, Riflemen, and Indian Wars in Texas 1840–1841* (Denton: University of North Texas Press, 2007), 45.

11. The original claim can be seen at https://tslarc.tsl.texas.gov/repclaims/142/14200374.pdf. The claim was not paid, and Buckman's widow Harriet filed for payment for it at the time she was resolving Buckman's estate in 1851, https://tslarc.tsl.texas.gov/repclaims/142/14200380.pdf. She was finally paid in 1853, https://tslarc.tsl. texas.gov/repclaims/142/14200381.pdf.

12. Karl von Sommer, *Bericht über meine Reise nach Texas im Jahre 1846 (The story of my trip to Texas in 1846),* (Bremen, Germany: Johann Georg Hesse, 1847. Available at Göttingen State and University Library, Germany; translation by the author.

13. Sorgel, *Sojourn in Texas*, 38.

14. Republic of Texas claim #6365, online at www.tsl.texas.gov/apps/arc/repclaims/viewdetails.php?id=68585. For Henry Raglin, see Thomas W. Cutrer, "Raglin, Henry Walton," *Handbook of Texas Online*, accessed February 2, 2016.

15. "Proceedings of the Board of Roads and Revenues of Harris County, January 17, 1844," *Telegraph and Texas Register* (Houston), February 14, 1844, 1, col. 1 , online at Portal to Texas History, http://texashistory.unt.edu.

16. Peterson, *The Road to Piney Point,* 24.

17. *Telegraph and Texas Register* (Houston), January 20, 1838, 3, col. 2, online at Portal to Texas History, http://texashistory.unt.edu.

18. Ibid., June 12, 1844, 2, col. 4.

19. Ibid., vol. 9, no. 48, ed. 1, November 27, 1844.

20. Peterson, *The Road to Piney Point,* 27.

21. Probate of Buckman Canfield Estate, Harris County Probate Records, vol. K, 293–309. This slave sale is fully described in the Probate of Buckman Canfield Estate, Harris County Probate Records, vol. F, 558–559.

22. Probate of Buckman Canfield Estate, Harris County Probate Records, vol. F, 557–559.

23. Marriage dates provided by Texas Marriage Index , based upon Harris County marriage licenses, via www.ancestry.com: Harriet Canfield married James J. Todd, January 22, 1845, Harris County, Texas; Harriet E. Todd married Benjamin Moore George, April 5, 1846, Harris County, Texas.

24. Genealogical notes provided by Canfield descendant Leilani Morse Cross, personal communication, 2014, and by her posts on the Canfield family tree at www.ancestry.com.

25. *Democratic Telegraph and Texas Register* (Houston), October 12, 1848, 1, col. 4–5, online at Portal to Texas History, http://texashistory.unt.edu.

26. Ibid., July 12, 1849, 3, col. 2.

27. *Catalogue of Machinery Manufactured by the Westinghouse Company* (Schenectady, N.Y.: F. Clymer, 1886).

28. *Democratic Telegraph and Texas Register* (Houston), July 12, 1849, 4, col. 4.

29. Harris County Deed Records, vol. T, 312, 314.

30. *Family history notes of Nancy Caroline Thornton, in Mrs. Arch B. Marshall, Forebears and Descendants of an Early Houston Family* (Houston: Privately published, 1975), 278. (Note that the 1850 census information was supposed to be given as of June 1, 1850, but the enumerator actually visited this family nearly eight months later, on January 24, 1851, so it is not certain which date was used in giving the answers.)

31. Jeannette Morse Hollady, "Family Facts as Related in My Hearing as a Child and Some of My Knowledge and Experience," in Marshall, *Forebears and Descendants,* 20, copy at Clayton Library, Houston Public LIbrary.

32. "Hotchkiss Premium Vertical Waterwheel," published in Montgomery, Alabama, February 20, 1846, original in an Alabama museum, online at www.bostonraremaps.com/inventory/power-to-the-people/.

33. Janet Wagner, personal communication, 2014.

34. Trevia Beverly, personal communication, March 8, 2015. The Cambeaux marker indicates one of several graves on the restaurant grounds known to Barbara Vargo, a co-owner, as indicated in a letter from Rod Crosby to Trevia Beverly dated August 25, 2012. The Vargo's groundskeeper, Manuel Gamboa, signed an affidavit on August 1, 2012, stating that "While building the gardens at Vargo's Restaurant [I] removed a gravestone which I took to my house. I also covered several other graves with dirt and planted Azaleas on their tops. This happened approximately in 1968." These documents are in Mrs. Beverly's personal files.

35. Chester W. Geue, *A New Land Beckoned: German Immigration to Texas, 1844–1847* (Baltimore: Genealogical Publishing Company, new and enlarged ed., 1982,), List of immigrants, 81, online at www.ancestry.com.

36. Personal correspondence from Mary Silliman (Sunshine) Eatwell Cook to Marie (Mrs. Arch B.) Marshall, ca. 1970. Cook was unaware that Leander Batke had passed away when

she wrote these notes, which were her transcriptions of what her mother had told her many years earlier.

37. Harris County Probate Records, vol. K, 293–294.

38. United States Census, Harris County, 1850, Schedule 2 (slave schedule), 607.

39. Martha Menchaca, "The Anti-Miscegenation History of the American Southwest, 1837 to 1970: Transforming Racial Ideology into Law," *Cultural Dynamics* 20, no. 3 (2008): 279–318.

40. Texas Marriages, 1837–1973, shows L. A. Betke marrying G. H. Carter in 1882 in Harris County, Texas; Texas Death Certificates, 1903–1982, shows Louise E. Carter (July 27, 1857–October 30, 1932, died in Houston, buried at Rosewood Park Cemetery, Heights), both online at www.ancestry.com. Louise's headstone is listed as Findagrave.com Memorial #102979429.

41. Texas Death Certificates, 1903–1982 for Leander Betka (August 20, 1860–July 31, 1926, died and buried at Hempstead, Texas) and Miss Emma Batke (September 8, 1859–November 21, 1938, died in Houston, buried at Rosewood Park Cemetery, Heights), both online at www.ancestry.com.

42. Findagrave.com Memorial #33754972, Hempstead Cemetery, Hempstead, Waller County.

43. Hollady, "Family Facts," in Marshall, Forebears and Descendants, 20–24.

44. Ibid.

45. Albert C. Timme, personal conversation with Leilani Morse Cross, 2000.

46. "P. C. Dunn Home Burned," *Houston Daily Post*, January 14, 1912, 15, col. 5.

6. German Immigration to Upper Buffalo Bayou

1. (probably Herman Charles Rummel), *History of Spring Branch, 1837–1937* (Houston: Privately published, 1937), Archives of Clayton Library, Houston Public Library.

2. Hugh E. Meredith, "Ernst, Johann Friedrich," *Handbook of Texas Online*, Texas State Historical Association.

3. Frederick Law Olmstead, *A Journey through Texas, or , A Saddle Trip on the Southwestern Frontier, with a Statistical Appendix* (Dix, Edwards, 1857; repr. Austin: University of Texas Press, 1978), 140–141.

4. Sarah H. Emmott, *Memorial Park: A Priceless Legacy* (Houston: Herring Press, 1992), 10. Also Louis F. Aulbach, Linda C. Gorski, and Robbie Morin, *Camp Logan: A World War I Emergency Training Center* (Houston: Louis Aulbach, Publisher, 2014), 79.

5. Moritz Tiling, *History of the German Element in Texas from 1820–1850, and Historical Sketches of the German Texas Singers' League and Houston Turnverein* (Houston: Moritz Tiling, Publisher, 1913), 24–29.

6. Robert Kleberg, in Tiling, *History of the German Element*, 25–27.

7. Stephen F. Austin's *Register of Families*, vol. 2, 93, March 20, 1835, online at www.ancestry.com.

8. Abstract 642, file number 000222, Heirs of John Reinermann (deceased): General Land Office, Austin, Texas.

9. Abstract 649, ibid.

10. Abstract 642, ibid.

11. Aulbach et al., Camp Logan, 79. This book is a welcome resource on the genealogy and history of the Reinermann clan, and Aulbach credits the help of David Hornburg in his research.

12. Emmott, *Memorial Park*, 10.

13. Abstract 644, file number 000054, Heirs of John Reinermann (deceased): General Land Office, Austin, Texas.

14. Gifford E. White, 1840 Citizens of Texas, vol. 2 (tax rolls), (Austin, Tex.: Author, 1983–88), 72.

15. Harris County Deed Records: Anna and Henry Reinermann to McHenry Winburn, March 17, 1838; Heirs of Heinrich Reinermann to Executors of McHenry Winburn, May 25, 1849. Also see Aulbach et al., Camp Logan, 80.

16. David Hornburg, personal communication, 2016.

17. Aulbach et al., Camp Logan, 80–81. Also Bernice Mistrot, "Clement's Corner," Newsletter, Washington Cemetery Historic Trust 25, no. 3 (August 2001): 1.

18. Harris County Probate Records, Petition of Louisa Bethje, Guardian, in Estate of Henry Reinermann, October 15, 1849. Also see Aulbach, *Camp Logan*, 80.

19. Aulbach, *Camp Logan*, 79–81.

20. Anonymous, "Oldest House Well Preserved: Built in Early '30s by John Reinermann," *Houston Chronicle*, August 4, 1915.

21. Aulbach et al., *Camp Logan*, 81.

22. Findagrave.com, Glenwood Cemetery, Houston, Texas.

23. Suzanne Turner and Joanne Seale Wilson, *Houston's Silent Garden: Glenwood Cemetery, 1871–2009* (College Station: Texas A&M University Press, 2010), 19.

24. Wolfram M. Von-Maszewski, trans., *Voyage to North America 1844–45: Prince Carl of Solms's Texas Diary of People, Places, and Events* (Denton: German-Texas Heritage Society and University of North Texas Press, 2000), 81.

25. William Henry Plageman family tree, www.ancestry.com.

26. Dilue Rose Harris, "Reminiscences of Mrs. Dilue Harris," *Southwestern Historical Quarterly* 4 (1900): 107.

27. Author unknown, *History of Texas, southwest, excerpt in Trevia Wooster Beverly, Habermacher Cemetery* (unpublished manuscript), 1998.

28. Von-Maszewski, *Voyage to North America*, 88–89. Also see Harris County Tax Rolls, 1837–1910, microfilm roll 1, taxes for 1841 on p. 10, taxes for 1843 on p. 8A, taxes for 1844 on p. 10, and taxes for 1845 on p. 7A.

29. Aulbach et al., *Camp Logan*, 18–20.

30. Daughters of the Republic of Texas, 116.

31. Confederate Pension Applications, 1899–1975, Collection #CPA16526, roll 388: Pension File Nos. 01760 to 01837, Application Years 1899 to 1899, Texas State Library and

Archives Commission, Austin.

32. Harris County, Map of the Old San Felipe Road, ca. 1890, William Bauer surveyor, Harris County Archives.

33. William Henry Plageman family tree, www.ancestry.com.

34. Abstract 356, Harris County (Joseph Habermacher), General Land Office, Austin.

35. Record of Appointment of Postmasters, 1832–1971, NARA Microfilm Publication M841, 145 rolls. Records of the Post Office Department, Record Group no. 28, Washington, D.C.: National Archives.

36. Aulbach et al., *Camp Logan,* 20–21.

37. William Henry Plageman family tree, www.ancestry.com.

38. The deed was filed in 1843. Harris County Deed Records I:188, filed 23 December 1843.

39. Wedding of James Crawford and Elizabeth Hogan, March 18, 1841. Tennessee State Marriages, 1780-2002 [database on-line]. Provo, UT, USA: Ancestry.com Operations Inc, 2008.

40. Janet K. Wagner, personal communication, 2014.

41. James Johnson Crawford Probate, October 22, 1844, Archives of the Harris County Clerk, Probate Records F:552-555 and 572-574.

42. "Administrator's Sale," *Houston Telegraph and Texas Register,* November 27, 1844.

43. Lyons purchase, Harris County Deed Records L:45, signed December 4, 1844. Kolbe purchase, Harris County Deed Records K:559, signed July 3, 1846.

44. A copy of the original agreement, signed on 23 December 1845, is in the possession of Kolbe descendant Nelda Blackshere Reynolds.

45. Chester William and Ethel H. Geue, eds., *A New Land Beckoned: German Immigration to Texas, 1844-1847* (Genealogical Publishing Co., 1972), 111. Also, Patsy Fox Andrews, ed.: Fifty Years, 1955-2005 (City of Spring Valley History Project, online at www.freepages.history.rootsweb.ancestry.com; retrieved September 2014).

46. Kolbe descendant Nelda Blackshere Reynolds, personal communication, 2016.

47. Patsy Fox Andrews, op. cit.

48. For example, see the "History of Spring Branch Oaks," by the Spring Branch Oaks Civic Association, online at www.springbranchoaks.com. Retrieved July 2016.

49. Kolbe descendant Nelda Blackshere Reynolds, personal communication, 2016.

50. Harris County Deed Records I:142, signed July 8, 1852.

51. Harris County Deed Records 77:311, signed November 16, 1888.

52. Houston City Directories of 1888-1900; copies in Metropolitan Research Center, Houston Public Library.

53. Anonymous, *Brief History of Spring Branch* (Super Neighborhood 85, Spring Branch Central, online at www.houstontx.gov/superneighborhoods/profiels/SN_85, accessed September 2014).

54. "Liste der Begraebrifs Plaetze des St. Petri Friedhofes" (List of burial grounds of St. Peter Friedhofes), 1856, from the personal files of Nelda Blackshere Reynolds.

55. "List of unconditional Land Certificates opened by the Bureau of Land Commissioners for Harris County from the 2d day of June A.D. 1845 until the 4th day of August A.D. 1845"; General land Office, Austin, Clerk Returns file no. 000020.

56. "Categories of Land Grants in Texas, " General Land Office, Austin, online at www.glo.texas.gov.

57. 1838 Passenger list on the sailing ship Cuba from Galveston to New Orleans: The National Archives at Washington, D.C.; Washington, D.C.; Work Projects Administration Transcript of Passenger Lists of Vessels Arriving at New Orleans, Louisiana, 1813–1849.

58. Moritz Tiling, History of the German Element in Texas from 1820–1850 (Houston: 1913), 49.

59. "Ida Schroeder Warwick Remembers . . . Growing Up on the Farm," *Hedwig Village Gazette,* July 4, 1986, 6.

60. Lena Rummel Dornberger, "Early Life in Texas, from C. W. Rummel's Diary," in *A Goodly Heritage: The Story of Carl Siegismund Bauer and Carl Wilhelm Rummel,* ed. Isla Bauer Maler, 3rd edition (Privately published, 1995), 61.

61. Evelyn Schroeder Kingsbury, personal communication, 2016.

62. Agreement of Jacob Schroeder with Dorothea, Heinrich and Frederich Schroeder, April 9, 1858; Harris County Deed Records vol. U, 171.

63. Harris County Deed Records with Jacob Schroeder as Grantor, 1866–1875.

64. Melissa M. Peterson, ed., *The Road to Piney Point* (Houston: Piney Point Village Historic Committee, 1994), 40. Also see "John D. Taylor Original Survey: Schroeder Land Once Austin's," *Hedwig Village Gazette,* July 4, 1986, 7.

65. "John D. Taylor Original Survey: Schroeder Land Once Austin's, " 7.

66. "A City Hall to Call Its Own?" *Houston Chronicle,* June 29, 1992, 14a; "Community saves historic structure in Piney Point," Houston Chronicle, January 6, 1993, "This Week" section. Also see "125 Year Old Home First in Mirror Series," *Houston Post,* January 30, 1974, "Today" section, 8.

67. "John D. Taylor Original Survey: Schroeder Land Once Austin's," .7.

68. Lauren Jodoin, Carl Siegismund Bauer, www.fayettecountyhistory.org, accessed September 2014.

69. Aulbach et al., *Camp Logan,* 44. Also Anonymous, *Bauer Family* (Fayette County Texas Heritage, Curtis Media, 1996), 26–27.

70. Andrews, *Fifty Years.*

71. Unknown grandson of Wilhelm Rummel (perhaps Herman Charles Rummel), 1937, *History of Spring Branch, 1837-1937.* Archives, Clayton Genealogical Branch of the Houston Public Library.

72. Louis C. Rummel, "Memories of My Early Life," in *A Goodly Heritage: The Story of Carl Siegismund Bauer and Carl Wilhelm Rummel*, ed. Isla Bauer Maler, 3rd edition (Privately published, 1995), 70.

73. Unknown grandson of Wilhelm Rummel (probably Herman Charles Rummel), *History of Spring Branch, 1837–1937* (1937), Clayton Library, Houston Public Library.

74. Harris County Deed Records, 1851, vol. P, 282.

75. Karen Herridge, *Spring Branch Heritage* (Houston: Wakebook Press, 1998), 15–16, copy at Clayton Library, Houston Public Library.

76. Herridge, *Spring Branch Heritage*, 16.

77. Cynthia A. Thornton, *The Times of Round Top* (AuthorHouse, 2013), 227.

78. William J. Luthe, *The Story of St. Peter Church: (1946)*, 2–3, online at ourfamilyaustin.wikispaces.com, accessed September 2014.

79. Spring Branch History, Spring Oaks Community website, www.springoaks.org.

80. Isla Bauer Maler, ed., "August Bauer," in *A Goodly Heritage: The Story of Carl Siegismund Bauer and Carl Wilhelm Rummel*, 3rd edition (Houston: Privately published, 1995), 32.

81. Unknown grandson of Wilhelm Rummel, *History of Spring Branch.*

82. Watson family tree, www.ancestry.com. Also see Lena M. Sauer death certificate, July 19, 1928, Texas Death Certificates, 1903–1982, accessed on ancestry.com.

83. Herridge, *Spring Branch Heritage*, 16–17.

84. Luthe, *The Story of St. Peter Church*, 4.

85. Thornton, *The Times of Round Top*, 227–229.

86. "Bauers Continue Travelling Sawmill Business Under Herman's Hands," *Hedwig Village Gazette*, July 4, 1986, 9.

87. "Ancestral Legacy: Bauers in Lumber Since 1870s," *Hedwig Village Gazette*, July 4, 1986, 8-9.

88. Heinrich Friedrick Bernhard Ahrenbeck family tree, www.ancestry.com.

89. Harris County Deed Records, vol. T, p. 312, 123 acres John Forrester to W. Ahrenback & Brother; Daniel & William Ahrenback to S. D. Hewes, vol. T, p. 314.

90. William J. Miller, *The Story of My Life, by a Born Texan*, www.rootsweb.ancestry.com/~txaustin/Pioneers/Miller.htm

91. Marie Neuman Gray and Virginia Stahman Snider, personal communication, 2015. Also Gray family tree, www.ancestry.com.

92. Harris County Deed Records of 1849, vol. O, 337, and 1856, vol. P, 697.

93. George E. Wolf, 1987–2001, Hillendahl Cemetery, in Cemeteries of Texas, www.cemeteris-of-tx.com. Also, U.S. Federal Census Mortality Schedules Index, 1850–1880, entry for Henry Hillendahl, 1870, ID# 197-149981; and Gray family tree, www.ancestry.com.

94. Ethel Geue, *New Homes in a New Land: German Immigration to Texas, 1847–1861* (Baltimore: Genealogical Publishing Company, 1970).

95. Most of the information on the Beinhorn family came from Charles Arthur Beinhorn Jr. and Louise Haggenos Beinhorn, Our Time Line, unpublished family history notes in the files of Nelda Blackshere Reynolds.

96. Marie Neuman Gray, personal communication and family history data, 2015.

97. "Addicks Reservoir," *Handbook of Texas Online*, www.tshaonline.org/handbook/online/articles/roa03, accessed October 14, 2014.

98. Andrea R. Stahman (now Andrea Stahman Burden), *Bear Creek: A Case Study in Locating Historic Site Remains in Southeast Texas*, MA thesis, Graduate School of Texas A&M University, 2004, 155 p.

99. Andrea R. Stahman, 155p.

100. Ibid., 50–53.

101. Marks Family Papers, LH7 Ranch, Barker, Texas, as quoted by Deborah Lightfoot Sizemore, The LH7 Ranch in Houston's Shadow (Denton: University of North Texas Press, 1991), 1–2.

102. E. H. Marks, as quoted in Sizemore, The LH7 Ranch, 3.

103. Sizemore, *The LH7 Ranch*, 3.

104. Ship Passenger Lists, Port of Galveston Texas 1846–1871 (Easley, S.C.: Southern Historical Press, 1984), 131p.

105. Early marriages of Austin County, 1824–1920, Grooms, RootsWeb, www.ancestry.com.

106. Sophia Striepe, file no. 129, Abstract 740, General Land Office, Austin.

107. Sizemore, *The LH7 Ranch*, 4.

108. Marie Neuman Gray, personal communication, 2015.

109. Ibid.; also Louis F. Aulbach, *Buffalo Bayou, an Echo of Houston's Wilderness Beginnings* (Houston: Louis Aulbach, Publisher, 2012), 20.–24.

110. Stahman, *Bear Creek*, 70–78.

111. Ibid., 70–78.

112. Ibid., 70–78. Also Bob&Salle2012 family tree, www.ancestry.com.

113. Stahman, *Bear Creek*, 88–90.

114. Ibid., 89–96, 117–133.

115. Ibid., 97–98.

116. Marie Neuman Gottfried, *The Descendants of Friedericke Beckendorff Kobs*, vol. 2 (Brookshire, Tex.: M. N. Gottfried, 1989); genealogical and historical materials assembled by Marie Neuman Gottfried, Pattison, Texas.

117. Ross Fields, Martha Doty Freeman, and Steven M. Kotter, *Inventory and Assessment of Cultural Resources at Addicks Reservoir, Harris County, Texas, Reports of Investigations* no. 12 (Austin: Prewitt and Associates, 1983); also Harris County Deed Records, vol. X, 271.

118. Margaret Ann Howard and Martha Doty Freeman, *Inventory and Assessment of Cultural Resources at Bear Creek Park, Addicks Reservoir, Harris County, Texas, Report of Investigations*

no. 24 (Austin: Prewitt and Associates, 1983), 82–83.

119. Margaret H. Edwards, *The Story of Madge Golbow Hopkins* (unpublished family history, undated), 28, copy at U.S. Army Corps of Engineers Addicks-Barker field office. Also see Gottfried, *Descendants of Friedericke Beckendorff Kobs*.

120. Gottfried, Descendants of Friedericke Beckendorff Kobs. The deed specifying the construction of the new home is in Harris County Deed Records, vol. 9A, 177–179.

121. Harris County Deed Records, vol. M, 462–463.

122. Edwards, Story of Madge Golbow Hopkins. Also see Fields et al., *Inventory, Addicks Reservoir,* Report 12.

123. Genealogical and historical materials assembled by Marie Neumann Gottfried, Pattison Texas.

124. Howard and Freeman, Inventory, Addicks Reservoir, Report 24, 74.

125. Ibid., 78.

126. Ibid., viii, 27.

127. Taped interview with Joe Golbow, March 18, 1982, in Edwards, Story of Madge Golbow Hopkins.

128. Genealogical and historical materials assembled by Marie Neuman Gottfried, Pattison Texas.

129. Edwards, Story of Madge Golbow Hopkins.

130. Ibid., 94–97.

131. Maxine Sullivan and Annette M. Parker, *The Schulz Family* (unpublished family history), 1984, copy at U.S. Army Corps of Engineers Addicks-Barker field office.

132. Ibid, 33–35.

133. Ibid, 146,

134. Ibid., 181–189.

135. A family record of the life of Mr. and Mrs. Frederick Kobs, family history prepared by Marie Neuman Gray, in the files of Martha Doty Freeman.

136. Fields et al., Inventory, Addicks Reservoir, Report 12.

137. A family record of the life of Mr. and Mrs. Frederick Kobs, family history prepared by Marie Neuman Gray, in the files of Martha Doty Freeman. Also see Garrett Kobs, Kobs-Hawkins-Garrett Family Tree, www.ancestry.com.

138. Ross C. Fields, Martha Doty Freeman, and Stephen M. Kotter, "Inventory and Assessment of Cultural Resources of Addicks Reservoir, Harris County, Texas, Report of Investigations no. 22" (Austin: Prewitt and Associates, 1983), , 168–169.

139. Marie Neuman Gray, German Families of Bear Creek, west Harris County, Texas (presentation to Texas German Society), 2003.

140. Margaret Hopkins Edwards, "History of Bear Creek," CF (Houston Cy-Fair Proud) Magazine, March–April 1988, 8.

141. Bear Creek Methodist Church and Cemetery, State of Texas Historical Marker. Also, "Centennial 1879–1979" pamphlet, Addicks United Methodist Church, Houston.

142. Stahman, *Bear Creek*, 49.

143. "New Dams to Bring Profit and Safety," Houston 38 (September 1948): 103.

144. D. H. Stover to Teresa Wolf, deed, September 25, 1838, Harris County Deed Records.

145. Gustav Dresel, *Gustav Dresel's Houston Journal: Adventures in North America and Texas, 1837–1841, ed. Max Freund* (Austin: University of Texas Press, Austin, 1954), 77.

146. Dresel, *Houston Journal,* 95.

147. John B. Glasgow–Theresa Wolf marriage, June 15, 1842, in Harris County Court Records, FHL microfilm # 0025221, www.ancestry.com.

148. As quoted in Dresel, *Houston Journal,* 143. Translation from Solms-Braunfels Archives Transcripts, LXIII, 176.

149. Johann Heinrich "John" Ojemann, Findagrave.com, Vollmer Cemetery.

150. Henry Vollmer and Kate Vollmer, Findagrave.com, Vollmer Cemetery.

151. Conrad William Sauer Sr., Findagrave.com, Vollmer Cemetery.

152. Walker Richard Gray Jr., Hillendahl descendant, personal communication, 2016.

153. Hermann Friedrich Niemann and Catherine Maria Kabbes Niemann, Findagrave.com, Vollmer Cemetery.

154. Findagrave.com, St. John Evangelical Lutheran Cemetery, Houston.

155. Mrs. Noel (Brown) McClure, "The Legacy of a Wilderness Church," *Genealogical Record,* September 1986, 175–177, copy at Clayton Library, Houston Public Library.

156. "The White Oak Shoot," *Houston Post,* May 15, 1887.

157. McClure, "Legacy of a Wilderness Church," 176.

158. The Heritage Society, http://www.heritagesociety.org/stjohnchurch/.

159. Betty L. Chapman, "German Immigrants Had Big Bering on City Development," *Houston Business Journal,* August 23 2009.

160. Ibid.

161. Moritz Tiling, *History of the German Element in Texas from 1820–1850, and Historical Sketches of the German Texas Singers' League and Houston Turnverein* (Houston: Moritz Tiling, Publisher, 1913) 88.

162. Ibid., 89.

163. Ibid., 90.

164. William Bammel, in Bering family tree, Familytreemaker.com.

165. Harris County Deed Records, vol. 36, 119 (1886) and vol. 45, 19 (1889).

166. Tiling, *History of the German Element,* 125.

7. The Morse Family of Pleasant Bend Plantation

1. Bernice Mistrot, Harris County Historical Commission, personal communication, 2015.

2. From a history of Leon County, Texas, http://genealogytrails.com/tex/pineywoods/leon/history1.html.

3. Marvel McFarland marriage, in Texas, Marriage Collection, 1814–1909 and 1966–2011, online database (Provo, Utah: Ancestry.com Operations, 2005). Also Texas, Muster Roll Index

Cards, 1838–1900, online database (Provo, Utah: Ancestry.com Operations, 2011).

4. Cassie McFee Reeder, *Through the Years: An Autobiography* (unpublished family manuscript), 1973, 10–17.

5. Janet Wagner, Historical Document Review, Reserve B within William White Patent 836, Harris County, private report (Houston: J. K. Wagner & Company, 1993), 20p.

6. The State of North Carolina to the Use of C. W. Buckley v. Henry G. Hampton, North Carolina Reports, vol. 23: Cases Argued and Determined in the Supreme Court of North Carolina from June Term 1840 to June Term 1841 (NC State Printers, 1913).

7. Michael L. Marshall, *Kernersville Letter: Stage Lines and Kernersville* (Kernersville, N.C.: People's Press, March 13, 1884), online at http://www.forsythnchistory.com/files/kernersville_stageline.pdf.

8. Harris County Deed Records, vol. 3, 537.

9. Unpublished notes "Written by Mrs. Daisy Crump Furlow who lived at 907 Hays St. San Antonio Texas," from the files of McFee relative Allyne (Mrs. Allen) Reeder.

10. Wagner, *Historical Document Review*, Reserve B.

11. Craig H. Roell, "Shearn, Charles," *Handbook of Texas Online*, Texas State Historical Association, accessed January 2, 2014. Also Anonymous, *History of Texas, Together with a Biographical History of the Cities of Houston and Galveston* (Chicago: Lewis Publishing Company, 1895), 345–347.

12. Janet Wagner, *Buffalo Bayou Historical Vignettes, 1825–1928, Report for Buffalo Bayou Partnership* (Houston: J. K. Wagner & Company, 1998), 6.

13. Roell, "Shearn, Charles."

14. Jesse A. Ziegler, *Wave of the Gulf, Ziegler's Scrapbook of the Texas Gulf Coast* (San Antonio: Naylor Company, 1938), 275. Also, "T. W. House", in History of Texas, together with a biographical history of the cities of Houston and Galveston (Chicago: Lewis Pub. Co., 1895), 313-317.

15. Anonymous, *History of Texas, Together With a Biographical History of the Cities of Houston and Galveston* (Chicago: Lewis Publishing Company, 1896), 346.

16. Cheryl Ferguson, "History of River Oaks:" online website of River Oaks Elementary Alumni, www.riveroaksalumni.org/portfolio/history-ro/. Accessed June 2016. Also see Art Stricklin, 2005, *Links, Lore and Legends: The Story of Texas Golf:* Taylor Trade Publishing, pp. 26-27.

17. Mrs. Arch B. Marshall, Forebears and Descendants of an Early Houston Family (Houston: Privately published, 1975), 1–7, copy at Clayton Library, Houston Public Library.

18. Jackson Turner Main, *Society and Economy in Colonial Connecticut* (Princeton, N.J.: Princeton University Press, 1983), 177, table 5.1, as quoted in Slavery in Connecticut, online at www.slavenorth.com.

19. Sammy Way, "South Main Street Holds Important History," Sumter Item, September 18, 2011, online at http://theitem.com/stories/south-main-street-holds-important-history,52695.

20. Letter of Marcus Deforest to John B. Miller, February 28, 1831, in Selected Items from the Miller-Furman-Dabbs Family Papers, University of South Carolina, June 7, 2011, online at https://library.sc.edu/socar/mnscrpts/MillerFurmanDabbs.pdf.

21. Anne King Gregorie, *The History of Sumter County* (Sumter: Library Board of Sumter County, 1954), 151.

22. Grace's maiden name, Baldwin, and birthplace, Connecticut, are known via the Texas death certificate of her daughter, Elizabeth A. (Morse) Grant, who died in San Antonio on December 23, 1920.

23. *Laws of the State of Mississippi, Embracing All Acts of a Public Nature* (Jackson: State of Mississippi, 1838), 858–859.

24. Jack D. Elliott Jr., "Colbert, Barton, and Vinton, Extinct Tombigbee River Towns," online at Lowndes County Mississippi History and Genealogy, www.lowndes.msghn.org.

25. Probate Court M126, Harris County, Texas, Will Book Q, p. 447, August 29, 1865.

26. Elliott, "Colbert, Barton, and Vinton".

27. From John L. Allen, December 17, 1845, in *The Papers of Jefferson Davis* (Baton Rouge: Louisiana State University Press, 1975), vol. 2, p. 110.

28. Elliott, "Colbert, Barton, and Vinton."

29. Ibid.

30. U.S. Census of 1850, Lowndes County, Mississippi, Schedule 2, p. 107.

31. Moritz Tiling, *1913, History of the German Element in Texas from 1820–1850* (Houston: Moritz Tiling, Publisher, 1913), 123.

32. From unpublished research of Janet Wagner, Harris County Deed Records, O/609; Q/57; P/597; W/347; A/836; Z/188; I/164.

33. Hunter vs. Morse, 1879, in Cases Argued and Decided in the Supreme Court of the State of Texas, vol. 49, 219–235.

34. Janet Wagner, personal communication, 2014.

35. Harris County, Minutes January Term 1866, Book E, p. 296; Estate, pp. 447–449.

36. *Houston Weekly Telegraph*, August 18, 1858, 1, col. 6, http://texashistory.unt.edu/ark:/67531/metapth236005.

37. Houston Weekly Telegraph, May 25, 1859, 2, col. 3, http://texashistory.unt.edu/ark:/67531/metapth236043.

38. Mississippi State Census, 1850, p. 1076.

39. Harris County tax records for 1856, Clayton Library, Houston.

40. C. Allan Jones, *Texas Roots: Agriculture and Rural Life Before the Civil War* (College Station: Texas A&M University Press, 2005), 139.

41. Peter Kolchin, *American Slavery 1619–1877* (New York: Hill and Wang, 1993), xiii.

42. Jones, *Texas Roots*, 139.

43. Ibid.

44. Thomas Affleck, *Affleck's Southern Rural Almanac, and Plantation and Garden Calendar for 1860,* 134, as quoted in Jones, *Texas Roots,* 145.

45. T. R. Fehrenbach, *Lone Star: A History of Texas and the Texans:* (1968; Cambridge, Mass.: Da Capo Press, 2000), 305.

46. Ibid., 307.

47. *Houston Weekly Telegraph* 21, no. 51, March 5, 1856.

48. *Houston Weekly Telegraph* 24, no. 1, March 24, 1858.

49. Findagrave.com, Hewins Cemetery, Sheffield, Massachusetts.

50. The obituary of Lovett's son, George L. Taft, stated that Lovett was a cousin of William Howard Taft's father, Alonzo Taft: "George L. Taft Funeral Friday; Death takes cousin of Late President, William H. Taft," *San Antonio Express,* May 26, 1932.

51. Melissa M. Peterson, *The Road to Piney Point* (Houston: Piney Point Village Historic Committee, 1994), 30. Also Wm. A. Morse with A. Groesbeck, A. H. Coleman, David H. Paige agreement: Harris County Deed Records, June 20, 1861, vol. Y, 334 (hereafter Morse et al., agreement).

52. G. S. Hardcastle to Wm. A. Morse and others, Harris County Deed Records, February 3, 1858, vol. V, 3.

53. Morse et al., agreement.

54. William Rogers to Groesbeck, Morse, Coleman and Paige, Harris County Deed Records, August 25, 1860, vol. X, 341.

55. George C. Werner, "Houston and Texas Central Railway," *Handbook of Texas Online,* accessed March 13, 2016.

56. Morse et al., agreement.

57. Julia Beazley, "Harris, John Richardson," *Handbook of Texas Online,* accessed March 13, 2016.

58. By the time of the agreement to dissolve William Morse & Company, all but 200 acres of William Morse's 742 acres in tracts 5 and 6 of the Taylor league land had been sold off in this manner. Morse et al., agreement.

59. Morse et al., agreement.

60. David H. Paige to S. S. Munger, Harris County Deed Records, January 5, 1866, vol. 2, 244, and David H. Paige to S. S. Munger, February 26, 1867, vol. 5, 40.

61. Memoir of James Jenkins, 1842, in Marion County South Carolina Genealogy and History, online at www.sciway3.net.

62. Nathan Bangs, *A History of the Methodist Episcopal Church,* Volume 4 (1829–1840), (New York: G. Lane and P. P. Sandford, Publishers, 1841), 28.

63. Minutes of the Annual Conferences of the Methodist Episcopal Church for the Years 1829–1839 (New York: T. Mason and G. Lane, Publishers, 1840), 245, 308, 309, 372. Ecclesiastical Register for 1834, in *The American Quarterly Register*, conducted by B. B. Edwards of the American Education Society (Boston: Perkins and Marvin, Publishers), vol. 5, 195.

64. Marshall, *Forebears and Descendants,* 10–13.

65. Research from the Morse Society, www.morsesociety.org.

66. Research from www.ancestry.com: Captain Josiah Jones family tree, and *The Ancestors of My Daughters: Bodges Soldiers in King Philip's War,* 260; Middlesex Deeds vol. IX, 336; *Drakes History of Middlesex County,* vol. II, 454, 490, 499.

67. A. S. Salley Jr., *History of Orangeburg County* (Orangeburg, S.C.: R. Lewis Berry, Printer, 1898), 471–486.

68. Marshall, *Forebears and Descendants,* 31.

69. *Houston Weekly Telegraph,* June 30, 1858, 1, col. 2,http://texashistory.unt.edu/ark:/67531/metapth235999.

70. *Houston Weekly Telegraph,* August 10, 1859.

71. "Strayed or Stolen" (advertisement), *Houston Weekly Telegraph,* December 22, 1859.

72. Anonymous, *History of the Bering Memorial Methodist Episcopal Church South* (Houston: Privately published, 1937), 2–3, 6–8.

73. Cassanndra McFee to Sophronia R. Parker, 1866, Harris County Deed Records, vol. 2, 500.

74. William H. Keeling journal, in Celia Hough Morse, Civil War Diary, unpublished manuscript, transcribed by Janet K. Wagner, 1993. A copy is in the author's personal files.

75. Joseph B. Taft, Findagrave.com Memorial# 2995871.

76. Janet Wagner, *Interments in the Morse-Bragg Cemetery, Research for DeLange, Hudspeth and Pitman, LLP* (Houston: J. K. Wagner & Company, 1995).

77. "Another Great Fire in Houston," *Houston Weekly Telegraph,* March 13, 1860, 1.

8. The Civil War Years

1. T. R. Fehrenbach, *Lone Star: A History of Texas and the Texans* (1968; New York: Da Capo Press, 2000), 328.

2. Gregg Cantrell, "Sam Houston and the Know-Nothings: A Reappraisal," *Southwestern Historical Quarterly* 96 (July 1992–April 1993): 333.

3. Fehrenbach, *Lone Star,* 329.

4. "Mass Meeting of Harris County," *Houston Weekly Telegraph,* December 4, 1860, 1.

5. James I. Haley, *Sam Houston* (Norman: University of Oklahoma Press, 2004), 390–91.

6. Burleson, Mrs. Georgia J., comp., "Part IV. Addresses and Articles of Dr. Burleson: General Sam Houston: Address Delivered Before the Texas Legislature, March 2, 1893, At the Memorial Services of the One Hundredth Anniversary of the Birth of Gen. Sam Houston, and the Fifty-Seventh of Texas Independence," *The Life and Writings of Rufus C. Burleson,* D.D., LL.D. (1901), 579.

7. "Public Meeting," *Houston Tri-Weekly Telegraph,* November 10, 1860, 2.

8. J. S. Taft, Houston, Harris County, Texas, in 1860 U.S. Federal Census–Slave Schedules, online database (Provo, Utah: Ancestry.com Operations, 2010).

9. *Houston Tri-Weekly Telegraph,* August 21, 1861, 2.

10. (probably Herman Charles Rummel), *History of Spring Branch, 1837–1937* (Houston: Privately published, 1937),

Archives of Clayton Library, Houston Public Library.

11. James O. Moore, *The Men of the Bayou City Guards* (Company A, 5th Texas Infantry, Hood's Brigade), MA thesis, University of Houston at Clear Lake, 1988 20.

12. Margaret Wood, *Civil War Conscription Laws*, 2012, Library of Congress, Law Librarians of Congress Blog, online at www.blogs.loc.gov/law.

13. "Harris County at War," *Houston Weekly Telegraph*, August 14, 1861.

14. Texas, Muster Roll Index Cards, 1838–1900, online database (Provo, Utah: Ancestry.com Operations, 2011), original data (Confederate, Union, Texas Rangers) from Texas State Library and Archives Commission, Austin.

15. Texas, Civil War Muster Roll Index Cards for W. H. Silliman, Texas State Library and Archives Commission, http://interactive.ancestry.com/2059/32622_1020703347_0023-00863/11547; also NARA M323, Compiled Service Records of Confederate Soldiers from Texas Units, H. W. Silliman, Eighth Cavalry (Terry's Regiment, First Rangers, Eighth Rangers), https://www.fold3.com/image/10638574/, both accessed September 9, 2015.

16. Mel Wheat, 8th Texas Cavalry, Terry's Texas Rangers, online at keathleywebs.com.

17. Ibid.

18. Robert Franklin Bunting, *Our Trust Is in the God of Battles: The Civil War Letters of Robert Franklin Bunting, Chaplain, Terry's Texas Rangers*, C.S.A. (Knoxville: University of Tennessee Press, 2006), 370.

19. Texas, Muster Roll Index Cards, 1838–1900, online database (Provo, Utah: Ancestry.com Operations, 2011).

20. Mel Wheat, 8th Texas Cavalry, Terry's Texas Rangers, online at keathleywebs.com.

21. Texas Civil War Muster Roll Index Cards for J. [sic] B. Silliman, Texas State Library and Archives Commission, http://interactive.ancestry.com/2059/32622_1020703347_0023-00863/11547; also NARA M323, Compiled Service Records of Confederate soldiers from Texas Units, J. B. Silliman (also recorded as I. B. Silliman), age 20, Private, Co. A, 2nd Infantry Battalion, Waul's Legion (Infantry, Cavalry, and Artillery), https://www.fold3.com/image/15526579/, both accessed September 9, 2015. Note that the final card in the latter file is misfiled: it belongs to Sgt. J. G. Selman, Co. C, a resident of Cherokee County, not to Pvt. I. B. Silliman, Co. A, a resident of Harris County.

22. David S. Pettus, transcriber, Diary of Edwin E. Rice; April 15, 1862–April 5, 1863, original document, Rosenberg Library, Galveston, Texas.

23. Wolfram M. Von-Maszewski, "German Letters & Diaries from Waul's Texas Legion," presented at the conference The Civil War in Texas: Changing Interpretations after 150 Years, Victoria, Texas, October 20, 2011.

24. Pettus, Diary of Edwin E. Rice, and Maszewski, "German Letters & Diaries."

25. Robert Voigt, Diaries and Letters, Box 3K/123, Dolph Briscoe Center for American History, University of Texas at Austin, as quoted by Von-Maszewski, "German Letters & Diaries."

26. Von-Maszewski, "German Letters & Diaries."

27. Waul's Texas Legion in the Battle of Vicksburg: from a course entitled "American Civil War, Furman University.

28. David G. Martin, *The Vicksburg Campaign, April 1862–July 1863* (Cambridge, Mass: Da Capo Press, 1990), 236 p.

29. Robert Janak, The Czechs of Company D, online at www.janakstexasczecharticlesandphotos.com/the-czechs-of-company-d-3/, accessed December 2014.

30. John Richard Lundberg, *Granbury's Texas Brigade, C.S.A.: The Color Brigade of the Army*, MA thesis, Texas Christian University, Fort Worth, 2005, 36–40.

31. Ibid., 64–86.

32. United Daughters of the Confederacy, "John Wesley Thornton," entry in Patriot Ancestors' Album, (Turner Publishing Company, 1999).

33. Mrs. Arch B. Marshall, *Forebears and Descendants of an Early Houston Family* (Houston: Privately published, 1975), 162, copy at Clayton Library, Houston Public Library.

34. United Daughters of the Confederacy, "John Wesley Thornton."

35. David Paul Smith, *Frontier Defense in the Civil War* (College Station: Texas A&M University Press, 1992), 19–25.

36. Robert Dunnam, "Frontier Regiment," *Handbook of Texas Online*, Texas State Historical Association, accessed January 07, 2015..

37. Richard B. McCaslin, "Bourland, James G.," *Handbook of Texas Online*, accessed January 07, 2015.

38. Smith, *Frontier Defense*, 122–126.

39. Rudolph L. Biesele, "German Attitude toward the Civil War," *Handbook of Texas Online*, accessed January 08, 2015.

40. William Henry Plageman family tree, www.ancestry.com.

41. William Henry Plageman family tree, www.ancestry.com.

42. Stephen and Thomas Habermacher entries, in Texas, Muster Roll Index Cards, 1838–1900, online database (Provo, Utah: Ancestry.com Operations, 2011).

43. C. Habermacher entry, ibid.

44. August Marks, H. Marks, and Albert Marks, entries, ibid.

45. Maudeen Marks, notes, as quoted in Deborah Lightfoot Sizemore, *The LH7 Ranch in Houston's Shadow* (Denton: University of North Texas Press, 1991), 4.

46. Sizemore, ibid., 4. Also "3 Prize Guns Stolen from Ranch Exhibit," *Houston Press*, November 28, 1956.

47. Sizemore, ibid., 22–24.

48. Ernst Kobs IV, notes on www.militaryhistoryonline.com/genealogy, accessed February 2015.

49. Karen Herridge, *Spring Branch Heritage* (Houston:

Wakebook Press, 1998), 16–17, copy at Clayton Library, Houston Public Library.

50. Lena Rummel Dornberger, "Early Life in Texas, from C. W. Rummel's Diary:" in Isla Bauer Maler, ed., *A Goodly Heritage: The Story of Carl Siegismund Bauer and Carl Wilhelm Rummel* (Privately published, third edition, 1995) p. 63.

51. Maxine Sullivan and Annette M. Parker, *The Schultz Family* (unpublished family history), 1984, 146, copy at U.S. Army Corps of Engineers Addicks-Barker field office.

52. Andrea R. Stahman, *Bear Creek: A Case Study in Locating Historic Site Remains in Southeast Texas*, MA thesis, Graduate School of Texas A&M University, 2004, 155p. For Theodore W. Hillendahl, see Alabama, Texas and Virginia Confederate Pensions, 1884–1958, Pensions files nos. 41536–41570, application in 1925.Also see National Park Service, in U.S. Civil War Soldiers, 1861–1865, online database (Provo, Utah: Ancestry.com Operations, 2007), M227, roll 17.

53. Richard G. Lowe, *Walker's Texas Division* (Baton Rouge: Louisiana State University Press, 2004).

54. Stahman, Bear Creek.

55. National Park Service. U.S. Civil War Soldiers, 1861-1865 [database on-line]. Provo, UT, USA: Ancestry.com Operations Inc, 2007, M227, Roll 3.

56. Chester William and Ethel H. Geue, eds., *A New Land Beckoned: German Immigration to Texas, 1844-1847* (Genealogical Publishing Co., 1972), 54. Also FindAGrave.com, Memorial# 35169665.

57. National Park Service. U.S. Civil War Soldiers, 1861-1865 [database on-line]. Provo, UT, USA: Ancestry.com Operations Inc, 2007.

58. Alwyn Barr, "Confederate Field Artillery," *Handbook of Texas Online,* accessed March 19, 2016. Also, Gary D. Bray, May 13, 2007, 4th Field Battery, Texas Light Artillery, The Texas in the Civil War Message Board, www.history-sites.com.

59. Charles Arthur Beinhorn, Jr. and Louise Haggenos Beinhorn, Our Time Line: unpublished family history notes in the personal files of Nelda Blackshere Reynolds.

60. Matzke descendant Marie Neuman Gray, personal communication, 2015.

61. Ibid.

62. Ludwig Koch, in *U.S. Civil War Soldiers, 1861–1865*, online database (Provo, Utah: Ancestry.com Operations, 2011).

63. Alwyn Barr, "Confederate Heavy Artillery," Handbook of Texas Online, accessed February 02, 2015.

64. Margaret H. Edwards, *The Story of Madge Golbow Hopkins* (unpublished family history, undated), 9–13, copy at U.S. Army Corps of Engineers Addicks-Barker field office.

65. Ibid., 13–15.

66. Copy of signed agreement between Sophia Striepe and Albert Marks, Harris County, June 29, 1874, Marks Family Papers, as quoted in Sizemore, The LH7 Ranch, 4–5.

67. Bernice Mistrot, "Clement's Corner," *Newsletter,* Washington Cemetery Historic Trust 25, no. 3 (August 2001): 1.

68. Frederick Reineman, 2nd Regiment, Texas Infantry, National Park Service, in U.S. Civil War Soldiers, 1861–1865, online database (Provo, Utah: Ancestry.com Operations, 2007), M227, roll 30.

69. Joseph E. Chance, "Second Texas Infantry," *Handbook of Texas Online,* accessed March 14, 2016.

70. Mistrot, "Clement's Corner."

71. Battle of Shiloh, National Park Service, Shiloh National Military Park, http://www.nps.gov/shil/learn/historyculture/shiloh-history.htm, accessed March 14, 2016.

72. "Papers of the Reinermann, Sandman, Bethje and Quensell families of Harris County, 1841–1917," MS 339, Woodson Research Center, Rice University, Houston.

73. Frederick Reineman, Compiled Service Records, Confederate Army, accessed on March 13, 2016 via Fold 3, online at www.ancestry.com.

74. David Hornburg, personal communication, March 2016.

75. T. Michael Parrish, "Rogers, William Peleg," *Handbook of Texas Online*, accessed March 15, 2016. William Rogers was born in Georgia, when his parents were visiting there from their home in Alabama.

76. Texas, Muster Roll Index Cards, 1838–1900, online database (Provo, Utah: Ancestry.com Operations, 2011).

77. Parrish, "Rogers, William Peleg."

78. Eleanor Damon Pace, ed., "The Diary and Letters of William P. Rogers, 1846–1862," *Southwestern Historical Quarterly* 32, no. 4 (April 1929): 286–288.

79. Parrish, "Rogers, William Peleg"; also Joseph E. Chance, *The Second Texas Infantry: From Shiloh to Vicksburg* (Austin: Eakin Press, 1984).

80. Jesse Ables and Luann Parrish, *Images of America: Corinth* (Mount Pleasant, S.C.: Arcadia Publishing Company, 2012), 31.

81. "Eureka Mills," *Houston Daily Times,* September 25, 1868.

82. David G. McComb, *Houston: A History* (1969; Austin: University of Texas Press, 1981), 55.

83. Eugene M. Ott Jr. and Glen E. Lich, "First Texas Cavalry, USA," *Handbook of Texas Online,* accessed March 07, 2016.

84. *Houston Tri-Weekly Telegraph,* August 25, 1865, 7, col. 2.

85. *Houston Tri-Weekly Telegraph,* August 26, 1865.

86. "Harris County at War," *Houston Weekly Telegraph* 27, no. 22, August 14, 1861.

87. George W. Cable, "New Orleans Before the Capture," *Century Illustrated Monthly Magazine* 29 (November 1884–April 1885): 918.

88. "Hay & Morse Wholesale & Retail Druggists," Advertisement, *Houston Weekly Telegraph*, 27, no. 4, April 9, 1861.

89. James Orville Moore, *The Men of the Bayou City Guards (Company A, 5th Texas Infantry)*, MA thesis, University of Houston at Clear Lake, 1988.

90. *Galveston Weekly News* 18, no. 30, Ed. 1, October 8, 1861.

91. Moore, *Men of the Bayou City Guards.*

92. "Harris County in the War," *Houston Tri-Weekly Telegraph*, March 26, 1862.

93. Celia Hough Morse, *Civil War Diary*, unpublished manuscript, transcribed by Janet K. Wagner, 1993.

94. Moore, *Men of the Bayou City Guards*, 45.

95. "The Texas Brigade in Virginia," *Houston Tri-Weekly Telegraph*, October 3, 1862.

96. "Special Correspondence," *Houston Weekly Telegraph*, September 29, 1862.

97. Moore, *Men of the Bayou City Guards*, 54.

98. Ibid., 55.

99. Ibid., 59.

100. *Houston Tri-Weekly Telegraph*, February 25, 1863.

101. Mrs. Arch B. Marshall, *Forebears and Descendants of an Early Houston Family* (Houston: Privately published, 1975), 19.

102. Edward B. Williams, *Hood's Texas Brigade in the Civil War* (Jefferson, N.C.: McFarland & Company, Publishers, 2012), 160–162, 261.

103. Moore, *Men of the Bayou City Guards*, 71–73.

104. Samuel D. Miller, First Lieutenant, Comdg. Seventy-third Pennsylvania Vols, Series 1—Volume 31 (Part II), 370–371, referenced in Find A Grave Memorial # 2995871.

105. Moore, *Men of the Bayou City Guards*, 76–78.

106. Marshall, *Forebears and Descendants*, 14–15.

107. Moore, *Men of the Bayou City Guards*, 83.

108. Terry's Texas Cavalry: in John F. Walter, 1981, *A history of Texas Units in the Civil War:* manuscript at the Historical Research Center, Texas Heritage Museum, Hill College, Hillsboro, Texas.

109. Houston City Directory, 1866.

110. *Houston Weekly Telegraph*, October 26, 1864, 2.

111. Moore, *Men of the Bayou City Guards*, 70–76.

112. Ibid., 86–88.

113. Joe Polley (Co. F, 4th Texas), *A Soldier's Letters to Charming Nellie* (1908; repr. Gaithersburg, Md.: Butternut Press, 1984), 264.

114. Ibid., 258.

115. Moore, *Men of the Bayou City Guards*, 94–96.

116. Ibid., 70–77.

117. *Houston Tri-Weekly Telegraph*, January 22, 1864.

118. Advertisement for McKinstry and Connick, *Houston Tri-Weekly Telegraph*, June 5, 1863.

119. Minutes of Houston City Council Proceedings, 1865. This document, on microfilm at the Houston Public Library, shows that about 15 years of council minutes are missing. The minutes of the first city council meeting under Federal control, in June 1865, state that Federal soldiers burned the papers while quartered in council chambers.

120. *Houston Tri-Weekly Telegraph*, February 25, 1863.

121. *Houston Tri-weekly Telegraph*, January 25, 1865, 1.

122. "Presentment of the Grand Jury, CS District Court," *Galveston Daily News*, March 8, 1865, 1, cols. 4–5.

123. *Galveston Daily News*, April 13, 1865, 2, col. 5.

124. David G. McComb, *Houston: A History* (1969; University of Texas Press, Austin, 1981), 54. The quote is from the *Galveston Daily News*, June 4, 1865.

125. (probably Herman Charles Rummel), *History of Spring Branch, 1837–1937* (Houston: Privately published, 1937), Archives of Clayton Library, Houston Public Library.

9. Reconstruction and African American Migration

1. Texas State Library, https://www.tsl.texas.gov/ref/abouttx/juneteenth.html.

2. T. R. Fehrenbach, *Lone Star: A History of Texas and the Texans:* (1968; Cambridge, Mass.: Da Capo Press, 2000), 395–396.

3. Cary D. Wintz, "Fourth Ward, Houston," *Handbook of Texas Online*, Texas State Historical Association, accessed December 16, 2015.

4. *Houston Tri-Weekly Telegraph*, Monday, July 10, 1865, 3, col. 3. General Orders 1 and 3.

5. Introduction, Howard Beeth and Cary D. Wintz, eds., *Black Dixie: Afro-Texan History and Culture in Houston* (College Station: Texas A&M University Press, 2000), 19–20.

6. Cecil Harper Jr., "Freedmen's Bureau," *Handbook of Texas Online*, accessed December 16, 2015

7. Scott L. Stabler, "Free Men Come to Houston: Blacks during Reconstruction," *Houston Review* 3, no. 1 (2012): 43, 73.

8. Charles Griffin to Otis Howard, June 16, 1867, O. O. Howard Papers, Bowdoin College, Brunswick, Maine, as quoted by Scott L. Stabler, "Free Men Come to Houston," 42.

9. Merline Pitre, 1992, "Richard Allen: The Chequered Career of Houston's First Black State Legislator," in Howard Beeth and Cary D. Wintz, eds., *Black Dixie: Afro-Texan History and Culture in Houston:* (College Station: Texas A&M University Press, 2000), 74–75.

10. Stabler, "Free Men Come to Houston," 75–76.

11. Mary Louise Passey, *Freedmantown: The Evolution of a Black Neighborhood in Houston, 1865–1880,* MA thesis, Rice University, Houston, 1993, 227p.

12. Houston Heritage Society, "Fourth Ward Cottage," unpublished historical notes, 17p. Also see www.heritagesociety.org/fourth-ward-cottage.

13. Dr. Howard Jones, *The Red Diary: A Chronological History of Black Americans in Houston and Some Neighboring Harris County Communities, 122 Years Later* (Austin: Nortex Press, 1991), 28. Also website of Trinity United Methodist Church, www.aframnews.com/trinity-united-methodist-church-2600-holman-street-houston-texas-77004/.

14. A Brief History, Antioch Downtown, www.ambchous-

ton.org.

15. Anonymous, *The Red Book of Houston: A Compendium of Social, Professional, Religious, Educational and Industrial Interests of Houston's Colored Population* (Houston: SoTex Publishing Company, 1915), 72–77.

16. Beeth and Wintz, *Black Dixie,* 88, and U.S. Federal Census data.

17. Allan Turner, "Congregation Marks 150 Years of Faith," *Houston Chronicle*, March 5, 2015, A1, A7. Also see deed at Harris County Deed Records, vol. 29, 409, Harriet George to Trustees of the Pilgrim's Rest Baptist Church.

18. History of Pilgrim's Rest Missionary Baptist Church, www.pilgrimrest.net.

19. 1867 Voter Registration Lists, Harris County, reel 6, lines 1046–1066, June 25, 1867, online at www.ancestry.com.

20. Dr. Diana Lynn Severance, "History of the Kohrville Community and the Kohrville School," ca. 2003, online at Wikipedia, entry for Kohrville, Texas. Also see 1870 U.S. Federal Census for Harris County; "An Application for a Texas State Historical Marker for Amos Cemetery, " Harris County Historical Commission (unpublished); and Trevia Wooster Beverly, "The Bottoms Cemetery, Lakewood Subdivision, Kohrville Community of Harris County, Texas" (unpublished manuscript in files of Trevia Beverly), 2005.

21. Kim Morgan, "Piney Point Church to Celebrate 145 Years of Memories; Church's First Congregation Were Freed Slaves from the South," *Houston Chronicle,* March 7, 2010, This Week section, 4.

22. Severance, "History of the Kohrville Community."

23. Turner, Congregation Marks 150 Years."

24. Texas Voter Registration Lists, 1867-1869, www.ancestry.com. Entry for David McGee on June 25, 1867.

25. Anonymous, 1996, *McGee Chapel Missionary Baptist Church, Historical Book, 1876-1996* (Houston: privately published, 1992), p. 21-22.

26. United States Federal Census, 1880, Subdivision 13 #84, Harris, Texas; Archive Collection T1134; Roll 27; Page 19, Schedule Type: Agriculture.

27. History of McGee Chapel Missionary Baptist Church, online at mcgee.gilbcomm.com. Also, Anonymous, *McGee Chapel Missionary Baptist Church,* 21-25. Also, Texas Death Certificates, 1903-1982, for P. A. McGee, died March 3, 1925.

28. See discussion, chapter 7.

29. 1867 Voter Registration Lists, reel 6, line 1046, June 25, 1867: "Jordan Banks, res. Houston, Harris, TX; 7 yr in state, 7 yr in county, colored, signed (his mark)."

30. William Hunter to Trustees of the Baptist Church, filed 1896, Harris County Deed Records, vol.95, 549.

31. Ibid., 464.

32. M. Alena Allen et al. to Harris County, filed 1899, Harris County Deed Records, vol. 111, 24.

33. River Oaks Corporation to Trustees of the Lovely Canada Baptist Church, filed 1938, Harris County Deed Records, vol. 1143, 343.

34. Hannah P. Morse married J. T. Hunt, April 3, 1867, in *Texas Marriages, 1837–1973,* FamilySearch, https://familysearch.org/ark:/61903/1:1:FXQ3-7WT, accessed January 17, 2016.

35. H. Hurt married H. F. Silliman, July 19, 1874, Harris Co., TX, in *Texas Marriages, 1837–1973,* FamilySearch, https://familysearch.org/ark:/61903/1:1:FXQ3-LM5, accessed January 17, 2016.

36. Mrs. Arch B. Marshall, *Forebears and Descendants of an Early Houston Family* (Houston: Privately published, 1975), 69, copy at Clayton Library, Houston Public Library.

37. Harris County Deed Book 29, 499–500, March 14, 1884.

38. Melissa M. Peterson, ed., *The Road to Piney Point* (Houston: Piney Point Village Historic Committee, 1994), 29.

39. See Chapter 7, this volume. Also see the documentation for the Harris County Historical Marker titled "The Morse-Bragg Cemetery," to be posted in 2016 online at http://www.historicalcommission.hctx.net/.

40. Marshall, *Forebears and Descendants,* 10–15.

41. The circumstances of his death are unknown, and the date is from State Masonic records. It seems plausible that like so many other returning soldiers, he may have had either wounds or illnesses related to the long war years spent outdoors and/or in battle.

42. Fehrenbach, *Lone Star,* 419.

43. Order for Grace Morse as Administratix of the Agur Morse Estate, August 29, 1865, Harris County Deed Records, vol. Q, 447.

44. Harris County Deed Records, 1869, vol. F, 607.

45. An additional 370-acre tract in the White survey had been sold to Benjamin A. Bragg before Agur Morse died, and it is not listed in Agur Morse's probate inventory.

46. Subdivision of part of the A. C. Reynolds league and of the William White one third league, January 27, 1871; Harris County Deed Records, vol. 9A, 499.

47. Harris County Deed Records, 1871, vol. 9B, 623–626.

48. Cassandra McFee to Sophronia R. Parker, March 30, 1866; Harris County Deed Records, vol. 2, 500. Mrs. Grace G. Morse to W. A. Parker, Sept ember13, 1872, Harris County Deed Records, vol. 17, 148.

49. Harris County Deed Records, vol. 87, 288, and vol. 20, 363.

50. Harris County Deed Records, vol. 13, 382, and vol. 17, 39.

51. *Galveston Daily News*, September 25, 1889, 3.

52. Harris County Deed Records, vol. 229, 377, no. 47524.

53. Janet Wagner, personal communication, 2014.

54. Mr. Taft, Postmaster, in *Houston Tri-Weekly Telegraph,* July 5, 1865, 4. Also, Houston City Directory for 1866 (Dallas: L. Polk, 1866).

55. *Houston Tri-Weekly Telegraph,* July 5, 1865, 4.

56. Ward Family Tree with numerous cited references, www.ancestry.com, accessed May 2016. Also Jas. S. Taft, *Washington Deaths,* 1883–1960, www.ancestry.com.

57. *Janet K. Wagner, Morse-Bragg Cemetery, Chronology: Dateline William White League*, private manuscript, 1992, and unpublished research notes, 1993.

58. United Stated Census, 1870, Schedule of Industry.

59. Harris County Death Records, no. 39.

60. Harris County Deed Records, vol. 13, 348, July 3, 1874.

61. Harris County Deed Records, vol. 12, 681, July 3, 1874.

62. J. K. Wagner & Company, *Interments in the Morse-Bragg Cemetery,* Research done for DeLange, Hudspeth and Pitman, LLP (Houston: J. K. Wagner & Company, 1995), 22p.

63. Marshall, *Forebears and Descendants*.

64. Most of the causes of death for burials at Morse-Bragg are taken from Wagner, *Interments, Morse-Bragg Cemetery.*

65. Wagner, "Historical Development of Buffalo Bayou."

66. Ibid.

67. Wagner, *Interments, Morse-Bragg Cemetery.*

68. State of Texas stone memorial to "Thaddus Constantine Bell" at Columbia Cemetery, West Columbia Texas, 1936. Bell's wife, Elizabeth Cayve Bell (1830-1864) and his father, Josiah Hughes Bell (1791-1838) are buried at that cemetery. Also see *The Handbook of Texas,* Texas State Historical Association, entry on Josiah Hughes Bell.

69. *The Handbook of Texas,* Texas State Historical Association, entry on Josiah Hughes Bell, with information from James A. Creighton, *A Narrative History of Brazoria County* (Angleton, Texas: Brazoria County Historical Commission, 1975), and Andrew Phelps McCormick, *Scotch-Irish in Ireland and America (1897)*.

70. Andrew Phelps McCormick, 1897, *Scotch-Irish in Ireland and America.* Unpublished family manuscript, p. 128.

71. List of Communicants, First Presbyterian Church of Houston. On microfilm, Houston Metropolitan Research Center, Houston Public Library.

72. Andrew Phelps McCormick, *Scotch-Irish in Ireland and America (1897)*.

73. Register of Deaths, 1871, First Presbyterian Church, Houston Texas; Houston Metropolitan Research Center, Houston Public Library.

74. Notes on 1936 Centennial Markers: online at http://www.thc.state.tx.us/preserve/projects-and-programs/state-historical-markers/1936-texas-centennial-markers

75. Bob Arnold and Alan Bell, Bell descendants, personal communication 2014. Also Jamie Murray, Brazoria County Historical Museum, personal communication, 2014.

76. Harris County Deed Records, vol. 2, 500).

77. *Janet K. Wagner, Morse-Bragg Cemetery, Chronology: Dateline William White League,* Private manuscript, 1992, and unpublished research notes, 1993.

78. Harris County Deed Records, 1872, vol. 11, 599.

79. "Houston," *Galveston Daily News,* September 12, 1872.

80. "Dolly Varden (costume)," Wikipedia.

81. Reeder, *Through the Years.*

82. J. B. Munger, *The Munger Book: Something of the Mungers, 1639–1914* (Tuttle, Morehouse & Taylor Company, 1915), 100, online at ancestry.com.

83. David H. Paige to S. S. Munger, Harris County Deed Records, January 5, 1866, vol. 2, 244.

84. *Houston Tri-Weekly Telegraph*, May 2, 1866, 3, col. 1.

85. "Cotton and Wool Factories in Texas," in *The Texas Almanac for 1870, and Emigrant's Guide to Texas,* 173, online at Portal to Texas History, http://texashistory.unt.edu.

86. *The Texas Almanac for 1867 with Statistics, Descriptive and Biographical Sketches, etc., Relating to Texas* (Galveston: W. Richardson & Company, 1867), 237, online at Portal to Texas History, http://texashistory.unt.edu.

87. "Cotton Manufacturers in Texas," *DeBouw's Review, Dedicated to the Restoration of the Southern States* (Journal), vol. 4 (1867): 265.

88. *Houston Tri-Weekly Telegraph,* November 5, 1867, 36, col. 3.

89. *Houston Tri-Weekly Telegraph,* October 29, 1868, 8, col. 4.

90. "Cotton and Wool Factories in Texas," 173, *Houston Tri-Weekly Telegraph,* June 29, 1866, 4, col. 2.

91. *Houston Tri-Weekly Telegraph,* May 23, 1872, 4, col. 2.

92. Louis F. Aulbach, Linda C. Gorski, and Robbie Morin, *Camp Logan: A World War I Emergency Training Center* (Houston: Louis Aulbach, Publisher, 2014), 83.

93. Dr. S. O. Young, *A Thumbnail History of the City of Houston, Texas, 1836–1912* (1912; repr. Ingleside, Tex.: Copano Bay Press, 2010), 135.

94. www.Findagrave.com.

95. Bernice Mistrot, "Clement's Corner," *Newsletter, Washington Cemetery Historic Trust,* 25, no. 3 (August 2001): 1. Also Aulbach et al., *Camp Logan,* 81.

96. Marshall, *Forebears and Descendants,* 67–68.

97. George C. Werner, "Buffalo Bayou, Brazos and Colorado Railway," *Handbook of Texas Online,* accessed January 17, 2015.

98. Deborah L. Sizemore, *The LH7 Ranch in Houston's Shadow: The E. H. Marks Legacy from Longhorns to the Salt Grass Trail* (Denton: University of North Texas Press, 1991).

99. Mrs. Glen T. Bundick, "Oldest Buffalo Bayou Home Rich in History," *Houston Chronicle,* February 13, 1949.

100. Sizemore, *The LH7 Ranch.*

101. E. H. Marks, 1967 interview, as quoted in Sizemore, *The LH7 Ranch,* 6.

102. David G. McComb, *Houston: A History* (1969; Austin: University of Texas Press, 1981), 54–55.

10. A Cattle Kingdom along the Bayou

1. Francis R. Lubbock, *Six Decades in Texas, or, Memoirs of Francis Richard Lubbock* (Austin: Ben C. Jones & Company,

1900), 126.

2. Ken Hoffman, "Time for What Might be a Hurtful History Lesson about Houston," *Houston Chronicle*, March 24, 2015, E1–E2.

3. Edward Nicholas Clopper, *An American family; Its Ups and Downs through Eight Generations in New Amsterdam, New York, Pennsylvania, Maryland, Ohio, and Texas, from 1650 to 1880* (Cincinnati, 1950),182–190.

4. Celia Hough Morse, *Civil War Diary*, unpublished manuscript, transcribed by Janet K. Wagner, 1993.

5. Cassie McFee Reeder, *Through the Years* (unpublished autobiography), 1962, McFee-Reeder family files.

6. H. F. McDanield and N. A. Taylor, *The Coming Empire, or Two Thousand Miles in Texas on Horseback* (New York: A. S. Barnes & Company, 1877), 11–12.

7. Reeder, *Through the Years*.

8. Reeder, *Through the Years*.

9. McDanield and Taylor, *The Coming Empire*, 16–17.

10. Lubbock, *Six Decades in Texas*, 122.

11. Lubbock, *Six Decades in Texas*, 126.

12. Lubbock, *Six Decades in Texas*, 127–128.

13. Lubbock, *Six Decades in Texas*, 136–137.

14. Lubbock, *Six Decades in Texas*, 138.

15. Andrew Forest Muir, ed., "Diary of a Young Man in Houston, 1838," *Southwestern Historical Quarterly* 53 (July 1949-April 1950): 294–303.

16. Francis R. Lubbock, *Six Decades in Texas*, 138–139.

17. E. H. Marks, 1967 interview, as quoted in Deborah L. Sizemore, *The LH7 Ranch in Houston's Shadow* (Denton: University of North Texas Press, 1991), 6.

18. Alecya Gallaway, *Saltgrass Cattlemen* (unpublished manuscript), 2003, archives, League City Public Library. This manuscript was prepared for a presentation at the Texas State Historical Convention, 2003.

19. Mickie Baldwin, "White, James Taylor," *Handbook of Texas Online*, Texas State Historical Association, accessed January 13, 2016.

20. Anonymous ["M. Fiske"], *A Visit to Texas: Being the Journal of a Traveller Through Those Parts Most Interesting to American Settlers* (New York: Goodrich and Wiley, 1834; repr. ed. Robert S. Gray, Houston: Cordovan Press, 1975), 76–80.

21. Gallaway, *Saltgrass Cattlemen*, 9–12. Also see Allen C. Coward in *Taylor Family Tree*, posted by hughtaylor80, www.ancestry.com.

22. Gallaway, *Saltgrass Cattlemen*, 10–11. Also Allen Cowherd listing in U.S. Federal Census for 1850, Galveston County.

23. Gallaway, *Saltgrass Cattlemen*, 11.

24. Information from displays, Butler Longhorn Museum, League City, Texas.

25. Alecya Callaway, notes in the archives of Butler Longhorn Museum. Also see notes by Floyd Lanny Martin for FindAGrave memorials for Thomas Caldwell, Phillips Memorial Cemetery, Galveston County, Texas, www.findagrave.com.

26. Priscilla T. Graham, *Highland Tank: Our Settlement* (Lulu.com, 2016); also see Alecya Gallaway, "Butler Longhorn Cowboys on the Chisholm Trail," in *Butler Breeder's Invitational Select Heifer Offering* (Lockhart, Texas, 2006), online at www.butlertexaslonghorns.com/catalog/2006/heifer/catalog1.html.

27. Alecya Gallaway, personal communication, 2016.

28. Charles Moreau-Harper, *Cattle Trails of the Prairies* (New York: Scribner, 1892), 732–734.

29. W.R. Baker to George W. Butler, Harris County Deed Records vol. 4, 88. January, 1867.

30. *Texas, Voter Registration Lists, 1867–1869*, online database (Provo, Utah: Ancestry.com Operations, 2011).

31. Burke to Coward, Harris County Deed Records, vol. 5, 8. February, 1867.

32. Anita Butler, great-granddaughter of George W. Butler, personal communication, January 18, 2016.

33. The Big Roundups (display), Butler Longhorn Museum, League City, Texas.

34. Schiebler sold his 50 percent interest in this tract when he was exiting the partnership in 1873; Harris County Deed Records, vol. 11, 941. The tract had earlier been purchased by Coward and Butler; Harris County Deed Records, vol. 9A, 442.

35. Alecya Gallaway, "Butler Longhorn Cowboys on the Chisholm Trail."

36. Harris County Deed Records, vol. 8, 337.

37. Alecya Gallaway, "Butler Longhorn Cowboys on the Chisholm Trail."

38. Anita Butler, personal communication, January 18, 2016.

39. Alecya Gallaway, "Butler Longhorn Cowboys on the Chisholm Trail."

40. Harris County Deed Records, vol. 11, 758. Butler is listed in the *Houston City Directory of 1873* as residing on San Felipe Road; copy in Houston Public Library.

41. Valma D.Fischer, *History of the Perkins Family* (unpublished manuscript), 1982.

42. U.S. Census, 1900, Galveston County, Texas. Also see Taylor Family Tree, posted by hughtaylor80, www.ancestry.com.

43. Vera Bell Gary, LaMarque, Texas, personal communication, 2016.

44. Alecya Gallaway, "Butler Longhorn Cowboys on the Chisholm Trail."

45. Melodey Mozeley Hauch, *Pioneer families of the 1867 Settlement, Texas City, Texas* (La Marque, Texas: African American Historic Preservation Committee, Inc., 2016), 2-15.

46. Alecya Gallaway, notes in the archives of Butler Longhorn Museum. Also see notes by Floyd Lanny Martin for FindAGrave memorials for Thomas Caldwell and Calvin Bell Sr., Phillips Memorial Cemetery, Galveston County, Texas, www.findagrave.com. For more information on The Settlement,

see Black cowboys/Bell family, Texas City Library, online at http://www.texascity-library.org/history/development/bells.php.

47. Moreau-Harper, *Cattle Trails of the Prairies*, 733–734.

48. Harris County Deed Records, vol. 9A, 642.

49. Gallaway, *Saltgrass Cattlemen*, 12.

50. *Galveston Daily News*, 1878, as quoted in The Big Roundups (display), Butler Longhorn Museum, League City, Texas.

51. Harris County Deed Records, vol. 11, 941, 942.

52. Heather Green Wooten, Ph.D., History of League City, online at www.leaguecity.com.

53. Deborah Sizemore, "Milby Butler, 1889–1971: The Butler Longhorns Live On," Butler Texas Longhorns website, www.butlertexaslonghorns.com. Also see the website of the Butler Longhorn Museum, League City, Texas, www.butlerlonghornmuseum.com.

54. Anonymous, *History of Texas, Together with a Biographical History of the Cities of Houston and Galveston* (Chicago: Lewis Publishing Company, 1895), 443–444.

55. Harris County Deed Records M:487; 3:367.

56. Colette Marie Baker Herzog, "Biography of George Frederick Baker," in *Daughters of the Republic of Texas*, vol. 1 (Paducah, Ky.: Turner Publishing Company, 1995).

57. Harris County Deed Records, vol. J, 472.

58. Herzog, "Biography of George Frederick Baker."

59. Harris County Deed Records, vol. J, 578.

60. Harris County Deed Records, vol. J, 471, 578; vol. O, 205; vol. P, 543. Also see Audrey Barrett Cook, *Obedience Smith (1771–1847): Pioneer of Three American Frontiers* (Houston: Early Publishing Company, 2008), 176–177.

61. Harris County Deed Records, vol. R, 22; the Boercher purchase of the slaughterhouse property is in vol. P, 72, and the Frome purchase is in vol. W, 64.

62. Protected Landmark Designation Report, Baker-Meyer Building, 315 Travis Street, City of Houston Planning and Development Department, Archeological and Historical Commission, June 8, 2010.

63. Anonymous, *History of Texas*, 443.

64. Henry D. & Frances T. McCallum, *The Wire that Fenced the West* (Norman: University of Oklahoma Press, 1965).

65. Dr. S. O. Young, *A Thumbnail History of the City of Houston Texas, 1836–1912* (1912; repr. Ingleside, Tex.: Copano Bay Press, 2010), ch. 8.

66. 1870 U.S. Census, Agricultural Survey, 1870, Harris County.

67. Deborah Sizemore, *The LH7 Ranch in Houston's Shadow* (Denton: University of North Texas Press, 1991).

11. A Transition to Modern Time

1. *Remembrances of Jeannette Morse Hollady, in Mrs. Arch B. Marshall, Forebears and Descendants of an Early Houston Family* (Houston: Privately published, 1975), 20, copy at Clayton Library, Houston Public Library.

2. Mrs. Glen T. Bundick, "Oldest Buffalo Bayou Home Rich in History," *Houston Chronicle*, February 13, 1949, 8–9.

3. Shepherd Drive was chosen as the eastern boundary for the 1880 census tally, because of rapid exurban growth in the areas east of Shepherd Drive by the 1880s. It was partly this growth that drove out the cattle industry that had existed along San Felipe road between modern Shepherd Drive and the Fourth Ward, as discussed in the last chapter.

4. William Hunter to Jordan Banks, Harris County Deed Records, vol.92, 549, filed 1896.

5. See Agricultural Schedule, 1880 federal census.

6. See, for example, maps of X. Ben Wu and Daniel Z. Sui, Texas A&M University, GIS-based Lacunarity Analysis for Assessing Urban Residential Segregation, Esri User Conference, 2002, online at www. proceedings.esri.com/library/userconf/proc02/pap0667/p0667.htm.

7. See Figure 8.4 and discussion, Chapter 7.

8. George C. Werner, "Texas Western Railway," *Handbook of Texas Online*, Texas State Historical Association, accessed January 22, 2016.

9. Harris County Deed Records, vol. 22, 746–762.

10. These stops are depicted on a map of Harris County published in 1888 by the Immigration and Development Association of Harris County, as part of a "Home-Seekers' Journal." From personal files of the late Charles Kruse, and of Christine Brown, U.S. Army Corps of Engineers, Houston.

11. Maudeen Marks, as quoted by Deborah L. Sizemore, *The LH7 Ranch in Houston's Shadow* (Denton: University of North Texas Press, 1991), 8. Also Carol Adams, *Historic Katy: An Illustrated History* (HPN Books, 2013).

12. Bundick, "Oldest Buffalo Bayou Home Rich in History."

13. H. F. McDanield and N. A. Taylor, *The Coming Empire, or Two Thousand Miles in Texas on Horseback* (New York: A. S. Barnes & Company, 1877), 10.

14. *Houston City Directory, 1890–1891*, 76.

15. Jim Vollmar and the Rosenberg Railroad Museum, *Railroads of Fort Bend County* (Charleston, S.C.: Arcadia Publishing, 2010), 89.

16. George C. Werner, "Houston Tap and Brazoria Railway," *Handbook of Texas Online.*

17. "Map of the Old San Felipe Road from B. A. Bragg's Farm to Waller-County Line at Cane Island," ca. 1890, surveyed by Wm. Bauer, drawn by H. H. Bruns, Archives of the Harris County Clerk.

18. Alan Krell, *The Devil's Rope: A Cultural History of Barbed Wire* (London: Reaktion Books, 2002), 28.

19. Cassie McFee Reeder, *Through The Years* (unpublished autobiography), 1962, McFee-Reeder family files; Sizemore, *The LH7 Ranch.*

20. Bundick, "Oldest Buffalo Bayou Home Rich in History."

21. "Map of New San Felipe Road from Webster Street to Lamar Place and northwest Corner of Mrs. Bragg's Farm," February 8, 1889, surveyed by J. J. Gillespie, drawn by H. H. Bruns, Archives of the Harris County Clerk.

22. "M. L. Westheimer, August 22, 1831–August 2, 1905," www.findagrave.com. Also, "M. L. Westheimer, Old and Respected Citizen of City Dead," *Houston Daily Post,* August 3, 1905, 4, col. 4; also "Funeral," *Houston Daily Post,* August 4, 1905, 4, col. 5.

23. Lionel M. Schooler, "Westheimer, Mitchell Louis," *Handbook of Texas Online*, accessed October 23, 2015.

24. See "Map of New San Felipe Road from Webster," Archives of the Harris County Clerk.

25. Reeder, *Through the Years.*

26. Ibid.

27. Anonymous, *History of Texas,* 695-696..

28. Melissa M. Peterson, ed., *The Road to Piney Point* (Houston: Piney Point Village Historic Committee, 1994), 29.

29. Remembrances of Jeannette Morse Hollady, 19.

30. Peterson, *The Road to Piney Point,* 31.

31. Mrs. Arch B. Marshall, *Forebears and Descendants of an Early Houston Family,* 20–21. Copy at Clayton Library, Houston Public Library.

32. Mary Luna Thornton Morse to Nancy Thornton, May 10, 1895; letter in the private collection of the author.

33. Marshall, *Forebears and Descendants,* 21.

34. Peterson, *The Road to Piney Point,* 68.

35. Marshall, *Forebears and Descendants,* 23–24.

36. Reeder, *Through the Years.*

37. Marshall, *Forebears and Descendants,* 21. In 1890 Harriett George sold to Zac Alford, probably the father of the Alford boys in Holladay's story, sixteen and one half acres of land out of the nearby Smalley Tract, for five dollars (*Galveston Daily News,* March 14, 1890, 3, col. 2).

38. Reeder, *Through the Years.*

39. Peterson, *The Road to Piney Point,* 57.

40. Reeder, *Through the Years.*

41. Reeder, *Through the Years.*

42. Peterson, *The Road to Piney Point,* 45 and 58.

43. Reeder, Through the Years.

44. Austin County Deed Records, vol. B, 306.

45. Letter from Nancy Caroline Thornton to Florence Thornton, 1891, Morse family archive, collected by Mrs. Arch Bruce Marshall and now in the care of the author.

46. Bundick, "Oldest Buffalo Bayou Home Rich in History."

47. Marshall, *Forebears and Descendants*, 23.

48. Trevia Wooster Beverly, *At Rest: A Historical Directory of Harris County, Texas, Cemeteries (1822–2001) Including Burial Customs and Other Interesting Facts, With a Listing of Past and Present Communities, Funeral Home and Monument Companies,* 2nd edition, from 370 to 509 cross-indexed listings (Houston: Tejas Publications & Research, 2001).

49. Remembrances of Jeannette Morse Hollady, in Marshall, *Forebears and Descendants,* 23.

50. *Houston City Directory,* 1901, 1903, 1905.

51. Kathy Monaghan Phillips, personal communication, 2014.

52. Marshall, *Forebears and Descendants,* 23.

53. Mortuary, Mrs. Harriett George, *Galveston Daily News,* January 6, 1892, 3, col. 2.

54. Marshall, *Forebears and Descendants,* 23.

55. Peterson, *The Road to Piney Point,* 67–68.

56. Jeannette Morse Hollady, "Family Facts as Related in My Hearing as a Child and Some of My Knowledge and Experience," in Marshall, *Forebears and Descendants,* 20–24.

57. Albert C. Timme, personal conversation with Leilani Morse Cross, 2000.

58. "P.C. Dunn Home Burned," *Houston Daily Post,* January 14, 1912, 15, col. 5.

59. Reeder, *Through the Years.*

60. Ibid.

61. Claudia Hazlewood, "Alief, Tx," x, accessed February 16, 2015. Also, "Alief Texas," www.wikipedia.org.

62. Jim Vollmar and the Rosenberg Railroad Museum, *Railroads of Fort Bend County* (Charleston, S.C.: Arcadia Publishing, 2010), 97.

63. Andrea R. Stahman, *Bear Creek: A Case Study in Locating Historic Site Remains in Southeast Texas,* MA thesis, Graduate School of Texas A&M University, 2004, 49–53.

64. Ibid., 48–54.

65. Vollmar and Rosenberg Railroad Museum, *Railroads of Fort Bend County,* 117.

66. Henry Schaper Lease to Spring Branch Schutzen Company, December 21, 1876, Harris County Deed Records.

67. Stahman, *Bear Creek,* 50–52.

68. Ibid., 51–53. Also see Sizemore, *The LH7 Ranch,* 69–72.

69. Ross Fields, Martha Doty Freeman, and Stephen M. Kotter, *Inventory and Assessment of Cultural Resources at Addicks Reservoir, Harris County,* Texas, Reports of Investigations no. 12 (Austin: Prewitt and Associates, 1983).

70. Joe Holley, "Today's Cypress Squeezes Out Fabled Dance Hall: Harris County's Oldest Saloon, Dance Hall Hosts Last Hurrah after Lifetimes of Memories," *Houston Chronicle,* January 2, 2016, online at www.chron.news, article 67232039.

71. Diana J. Kleiner, "Hillendahl, Tx," *Handbook of Texas Online,* http://www.tshaonline.org/handbook/online/articles/hrhmw, accessed October 02, 2014.

72. Children's letters, *Houston Post,* June 18, 1892.

73. Ross Fields, Molly Ficklen Godwin, Martha Doty Freeman, and Susan V. Lisk, *Inventory and Assessment of Cultural Resources at Barker Reservoir, Fort Bend and Harris Counties, Texas* Reports of Investigations no. 40, (Austin: Prewitt and Associates, 1986), 22–31.

74. Atha Marks Dimon, "Barker, Tx," *Handbook of Texas*

Online. Also Harris County Map Records, vol. 1, no. 10.

75. Fields et al., *Inventory, Barker Reservoir,* 22–32.

76. Interview of Mrs. Fisher (daughter of midwestern farmer John Wendling) by Martha Doty Freeman, December 15, 1984, Barker, Texas. The original notes are with Martha Freeman.

77. Ibid.

78. Martha Doty Freeman and Joe C. Freeman, Marks Ranch Headquarters, Harris County Texas, Historic American Buildings Survey Documentation, Austin, Texas, prepared for the Estate of Maudeen Marks, 2012p. 13.

79. Sizemore, *The LH7 Ranch,* 52.

80. Ibid.

81. Freeman and Freeman, *Marks Ranch Headquarters.*

82. Harris County Deed Records, vol. 44, 638; vol. 53, 425; vol. 48, 328.

83. Meyer M. Levy, Bleasdale Family Tree with relevant sources, www.ancestry.com.

84. *Harris County Deed Records,* vol. 89, 241.

85. Stahman, *Bear Creek,* 54.

86. Sizemore, *The LH7 Ranch,* 33.

87. Claudia Hazlewood, "Alief, Tx," *Handbook of Texas Online,* accessed February 16, 2015.

12. Epilogue

1. *Road Map of Houston,* 1937, University of Houston Digital Library.

2. Renee Kientz, "Once upon a Time: Tiny Cemetery on Busy Long Point Last Trace of Hillendahl Family Farm," *Houston Chronicle,* August 8, 1999, Lifestyle section, 1.

3. Kientz, "Once upon a Time."

4. Evelyn Schroeder Kingsbury, personal communication, 2016.

5. Mrs. Noel (Brown) McClure, "The Legacy of a Wilderness Church," *Genealogical Record,* September 1986, 175-177, copy at Clayton Library, Houston Public Library.

6. The Heritage Society, online at www.heritagesociety.org stjohnchurch/.

7. See discussion, Chapter 9.

8. John Nova Lomax, "What Is Happening to Texas's Dance Halls? The Historic Tin Hall Closes its Doors at the End of the Year," *Texas Monthly,* 2015, online at www.texasmonthly.com.

9. Erin Mulvaney, "Fulshear Growing Pains Hit Ballot," *Houston Chronicle,* November 3, 2013.

10. Dan M. Worrall, An Application for a Harris County Historical Marker for the Morse-Bragg (Pleasant Bend) Cemetery, 2014, Harris County Historical Commission archives.

11. Brant family tree, www.ancestry.com.

12. Kientz, "Once upon a Time."

13. Paris Achen, "Birth of a Community: Historic Church Plays a Big Role in the Creation of Spring Branch," *Houston Chronicle,* October 10, 2002, This Week section, 1.

14. Clodine: The West Houston Archives, online at www.westhoustonarchives.org.

15. "A city hall to call its own?:" *Houston Chronicle,* June 29, 1992, p. 14a; "Community saves historic structure in Piney Point:" *Houston Chronicle,* January 6, 1993, in "This Week" section. Also see "125 Year Old Home First in Mirror Series:" The *Houston Post,* January 30, 1974, "Today section," p. 8.

16. Lane Hillendahl Family Tree, www.ancestry.com.

17. Margaret H. Edwards, The Koch-Golbow Homestead Research, supplement to her biography of her mother, *The Story of Madge Golbow Hopkins* (unpublished family history, undated), copy at U.S. Army Corps of Engineers Addicks-Barker field office. Also, Margaret H. Edwards, *The Story of Madge Golbow Hopkins* (unpublished family history, undated), 28.

18. David Hornburg, information on Vollmer Cemetery and Johann Ojemann, www.findagrave.com.

19. "The Blue-Light Cemetery,"*Suburbia Reporter,* August 1975.

20. Andrea R. Stahman, *Bear Creek: A Case Study in Locating Historic Site Remains in Southeast Texas,* MA thesis, Graduate School of Texas A&M University, 2004, 129–130.

21. Groschke Cemetery on Pine Forest Road, anonymous file, U.S. Army Corps of Engineers.

22. Cemeteries in Addicks Reservoir, anonymous file, U.S. Army Corps of Engineers, Addicks-Barker field office.

23. Deed, Harriet George to Trustees of the Pilgrim's Rest Baptist Church, March 25, 1884, Harris County Deed Records, vol. 29, 409.

24. "Congregation Marks 150 Years of Faith," *Houston Chronicle,* March 3, 2015, 1.

25. Trevia Beverly, *At Rest: A Historical Directory of Harris County Texas Cemeteries (1822-2001)* (Houston: Tejas Publications & Research, 2001), Cemetery no. 374.

26. *Burial Sites of Harris County, Texas,* online database, rootsweb.ancestry.com; also see Beverly, At Rest, Cemetery no. 324. The Morse burials there are described in Mrs. Arch B. Marshall, *Forebears and Descendants of an Early Houston Family,* (Houston: Privately published, 1975), 23, copy at Clayton Library, Houston Public Library.

27. Trevia Beverly, personal communication, March 8, 2015.

28. Christine Brown and Janet Wagner, personal communication, 2015.

29. Memorial Park Master Plan, 2015, Memorial Park Conservancy, www.memorialparktomorrow.org, accessed April, 2015.

30. David G. McComb, *Houston: A History* (1969; repr. Austin: University of Texas Press, 1981), 192.

31. Addicks and Barker Reservoirs, informational brochure,

n.d., U.S. Army Corps of Engineers, Galveston District.

32. 2009 Master Plan, Addicks and Barker Reservoirs, U.S. Army Corps of Engineers, Galveston District, Galveston, Texas: online at www.swg.usace.army.mil/Portals/26/docs.

33. Anonymous ["M. Fiske"], *A Visit to Texas: Being the Journal of a Traveller through Those Parts Most Interesting to American Settlers* (New York:, Goodrich and Wiley, 1834), 186, 158-159; a extended extract is given in Chapter 1.

34. About Us, Katy Prairie Conservancy website, www.katyprairie.org, accessed April 2016.

35. Jaime González, Katy Prairie Conservancy, personal communication, 2016.

36. Information on these programs is available online at www.historicalcommission.hctx.net/

INDEX

About the Author

Dan Michael Worrall has been a member of the Harris County Historical Commission since 2014, working on a project to bring historical markers to significant sites in western Harris County. He is also a director of the Morse-Bragg Cemetery Association, and worked to save and protect that nineteenth-century graveyard from development. That task has recently been accomplished, and the cemetery, replete with a new obelisk and a Harris County historical marker, is now a Harris County park. Dan is one of a fifth generation of his family to live in the Houston area, and some of his ancestors could be found at Pleasant Bend, Piney Point, and Wheaton's Ford along the San Felipe Trail, among other places.

He is a retired geologist, and held various exploration, research, and management roles during his career with Shell Oil Company. He holds a Bachelor's Degree from Rice University, a Master of Arts in Teaching from Northwestern University, a Master of Arts in geology from the University of Wyoming, and a PhD in geology from the University of Texas at Austin.

Dan has a number of geologic publications from earlier years. In retirement, he has written a number of books on the social history and usage of the concertina, a Victorian musical instrument that has gained global favor in traditional music circles in recent years. This book marks his first venture into Texas history.

Made in the USA
Lexington, KY
02 December 2017